Deborah Cuccia

There are two German States and two must remain?

HISTORISCHE EUROPA-STUDIEN
HISTORIC EUROPE STUDIES

Geschichte in Erfahrung, Gegenwart und Zukunft
History in Experience, the Present and the Future

herausgegeben vom
Institut für Geschichte
der Stiftung Universität Hildesheim
unter der Leitung von Michael Gehler

edited by
the Institute of History
University of Hildesheim
directed by Michael Gehler

Band 22
Volume 22

Deborah Cuccia

There are two German States and two must remain?

Georg Olms Verlag
Hildesheim · Zürich · New York
2019

Deborah Cuccia

There are two German States and two must remain?

Italy and the long Path from the
German Question to the Re-unification

Georg Olms Verlag
Hildesheim · Zürich · New York
2019

Gefördert durch Mittel der Stiftung Universität Hildesheim

Bibliografische Information der Deutschen Nationalbibliothek

Die Deutsche Nationalbibliothek verzeichnet diese Publikation in der Deutschen
Nationalbibliografie; detaillierte bibliografische Daten
sind im Internet über *http://dnb.d-nb.de* abrufbar.

© Georg Olms Verlag AG, Hildesheim 2019
Gedruckt auf säurefreiem und alterungsbeständigem Papier
Umschlagentwurf: Anna Braungart, Tübingen
Herstellung: KM-Druck, 64823 Groß-Umstadt
Printed in Germany
www.olms.de
ISSN 1869-1196
ISBN 978-3-487-15810-5

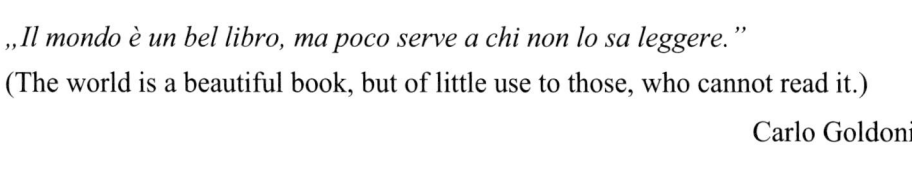

„Il mondo è un bel libro, ma poco serve a chi non lo sa leggere."
(The world is a beautiful book, but of little use to those, who cannot read it.)

Carlo Goldoni

Contents

Vorwort by Michael Gehler

1. Es war nicht nur Andreotti!

Die Äußerung des italienischen Regierungschefs Giulio Andreotti, „Es gebe zwei deutsche Staaten, und zwei müssten es bleiben", hatten die deutsch-italienischen Beziehungen bereits im September 1984 negativ berührt. Ende November 1989 äußerte sich der italienische Christdemokrat nochmals ähnlich. In einem Gespräch mit Gorbatschow bezeichnete Andreotti die deutsche Einigung als nicht aktuell. Diese Stellungnahmen prägten klischeehaft und verkürzt das Bild von Italiens Haltung zur deutschen Einigung von 1990 als markantester Einschnitt der europäischen Nachkriegsgeschichte.

Das Thema als solches gehört zu den am besten dokumentierten Forschungsanliegen der europäischen Zeitgeschichtsschreibung. Der Befund gilt zumindest für den inneren deutsch-deutschen Einigungsprozess wie auch für die Reaktionen der für Berlin und Deutschland als Ganzes zuständigen Vier Mächte (die USA, die UdSSR, Frankreich und Großbritannien). Der 9. November 1989 steht jedoch mit der Öffnung des Grenzübergangs in Berlin Bornholmer Straße für eine Zäsur auch in den Beziehungen des neuen Deutschlands zu seinen europäischen Partnern im Rahmen der Europäischen Gemeinschaften. Die französischen und britischen Beobachtungen, Perzeptionen und Reaktionen auf die sich vollziehende deutsche Einheit sind durch eine Reihe von Studien hinreichend untersucht worden. Was allerdings noch fehlt sind Untersuchungen über mittel- und unmittelbaren Nachbarstaaten und hierbei auch Italien. Bisher vielfach bekannt und weidlich zitiert sind vereinzelte Aufsätze über die kritisch-negative Äußerung von Italiens Ministerpräsident 1989, aber diese ist nur eine Momentaufnahme. Das italienische gesamte Verhalten war komplexer und umfassender als das seines Regierungschefs.

2. Einführung in das Werk. Methode, Quellenlage und Archive

Es war ein zentrales Anliegen dieses Buchprojekts, die verschiedenen Phasen der Entwicklung vom Herbst 1989 bis zur deutschen Einheit 1990 zu beleuchten, aber auch die Vorgeschichte vom Ende der 1970er bis in die 1980er Jahre einzubeziehen, wobei es nicht nur um das „offizielle" staatliche, sondern auch um das „inoffizielle" Italien ging. Dabei war neben Diplomatie auch auf die Journalistik, den Parlamentarismus, das Parteienspektrum, die Schriftsteller und Wissenschaft in einem umfassenden Mehrebenen-Exkurs einzugehen. Das Gewicht der langen Geschichte („longue durée") ist damit berücksichtigt, um die Rolle Italiens in der Zeit der deutschen Einigung besser zu verstehen.

Besonders wichtig war es hierbei auch, dass begriffliche Klarheit geleistet wird und Unterscheidungen hinsichtlich der verschiedenen und dabei auch abweichenden Terminologien, geschaffen werden, wie z. B. „Deutschlandfrage",

„deutsche Frage", „Einigung", „Vereinigung", „Wiedervereinigung". Dabei reflektiert Deborah Cuccia auch, was unter der Bedeutung des Worts „Mitteleuropa" verstanden wurde und zu verstehen ist.

Es handelt sich hierbei um keine rein bilaterale Geschichtsbetrachtung, sondern um eine Mehrebenen-Darstellung – zwischenstaatliche, interregionale, interinstitutionelle, kulturpolitische sowie medienspezifische und multinationale Ebene – auf der Grundlage verschiedenster Archive (u. a. in Berlin, in Bonn-St. Augustin, in Paris, in Nantes, in Rom und in Florenz). Besonders verdienstvoll ist es, dass aus den Quellen die Originalzitate nicht nur im Text aufscheinen, sondern auch die entsprechende Übersetzung in den Fußnoten ausgewiesen ist, was die Nachvollziehung ihrer Authentizität und Originalität ermöglicht.

3. Relevante Inhalte

In einer „Tour d'horizon" geht die Autorin auf die Vorgeschichte des Verhältnisses zwischen Italien und Deutschland im Zeitraum von 1979 bis 1988 ein, wobei verschiedene relevante Themen berührt werden wie die Entwicklung vom Europäischen Währungssystem (EWS) zum NATO-Doppelbeschluss und der Umgang von Giulio Andreotti und Francesco Cossiga mit einem in Bewegung geratenen und immer unruhiger gewordenen Deutschland, wobei in Bezug auf den letzteren Aspekt die Verfasserin der Frage nachgeht, ob es eine Neubestimmung der italienischen Position in der Bewertung der deutschen Frage gegeben hat. Der Genscher-Colombo Plan von 1981 wird als ein in zweifache Hinsicht Traum begriffen, wobei Deborah Cuccia Grenzen und Möglichkeiten dieses deutsch-italienischen Paars ausleuchtet. Die Integration Europas, wie auch der Entspannungsprozess in Europa, boten ideale Rahmenbedingungen, um allfällige italienische Kritiken und Vorbehalte abzuschwächen oder gar aufzulösen.

Im zweiten großen Teil ihrer Studie nähert sich Frau Cuccia dem engeren Fragenkreis ihres Themas. Hier geht es um „Italien zwischen deutscher Frage und ‚gemeinsamen europäischen Haus' in den Jahren 1989/90". Es setzt ein mit dem Herbst 1989: „Das Unglaubliche wurde möglich: Vom Unbehagen zur Suche nach einer Strategie." Dabei thematisiert die Verfasserin das von Gorbatschow propagierte „gemeinsame europäische Haus".

4. Der Kern des Werkes

Der sogenannte „Fall der Berliner Mauer" bewirkte vor diesem veränderten Hintergrund vielschichtige Reaktionen, die differenzierter waren als die von alten Befürchtungen und Vorurteilen geprägte Haltung von Andreotti lange Zeit anzunehmen gestattete: Trotz der altbekannten Sorgen vor einem zu starken Deutschland transportierten die Pressekommentare weit weniger Gefühle der Angst als vielmehr eine Grundstimmung, die die Autorin als „kollektive

Umarmung" begrifflich zu fassen versucht, wobei sie das ganze Ausmaß an positiven Veränderungen in der italienischen Perzeption Deutschlands verdeutlicht. Sie unterlässt es dabei nicht herauszuarbeiten, dass die italienische Presselandschaft einen durchwegs elitären Charakter hatte und die Zahl der Leserinnen und Leser weit bescheidener ausfiel als in anderen Ländern Europas.

Abgesehen von den Printmedien ist auffallend, dass auch politische Kreise, die die deutsche Wiedervereinigung noch Mitte des Jahres 1989 für nicht aktuell hielten, differenziert reagierten: Je nach politischer Couleur kann die Autorin verschiedenartige Wahrnehmungen, aber auch Vereinnahmungen für die jeweilige eigene politische Klientel und die jeweiligen innenpolitischen Zielsetzungen identifizieren. Die Democrazia Cristiana (DC) hinterließ beispielsweise den Eindruck, als habe sie den 9. November ohne jegliche Erwartung erleben müssen, von einer Vorahnung oder gar Vorbereitung gar nicht zu sprechen. Sie wurde von der Entwicklung völlig überrascht. Bemerkenswert aufgeschlossen waren die ersten Pressestellungnahmen von Staatspräsident Francesco Cossiga, was für Deborah Cuccia nicht verwunderte. Cossiga war einer der wenigen Politiker Italiens, der über gute Kenntnisse der deutschen Geschichte, Kultur und Sprache verfügte und ein spezielles Maß an Feingefühl für die innerdeutsche Situation aufbrachte. Weit weniger aufgeschlossene und vorbelastete war die Position des Ministerpräsidenten Andreotti mit seiner oben bereits zitierten Meinung.

Am Palazzo Chigi, an der Farnesina, wie auch das italienische Außenministerium genannt wird, sah man sich infolge der Veränderungen in Deutschland gezwungen, eine neue Strategie auf integrationspolitischer, transatlantischer und mitteleuropäischer Ebene zu entwickeln, um die Bedingungen und Konsequenzen der deutschen Einigung im Rahmen der Europäischen Gemeinschaften, der NATO und der KSZE neu zu gestalten. Als sich jedoch der Kontext der „Zwei-plus-Vier"-Verhandlungen seit Februar 1990 abzeichnete, d.h. weder die NATO noch die KSZE als entscheidendes Forum in Frage kam und somit Italien keine Akteursrolle einnehmen würde (Deutschlands Außenminister Genscher ließ seinen Amtskollegen Gianni De Michelis nicht gerade schmeichelhaft wissen, dass er nicht „part of the game" sei), waren zwei Folgen für das römische Selbstverständnis absehbar.

Der traditionelle Minderwertigkeitskomplex der italienischen Politik, auf der europäischen Ebene als mittlerer Staat nicht auf gleicher Augenhöhe mit Frankreich und Großbritannien agieren zu können, machte sich alsbald schmerzlich bemerkbar. Dies wurde durch eine zweite Reaktion zügig zu kompensieren versucht: Die Öffnung des Ostens sollte nun für Italien die Chance bieten, das schon seit den 1980er Jahren verfolgte Ziel einer Vermittlerrolle zwischen Donau- und Mittelmeerraum zu spielen, v.a. durch die Eroberung neuer Märkte der eigenen Wirtschaft weitere Absatzräume zu erschließen. Nach der

Bundesrepublik und nur knapp nach Österreich war Italien drittwichtigster Handelspartner Ungarns jenseits des „Eisernen Vorhangs" gewesen. Dieser Anteil sollte nun noch gesteigert werden.

Das änderte nichts an der Tatsache, dass die Bundesrepublik mit mehr als 21 % der italienischen Importe außerwirtschaftlich am relevantesten für Italien war.

Von einer einheitlichen Meinung Italiens kann nicht gesprochen werden wie die Autorin überzeugend nachweist.

Aufgrund der unterschiedlichen geschichtlichen, gesellschaftlichen und wirtschaftlichen Entwicklungen des Landes ist es notwendig, von multiplen Reaktionen der „verschiedenen Italien" sowohl innerhalb als auch außerhalb seines politischen Spektrums auszugehen. Wie Deborah Cuccia nachweist, änderte sich die Wahrnehmung Deutschlands durch Italien nach Ende des Zweiten Weltkriegs mehrfach maßgeblich. Diese Vorgänge verliefen langsam und nicht linear. Erst seit den 1980er Jahren entwickelte sich eine facettenreiche Vorstellung von Deutschland in der italienischen Wahrnehmung, in der Ängste und Skepsis im Zeichen der deutschen Kriegsvergangenheit immer stärker zurücktraten. Dieser Paradigmenwechsel vollzog sich durch einen intensivierten Kulturaustausch. Die gemischten Gefühle wichen jenen aus Achtung, Respekt, Bewunderung und Wertschätzung, wobei das italienische Bewusstsein von der Fortexistenz der sogenannten „deutschen Frage" bestehen blieb.

Die Autorin hat mit ihrer Arbeit mehr als eine klassische diplomatie- und politikwissenschaftliche Studie vorgelegt, sondern vielmehr im Sinne von „Internationaler Geschichte" auch „soft factors" wie Gesellschaft, Kultur, und Publizistik einbezogen. Deborah Cuccia beantwortet in ihrer mehrgliedrigen und multiperspektivischen Analyse eine Reihe relevanter Fragen, so zum Beispiel nach den Akteuren und den Spannungen in Italien ebenso wie nach den Ängsten, Erwartungen und Hoffnungen, die die deutsch-deutsche Entwicklung auslöste. Dabei geraten nicht nur Politik und Diplomatie, sondern auch Medien und Wirtschaft in den Fokus.

Die Verfasserin eröffnet auf diese Weise gänzlich neue Einblicke in die Ambivalenzen des zu Ende gehenden Kalten Kriegs in Europa im Allgemeinen und der deutsch-italienischen Beziehungen im Besonderen.

Ihre Studie besticht durch eine originelle Behandlung des Stoffs, die Vielfalt an mehrsprachigen Quellen sowie den interdisziplinären und zugleich multidisziplinären Forschungsansatz. Fragen des Kulturtransfers werden dabei behutsam beantwortet. Dadurch wird eine innovative Forschungsleistung erbracht.

6. FAZIT: Eine Absage an politikgeschichtliche Engführung

Deborah Cuccia kann durch ihre Studie nachvollziehbar und überzeugend die von der bisherigen deutsch-italienischen Forschung aufgestellten These in Frage stellen, dass die Zäsur des „Mauerfalls" in den deutsch-italienischen Beziehungen zur „schleichenden Entfremdung" zwischen Deutschland und Italien beigetragen habe. Dieses Bild ist in seiner Monokausalität, Reduzierung und einseitigen Tendenz so nicht mehr aufrechtzuerhalten. Während die italienischen Positionen vor der deutsch-deutschen Einigung von politischer Vorsicht und Zurückhaltung sowie auch von gleichsam eingefrorenen Stereotypen charakterisiert gewesen seien, so die fragliche These, hätten sich die Beziehungen nach dem „Mauerfall" merklich abgekühlt, was die Autorin zwar für die Regierungsebene auch bestätigen kann.

Die Erklärungsansätze für die „Entfremdung" erkennt die Verfasserin jedoch weniger in einem eventuell noch immer konfliktbelasteten zwischenstaatlichen Verhältnis zu Deutschland. Sie macht dafür vor allem eher innenpolitische Gründe verantwortlich: In den 1990er-Jahren waren es innenpolitische Affäre und Skandale sowie tiefgreifende wirtschaftliche Reformen vor dem Hintergrund der Maastricht-Kriterien und der Vorbereitung der Einführung des Euros, die die politischen Kräfte absorbierten. Dieser komplexe Vorgang blockierte den Blick über die Alpen und beeinträchtigte nicht nur die Zusammenarbeit mit Deutschland, sondern auch jene mit anderen EU-Partnern. Eine ganz andere Wirkung entfaltete die von der bisherigen Forschung unbeachtet gebliebene interregionale Kooperation, vor allem die wirtschaftliche Zusammenarbeit zwischen dem Nordosten Italiens und Bayerns im lokalen kulturellen Austausch als auch in der Vertiefung von politischen Kontakten auf der Ebene der Regionalisierung, wobei von den entsprechenden Medien ein positiv besetztes Deutschland artikuliert wurde. Klassische Stereotype waren teilweise durch neue Vorstellungen substituiert worden. Die Auffassung von der „schleichenden Entfremdung" kann also laut Deborah Cuccia nicht einmal für den Bereich der Regierungspolitik insgesamt gelten, sondern auch nur eingeschränkt während sich für den kulturellen und wirtschaftlichen Bereich keineswegs Tendenzen der Verschlechterung nachweisen lassen.

Die Autorin stellt ihre gut untermauerte These der Auffassung entgegen, dass es sich an Stelle einer Entfremdung zwischen Deutschland und Italien vielmehr um eine verpasste Gelegenheit der Revitalisierung und folglich einen „Dornröschenschlaf der Beziehungen" gehandelt habe.

Eine neue Dimension des zwischenstaatlichen Verhältnisses ist durch die sogenannte „Euro-Krise" zwischen Berlin, Rom und Brüssel eingetreten. Die fehlende Möglichkeit, wie noch in früheren Zeiten, in Zeichen der Wirtschaftskrise die Lira abzuwerten, um die italienischen Exporte weiterhin zu ermöglichen, ist durch den Eintritt Italiens in den Euro-Raum unmöglich geworden. Daneben hat auch die deutsche Sparpolitik im Zeichen der Rettungspakete für angeschlagene Euro-Länder zunehmend in Südeuropa zu Verstimmungen, ja bis zu Verwerfungen geführt. Vor diesem Hintergrund hat sich in Italien eine mitunter sehr deutschlandkritische – auch fast schon EU-feindliche – Stimmung in breiteren Kreisen der Bevölkerung, aber auch in akademischen und intellektuellen Eliten ergeben. Dies wiederum wäre ein eigenes neues Thema, welches in dieser Studie nicht mehr berührt werden konnte, aber es zeigt, dass das Klima und die Stimmungen zwischen Staaten immer wieder Veränderungen unterworfen sind.

Deborah Cuccia ist eine europäische Kollegin par excellence. Sie studierte nicht nur Geschichte, sondern auch Fremdsprachen, u. a. an der Universität in Florenz.

Als Nachwuchswissenschaftlerin decken ihre akademischen Interessen ein weites Feld ab und umfassen die Geschichte der internationalen Beziehungen, sowie die Geschichte des europäischen Integrationsprozesses unter besonderer Berücksichtigung Deutschlands und Italiens, aber auch die Geschichte der Sowjetunion in den 1980er Jahren. Als Stipendiatin des Deutschen Akademischen Austauschdienstes (DAAD) hat sie in zahlreichen deutschen Archiven für ihre Studie recherchiert. All das kam ihrer nun als Buchform vorliegenden Dissertation sehr zugute.

Es bleibt nur noch dem Werk, die Verdienste und Aufmerksamkeit zu wünschen.

Hildesheim, im März 2019   Michael Gehler

Man muss das Gestern kennen, man muss auch das Gestern denken, wenn man das Morgen gut und dauerhaft gestalten will. (Konrad Adenauer)

Preface

A correct understanding of the mesmerizing effects resulting from the 1989 events behoves us to consider both the quantity and the quality of the succession of developments that had took place long before the fall of the Berlin Wall.

New Year of 1989 started embedded in negotiations between the independent trade union Solidarnŏsć[1] and the Polish Communist party. In April, the outcome of these negotiations became public: the independent union had been legalized and authorized to participate in the coming elections on 4 June. Subsequently, on 24 August, Tadeusz Mazowiecki gave birth to the first non-communist government of Central-Eastern Europe.

Furthermore, on 27 June, with a decidedly symbolic gesture, the Austrian and Hungarian Foreign Ministers, Alois Mock and Gyula Horn, cut the barbed wire that until that moment had kept their countries apart.[2] Not even two months later, on 19 August, the so-called "Pan-European picnic" was celebrated for the symbolic opening of the frontier. At last, on 23 August, the Hungarian government opened the Austrian border. A growing number of Eastern German citizens started flooding towards Austria, being this their first stop before their final destination: the Federal Republic of Germany.[3]

---

[1] Among the many works concerning this subject, see, in particular, Michael Gehler, 1989 Ambivalent Revolutions with different Backgrounds and Consequences, in: Wolfgang Mueller/Michael Gehler/Arnold Suppan (eds.), The Revolutions of 1989. A Handbook (Österreichische Akademie der Wissenschaften/Philosophische Historische Klasse/Institut für Neuzeit- und Zeitgeschichtsforschung), Wien 2015, pp. 587–604; Jeryz Maćków, Polen im Umbruch: Die Wahlen 1989. Politische Hintergründe, Verlauf, Analyse, in: *Zeitschrift für Parlamentsfragen* 20 (1989), n. 4, pp. 561–580; Leonid Luks, Katholizismus und politische Macht im kommunistischen Polen 1945–1989. Die Anatomie einer Befreiung, Köln – Weimar – Wien 1993; Mieczyslaw F. Rakowski, Es begann in Polen. Der Anfang vom Ende des Ostblockes, Hamburg 1995; Pierre Grosser, L'année où le monde a basculé, Paris 2009; Sara Tavani, Muddling Through the European Bloc System: The Evolution of Italian-Polish Relations over the 1970s and 1980s, in: Wilfried Loth/Nicolae Păun (eds.), Disintegration and Integration in East-Central Europe 1919-Post 1989, Baden-Baden 2014, pp. 147–168.
[2] See Michael Gehler, Die Umsturzbewegungen 1989 in Mittel- und Osteuropa, in: *Aus Politik und Zeitgeschichte* (2004), B 41–42, pp. 36–46. See also Maximilian Graf, Österreich und das Ende der DDR, in: Michael Gehler/Maximilian Graf (eds.), Europa und die deutsche Einheit. Beobachtungen, Entscheidungen und Folgen, Göttingen 2017, pp. 259–294.
[3] Hereafter the German term *Bundesrepublik* will be used referring to the Federal Republic of Germany. For its Eastern counterpart the German acronym DDR (Deutsche Demokratische Republik) will be used.

On 7 October, the Hungarian Communist Party modified its own denomination into the Hungarian Socialist Party. It was the first Central-Eastern European communist party to disappear. The Parliament adopted a regulation to foresee the implementation of multiparty elections.

Meanwhile, on 17 July, Austria applied for membership within the European Economic Communities.[4] In such a climate of rapid and far-reaching changes a four-cornered initiative, known as the *Quadrangolare*, was conceived in Budapest by the then Foreign ministers Gianni de Michelis in Italy, Gyula Horn in Hungary, Alois Mock in Austria and Budomir Loncar in Yugoslavia. On 2 November, an informal meeting among Gianni de Michelis and the presidents of the regions and autonomous provinces members of the *Alpe Adria* (the Alps-Adriatic Working-group) and of the Adriatic initiative had already defined its specific features.

Later on, a pacific group of students demonstrating in the streets of Praga was charged by local police forces. This particular event marked the beginning of what was later known as the *Velvet Revolution*. In the following days public demonstrations in Praga escalated and on 28 November the Czech Communist Party had to relinquish its sole control over political power. As a result, the communist leader Gustav Hasák tendered his resignation.[5]

By the end of the year, the images of the outbreak of violence in the Rumanian city of Timisoara had hit worldwide headlines. They reached their climax on Christmas day with the public execution of the political leader and president, Nicolae Ceauşescu, and of his wife.[6]

In October, in striking contrast with this changing climate, the Eastern German government celebrated, at great expenses, its fortieth anniversary. One of the most popular allegories of that time represented two young women running side by side; one of them carrying the French banner and the other a flag with the hammer and sickle on the German colours. Underneath this picture, two dates were marked: 1789–1989. The similarity outlined between the French Revolution and the establishment of a communist regime in Eastern-Germany was palpable.[7]

---

[4] Hereafter the acronym EEC will be also used.

[5] See, for example, Steven Saxonberg, The Fall. A comparative Study of the End of Communism in Czechoslovakia, East Germany, Hungary and Poland, Amsterdam 2001.

[6] See, for example, the "Atti della giornata di studi": Italia, Romania e Europa centro-orientale. Diplomazia culturale e imperativi geopolitici da Versailles ai nostri giorni (Facoltà di Lettere e Filosofia dell'Università di Perugia), 22 November 2015. See also Ovidiu Pecican, Integration as Disintegration. Some Remarks on the Romanian Case viewed by Emil Cioran, in: Wilfried Loth/Nicolae Păun (eds.), Disintegration and Integration in East-Central Europe, pp. 352–356.

[7] See Alberto Indelicato, Memorie di uno Stato Fantasma: Berlino 1987–1990, Berlino 2004, p. 145.

Still, a very different similarity rapidly took its place. Meanwhile, dissatisfaction creeping among German citizens had been, indeed, increasing at a brisk
pace. Popular demonstrations at Alexanderplatz on 4 November were but the first
clear sign of the approaching overcoming of the state division.

Faced with these events, a press conference was quickly organized over the
afternoon of the 9 November at a local press centre with the participation of the
DDR government spokesman, Günther Schabowski. At 06.53 p.m., in a room
crammed with reporters, Riccardo Ehrman, an ANSA correspondent[8], asked a
question, which caused great annoyance to Günther Schabowski. Riccardo Ehrman had asked if the authorization for private travels abroad was a mistake. The
question raised was deliberately provocative. Approximately ten days before a
new law had authorized DDR citizens in possession of a passport and a visa to
travel abroad. Still, major difficulties in complying with both these requirements
let many observers to believe that the announcement was nothing more than pure
propaganda. After an awkward moment, Schabowski first attempted to deny the
allegations, then he took out a small piece of paper and started reading an announcement. According to what he read, DDR citizens had the right to cross the
border if in possession of identity papers, and no previous authorization of policy
forces was needed. His reaction unfolded a number of other questions, first and
foremost if this announcement applied to West Berlin, and since when.[9] Under
growing pressure, Schabowski confirmed that what had been said also included
the border crossings into West Berlin and "ab sofort", hence immediately.[10]

Despite rising tensions within the DDR, European governments and their
leaders were taken by surprise when Eastern-German citizens began to pour into
Berlin security checkpoints. Knocking the first brick out of the Berlin Wall along
the Bornholmerstraße sealed the commencement of the path towards re-unification. It was the night of 9 November 1989.

Those pictures literally travelled around the world. More than any other frontier, the division of Berlin – and the Berlin Wall as its physical representation –
epitomized in people's mind the ultimate sign of the division of Europe into
spheres of influence. More than any other event in Central-Eastern Europe, its
demolition contributed to reshape both geographical and ideological maps.

It is debatable whether this spectacular event represented a real hiatus in international history and in European history, especially as regards developments

---

[8] From 1976 correspondent in Berlin of the ANSA (*agenzia giornalistica italiana*, the Italian news
agency).
[9] The question, whether the announcement applied to Berlin West and since when, was raised by
Peter Brinkmann, correspondent in Berlin of the German newspaper *Bild*. See Ewald König,
Menschen Mauer Mythen, Halle 2014, pp. 183–185.
[10] As a result of the information sent by its correspondent in Berlin, the Italian ANSA was able to
spread the news of the fall of the Berlin Wall thirty-one minutes before other competing agencies.

in Germany and in the foreign policies of other European states. Regardless of our position towards this issue, it appears difficult to deny that the fall of the Berlin Wall and the following process of the German re-unification captured the attention of millions of viewers, ranging from present-day observers to prominent journalists, social and political scientists and legal experts.

The so-called *"German events"* have been a constant source of interest in social sciences in their entirety from the beginning of the 1990s. Early studies gave priority to internal aspects, such as social changes resulting from rapprochement between the former Western and Easter Germanies, adjustments in political and election systems, as well as legal adjustments whose implementation was an essential prerequisite to the ongoing transition.[11]

Nevertheless, it did not take long before historical studies of the events were conceived as well.[12] Straddling between the end of the 1990s and the beginning of the following decade, the main research focus was either on the relationship between Eastern and Western Germany, or on the role played by the Superpowers. From the mid 1990s, historical research has begun, however, to turn its attention to new topics which concerned both the possibilities created on the European stage by such far-reaching changes, and the contribution to the abovementioned dynamics of other European players. To be more precise, until the mid-Noughties publications dealing with the contribution of either of the United States of America, or of the Soviet Union had had the lion's share. Although other European actors, especially France, were not neglected, the focus of research mainly dealt with old fears such as the well-known Rapallo-complex.

Only in the last few years the discussion has been prompted by new outlooks. France and Great Britain have been the object of challenging works[13], many of them trying to provide a deeper insight into the reactions arising from the German events not only in the realm of politics and diplomacy, but also from an economic,

---

[11] Among the works published in Italy, see, for example, Elia Bosco, La nuova Germania: Società, istituzioni, cultura, politica dopo la riunificazione, Milano 2001. See also Gian Enrico Rusconi, Capire la Germania: Un diario ragionato sulla questione tedesca, Bologna 1990. Among the works written in a popular or journalistic style, see, for example, Alfredo Venturi, Il Novecento visto da Berlino: Il futuro è passato di qui, Milano 2004.

[12] See, for example, Tilo Schabert, Wie Weltgeschichte gemacht wird: Frankreich und die deutsche Einheit, Stuttgart 2002.

[13] See, for example, Frédéric Bozo, Mitterrand la fin de la guerre froide et la réunification allemande, Paris 2005. See also Frederike Schotters, 1984: François Mitterrand und die Suche nach Auswegen aus dem Kalten Krieg, in: Markus Berhardt, Wolfgang Blösel/Stefan Brakensiek/Benjamin Scheller, Möglichkeitshorizonte. Zur Pluralität von Zukunftserwartungen und Handlungsoptionen in der Geschichte, Frankfurt am Main 2018, pp. 295–318. See, as well, Frederike Schotters, Frankreich und das Ende des Kalten Krieges: Gefühlsstrategien der équipe Mitterrand 1981–1990 (Studien zur Internationalen Geschichte, Band 44), München 2019.

cultural and mass media point of view. Similar endeavours have only more recently been made for smaller European countries, such as Austria and Hungary.[14]

It is precisely in these recent developments that the idea of Italy as the object of this study has been conceived. Why focus our attention on Italy rather than on another European state?

Several arguments lie behind this preference and they cannot be merely traced back to my nationality.

Firstly, the depth and the "specific weight" of the relationship forged between Rome and Bonn throughout the last fifty years makes this choice extremely attractive. Indeed, from the earliest years following the end of the Second World War Italy has been developing a close and complex interaction with the Federal Republic of Germany first at a bilateral level[15], then in the context of the European Integration process.[16]

Moreover, it should be added that even before evolving in modern national states, Italy and Germany had given birth to a network of intricate economic and cultural interactions, which bequeathed deep traces in the German and Italian collective imagination. Italy, for instance, is often perceived by Germans wrapped in the aura of the eighteenth-century Goethe's vision, as "Das Land wo die Zitronen blühen".[17] Its historical, cultural and musical heritage, as well as its many artistic riches, enjoy great standing and high praises, while the contemporary social and political reality is often observed with a mixture of suspicion, aloofness and even mockery. Germany is, in turn, described in Italy as the em-

---

[14] Among recent works, see, for example, Wolfgang Mueller/Michael Gehler/Arnold Suppan (eds.), The Revolutions of 1989. A Handbook (Österreichische Akademie der Wissenschaften/Philosophische Historische Klasse/Institut für Neuzeit- und Zeitgeschichtsforschung), Wien 2015. See also Michael Gehler, Bonn – Budapest – Wien: Das deutsch-österreichisch-ungarische Zusammenspiel als Katalysator für die Erosion des SED-Regimes 1989–1990, in: Andrea Brait/Michael Gehler (eds.), Grenzöffnung 1989: Innen und Außenperspektiven und die Folgen für Österreich (Schriftenreihe des Forschungsinstituts für politisch-historische Studien der Dr. Wilfried-Haslauer-Bibliothek Salzburg), Wien – Köln – Weimar 2014, pp. 135–162.

[15] In this context, it is interesting to remark that the first Western German embassy abroad was established in Rome, and that Chancellor Konrad Adenauer chose Italy as destination of his first state-visit in a foreign country.

[16] See, for example, Maddalena Guiotto, La tradizione europeista dei partiti cristiano-democratici: CDU/CSU e DC negli anni Cinquanta. See also Pietro Scoppola, Alcide de Gasperi e Konrad Adenauer; both in: Gian Enrico Rusconi/Hans Woller (eds.), Italia e Germania 1945–2000: La costruzione dell'Europa (Collana Istituto Trentino di Cultura), Bologna 2005, pp. 153–191.

[17] „Kennst du das Land wo die Zitronen blühn, im dunklen Laub die Goldrangen glühn, ein sanfter Wind vom blauen Himmel weht, die Myrte still und hoch der Lorbeer steht, Kennst du es wohl? Dahin Dahin! Möcht ich mit dir, o mein Geliebter ziehn! [...]" quotation from Goethe's masterpiece "Wilhelm Meisters Lehrjahre".

bodiment of the "Sekundärtugend"[18], a country ruled by order and discipline, whereas its political and economic system is the object of mixed reactions dithering between admiration and sheer refusal. A study of the Italian reaction to the fall of the Berlin Wall and the successive process of re-unification should allow us to understand which stereotypes were still present at the end of the 1980s and, above all, how and how much they influenced Italian perceptions and reactions.

Secondly, we have to take into account the context in which this interaction between Italy and Germany took place. No state or entity governed by international law can operate in isolation. On the contrary, its actions are affected by – and forge in turn – the space where such interaction takes place. Therefore, the relationship between Rome and Bonn (and after the re-unification between Rome and Berlin) is inseparable both from the kind of international framework it is embedded in, and from the great questions related to the future of the European integration. We are dealing with two states in which, after the Second World War, the "European faith" became a pillar of international projection. The decades that elapsed between the creation of the first European cooperation structures and the signing of the Maastricht Treaty were constellated by close collaboration and by a high complementarity of interests between Rome and Bonn. Before the difficulty of dealing with the various stages of the complex issue involved, a short preface should define the subject in a few graphic details without going any further, the chapters that follow will analyse more accurately its main turning points.

At a first glance, the initial steps of the integration process were marked by the similarities shared by the two countries in their vision of Europe. Besides being the cradle of federalist movements, one must bear in mind that both Italy and Germany shared – at the beginning of the 1950s – the common goal of flanking an economic cooperation with a military cooperation, in view of the creation of a European political community. The EDC plan turned out to be a failure. The desire to favour the development of an integration model not confined to a merely economic issue – thus enhancing a vision of Europe going beyond a customs union or a simple space of economic cooperation – remained, however, a core element linking important segments of the political élites in both countries. Nearly thirty years after the failure of the EDC plan, the initiative for a European-Union,

---

[18] By the definition "middle class-values" or, in German, *Sekundärtugend*, we imply a set of specific features traditionally associated by Italians to Germans, such as diligence, faithfulness, obedience, discipline, punctuality and sense of duty. It is a concept, which played a central role in the *Positivismusstreit* of the 1970s and it was used in opposition to the so-called primary or cardinal virtues (a quartet set of virtues recognized in the writings of Classical-Antiquity, in particular by Plato, and later developed in the Christian tradition): Justice, courage, temperance and prudence. The word *Positivismusstreit* is related to the epistemologic debate between the scholars of Karl Popper and of Theodor Adorno.

better known as Genscher-Colombo project, displayed the common will to give new impetus to the integration process in areas such as the security policy and the culture cooperation, to favour a substantial review of internal decision-making processes and last, but not least, to intensify the European Political Cooperation[19], ensuring its better and more efficient coordination with the existing EC structures.

Lastly, this case study allows us to gain a better understanding of the Italian Foreign policy and of the Italian society at the end of the Cold War and on the threshold of the breakdown of the political system known as the *Prima Repubblica*.[20] These are some among the main reasons why this subject has been chosen.

Before going further into details, I would like to thank the many archivists I got in touch with during these years of research; without their valuable help it would have been impossible for me to complete this study.

In Italy, I am grateful to Luciana Devoti, Simona Panunzi and Concetta Argiolas from the archives of the *Istituto Sturzo*, to Giovanna Bosman and Cristina Pipitone of the *Fondazione Gramsci*, to Paolo Evangelisti of the historical archive of the Italian *Camera dei Deputati* and last, but not least, to the staff of the Historical Archives of the European Union located at Villa Salviati in Florence. I am also very grateful to Pasquale Chessa for the kindness with which he welcomed and supported my application to access Francesco Cossiga's private archive (which is at present still officialy closed).

While some of this work is based on diplomatic documents available in Italy, I also had to do primary research in archives in other corners of Europe. In France all my gratitude to Ariane Morai-Abreu of the *Archive du Ministère des Affaires étrangères Paris La Courneuve*, to Eric Lechevallier at the *Centre des Archives diplomatiques de Nantes*, and in Germany to Angela Keller Kühne of the archive of the *Stiftung Konrad Adenauer*. In Paris and Berlin, Jean-Charles Bédague and Maximilien Girard of the French *Archives Nationales,* and Birgit Kmezik of the *Politisches Archiv des Auswärtigen Amtes*, were wonderfully supportive in helping me in finding my way in the documents and in providing access to hitherto

---

[19] Hereafter the acronym EPC will be also used.

[20] The expression *First Republic* is controversial both in its contents and in its use. The transition from the First to the Second Republic was not the result of the adoption of a new constitutional text. The expression "Seconda Repubblica" points at the discrepancies of the phase after the political scandals of the period 1992–1994, whereas the term "prima Repubblica" refers to the period 1948 up to 1992/1994. Three events were the doorway to the second Republic, namely, in addition to the abovementioned scandals, the new electoral law of 1993 and the election of Silvio Berlusconi in 1994. The expression has been used by prominent journalists and politicians. Among the lattest, the President of the Italian Senate Pera in 2002, and Prime Minister Giuliano Amato. See, in particular, Giorgio Galli, I partiti politici italiani (1943–2004), Milano 2004. See also Friederike Hausmann, Die Deutschen und ihre Nachbarn: Italien, München 1999, pp. 197–207.

untapped sources. Last, but not least, I would also like to thank the *Deutsch-Italienische Gesellschaft Hildesheim* and its president, Dr. Christian Vogel.

Still, my primary debt of gratitude is to both my tutors, Michael Gehler from the *Stiftung Universität Hildesheim* and Maria Eleonora Guasconi from the *Università di Genova* for their valuable recommendations and continuous support while helping to shape this study throughout these last years.

I would also like to express my gratitude to the language lectors of the University of Florence and of the University of Florence Language Centre. Among them my heart goes to Christiane Colinet and Isabelle Maingain, to German language lectors (Petra Brunnhuber, Andrea Geselle, Claudia Roos and Karin Uhl), and to Spanish lectors (Aurea Alacreu, Olga Mictil, Mónica Aragones Molina and Maria de los Reyes Rodríguez). The support of the German and French lectors was indeed invaluable in letting me share their love for these two languages and in supporting me in getting a stock of knowledge which has been an essential precondition to this work. I also thank Spanish lectors for granting me plenty of opportunities to work with them into the organization of seminars and workshops dealing with historical issues, as it allowed me to improve my language skills and to get useful teaching experience as well.

I own another debt of gratitude to the many diplomats, journalists and experts who very kindly accepted to be interviewed for this study on Germany and Italy.

I am also deeply indebted to Elisa Anastassopulos for reading parts of this work as it was being prepared and last, but not least, to my sister Denise for her continuous support even by sheer presence, for her suggestions and love.

This book is dedicated to the memory of my beloved mother whose affection, teaching and example have always been with me through the years. She taught me about the value of history, that only by knowing the past we can understand the present and shape the future.

Florence/Hildesheim, Winter and Spring 2019

I. Introduction

1. Objectives, State of the Art and Methodology

As anticipated in the preface, the process of the German "*Reunification/Unification*" is the main subject of this study. Its specific focus lies on the Italian actions and reactions to this event.

This subject choice must be read and understood in light of the existing literature, of the state of the art at the Italian and European level, and of the new directions research has taken during these last few decades. Today, although thirty years have elapsed, it can still be considered as a matter of interest and debate both the disintegration of the Berlin Wall on the one hand – to which Eastern German citizens contributed with their unfaltering pressure to change the status quo – and the events which led to the recreation of a unified German state in the heart of Europe on the other.

From the end of 1989, the governments and diplomacies of the Continent had slipped into a state of constant turmoil, which lasted until spring of 1990 and, in some cases, even until the summer of the same year. Such developments brought to light diverging interests, fears, doubts, aspirations, and new ideas of all those involved. There were many reactions to these events; at times positive, at times negative, but none neutral. In Europe, the admiration for the results achieved by the pressure of popular protests in Eastern Germany went hand in hand with the perception of a historical duty to support the right to self-determination of the German people without creating obstacles to this path. This admiration was though also merged with concerns about potential imbalances which could result from a united Germany wielding an excessive economic and political clout within the European Communities.

The firm and prolonged oppositional stance adopted by the British Prime Minister, Margaret Thatcher, the initial hesitations of the French *Président de la République* François Mitterrand, and the guarded approach of the Italian *Presidente del Consiglio* Giulio Andreotti, were already widely known by contemporaries as far back as 1990. However, throughout the following years new studies have allowed for a better understanding of some of these reactions both at an official level as well as in the light of public opinion stances. Initial assumptions were softened and reviewed and some general statements were better defined, thus reflecting a deeper understanding of the interaction of multiple international factors. Such thorough comprehension of the constraints imposed by the existing international and European framework went hand in hand with efforts to take proper account of the personality of some political players who had a pivotal role within the process, of the values and interests which had led their actions in the broader context of both their biographical profiles, and of their political affiliation.

To begin with, in 1998 the collection of documents of the German Chancellery "Sonderedition aus den Akten des Bundeskanzleramtes" was published.[1] Unique of its kind until that moment, this collection contains more than 1600 pages of documents. They provide a greater understanding of the contribution made by the Chancellor, along with his closest advisors, to the transformation process in Central and Eastern Europe, and in particular to the chain of events which paved the way for the establishment of a German unified state between 1989 and 1990.

On the contrary, the contribution of other German players, such as the Federal Ministries – the Foreign Office, but also the Treasury Department, the Ministry for Economic Affairs, the Ministry of Justice and that of Defence – became relegated to a second place. This was due to a lack of documents on which to initiate a study of the same standard of quality and reliability as the one on the Chancellor. One of the main reasons explaining this issue has lied on the initial decision of the German Foreign Office archive[2] to stick, without exceptions, to the basic "thirty-year rule" both as regards files of the Bundesrepublik and of the *Ministerium für Auswärtige Angelegenheiten*.[3] This position was partially modified in 2009 when hundreds of diplomatic records, mostly covering the two-year period 1989–1990, were declassified. One year later the publication of a selection of these records[4], edited by Andreas Hilger, shed new light on the talks between the then German Foreign Minister, Hans-Dietrich Genscher, and his Soviet counterpart, Eduard Shevardnadze. In broader terms, this publication also shed new light on the Bundesrepublik-URSS couple, thus strengthening among scholars the awareness of its importance.

It did not take long before other European archives embraced the same stance. In 2006 a Polish collection of diplomatic documentation was published[5] under the direction of Włodzimierz Borodziej. It was meant not only to provide a better understanding of the contribution of the Government and of the Foreign Office in Warsaw to the 1989 events, but also to enrich a literature that until that moment had mainly been confined either to the analysis of the inter-German interaction, or to the assessment of the cooperation established between the German Chan-

[1] See Hanns Jürgen Küsters/Daniel Hofmann (eds.), Deutsche Einheit: Sonderedition aus den Akten des Bundeskanzleramtes 1989/1990, München 1998.
[2] Hereafter also indicated as "Politisches Archiv des Auswärtigen Amts", or, alternatively, by the acronym PA AA.
[3] Official denomination of the Foreign Office of the then DDR, hereafter the acronym MfAA will be also used.
[4] Andreas Hilger (ed.), Diplomatie für die deutsche Einheit, Dokumente des Auswärtigen Amts zu den deutsch-sowjetischen Beziehungen 1989–1990, Hamburg 2011.
[5] Włodzimierz Borodziej (ed.), Polska Wobec zjednoczenia Niemiec 1989–1991 Dokumenty dyplomatyczne, Warsaw 2006.

cellor, Helmut Kohl (1982–1998), and the US President, George W. Bush (1989–1993). However, the language barrier provided by a text written in Polish and the lack of translations has actually limited its influence to the local academic community.

Three years later, on the occasion of the Second Anniversary of the 1989 events, the British collection "German Unification 1989–1990"[6] was published in London. Benefiting of a wide circulation within the scientific community shortly after its release, its influence was by far greater than that of the Polish collection. The "German Unification 1989–1990" provided an extensive overview of the talks between the British Prime Minister, Margaret Thatcher (1979–1990), and the leading personalities of the Bundesrepublik establishment. It also outlined the role played by the British Foreign Minister, Douglas Hurd (1989–1995), and the *Commonwealth and Foreign Office* which he led.

At a closer glance this collection seems to serve a double purpose. On the one hand, the huge number of records provided could support historians with the task of softening the widely spread feeling that Britain had strongly opposed the process of the German re-unification.

On the other hand, it seems plausible to affirm that the collection also aimed at stressing the presence of a certain degree of scepticism within other European countries as well, above all that of France. As regards the first purpose, the choice of documents published by England stresses the existing discordance between the strongly negative stance of the Prime Minister – which is hardly confutable – and the positive attitude embraced by the Commonwealth and Foreign Office.

---

[6] Patrick Salmon/Keith Hamilton/Stephen Twigge (eds.), Documents on British Policy Overseas: German Unification 1989–1990, Series III, Volume VII, London 2010.

Karikatur: „Maggie Liebling, bist Du nicht pessimistisch wegen der Wiedervereinigung?" ‚Unbekannt

Fig. 1: Caricature: "Dear Maggie, dont't you think you are too worried about the Reunification?"
Anonymous author, 1990

As for the second point mentioned – the scepticism displayed by France – a brief explanation is necessary. Although in 2009 French archival documents were still not accessible for researchers, during previous years some exhaustive studies[7] concerning the French attitude had been published. Among their authors were some of the most prominent personalities of the European academic community like Tilo Schabert and Frédéric Bozo. During the last period of François Mitterrand's presidency, under exceptional circumstances, professor Tilo Schabert had been granted access to a huge amount of records before their relocation from the *Palais de l'Elysée* (the headquarters of the French President) to the premises of the *Archives Nationales*. As a result, Tilo Schabert had developed an account of the events confuting some traditional historical references, first and foremost, by reversing the hypothesis that the French President had opposed the possibility of a German state re-unification.

Hence, it seems that the British collection tried to demonstrate the following: although the French reactions could not be put at the same level of Margaret Thatcher's negative stance, they had often been haunted by the same fears and doubts as those of the Commonwealth and Foreign Office.

Soon afterwards French archives as well were, at least partially, declared accessible. As in the Polish and British case, a collection of records was conceived, under the direction of Maurice Vaïsse and Christian Wenkel.[8] It suffered, however, from the lack of permission to publish even extracts of the documents col-

---

[7] See, in particular, Tilo Schabert, Mitterrand et la réunification allemande : Une histoire secrète (1981–1995), Paris 2005 and id., Wie Weltgeschichte gemacht wird: Frankreich und die Deutsche Einheit, Stuttgart 2002.
[8] Maurice Vaïsse/Christian Wenkel (eds.), La diplomatie française face à la réunification allemande (d'après des archives inédits), Paris 2012.

lected at the *Archives Nationales* concerning the meetings between François Mitterrand and other European leaders. Hence, the authors could but provide a commentary of the impression they got from them.

As far as Russia, the former Soviet Union, is concerned, the access to archival documents was and still is difficult.[9] The decision of the Gorbačëv Foundation to release a significant amount of the acts[10] entrusted to its care has provided, however, not only a deeper knowledge of Michail Gorbačëv's view and approach to the "German question" and the process of re-unification, but also a first insight into many – until that moment – unknown aspects of the German-Soviet relationship in the final phase of the Cold War. The keen interest the scientific community had taken in a set of documents that had the potential to substantiate the analysis and to ease the understanding of the issue, along with a prompt translation into German[11], ensured a wider dissemination compared with the abovementioned Polish collection of records.

This was followed by the release by the US *National Security Archives* of new primary sources on the last years of the Cold War [12] and by Gerhard A. Ritter's essay publication.[13]

Finally, the collection edited by Heike Amos and Tim Geiger on behalf of the *Institut für Zeitgeschichte* in 2015 should also be mentioned.[14] The authors provided the reader with an accurate introduction leading through the assessment of a remarkable amount of diplomatic records recently declassified by the PA AA. Besides further enriching the literature with new insights into the role played by the *Auswärtiges Amt*, such records have also allowed the scientific community to broaden the analysis to the contribution of the MfAA and to deepen the understanding of the developments within the 2+4 negotiations. Furthermore, they have paved the way for nearly uncharted research paths, closely exploring the

---

[9] Thanks to special authorisations new collections have been, however, published throughout these last few years. See, in particular, Stefan Karner/Mark Kramer/Peter Ruggenthaler (eds.), Der Kreml und die Wende 1989. Interne Analysen der sowjetischen Führung zum Fall der kommunistischen Regime: Dokumente (Österreichisches Ludwig-Boltzmann-Institut), Innsbruck – Wien – Bozen 2014.

[10] Alexander Galkin (ed.), *Михаил Горбачев и гирманский вопрос, сборник документов* 1986–1991, Moskva 1996.

[11] Andreas Hilger (ed.) Joachim Glaubitz (translator), Michail Gorbatschow und die deutsche Frage: Sowjetische Dokumente 1986–1991, München 2011.

[12] See the documents published in: http://nsarchive.gwu.edu (last accessed 9.2.2016).

[13] Gerhard A. Ritter, Hans-Dietrich Genscher, das Auswärtige Amt und die deutsche Vereinigung, München 2013.

[14] Horst Möller/Ilse Dorothee Pautsch/Gregor Schöllgen/Hermann Wentker/Andreas Wirsching (eds.) Heike Amos/Tim Geiger (edited by), Die Einheit: Das Auswärtige Amt, das DDR-Außenministerium und der Zwei-plus-Vier Prozess (im Auftrag des Instituts für Zeitgeschichte Berlin – München), Göttingen 2015.

contribution – or lack of contribution – offered by states which were not invited to take part in the 2+4 negotiations.[15]

Therefore, it is not surprising that historical research blossomed in this environment. The support of so many heterogeneous collections of diplomatic documentation, even without considering the many autobiographical books historians can access, have offered an excellent study framework. In addition, the activism of an increasing number of national archives in granting access to untapped sources have ensured a constant supply of new diplomatic files, thus further nurturing the interest for events whose intrinsic importance is undisputable, both in terms of international and European dynamics.[16]

The result has been the accumulation of a rich set of books, essays and articles that provide a broad overview on the domestic German problems, the role played by the Superpowers, and by both France and Great Britain.[17]

By contrast, if we turn our attention to the state of the art concerning the contribution of other European partners of Germany, above all Italy, the situation is far less satisfactory. From a historical perspective, it is still an arduous task to deal in a balanced way with the policies pursued in Italy during the last decade of the Cold War. The number of publications focusing on the Italian foreign policy in the 1980s is, in fact, relatively small[18], and the debate about the relationship

---

[15] Among the works concerning the role played by other European states, see, for example, Michael Gehler, Bonn-Budapest-Wien: Das deutsch-österreichisch-ungarische Zusammenspiel als Katalysator für die Erosion des SED-Regimes 1989–1990, in: Andrea Brait/Michael Gehler (eds.), Grenzöffnung 1989: Innen und Außenperspektiven und die Folgen für Österreich (Schriftenreihe des Forschungsinstituts für politisch-historische Studien der Dr.-Wilfried-Haslauer-Bibliothek), Salzburg 2014, pp. 135–162.

[16] See, for example, Andreas Rödder, Deutschland einig Vaterland: Die Geschichte der Wiedervereinigung, München 2009. Klaus Hildebrand, Probleme und Perspektiven der Forschung zur deutschen Einheit 1989/1990, in: *Vierteljahrshefte für Zeitgeschichte* 52 (2004), pp. 193–210; Markus Driftmann, Die Bonner Deutschlandpolitik 1989/1990: Eine Analyse der deutschlandpolitischen Entscheidungsprozesse angesichts des Zerfalls der DDR, Münster 2005; Andreas Rödder, Zeitgeschichte als Herausforderung: Die deutsche Einheit, in: *Historische Zeitschrift* 286 (2008), pp. 289–339.

[17] Tilo Schabert, Mitterrand et la réunification allemande; Frédéric Bozo, Mitterrand la fin de la guerre froide et la réunification allemande; Yvonne Klein, Obstructive or promoting? British Views on German Unification 1989/1990, in: *German Politics* 5 (1996), pp. 404–431; Norman Himmler, Zwischen Macht und Mittelmaß: Großbritanniens Außenpolitik und das Ende des Kalten Krieges. Akteure, Interesse und Entscheidungsprozesse der britischen Regierung 1989–1990, Berlin 2001; Frank Costigliola, An arm around the shoulder: The United States, NATO and the German Reunification 1989–1990, in: *Contemporary European History* 3 (1994), pp. 87–110.

[18] See, in particular, Ennio di Nolfo, La politica estera italiana negli anni Ottanta, Bari – Roma 2003. See also Giuseppe Romeo, La politica estera italiana nell'era Andreotti 1972–1992, Soveria Mannelli 2000; see also Antonio Varsori, L'Italia e la fine della guerra fredda. La politica estera dei governi Andreotti 1989–1992, Bologna 2013.

between Italy and Germany in the same time-period is even narrower.[19] Among the various angles from which the network of relations forged between Italy and Germany could be observed, the process of re-unification is still, in many respects, an underdeveloped line of investigation.[20]

Over the years the main obstacles impeding the fieldwork can be traced back to the almost complete lack of access to the archive of the Italian Foreign Ministry and also, partly, to a certain reluctance to deal with a subject intertwined with the rapidly changing Italian political conditions at the end of the 1980s, hence liable to be contaminated by negative value judgments about most of the political personalities of that time. At the beginning of the 1990s members of the most influential Italian parties were the target of the inquiries of judges, which were echoed in the national and international press, and which disrupted the entire political system. This was followed by a sort of *damnatio memoriae* whose effects are still relevant.

This gap has, therefore, mostly been filled by prominent journalists and political experts whose volumes, although rich in details, fall into the category of popular articles, political journalism or memoirs, rather than in the field of historical research.[21] The only exceptions are a few essays, mostly written by non-Italians, dealing with some specific issues of the Italian approach, such as the reaction of the national press.[22]

Another serious obstacle is created by there being not one single Italian approach, but rather a number of different approaches within Italy. This ramification of positions has brought about the terms "Italian approaches", or even "the approaches of different Italies". Both these definitions try to describe the complexity of the Italian situation in 1989. Regional and local differences were and

---

[19] Among the few works dealing with the research field "the Italo-German couple in the 1980s" see Luigi Vittorio Ferraris, Deutsch-italienische Beziehungen in den 1980er Jahren. Aufzeichnungen aus italienischen diplomatischen Akten, in: Michael Gehler/Maddalena Guiotto (eds.), Italien Österreich und die Bundesrepublik Deutschland in Europa. Ein Dreiecksverhältnis in seinen wechselseitigen Beziehungen und Wahrnehmungen von 1945/1949 bis zur Gegenwart, Wien – Köln – Weimar 2012, pp. 243–262.

[20] With the remarkable exception of the contribution provided by Antonio Varsori, Italy the East European Revolutions and the Reunification of Germany, in: Wolfgang Mueller/Michael Gehler/Arnold Suppan (eds.), The Revolutions of 1989, pp. 403–418.

[21] Among the volumes falling into the category of popular articles and political journalism, see, for example, Alfredo Venturi, Il Novecento visto da Berlino. See also Massimo Nava, Germania Germania: Dalla notte del Muro alla Riunificazione, Milano 1990. As far as memoirs are concerned, see, for example, Alberto Indelicato Memorie di uno stato fantasma: Berlino 1987–1990, Berlin 2004

[22] See, for example, Eva Sabine Kuntz, Konstanz und Wandel von Stereotypen: Deutschlandbilder in der italienischen Presse nach dem Zweiten Weltkrieg (Italien in Geschichte und Gegenwart Band 9), Frankfurt am Main 1997, pp. 347–368.

are widespread in Europe, and not just in Italy; still, the issue is for many reasons more acutely pronounced south of the Alps than in France or in Great Britain.[23]

To tackle the problem concerning the complex Italian archival situation it became necessary to opt for a strategy of diversification of sources to include both national and foreign records, such as the latest available German and French documents. In Italy, it has been possible to consult the archives of some of the then most influential political parties and records entrusted to private foundations. Both the *Partito Comunista italiano*[24] and the *Democrazia Cristiana*[25] archival material, respectively retained at the Gramsci Institute and at the Sturzo Institute, have been of limited real help to ensure the fruitful development of the research.[26] Far more valuable was the contribution provided by the *Andreotti Archives*, also kept at the Luigi Sturzo Institute. The choice to consult the Andreotti archives arose from the observation that the figure of Giulio Andreotti not only left his unique personal imprint on nearly half a century of Italian political history, but he also was, without interruptions, Italian Foreign Minister from 1983 to 1987 and in 1989 had the post of *presidente del Consiglio*. Francesco Cossiga's documents, entrusted soon after his death to the historical archive of the *Camera dei Deputati*, were also very enlightening.

In addition to the documents collected in Italy, access was also granted to the French diplomatic records, both at the Archives of the Foreign Ministry (in Paris La Courneuve[27] and in Nantes[28]), and at the National Archives [29], and it was also

---

[23] The path which led to the birth of a modern state with a centralized government, especially in France, probably allowed to reduce local disparities, which in Italy are deeply rooted.

[24] Hereafter the acronym PCI will be also used.

[25] Hereafter the acronym DC will be also used.

[26] As far as the records of the Italian Communist Party are concerned, the sections *Comitato centrale*, *Direzione*, *Segreteria* and *Estero* in the period between 1979 and 1989 were consulted. In accordance with the "thirty-year-rule" enforced at the Gramsci Institute, full access to records was granted up to the year 1985, whereas after that date only partial access was possible. Furthermore, another objective limit overlaps with the previous one due to the application of a "thirty-year rule". Regardless of the time-constraints, as we move towards the end of the 1980s the size of the material kept at the Institute shrinks dramatically. Even greater were the hurdles faced at the Luigi Sturzo Institute. It could provide but an incomplete picture of the party's foreign projection in the 1980s as a result of both of the limited data available and of the lack of a widespread debate over Foreign policy's issues within the party.

[27] On the premises of the archive of the French Foreign Ministry in Paris la Courneuve I had access to the diplomatic records gathered in the sections *Bureau d'ordre Europe* 1981–1985 and *Bureau d'ordre Europe* 1986–1990, sub-sections Italy, Germany (Federal Republic and Democratic Republic), Austria, Hungary, Europe, EEC and CoE.

[28] On the premises in Nantes I had access to the "archives rapatriées", records produced by the French embassies abroad (in my case the French embassy in Rome, Bonn, Berlin and Budapest). See the bibliography for further information.

[29] At the French "Archives Nationales", it was possible to have access to diplomatic records concerning François Mitterrand's presidency (especially the meetings and talks between the French

possible to consult the German diplomatic records at the Archive of the Foreign Office in Berlin.[30]

The chance to make use of both Italian records and of foreign diplomatic documents has offered at least two major benefits. On the one hand, a diversification of sources has granted the opportunity to partially overcome the deficiencies due to the lack of access to many Italian archives, and to fill some of the "gaps" still affecting the Italian records already open to consultation. On the other hand, it has also provided the opportunity to observe how the Italian foreign policy was viewed from other countries.

French and German diplomatic sources, far from being just a means to an end, meaning an instrument to overcome the deficits still affecting the Italian archives, proved to be a significant contribution to develop a broader overview. This is because it must be assumed that each state, regardless how large or influential it might be, does not operate in isolation, but rather under the impact of material constraints, human resources, as well as of external stress and pressures.

In this perspective, foreign archival sources have allowed first to cast a glance at how European partners evaluated Italy's moves, and then to assess the effects of these evaluations in the framing of an Italian response strategy suitable to cope with the process of the German re-unification. This last remark lays itself open to a controversial debate regarding the very nature of the Italian foreign policy, whether this country was able to establish and support a great political design, or if it merely confined itself to conduct diplomatic relations with its partners. Such a broad debate will be reflected in this text insofar as the information that has been gathered on the 1989–1990 events will open up the discussion on the position of Rome, if Rome was able to give birth to a far-reaching proposal, whether such a proposal was accepted by its partners and, if so, to what extent.

Some further remarks must be devoted to the French records. If it is comparatively straightforward – in the context of the chosen research object – to understand the choice to make use of the available German archival toolbox, it appears much less clear why it seemed advisable to resort to the French archival sources

---

President and the Italian Prime Minister from November 1989 up to the beginning of the following spring and the French approach to the Genscher-Colombo plan). As far as the acts making up the archive Mitterrand are concerned, no general finding aids are at present provided. It is, therefore, compulsory to get a special authorization regardless of the number of years elapsed. After first contacts with the responsible person from the archive a limited number of files (among a list compiled by the responsible person himself) was selected and a formal request, "demande de dérogation", was made.

[30] In Berlin, full access to records dating back more than thirty years was granted. This means documents up to 1984. As for the period between 1985–1990, whereas some files were accessible as part of the records declassified in advance, the majority of records concerning Italy are still not open to consultation. It was, therefore, necessary to make a formal request of access, which was accepted in its entirety.

too. Further into the text this issue will be put in the right perspective and given some better context. At this point it is possible, however, to briefly mention the limits resulting from a strictly bilateral analysis, even taking into account the international constraints. On the one hand, a bilateral approach has been rendered increasingly obsolete by a political environment of growing European integration. On the other, throughout the second half of the 20th century France had always been such a fundamental frame of reference for Rome and Bonn that at certain times there were even talks of a triangular relationship between these three players.

In addition to the documents personally collected at the archives visited, German, French, Soviet, Austrian and British collections of diplomatic documentation have also been a valuable source of information.[31]

Still, the sole support of archival material would not have been sufficient to ensure a full picture of the Italian approach, it being the combined effect of different inputs. Therefore, the analysis was also supplemented by additional data gathered through interviews with diplomats and experts[32], by the use of memoirs, and of the Italian and German press. Recent developments in historical research have shown that a concomitant recourse to all these different sources can prove extremely useful in expanding the analysis by emphasizing some points which the diplomatic act might sometimes leave in the shade. Foreign policy rests on a set of both external and internal inputs resulting from the episteme of the diplomats, as well as from the "doxa", the opinion of the events provided by the media.

---

[31] See the bibliography at the end for a comprehensive list of all the collections of records the author has resorted to.

[32] The interviewees were chosen among the so called "privileged witnesses" (that is among senior figures being involved in the Italo-German relationship). For the purposes of this research they were grouped into two categories: diplomats and politicians on the one side, journalists on the other. As for the first group the framework of a semi-structured interview was applied. While a structured interview has the same rigorous set of questions for all interviewees and does not allow any diversion, a semi-structured interview is open, allowing new ideas to be brought up during the interview following what the interviewee says. It allows, therefore, to place greater value on the specific position occupied by the interviewee. However, the interviewer, even in a semi-structured interview, has a framework of themes that must be explored, a sort of guide composed by a set of questions that can be asked in different ways for different participants. Interview guides help to focus the interview on the topics at hand without constraining interviewees to a particular format. Such interviews are also open for further questions to develop during the course of the interview, based on the interviewees' responses. This freedom also helped to tailor the questions to the interview situation. As for the second group, unstructured interviews (interviews in which questions are not prearranged) seemed preferable, as the author already had the articles written by the interviewees and wished to informally discuss their implications to collect further data. The form of the unstructured interview varies widely. In this research some general ideas were prepared in advance according to the kind of topics the journalist had chosen in his articles. Unstructured interviews tend to be more informal and free than structured ones, much like an everyday conversation.

Furthermore, it is enforced by men living in a defined space and time-period, therefore acting according to their specific historical, psychological, cultural and political "inheritance".

As far as the many and different positions that were created in Italy on the wave of 1989 events are concerned, the field of research had to be organized on two fundamental elements, namely the "Italia ufficiale" (official Italy) and "Italia non ufficiale" (non-official Italy). In this way, the research reflects an orientation, which has become increasingly popular in recent years, that includes a more global vision of social, cultural, economic and political realities, as well as the necessity to take into account new phenomena.

The first cornerstone – official Italy – consists of a varied group of political parties[33], leading political figures, Parliament, Foreign Ministry and Government. Even broader is the second one, the non-official Italy, which includes the economic and cultural realm, as well as the press.

Particular attention will be also paid to the question of whether the perception by the "Italia non ufficiale" mirrored the attitude of the Italian public opinion, and if so, how and to what extent. To understand how this phenomenon of "the perception of the German re-unification process" affected the Italian public opinion it is necessary to replace, in some specific paragraphs, a qualitative method of analysis with a quantitative analytical method, by virtue of the findings produced by opinion surveys such as the Eurobarometer.[34]

Besides, it is desirable, for reasons of both clarity and rationalisation, to address firstly the reaction of the "Italia ufficiale", and then to move to the perception of the so called "Italia non ufficiale." Although these are matters which must be dealt with separately, this choice does not, in any way, imply that they evolved without intercommunication and without influencing one another. In order to emphasise the level of interaction existing between them, some cross sections are to be provided in each Chapter where primary diplomatic sources and the press are analysed in parallel.

Before dealing with the last issues of this introductory chapter, that is the levels of analysis and the definition of both the time boundaries and the framework of this work, some further remarks must be devoted to the research methodology adopted.

The aim pursued by historians cannot be confined to merely providing a clear as possible description of the events. As a picture restorer who, by virtue of scrupulous work, slowly removes the patina of time to restore a work of art to its

---

[33] This research work mainly deals with the most influential Italian political parties of that time: The "Democrazia Cristiana" (DC), the "Partito Socialista italiano" (PSI) and the "Partito Comunista italiano" (PCI).

[34] See, in particular, Eurobarometer n. 32, 33, 34 (November 1989/December 1990).

former beauty, so also the historian, by using his specific toolbox, which consists of the primary resources he is working on, tries to remove the patina of time and to detect the causes underlying past events in order to rescue them from oblivion. Thus, the path for the historian lies in first identifying and mapping the root causes[35] of specific events, and then providing an interpretation of their role. In this manner it is possible either to move from a general hypothesis – whose correctness is questioned by the scholar in light of the available sources – or to address a specific question raised at the beginning of the text. This work opted for the second option over the first.

The chapters that follow do not aim to support the hypothesis that Italy had either an active or a passive role in the context of the German events. On the contrary, they aim to shed some light on the Italian actions and reactions by, *firstly*, discussing the goals, both material and immaterial, and by examining the internal and external pressures that have had an influence on these actions.

Finally, the position of Italy's partners on all this is taken into account. As a result, some hypothesis on the consequences of these actions and reactions on the bilateral relationship between Italy and Germany in the broader context of the European integration process will be formed, both in the short and in the medium term.

A multi-level approach was embraced in order to succeed in this objective. In the background of the research, the constraints resulting from the international framework, along with the most important political and social internal variables, were carefully taken into account.[36] As far as Italy is concerned the influence of the domestic political dynamics was particularly pronounced in the 1980s. At that

---

[35] The abovementioned approach to history is ideally related to the strict standards of evidence-gathering and analysis of causes and effects introduced into historical research by Thucydides. The Greek historian Thucydides countered the challenge posed by a traditional approach to history deeply influenced by disciplines such as geography and ethnography as source of moral lessons with a thorough study of the causes of past events and of individual and collective motives. Deeply influenced by the methods and thinking of early medical writers, especially Hippocrates of Kos, Thucydides tried to apply some of their teachings to his analytic method insofar as he made a clear distinction between facts, causes and motives. The *facts* were the superficial marks (the symptoms) of deeper causes (the illnesses) and they were to be pieced together in the most detailed manner possible to comprehend their causes. There were two sets of possible *causes*: apparent causes and root causes. Each historian, according to Thucydides, had to undertake the task of firstly distinguishing between apparent and root causes, then leaving aside the apparent causes and putting the root causes in the right perspective for thorough analysis. As for the motives, Thucydides described them as the unchangeable physics of man. Finally, as the doctor was interested in illnesses to treat them, so the historian had to mainly focus on processes of crisis rather than in political balance.

[36] The importance of the social constraints on historical research developments has been, for instance, acutely emphasised by Elisabeth Röhrlich in her study on the Austrian chancellor Bruno Kreisky. See Elisabeth Röhrlich, Kreiskys Außenpolitik: Zwischen österreichischer Identität und internationalem Programm, Vienna 2008, p. 16.

specific moment, for the first time since the end of the Second World War, a non-Christian-Democrat politician was appointed as President of the Republic and, soon after, the same happened with the appointment of the new Prime Minister.[37]

Based on these elements and in light of both the state of the art previously depicted and the new directions taking shape throughout these last few years, it seemed appropriate to consider the research areas chosen – the "Italia ufficiale" and the "Italia non ufficiale" – through the prism of three different levels of analysis.

The European level of analysis is the first to be selected. During the two decades that preceded the beginning of the 1980s, the constant and progressive transfer of powers, and in particular of economic competences, from Members States to the European Community, had had far from negligible effects on the way European states interacted among themselves. The Eighties marked the beginning of a phase of enhancement in the integration process: The Milan European Council, the approval of the Single European Act and, last but not least, the impetus given by the European Commission are its most prominent stages. Besides, it should not be forgotten that the Davignon report, published on 27 December 1970, set the stage for the establishment of the EPC, an informal consultation mechanism among the Member States. Its inherent limitations and weaknesses notwithstanding, above all its intergovernmental nature, the EPC rapidly established itself as an important mechanism that had the potential to foster the creation of deeper and more efficient forms of coordination, and to slowly set in motion a process of harmonization of the Foreign policy tools and targets pursued by the Member States.

The second level of analysis chosen can be described as an "approccio bilaterale flessibile" (a flexible bilateral approach). Namely, a bilateral approach enriched with specific references to the role played by France, Austria and the so-called Italian Ostpolitik.[38] The interaction between Rome and Bonn in the 1980s

---

[37] This statement is not fully correct, as, soon after the end of the Second World War, Ferruccio Parri, leading figure of the *Partito d'Azione*, had been appointed Prime Minister (between June and December 1945). The political party Ferruccio Parri belonged to enjoyed high standing by virtue of its significant contribution to the Resistance movement. Its political influence, however, was more limited and slowly decreased as time passed. Nevertheless, if we consider the time-period following the end of the war as a transitional phase, as neither the peace treaty had been signed nor the issue concerning the form of government had been solved, the statement (not unusual in foreign diplomatic documents) that Giovanni Spadolini was, in 1981, the first non-Christian-Democrat appointed Head of Government in the history of the Italian Republic appears to be more understandable.

[38] See Sara Tavani, Alle origini della Ostpolitik italiana: L'evoluzione della politica orientale del centro-sinistra organico di Aldo Moro, in: Daniele Mezzan/Renato Moro (eds.), Studiare Aldo Moro per capire l'Italia, Soveria Mannelli 2014, pp. 467–488.

was, in fact, under continued stress due to the challenge posed by the strengthening of the Franco-German couple, by the inconsistency created by internal ups and downs of the "vertenza alto-altesina" after the signing of the De Gasperi-Gruber agreement [39] (the South Tyrolean question finally settled in 1992) and, last but not least, by the new dynamics arising from a greater Italian commitment in Central-Eastern Europe.

> «In coincidenza con l'avvento di Gorbačev alla guida dell'URSS, l'azione del governo italiano si è caratterizzata per un'attenzione crescente verso l'Europa orientale nel convincimento che il passaggio della titolarità del potere [...] costituisse un fatto innovativo destinato ad avere incisive ripercussioni nel mondo intero [...]».[40]

This commitment was mirrored in an increasingly close relationship with Moscow, in a growing interest in strengthening and deepening the political, economic and cultural ties with the countries belonging to the Warsaw Pact (among them the DDR, which was officially recognised by Italy in 1973), and in a strategy of regional and local integration by means of cooperation structures like *Alpe Adria*.[41]

The individual level of analysis was the third and the last one to be selected. In recent years scholars have displayed a growing penchant for either biographical essays of leading political figures, or, even more often, for historical essays complemented with extensive biographical references.[42] This is, indeed, a rather recent development at odds with a long lasting tradition prone to confine biographical studies within the frontiers of popular articles and political journalism. Biographical essays tended, in fact, to be anecdotal and to focus on psychological factors, whose objective importance and specific weight were not easy to measure

---

[39] See Mario Toscano, Storia diplomatica della questione dell'Alto Adige (XXIII), Bari 1967, pp. 339–402. See Ruggero Moscati, L'accordo de Gasperi Gruber, in: *Rivista Storia e Politica* XIII (1972), n. 4, pp. 401–422. See also Luciano Monzali, Giulio Andreotti e le relazioni italo-austriache 1972–1992, Merano 2016, pp. 1–3.

[40] "After the coming to power in the Soviet Union of Gorbačëv, the Italian foreign policy distinguished itself through a growing interest for Eastern Europe rooted in the belief that this transfer of power [...] was an innovation destined to exert a powerful influence all over the world". See Ruolo dell'Italia verso l'est europeo nella seconda metà degli anni Ottanta, appunto del Ministero degli Esteri, not dated (approximately it can be situated in autumn 1989). Istituto Luigi Sturzo (hereafter ILS), Archivio Carte Andreotti (hereafter AGA), section Europe, box (hereafter b.) 383.

[41] For further information on the local cooperation frameworks promoted by Italy in the 1970s and the 1980s see Liviana Poropat, Alpe Adria e iniziativa centro-europea: Cooperazione nell'Alpe Adria e nell'area danubiana, Napoli 1993.

[42] See, for example, Lothar Gall, Bismarck. Der weiße Revolutionär, Frankfurt am Main 1981. See also Hans-Peter Schwarz, Adenauer. Der Aufstieg. 1876–1952, Stuttgart 1986.

within an historical perspective.[43] This trend demonstrates the strong reluctance to accept biographical essays into the family of history. Recently, however, scholars have slowly begun to overcome this prejudice, by combining a biographical approach with a rigorous analysis and with a strict definition of the object of research.[44]

This specific study does not belong, strictly speaking, to the biographical genre. Still, it makes extensive use of references from the biographical profiles of some of the Italian and German leading political figures in the chosen time-frame, and it also bears in mind their respective education paths and political environment. The influence of individual factors proves to be even more significant in the absence of institutionalized structures for regular coordination and consultation which enables political partners to pursue their common objectives in a consistent and stable manner. In such cases, the "Männerfreundschaft", namely the friendship and the affinity among political players, can help accelerate, slow down or even ease specific developments.

1.1 Defining the Time Boundaries of the Research Field

This research project was originally meant to focus, within a strictly bilateral approach, on the Italian perceptions and their reactions towards the German events, which I felt needed to be investigated now that new archival sources are available. Firstly, Italian fears and expectations were to be addressed; then, the changing process of the relationship between Rome and Bonn from 9 November 1989 until 3 October 1990 was to be critically discussed. All the information provided by the documents collected, together with the specific issues they highlighted, have turned, however, the subject of this work into something broader: a study of the Italian vision of the "deutsche Frage" from 1979 up to the re-unification. Its temporal perspective has therefore shifted backwards, from 1989–1990 to the 1980s as a whole. Besides this, it became necessary, as previously discussed, to consider more than one level of analysis.

At a closer glance, it also became clear that Italy's reactions to the 1989–1990 dramatic transformations revealed themselves as being part of a set of events associated with a peculiar awareness of the "German question"[45], which is deeply rooted in the past. Therefore, I found it impossible to understand the prime causes

---

[43] As for the controversial relations betweeen psychology and historical research, see, in particular, Josef Rattner (ed.), Geschichte und Psychoanalyse, Würzburg 2010.

[44] See, for example, Thomas Etzemüller, Die Form Biographie als Modus der Geschichtsbeschreibung, in: Michael Ruck/Karl-Heinrich Pohl, Regionen im Nationalsozialismus, Bielefeld 2003, pp. 79–90, 71.

[45] See, in particular, Wolf D. Grüner, Die deutsche Frage. Ein Problem der europäischen Geschichte seit 1800, München 1992.

of the Italian reactions, and not merely the apparent ones, without accurately exploring the main trends of the Italo-German couple in the 1980s.

To summarize, the focus of this work is set on the time period between 1979
and October 1990, although the Italian reactions to the 1989–1990 events will not
be neglected. This is not, of course, to say that the developments before 1979 are
unimportant for a comprehensive overview of the Italo-German relationship, but
only that after 1979 the conditions and the capabilities had reached a stage which
is central to the set objectives. Hence, it seems advisable to deal with the dynamics before 1979 and after 1990 only if strictly necessary to the overall understanding of the chosen object.

1.2 Defining the Framework of the Research Field

The text is divided into some preliminary chapters, a second part dealing with the
relationship between Italy and Germany from 1979 to 1988, and a third section
providing a discussion of the Italian reactions after the fall of the Berlin Wall.
The postface concludes this overview by dealing with the notion of *schleichende
Entfremdung* (creeping estrangement) between Italy and Germany, which was
introduced by the Italian expert Gian Enrico Rusconi and which is to be used for
the examination of the Italo-German couple after the re-unification.

In this first part of the research, chapter one depicts the objectives, the state
of the art, the chosen methodology and the levels of analysis. The following chapter discusses some issues of terminology, briefly deals with the historical background of the Italo-German relationship before the Second World War (in close
association with the problem of the frontiers as core element of the *deutsche
Frage*), and finally proposes some explanations of the terms used. Clearly, this is
an important issue as well. The meaning and the context in which the key terms
"Reunification", "Mitteleuropa" and "German question" are used must be fairly
addressed before going into further details.

In the second part of the study chapters four, five and six consider the changing patterns of the Italo-German relationship from 1979 until the end of 1988
through the prism of the three levels of analysis chosen, firstly by looking at Foreign policy and government issues, then at the perceptions of the press and, finally, at the cultural relations involved. Within a chronologically organized
framework each paragraph highlights the specific importance of a different key
moment. Although absolute priority is given to the interaction between Italy and
the Bundesrepublik, the DDR and the Italian Ostpolitik will be briefly addressed
whenever necessary to better comprehend the Italian vision of the "German question".

Part three looks at the reactions of the "Italia ufficiale" and the "Italia non
ufficiale", a specific focus lying on the Italian mitteleuropean policy and on the
Quadrangolare initiative which was part of the strategy developed to cope with

the dynamics unleashed by the fall of the Wall. In this third section, which considers the time-period between November 1989 and October 1990, the events are divided into three different groups according to the main turning points of the Italian stance. Chapter seven covers the time-period up to the end of November 1989, whereas chapter eight deals with the events taking place from November 1989 until February 1990. Chapter nine outlines the developments from spring 1990.[46] At the beginning of each one of these chapters a short presentation of the most prominent domestic German events and international dynamics is provided in order to set the Italian stance in its historical environment, thus giving us better tools to comprehend its causes and let the peculiar aspects which distinguished the Italian stance from the approach of other European countries come to the surface. Among these peculiar aspects, one of the most complex to address is the marked inter-connection linking the perception of the German question to the domestic tribulations of the Soviet Union, and to the changing process within the Eastern bloc.

This third section revolves around three main questions. Firstly, it is necessary to discuss whether Italy had a full picture of the evolutionary stage reached by the countries beyond the Iron Curtain in general, and the DDR in particular, during the years immediately preceding 1989. Secondly, it is interesting to investigate whether, during the few months preceding November 1989, a certain feeling, even if a vague one, of the approaching German upheaval was being spread, and, if so, to what extent and in which political and social contexts. Finally, our last field of research concerns not only the Italian worries, but also the hopes and expectations associated with the changes that the process of re-unification had unleashed.

In the months preceding the fall of the Wall, the Italian diplomacy had paid constant and growing attention to the turmoil spreading in Central-Eastern Europe.[47] Still, the conclusion reached was that this state of turmoil had not the po-

---

[46] In her essay, Frankreich und das vereinigte Deutschland: Interessen und Perzeptionen im Spannungsfeld, Valérie Guérin Sendelbach divided the process of re-unification in three different phases according to the trends of the French reactions. Her choice can be easily applied to the description and discussion of the Italian stance as well, provided that some specific points are firstly cleared up in light of the different international profile the two countries kept and of the approach to the "German question" they had developed. These caveats notwithstanding, the "10-Punkte Erklärung" and the Ottawa summit seem to embody for both countries the most important turning-points during the time-period considered. The first of these events had, for both France and Italy, in many ways, similar repercussions, whereas the second event affected them differently. It provided France with the chance to strengthen its influence on the German domestic dynamics, while Italy received a severe setback for its ambitions.

[47] Hereafter the acronym MAE or, as an alternative, the word "Farnesina" will be also used.

tential to threaten, at least in the short term, the survival of the DDR, as the Soviet Union did not intend to accept a fundamental change of the German situation.[48]

The fall of the Wall marked, however, the beginning of a phase clouded with doubts and higher uncertainty. During the month of November several attempts to make sense of the real extent of what had happened unfolded. In order to rise to the challenge so abruptly triggered by this social and political earthquake, politicians had to summon up all the energy and inventiveness they had. Making use of a theatre metaphor [49], politicians and decision-makers in the most important European and non-European capitals could be compared with actors who unexpectedly had to act in a drama whose text they ignored. The actors themselves were in charge of the direction of a play with improvised dialogues, whose plot was unfolding on the European stage. Among the Italian "actors" involved in this drama, Prime Minister Giulio Andreotti is the political figure on whom there was far more debate and on whom there have been written far more essays. His contribution – or lack of contribution – to the process of re-unification has quickly become something of a legend. Rumours spread that the Italian Head of Government ranked amongst those political leaders busy writing a plot able to block the German changing process or, where that not possible, at least to slow down its speed for as long as possible. This feeling, apparently confirmed by the sentences Giulio Andreotti himself had uttered in September 1984, is up to the present day widespread both among the general public and the scientific community: *Esistono due stati germanici e due stati germanici devono rimanere?*[50]

The abovementioned statement has been quoted in the title of this research. The question mark added at the end stresses the need to deconstruct the sentence and then give it some better context in order to be able to discuss its possible meanings. The next step involves a better placement on the German re-unification stage not only of the role of Giulio Andreotti, but also of other less well-known Italian influential actors, of co-stars and of movie extras. The sentence uttered by Giulio Andreotti in 1984 was, therefore, also added to the title as a controversial starting point aiming at showing from the very beginning that the approach of the Italian Prime Minister was not necessarily representative of his country in its entirety.

---

[48] See Doc. 54 *Из беседы М.С. Горбачева с Дж. Андреотти Рим, 29 ноября 1989 года*, Rome 29.11.1989, in: *Михаил Горбачев и гирманский вопрос, сборник документов* 1986–1991 (collection of Soviet records).

[49] A similiar metaphor was used by Tilo Schabert in dealing with the process of the German re-unification. See Tilo Schabert, Mitterrand et la réunification allemande, pp. 8–9.

[50] "There are two German states and two German states must remain". See Queste le frasi all'origine del caso, in: *Repubblica*, 16.9.1984, p. 3.

The transition to the following phase was symbolically sanctioned on 28 November when the German Chancellor presented its Ten-Point Plan to the Bundestag. The closest allies of Germany, the Auswärtiges Amt and its Foreign Minister, and even many among the advisors of Kohl, were kept out of the loop until the day of the statement. For Italy, this transition was also symbolically sanctioned through the state visit of the Soviet leader to Rome the day after[51], on 29 November 1989. This was the beginning of a stage when, once faced with the fact that the completion of the ongoing process was inevitable, the Italian government tried to develop a strategy that would result both coherent and effective. This second phase was marked by important steps such as the European Summit in Strasbourg in December 1989, the meeting among Christian-Democrats leaders in Pisa on 17 February, and the NATO Summit in Ottawa at the end of the same month. Although Italian politicians were not always best characterised for their congruity, it seems that throughout these months they did reach a certain degree of conformity in their views towards the main objectives of Foreign policy.

The end of the Ottawa Summit, the beginning of the 2+4 negotiations (to which Italy was not invited to participate), and the implementation of free political elections in the DDR were the bell for the third and last round. The 2+4 negotiations, together with the steps taken to accelerate the process of European integration, were the driving forces of this third and last stage, whose end was marked by the rebirth of a united German state on 3 October 1990.

The postface provides a discussion of some concepts and theories proposed in the aftermath of this event to make sense of the new trends in the relationship between Rome and Berlin, which the implosion of the Soviet behemoth had thrown open.

---

[51] See Hanns Jürgen Küsters/Daniel Hofmann (eds.), Deutsche Einheit: Sonderedition aus den Akten des Bundeskanzleramtes 1989/1990, München 8. Juli 1998, introduction. The negative judgment that the authors expressed about the Ten-Point Plan was confirmed in the interviews with many Italian diplomats. Ambassador Cavalchini, close advisor of Prime Minister Andreotti, remarked that Kohl acted with great determination, perhaps even with impetuousness, seen the reactions to his famous Ten-Point Plan on 28 November, which were the object of a long debate at the European Council and before that at the Nato Summit in Brussels organized after the meeting in Malta. It was not only about Margaret Thatcher and her personal opinions, Mitterrand as well was disappointed and vexed as Kohl had never hinted to his decision to present this statement and everything had been carried out very discreetly. See the authors' interview with ambassador Luigi Guidobono Cavalchini (5.2.2016).

2. Terms burdened with Meanings

Any scientific study should start by defining the core concepts used in the text. Dealing with the "German events" requires both an explanation of the meaning of the expression *deutsche Frage*, and a discussion about its historical evolution. This is important in order to comprehend the specific weight this expression came to carry in the Italian perceptions.

A wide range of literature can be found about the role played by the "deutsche Frage" in the history of international relations. From this though, it does not follow that, together with a number of common features, each European country did not have its own set of critical elements, which resulted from its geographical and political specific conditions as well as from its historical inheritance.

In addition to explaining the *deutsche Frage*, the choice of the term *Mitteleuropa* used to describe the 1989–1990 events must also be addressed, discussed and contextualized.

2.1 The *deutsche Frage*

The expression *deutsche Frage* refers to a thorny issue that has dominated the history of international relations since the dawn of the 17th century.[1] In that hectic moment of European history, the notion of a universal empire had not completely disappeared, even though it was under growing pressure from the emergence of new players on the international stage: the modern states which were the result of a process of border definition and of centralization of the attributes of sovereignty.

In 843 a.C., the Treaty of Verdun[2] had not bequeathed to Central Europe the equivalent of a Capetingian authority. In other words, it had not given a territorial basis endowed with at least some unifying elements. The Ottonian Empire, even at its zenith, lacked the features of a coherent political entity. Since pre-modern history the Holy Roman Empire was, in fact, the result of both a marked internal competition between different jurisdictions, and the consequence of a clear lack of control of its structures by the state. Due to the inability of the ruling monarchs to impose their authority on their vassals, this fragmentation of sovereignty already existed, de facto, during the High Middle Ages. It was not though until 1356 that it found a legal basis, the so-called *Goldene Bulle*.[3]

---

[1] See Lucien Bély, Les relations internationales en Europe XVII-XVIII siècles, Paris 1992.
[2] See Jean Picq, Une histoire de l'Etat en Europe, Paris 2009, chapters (hereafter ch.) 2 and 3.
[3] According to the imperial decree known as *Goldene Bulle* (Golden Bull in English) the emperor was chosen by seven prince-electors: the archbishop of Mainz, Cologne and Trier, the Count Palatin of the Rhine, the Duke of Saxony, the Margrave of Brandenburg and the King of Bohemia (the House of Habsburg, omitted in this original list of prince-electors, succeeded the kingdom of

Consequently, according to Jean Picq, at the dawn of modern history neither the French model of concentration and centralisation of power, nor the English approach to harmonisation by virtue of common law, can help us understand the complex dual system that regulated the interaction between the imperial and the local authorities.[4]

It is not easy, in fact, to define what the Holy Roman Empire actually was on the eve of Modern Age. It was certainly a structure with marked universalistic aspirations, built on a feudal inheritance forged through Medieval times. But it had also been subjected to a process of progressive territorial reduction and rearrangement. Although at the beginning of the 16th century the Empire still encompassed several non-German-speaking lands, it also started identifying itself primarily with a space defined by a common language[5], as it can be understood[6] since 1512 by the use of the term "Holy Roman Empire of German Nation".

In 1648, the Münster and Osnabrück peace treaties (commonly known as the peace of Westphalia) further accentuated this domestic fragmentation by giving it a new legal basis. For the first time in history the "German question" dominated the negotiations of a peace treaty. This was because the underlying issue was to define what characteristics, and what weight, the German people – which were at the heart of Europe – should bear. And in reality the question was therefore also about what structure the German territory would take. It became of the utmost importance to strike a lasting balance within the Empire as this would become an essential prerequisite for a balanced European system. This necessity has from then on become a recurring feature in the history of international relations.[7]

Bohemia starting from the 16th century, and since then it influenced the election of the next emperor). From the 14th century these prince-electors had basically the power of a monarch on their lands (which the emperor had not the power to dissolve) as they were entitled to impart justice without prior authorization or subsequent imperial ratification.

[4] See Jean Picq, Une histoire de l'Etat en Europe, p. 212.

[5] The German word "deutschsprachiger Raum", refers to a territory where the German language is spoken. This concept had a pivotal role within the German Romantic movement, especially with regards to the discussion about features and both material and ideal borders of a German nation. Nowadays, the "deutschsprachiger Raum" comprises Germany, Austria, part of Switzerland and the microstate Liechtenstein. Besides, those regions where the majority of the population speaks German as a first language can be also considered as being part of the "deutschsprachiger Raum". For instance, South Tyrol, part of Belgium, Luxembourg and Denmark.

[6] See Georges-Henri Soutou, Une histoire tourmentée : Allemagne unie ou désunie, in: *Questions internationales* 54 (mars-avril 2012), pp. 8–19.

[7] France was at the centre of the peace conference trying to persuade its partners that it was of the utmost importance to address the German issue. This approach was a direct expression of the concerns prompting its foreign policy after the treaty of Chambord: "Tenir sous main les affaires de l'Allemagne dans la plus grande difficulté qu'on pourra" (according to the translation proposed by Werner Rouget: die deutschen Angelegenheiten unter der Hand im Zustand der größtmöglichen Schwierigkeiten halten). A large number of experts attribute this statement to a royal counsellor of

According to the Westphalian peace settlement, the Holy Roman Empire of German Nation was inclusive of more than three hundred – among small and large – political entities which were represented at the Imperial Diet.[8] These political bodies that composed the Holy Roman Empire of German Nation were converted through the peace treaty into sovereign states, henceforth not just de facto, but also de jure, possessing almost unlimited discretion to enter into alliances (jus foederis), to declare war, and to sign peace treaties (jus belli ac pacis). The Westphalian treaty provisions gave birth to a kind of political organisation qualified by the German jurist Samuel von Pufendorf[9] as a "monstrum juridicum".[10]

The warning signs of the emergence of a German problem can be detected as far back as the first half of the 17th century, and yet this issue cannot be properly addressed in a modern sense before 1806/1815. These two dates have a truly symbolic meaning. In 1806, the Holy Roman Empire of German Nation was dissolved by the will of Napoleon I, and in 1815, the Congress of Vienna came to its end. To address the German question in a modern sense two prerequisites are indispensable: The loss of the imperial dimension, and the existence of modern nation-states which would act in an international framework with defined characteristics.

The process which led to the creation of a modern nation-state in the heart of Europe was, however, a slow and conflicting path for both historical reasons and for the lack of distinct natural barriers in the Northern part of the German speaking area. In the mid-19th century, the creation of a nation-state was still a process in the making, whereas local realities retained their competitive position. In this regard, it is interesting to recall the obstacles faced by Otto von Bismarck in his rise to political power. Despite the fact that the Prussian *Ministerpräsident* intended to enable the emergence of a strong and homogenous German state, he did

---

the French King Henry II (during the negotiations of the abovementioned treaty of Chambord in 1552). See Werner Rouget, Schwierige Nachbarschaft am Rhein: Frankreich-Deutschland, Bonn 1998, p. 15.

[8] Thus, France averted the German danger which had haunted its foreign policy from the previous century when the Emperor Charles V, by virtue of a skilful marriage strategy, had nearly succeeded in creating a universal monarchy. It appeared, therefore, necessary for France to capitalize on the opportunities offered by the negotiations, with a view to prevent further disturbances and risks of encirclement coming from Imperial forces.

[9] Samuel von Pufendorf (1632–1694) was a well-known German jurist, political philosopher, economist, historian and statesman. Among his achievements as a writer, *De statu imperii Germanici liber unus* (1667) and *De statu imperii Germanici* (Amsterdam 1669).

[10] The kind of political organisation defined by the peace treaties could not be explained using the interpretive framework of sovereignty provided by the French philosopher Jean Bodin. According to this framework, alliances between states were the first step either to pool together resources to enable a cooperation among sovereign independent political entities, or to subordinate these bodies on the path of becoming a new state to a superior authority.

not opt for a Prussification policy, but rather fell back on a complicated operation consisting in the progressive transfer of the Prussian political practice over to the local substratum.

Neither the Congress of Vienna [11], which tried to solve the "German question" by creating a confederation on what remained of the "Holy Roman Empire of German Nation" (the *Deutscher Bund*, an association of thirty-nine sovereign states chaired by the emperor of Austria), nor the Prussian victory at Königgrätz[12] in 1866, which resulted in the dissolution of the Confederation and in the subsequent creation of two German-speaking political entities (a federal state with Berlin as its city-capital and a multination empire with Vienna as its political capital), and not even the settlement defined at the end of the First World War, managed to find a lasting and successful solution to this long-standing problem.

In the interwar period, the United States of America turned, partially, once again inwards, towards political isolation.[13] During this period, none of the European major powers were able to propose a strategy to put the "deutsche Frage" on the pathway to a final solution. Europe dithered between the choice, actively supported by France, of imposing punitive measures which would marginalize the Republic of Weimar, and of embarking in an ambiguous cooperation approach with the German political élite. Even the strategy of appeasement – the foreign policy of making political and material concessions to the enemy – applied by the British government towards Nazi Germany, was just as ambiguous. In 1939, the question of the role and weight of Germany within the international and European framework, came back once again with even greater intensity and violence.

By the end of the Second World War, the issue was, therefore, back on the negotiating table, fundamentally unresolved. Italy was by then a divided, war-torn country whose "cobelligerance" became recognized by the Allies only with great reluctance. It would appear reasonable to assume that Italy could provide but a limited contribution to the definition of the post-war conditions imposed to the defeated countries.

> „Die italienische Regierung konnte sich den Luxus einer eigenständigen Deutschlandpolitik zu diesem Zeitpunkt nicht leisten […] An den verschiedenen Konferenzen der Alliierten, als das Deutschlandproblem diskutiert wurde, partizipierte Italien nicht und konnte deshalb keine direkte Einflussnahme ausüben. Die italienische Regierung verfügte nicht wie General de Gaulle über eine Reihe bereits

---

[11] June 1814-July 1815.
[12] Also Sadowa.
[13] See, in particular, Klaus Schwabe, Weltmacht und Weltordnung: Amerikanische Außenpolitik von 1898 bis zur Gegenwart. Eine Jahrhundertgeschichte, Paderborn 2006.

während des Krieges entstandener Lösungsvorschläge zur deutschen Frage [...]."[14]

It is, in fact, difficult to disagree with the statement of Charis Pöthig that, by the end of the war, Italy could not afford the luxury of producing a German policy, or, supposing Italy had one, persuade the Allies to give it credit.

The question arises as to whether it may be concluded that Italy did not possess a specific vision of the German issue. If we rely, to challenge this assumption, on the guidelines provided by policy papers or programme documents that Italy could have drawn during the war, our expectations are bound to be disappointed, as no such paperwork exists. Looking for programme documents on the German issue would presuppose Italy had developed a specific view of the subject, which was not the case[15], both for contingent reasons and for sound historical considerations. Italy was not only a defeated country, but it also was a "late-born" nation-state whose intrinsic weaknesses had impaired its ability to exert significant influence on the great international issues.

Italy had, therefore, not been capable to develop a vision of the German question comparable either to the approach of the British government, which held the power of preserving the balance of power on the Continent for more than a century, or to the French stance, which was deeply influenced by the necessities imposed by sharing a border with Germany.[16] Strictly speaking, Italy was not a neighbouring country of Germany. Still, Italy shared a common border with Austria, that is with the *deutschprachiger Raum,* and had therefore specific concerns

---

[14] "At that stage the Italian Government could not afford the luxury of an independent German policy [...] Italy did not participate in the conferences where the Allied Powers discussed the German problem and it was, therefore, unable to materially affect their outcome. Unlike General de Gaulle, the Italian Government could not rely on a series of proposals drawn up during war-time in order to address the *deutsche Frage* [...]". See Charis Pöthig, Italien und die DDR, Die politischen ökonomischen und kulturellen Beziehungen von 1949 bis 1980, Frankfurt am Main 2000, pp. 49–50.

[15] "Non vi era una percezione uniforme della questione tedesca. Allora la maggioranza dell'opinione pubblica non pensava che il mondo bipolare diviso dalla cortina di ferro potesse aver presto termine. Si era convinti che le due Germanie sarebbero continuate ad esistere come due stati tedeschi separati" (Italy lacked an homogenous vision of the German question. The majority of the public opinion could not believe that the world as it was divided by the Iron Curtain could come to an end. We were persuaded that Germany would continue to be divided in two states). See the author's interview with Ambassador Leonardo Visconti di Modrone (22.3.2016).

[16] As for the French perspective, see Werner Rouger, Schwierige Nachbarschaft am Rhein: Frankreich-Deutschland, Bonn 1998. See also Hans-Georg Ehrhart, Die deutsche Frage aus französischer Sicht (1981–1987). Frankreich zwischen deutschlandpolitischen Befürchtungen, sicherheitspolitischen Nöten und europäischen Hoffnungen, München 1988.

aimed at effectively counteracting the Austrian diplomatic efforts to regain control of the *Alto Adige-Südtirol* (South Tyrol).[17]

In this context, it cannot either be overlooked the fact that Austria, like Germany, was occupied by foreign troops. As neither can we forget that both its political status and the nature of its future relations with Germany had not been clearly defined in the immediate aftermath of the conflict. This political uncertainty left, in fact, extensive room for fears that the German speaking countries could proceed on the path towards unification.[18] It was only from the mid-1950s, after the signing of the State Treaty and the passing of the Declaration of Neutrality, that Austria launched a Foreign policy based on the promotion of those specific political, cultural, as well as social and economic features most suitable to stress its identity, hence to distinguish itself among "other German speaking states".[19]

> „Für die Entwicklung der österreichischen Identität nach 1945 waren die Abgrenzung von Deutschland und die Distanzierung von allem ‚Deutschen‘ essentiell. Alle drei Argumente (Opferstatus, Weiterbestand sowie Unabhängigkeit Österreichs) spielten in der (Außen-) Politik Kreiskys eine besondere Rolle, wobei die Verantwortung für persönliche und institutionelle Involvierungen in die Verbrechen des Nationalsozialismus auf Deutschland (bzw. das, was davon übrig blieb) abgewälzt werden sollte […].“[20]

It was a far-reaching strategy, firstly aimed at targeting Western partners, and then, from the mid-1980s, seeking to include Central-Eastern Europe as a whole, which found in Italy a receptive hearing.

We can, as a result, draw the conclusion that Italy had not produced a vision of the *Deutschlandfrage* (the question of Germany), a German policy stricto senso, but it had a German policy in a broader sense. In other words, Italy had to affirm specific demands regarding the *deutsche Frage* (the German question),

---

[17] See Umberto Corsini, Problemi di un territorio di confine: Trentino e Alto Adige dalla sovranità austriaca all'accordo de Gasperi-Gruber, Trento 1994.
[18] See Michael Gehler, Österreichs Außenpolitik der Zweiten Republik, Innsbruck – Wien – Bozen 2005.
[19] See Ibid., pp. 564–568.
[20] "After 1945 the distinction from Germany and the dissociation from all what was 'German' was essential for the development of an Austrian identity. All three arguments (status of victim, survival and independence of Austria) had a special role in Kreisky's Foreign policy, wherein the burden for personal and institutional involvement in the crimes of National Socialism should be passed onto Germany (or rather on what remained of it) […]". See Michael Gehler, Bruno Kreisky Italien und die deutsche Frage, in: Michael Gehler/Maddalena Guiotto (eds.), Italien Österreich und die Bundesrepublik Deutschland in Europa: Ein Dreiecksverhältnis in seinen wechselseitigen Beziehungen und Wahrnehmungen von 1945/49 bis zur Gegenwart, Wien 2012, pp. 173–208.

seen as the rearrangement of the area lying in the heart of Europe.[21] At the end of the war, this specific interest went hand in hand with a more general demand for security and inner European cooperation. In the pursuit of these goals, Italy found from the very beginning an important partner in Western Germany.

The fact that Italy had not been directly involved in the decisions taken by the Allies with regards to Germany is susceptible to a range of diverse interpretations, several among them not entirely negative. Quoting once again Charis Pöthig, Italy could not, by any means, afford the luxury of envisaging its own *policy of Germany* to assert at the negotiating table. However, this also meant that Italy was not tied to the same strings that more influential countries had to accept.

This situation gave Italy the opportunity, somewhat neglected in historical research, to set, with a certain degree of independence, the limits of its *German policy*, to implement it, and to pursue its full realization with all the flexibility that the new international framework allowed. In the following years, its not being at the winner's table paradoxically entailed the advantage, as compared to Paris or London, of greater room for manoeuvre. This space became usable in the definition of the relationship with the recently created Western German State.

2.2 Unification or Reunification?

The expression re-unification has purposely been presented hyphened in this text. This choice is the result of the many difficulties that have been encountered in settling on one definition over another.

Wiedervereinigung, Vereinigung, Einigung, deutsch-deutscher Einigungsprozess, deutsch-deutscher Transformationsprozess, deutsche Einheit and *deutsche Wende*[22] are only some of the words most frequently used to identify the 1989–1990 events. Among them it is necessary to distinguish between those terms used as far back as 1990 to indicate the German developments, such as *Wiedervereinigung, Vereinigung* or *Einigung,* and those terms elaborated, *a posteriori*, for definition purposes.

---

[21] See Luigi Vittorio Ferraris, Deutschland, Österreich und Italien als Eckpfeiler im Aufbau Europas, in Ibid., pp. 47–62. Former Italian Ambassador in the Bundesrepublik, Luigi Vittorio Ferraris (1980–1987), highlighted the degree of entanglement between Italy and the German speaking area. He also highlighted that until recent times Italy, unlike France, had drawn no clear distinction between Austria and Germany. During the 19th century, the emergence of a riper National conscience supported the perception, slowly growing within the cultural and political élite, that two political bodies coexisted in the heart of Europe, Austria being the major obstacle to the path of national unification. By contrast, the relationship between Italy and Prussia (after 1871 Germany) was fundamentally non-conflictual until the First World War, and some wings within the then Italian political parties and the local bureaucracy had frequent exchanges with their counterparts in Berlin.
[22] The expression was coined by Egon Krenz and it is nowadays widely spread in the former Eastern Germany.

This analysis will focus on assessing the three lexemes most popular in 1989, and it will start by defining their meaning.[23] Our semantic field includes the three nouns *Wiedervereinigung, Vereinigung, Einigung,* together with their three corresponding verbs, which are as important as the nouns as far as their communicative purpose is concerned.

First of all, the verbs will be discussed, in order to properly identify common semantic elements among the lexemes selected. All three verbs share the same root: the adjective *einig* (united). The verbs *einigen* and *vereinigen* have the meaning of "etwas zu seiner Einheit verbinden, sich zu einer Einheit zusammenschließen", in other words they identify the process which allows to reach a certain state, the *Einheit* (unity). Both terms may be used to indicate the process leading to political unity; still, in this specific context, the verb *vereinigen* is mostly employed. The term created by joining together the verb *vereinigen* and the preposition *wieder* indicates the act of bringing together in a single political unit two or more states which were previously divided.[24]

During the time-period in which Germany was a divided country considerable differences have dominated the approach taken in Germany and abroad regarding the basis of the political separation and its potential future course.

Unlike the DDR, which at the beginning of the 1970s chose to abandon the objective enshrined in its constitution, being a "schrittweise Annäherung der beiden deutschen Staaten bis zu ihrer Vereinigung auf der Gundlage der Demokratie und des Sozialismus", the Bundesrepublik preferred to stick to the clause written into the preamble to the German *Grundgesetz* of 23 May 1949: "Das gesamte Deutsche Volk bleibt aufgefordert, in freier Selbstbestimmung die Einheit und Freiheit Deutschlands zu vollenden."

It cannot be denied that this clause did not have the same political clout or the same status in each government from the end of the 1940s. Still, the clause in question was never formally modified after 1949.[25] On the contrary, the idea of a separation of the German territory as opposed to the goal of a future reunification slowly took root in the East, having one of its first public recognitions in the article written by Hermann Axen in 1970.[26] However, it was necessary to wait two more years before the Central Committee officially affirmed that differences in social structures had so deeply affected the very essence of the German nation,

---

[23] In this respect see the Deutsches Universal Wörterbuch Duden 7. Auflage, Mannheim, Duden Verlag, 2007.

[24] See Dieter Herberg and others (eds.), Schlüsselwörter der Wendezeit, Wörterbuch zum öffentlichen Sprachgebrauch 1989–1990, Berlin 1997, ch. 14 p. 390.

[25] See Werner Weidenfeld/Karl-Rudolf Korte (eds.), Handwörterbuch zur deutschen Einheit, Frankfurt – New York 1992.

[26] *Neues Deutschland*, 14.9.1970.

that the idea itself of a united German nation needed to be overcome.[27] Based on these ideological transformations, the constitutional text was modified in 1974. References to the terms "Germany", "German nation", and above all "Ver-einigung", were all carefully deleted, while the "socialist" nature of the DDR was further accentuated.

When the Western and Eastern constitutional texts are compared, it appears even more clearly that in the German *Grundgesetz* no reference to the existence of two German states had ever been included. On the contrary, Germany was presented as a single entity whose people were invested with the historical duty of fulfilling unity and freedom. Although the lexeme "reunification" appeared neither in the DDR Constitution (until 1974 the term *Vereinigung* was used), nor in the *Grundgesetz* (where the lexeme *Einheit* had been selected), after the end of the conflict it quickly became the main point of reference in the ongoing debate.[28] Throughout the years this word became frequently subjected to heated discussions, and not less to violent attacks, as the following statements uttered by Chancellor Willy Brandt seem to confirm:

> „Lange wurde aus dem Grundgesetz eine Pflicht zur Wiedervereinigung abgeleitet. In Wirklichkeit spricht die Präambel von der Verpflichtung des gesamten deutschen Volkes in freier Selbstbestimmung die Einheit in Frieden und Freiheit Deutschlands zu vollenden. Das war anders und mehr als fiktives […]. Aber die Verwirrung der Begriffe war beträchtlich. Aus Einheit wurde Wiedervereinigung […]".[29]

The actions and reactions of the European partners of Germany must be read and understood in light of these linguistic issues and of the ambiguity implied by the terms used.

As far as Italy is concerned, the debate just outlined casts a rather feeble light on the national political life. After the end of the Second World War, and throughout the entire period of the German state-division, "riunificazione" (reunification) was, in fact, the predominant lexeme of the Italian debate. As time passed, especially after the signing of the Helsinki Final Act, the term was being mainly used

---

[27] Report of Erich Honecker to the VI central committee of the SED, 1972. See Alberto Indelicato, Memorie di uno stato fantasma: Berlino 1987–1990, Berlin 2004.

[28] See Dieter Herberg (ed.), Schlüsselwörter der Wendezeit, ch. 14.

[29] "For a long time a duty to 'Reunification' was derived from the *Grundgesetz* (Basic Law). In reality, the preamble only refers to the obligation of the German people to peacefully accomplish, by free self-determination, the unity and freedom of Germany. That was different and more fictional than real […] But the confusion of terms was considerable. Unity turned into Reunification". Willy Brandt, Erinnerungen, Berlin 1990. Quoted in Konrad Löw, …bis zum Verrat der Freiheit: Die Gesellschaft der Bundesrepublik und die DDR, Langen Mueller, 1994, p. 97.

as synonym of an academic hypothesis rather than a real possibility, at least in the short/medium term.[30] Furthermore, until 1989 this word was subjected in the Italian debate to a fundamental inherent ambiguity. It could, indeed, imply both a possible reunion between the two German states created at the end of the conflict, and – on the other end – the rebirth of a German political body which would respect the old external borders in existence until 1937. The ruling of the German Constitutional Court given in 1973 further complicated an already unclear matter.[31]

According to the Italian government, a correct understanding of the German question in its fundamental political and legal aspects required a thorough analysis of the Grundgesetz preamble and of the articles 23 and 146. It also required to consider the abovementioned ruling of the Court sitting in Karlsruhe, from which it could be inferred that the *Reich* had survived military defeat in 1945. The Reich had not, therefore, ceased to exist, neither after the surrender of May 1945, nor as result of military occupation.[32] The 1973 constitutional Ruling seemed to confirm what could be deduced from the *Grundgesetz*, that the *Reich* existing in 1937 had not lost its international personality.[33] Furthermore, the Bundesrepublik was

---

[30] The interview with ambassador Cavalchini (5.2.2016), confirms the feeling that both the Italian diplomacy and the Italian public opinion were inclined to believe that Germany would remain a divided country.

[31] See, in particular, Der Grundlagenvertrag vor dem Bundesverfassungsgericht. Dokumentation zum Urteil vom 31. Juli 1973 über die Vereinbarkeit des Grundlagenvertrags mit dem Grundgesetz, edited by Presse und Informationsamt der Bundesregierung, Karlsruhe 1975. Dieter Blumenwitz, Die Christlich-Soziale Union und die deutsche Frage, in: Hanns-Seidel Stiftung (ed.), Handbuch zur deutschen Einheit 1949–1989–1999, Bonn 1999, pp. 417–430.

[32] On the basis of the abovementioned legal assumptions, Rome estimated that the government in Bonn had at first presumed that the winning powers would solve the German issue by granting to the people living in the occupied areas to fulfil their wish to remain part of a single German state. Once this illusion faded, the Federal Government had abandoned this guarded approach, opting for a new strategy. Although the reunification was still, theoretically, the ultimate goal to reach, in everyday practice it was generally accepted that its realisation would require a rather long time.

[33] The Ruling of the Constitutional Court must be also understood in light of both the transition that shaped German politics, and of the opposition within German politics itself. These resulted firstly from the Treaty of Moscow of 12 August 1970, which contained a letter regarding the German unity, and then from the main treaty between the two German states: The Vertrag über die Grundlagen der Beziehungen zwischen der Bundesrepublik Deutschland und der Deutschen Demokratischen Republik. Once the treaty with the Soviet Union was ratified in Parliament on 17 May 1972, the Social Democratic Party had undertaken negotiations with the DDR for the formulation of a treaty on the relationship between the two German states for as long as they would be separate. In Parliament, notwithstanding the strong opposition to this project by the Christian Democratic Party, the treaty between the Bundesrepublik and the DDR was voted through and took effect on 21 June 1973. Because of the pressure created by the Bavarian faction of the Christian Democratic Party (CSU), the Constitutional Court was asked to review the compatibility between the Treaty and the clause of the preamble in the Fundamental Law of 1949. The Constitutional Court upheld the compatibility between the two legal documents, and it also went on to comment on the legal

not to be considered a successor state but the same state, even if it did not share the same territorial extent.[34]

The rapid changes occurring from November 1989 had further increased, both in the central government and in the Italian press, the worries and fears concerning the ambiguity of the "reunification" notion in light of the 1973 ruling.

The use of this term allowed the press to draw from a rich linguistic heritage and an equally rich historic resource pool, as the term lent itself to different representations of the events. In other words, its use hinted both at the duty to support a process generated by a historical turning-point, which could pave the way for the rebirth of the German nation after ages of forcible separation, and at the risks of a potential destabilisation that a redefinition of the German frontiers may cause.

From a strictly legal point of view the process leading to the creation of a united German state was a process of incorporation. This is the process when a state, in our case the Bundesrepublik, replaces another, and fully exercises its sovereignty on the territory of this second state, in our case the DDR, which consequently ceases to exist.[35] The use of either a legal notion, of the word Vereinigung, or of one of the notions established in retrospect for definition purposes, would allow us to avoid the contradictions implied by the lexeme "reunification".

Still, this would also mean the loss, *tout court*, of irreplaceable raw material, with emotional, linguistic and historical features, which has been bequeathed to posterity. Lastly, the term reunification was the most currently used in 1989/1990 both in Italy and in Germany.[36]

As a result, it has seemed appropriate to choose the term "reunification" to address the German events and to use it critically, fully aware of the risks this implies. The hyphen between the preposition and the verb graphically embodies such awareness.

2.3 Mitteleuropa

"Mitteleuropa" is a German term which enjoyed great popularity in the 1980s and in the 1990s. Over time, it entered into everyday use, and it was also adopted in other languages, for instance in Italian, as a loanword. It is made up from the German words *Mittel* and *Europa*. It may be fairly straightforward to provide a

---

nature of the Bundesrepublik, and of its relationship with the Reich. For the role of the CSU and the Constitutional Court, see Franz Josef Strauss, Erinnerungen, Berlin, 1989.

[34] See Urteil des Bundesverfassungsgerichtes vom 31.7.1973 zum Grundlagenvertrag zwischen der BRD und der DDR, Aktenzeichen 2 BvF 1/73.

[35] On this subject see Antonio Cassese, Diritto internazionale, Bologna 2006

[36] See Hanns Jürgen Küsters, Helmut Kohl die CDU und die Wiederherstellung der deutschen Einheit, in: Michael Gehler/Maximilian Graf (eds.), Europa und die deutsche Einheit. Beobachtungen, Entscheidungen und Folgen, Göttingen 2017, pp. 27–42.

translation of this expression, but it is far more complicated to identify beyond doubt its field of application from a geographical, historical, political and cultural perspective.

From a geographical point of view, the term Mitteleuropa usually refers to a variable group of states and regions. Two conflicting schools of thought, the Anglo-Saxon school and the Continental one, propose two different criteria for its definition.

The Anglo-Saxon one identifies its main axis in an imaginary line from Trieste to Tallin. According to this definition, the expression Mitteleuropa groups together several political entities – for instance Poland, the former Czechoslovakia, Hungary and Austria – which lie between Germany and Russia, being respectively its Western and Eastern border. A large number of Anglo-Saxon scholars also argue that Germany, unlike Russia, should be considered a part of the Mitteleuropean space.

The second school of thought, the Continental one, argues that the notion *Mitteleuropa* includes in its broader sense not only those areas once controlled by the Habsburg Empire, but also Germany, Poland and Switzerland. Furthermore, some of its scholars even take into account the entire extension of the area under German cultural influence at the beginning of the 20th century, and that under the Habsburg influence until 1918, thus also including into Mitteleuropa the Baltic Republics and Croatia.[37]

In this specific meaning, the geographical criterion is supplemented by a linguistic approach: Mitteleuropa is in this case considered a synonym of the "deutschsprachiger Raum", the area in which the German language and culture disseminated up to Modern Age. If, instead of joining the geographical criterion with a linguistic approach, we rather supplement it with one based on differences of religions, it becomes possible to identify the Eastern border of Mitteleuropa in the ideal dividing line between the Catholic and the Orthodox areas.

Surely, this second vision is of great value in identifying in a clearer way the Eastern border of Mitteleuropa by stressing the German-Russian divide, but it has the inconvenience of offering no instruments to clearly define its Western and Southern borders.

In dealing with the search of a geographical definition of Mitteleuropa the publications of the *Institut für den Donauraum und Mitteleuropa* also retain a certain importance.[38] Accordingly, Mitteleuropa should be regarded as an expression to indicate the territories belonging to the Danube river basin. In this case, its borders are therefore Austria in the West, Ukraine in the East, Poland in the

---

[37] See Thomas Row (ed.), Does Central Europe still exist? (Favorita Papers of the Diplomatic Academy of Vienna), Vienna 2006.
[38] See http://www.idm.at/ (last consulted 14.6.2018).

North, and Serbia in the South. It follows that Italy and Germany are only to be partially included in this notion of Mitteleuropa.

In 1999, the *Meyers Großes Taschenlexikon* proposed a geographical definition, which, unlike the abovementioned hypotheses, included all former territories of the Austrian-Hungarian Empire, Germany in its entirety, Switzerland, even Romania, but it left out Italy.[39]

Finally, in its narrower sense, the expression Mitteleuropa encompasses the geographical area within the ideal line that joins together the cities of Munich, Dresden, Cracow, Budapest, Zagreb, Trieste, and it has its focal point in Vienna.

Each approach mentioned is, however, inadequate in providing a convincing definition of Mitteleuropa. The reason of such difficulties can be linked to the geographical elements of Mitteleuropa. These have traditionally been matched by a historical and political dimension which are associated with marked emotional reactions. This further complicates any attempt of providing a definition of the term.

Historically, it was not until the mid-19th century that the expression Mitteleuropa enjoyed growing attention. This was indeed the moment when, on the ashes of the dissolution of the "Holy Roman Empire of German Nation", different concepts and plans concerning "Mitteleuropa" were conceived, their main objective was to both fill the economic and political vacuum left by the end of the Empire, and to rise to the challenge issued by the British industrialisation.

The work of Friedrich Naumann published in 1915 is usually considered as the first mature attempt of using the notion for political purposes. At the end of the war, Naumann proposed to create a confederation stretching from the Baltic until the Balkans under the economic, cultural, and political hegemony of Germany. Still, in the middle of the previous century, the Austrian Foreign Minister had already used the notion of Mitteleuropa with political aims in launching a plan for the creation of a Mitteleuropean confederation, as opposed to the custom union controlled by Prussia. At the end of 1848, the Austrian Head of Government, Fürst von Schwarzenberg[40], had also proposed a Mitteleuropean plan.

In the 19th century, the idea of Mitteleuropa was, however, mainly related to the rivalry between Austria and Prussia for hegemony on the German area, whereas during the following century this notion was gradually absorbed by the German geopolitical school of thought. In the first half of the 20th century the expression Mitteleuropa also slowly acquired marked ideological connotations which mirrored the tribulations and the inherent difficulties of the Republic of Weimar, and the uncertainty which followed the dissolution of the Austrian-

---

[39] See Meyers Großes Taschenlexikon, Mannheim – Leipzig 1999, vol. 15, p. 30.
[40] See Michael Gehler, Deutschland als neue Zentralmacht Europas und seine Außenpolitik, in: Michael Gehler/Paul Luif/Elisabeth Vyslonzil (eds.), Die Dimension Mitteleuropa in der Europäischen Union (Historische Europa Studien), Hildesheim 2015, pp. 25–78.

Hungarian Empire. On the one hand, in those years a plethora of different proposals, which did not encompass Germany, were formulated in order to ensure
some sort of coordination among the recently created Eastern European states. In
1918, the Rumanian leader Ionescu and his Polish counterpart proposed the idea
of creating a confederation in Central-Eastern Europe, the Central-European
democratic Union, which would include all states between Germany and Russia.
Both this proposal, as well as the idea of the Hungarian professor Elemer Hantos
and the Slovak statesman Milan Hodža to create a confederation of the Danube,
turned out to be a failure. On the other hand, the coming to power of the Nazi
sealed the connection between the notion Mitteleuropa and the concept so cherished by the geopolitical school led by Karl Haushofer: *Lebensraum*.

The Second World War wiped out the very essence of the cultural and economic bonds, which had blossomed throughout the previous centuries under the
German hegemony. The Cold War and the application beyond the Curtain of the
strict system of Real Socialism further deepened the chasm. Besides, the instrumental use made by the Nazi-regime of the word Mitteleuropa suggested at first
to be extremely cautious in referring to it.

It was, therefore, not until the 1970s and above all the 1980s, that the notion
Mitteleuropa was fully rediscovered. Back then, the perspective dithered between
nostalgia for the past and the desire to create new political platforms. However,
at first its use was strictly limited to the cultural field to refer to the many cultural,
literary and musical expressions – as the works of Ludwig Wittgenstein, Robert
Musil, Arthur Schnitzler, Hugo von Hofmannsthal, Rainer Maria Rilke, and
Franz Kafka – which had blossomed in the Austrian-Hungarian melting pot at the
turn of the previous century.

By the mid-1970s, the work on Mitteleuropa of the Italian historian Claudio
Magris[41] started to have a certain success even beyond the national borders. Some
years later, another Italian historian native of Trieste, Arduino Agnelli, also published a successful book on the origins of the notion Mitteleuropa.[42] All this was
also made possible by a set of initiatives which were introduced to value and
enhance cooperation among Italian, German and Austrian scholars. Examples are
the establishment in Gorizia of an institute for Mitteleuropean cultural meetings,
and the *Italo-German Institute* in Trent.[43]

Additionally, in Italy this process of rediscovery found an extremely fertile
soil and a receptive audience as was confirmed by the 1985 conference hosted by
the University of Pavia.[44] In this conference, Mitteleuropa was presented and

---

[41] Claudio Magris, Il mito asburgico nella letteratura austriaca moderna, Torino 1963.
[42] Arduino Agnelli, La genesi dell'idea di Mitteleuropa, Milano 1971.
[43] Nowadays known as *Istituto storico italo-germanico/Italienisch-Deutsches Historisches Institut*.
[44] See the "atti del convegno" edited by Maria Enrica d'Agostini/Marino Freschi, Mitteleuropa
storiografia e scrittura, Pavia 1985.

discussed as a geographical and historical notion forged on the experience of the Austrian-Hungarian Empire, as an economic potential space for cooperation among the companies of the Danube river basin on both sides of the Curtain, and also as a box to house the potential unleashed by the human and cultural developments in the Eastern Bloc, especially after 1985.

The notion Mitteleuropa will here be used with the specific meaning proposed in Italy between the 1970s and the 1980s, as a synonym of the Danube river basin, whereas the notion Eastern Europe will be used to refer to the European countries under the Soviet hegemony. The broader expression Central Europe will be used to address the whole area lying between the Russian border and the German Western border.

3. Some Preliminary Remarks

On 15 June 1951, Konrad Adenauer, the German Chancellor, travelled to Rome on an official State visit. This represented an important step forward in strengthening the official ties between the Italian and the German governments.

Certainly, after the Second World War France had become a central element of the Italian Foreign policy affairs, as it was, for instance, a supporter of the opportunity to admit Italy in the Atlantic Alliance.[1]

Still, it is equally true that Italian politics and diplomacy, though with contradictory feelings, did not ignore the possibility to start a parallel process of closer cooperation with Bonn. Some among the reasons behind this stance can be identified in the wish of Rome to prevent an excessive subordination to Paris, and also in the hope that the fear of an axis between Rome and the newly created German Federal Republic would induce French policy makers to an attitude of greater flexibility.[2]

By contrast, the hypothesis that in the 1950s Rome feared a dangerous rapprochement between Paris and Bonn is far less convincing.[3] The periodization recommended by the well-known historian Georges-Henri Soutou[4] considers the years of the French Fourth Republic as a period free from concerns of this nature, a phase in which the Italian diplomacy looked favourably to a progressive overcoming of the traditional Franco-German rivalry.[5]

The choice of strengthening the ties with the newborn Western German State also gave Italy a number of benefits which confirm that this determination was not the sole result of the instrumental need of Rome to create more favourable conditions in order to improve its relationship with Paris.

---

[1] See Antonio Varsori, La classe politique italienne et le couple franco-allemand, in: *Revue d'Allemagne et des pays de langue allemande*, 2 (1997), volume 9, pp. 243–244.

[2] See Bruna Bagnato, L'Italia, la Francia e «una subalternità leggera» 1947–1958, in: Leopoldo Nuti/Massimiliano Guderzo/Bruna Bagnato (eds.), Nuove Questioni di Storia delle Relazioni Internazionali, Roma – Bari 2015, pp. 5–31, 16–17.

[3] See Tiziana Di Maio, Alcide De Gasperi e Konrad Adenauer. Tra superamento del passato e processo di integrazione europea (1945–1954), Torino 2004, pp. XV-XVI.

[4] See Georges-Henri Soutou, L'Italie et le couple franco-allemand, in: Antonio Varsori/Piero Craveri (eds.), L'Italia nella costruzione europea: Un Bilancio Storico, Milano 2009, pp. 43–66, 43.

[5] It would be incorrect to speak of a Franco-German couple in the absence of some specific conditions: the weakening of the French colonial projection, and the coming to power of Charles de Gaulle, together with the beginning of the Fifth Republic and the failure of the Fouchet Plan. In addition, before the beginning of the 1960s, Charles de Gaulle was not a great supporter of a closer cooperation with Bonn. Even if the foundations for a closer cooperation between Paris and Bonn were laid in the 1950s, it would not be correct either to speak of the existence of a Franco-German couple in the 1950s or to affirm that Rome feared its emergence. It was not until the 1960s and especially the 1970s that Italy showed a growing concern regarding the increasing cooperation between France and Germany.

Only if we understand these motivations and benefits, can we define an appropriate framework for the interpretation of the Italian-German relationship. For the correct interpretation of this framework, the methods and the channels by which this relationship took shape are equally interesting. They laid the foundations upon which the relations between these two countries were based until the last decade of the bipolar confrontation. These foundations, as well as the most relevant weaknesses of the Italo-German couple, remained substantially unchanged until the 1980s. It is, therefore, necessary to provide a brief analysis of some turning-points in the evolution of the Italian-German relationship in the 1950s.

This chapter will first address the reactions of the Italian press to the state visit of Adenauer, which, after the War, can be considered the moment of closest rapprochement between the two countries. Then, it will focus on the political and diplomatic issues that gradually paved the way for this visit.

3.1 The *deutsche Frage* taking shape

The most prominent Italian newspapers[6] paid significant attention to the state visit of Adenauer and to the personality of the German leader.

Particular enthusiasm was expressed in the articles written by journalists of the conservative newspaper *Corriere della Sera*.[7] Giorgio Sansa[8], the Italian correspondent in Germany, presented the meeting with an article emblematically entitled "Fedele all'Occidente"[9] (Faithful to the West). He wrote that the statesman visiting Rome could be considered, after just two years in office, as one of the most eminent and respected personalities of international politics.

In the previous years, the Turin newspaper *La Stampa* had usually had a critical stance towards its German neighbour. Still, in 1951, it also expressed positive

---

[6] The conservative *Corriere della Sera*, the liberal *La Stampa* and the *Repubblica*. In this chapter, as well as in the following chapters, not all articles, only a selection of the most relevant among them in the field of politics, economy and culture published on Germany in these newspapers, will be discussed. These articles were collected thanks to the support of both the on-line archives of the abovementioned newspapers and the "Presseabteilung" of the Konrad Adenauer Foundation in Bonn/Sankt Augustin.

[7] In the weeks before and after the state visit of Konrad Adenauer, the Turin newspaper *La Stampa* published more articles on Germany than the *Corriere della Sera*. Still, the latter dedicated a larger proportion of its articles on Germany to Adenauer. One third of the articles on Germany published by *La Stampa* concerned Adenauer, whereas half of the articles published in its Milan opponent referred to the Chancellor.

[8] Unlike the majority of the then Italian journalists, Giorgio Sansa had in-depth knowledge of Germany. From the mid-1920s up to the beginning of the following decade, he had worked in Vienna for the Italian Newspaper *Resto del Carlino*. In the 1930s, he had worked in Berlin and Paris for the Turin newspaper *La Stampa*.

[9] Giorgio Sansa, Fedele all'Occidente, *Corriere della Sera* (herafter, *CdS*), 14.6.1951, p. 1.

judgments, though less enthusiastic, on the results of the official visit of Konrad Adenauer. Its journalist Italo Zingarelli[10] had lavished words of praise on the personality of the German Chancellor, on his role on the international scene, and on his friendship with his Italian counterpart, Alcide De Gasperi.

In the weeks before and after this state visit, the articles published in the Italian press, both in the conservative newspapers and in the liberal ones, were dominated by two key terms in association with Germany: European loyalty and rootedness in the common Christian (Catholic) tradition. The contrast with the comments published two years before, in 1949, in which "nationalism" was still the most recurrent term in association with Germany, was very sharp.

Adenauer appeared to the Italian press, and in particular to the conservative media, as reassuring as the dimensions of Western Germany.[11] In the description provided by the Milan newspaper *Corriere della Sera*, Western Germany was presented as an "Enlarged Rheinland". Its Catholic faith was as strong and rooted as its desire to achieve a useful and necessary reconciliation with the French partner. By 1951, unlike the *Corriere della Sera*, *La Stampa* had not given up the use of the term nationalism when it referred to Germany. Still, its connotations assumed positive shades, insofar as they were related to the political course of the German Chancellor.[12]

These brief comments must not lead to the conclusion that the beginning of the Fifties marked a radical change in the Italian vision of Germany, or that the nationalistic and military associations related to Germany had been definitively overcome. On the contrary, the Italian press showed a tendency to a provisional identification between the new Germany and its Chancellor.

This tendency had two interesting implications for the developments, which were to follow. On the one side, a "Rheinisch" vision of Germany found a certain echo in the then Italian press. The new dimensions of the German ally, reduced almost entirely to its South-Western regions, perceived as Catholic and Latin, were reassuring, especially when considered in the context of an increasing

---

[10] Italo Zingarelli, Ritratto di Adenauer, *La Stampa*, 14.6.1951, pp. 1, 3.

[11] "Egli è figlio della parte 'romana' della Germania. E nato e cresciuto sulla riva sinistra del Reno, dove presero stanza duemila anni fa i legionari, portandovi la viticoltura e dove la chiesa cattolica fu sempre forte". (He is a son of the 'Roman' part of Germany. He was born and grew up on the left bank of the Rhine, where two thousand years ago the Roman legionnaires arrived, and they brought wine-growing with them. The Catholic Church has always had a strong influence on the area), Fedele all'Occidente, *CdS*, 14.6.1951, p. 1.

[12] See Italo Zingarelli, Ritratto di Adenauer, *La Stampa*, 14.6.1951, p. 1.

European integration.[13] On the other side, an allied country was essentially de-scribed through the lens of its first citizen.

At the beginning of the Fifties, the approach of the Italian press could appar-ently hint at a widespread "Germanophilia". This was even more evident when compared with the negative judgments that still dominated the articles published by the French newspapers. A closer study allows, however, to show how the roots of this "German fever"[14] were unfulfilled and fragile. The positive remarks about the Chancellor were rarely extended to the German people in its entirety: "Gli alleati vedono Adenauer procedere a notevole distanza dal resto del popolo tede-sco [...] spesso viene da dubitare della sincerità dei tedeschi, ma nessuno dubita di Adenauer".[15]

This human component also had a significant role at a political level, as it embodied one of the three pillars on which the Italian-German couple was based.

In his memoirs, the German Chancellor recalls that he shared a sincere friend-ship with the Italian statesman, Alcide De Gasperi. This was based on the aware-ness that both of them had a historic duty to fulfil which the common Christian heritage had bestowed on the European people.[16] Even if this friendship between the Italian and the German Christian-Democrat politicians was truly deep, it is not enough to justify the choice of Rome as the destination of the first official visit of the German leader, especially if it is taken out of its political context.

The main biographer of Adenauer, Hans-Peter Schwarz, provides a simple answer to this problem: in 1951, Italy was the only European country in which Adenauer would be welcomed unreservedly.[17] Still, this statement by Hans-Peter Schwarz takes only partially into account the fact that, despite a certain caution imposed by the recent past, since 1947, the Italian political class had shown a growing penchant for the Bundesrepublik as a possible interlocutor.

Throughout the last few years, the results of several in-depth studies have revealed the existence of a complex path that led to a gradual rapprochement and to a closer cooperation between Bonn and Rome, which culminated in the state

---

[13] See, for example, Giuseppe Piazza, L'Europeo Adenauer, *Giornale d'Italia*, 15.6.1951, Luciano Morante, Dichiarazioni di Adenauer in partenza per Roma, *La Stampa*, 13.6.1951, p. 5. See also Tito Sansa, Italia e Germania per l'Unità europea, *CdS*, 17.6.1951, p. 1.

[14] This term "fièvre germanophile" was used by Pierre Guillen in his essay, *L'Italie et le problème allemand 1945–1995*, to depict the Italian climate at the beginning of the 1950s.

[15] "The allies see Adenauer proceed at a considerable distance from the rest of the German people [...] one can often be tempted to doubt the sincerity of the Germans, but no one doubts Adenauer". See Giorgio Sansa, Adenauer arriverà oggi a Roma, *CdS*, 14.6.1951, p. 1. See also Giorgio Sansa, Nel Parlamento di Bonn si danno feste da ballo, in which the journalist affirmed that Adenauer was a democrat who led a country that could not comprehend what democracy actually was.

[16] Konrad Adenauer, Erinnerungen 1955–1959 (vol. III), Stuttgart 1967, p. 259.

[17] Hans-Peter Schwarz, Konrad Adenauer der Aufstieg 1876–1952 (vol. I), Stuttgart 1986, p. 866.

visit of the German Chancellor in 1951, and in that of the Italian Prime Minister to Bonn during the following year.[18]According to the Italian expert, Gian Enrico Rusconi, the Note submitted on 13 March 1947 to the four occupying powers may be considered as the first sign of a genuine Italian interest in the fate of Germany.[19] In this note, Rome exposed for the first time its own point of view on the question of Germany, which was described as „vital for the future of Europe". Based on its state of co-belligerence which the Allies had reluctantly recognized, Italy was trying to influence the negotiating process regarding a solution of the German issue.[20] The note seemed to fall into the strategy of the then Foreign Minister, Count Carlo Sforza, and of the Italian Prime Minister, Alcide De Gasperi. Both of them wished for a swift reintegration of Germany in the international and European community.[21]

Still, this strategy was subjected to serious criticism and was far from having consensus both in the government[22] and among Italian diplomats. For instance, the then Italian Ambassador to Paris, Pietro Quaroni, did share the need to fully reintegrate Western Germany into the community of free nations, in order to avoid the emergence of a new explosion of violence. He also considered this path as a necessary contribution to the rebirth of the Continent. He was nonetheless extremely skeptic about the real ability of his government to influence the ongoing negotiations. He, therefore, suggested to refrain from any attempt in this direction.[23]

---

[18] See, in particular, Tiziana di Maio, Alcide De Gasperi e Konrad Adenauer. Tra superamento del passato e processo di integrazione europea (1945–1954), Torino 2004. See also Maddalena Guiotto/Johannes Lill, Italia-Germania Deutschland-Italien 1948–1958 Riavvicinamenti Wiederannäherungen, Firenze 1997. See as well Piero Craveri, Europeismo e federalismo nel pensiero e nell'azione di Alcide de Gasperi, and Federico Scarano, Antonio Segni, Konrad Adenauer e l'integrazione europea, in: Piero Craveri/Antonio Varsori (eds.), L'Italia nella costruzione europea. Un bilancio storico (1957–2007), Milano 2009, pp. 335–348, 369–394.

[19] See Gian Enrico Rusconi, Germania Italia Europa: Dallo Stato di Potenza alla Potenza Civile, Torino 2003, pp. 224–225.

[20] See Livio Zeno, Il Conte Sforza ritratto di un grande diplomatico, Milano, Monnet new edition printed in 2000.

[21] See Carlo Sforza, Cinque anni a Palazzo Chigi. La politica estera italiana dal 1947 al 1951, Firenze 1952.

[22] Concerning the stance of Foreign Minister Carlo Sforza, opinions differ. Some scholars suggest that he fully shared the desire of Alcide De Gasperi to cooperate more closely with the Bundesrepublik. On the contrary, other scholars, for instance Alain Quagliarino, have stressed the "latin component" of his approach to foreign politics. Alain Quagliarino has also signalled his preference for the "latin sister" (France) and his reservations about the "barbarians" from the North. See Alain Quagliarino, La question allemande dans les relations franco-italiennes de 1951 à 1954, in: *Mélange de l'Ecole française de Rome. Italie et Méditerranée* 2 (1992), volume 104, p. 880.

[23] See Charis Pöthig, Italien und die DDR, Frankfurt am Main 2000, p. 50.

The Italian representative in London was also in favour of a reintegration of Germany in the community of states, but he was also more optimistic about the capacity of his country to have an influence on the ongoing negotiations.[24] By contrast, the Italian General-Consul in Hamburg, Guido Relli, remarked that the division which was taking shape on the German soil, though painful, would be beneficial for the West in its entirety.[25] In Moscow, Manlio Brosio still considered, in 1947, Germany as a threat to everyone, including Italy, and he, therefore, suggested the application of strict international control. In light of such different opinions and of the strong left-wing opposition to a rapprochement, the increasingly close relationship between Western Germany and Italy took the shape of frequent contacts between the Italian and the German Christian-Democratic parties.[26]

In June 1949, the Italian Foreign Minister commented to the then secretary of the DC, Paolo Emilio Taviani, his satisfaction with the network of exchanges that had been established during the previous two years between the Italian DC and the German CDU. This had been possible both in the context of the *Nouvelles Equipes Internationales*[27], and thanks to the mediation of Austrian and Bavarian politicians. He also recommended to further strengthen cross-border relations between parties belonging to the same "family".

Surely, the contacts with the CDU – especially with politicians of the Rhineland – which mainly blossomed within European and international programmes of cooperation, were an important contribution to the rapprochement between Rome and Bonn. Still, the role played by the Bavarian Christian-Democracy[28] was even more significant, especially in the early stages of this process. The ties of the latter with the Italian Christian-Democracy were favoured by their geographical proximity, by their many cultural affinities, and also by their common economic interests.

In addition, starting from 1949, the contribution of the Italian General-Consul in Munich cannot either be overlooked. In his capacity of Consul, Baron

---

[24] See Christian Vordemann, Deutschland-Italien 1949–1961: Die diplomatischen Beziehungen (in Geschichte und Gegenwart volume III), Frankfurt am Main 1994.

[25] See Charis Pöthig, Italien und die DDR, p. 51.

[26] See Tiziana Di Maio, Alcide De Gasperi und Konrad Adenauer. Zwischen Überwindung der Vergangenheit und europäischem Integrationsprojekt 1945–1954 (Geschichte und Gegenwart 34), Frankfurt am Main 2014.

[27] See Michael Gehler, Adenauer's idea on Europe and on Western European Integration Policy within the Context of Private and Political Networks, in: Jean Dominique Durand (ed.), Christian Democrat Internationalism. Its action in Europe and worldwide from post World War II until the 1990 (volume II The developments [1945–1979] the role of parties, movements, people), Frankfurt am Main 2013, pp. 201–241.

[28] Hereafter, also CSU.

Francesco Malfatti, back then a young Italian diplomat, often acted as a "bridge" between the CSU and the Christian Democratic groups close to the Catholic Action. From 1947 to 1949, frequent Party Congresses, religious pilgrimages, visits to the Vatican, as well as fairs and cultural exhibitions offered plenty of opportunities to reinforce political relations, and to pave the way for a rapprochement between Rome and Bonn. Hans Ehard, Hanns Seidel, Josef Müller and Heinz Heggenreiner were some among the most important interlocutors of the DC.[29] In September 1949, Hanns Seidel[30], the Bavarian Minister of Economy, attended the fair of Bolzano. During his Italian journey, he had talks in Trento with the Italian Prime Minister and in Rome with the then Minister of Finance, Ivan Matteo Lombardo.

The interest of the Bavarian politician in improving relations with Rome was not only expressed by his many trips to Italy, which followed the journey of the year 1949, but also by his support to the appointment of Heinz Heggenreiner – a member of the CSU with good contacts in the Italian capital – as advisor of the German Consul to Rome, Clemens von Brentano.[31]

In light of these new conditions and ambitions, the first of the pillars on which the Italian-German couple would be henceforth based gradually took shape between 1947 and 1949: the *party pillar*. This definition stresses the significant role that the political parties, or to be more correct the Christian Democrats, had in laying the foundations for future relations. The party pillar was based on the assumption that Europe was Italy's primary need and that Germany was vital to Europe, in order to ensure the political and economic revival of the Continent.

Did the party pillar bring an added value to the Italo-German couple or did it rather represent its original sin? Several different answers are possible in light of the records available.

On the one hand, the party pillar did bring an added value, insofar as it allowed a deepening of the relationship in a flexible context and in the absence of

---

[29] See Thomas Schlemmer, Aufbruch, Krise und Erneuerung. Die Christlich-Soziale Union 1945 bis 1955, Oldenburg 1998. See also Hanns Seidel Stiftung (ed.), Josef Müller: Der erste Vorsitzende der CSU, München 1988.

[30] Hanns Seidel, member of the CSU since 1945, was the Bavarian Minister of Economy from 1947 to 1954 and from then until 1960 he was the president of the Land Bavaria. See, for example, Hans Ferdinand Groß, Hanns Seidel 1901 bis 1961. Eine politische Biographie, München 1992; Alfred Bayer/Manfred Baumgärtel (eds.), Weltanschauung und politisches Handeln. Hanns Seidel zum 100. Geburtstag (Sonderausgabe der Politischen Studien), Grünwald 2001. See also Stephan Deutinger, Hanns Seidel (1901–1961), in: *Zeitgeschichte in Lebensbildern* 11, Münster 2004, pp. 160–174.

[31] See Maddalena Guiotto, La tradizione europeista dei partiti cristiano-democratici: CDU/CSU e DC negli anni Cinquanta, in: Gian Enrico Rusconi/Hans Woller (eds.), Italia e Germania 1945–2000, Bologna 2005, pp. 153–178, 164.

the constraints that official visits impose. The Christian Democrats acted as a "drive belt", a cog in the transmission of the essential issues which were discussed at party level, and then in the government. This pillar also allowed to draw on a rich set of religious and regional resources.

The issue of the role that the Vatican played in the process of gradual rapprochement between the two countries would certainly deserve closer attention; here, it is however particularly important to stress that many members of the CSU had maintained close contacts with the Vatican since the years preceding the Second World War. Josef Müller, one of the main partners of Alcide De Gasperi, had become acquainted with Eugenio Pacelli[32] while the latter was Apostolic Nuncio in Munich. They had remained in close contacts after the War. CSU politicians often visited the Vatican in those years, especially on the occasion of the celebration of the Holy Year 1950. The year 1950 offered indeed a variety of opportunities for consultations between Bavarian and Italian deputies.

Still, these celebrations were not merely an opportunity for contacts with leading figures of the Bavarian Christian-democracy. We must also bear in mind that during these celebrations Heinrich von Brentano, Chairman of the CDU fraction in the German Parliament, met in the month of April monsignor Tardini and Monsignor Montini and, soon after, also Foreign Minister Carlo Sforza from the Italian Liberal Party. Last, but not least, up until the mid-1950s, the Bavarian regional government toyed with the idea of opening a diplomatic delegation to the Holy See. This ambition was based on a tradition that until 1918 had allowed Bavaria to maintain its representations abroad, despite the incorporation into the Reich in 1870.[33]

Regional resources should not be overlooked either. Ever since the end of the 1940s, the government and the Italian diplomacy had sensed that the Bundesrepublik Fundamental Law would endow the German *Länder* with broad competences and that they would, therefore, constitute the levers of the future economic and cultural choices. In light of these considerations, the Land Bavaria always had a significant mediating role between the "German world" and Italy, at first

---

[32] Eugenio Pacelli was elected Pope under the name of Pio XII. Many German priests were his closest advisors, for instance Robert Leiber and Ludwig Kaas. The latter had negotiated with Chancellor von Papen the Concordat between the Weimar Republic and the Catholic Church. Concerning Eugenio Pacelli and his vision of the German issue, see, in particular, Herbert Schambeck, Beiträge zum Leben und Werk anläßlich seines 20. Todestages, München 1979; Jean-Marie Mayeur, Pio XII e i movimenti cattolici in Europa, Bari – Roma 1984.

[33] See the note sent by the Auswärtiges Amt to its Embassy at the Vatican, 22.1.1951, PA AA, B 11, vol. ll9, quoted in Maddalena Guiotto, La tradizione europeista dei partiti cristiano-democratici, p. 165.

through political and religious channels and, since the early Seventies, also in the context of regional initiatives launched by Italy in the Mitteleuropean area.[34]

On the other hand, this party pillar also was a critical element of fragility, or, to use once again a religious metaphor, an original sin of the Italian-German couple. In 1951, the issues discussed at the party level could be quickly and easily conveyed to the Italian government. This was mainly due to favourable political conditions. In the following years, there were, however, signs of a growing weakening of the government led by Alcide De Gasperi. This weakening had pernicious consequences on a relationship whose institutionalized structures for coordination and cooperation either did not exist or were still at an embryonic stage.[35]

By the end of the 1940s, bilateral relations between Italy and the Bundesrepublik were also based on an economic and cultural pillar which introduced further elements of flexibility and informality. In the 1947 note submitted to the occupying powers, Italy had already expressed his fervent wish that Germany could be re-integrated in the community of nations as soon as possible, in order to have the opportunity to do business with it. Unlike the ups and downs which the political ties between Italy and Germany went through after 1949, a close economic and cultural interconnection can be considered a long term factor. A great level of complementarity between the industries of the two countries also helps to understand the reasons why the Bundesrepublik, despite the military defeat of Germany and the loss of the Eastern territories, quickly became one of the main trading partners of Rome.[36] By the end of 1949, the Bundesrepublik had achieved and even exceeded the level of pre-war German production, and unemployment had been brought down to 11 %. With regards to exports, the Bundesrepublik was, after the United States, the largest trading partner of Italy.[37] As regards imports as well, Bonn was the second largest partner of Italy.[38]

---

[34] Communauté de Travail Alpe Adria, télégramme Rome n. 175, 21.2.1990. Archive du Ministère des affaires étrangères (hereafter AMAE), inva1935, Direction Europe, Série Autriche, carton 6176, sous-série 13, dossier 7, période 1986–1990.

[35] The German Ambassador to Rome, Klemens Von Brentano, could count on the sole support of the former Consul of the Third Reich to Florence and on two advisors. When Adenauer visited Rome, Bonn had opened only one consulate in Italy, in Milan. The possibility to open a second consulate, in the city of Palermo, was still an object of discussion. No German cultural association existed in Italy, with the only exception of Rome. Only one German lector was employed in Italy, in the University of Venice.

[36] In 1951, according to ISTAT data, the Bundesrepublik was the second largest trading partner of Italy. See ISTAT, Statistiche del Commercio con l'Estero (Foreign Trade Statistics), Series II, n. 12.

[37] See Luciano Tosi, Politica ed Economia nelle Relazioni Internazionali dell'Italia del Secondo Dopoguerra, Roma 2002.

[38] See Maximiliane Rieder, Deutsch-Italienische Wirtschaftsbeziehungen. Kontinuitäten und Brüche 1936–1957, Frankfurt am Main 2003.

Even if at the beginning of the 1950s bilateral-exchanges were enjoying strong economic growth, the number of the German chambers of commerce did not increase significantly. The first *Anwerbevertrag* was not signed until 20 December 1955.[39] In the early stages of the Italian-German rapprochement, both governments favoured, in fact, the contribution of private and semi-private ventures.

Cultural exchanges also blossomed within a complex network of private and semi-private initiatives. Even if, by the end of the 1940s, cultural relations still lacked efficient institutionalized structures of coordination, they could rely on a number of elements of continuity in cultural transference that the war years had only partially affected. The number of German books published in Italy was not comparable with pre-War figures, and yet, the result was not negligible.[40] The participation of German experts, on an individual basis, in Italian conferences was also remarkable, as well as the number of German journalists who worked in Rome. Twelve German correspondents had been sent to Rome, whereas only three French journalists worked in the Italian capital city.

---

[39] The making of the Italian-German relationship must be also considered in light of the Italian necessity to favour the migration of part of its workforce towards other European countries. In the short term, this migration could offer major advantages. It would reduce unemployement at home – together with its social consequences – and it would improve the national balance of payments. In 1946/1947, Italy had signed agreements for "workforce exchange" with Switzerland, France, Belgium and the United Kingdom. These agreements had only partially addressed the problem. This was due to the economic difficulties these countries were going through, and to their reluctance to accept foreign workers for long periods of time. The Bundesrepublik appeared as the ideal partner to ease the problem of unemployment in Italy. Besides, the migration of part of the Italian workforce towards Germany would also compensate for the significant decline of Italian exports towards Germany by the end of 1952. Negotiations proved, however, lengthy. Bonn wanted to be sure to be capable of absorbing the supply of labour arriving from the "Eastern territories" before signing an agreement with Italy. In addition, Bonn was also concerned with the social implications of this transfer of workforce. Italian workers were, at first, addressed as *Gastarbeiter* (literally, guest workers). This stresses that, at first, the stay of Italian workers was considered to be of a temporary nature. See Federico Romero, Emigrazione e Integrazione 1945–1973, Roma – Bari 1991. See also Bettina Severin-Barboutie, Die Fremdwahrnehmung von Italienern und Türken in der Bundesrepublik, in: Oliver Janz/Roberto Sala (eds.), Dolce Vita? Das Bild der italienischen Migranten in Deutschland, Frankfurt am Main 2011, pp. 233–245. See as well Roberto Sala, Die Migrationspolitische Bedeutung der italienischen Arbeitswanderung in die Bundesrepublik, in: Jochen Oltmer/Axel Kreienbrink/Carlos Sanz Díaz (eds.), Das Gastarbeitersystem: Arbeitsmigration und ihre Folgen in der Bundesrepublik Deutschland und Westeuropa, in: *Schriftenreihe der Vierteljahrshefte für Zeitgeschichte Band* 104, Institut für Zeitgeschichte, München – Berlin 2012, pp. 71–88. See also ISTAT data http://www.emigrati.it/Emigrazione/DatiStatItalMondo.asp (last consulted 19.7.2016).

[40] See, in particular, Hans-Georg Schmidt-Bergmann, Zwischen Kontinuität und Rekonstruktion. Kulturtransfer zwischen Deutschland und Italien nach 1945 (Reihe der Villa Vigoni), Tübingen 1998.

Both partners shared the need to embed cultural and economic exchanges in a broader developing planning. Still, it was not until the mid-1950s that the framework of cultural cooperation assumed a more defined shape.[41] Both partners shared, in fact, the wish to avoid giving the impression that a special axis was taking shape between Rome and Bonn. At first, it was, therefore, extremely useful to rely on an intricate network of bottom-up and top-down commercial and cultural initiatives. These are the reasons why it is so difficult to draw a clear distinction between bottom-up initiatives, top-down initiatives and bottom-up initiatives which were indirectly supported by the two governments.

The *Goethe-Institut* represents a good example of the main features and contradictions within the Italian-German cultural network.[42] The Goethe Institutes were a direct offshoot of the central government. Still, unlike their counterparts in other Western European countries, they benefited of a larger organizational and decision-making autonomy. Culture could be a useful asset to promote the image of the Federal Republic abroad. The rich philosophical and literary heritage of Germany still enjoyed high standing in many cultural circles in Italy. Since their establishment, the Goethe Institutes acted as cultural circles *stricto senso*, political issues and recent controversial historical developments were usually excluded from their cultural programme. In Bonn's intentions, the cultural vitality of the new German State would gradually help to improve the image of Germany.

Still, in the 1950s, the achievement of this aim was significantly hindered by the persistence in large sectors of the Italian population of deep-rooted negative associations. Besides, left-wing intellectuals did not oppose the philosophical and literary heritage of Germany, but rather the desire to use it to enhance the profile and the capacity of attraction of the Bundesrepublik.

For decades, the vision of Germany was held hostage to a strong political polarisation. Conservative parties supported the image of the Bundesrepublik as a Catholic Republic, a "Latin" country, a sort of enlarged "Rhineland/Bavaria". Left-wing parties opposed it with the image of the DDR as a Socialist, Democratic and proletarian Republic.[43] Both images were presented as the antithesis of the Prussian military legacy, the first one in light of its different geographic dimension, the latter thanks to the positive influence of the Marxist/Leninist ideology. In both cases, an external element ensured the reliability of the new state: The European integration process in the West, and Moscow's role as a tutelary deity in the East.

---

[41] The first cultural agreement between Italy and Germany was signed on 8 February 1956 by the Italian Minister Martino and the German Minister von Brentano. It was not until December 1957 that it entered into force.

[42] See *Goethe-Institut* Inter Nationes, Murnau, Manila, Minsk. 50. Jahre Goethe Institut, München 2001.

[43] See Charis Pöthig, Italien und die DDR, p. 59.

The same tools were used to deepen the ties between Italy and the chosen German state: a party pillar together with an economic/cultural one. Ever since the 1950s, the Goethe Institutes were, in fact, in competition with the activities promoted by the Thomas Mann Centre. Economic exchanges with the Bundesrepublik were in competition with the creation of *de facto* relations with the DDR thanks to the support of the *Handelskammern*, which worked closely with the DIA[44] compensation system. Labour unions were the political counterpart of the contacts through the Vatican. The most sensitive issues regarding the perception of Germany were never raised in the debate, at least until the end of the Seventies.

In the 1950s, Italy seemed to lack personalities capable of fully understanding their German interlocutors. Alcide De Gasperi was a significant exception, as he not only had an excellent command of German, but he was also capable of greater sensitivity and understanding towards the "German speaking area". Firstly, he had spent his early years in the Austro-Hungarian Empire, where he had completed his studies first, and then had also participated actively in political life. In addition to the knowledge of the German language, there are further aspects of the biographical profile of De Gasperi which deserve close attention.[45]

On the one hand, the Habsburg Empire represented in the vision of De Gasperi a magnet, a microcosm which had allowed the cohabitation of peoples of different nationalities.[46]

On the other hand, it is equally important to stress that the experience of De Gasperi with the German-speaking world concerned one specific geographical area: the Austro-Bavarian one, where the Catholic Church and the conservative parties traditionally had a strong influence.[47] This set of elements made of De

---

[44] Deutscher Innen- und Aussenhandel.

[45] As for the life of De Gasperi, see the three volumes edited by Alfredo Canavero/Paolo Pombeni/Giovanni Battista Re/Giorgio Vecchio in 2009 on behalf of the De Gasperi Foundation. See also Maddalena Guiotto, Alcide De Gasperi a Vienna, Innsbruck e durante la guerra, 1902–1918, in: Maddalena Guiotto (ed.), A. De Gasperi. Scritti e discorsi politici, vol. I, Alcide De Gasperi nel Trentino asburgico (tomo 2), Bologna 2006, pp. 1831–2051; Franz Adlgasser, Die Mitglieder der österreichischen Zentralparlamente 1848–1918. Konstituierender Reichstag 1848–1918. Reichsrat 1861–1918. Ein biographisches Lexikon (Reihe Studien zur Geschichte der österreichisch-ungarischen Monarchie 33), Wien 2014; Adolf Kohler, Un uomo spinto dalle sue convinzioni: Alcide De Gasperi, in: Werner Weidenfeld/Adolf Kohler/Dieter Dettke (eds.), Un impegno per l'Europa: Konrad Adenauer, Alcide De Gasperi, Robert Schuman, Roma 1981, pp. 39- 63.

[46] In spite of this feeling of admiration, De Gasperi was not unaware of the weaknesses which had affected the Austrian-Hungarian empire. See Michael Gehler, Alcide De Gasperi und die Südtirolfrage im Lichte der österreichisch-italienischen Beziehungen 1945–1954, in: Klaus Brandstätter/Julia Hörmann (eds.), Tirol-Österreich-Italien. Festschrift für Josef Riedmann zum 65. Geburtstag, Innsbruck 2005, pp. 249–267, 253.

[47] In the 1950s, Bavaria was often presented as the very image of a Catholic country, a quiet and industrious state, so different from the Prussian "Pickelhaube" (spiked helmets). This association was also widespread beyond the Italian borders. In an interview with Michèle Weinachter, the

Gasperi an exception, not only within the then Italian political landscape, but, partially, also within his own party.

> «De Gasperi aveva un vantaggio che aveva appartenuto in gioventù prima alla Dieta di Innsbruck, poi al Parlamento plurinazionale di Vienna. Quindi aveva una capacità a misurarsi con questi problemi e anche a capire, cosa che qui molti non avevano perché non avevamo avuto nessuna esperienza. Quindi all'inizio [...] c'era un certo disinteresse, una certa disattenzione verso questi problemi».[48]

The third and last pillar of the Italian-German couple took shape in the early Fifties in the context of this close friendship, and of the cooperation which arose from it. It will be referred to as *personal pillar* or by the German term *Männerfreundschaft*. Is it possible to consider personal relations between leading political figures as a pillar which supported the relationship between Italy and Germany?

Undoubtedly, personal contacts between Italian and German leaders are less known and studied than those which have linked French and German politicians, starting with the relationship between Charles de Gaulle and Konrad Adenauer and continuing with the one between Helmut Schmidt and Valéry Giscard d'Estaing, and finally that between Helmut Kohl and François Mitterrand.

Nevertheless, the contacts between Italian and German leaders had a very significant role and their importance, even in the late 1970s, was enhanced by the lack of a solid legal basis that could guarantee a constant dialogue not only between Heads of State and Government and Foreign ministers, but also between technical ministers, senior civil servants and chief executives of economic agencies. In this context, the relationship between political parties, and the personal friendship between leaders played a significant role both in accelerating the cooperation between the two countries as in delaying it.

After 1952, the relationship between De Gasperi and Adenauer showed how the absence of solid structures prevented the two countries from capitalizing on

---

cousin of President Valéry Giscard d'Estaing affirmed: "[...] Un bout de la Bavière. L'Allemagne catholique tranquille, paisible et très différente de l'Allemagne des casques à pointe [...]". See Michèle Weinachter, Valéry Giscard d'Estaing et l'Allemagne. Le double rêve inachevé, Paris 2004, p. 27.

[48] "De Gasperi had an advantage. In his youth, he had been member of the Diet of Innsbruck first, and then member of the Plurinational Parliament in Vienna. Therefore, he had the ability to respond to these challenges and also to understand them. Many of us did not have this ability, because we had no experience with these things. In the beginning [...] there was a certain lack of interest, a certain alienation from these problems". See the interview Giulio Andreotti gave to Cinzia Rognoni Vercelli in Rome (11.12.1998), in: Voices on Europe, Oral History Collections, Historical Archives of the European Union (http://www.eui/HAEU/OralHistory/, last accessed 1.2.2016).

the results that the personal and the party pillars had allowed to reach, and to limit losses when one or both of these pillars were weakened or did not work properly.

At an economic level, by the end of 1952, growing problems came to the surface. Business relations between the two countries had been established so that the Italian monthly deficit would not exceed the 2.5 million dollars. In November 1952, the Italian deficit amounted to more than $ 40 million.[49] Italy, which did not intend to increase its creditor position in the EPU[50], thus harboured a specific interest to engage in commercial negotiations with Bonn, so that the deficit of the Italian balance of payments could be reabsorbed. Such interest, together with the German resistance to accept an increase of the Italian exports in sectors such as fruit, vegetables and wine, resulted in long and difficult negotiations, all in an atmosphere of growing misunderstandings.

Tensions concerned not only the economic field, but also the weakening of the Italian government and of the political clout of De Gasperi himself. This also favoured the re-emergence in the Italian press of anti-German feelings. The pardon granted to the former German Marshall Kesselring[51], as well as the tensions linked to the question of Trieste and especially to the South Tyrolean issue[52] added more fuel to the fire. In the mid-1950s and in the 1960s, the latter issue took dimensions that went beyond the boundaries of a national problem or of an Italian-Austrian bilateral disagreement. The German press took a clear stance in favour of the South Tyrol separatist movements. In September 1953, the president of the German Parliament, Hermann Ehlers, affirmed that Bolzano should still be called Bozen and that the South Tyrolean people were still part of the "Germanies". In an interview with the Roman newspaper *Il Messaggero* Adenauer did remark that the South Tyrolean issue was essentially an Italian internal problem, but his statements could only partially reduce the chasm that was building up.

The death of Alcide De Gasperi on 19 August 1954 symbolically embodied the end of the first season of the Italian-German relationship. What did this personal pillar leave in the Italian vision of the German issue?

Konrad Adenauer was not the first German politician with which De Gasperi had cooperated. Over the years, De Gasperi had already enjoyed a fruitful exchange of ideas with Josef Müller based on their common determination to support the enhancement of trade and of economic relations between their countries

---

[49] See Alain Quagliarino, La question allemande dans les relations franco-italiennes de 1951 à 1954, in: *Mélange de l'Ecole française de Rome. Italie et Méditerranée* 2 (1992), vol. 104, pp. 889–890.
[50] European Payments Union.
[51] The newspapers the *Popolo* and the *Quotidiano* (newspaper linked to the Catholic Action) were the only ones which did not write about such problems.
[52] See, in particular, Luciano Monzali, Giulio Andreotti e le relazioni italo-austriache. See also Michael Gehler, Alcide De Gasperi und die Südtirolfrage, p. 255.

in a continent which was perceived as a moral force.[53] Still, it was only with Konrad Adenauer that the Italian Prime Minister built up a strong relationship based on a common vision of Germany and of its role within Europe.[54]

In an effort to reconstruct the evolution of the relations between De Gasperi and Müller, Maddalena Guiotto has recalled how important the necessity to maintain the German national unity was for the Bavarian politician. Müller was persuaded that Germany was the Eastern front of the Western world, and that the German people had to stay together, even if that meant to embrace a neutralist vision or to come to terms with Moscow.[55]

On the contrary, De Gasperi and Adenauer fully shared a vision of Europe based on three principles: Atlantism and European integration, anticomunism and a sharp refusal of neutralist positions.[56] This produced a vision of Germany and of Europe which represented for nearly forty years a milestone of Italian political life and of its approach to the German issue.[57] What both statesmen shared was their unshakeable determination to work together for the creation of a *Carolingian* united Europe. The term Carolingian does not refer to a European project based on the Franco-German couple, because times were not ripe enough for that. It rather refers to the vision of a Continent whose ideal core lied along the banks of the Rhine River, and that embraced all the territories west of this river, the territories between the course of the Rhine and the Elba River, and those which lied South-West of the Upper Danube River. Such a vision was ideally connected with the extension of the Roman Empire under Charlemagne, of which Italy was

---

[53] See Josef Müller ad Alcide De Gasperi, 28 agosto 1948. ACSP, Nachlaß Müller, A.62, quoted in Maddalena Guiotto, Alcide De Gasperi a Vienna, p. 162.

[54] The relationship between Alcide De Gasperi and the German Chancellor was extremely complex. Undoubtedly, Alcide De Gasperi shared a sincere friendship with Konrad Adenauer, and he was also in very good terms with other CSU and CDU politicians. In 1954 a certain feeling of mistrust nonetheless still hovered over these human contacts. Paolo Taviani wrote in his diary: "De Gasperi teme i tedeschi. 'Non ti illudere-disse-aspetta che l'Austria e la Germania abbiano la piena indipendenza e poi vedrai'. Tacque a lungo, poi soggiunse quasi parlando a se stesso. 'Adenauer! Mah! Non saprei proprio se è un'eccezione, chissà che anche lui non sia come gli altri e si comporti così perché in questa contingenza non può fare altrimenti. Comunque antinazista lo è stato e nella democrazia crede sul serio'". (De Gasperi fears the Germans. 'Have no illusions! Wait until Austria and Germany regain their independence and you shall see what happens'. He kept quiet for a moment, and then he said, as if he were talking to himself. 'Adenauer! I really don't know if he is an exception, perhaps he is just like the others and he behaves in such a way because he has no alternatives. Anyway, he was sincerely against the Nazi and he truly believes in democracy'). See Paolo Emilio Taviani, I giorni di Trieste. Diario 1953–1954, Bologna 1998, p. 130. Quoted in Gian Enrico Rusconi, Germania Italia Europa, p. 221.

[55] Maddalena Guiotto, La tradizione europeista dei partiti cristiano-democratici, p. 163.

[56] See Gian Enrico Rusconi, Germania Italia Europa. Dallo Stato di Potenza alla Potenza Civile, Torino 2003, pp. 216–220.

[57] See, in particular, Frank R. Pfetsch, Die Außenpolitik der Bundesrepublik 1949–1992, München 1993, pp. 139–154.

an important part. The German division was an essential precondition for the re-alization of this European-project. A reunification based on a neutral choice was unacceptable, whereas the link with Western Europe was essential for Bonn.[58]

The Italian approach to the German issue assumed a definite shape only in the Fifties, and it was based on this unspoken – at least until 1984 – assumption that, given the circumstances, the division of Germany was the guarantee for Eu-ropean peace and integration. Henceforth, this vision was never challenged, even when, in 1973, Italy decided to establish diplomatic relations with Eastern Ger-many. We must bear in mind both the strategy pursued by the German govern-ment from 1969 which aimed at a progressive improvement of the relations with the Eastern German state, and also the transformations within the DDR, where the idea of a separation of the German territory as opposed to the goal of a future reunification was slowly taking roots at the beginning of the 1970s.

The sentences by Giulio Andreotti of September 1984 could have been ut-tered thirty years before by his mentor, Alcide De Gasperi: there existed two Ger-man states and they should remain so to guarantee peace in Europe. Was this perspective fundamentally unchanged in 1984? Did these sentences of the then Foreign Minister mirror the vision of his political party, of his government, or even of the Italian diplomacy?

---

[58] The choice of Adenauer to give up the goal of reunification was certainly due to his conviction that priority had to be attributed to the Western integration of his country. This conviction probably overlapped with a limited interest for the Eastern part of the country: "[...] Der gestandene Rhein-länder, der eher ein Westdeutscher, als ein Deutscher schlechthin sein wollte. Dem der Osten, auch der deutsche, fremd war. Er erzählte selbst: Im Zug nach Berlin habe er [...] immer das Gefühl gehabt hinter der Elbe höre Europa auf, und ab Magdeburg die Vorhänge zugezogen". See Willy Brandt, Erinnerungen, Frankfurt am Main 1989, p. 37. Regardless of our position towards this quo-tation, it is undeniable that Adenauer was not ready to come to terms with Moscow, in order to achieve reunification. His reaction to the Soviet note of 1952 fully confirms this statement. He refused to consider this note, even before the Allies could decide how to react and also before having tested the intentions of the Soviet leader. At present, it is difficult to affirm beyond doubt whether the note of Stalin was just a bluff to weaken the Western bloc – as the Italian Foreign Ministry believed – or whether it was a "verpasste Chance" for Germany. Peter Ruggenthaler sup-ported the first hypothesis, whereas the Austrian historian Rolf Steininger, supported the latter hy-pothesis. See Michael Gehler, Deutschland: Von der Teilung zur Einigung 1945 bis heute, Wien – Köln – Weimar 2010, pp. 143–148; Peter Ruggenthaler (ed.), Stalins großer Bluff. Die Geschichte der Stalin-Note in Dokumenten der sowjetischen Führung (Schriftenreihe der Vierteljahrshefte für Zeitgeschichte 95), München 2007; Rolf Steininger, Eine Chance zur Wiedervereinigung? Die Sta-lin Note vom 10. März 1952. Darstellung und Dokumentation auf der Grundlage unveröffentlichten britischer und amerikanischer Akten (Archiv für Sozialgeschichte Beiheft 12), Bonn 1986. See also Michael Gehler, Modellfall für Deutschland? Die Österreichlösung mit Staatsvertrag und Neutrali-tät 1945–1955, Innsbruck 2007, pp. 207–217. Some years later, Giulio Andreotti affirmed in an interview-book that his mentor, Alcide De Gasperi, and Konrad Adenauer had always inwardly been persuaded that the German frontiers should never again been questioned. See Giulio Andreotti, Intervista su De Gasperi, Roma – Bari 1977, p. 162.

These are some of the questions to which the following chapters will try and find an answer.

II. *TOUR D'HORIZON*: ITALY AND GERMANY

1979–1988

4. The First Stage of the Italo-German Relationship (1979–1984)

L'Europe est comme un rôti. Le rôti même ce sont la France et l'Allemagne, avec en accompagnement un peu de cresson de fontaine, l'Italie, et un peu de sauce, les Pays du Benelux.[1] (Charles de Gaulle)

"Europe is like a roast. France and Germany are the actual roast, with watercress on the side – that is Italy – and some dressing: The Benelux countries".

In this perspective, Italy presents itself as some sort of side dish made up of an annual plant, the watercress, easy to grow and pleasant to the taste.

Apart from this metaphor used by the French President, many different definitions have frequently emphasised the secondary role which Italy was supposed to play in the European integration process and, generally speaking, in international dynamics. Throughout the years, some of them have had a fair amount of success, for example that of Italy as "*Cenerentola d'Europa*" (the Cinderella of Europe), and Italy as "*Lunch Power*".

Does this image correspond to the real status of the country at the end of the 1970s, or to the perception Germany had of it?

This question is the core of the fourth chapter, where the presentation of the evolution of the Italo-German relationship in the 1980s will be addressed starting from 1979 and going through to 1989. As we shall see below, 1979 marked in fact a turning point compared to the previous dynamics and it is, therefore, far more representative than 1980.[2]

---

[1] With regard to this quotation of Charles de Gaulle, see Michèle Weinachter, Valéry Giscard d'Estaing et l'Allemagne. Le double rêve inachevé, Paris 2004, p. 66.

[2] The former Italian Ambassador to Bonn drew similar conclusions in one of his essays. See Luigi Vittorio Ferraris, Deutsch-italienische Beziehungen in den 1980er Jahren. Aufzeichnungen aus italienischen diplomatischen Akten, in: Michael Gehler/Maddalena Guiotto, Italien Österreich und die Bundesrepublik Deutschland in Europa: Ein Dreiecksverhältnis in seinen wechselseitigen Beziehungen und Wahrnehmungen von 1945/49 bis zur Gegenwart (Institut für Geschichte der Universität Hildesheim, Arbeitskreis Europäische Integration, Historische Forschungen, Veröffentlichungen 8), Wien – Köln – Weimar 2012, pp. 243–262, 246. The approach taken in this chapter is though partially different. Firstly, there is no doubt that in the period before 1979 there were growing tensions between Italy and Germany. However, this was not just a question of casualty, rather it is the consequence of unsolved issues and potential motives of rivalry that had been growing and growing and exploded mainly with the Kappler Affair (briefly quoted in the essay). The second difference consists in the main reasons for this change. Although this chapter shares the thesis in the essay of Ferraris of a crucial role played by the Italian involvement in the EMS, and by the Italian determination to share the NATO dual track decision, it does not agree with the central role attributed to the sole visit of President Pertini in the Bundesrepublik in September 1979. Surely, this state visit had an important symbolic role, but the importance of the frequent visits of Italian Prime Minister Francesco Cossiga should not be neglected.

Since autumn 1989, a series of events started to modify, at least partially, the interaction between the two states both at a bilateral and at a European level, which makes this date important too. During this decade two distinct periods can be identified, the first one covers the years 1979 to 1983–1984, and the second one the years from September 1984 until the beginning of 1989.[3] September 1984 has been chosen not in reference to the replacement at the head of the German Government of Helmut Schmidt by Helmut Kohl – which happened in 1982 – nor to the establishment of a new Italian government – which, in turn, took place in 1983 –. It rather points at the moment when Italian Foreign Minister Giulio Andreotti uttered the few words quoted in the title of this work.

Naturally, each periodization is only of an indicative nature, as it tries to set some boundaries in a flow of events in order to ensure greater clarity and consistency in the narrative. It identifies some specific moments which seem to be particularly relevant, and, among the different options available, September 1984 has been preferred because of the sentences of Giulio Andreotti. Their implications are the ideal basis for a preliminary assessment of the bilateral relationship between Italy and Germany, and of the Italian position on the German question.

4.1 From the EMS to the NATO Dual Track Decision:
Andreotti and Cossiga dealing with a worried Germany

According to Piero Craveri, the murder of Aldo Moro and the elections that followed were the embodiment of the end of the political system known as *Prima Repubblica* (First Republic).[4] Although this system actually survived 1979 and its political parties continued to exist until 1992, the opportunities to reform it were *de facto* exhausted.

Besides, in Piero Craveri's analysis, the political parties were by then, even if at different levels, aware of the imperative need of an institutional change. Still, there were no fitting responses to the challenge. The DC was ambiguous in its approach, whereas the PCI adamantly refused to bend to change. Bettino Craxi and the PSI tried to put the issue at the centre of the debate, but in the end they also proved to be incapable of altering the foundations of the system.[5]

---

[3] The first period will be the object of this fourth chapter, whereas the second period, from 1984 to 1988, will be the object of the fifth.

[4] See Piero Craveri, Dopo "l'unità nazionale" la crisi del sistema dei partiti, in: Simona Colarizi/Piero Craveri/Silvio Pons/Gaetano Quagliariello (eds.), Gli Anni Ottanta come Storia, Soveria Mannelli 2004, pp. 11–30, 11.

[5] See Agostino Giovagnoli, La crisi della centralità democristiana, in: Simona Colarizi/Piero Craveri/Silvio Pons/Gaetano Quagliariello (eds.), Gli Anni Ottanta come Storia, pp. 65–102, 86. See also various documents in Archivio storico della Camera dei Deputati (hereafter ASCD), Fondo Francesco Cossiga, Archivio con titolario 1944–2010, b. 62.

For more than a decade Italy suffered from an underlying layer of tension between attempts to restore some sort of "centrism", and feeble attempts to overthrow all the system. To make the picture worse, the main Italian political parties were more and more discredited, and this further accelerated the moral decay of the system.

German archival sources provide an equally worrying overview. From 1979 to 1984, each state visit was an opportunity to officially restate the excellent cooperation the two countries enjoyed, the absence of pending disputes, and the close affinities in the field of Foreign policy.[6] Still, in the shadow of such statements, the layer of tension underlying the Italian system and the moral decay within the DC caused a great deal of discussions in Bonn, and gave rise to a widespread feeling of concern.

The involvement of DC party officials in political and financial scandals, as well as in local administrative inefficiencies, were considered in Bonn old topics of discussion.[7] However, by the end of the 1970s new elements further complicated this picture, such as the rise of the Socialist Party[8] and the growing internal divide and disputes within the DC which significantly impaired its capability for external projection and action[9]:

> „Die politische Kraft der christdemokratischen Partei Italiens erschöpft sich heute weitgehend in solchen internen Auseinandersetzungen [...]. Die DC empfindet sich selbst als verwundbar und reagiert defensiv."[10]

During this time the modification of the internal balances of the DC in favour of "Southern recruits" also seemed to worry the German government, as it could render the dialogue between the countries even more difficult. Furthermore, the growing entrenchment of the Christian-Democratic party behind a Southern

---

[6] According to French sources, such official statements were nothing more than the expression of a lack of real interest in mutual cooperation. See Relations italo-allemandes, Ambassade de France en Italie, Gillet Martinet ambassadeur de France en Italie à son excellence Claude Cheysson ministre des relations extérieures, Rome, 27.12.1983. AMAE, inva1930, Direction Europe, Série RFA, carton 4907, sous-série 11, période 1981–1985.

[7] See Italienische Innenpolitik: Moralische Frage und Krise der DC, January 1981. Politisches Archiv des Auswärtigen Amts (hereafter PA AA), Bestand 26 (hereafter B), Bestellenummer (hereafter n.) 123280.

[8] See Regierungskrise in Italien, Aus Rom Diplo an Bonn AA, Fernschreiben N. 491, 29. 05.1981. PA AA, B26, n. 123280.

[9] See Regierungskrise in Italien, Aus Rom Diplo an Bonn AA, Fernschreiben n. 521, June 1981. PA AA, B26, n. 123280.

[10] "The political clout of the Italian Christian-Democrats is wearing thin in an increasing internal struggle. The DC has a growing feeling of being vulnerable and reacts defensively". See Italienische Innenpolitik, Moralische Frage und Krise der DC, January 1981. PA AA, B 26 n. 123280.

electorate gave rise in Germany and in France to reasonable doubts as to its resilience in the long term: "[…] Le poids du Sud dans les instances dirigeantes du parti est singulièrement renforcé […]".[11]

Criticism did not spare the PSI and its rising star, Bettino Craxi. The dynamic approach promoted by the new socialist leader might have genuinely aimed at creating an anti-communist and anti-clerical political force equipped with a platform suited to challenge the supremacy of the Christian-Democrats. Still, in the early Eighties this goal was a distant one, while the relationship with other secular forces of the country remained in many respects troubled.[12] Besides, the PSI was no exception to the general rule that party congresses mainly dealt with internal issues, such as electoral priorities, whereas Foreign policy issues remained on the sidelines. The forty-second Congress of the Italian Socialist Party in Palermo is a good example of what has just been stated. During this meeting, relevant topics such as security issues were not even addressed and the NATO dual track decision of December 1979 was just used as a means of standing out against the Communists.[13]

The conclusion could be drawn that Foreign policy issues would not be addressed unless they directly affected internal dynamics or leadership problems, both within the DC and in the PSI.

A far less worrying overview was apparently provided in Bonn with regard to the Italian Foreign policy. Despite this political immobilism at home, from the end of the 1970s Italy seemed eager to breathe new life into its international projection. While remaining faithful to the commitments – Atlanticism and Europeanism – which had been accepted by De Gasperi, its foreign policy started exploring new possibilities.[14]

The analysis of the causes of this new course was, however, less rosy. On several occasions, this increased activism seemed to be aimed at immediate success and satisfaction only. In other words, it was a mere question of being involved in the main international and European meetings.[15]

---

[11] "[…] the weight of the South within the management of the party is particularly enhanced […] ". See Le nouveau visage de la Démocratie Chrétienne (Gillet Martinet ambassadeur de France en Italie à son excellence le ministre des relations extérieures), Rome, 19.5.1982. AMAE, inva1930, Direction Europe, Série Italie, carton 5308, sous-série 2, dossier 9, période 1981–1985.

[12] See Italienische Innenpolitik, Moralische Frage und Krise der DC, January 1981. PA AA, B 26 n. 123280.

[13] See Italienische Innenpolitik, Botschaft der Bundesrepublik Deutschland an das Auswärtige Amt, Referat 203, April 1981. PA AA, B 26 n. 123280.

[14] See Giuseppe Romeo, La politica estera nell'era Andreotti (1972–1992), Soveria Mannelli 2000, p. 14.

[15] See Politischer Halbjahrsbericht Italien 1980, summer 1980. PA AA, B 26 n. 123280.

Although French diplomatic records also refer to these weaknesses while dealing with the Italian political system in this period, their role, for example as concerns the DC, was often put into a somewhat different perspective.[16] On the occasion of the fifteenth Congress of the DC in 1982, some signs of political renewal were, for example, detected.

> « Virage, transition, relance ? A l'issue du XVe Congrès de la DC [...] le bilan est loin d'être négligeable : la redistribution des cartes à l'intérieur du parti, le déclin des courants traditionnels [...] l'apparition au premier plan des visages nouveaux [...]. La méridionalisation de la DC mécontente certains [...] mais reflet assez fidèlement l'évolution de l'implantation du Parti ».[17]

Two years later, the failure to discuss international issues at the party Congress was justified on the basis of the specific history of the party. For more than forty years it had been keeping hold of the reins of political power, thus identifying its foreign policy priorities with those of the acting government.

> « Le XVIe Congrès de la DC n'a pas failli à la tradition. La situation internationale et la politique étrangère n'y ont eu droit qu'à la part du pauvre [...]. M. De Mita, qui ne passe pas pour un oracle en la matière a [...] consacré quelques paragraphes de son discours fleuve de cinq heures aux questions internationales.
> Mais M. Andreotti [...] l'actuel ministre des affaires étrangères, qui a axé son intervention sur les problèmes internes au parti ne s'y est beaucoup attardé. Il n'y a dans cette attitude rien de surprenant. La DC ne s'est jamais souciée d'élaborer en tant que parti ses propres conceptions théoriques de politique internationale dans la mesure où ayant de façon presque interrompue détenu le portefeuille des affaires

---

[16] This different approach does not imply that the French diplomacy was unaware of the growing political fatigue within the Italian political system and its main party, the DC. This can be confirmed by the remarks of the French Ambassador to Rome, Gilles Martinet: "La DC, un partito provinciale che esprimeva un'Italia profonda che non aveva né orgoglio nazionale, né apertura al mondo, salvo nell'America e, un po', nella Germania". (The DC: A provincial party, the expression of a country with neither national pride, nor openness to the world, except towards the US, and, a little, towards Germany). See Bruna Bagnato, L'Italia vista da Palazzo Farnese: la missione di Gilles Martinet (1981–1984), in: Ennio di Nolfo (ed.), La politica estera italiana negli anni Ottanta, Bari – Roma 2003, pp. 225–283, 238–239.
[17] "Change of direction, transition or relaunching? At the end of the 15th DC congress [...] the outcome is far from being negligible: the redistribution of the cards within the party, the decline of the traditional factions [...] the emerging on the stage of new faces [...]. The Southernization of the DC displeases some people [...], but it mirrors faithfully enough the internal evolution of this party". See Le nouveau visage de la Démocratie Chrétienne, Gillet Martinet ambassadeur de France en Italie à son excellence le ministre des relations extérieures, 19.5.1982. AMAE, inva1930, Direction Europe, Série Italie, carton 5308, sous-série 2, dossier 9, période 1981–1985.

étrangères depuis quarante ans, elle s'est très largement identifiée aux options des gouvernements successifs [...] ».[18]

The evaluations of Bonn and Paris on Italian politics vary even more widely, if we consider the remarks about the Italian Socialist Party and its Congress in Palermo in 1981:

> « Les conceptions exprimées par M. Craxi méritent attention, tant en raison de la nouveauté du ton employé, que du caractère déterminant de l'influence qu'exerce le PSI au sein du gouvernement [...] Au total Craxi a abordé les questions internationales sous un jour nouveau en Italie : Aux références rituelles et commodes à l'Alliance Atlantique et à la Communauté Européenne [...] il a substitué une affirmation du rôle international de l'Italie. Cette innovation concerne davantage les attitudes que le contenu de la politique étrangère, mais est significative du nouveau style que le secrétaire général socialiste s'efforce d'instaurer [...] ».[19]

Why was Bonn so alarmed by the Italian inner situation?

Once again the interpretative framework proposed in chapter three may offer useful tools in order to better understand the nature of Bonn's concerns.

Firstly, it is necessary to recall the importance, since the 1950s, of the "party pillar" in the relationship between Italy and Germany, and the significance of the DC as a "point of contact". Throughout the years, even after De Gasperi's death and the end of the "centrism", the DC had retained a leading role on the Italian political stage, and its members had been key interlocutors for the Bundesrepublik.

---

[18] "The sixteenth Congress of the DC did not break with tradition. The international situation and Foreign policy played second fiddle [...]. De Mita, who in this field is certainly not an oracle [...] at least devoted some paragraphs of his interminable speech of five hours to the international situation, whereas Andreotti [...] at present Italian Foreign Minister, focused on problems within the party instead of lingering over Foreign policy issues. There is nothing surprising in this approach. The DC never concerned itself as a party with the formulation of an international theoretical framework. It has been in control, nearly without interruptions, of the foreign portfolio for forty years, thus identifying its position with that of the acting government". See Congrès de la DC. Questions de politique étrangère, Ambassade de France en Italie le chargé d'affaires à son excellence le ministre des affaires étrangères, 06.3.1984. AMAE, inva1930, Direction Europe, Série Italie, carton 5308, sous-série 2, dossier 9, période 1981–1985.

[19] "The notion expressed by Craxi deserves our attention, both because of the new tone he set and because of the decisive influence of the PSI on the government [...] Overall, Craxi addressed international issues in a different light for Italy. He replaced traditional and convenient references to the Atlantic Alliance and to the European Community [...] with the affirmation of the Italian role in the world. This innovation concerns more the external approach than Foreign policy contents. Still, it is the signal of the new style that the General Secretary strives to establish". Ambassade de France en Italie, Jacques Senart ambassadeur de France à son excellence le ministre des affaires étrangères, 28.4.1981. AMAE, inva1930, Direction Europe, Série Italie, carton 5308, sous-série 2, dossier 9, période 1981–1985.

Secondly, it must not be neglected that between 1978 and 1979 the EMS[20] and the problem of Euromissiles were of a quite crucial importance when it came to assessing the German approach to international politics. Italy was a key factor both within the EMS and in the context of the euromissiles issue. In addition, in light of the no-accession of the United Kingdom to the EMS, Italy's participation grew in importance[21], as Filippo Maria Pandolfi[22] recalled in an interview to the newspaper *Eco di Bergamo*:

> «[…] Il mio rapporto con Schmidt trae origine dalla sua determinazione, condivisa con il presidente francese Giscard d'Estaing, di porre fine alla caotica fluttuazione delle monete europee, determinatasi con l'abbandono del sistema di cambi fissi deciso da Nixon nell'agosto 1971, e di introdurre un regime di fluttuazione limitata e controllata. In Italia aveva iniziato la sua attività, il 16 marzo 1978, giorno del rapimento di Moro, il terzo governo Andreotti [...] Nel precedente governo ero ministro delle Finanze, nel nuovo divento ministro del Tesoro. La consumata cautela di Andreotti finì per lasciare a me il bandolo della trattativa, pubblica o riservata secondo i casi, con il cancelliere Schmidt [...].
> Nel caso della trattativa di cui parliamo, Schmidt si serviva di uno strettissimo ed autorevole collaboratore, Manfred Lahnstein, allora Segretario di Stato alla cancelleria federale e in seguito ministro delle Finanze. Almeno una volta al mese veniva in Italia. Un paio di volte venne a Bergamo. Lo ricordo qui, nel mio studio, proprio qui dove ora è seduto lei: mi parlò di un incontro con Craxi, deludente [...] *Dopo il rifiuto inglese, senza l'adesione italiana non sarebbe nato lo Sme, questo è certo [...]*».[23]

---

[20] European Monetary System.

[21] See the interview that Giulio Andreotti gave to Cinzia Rognoni Vercelli in Rome (11.12.1998), in: Voices on Europe, Oral History Collections, Historical Archives of the European Union (http://www.eui/HAEU/OralHistory/, last consulted 1.2.2016). In the interview Giulio Andreotti made explicit reference to the pressions of the Franco-German couple, particularly of his French counterpart, President Valéry Giscard d'Estaing, and of the German Chancellor, Helmut Schmidt, to persuade Italy to enter the EMS as quickly as possible (with a view to preventing speculations and monetary disorder).

[22] Born in Bergamo in November 1927, Filippo Maria Pandolfi was Finance Undersecretary in the governments of Aldo Moro from 1974 until July 1976. In 1976, in the third Andreotti government, he became Minister of Finance, and then he was appointed Minister of Treasury, from 1978 until 1979, into the government lead by Giulio Andreotti, and from 1979 until 1980 into Francesco Cossiga's first and second government.

[23] "[…] My relationship with Schmidt has its roots in his determination, shared with French President Valéry Giscard d'Estaing, to put an end to frenzied currency fluctuations, which had followed the collapse of the Bretton Woods system. In Italy, the third government under the leadership of Giulio Andreotti had started working on 16 March 1978, the same day of Aldo Moro's kidnap. […] In the previous government I was the Minister of Finance, in this one Minister of Treasury. Andreotti's consummate skills and well-known prudence resulted in me dealing with Schmidt about the whole issue […]. During the negotiations Schmidt could rely on a very close and influential advisor, Manfred Lahnstein. At that time, he was Secretary of State at the Chancellery; later on he became

Political tensions were likely to have negative effects not only on the internal Italian balance, but also on the economic reform the country had to implement to stay in the EMS.[24] Therefore, concerns about the Italian political health mirrored, at first, the fact that instrumentally the Mediterranean country was vital to the course France and Germany were beginning to outline. A trustworthy political leadership was considered as an essential prerequisite to overcome the serious economic situation Italy was facing in the 1970s.[25]

Between summer 1973 and the summer of the following year, Italian economic difficulties had, in fact, imposed exceptional policy measures, such as substantial international loans, and these from Germany in particular. As a result, Italian gold reserves had decreased.[26] A marked slowdown in the economic growth rate, the consequences of a global recession, the Italian labour rigidity and the lack of market confidence, all triggered a solvency crisis which resulted in massive exchange rate pressures that the Italian gold reserves could not absorb.

To all this, we must also add the depreciation of the local currency, the lira, which between 1976 and 1980 lost nearly half of its value. In 1980, the balance of payments' deficit was estimated at 40 million Deutsche Mark, while the lira had lost 6 % of its value against the ECU (European currency unit).[27]

Minister of Finance. At least once a month Schmidt used to come to Italy. A couple of times he also came to Bergamo. I remember it well; he was sitting here in my office, on the spot you are sitting now. He told me about a meeting he had had with Craxi, disappointing […] *After the British refusal, the EMS would have never been created without Italy, that's for sure* […]". See the interview of Franco Cattaneo to the Italian newspaper *Eco di Bergamo*. It was published on Monday 23 September 2013 in the article "Pandolfi racconta la Germania. I miei anni con Schmidt e Kohl", in: http://www.ecodibergamo.it/stories/Homepage/395105_pandolfi_racconta_la_germania_i_miei_anni_con_schimdt_e_kohl/?mediaon.trackers.autorefresh.Homepage (last consulted 31.7.2016).

[24] See Duccio Basosi/Giovanni Bernardini, The Puerto Rico Summit of 1977 and the End of Eurocommunism, in: Leopoldo Nuti, The Crisis of the Détente in Europe from Helsinki to Gorbachev 1975–1985, Londra 2008, pp. 256–267. See also Antonio Varsori, Puerto Rico 1976: Le potenze occidentali e il problema del comunismo in Italia, in: *Ventunesimo Secolo* VII (2008), n. 16, pp. 89–121.

[25] In the 1970s this complicated Italian economic situation was intertwined with the electoral successes which the PCI achieved, and also with the increasing popularity of eurocommunism. Chancellor Helmut Schmidt himself revealed some weeks after the Puerto Rico Summit that during that meeting the "Italian issue" had been discussed with the US, Great Britain and France. He had promoted the idea (he had already expressed it in 1974) that the communist party's no-accession to political power had to be considered as a prerequisite for providing financial aid. See Duccio Basosi/Giovanni Bernardini, The Puerto Rico Summit of 1977, p. 262. Chancellor Schmidt's declarations provoked a great scandal in Italy, which also involved France and Great Britain.

[26] See Mauro Campus, Il governo del «vincolo esterno»: interazione, compatibilità e limiti del sistema economico italiano nella crisi degli anni Settanta, in: Leopoldo Nuti/Massimiliano Guderzo/Bruna Bagnato (eds.), Nuove Questioni di Storia della Relazioni Internazionali, Roma – Bari 2015, pp. 266–294, 278–279.

[27] Politischer Halbjahresbericht Italien 1980, summer 1980. PA AA, B 26 n. 123280.

Besides, the internal decay of the DC and its southernization led to a growing sympathy within the national business community towards the Republicans and the Socialists of the PSI.[28] Did Bonn consider it possible, in 1979, to find reliable political and economic partners within the socialist realm?

The German Federal decision-makers were seriously worried about the potential consequences that a government led by the Socialists might result in, as can be confirmed by the meeting between Chancellor Helmut Schmidt and Italian Prime Minister Giulio Andreotti at *Palazzo Chigi* on 10 July 1979.

„Nach der Begrüßung gab Ministerpräsident Andreotti seiner Freude darüber Ausdruck, den Bundeskanzler in einem besonders heiklen Moment der Regierungsbildung sehen zu können. Es würden Anstrengungen unternommen, um zu einer Koalition zu finden, die bereit sei, sich in bezug auf die wichtigsten Fragen, d.h besonders die wirtschaftlich-finanziellen Probleme [...] einzusetzen.
Auf die Frage des Bundeskanzlers, ob er meine, daß Craxi eine Regierung bilden könne, antwortete Andreotti, Craxi habe den Auftrag dazu erhalten, die Bildung einer Regierung erscheine jedoch noch schwierig.
Der Bundeskanzler stellte die Frage, ob es nicht zu einer Minderheitsregierung Andreottis kommen könnte. Andreotti verneinte dies [...]. Der Bundeskanzler schilderte sodann den Eindruck, den er von Craxi nach zwei Begegnungen habe: 1) Craxi selbst strebe eine Koalition mit der DC an, aber er habe Schwierigkeiten innerhalb seiner Partei 2) sei ihm (Bundeskanzler) aufgefallen, daß Craxi keine ausreichenden Kenntnisse auf ökonomischem Gebiet besitze. Er (Bundeskanzler) habe das Gespräch absichtlich auf den Pandolfi-Plan gebracht und dabei festgestellt, daß Craxi nicht genügend davon verstehe. In einer von Craxi geführten Regierung müßten die wirtschaftspolitischen Ressorts auf jedem Fall in fachkundige Hände gelegt werden [...].
Er (Bundeskanzler) habe Craxi deutlich gesagt, falls es nicht gelinge eine Koalitionsregierung [...] zustande zu bringen, so habe er – Craxi – die Verantwortung dafür zu tragen, wenn Italien später in die Hände kommunistischer Regierungen falle [...] Craxi scheine guten Willen zu besitzen, aber nicht genügend Kraft zu haben."[29]

---

[28] See Italienische Innenpolitik, Moralische Frage und Krise der DC, January 1981. PA AA, B 26 n. 123280.

[29] "After the usual welcome, Prime Minister Andreotti expressed his delight in meeting the Chancellor during such a difficult stage as was the formation of the government. He affirmed that efforts had been made to put together a coalition which could deal with the most important issues [...] such as economic and financial problems. As for the question raised by the Chancellor, as to whether Craxi had the ability to form a government, Andreotti commented that Craxi had received the mandate, but the actual formation of a government was still a difficult task. The Chancellor asked whether Andreotti could build a minority government. Andreotti gave a negative answer [...]. The Chancellor depicted the impression which he had of Craxi after two meetings: 1) Craxi strives for a coalition with the DC, but he has difficulties within his own political party 2) The Chancellor has also noticed that Craxi has no in-depth knowledge in the economic field. In a government led by

The participation of the PSI into the next government could result, according to German experts, in a more flexible economic approach either for political ends or for a lack of adequate knowledge. This would though defeat the objective that the so-called *Pandolfi Plan*[30] had outlined.

It was, therefore, of the utmost importance to be able to rely on dependable partners. Until 1979, all these partners belonged to the DC, Prime Minister Giulio Andreotti and his Minister of Treasury Filippo Maria Pandolfi being the most influential among them.

Without wishing to emphasise the human dimension too strongly, it seems that the good cooperation between the German Chancellor and the Italian Prime Minister allowed both countries the opportunity to interact in an atmosphere of confidence. It was a considerable asset for both Italy and Germany[31], considering that this was a period of significant social tensions.[32] This "friendship" stood the test of time despite frequent moments of institutional and political tensions[33], and

---

Craxi, the control of the economic resorts should remain in the hands of competent people [...]. The German Chancellor plainly told Craxi that if he failed to build a government, he would be responsible if the Communists seized power in Italy. Craxi seems to have good intentions, but not enough strength". See Doc. 206, Gespräch des Bundeskanzlers Schmidt mit Ministerpräsidenten Andreotti, VS-vertraulich (confidential), Rom, 10.7.1979, in: Akten zur Auswärtigen Politik Deutschland (hereafter AAPD) 1979 Band 2, ed. by Michael Ploetz/Tim Szatkowski/Ilse Dorothee Pautsch, München 2011. In the two previous years Helmut Schmidt and Bettino Craxi had met twice, during December 1977 on the occasion of an official state visit in Rome and during May 1979 in Bonn.

[30] In August 1978, the Minister of Finance Pandolfi presented the draft of a three-year reform programme, which the German Federal Ministry analysed from October 1978. The Federal Ministry gave an overall positive assessment, as the plan proposed appropriate measures to tackle the problems not just in the short term.

[31] See, for example, Federico Scarano, Le Relazioni con la Repubblica Federale di Germania e la questione tedesca, in: Francesco Lefebvre D'Ovidio/Luca Micheletta (eds.), Giulio Andreotti e l'Europa, Roma 2017, pp. 27–46, 35.

[32] This close cooperation had been evolving throughout the years based not only on common economic interests, but also on a shared determination to defeat the wave of political terrorism shaking the two countries. In December 1977 political terrorism had been, for the first time, the object of bilateral consultations (at Valeggio sul Mincio, a place near Verona). The occasion for such meeting was the political crisis, which in Germany followed the abduction of Hanns Martin Schleyer, president of the Federation of German Industries. Andreotti expressed his thoughts at the meeting of Valeggio sul Mincio: "große Bewunderung für die Art und Weise, wie dieser, die Dinge geführt habe". See Doc. 345, in: AAPD 1977 Band 2, ed. by Amit das Gupta/Tim Geiger/Matthias Peter/Fabian Hilfrich/Mechthild Lindemann, München 2008, pp. 1650–1666. Concerning the importance of the cooperation between Helmut Schmidt and Giulio Andreotti, see also the author's interview with Ambassador Ferdinando Salleo (28.10.2016).

[33] See, for example, Con grande Amicizia, *Der Spiegel* n. 50/1977. The title of the article published by the German magazine *Der Spiegel* refers to the dedication Giulio Andreotti wrote in the book (a collection of writings of Marco Aurelio, one of the philosophers whom the Chancellor appreciated the most) he gave Helmut Schmidt as a present: "Con grande amicizia e ammirazione".

despite the intransigence of the German leader who was faced with Italian hesitations.

> «[…] L'incontro decisivo per lo SME avvenne il 1° novembre a Siena. Apparentemente una tranquilla visita turistica, con i protagonisti accompagnati dalle mogli. In realtà, un lungo incontro notturno in prefettura. Un incontro a quattro, durato fino a poco prima delle tre: il presidente del Consiglio Andreotti, il governatore della Banca d'Italia Baffi ed io, da una parte, Schmidt, solo, dall'altra. Ne ho un ricordo vivissimo. Un cancelliere duro e intransigente, davanti ai silenzi di Andreotti e alle esitazioni di Baffi».[34]

It might come as a surprise that two men who did not belong to the same political family and had a rather different background could reach such a good understanding.[35]

It is well known that Chancellor Schmidt belonged to the right wing of his party. Still, a shared desire to pursue common goals seemed to be far more relevant than the sheer political affiliation to one group or another. The 1979 meeting of Palazzo Chigi was, in fact, organized in a moment when Italy and Germany were increasingly sharing the same basic approach on détente and security issues.

All things considered, by the end of the 1970s Italy was undoubtedly something of a problem for Bonn, but its role was far from negligible. In light of the Italian inner difficulties, the weakening of the "party pillar" and of the "economic pillar" indirectly strengthened the importance of the "human pillar"[36], i.e. the

---

[34] "[…] the decisive encounter for the EMS took place in Siena in November. Apparently, it was just a pleasant tourist visit, the participants having come with their wives. However, the truth was that they had come for a special meeting in the local *prefettura*. The meeting lasted until nearly 3.00 in the morning. Four people were present: Prime Minister Andreotti with the Governor of the Bank of Italy, Baffi and I on one side of the table, Chancellor Schmidt, alone, on the other. I remember it very well. Schmidt was tough and uncompromising, whereas Baffi hesitated and Andreotti remained silent".
http://www.ecodibergamo.it/stories/Homepage/395105_pandolfi_racconta_la_germania_i_miei_anni_con_schimdt_e_kohl/?mediaon.trackers.autorefresh.Homepage, (last consulted 31.7.2016).
[35] Concerning the relationship between Andreotti and Schmidt see the personal recollections of the two politicians: Helmut Schmidt, Die Deutschen und ihre Nachbarn, Berlin 1992, p. 365 and Giulio Andreotti, Diari, p. 73. See also Federico Scarano, Le Relazioni con la Repubblica Federale di Germania e la questione tedesca, pp. 31–32.
[36] Concerning the importance of the human element: "Surtout sur le plan politique […] M. Schmidt homme du Nord, protestant et au caractère hautain […] n'avait guère de considération pour l'Italie et ses dirigeants, sauf Andreotti […]". (Especially at a political level […] Schmidt was a Northerner, a Lutheran and a haughty man […] he did not think much of Italy and its politicians, with the only exception of Andreotti). See Les Relations italo-allemandes, Gillet Martinet ambassadeur de France en Italie à son excellence Claude Cheysson ministre des relations extérieures, Rome, 27.12.1983. AMAE, inva1930, Direction Europe, Série RFA, carton 4907, sous-série 11, période 1981–1985, Ambassade de France en Italie. On this point many different amusing anecdotes have been told

relationship between the German Chancellor and Giulio Andreotti at first, and then also with his successor to the post of Prime Minister, Francesco Cossiga.[37]

Within this framework, two items are yet to be discussed. On the one hand, the question arises as to whether in 1979 Italy shared the interest to work more closely with Bonn. On the other hand, we have to wonder whether this interest had an instrumental or ancillary character. The answer to both questions is a positive one.

The adhesion to the EMS allowed Italy to avoid the danger of being left outside the core group of countries that created a zone of economic and monetary stability in Europe.[38] Likewise, the government's decision to station Cruise missiles on Italian soil demonstrated the desire to increase the strategic size of the country.[39] In the framework of the Italo-German relationship the EMS can be treated, therefore, as a marriage of convenience through which Germany gained a surplus in its trade, while Italy expected that the obstacles to its participation on an equal footing had been, at least partially, removed. In order to achieve these aims, Germany as a partner was a sensible choice. This does not necessarily mean that the *Farnesina* was totally unaware of the difficulties and weaknesses affecting this marriage of convenience celebrated between 1978 and 1979.

In previous years, the Kappler Affair[40], and the tensions related to the wave of terrorist attacks in both countries – emphasised by the disinformation of the

---

throughout the years. Helmut Schmidt, for example, had allegedly said in 1975 that the Italian tank had one forward gear, but two reverse speeds. See the author's interview with Ambassador Ferdinando Salleo (28.10.2016). In a brief exchange of views (Berlin 28.9.2017) with Horst Teltchik, Schmidt's dim opinion of Italy as a partner and of its politicians was fully confirmed. The same applies to many of his interlocutors in other Western countries, with the remarkable exception of Valéry Giscard d'Estaing and Jacques Chirac.

[37] The exchange of letters between Schmidt and Cossiga (held in the Cossiga archive) shows that a good relationship had also been established between the German Chancellor and the successor of Andreotti as Prime Minister. See, for example, Lettera di Francesco Cossiga a Helmut Schmidt, Rome, 2.11.2007. ASCD, Fondo Francesco Cossiga, archivio con titolario 1944–2010, b.24.

[38] Still, this determination to become part of the EMS was not correlated to an equally strong determination to adapt the national economy to the new monetary environment. It was rather a political choice, whose economic consequences were only partially softened by the negotiating skills of the Minister of Finance and of the Governor of the Bank of Italy. See in particular Peter Ludlow, The making of the European Monetary System, London 1982. See also Mauro Campus, Il governo del «vincolo esterno»: interazione, compatibilità e limiti del sistema economico italiano nella crisi degli anni Settanta, pp. 268–269.

[39] See, in particular, Leopoldo Nuti, La sfida nucleare. La politica estera italiana e le armi atomiche 1945–1991, Bologna 2007. See of the same author: Leopoldo Nuti, The origins of the 1979 Dual Track Decision-A Survey, in: Leopoldo Nuti (ed.), The Crisis of the Détente in Europe from Helsinki to Gorbachev 1975–1985, London 2008, pp. 57–81.

[40] In August 1977, Herbert Kappler, tried by an Italian military tribunal in 1948 and sentenced to life imprisonment, escaped from the hospital where he had been moved due to sever health

German public opinion concerning the Italian social situation and the resulting reaction of the Italian press – had lead to a spiral of misunderstandings. It was certainly the result of heterogeneous issues; nevertheless, an important role was played by the fact that both the Italian public opinion and part of its political élite were prone to explain the anti-communist approach of the Federal Republic as nothing else than a reactionary feeling. This was either as a result of a lack of knowledge or of a lack of specific political priorities. In addition, different economic conditions[41] and equally different definitions of the notion of the rule of law and individual liberty deepened the divide.[42]

Since the early 1950s, in its German policy the Italian government had been pursuing a strategy based on the achievement of common goals, although not always successfully. This self-sustaining spiral of misunderstandings was a source of increasing concern in Rome as it could damage not only the economic exchange between Italy and the Federal Republic, but also their diplomatic cooperation at a delicate stage. In 1979, much more than the previously discussed interests were at stake. In Rome, the feeling that the Franco-German couple was losing some of its edge was increasing. As a result, it was possible that Bonn might have been more receptive to the opportunity of strengthening the links with its Southern partner.

"L'Italie a eu régulièrement tendance a exagéré la solidité et l'exclusivité du couple franco-allemand [...]".[43] This is the sentence with which the French historian Georges-Henri Soutou opens his essay on the Italian vision of the Franco-German couple. In 1979, a bumpy past stood behind the relationship between Paris and Bonn. Despite the overall understanding eventually reached between Konrad Adenauer and Charles de Gaulle, Germany had never embraced neither the French model of "*l'Europe des nations*", nor the Fouchet Plan as its institutional transposition. On the contrary, it had remained true to an original Monnet approach. Later on, in the era Brandt-Pompidou, the Franco-German couple was certainly built on a shared geopolitical vision of Europe. Still, it lacked a certain political and emotional kinship. It also seems that the French President distrusted

---

conditions with the help of his second wife. During the following weeks and months, this was the subject of heated controversy both in the national press and within the Government. For further information, see the section of chapter 6 dealing with the press.

[41] See Nota, Ministero degli Affari Esteri DG Affari economici, Rome, 4.7.1978. ILS, AGA, section Europe, b. 356.

[42] It seems that in Germany the possibility to restrict individual liberties if imperative collective needs demanded it was more generally accepted than in Italy. See Johannes Hürter, Anti-Terrorismus Politik. Ein deutsch-italienischer Vergleich 1969–1982, in: *Vierteljahrshefte für Zeitgeschichte* 57 (2009), Heft 3, pp. 329–348.

[43] See Georges-Henri Soutou, L'Italie et le couple franco-allemand, in: Antonio Varsori/Piero Craveri (eds.), L'Italia nella costruzione europea, pp. 43–66, 43.

certain implications of Brandt's Ostpolitik. Georges Pompidou was more in tune with Britain and its Prime Minister, Edward Heath, than his predecessor had ever been.

It seems, therefore, that Italy tried to conceal its own political limitations by indulging itself in the thought of the unbreakable bond between its Northern neighbours that limited its space for manoeuvre.[44] It is, however, difficult to deny that the accession to power of Valéry Giscard d'Estaing marked the beginning of a new season in the interaction between Bonn and Paris. Several clues point in this direction.

First of all, Helmut Schmidt and Valéry Giscard d'Estaing had had a very similar education and political background. This goes hand in hand with the fact that they shared from the very beginning of their political mandate the same vision of Europe and the same goals, especially in the economic and monetary field. This was the ideal basis for an extremely close relationship and for increasingly frequent exchanges of opinion both officially and alongside regular channels.

Besides, they showed political foresight in the choice of their principal advisors, and in their use of the press and of the mass media to promote their view of the Franco-German couple in order to enhance its rootedness in the respective public opinions.[45]

Nevertheless, even the Franco-German couple had its own *Achilles' heels* during the presidency of Giscard d'Estaing, namely strategic and defence issues.[46] This is where Rome sensed that through enhanced cooperation with Italy

---

[44] Ibid., pp. 43–44. To mitigate negative consequences, Italy tried either to associate itself with the initiatives proposed by this couple, or to convert them into multilateral plans.

[45] See, for example, Dieter Menyesch/Bérénice Manac'h, France-Allemagne Deutschland-Frankreich Relations internationales et interdépendence bilatérale 1963–1982, Münich 1980; Henri Ménudier, Le couple franco-allemand en Europe, Paris 1993; Henri Ménudier, Das Deutschlandbild der Franzosen in den siebziger Jahren. Gesammelte Aufsätze, Bonn 1981; Alfred Frisch, Les relations franco-allemandes: Une amitié solide et fragile à la fois, in: *Dokumente* (September 1976), Documents 31 (4–5), pp. 5–17; Michèle Weinachter, Valéry Giscard d'Estaing et l'Allemagne. Le double rêve inachevé, Paris 2004.

[46] In 1974, the stock of knowledge in the field of defence of the French President was scanty compared to his expertise in economic and monetary issues. This was even more evident if we consider the "defence background" of his German counterpart, Schmidt, who had been for instance Minister of Defence from 1969 to 1972. In this regard the reasoning proposed by Michèle Weinachter is extremely interesting. He affirms that from the very beginning of his presidential mandate Giscard showed a strong willingness to compensate his poor defence expertise. In so doing he reached, according to Weinachter, peculiar conclusions, which were hardly compatible with the Gaullist defence approach adopted by France. Therefore, the French President sympathised with Schmidt's fears and worries, unlike the majority of the French political élite. Such sensibility, rather peculiar in a French politician, did not leave any significant trace in the official diplomatic records. Michèle Weinachter reached, therefore, his conclusions mainly on the basis of a series of interviews with important German and French personalities, including Valéry Giscard d'Estaing himself. Officially, France remained true to its traditional Gaullist defence approach.

Bonn might gain some useful tools to counterbalance the concerns of the public opinion and to better assert itself on the European stage.[47] Italy would, in turn, benefit from an additional support, while striving against political and economic bottlenecks, to strengthen its international and European projection.[48]

4.2 The NATO Dual Track Decision and Francesco Cossiga: An Updating of the Italian Vision of the German Question?

> *Er (Francesco Cossiga) ist entschlossen das ganze Gewicht seiner Regierung für die kommende NATO Entscheidung in die Waagschale zu werfen.[49]*
> (Francesco Cossiga)

During the 28 October 1977 inaugural address at the International Institute for Strategic Studies, Helmut Schmidt warned of the risks posed by the deployment of the Soviet intermediate-range ballistic missiles known as SS-20.

Briefly and simply, the German Chancellor reminded his audience that the USA were not in possession of appropriate weapons to fire back, unless they resorted to their intercontinental missiles, which would have triggered a mutually assured destruction.[50] This led to a creeping feeling of insecurity, together with the risk of questioning the nuclear guarantee provided by the American super-power. [51]

In his London speech Schmidt did not propose, at least as a first option, a Western deployment of new generation intermediate-range missiles, but rather recommended to discourage the Soviet Union by including the SS-20 in the on-going SALT II negotiations for armament control. In this sense, the German

---

[47] See Lettera di Francesco Cossiga a Helmut Kohl, Rome, 30.7.1998. ASCD, Fondo Francesco Cossiga, archivio con titolario 1944–2010, b.24. This letter provides useful information on the great importance attached by Rome to the improvement of its relationship with Bonn as an essential part of the overall development of Europe.

[48] See, among others, Discorso del presidente del Consiglio On. Cossiga al XIV congresso della DC, 15–20.2.1980. ASCD, Fondo Francesco Cossiga, archivio 1965–1985, b. 4.

[49] "Regarding the approaching NATO Council, he (Francesco Cossiga) is determined to throw the full institutional weight of his government into the balance". Quotation from the report of the meeting between Francesco Cossiga and Helmut Schmidt in October 1979.

[50] See Helmut Schmidt, Menschen und Mächte, Berlin 1999, p. 230.

[51] See, in particular Tim Geiger/Philipp Gassert/Hermann Wentker (eds.), Zweiter Kalter Krieg und Friedensbewegung. Der NATO-Doppelbeschluss in deutsch-deutscher und internationaler Perspektive, München 2011.

leadership tried to put pressure on US President Jimmy Carter but, eventually, did not have any success.[52]

Only during the autumn of 1978 a solution to this impasse was found[53] and, soon after, it was made public at the 5–7 January 1979 summit at Guadalupe.[54] What was later known as the "NATO dual track decision" consisted on putting pressure on the Soviet Government. This was done by threatening the deployment of Pershing missiles as to induce the Soviets to stop deploying their own ballistic missiles and to remove the existing SS-20s. In the case of a non satisfactory response from the Soviets, NATO was ready to proceed with the effective deployment of Pershing missiles.

Although the focus of this work does not allow in-depth investigation of the NATO decision, it is nonetheless important to understand what influence it had on the relationship between Bonn and Rome. According to Leopoldo Nuti, this decision should, in fact, be considered as a key point to understanding the change in the international scenario between the Seventies and the Eighties, the change in Italian internal politics, and the redefinition of an Italian foreign policy which now aimed at giving new strength to the Italian international role.[55]

During the Guadalupe Summit[56], the risks linked to the so called "German singularity" had been evident, i.e. a situation in which only Germany would have supported the NATO decision.[57] The German Chancellor had been fearing such

---

[52] See Helga Haftendorn, Sicherheit und Stabilität: Außenbeziehungen der Bundesrepublik zwischen Ölkrise und NATO-Doppelbeschluss, München 1986, p. 25. See also Matthias Schultz, The Strained Alliance. U.S.-European Relations from Nixon to Carter, Cambridge 2010. See Leopoldo Nuti/Frédéric Bozo/Marie-Pierre/Berndt Rother, The Euromissile Crisis and the End of the Cold War, Stanford 2015.

[53] See Valéry Giscard D'Estaing, Le pouvoir et la vie. L'Affrontement, Paris 1991, p. 365, quoted in Michèle Weinachter, Valéry Giscard d'Estaing et l'Allemagne, p. 209.

[54] As for the Guadalupe summit and the German position see, in particular, Doc.1 Gespräch des Bundeskanzlers Schmidt mit Premierminister Callaghan, Präsident Carter und Staatspräsident Giscard d'Estaing auf Guadeloupe, 5.1.1979, in: AAPD, 1979 Band 1, München 2011.

[55] See Leopoldo Nuti, L'Italia e lo schieramento dei missili da crociera BGM-109 G "Gryphon", quoted in: Simona Colarizi/Piero Craveri/Silvio Pons/Gaetano Quagliarinello, Gli Anni Ottanta come Storia, p. 119. The same essay can be found in Ennio di Nolfo (ed.), La politica estera italiana negli anni Ottanta, Bari – Roma 2003, pp. 41–75.

[56] The importance of the psychological effect provoked in Italy by this exclusion is confirmed in the interview Francesco Cossiga gave to Clio Pedone (27.11.2009): "Da presidente del Consiglio condividevo appieno le preoccupazioni dei tedeschi sull'aggressività sovietica e un po' deluso per l'esclusione del nostro paese dal vertice della Guadalupa decisi di cercare per l'Italia un ruolo da protagonista […]". (As Prime Minister I shared German concerns regarding the Soviet aggressiveness and I was also a little disappointed by the exclusion of our country from the Guadalupe summit. So, I was determined to put Italy in the position of playing a central role). See Clio Pedone, Cossiga, L'uomo che guardò oltre il Muro, Soveria Mannelli 2013, pp. 74–78.

[57] See Doc. 219, Gespräch des Bundesministers Genscher mit dem amerikanischen Außenminister Vance, Washington, VS-vertraulich, 9.8.1979, p. 1956, in: AAPD, 1979 Band 2, München 2011.

a scenario since the first half of 1979 and this was one of the main issues discussed during his meetings with the Italian President of the Republic, Sandro Pertini. In the meantime, consultations were still ongoing in Italy for the definition of a new government.

According to the report of these visits provided by Lelio Lagorio[58], the Italian President reassured the German Chancellor about the Italian willingness to support the Federal Republic:

> «Alla sfida del Cremlino reagì per prima la Germania [...] o, meglio ancora, il cancelliere Helmut Schmidt in prima persona. [...] Ma Schmidt aveva un problema "Non voglio – diceva – che la Germania sia il solo paese che accetta un riarmo atomico. Se non c'è un'altra grande Nazione in Europa che è solidale con la Germania non se ne fa di niente. E non parlatemi della Francia e della Gran Bretagna: Sono già due potenze nucleari e per loro con gli euromissili non cambia molto". O l'Italia dunque o nulla. Ma l'Italia era un problema. Lungamente negletta sullo scenario internazionale [...] militarmente negligente, estromessa dai vertici dei grandi [...] l'Italia era difficile da classificare come un alleato [...] Ma Schmidt non aveva alternative o l'Italia o nulla. Pertini [...] a Schmidt assicurò a conclusione di un colloquio "L'Italia non lascerà sola la Germania. [...]"».[59]

In addition to the assurances given by President Pertini, the July 1979 meeting between the German Chancellor and Francesco Cossiga, shortly before Cossiga's appointment as Prime Minister, was also a significant step on Italy's way to deployment.[60] The Italian diplomatic records already open to consultation do not provide, however, any evidence to support the report of Lelio Lagorio, with the only exception of some vague mention of the shared desire, expressed during

---

[58] Born in Trieste on 9 November 1925, Lelio Lagorio was mayor of Florence in 1965 and in the following years he was president of the "Regione Toscana". From April 1980 until August 1983 he was Minister of Defence.

[59] "Germany was the first country to react to the challenge issued by the Kremlin [...] or, better still, it was Chancellor Helmut Schmidt himself to react. [...] Still, Schmidt had a problem 'I do not want – he said – Germany to accept a nuclear deployment alone. If it is not supported by another great European Nation, we give up. And do not mention France or Great Britain: they are nuclear states already, for them the euromissiles are not such a great change'. Italy or no one else. But Italy was something of a problem. For a long time neglected on the international stage [...] militarily negligent, excluded from the summits of the big states [...] it was difficult to consider Italy as an ally [...] but Schmidt had no other choice, either Italy or nothing. [...] Pertini [...] to Schmidt said at the end of the meeting 'Italy does not intend to leave Germany alone' [...]". See Lelio Lagorio, La sfida del Cremlino, in: Ennio di Nolfo (ed.), La politica estera italiana negli anni Ottanta, pp. 85–86.

[60] See Clio Pedone, Cossiga l'uomo che guardò oltre il Muro, pp. 56–66.

Sandro Pertini's official state visit to Bonn in September 1979, to intensify bilateral scientific cooperation.[61]

When more Italian records are finally accessible for researchers, it will be possible to provide a more detailed reconstruction of these events. Still, the already published German records, together with the valuable support of the interviews, allow us to draw an overview of the Italo-German path to the NATO dual track decision. Furthermore, with specific regard to Sandro Pertini's state visit in September 1979 and his exchange of views with Chancellor Schmidt, German diplomatic documents provide a record of the events, which partially support the statements made by Lelio Lagorio:

> „Bundeskanzler: Diese Waffen dürfen nicht nur auf deutschem Territorium stationiert werden, um Deutschland nicht unter den Verbündeten in eine singuläre Rolle zu drängen. Denn die Allianz darf in einem so wesentlichen Bereich des Vertrages nicht zu einer deutsch-amerikanischen Allianz herabsinken […] eine Stationierung nur auf deutschem oder britischem Territorium reicht für uns nicht aus, da unsere Lage nicht mit der des Kernwaffenstaates Großbritanniens verglichen werden kann. In dieser Frage wurde er von seinem Freund Valéry Giscard d'Estaing unterstützt […] Pertini betont, daß die Deutschen nicht allein den Preis für Frieden und Entspannung in Europa zahlen können."[62]

The risk of a "German singularity" was evident in the words uttered by the Chancellor, but, compared to Lelio Lagorio's statements, a more complex reasoning concerning the allies Germany could have relied on was provided. Neither

---

[61] See Al Cancelliere della Repubblica Federale tedesca, Bonn, 18.9.1979, pp. 198–200, in: Simone Neri Serneri/Antonio Casali/Giovanni Errera (eds.), Scritti e Discorsi di Sandro Pertini, Volume II 1964–1985, Fondazione di Studi Storici Filippo Turati/Presidenza del Consiglio dei Ministri Dipartimento per l'Informazione e l'Editoria, Roma 1979. See also Visita del Presidente della Repubblica Pertini (18–22 September), in: 1979, Testi e documenti sulla politica estera dell'Italia, Roma 1981. The only motive of evident conflict in an overall fruitful visit was the exchange of views between Pertini and Strauss in Munich. They mainly discussed the issue of the Italian "Gastarbeiter". According to Strauss, the Bavarian Government intended to provide the sons and daughters of the Italian "Gastarbeiter" with Italian schools "to prevent them from losing touch with the Italian language and culture, which would make their return to Italy difficult". By contrast, President Pertini believed that it was of the utmost importance to grant full integration to these second-generation migrants into the society they already lived in.

[62] "Chancellor: These arms should not be stationed only on the German territory, which would eventually isolate Germany. In such an essential matter for the Treaty, the Alliance should not be lowered to an American-German alliance […] A deployment on the German or British territory is not enough for us, as our specific status is not comparable to that of the nuclear state of Great Britain. On this matter he was supported by his friend Valéry Giscard D'Estaing […] Pertini affirmed that the Germans should not be left alone to pay the price for freedom and détente in Europe". See Doc. 272 Gespräch des Bundeskanzlers Schmidt mit Staatspräsident Pertini", VS-NfD, Bonn, 19.9.1979, in: AAPD, 1979 Band 2, München 2011.

France, nor the United Kingdom, though for different reasons, could meet Bonn's requirements.[63] Great Britain was a nuclear power, and one might also add a non-continental one, and both these elements combined together gave it a special status. As far as France was concerned, Valéry Giscard d'Estaing seemed at least to sympathise with his German counterpart, which would corroborate Michèle Weinachter's argument as to the divide between the personal approach of the French President and the official position of his country.[64]

Still, nothing was said about the assurances given by President Pertini. To find some evidence we must consider the meeting taking place at the beginning of the following month at the chancellery in Bonn between Helmut Schmidt and Francesco Cossiga.[65]

During this meeting, Francesco Cossiga, by then Italian Prime Minister [66], not only reaffirmed that Italy had not the slightest intention of leaving its German ally alone, "Wir werden Deutschland nicht allein lassen"[67], but he also made explicit mention to the assurances given by President Pertini some months before "Cossiga wiederholt zur anstehenden NATO-Entscheidung die Aussage Pertinis, daß Italien die Bundesrepublik Deutschland in dieser Frage nicht allein lassen wird".[68]

The appointment of Francesco Cossiga as new Prime Minister contributed to the beginning of a new chapter in the history of the relationship between Rome and Bonn, its first steps being intertwined with the dual track decision.[69]

---

[63] In corroboration of this statement, see also Clio Pedone, Cossiga l'uomo che guardò oltre il Muro, p. 76, in particular the interview with Francesco Cossiga: "Helmut Schmidt mise una condizione inderogabile: che a ospitare i missili, oltre che la RFT, dovesse essere anche un'altra potenza occidentale. Non il Regno Unito, che aveva già un proprio arsenale nucleare, e neppure la Francia, quindi la scelta era obbligata tra l'Italia, la Danimarca, i Paesi Bassi e il Belgio. Fatto sta che questi ultimi dissero di non essere affatto disposti [...]". (Helmut Schmidt imposed a no-negotiable condition: Besides the Bundesrepublik, another European state had to agree to host the missiles. Not the UK, it already had its own nuclear arsenal, not France, therefore there was no other choice. It was either Italy or Denmark, the Netherlands or Belgium. The fact is that all of them expect for Italy refused [...]).

[64] See footnote 46 chapter 4.1.

[65] See Doc. 288 Gespräch des Bundeskanzlers Schmidt mit Ministerpräsident Cossiga, VS-vertraulich, Bonn Bundeskanzleramt, 9.10.1979, from 10.40 a.m. to 03.45 p.m., in: AAPD, 1979 Band 2, München 2011.

[66] After Franco Maria Malfatti resigned, Cossiga was also caretaker Foreign Minister from 24 November 1979 to 14 January 1980.

[67] See Doc. 288 Gespräch des Bundeskanzlers Schmidt mit Ministerpräsident Cossiga, VS-vertraulich, Bonn Bundeskanzleramt, 9.10.1979, from 10.40 a.m. to 03.45 p.m., in: AAPD, 1979 Band 2, München 2011.

[68] See Ibid.

[69] See Lettera di Helmut Kohl a Francesco Cossiga, Bonn, 16.7.1998. ASCD, Fondo Francesco Cossiga, archivio con titolario 1944–2010, b.24.

Helmut Schmidt's *Erinnerungen* contains no such enthusiastic comments regarding Francesco Cossiga as Margaret Thatcher's memoirs reveal:

> "I had already had dealings with Sig. Cossiga in 1979 when the Schild family, my constituents, were kidnapped in Sardinia. I had found him highly competent and deeply concerned. He was also a man of principle, as his earlier resignation as Minister of Interior after the murder of the former Christian Democrat leader Aldo Moro showed[70], and as I already knew him to be from my own experience. Italian politics and Italian politicians do not evoke much understanding or sympathy from the British, or indeed from the Italians, and I confess to sharing some of that disenchantment. But Francesco Cossiga was himself a sceptic about the usual Italian practices. He was the nearest thing to an independent in Italian politics; in negotiations he always played a straight hand; he could be relied upon his word, as he did over the stationing of Cruise missiles in Italy [...]".[71]

Nevertheless, Schmidt often praised the Italian politician during interviews and in articles published in the press, both during his mandate and in the following years:

> „Cossiga ist ein Europäer nicht bloß aus Pragmatismus oder aus schlichter Notwendigkeit, sondern aus innerer Überzeugung. [...] Cossiga ist ein Staatsrechtler, zugleich ein gebildeter, sprachenkundiger Mann. Und er ist – wie sein Rücktritt als Innenminister nach dem Mord an Aldo Moro zeigte – ein Mann von Charakter. Er redet seinen Landesleuten nicht nach dem Munde, er redet nicht nur von ihren Rechten, sondern auch von ihren Pflichten. Er ist kein Draufgänger, sondern vorsichtig, kein parteipolitischer Taktiker, sondern umsichtig und weitsichtig. Wenn Cossiga in diesen Tagen nach Deutschland kommt, so trifft er viele Freunde. Insofern ist Francesco Cossiga auch bei uns *zu Hause*."[72]

For the German Chancellor, Francesco Cossiga was a partner who ensured political continuity in the midst of international changes. The stock of knowledge

---

[70] The choice of Francesco Cossiga to resign after the brutal death of the Christian-Democrat leader and friend Aldo Moro had a strong impact abroad, as Margaret Thatcher noticed in her Memoirs. See also the remarks of the then US Ambassador to Italy in: Richard Newton Gardner, Mission Italy. Gli anni di piombo raccontati dall'ambasciatore americano a Roma 1977–1981, Milano 2004.

[71] See Margaret Thatcher, The Downing Street Years 1979–1990, New York 1993, pp. 82–83.

[72] "He is a European not merely to suit his pragmatism or out of sheer necessity, but rather out of inner conviction. [...] Cossiga is a constitutional jurist and at the same time he is a learned man, well-versed in languages. He is also a man of character, as his resignation as Interior Minister demonstrates. He does not say to his compatriots what they want to hear, he does not just talk about their rights, but also about their duties. He is not a daredevil, he is rather cautious; he is not a party-political tactician, he is rather prudent and far-sighted. When Cossiga visits Germany, he will meet many friends. In this respect Francesco Cossiga is here *at home*". See Helmut Schmidt, *die Zeit*, 18.4.1986. Konrad Adenauer Stiftung St. Augustin Archiv für Christlich-demokratische Politik (hereafter ACDP), Abteilung Pressedokumentation, file: Francesco Cossiga, press cutting.

Cossiga could rely on was probably far more than Bonn would have ever expected from a successor of Andreotti and last, but not least, Cossiga had a sharp and rather peculiar feeling for Germany compared to the approach of the majority of the Italian political establishment.

Henry Kissinger allegedly said that the new Italian Prime Minister did not look like a Christian-Democrat at all[73], even if by 1979 the Sardinian politician had a record of active involvement within the DC (as Flaminio Piccoli[74] used to remark), which was also a sign of continuity for Bonn.

Born in Sassari 26 July 1928, Cossiga had become, at the young age of seventeen, a member of the Christian-Democratic party. At first Cossiga chose an academic career as teaching assistant in Constitutional law to Professor Guarino, but later decided to abandon such a career to devote himself entirely to politics.[75] His political offices as Undersecretary of Defence in the governments Moro III, Leone II, Rumor I and Rumor II[76] are well known, though he is perhaps better known for his appointment in February 1976 as Interior Minister and his resignation from this two years later after the murder of his friend and Italian leader Aldo Moro. On the contrary, other milestones of his political career are less known, for example his appointment in the government Moro IV as Minister without a

---

[73] See Stefano Folli, Cossiga democristiano d'Occidente, in: *Il Sole24Ore,* 18.8.2010. http://www.ilsole24ore.com/art/commenti-e-idee/2010-08-18/democristiano-occidente-085830_PRN.shtml (last consulted 15.5.2016).

[74] Flaminio Piccoli was born in December 1915 in Kirchbichl, a small village of the Austrian Tyrol. At the end of the War he moved with his family to Trento, where some years later he was also very active in the Catholic movement, keeping in close touch with one of its most charismatic figures, the archbishop Celestino Endrici. In 1938 he graduated in Foreign Languages and Literature from the University of Venice. From the very beginning of his political career he was on very friendly terms with Alcide De Gasperi, although Piccoli was more than thirty years his junior. From 1980 to 1982, while he was secretary of the Christian Democratic party, he often praised Francesco Cossiga as a man of strong political and religious principles (as his activism at a young age in the FUCI confirmed). See ILS, Fondo Democrazia Cristiana, Corrispondenza Estera, Sezione Flaminio Piccoli 1980–1982, various documents. In addition, Flaminio Piccoli seemed to believe that Cossiga had had a stabilizing influence on Italian politics both at home and abroad, thus allowing a more balanced assessment of facts and unresolved issues. See Cesare Golfari, Cossiga due Forlani uno. Gli anni del preambolo, Varese 1982, p. 8.

[75] See Lettera di Francesco Cossiga a François Bayrou, Rome, 17.7.2004. ASCD, Fondo Francesco Cossiga, archivio con titolario 1944–2010, b.24. Some useful information can be gathered from this document. Cossiga belonged to a Sardinian, republican, anti-fascist family with strong Catholic and Liberal beliefs. He became at an early age member of the "Azione Cattolica italiana", at first as member of the "Gioventù d'Azione Cattolica", and later on in the "Federazione Universitaria Cattolica italiana" as advisor to *Monsignor Giovanni Battista Montini*. After the Second World War he represented the "Federazione Universitaria Cattolica italiana" at the "Bureau International di Pax Romana" in Freiburg.

[76] From 1966 to 1970.

portfolio for administrative reform of the public sector.[77] As such he promoted the creation of what later became the "Scuola Superiore per la Pubblica Amministrazione":

> «Cossiga è stato [...] ministro della Riforma della Pubblica Amministrazione, pochi lo ricordano in tale veste, anche perché, in effetti, ricoprì l'incarico per un periodo molto breve. All'epoca io ero vicecapo di gabinetto al Ministero e ricordo con precisione alcuni aspetti dell'azione riformatrice svolta da Cossiga nella burocrazia italiana [...] Cossiga riuscì a portare a termine la negoziazione per la scala mobile [...] mise molto ordine nelle carriere pubbliche e nella Pubblica Amministrazione, avviò la Scuola Superiore della Pubblica Amministrazione e, sempre in quegli anni iniziò la smilitarizzazione della polizia [...]».[78]

It is even less widely known that, as Interior Minister, Francesco Cossiga had the opportunity to attend some training courses on counter-terrorism, both in Germany and in the United Kingdom.

This overview, albeit short, provides a vital piece of information which clarifies the kind of expertise and the wealth of experience Cossiga could rely on from his first contacts with Bonn.

First and foremost, his appointment meant political continuity, although he was not very familiar with economic issues.[79] Secondly, along with legal training, Cossiga had comprehensive and consistent expertise in the field of security and defence, which gave him some common ground with the German Chancellor. Furthermore, during the 1970s, he had been developing a marked sensibility for counter-political terrorism and a strong feeling for its concrete manifestations in Germany. Last, but not least, he was one of the few Italian politicians to be aware of the weaknesses of the National administrative network. This was much more than Helmut Schmidt had hoped for in July 1979. Namely an overall continuity in Italian politics, or, if the worst came to the worst with a Socialist Prime Minister, the stability which comes from keeping the economic levers in the hands of trustworthy partners. In 1979, this need was overshadowed by another crucial

---

[77] See Clio Pedone, *Cossiga l'uomo che guardò oltre il Muro*, ch.1, par. 2, p. 17.

[78] "Cossiga was [...] Minister for the administrative Reform of the public sector, although very few people remember him in this capacity, actually he had this responsibility for a short time. I was deputy head of cabinet back then, therefore I remember the exact details of Cossiga's reform policy [...] Cossiga carried out the negotiations on the sliding wage scale [...] he brought some order to public careers and in public administration, he launched the 'Scuola Superiore della Pubblica Amministrazione' and in the same period he also engaged in the demilitarisation of the local police forces [...]". See the interview Senator Luigi Zanda gave to Clio Pedone (14.3.2011). For the text of the interview see Clio Pedone, *Cossiga l'uomo che guardò oltre il Muro*, pp. 79–82.

[79] Cossiga tried and compensated for it by confirming Filippo Maria Pandolfi's assignment as Minister of Treasury, which also greatly reassured the government in Bonn.

need, in that the hypothetical partner should also be reliable as regards the issue of euromissiles. Cossiga seemed to be the answer to both prayers:

> «La decisione degli euromissili fu una delle più importanti che prese Cossiga sul piano internazionale grazie tra l'altro ad una buona amicizia con Helmut Schmidt e con Van Agt (con i quali avevano collaborato da ministro degli Interni). Fu decisiva questa scelta di Cossiga, perché la Germania si sentì appoggiata, non potevano prendere questa decisione da soli, cercavano aiuto e l'aiuto lo trovarono nell'Italia e in Francesco Cossiga [...]. Il fatto di aver deciso per gli euromissili ha determinato poi lentamente il ripiegamento dell'URSS sulle proprie posizioni e tutti i cambiamenti che hanno portato al crollo dell'URSS».[80]

Moreover, the long and detailed interview with Ambassador Ludovico Ortona sheds some light on a further point belonging to that category of elements usually relegated to the sidelines of diplomatic records:

> «[...] tra l'altro aveva un'impostazione un po' atipica per un democristiano, perché in effetti i democristiani erano molto avanti nella zona grigia, non era decisionisti o lo erano a fatica, erano piuttosto propensi al compromesso. Non che Cossiga non lo fosse, ma era piuttosto decisionista e questo suo decisionismo era molto apprezzato nel mondo politico tedesco e britannico. Tanto è che Cossiga ha avuto rapporti con molti uomini politici tedeschi a cominciare da Helmut Schmidt per tutta la questione nel 1979 degli euromissili [...]».[81]

---

[80] "Internationally the choice regarding euromissiles was one of the most delicate Cossiga ever made. This was also possible thanks to his good friendship with Helmut Schmidt and Van Agt (they had worked side by side as Interior Ministers). This choice had a decisive role, because Germany had the feeling of being supported. Germany could not act on its own; it was looking for help, which it found in Italy and in Francesco Cossiga. This was also one of the causes of the Soviet rollback and of the changes leading to the demise of the communist behemoth". Author's interview with ambassador Ludovico Ortona (22.3.2016). See also Intervento alla Camera dei Deputati: dibattito sugli euromissili. ASCD, Fondo Francesco Cossiga, archivio 1965–1985, b.4, fascicolo 33. As for the last statement made by ambassador Ortona see also Lettera di Francesco Cossiga al presidente Rau, Rome, 8.4.2002; ASCD, Fondo Francesco Cossiga, archivio con titolario 1944–2010, b.24.

[81] "Besides, he (Cossiga) had an unusual approach for a Christian-Democrat, as the members of his party often moved into a grey area. In other words, they were not great decision-makers, they had difficulty in taking decisions, they were more willing to compromise. Cossiga was not against compromise, but he was also a volunteer by nature, and this approach was appreciated both in Germany and in Great Britain. It is, therefore, not a surprise that Cossiga had good relations with many German politicians, starting with Helmut Schmidt regarding the issue of euromissiles in 1979 [...]". In author's interview with ambassador Ludovico Ortona. The US Ambassador to Rome, Richard Newton Gardner, indirectly confirmed this statement. He used to say that Cossiga gave the impression of an open-minded, frank, spontaneous and outgoing man, who did not avoid problems. Besides, unlike Andreotti, he seemed to believe in what he said. See Richard Newton Gardner, *Gli anni di piombo raccontati dall'ambasciatore italiano a Roma*, pp. 305–308.

If we carefully consider the topics of discussion at the meetings between the Chancellor and the Prime Minister, starting from the autumn of 1979[82], there is more to be found than a mere confirmation of what came to light through the interviews and the analysis of the biographical profiles of the protagonists. The records show, in fact, an Italian willingness to go beyond a mere display of solidarity with the German Federal Republic:

> „Bundeskanzler betont zu Beginn, daß er sich ganz außerordentlich über den Besuch von Cossiga freut [...] Zum deutsch-italienischen Verhältnis in der Gegenwart gehört diese enge Zusammenarbeit [...]. Staatspräsident Pertini hat bei seinem Besuch in Deutschland einen tiefen Eindruck nicht nur auf die Gesprächspartner, sondern auch auf die gesamte deutsche Öffentlichkeit gemacht.
> Cossiga dankt für die freundliche Begrüßung. Staatspräsident Pertini hat sich begeistert über den Empfang durch das deutsche Volk, den Bundespräsidenten und insbesondere den Bundeskanzler geäußert. Er mißt den bilateralen deutsch-italienischen Beziehungen im gemeinsamen Rahmen von NATO und EG allergrößte Bedeutung bei. [...] Er wird sich voll dafür einsetzten, sie weiter aufzubauen [...] Cossiga schlägt vor bei künftigen deutsch-italienischen Konsultationen der Regierungschef auch Minister der beiden Kabinette hinzuziehen [...]."[83]

After the usual greetings and a short mention of the history of the Italo-German relationship in the past, the 9 October 1979 Bonn meeting between Schmidt and Cossiga mainly focused on three central issues.

The first two issues concerned East-West relations, along with the Soviet internal changes and the problems arising from the dual track decision. According to the German and Italian comments, the Netherlands appeared to be extremely

---

[82] With reference to the issues here discussed, the most interesting meetings took place in Bonn on 9 October 1979, in Hamburg on 26 April 1980 and in Rome between 15 and 16 May 1980. In addition, many telephone conversations complete this picture (unfortunately in this last respect information provided by the records is rather scanty). Ambassador Ferdinando Salleo recalled in the interview given to the author that Chancellor Schmidt was in the habit of meeting Cossiga quite frequently in the autumn of 1979. Such meetings often took place during the so called "after hours" at the Italian Embassy in Bonn.

[83] "The Chancellor started by underlining his great pleasure with Cossiga's visit [...] at present this close cooperation forms part of the Italo-German relationship [...] During his state-visit to Germany President Pertini made a lasting impression both on his interlocutors and on the German public at large. Cossiga thanked back for the welcome he received. President Pertini spoke in the highest terms about the way he was received by the German people, by the German President, and above all, by the Chancellor. He attaches a great importance to the Italo-German relationship in the framework of NATO and of the EC. [...] He is ready to fully commit himself to further strengthen them. [...] Cossiga proposes to also admit Ministers of both governments to participate in the next bilateral consultations". See Doc. 288, Gespräch des Bundeskanzlers Schmidt mit Ministerpräsident Cossiga, VS-vertraulich, Bundeskanzleramt, Bonn, 9.10.1979, from 10.40 a.m. to 03.45 p.m., in: AAPD, 1979 Band 2, München 2011, p. 1415.

vulnerable to Soviet propaganda, because of the strong influence of pacifist movements on its public opinion and the intrinsic weakness of a government that could not rely on a strong majority in Parliament.

A specific focus was then devoted to the changes within the Italian Socialist Party and to the approach of its leader, Bettino Craxi, to the pending international problems. In the opinion of the Italian political leader, active support and "guidance" from the German Socialists for the evolution within the PSI could ease the Italian decision-making process regarding euromissiles.[84]

The third and last issue of discussion concerned both the difficulties in organizing the Summit of Venice – it being planned for the following year and it being a crucial step for the German chancellor – and the layer of tension within the EEC. The EEC faced the challenge of narrowing the economic gap between the Member States without overlooking the task of supporting a significant transformation of the then Common Agricultural Policy (CAP). This last issue was also the main link between this meeting and the ones which followed during spring 1980.[85]

Between the end of 1979 and the beginning of 1980 the attention of the Italian Prime Minister was, in fact, also focused on the CAP[86], whose burden for Italy was bound to increase with the accession of new Mediterranean States.[87]

The suggestions made during this summit to improve bilateral relations between Rome and Bonn are not less interesting than the international issues discussed. The previous quotation shows for instance a recurring feature of the two governments led by Francesco Cossiga between 1979 and 1980, namely the strong desire to favour a participation of the ministers of both countries in the regular Italo-German summits of political leaders. Schmidt seemed to appreciate the hint, in so far as the Interior and Foreign Ministers, the Ministers of Economy, Finance and Research could be invited to participate in these meetings on a regular basis.[88]

---

[84] See Ibid., pp. 1417–1418.

[85] During spring 1980, the lack of a compromise on the inner reform of the CAP seemed to worry the Italian government also for its potential consequences on the credibility of the European Economic Community on the international stage. See Doc.132, Gespräch des Bundeskanzlers Schmidt mit Ministerpräsident Cossiga, VS-NfD, Gästehaus des Hamburger Senats, Hamburg, 26 April 1980, in: AAPD, 1980, Band I, München, 2012. See also Seminario della DC sulla politica estera intervento di Francesco Cossiga, Firenze, 5.5.1980. ASCD, Fondo Francesco Cossiga, archivio 1965–1985, b.5.

[86] See Doc. 30, Telefongespräch des Bundeskanzlers Schmidt mit Ministerpräsident Cossiga, VS-vertraulich, January 1980, from 01.55 to 02.40 p.m., in: AAPD, 1980 Band I, München, 2012.

[87] See Doc. 288, Gespräch des Bundeskanzlers Schmidt mit Ministerpräsident Cossiga, VS-vertraulich, Bundeskanzleramt, Bonn, 9 October 1979, from 10.40 a.m. to 03.45 p.m., p. 1422, in: AAPD, 1979 Band 2, München 2011.

[88] "The suggestion made by Cossiga was crowned with success during the following meetings. See Dichiarazione del Presidente del Consiglio a seguito degli incontri con il Cancelliere della

It was, on the contrary, far more complicated to accept the Italian suggestion to also include the Ministers of Defence as a precondition for a more efficient exchange of information, in the short term, and a closer cooperation in defence and security issues in the medium and long term. The German reluctance to follow this path can probably be explained in the light of the needs and conditions of its partnership with France, whose regular meetings with Germany did not involve the Ministers of Defence.[89]

Certainly, Francesco Cossiga was not the first Italian politician or diplomat to sense the necessity to improve the very nature of the relationship linking Rome to Bonn by widening the horizons as to involve decision-makers other than the Heads of Government.[90] It had been indeed a subject of discussion since the end of the De Gasperi era, whose political weight had been strengthened by the success of the partnership Schmidt-Giscard d'Estaing. Still, Francesco Cossiga was the first Head of Government to make this goal one of the priorities of his policy.[91]

Without wishing to reduce its intrinsic significance, the euromissile issue also presented an opportunity to strengthen the links between Bonn and Rome. As the meetings after December 1979 suggest, it would be a mistake to read and understand the significance of the relationship with Bonn merely on grounds of achieving the common goal of deployment.

Repubblica Federale di Germania Schmidt, Rome, 16.5.1980. ASCD, Fondo Francesco Cossiga, archivio 1965–1985, b.5, fascicolo 80: [...] Il Cancelliere è accompagnato dai Ministri delle finanze e dell'economia secondo quanto avevamo previsto nella mia ultima visita a Bonn e che cioè, così come avviene per gli incontri bilaterali tra il Cancelliere federale ed i Capi di Stato e di Governo di altri Paesi europei, anche con l'Italia gli incontri avvenissero contemporaneamente anche a livello di ministri [...] in generale abbiamo registrato una piena e larghissima identità di vedute fra il Governo Federale di Germania ed il Governo italiano per quanto riguarda i problemi di sicurezza, della distensione, della solidarietà con gli Stati Uniti d'America [...]". (The Chancellor came accompanied by the Ministers of Finance and Economy according to what we had decided during my last visit in Bonn. As it is custom in the summits between the German Chancellor and other European leaders, the meetings with Italy are also to include the participation of the ministers [...] Italy and Germany share the same vision concerning security issues, the détente and the solidarity with the United States of America [...]).

[89] See, among others, l'influence de la R.F.A en Italie, Ambassade de France en Italie, Gillet Martinet ambassadeur de France en Italie à son excellence Claude Cheysson ministre des relations extérieures, Rome, 29. 11 1983. AMAE, inva1930, Direction Europe, Série RFA, carton 4907, sous-série 11, période 1981–1985

[90] See lettera di Francesco Cossiga a Schroeder, 18.3.1999. ASCD, Fondo Francesco Cossiga, archivio con titolario 1944–2010, b.24.

[91] See Schmidt und Cossiga wünschen Ost-West Balance, dpa, October 1979, in: ACDP, Abteilung Pressedokumentation, Francesco Cossiga. The report highlights how important Cossiga's suggestion was, and the prompt acceptance by the Chancellor to include more ministers in the bilateral summits routine.

This marriage of convenience was born on the basis of instrumental needs on both sides. For Italy this meant the feeling of having a real chance to take advantage of the Franco-German defence disagreements together with the desire to strengthen its own influence in the "deutschsprachiger Raum" once the "vertenza altoatesina" had been solved.[92] In a few years it had, however, blossomed into something quite different. This was also the result of the determination of a new Prime Minister, whose background and approach to the German question made him an exception both within his own party and in the broader context of the Italian political realm.

> „Cossiga würdigt die Rolle der engen Begegnungen der Völker durch die Anwesenheit von italienischen Gastarbeitern in Deutschland […] Als Verfassungsrechtler hat er in Deutschland stets eine zweite geistige Heimat gesehen. Es gibt für ihn auch gewisse familiäre Wurzeln: Vor einer alten Tante hat er immer Süßigkeiten nur bekommen, wenn er sie auf Deutsch darum bat."[93]

By the end of the Seventies, it had become common practice on part of the Italian politicians to mention, during official bilateral summits, the influence that he huge number of Italian "Gastarbeiter" had on German society, and they used the role of the increasing flow of tourists as a useful link. It was, in contrast, far more unusual, both among politicians and diplomats[94], to call Germany a "spiritual home" or to have a good command of the German language.

---

[92] The agreement of November 1969 and the measures of the so called "pacchetto", which the commission "dei diciannove" (a commission composed of nineteen members) had been discussing since 1960, allowed a certain improvement in the "vertenza altoatesina" (the issue of South Tyrol). See, in particular, Luciano Monzali, Giulio Andreotti e le relazioni italo-austriache 1972–1992, Merano, 2015, pp. 9–10. These changes made a sort of "détente" in the relationship between Rome and Vienna possible, hence an enhanced flexibility in the Italian role in the Mitteleuropean area at the end of the 1970s. Such changes also had a positive influence on the regional cooperation structures, such as the Alpe Adria, created in 1978 (see chapter 5.2) and, though indirectly, on the relationship with Bonn. Italy had, indeed, suspected a German involvement in the wave of political terrorism in the 1960s in South Tyrol. See author's interview with Ambassador Alessandro Quaroni (12.2.2016). Lastly, the "pacchetto" also had the merit of paving the way for the removal of the Italian veto to the accession of Austria to the EC. See Moro a rappresentanze italiane a Bruxelles e Vienna, 7.12.1969. ILS, AGA, serie Europa, b.420.

[93] "He praised the close encounters of people through the presence of Italian 'Gastarbeiter'. As a constitutional jurist, he has always considered Germany a second spiritual home. There are also personal reasons. An old aunt always gave him sweets if he asked for them in German". See Doc. 288, Gespräch des Bundeskanzler Schmidt mit Ministerpräsident Cossiga, VS-vertraulich, Bundeskanzleramt, Bonn, 9 October 1979, from 10.40 a.m. to 03.45 p.m., p. 1414, in: AAPD, 1979 Band 2, München 2011.

[94] It is not easy to address the issue of the "presenza di germanisti" (meaning the existence of experts on Germany) and of the real knowledge of the German language of those in the ranks of Italian diplomats. Still, its influence on the relationship between Rome and Bonn in the 1980s is far from negligible. A few comments are, therefore, necessary at this stage. The information gathered

«Il tedesco è una lingua più difficile del francese, meno simile all'italiano, più lontana in un certo senso e perciò credo che fosse studiata meno del francese [...] La tendenza era quella di studiare il francese. Non c'erano moltissimi germanisti, anche se la cultura tedesca era conosciuta e studiata. [...] Il che significa che si è formata una classe diplomatica più orientata sul francese che sul tedesco. Però esiste in seno alla diplomazia una forte corrente di colleghi che parla benissimo il tedesco e che inevitabilmente finisce per andare in Germania [...]. I colleghi che sono stati a Bonn prima e a Berlino poi parlano tutti il tedesco. Luigi Vittorio Ferraris parlava bene il tedesco e Marcello Guidi era addirittura bilingue [...]».[95]

Knowledge of the German language, and more generally speaking, of foreign languages was, in fact, not widespread among Italian politicians, and for the majority of them it was no common practice to spend a period abroad before the actual beginning of their political career at the highest levels. Those who had a good command of the language, or at least were a little familiar with the political culture of the "German speaking area", were either born or had grown up in Trentino or South Tyrol, such as Alcide De Gasperi[96] and Flaminio Piccoli[97], or, at least had been involved in the negotiations concerning the South Tyrolean issue (vertenza altoatesina), as was Giulio Andreotti.[98]

---

through interviews with leading former Italian diplomats has shown the importance and the limitations of the existence of experts on Germany working at the Farnesina. Ambassador to Western Germany Pietro Quaroni complained in 1961 about the great difficulties of representing Italy in a country whose language a diplomat does not know. See, in particular, the author's interview with Alessandro Quaroni, son of Pietro Quaroni, both Italian diplomats. Further information is provided by German diplomatic records. The Eighties marked the beginning of a substantial improvement. The Ambassadors working in Bonn during that decade, Luigi Vittorio Ferraris from 1980 to 1987, Raniero Vanni d'Archirafi from 1987 to 1989 and Marcello Guidi from 1989 to 1992, had all a good command of German and an overall good knowledge of its culture. See Italienische Vertreter in der Bundesrepublik 1985–1990. PP AA, B 26 n. 140535.

[95] "The German language is more difficult than the French. It is less like Italian. In a sense, it is less familiar. I believe that this is the reason why French was more widely studied than German. There were not many experts on Germany, even if the German culture was known and studied. This means that Italian diplomats were more familiar with French. There is nonetheless a group of fellow diplomats who have a very good command of the language and they almost invariably spend part of their careers in Germany [...]. All my colleagues, first in Bonn and then in Berlin, speak German. Luigi Vittorio Ferraris spoke very good German and Marcello Guidi grew up bilingual [...]". See the author's interview with Ambassador Leonardo Visconti di Modrone, (referring to his fellow diplomats, Ambassador Visconti intended those colleagues who were in active service in the Eighties, Nineties and in the Noughties). For Ambassador Guidi see Botschafter Marcello Guidi 1989–1992. PP AA, B 26 n. 17358

[96] See ch.3.

[97] See footnote 74 ch. 4.2.

[98] Giulio Andreotti worked side by side with Alcide De Gasperi, who appointed him Undersecretary of the Prime Minister office (1947–1954). This close cooperation with De Gasperi gave Andreotti the unique change to widen his horizons to the political culture of the German speaking area through the thorny issue of the relationship between Italy and Austria, and then the even more important

As a result, the Italian vision of Germany and of the German question was usually filtered, and sometimes even deformed, by a sort of "magnifier", the South-Tyrolean lens and, more generally speaking, the Austrian lens. Cossiga was an exception not only because he had a good command of the language, but also because he was unaffected by such a limitation.

«Cossiga aveva una seria conoscenza, una conoscenza profonda, della lingua e della cultura tedesca e del mondo tedesco in genere. Ciò nasce probabilmente dal fatto che aveva imparato il tedesco da ragazzino. Non ricordo purtroppo bene, lui me lo spiegò, credo fosse una bambinaia, o piuttosto una zia».[99]

Opinions differ as to how the Prime Minister acquired a good knowledge of German. According to archival records and interviews which Cossiga himself gave on the subject, an old aunt was the first who made young Cossiga curious about the German speaking world.

«Giornalista: Lei è un po' un conoscitore della nostra lingua, ma anche della nostra cultura. Mi ha detto che già da giovane ha conosciuto la nostra cultura. Come sono avvenuti questi incontri?
Cossiga: Guardi l'incontro ha una doppia origine, un'origine familiare ed un'origine di scelta di studi. Ha un'origine familiare perché avevo una carissima zia che era tedesca, bavarese, la quale è stata la prima, ad introdurmi in modo molto semplice nella lingua tedesca. Quando passavo dei periodi con Lei, quando ero

---

South Tyrolean problem. In addition to being Undersecretary, Andreotti was, in fact, also in charge of the management of the body responsible for border issues, including the application of the 1946 treaty. Unlike many among his contemporaries, Andreotti showed a keen interest for the South Tyrolean issue. See, in particolar, Massimo Franco, Andreotti. La vita di un uomo politico, la storia di un'epoca, Milano, 2010; Mario Barone/Ennio di Nolfo (eds.), Giulio Andreotti, l'uomo il cattolico lo statista, Soveria Mannelli 2010. See also Giulio Andreotti, 1947. L'anno delle grandi svolte nel diario di un protagonista, Milano 2005 and Giulio Andreotti, De Gasperi visto da vicino, Milano 1985. See also the interview Giulio Andreotti gave to Cinzia Rognoni Vercelli in Rome (11.12.1998), in: Voices on Europe, Oral History Collections, Historical Archives of the European Union (http://www.eui/HAEU/OralHistory/, last consulted 1.2.2016). Lastly, see the interview Ambassador Alessandro Quaroni gave to the author: "[…] una conoscenza dei profondi legami tra Andreotti e la struttura del potere alto-atesino è necessaria…Andreotti passava sempre le vacanze a Merano […] in Alto Adige è una persona che ha una reputazione estremamente positiva e questo si riflette nella percezione austriaca, insieme al suo ruolo nell'ultima fase del negoziato con l'Austria […]". ([…] a knowledge of the deep links between Andreotti and the South-Tyrolean structures of power is indispensable…Andreotti frequently spent his holidays in Meran, […] in Alto Adige he had an extremely positive reputation, which was mirrored in the perception that Austria had of him, together with the role he played in the last stages of the negotiations with Austria […]).
[99] "Cossiga was proficient in German. He had a deep knowledge of the language and culture of the German speaking world. Probably, the reason was that he had learned it at a young age. Unfortunately, I do not remember very well, he (Cossiga) told me, perhaps it was a nanny or rather an aunt". See the author's interview with Ambassador Ludovico Ortona (22.3.2015).

giovane, mi ha insegnato il tedesco. Ho avuto nella sua casa la possibilità di leggere i suoi libri. Poi nella scuola ho continuato a studiare il tedesco. Mi ha affascinato questa lingua per la sua struttura logica. Io ho molte grammatiche tedesche. In più, poi, mi sono iscritto alla facoltà di Giurisprudenza e ho cominciato a studiare il diritto. Allora la conoscenza del tedesco era uno strumento di carattere tecnico».[100]

Another version suggests that Cossiga had a nurse who taught him German, but there is no information or evidence in the records to substantiate this statement. As for the German press, the influential *Frankfurter Allgemeine Zeitung* suggested that Cossiga had a German grandmother:

> „[…] Cossiga ist Deutschland und den Deutschen zugetan, nicht nur, weil er ein Mann von Kultur ist, sondern auch weil eine Großmutter aus Deutschland stammte. […].“[101]

We cannot rule out the possibility that more than one hypothesis may be true. Regardless of the one we choose, it is undeniable that from a young age he had a bond with Germany, which his studies further strengthened and deepened.

Language skills are an asset which should not be neglected, both as a tool to foster an atmosphere of confidence during bilateral meetings, and as an auxiliary facility to help proper understanding of the culture of the partner while dealing with him. In this perspective, it is noteworthy that some of the meetings between Francesco Cossiga and Helmut Schmidt took place only with the help of an "interpreter" if needed (which could allow a private face-to-face exchange of information as in that time so often happened between Giscard d'Estaing and Schmidt).

Furthermore, this early bond with Germany had also been reinforced in 1961 when Francesco Cossiga, back then a promising thirty-three-year-old deputy, had been selected to be head of the official delegation sent to Germany to monitor the election campaign. The Christian-Democratic parties of several Western European states, among them the Italian DC, were concerned about the resilience of

---

[100] See Intervista del presidente Cossiga con il signor Horst Schlitter del quotidiano tedesco Frankfurter Rundschau (the interview which Cossiga gave to Horst Schlitter from the German newspaper Frankfurter Rundschau), Rome, 1.8.1988. ASCD, Fondo Francesco Cossiga, archivio con titolario 1944–2010, Presidenza della Repubblica-Settennato 1985–1992, b.192, fascicolo 23.

[101] "Cossiga is devoted to Germany and to the Germans not only because he is a learned man, but also because his grandmother came from Germany". Heinz-Joachim Fischer, Der Mutigste der Gemäßigten, *Frankfurter Allgemeine Zeitung* (hereafter also *FAZ*), 25.6.1985, in: Konrad Adenauer Stiftung, St. Augustin, ACDP, Abteilung Pressedokumentation, file: Francesco Cossiga, press cutting. See also Hansjakob Stehle, Ein Moralist, der die Ohnmacht kennt, *die Zeit*, 28.6.1985, in St. Augustin, ACDP, Abteilung Pressedokumentation, file: Francesco Cossiga, press cutting.

the CDU and feared the consequences of a more influential and assertive Socialist Party. Officially, the Italian delegation had been sent to express solidarity with the party of Chancellor Adenauer. Unofficially, however, the delegation had been sent to closely follow the ongoing political developments. It was one of Cossiga's first "missions abroad"; it gave him the opportunity of being one of few foreign observers witnessing the erection of the Berlin Wall.[102]

As a result of this mix of skills and experiences the Italian Prime Minister had developed a vision where a "deutsche Frage" and a "Deutschlandfrage" coexisted. An overall interest for the German speaking world and, more generally, for Central-Eastern Europe (an area where both Italian and German potential influence was growing) is meant by the term "deutsche Frage". By the term "Deutschlandfrage" we mean more specifically Western Germany, its weight in International dynamics and, even more relevant, in European ones.

The political programme of Cossiga seemed to be animated by a raising desire to give new momentum to the interaction between Bonn and Rome by boosting bilateral cooperation through more frequent meetings, which would include a wide range of ministers, and also through increased security and defence coordination both within NATO and in the European Community. Being this scheme rather ambitious, especially in the light of the Italian economic and political weaknesses and difficulties, it is only logical to wonder whether it was feasible, and what kind of inheritance it left for the years to come. At the end of this subchapter two different types of conclusions can be drawn.

On the one hand, if we choose to draw our conclusions in light of the inheritance left for the following years, the balance-sheet is mainly negative. Cossiga remained in power for barely a year, nothing surprising if we consider the average lifespan of Italian governments. Still, the time in which he was entitled to lead his country was too brief for practical results to be achieved, such as the ones Giscard d'Estaing and Schmidt had reached. The only noteworthy exception is the decision leading to the deployment of Pershing missiles. A gradual erosion of Helmut Schmidt's political clout as a result of both a dissatisfied public opinion and marked tensions between the coalition partners, the SPD (*Sozialistische Partei Deutschlands*) and the FDP (*Freie Demokratische Partei*), also affected the chances of success of the abovementioned scheme.

Knowledge of German within the Italian political élite was and remained limited, while Cossiga's complex and comprehensive approach, where a *deutsche*

---

[102] See lettera di Francesco Cossiga a Helmut Kohl, 22.7.1993. ASCD, Fondo Francesco Cossiga, archivio con titolario 1944–2010, b.24. See also intervista del presidente Cossiga con il signor Andreas Srenk e la signora Rose Marie Borngasserper il quotidiano tedesco Die Welt (interview of Francesco Cossiga with Mr Andreas Srenk and Mrs. Rose Marie Borngasserper from the newspaper *Die Welt*), Rome, 10.12.1990. ASCD, Fondo Francesco Cossiga, archivio con titolario 1944–2010, Presidenza della Repubblica-Settennato 1985–1992, b.192, fascicolo 40.

Frage coexisted with a *Deutschlandfrage*, was an episode without follow-up. His vision was, therefore, significant not for its potential to spread, but merely as an expression of the peculiar role he had into the changing patterns of the Italo-German relationship, at first as Prime Minister and later on as President of the Republic.

On the other hand, if we choose to draw our conclusions in light of the feeling which observers had in 1980, the balance-sheet is not so negative. The commitment of the executive led by Francesco Cossiga to endorse the NATO dual track decision showed that Italy could be a reliable partner, and this is especially noteworthy in a phase when the Franco-German couple seemed to have lost some of its edge. Sandro Pertini and Francesco Cossiga, both as political figures and as individuals, were a catalyst for interest in the German press, which contributed to a slow but positive progress in this bilateral relationship, breaking the spiral of misunderstandings existing in 1977 and overcoming some of the stereotypes traditionally associated with the "*bel Paese*".

Furthermore, the second Cossiga government left another important inheritance in the shape of a Foreign Minister, Emilio Colombo, who in the following years made the news together with his German counterpart, Hans-Dietrich Genscher, for their major efforts in breathing new life into the European integration process. In retrospective it could be argued that all these combined efforts resulted in nothing else than a no legally binding solemn declaration. Still, in 1980 this could not be considered in any way a foregone conclusion.

It also left as inheritance a new Ambassador to Bonn, Luigi Vittorio Ferraris[103], the first of a series of diplomats leading the Italian embassy during the 1980s. All of them had good command of the German language, were appreciated in the German Foreign Ministry, and had a certain influence on the German press.

Lastly, the most relevant inheritance left to posterity was a dialectic between old stereotypes and new representations, and also between individual surges of interest and a greater determination to see enforced tangible measures which would lead to greater institutionalisation in the relationship with Bonn. This dialectic was destined to be the constant framework of interaction between Rome and Bonn in the 1980s.

---

[103] Luigi Vittorio Ferraris was appointed Ambassador to Western Germany in January 1980, during the second government led by Helmut Schmidt. According to German diplomatic records, both positive and far less enthusiastic conclusions can be drawn on his ability to attract the attention of the media, and, above all, on the opinions he expressed on Germany after the end of his appointment.

4.3 The Genscher-Colombo Plan, the Double Unrealized Dream: Potential and Limits of the Italo-German Couple

> *Im Laufe des Jahres 1981 traf ich mich häufig mit meinem italienischen Kollegen Emilio Colombo, der zu den großen Persönlichkeiten der italie-nischen Nachkriegspolitik gehört. Die Zusamme-nar-beit mit ihm gestaltete sich so freundlich und eng, dass ich es zuweilen bedauerte mich mit ihm nicht in einer gemeinsamen Sprache unterhalten zu kön-nen.*[104] (Hans-Dietrich Genscher)

This sub-chapter deals with the period between the second half of 1980 and 1983, and its focus is primarily on the draft "European Act". This Act, better known as the Genscher-Colombo Plan in reference to the names of its supporters, the German and Italian Foreign Ministers, is also known in France as "*project germano-italien*" or "*propositions germano-italiennes*"[105], and it has been selected as the main thread of this sub-chapter.

The so called Genscher-Colombo Plan has often been the subject of conflicting opinions for its provisions and their effectiveness, efficacy, relevance and impact on the specific needs required for successfully relaunching the integration process.[106] Still, within the framework of the relationship between Rome and

---

[104] "Throughout the year 1981, I have often met my Italian colleague, Emilio Colombo. He is one of the most prominent personalities of Italian post-War politics. The cooperation with him was so friendly and close, that I sometimes regretted that we were unable to communicate in a common language". See Hans-Dietrich Genscher, Erinnerungen, Berlin 1995, p. 363.

[105] See, for example, note sur le Projet Spinelli de Traité sur l'Union européenne, Ministère des affaires étrangères direction d'Europe, 02.2.1984. Archives Nationales de France (hereafter ANF), série 5 AG 4, archives de Pierre Morel (hereafter PM)/8, dossier 2 (the consultation was authorized thanks to a specific "derogation" (authorisation), which did not include the right of reproduction).

[106] The wide scientific literature existing on the subject of European integration has given limited consideration, especially in Italy, to this initiative, first and foremost in light of the poor results achieved through it. The contents of the interviews with leading Italian diplomats of that time have reinforced this overall negative impression. Speaking about the phases of the European integration process where the cooperation between Italy and Germany had a significant role, Ambassadors Pietro Calamia and Roberto Nigido mentioned the Conference of Messina in 1955, negotiations regarding the British accession at the beginning of the 1970s, the direct election of the European Parliament, the negotiations for enlargement to Spain and Portugal and, with even greater emphasis, the 1985 Milan Council. The Genscher-Colombo Plan came only second in this regard. Still, looking further into the matter, both interviews provided further points for reflection. Firstly, at a closer glance, it is undeniable that several contents of the Single European Act had been in a certain way anticipated by the initiative promoted by Hans-Dietrich Genscher and Emilio Colombo. Secondly and lastly, given the stalemates of the EC, it is noteworthy that such an ambitious initiative was

Bonn, this period was, as we shall later discuss, a phase of further rapprochement, of unprecedented cooperation after the death of Alcide De Gasperi in 1954, and the first – and probably also the last – coherent attempt to realise a double dream: the dream of strengthening the Italo-German couple so that it could also be one of the forces driving the revival of the integration process.

The joint Italo-German initiative had its roots in the convergence of two different backgrounds, namely the many economic, institutional and political bottlenecks affecting the EC at the beginning of the Eighties, and the slow but steady improvement of the relationship between Bonn and Rome. In order to grasp the meaning of the process leading to this project it is advisable, as a first step, to identify and contextualise those specific trends that enabled the merging of the two backgrounds which, apparently, had very little in common.

At the beginning of the 1980s, two recurring expressions had come to dominate the debate in the Bundesrepublik: The "Eurosklerose"[107] and the "Europamüdigkeit".[108] A well-known German caricaturist captured the attention of the public with a play on words, which mocked and exposed the state of growing fatigue affecting the European Communities.[109] The word *Europe* was divided into its constituent letters. Each one of them was associated with an expression symbolising the political stalemates in which Europe was bogged down: E equated with "*Euphorie*" (high spirits), U with "*Unmut*" (bad feeling), R with "*Resignation*" (resignation), O with "*Optimismus*" (optimism), P with "*Pessimismus*" (pessimism) and A with "*Apathie*" (inertia).

Within the ongoing debate, issues as the lack of democratic legitimacy of the European decision-making process and the need for greater involvement of the European Parliament were increasingly raised.[110] Decision-taking had, in fact,

---

proposed and equally noteworthy is the fact that it was the result of the cooperation between Rome and Bonn.

[107] This expression was probably coined by the president of the Kieler Institut für Weltwirtschaft, Helmut Giersch, who also made it popular with his namesake article published in *Wirtschaftswoche*, 12.8.1983.

[108] See Ulrich Lappenküper, Hans-Dietrich Genscher-Emilio Colombo und der Kampf gegen die „Eurosklerose", in: Michael Gehler/Maddalena Guiotto, Italien Österreich und die Bundesrepublik Deutschland in Europa. Ein Dreiecksverhältnis in seinen wechselseitigen Beziehungen und Wahrnehmungen von 1945/49 bis zur Gegenwart (Institut für Geschichte der Universität Hildesheim, Arbeitskreis Europäische Integration, Historische Forschungen, Veröffentlichungen 8), Wien – Köln – Weimar 2012, pp. 225–242.

[109] See Hans Werner Lautenschlager, Von der Genscher-Colombo-Initiative zum Vertrag von Maastricht, in: Klaus Kinkel (ed.), In der Verantwortung: Hans-Dietrich Genscher zum Siebzigsten, Berlin 1997, p. 568.

[110] Ulrich Rosengarten, Die Genscher-Colombo-Initiative. Baustein für die Europäische Union, Baden-Baden 2008, pp. 11–13.

become so slow to the point of being sclerotic. Besides, the mounting economic and financial difficulties, especially the problem of the Community's budget and of its own resources, had led in 1979 to the risk of a virtual paralysis in the normal functioning of the common mechanisms.[111] At that time, two thirds of the resources on which the Community could rely were absorbed by the CAP. Germany alone paid for approximately 30 % of this budget and firmly rejected to be further burdened, in the absence of structural reforms.[112] The frequent use of expressions such as "Zahlmeister" in the German national debate and in the media gave voice to this growing discontent.[113]

Foreign Minister Hans-Dietrich Genscher was fully aware of such risks, but he also feared that an EC, where neither the Common Market nor freedom of movement had achieved full implementation, would be reduced to the level of a mere customs union.[114]

Furthermore, economic and financial difficulties were not the sole source of inspiration for the speech he delivered in Stuttgart on 6 January 1981, on the occasion of the traditional FDP meeting, the *Dreikönigstreffen*.[115] Hans-Dietrich Genscher strongly felt the utmost importance of giving fresh impetus to Europe by putting forward reform proposals that also emphasised the political objective of European unification. The EC urgently needed wide-ranging political

---

[111] The adjustment mechanism created in 1975 in the face of the UK severe public deficit no longer applied after 1 January 1980. At the Dublin European Council of September 1979 the new British Prime Minister, Margaret Thatcher, had already given proof of the claims which she intended to lay in the months and years to come. See, for instance, Doc.132, Gespräch des Bundeskanzlers Schmidt mit Ministerpräsident Cossiga, VS-NfD, Gästehaus des Hamburger Senats, Hamburg, 26.4.1980, from 02.00 p.m., pp. 690–691, in: AAPD, 1980, Band I, München, 2012. Italy and the Bundesrepublik feared that irreconcilable discrepancies between France and the UK concerning budget issues might prevent the Community from overcoming its deadlock. See Antonio Varsori, L'Italia e l'integrazione europea: l'occasione perduta? in: Simona Colarizi/Piero Craveri/Silvio Pons/Gaetano Quagliariello (eds.), Gli Anni Ottanta come Storia, Soveria Mannelli 2004, pp. 155–184, 164; Pietro Calamia, La svolta europea del 1985. Il ruolo dell'Italia, in *Rivista di studi politici internazionali*, vol.79 n. 1 (2012), pp. 15–24.

[112] See Werner Weidenfeld, Europäische Einigung im historischen Überblick, in: Werner Weidenfeld/Wolfgang Wessels (eds.), Europa von A-Z. Taschenbuch der europäischen Integration, Baden-Baden 2016, pp. 15–54.

[113] Other expressions were equally popular to speak out on this growing dissatisfaction such as "Melchkuh", meaning the Bundesrepublik as the dairy cow of the Community. See Ulrich Rosengarten, Die Genscher-Colombo-Initiative, p. 18.

[114] See the 20 May 1980 speech delivered by Hans-Dietrich Genscher on the occasion of the twenty-fifth anniversary of the founding of the Deutsche Gesellschaft für Auswärtige Politik, in: Hans-Dietrich Genscher, Deutsche Außenpolitik. Ausgewählte Reden und Aufsätze 1974–1985, second edition, Stuttgart 1985, p. 246.

[115] The "*Dreikönigstag*" is the German word for Epiphany. As this FDP meeting usually took place on 6 January it was called "Dreikönigsgespräch" (meeting of the Epiphany). Genscher's speech is, therefore, sometimes also referred to as the "Epiphany Appeal".

reform[116], to buttress its external projection and its influence on international changes.[117]

> „[…] Unsere Sicherheit gewinnen wir aus dem westlichen Bündnis und der Europäischen Gemeinschaft. Hier allein finden wir auch das Fundament für unsere Politik gegenüber dem Osten. […] Europa braucht einen neuen politischen Impuls. Es braucht einen sichtbaren Schritt in Richtung auf die Europäische Union. Ich frage: Ist es nicht endlich Zeit für einen Vertrag über die Europäische Union? Um die schon vorhandene Verflechtung innerhalb der Europäischen Gemeinschaft und unter den 10 Mitgliedstaaten stärker in Richtung auf diese Union auszurichten. Um den inneren Zusammenhalt der Gemeinschaft zu stärken, damit die Gemeinschaft in die Lage versetzt wird, auch psychologisch die 1981/82 anstehenden schwierigen internen Probleme zu lösen. Um die Grundlagen für gemeinsames außenpolitisches Handeln zu festigen und damit das Gewicht der Gemeinschaft als Partner der USA und mit den USA zusammen in der internationalen Politik zu verstärken. Ziele einer Europäischen Union müssen sein: die Entwicklung einer gemeinsamen europäischen Außenpolitik, der Ausbau der Gemeinschaftspolitiken entsprechend den Verträgen von Paris und Rom, die Abstimmung im Bereich der Sicherheitspolitik, die engere Zusammenarbeit im kulturellen Bereich und die Harmonisierung der Gesetzgebung. Diese Forderungen sind alle nicht neu […] aber die Zeit ist reif, sie in die Wirklichkeit umzusetzen […] Das alles gilt für die Deutschen im geteilten Land in besonderem Maße. […].“[118]

In order to provide the Member States with the necessary tools to meet the new challenges set by these changing international dynamics, the German Foreign Minister argued for greater political cooperation, which could only be achieved through the creation of a *European Political Union*. Prime aims on this path were the definition of a common European Foreign policy and the extension of the Community's powers into new areas, defence and justice included.

---

[116] See Maria Eleonora Guasconi, L'Italia e la cooperazione politica europea nella prima metà degli anni Ottanta, in: Leopoldo Nuti/Massimiliano Guderzo, Bruna Bagnato (eds.), Nuove Questioni di Storia della Relazioni Internazionali, Roma – Bari 2015, pp. 57–80, 64.

[117] According to French records, both this project and the initiative promoted by Spinelli were based on similar assessments concerning the reasons of the European stalemates, i.e. both of them had an "institutional background". The initiative launched by Spinelli pursued, however, more ambitious objectives in comparison with the Italo-German plan. Spinelli tried, in fact, to alter the very foundations of the Communities, whereas Genscher and Colombo confined their ambitions to a reform process enshrined into the existing treaties. See note du directeur des affaires économiques, Ministère des affaires étrangères, Paris, 28.6.1984. ANF, série 5 AG 4, PM/8, dossier 2.

[118] See Freie Demokratische Korrespondenz, 06.1.1981, n. 2, Bonn: Pressedienst der Freien Demokratischen Partei. Hans-Dietrich Genscher, Deutsche Außenpolitik. Ausgewählte Reden und Aufsätze 1974–1985, second edition, Stuttgart 1985, p. 306. Text of the speech (and translation) in: http://www.cvce.eu/obj/rede_von_hans_dietrich_genscher_stuttgart_6_januar_1981-de-73cd40b0–7dce-479b8c7c-8404afe7c69e.html (last consulted 31.8.2016).

In his capacity as Foreign Minister, Hans-Dietrich Genscher was well placed to assess the risks and opportunities arising from the ongoing transformations. Based on his wealth of experience, it seemed only logical for Genscher to assume that the EPC was, by its very nature, not an adequate tool to support the kind of cooperation which the new international scenario demanded from the EC to continue as a credible partner.[119]

The EPC, established in 1970 on the basis of the Davignon report, was an informal arrangement to allow a certain degree of coordination of the foreign policies of Member States through a six-monthly meeting of their Foreign ministers.[120] A rather flexible institutional structure was matched by an extensive flexibility in the agenda. This intergovernmental cooperation mechanism worked alongside the EC, but it was not part of it. The Commission was invited to express its opinion if and only if matters within its competencies were concerned.[121] Despite its many intrinsic limitations, the existence of a mechanism of political coordination had played an important role in fostering an atmosphere of greater trust and solidarity among its participants. Thus, it had contributed to the success of the Conference of Helsinki, during whose negotiations the EPC had provided Member States with a useful framework to coordinate their efforts, which had been particularly noteworthy in the context of the principles enshrined in the so-called "third basket".[122]

The rapid deterioration of the international framework, the European inability to speak with one voice concerning, for instance, the Iranian crisis and the Soviet invasion of Afghanistan, and the increasing number of trouble spots all over the world persuaded the German Foreign Minister that time had come for a leap in quality. In his 1981 speech Genscher argued, in fact, for political reforms which would remove the artificial distinction between the cooperation within the European Communities and the foreign policy coordination. Unlike other initiatives, such as the one Altiero Spinelli was supporting, the ultimate goal was not to rebuild the Communities on new foundations, thus abandoning the "Monnet method", with its specific comunitarisation approach in European institutions and policy. On the contrary, following in the footsteps of the Monnet approach, it was

---

[119] See Hans-Dieter Lucas, Politik der kleinen Schritten-Genscher und die neue Europapolitik 1974–1983, in: Klaus Kinkel (ed.), In der Verantwortung: Hans-Dietrich Genscher zum Siebzigsten, Berlin 1997, pp. 85–113.

[120] This high level summit was flanked by a network of meetings at different levels, from the political directors to the desk level. Furthermore, a committee composed of political directors had been established with the task of defining the technical and operational conditions necessary for the high level summits to play their role.

[121] See Maria Eleonora Guasconi, L'Italia e la cooperazione politica europea, p. 59.

[122] See Deborah Cuccia, The Genscher-Colombo Plan: A forgotten page in the European Integration History, in: *Journal of European Integration History* 24 (1), January 2018, pp. 59–78

believed that a process based on concrete objectives and gradual changes, which would finally lead to the signing of a new treaty, was the best option.

Between the lines of this "Epiphany Appeal", it was not difficult to read the urgent importance the adoption of such reforms had for the Bundesrepublik, as outpost of the Western bloc. More than other Western German politicians Genscher was extremely receptive to the political barometer of the *other Germany*, where he was born and where he had spent his early life.[123] His speech was, therefore, also inspired by the ambition that in the future the EC could be a magnet for the countries beyond the Iron Curtain.[124]

The choice of the location where the Address was delivered was not left to chance. On the contrary, it embodied great symbolic value, as it took place in the same town, Stuttgart, in the same building and even in the same room where, on 6 September 1946, the US Secretary of State, James Francis Byrnes (July 1945-January 1947), had delivered the declaration which had paved the way for post-war (Western) German economic and political regeneration.[125] The occasion for the delivery of this message was the annual FDP meeting; Genscher, therefore, spoke in his capacity as liberal leader and not as Foreign Minister. This specific choice might seem odd, unless we consider its background very carefully. More than just the above-mentioned European situation had induced him to take the decision to deliver this speech.[126]

Firstly, he aimed to revitalize the interest of German public opinion in the European integration process, reawakening the interest of a population which, in the early Eighties, saw such a process as a synonym of uncertainty, and which was sensible to the appeal of pacifist propaganda. [127]

Secondly, the German Foreign Minister wanted to strengthen the influence of his own party, the FDP. In a period when tensions were increasing within the ruling coalition, he wanted to maximize its influence on issues such as European

---

[123] See, in particular, Hans-Dietrich Genscher, Erinnerungen, Berlin 1995, part I, ch. 1 and 2.
[124] See Doc. 253, Gespräch des Bundesministers Genscher mit dem italienischen Außenminister Colombo in Rom, VS-vertraulich, Rome, 11.9.1981, in: AAPD, 1981 Band II, München 2012.
[125] See Hans-Dietrich Genscher's speech in Stuttgart, in:
http://www.cvce.eu/obj/rede_von_hans_dietrich_genscher_Stuttgart_6_januar_1981-de-73cd40b0-7dce-479b8c7c-8404afe7c69e.html (last accessed 1.12.2017)
[126] It was possible to reach these conclusions after in-depth analysis and comparison of German and French archival records. See, in particular, PA AA, B26, n. 123280, 123281, 123282. See also Note du directeur des affaires économiques sur le plan Genscher-Colombo, Ministère des affaires étran-gères, direction Europe, comité interministeriel, 14.5.1982. ANF, série 5 AG 4, PM/8, dossier 2.
[127] See Note sur l'Union européenne, Ministère des Relations Extérieures, sous-direction d'Europe occidentale, 14.11.1981. AMAE 1930inva, Direction Europe, Série Italie, carton 5331, sous-série 11–1 11–6, période 1981–1985. See also Doc. 253, Gespräch des Bundesministers Genscher mit dem italienischen Außenminister Colombo in Rom, VS-vertraulich, Rome, 11.9.1981, in: AAPD, 1981 Band II, München 2012.

integration, over which the Christian Democrats had exercised a virtual monopoly from the 1950s. Only later had the SPD, led by Chancellor Schmidt, also started emphasizing its own European commitment by supporting efforts to give new momentum to the integration process. Such action, carried out through a strong cooperation with Valery Giscard d'Estaing, was mainly focused on economic and monetary issues rather than on institutional features.[128]

At first Genscher's initiative faced opposition. Many members of his own government were sceptical about the possibility of giving birth to a European Foreign policy which would include security elements.[129] Both Chancellor Schmidt and Defence Minister Hans Apel (1978–1982)[130] considered it utopian to even think of a real security policy for Europe.[131] It was evident that Genscher needed the support of another European partner, but it is not evident why such a partner should have been Italy.

With the exception only of the De Gasperi era, Bonn and Rome had never shared bonds as strong as those existing between Paris and Bonn. However, by 1981 the Franco-German couple was going through a difficult time, partly as a result of Mitterrand replacing Giscard d'Estaing as French President. If the relationship between President Mitterrand and Chancellor Schmidt[132] was not easy,

---

[128] See Ulrich Lappenküper, Hans-Dietrich Genscher-Emilio Colombo und der Kampf gegen die „Eurosklerose", p. 226.

[129] See Ulrich Rosengarten, Die Genscher-Colombo-Initiative, pp. 42–46.

[130] Hans Apel (25.2.1932- 06.2.2011 Hamburg) was a renowned German politician and Economist. Member of the SPD, he was *parlamentarischer Staatssekretär* at the German Foreign Ministry from 1972 to 1974, then he was Minister of Finance from 1978 and Minister of Defence from 1978 to 1982.

[131] See Wilfried Loth, L'Allemagne et l'Italie dans le processus de construction européenne: une coopération occasionnelle? in: Piero Craveri/Antonio Varsori (eds.), L'Italia nella costruzione europea. Un bilancio storico (1957–2007), Milano 2009, pp. 455–466, 464.

[132] Hubert Védrine witnessed such difficulties in his Memoirs: "À Bonn c'est avec regret que le Chancelier Helmut Schmidt, malade et amer, voit son ami Valéry Giscard d'Estaing avec lequel il a instauré la pratique des Conseils européens, progrès déterminant pour l'Europe […], être désavoué par les électeurs: lors des réunions de l'Internationale socialiste, il a sèchement reproché à François Mitterrand son alliance avec les communistes. […] En février 1981 Helmut Schmidt s'est inquiété, 'L'élection de François Mitterrand ? Ne me parlez pas de malheur'. […] En mai 1981, François Mitterrand n'a pas à proprement parler de politique allemande et ses rapports avec Helmut Schmidt sont plus que frais […] La gauche française reste alors très en arrière de la main sur la coopération franco-allemande. Peu sont ceux qui se souviennent des initiatives de Pierre Mendès France ou de Guy Mollet en faveur du dialogue franco-allemand. Quant au geste de la réconciliation franco-allemande […] par le général de Gaulle et le Chancelier Adenauer, ne se sentent pas tout à fait de cette famille-là". (In Bonn Chancellor Helmut Schmidt, ill and bitter, observes with regret his friend Valéry Giscard d'Estaing [together they instituted the tradition of the European Councils, an important step for Europe] being abandoned by French electors: on the occasion of the meeting of the Socialist Internationale, he curtly reproached Mitterrand his alliance with the Communists. […] During February 1981 Schmidt was preoccupied, speaking of the election of François Mitterrand he said 'Do not speak of such an unfortunate event'. […]. During May 1981 François

the situation was even worsened by the Communist involvement within the French government and the lack of interest showed for European integration.[133]

In a recently published book, the hypothesis has been formulated that in the 1970s the relationship with Paris had become a "*domaine ultraréservé*"[134] of the Chancellor, with a consequent marginalization of the role of his Foreign Minister. By assuming such a position as true, it would be easier to understand Genscher's interest in Italy as the most suitable partner for the initiative which he intended to take.

Last, but not least, by 1981, Italian Foreign Minister Colombo had for some time represented a reference point and was a model for Genscher's European politics. Colombo's reputation as a supporter of European integration from its very first steps, and the role he had played as European Parliament President (1977–1980), made him a strategic partner who could give credibility and support to the process Genscher was so keen to launch.

Born in Potenza on 11 April 1920, Emilio Colombo had started his political career after the Second World War, at first as Undersecretary for Public Works, then as Undersecretary and Minister for Agriculture, for Foreign Commerce, for Industry and as Minister of Treasury. Throughout those years he had always been an appreciated member of his Party, the DC, even without playing a leading role. At the beginning of the Eighties he had been appointed as Foreign Minister.

The European profile of Colombo[135] is, at the very least, equally interesting. Many people remember him in his capacity of European Parliament President.

Mitterrand never properly addressed the *politique allemande* and his relationship with Helmut Schmidt was rather cold [...] the French Left had fallen behind concerning the Franco-German cooperation. Very few remembered the initiatives promoted by Pierre Mendès France and Guy Mollet. As for the mark of reconciliation of general De Gaulle and Chancellor Konrad Adenauer, they did not belong to that family). See Hubert Védrine, Les mondes de François Mitterrand. À l'Élysée 1981–1995, Paris 1996, pp. 83–84, 128, 120–121.

[133] The communist participation in the French Government was a constant issue of discussion in the meetings of 1981 and 1982 between Genscher and Colombo. Even if there was criticism for the lack of French support in such a delicate moment for the European integration, the documents do not show a fear that such a situation could cause more extended consequences. The communist involvement in the Government did not seem to have induced any alarming change in the French foreign attitude, nor within other European communist parties. See Deutsch-italienische Außenminister-Konsultationen, Fernschreiben aus RomDiplo, VS-NfD, 17.7.1981. PA AA, B26, n. 123281, Similar conclusions were drawn during the Montebello meeting that took place on 20 July. Questioned by his Italian counterpart, the German Chancellor pointed out that what was happening in France was probably an attempt of getting control over the powerful French Labor Unions. See Vermerk über das Gespräch des Bundeskanzlers mit dem italienischen Ministerpräsidenten Spadolini bei Frühstück in Montebello, Montebello, 20.7.1981. PA AA, B26, n. 123282.

[134] See Michèle Weinachter, Valéry Giscard d'Estaing et l'Allemagne. Le double rêve inachevé, Paris 2004, p. 95.

[135] For a short overview of Colombo's political career, see: E morto il senatore Emilio Colombo, ultimo costituente ed ex-presidente del parlamento Ue, *Il Sole24Ore*, 25.6.2013, in:

Still, this was only the confirmation of the strong European commitment which he had shown throughout previous years, for instance as a capable mediator in situations such as the "empty chair crisis".[136]

Both in the scientific literature and in popular articles, the lack within the Italian political establishment of personalities capable of fully understanding their German counterparts has been frequently remarked and, sometimes, criticised. Still, even Germany seemed to be missing personalities capable of going beyond a superficial appreciation of the Italian cultural heritage. Hans-Dietrich Genscher was more than an extremely skilfull politician. He was also capable of greater sensibility and understanding than his predecessors had showed towards Italy: an exception with important consequences and implications.[137] He would follow with great interest the evolution of Italian internal changes and its Foreign policy. Besides, his memoirs show that he was able to fully understand the implications of phenomena such as Eurocommunism[138], or the difficulties faced by Italy at the end of the Seventies, without the prejudices usually characterizing his country-men.[139] In 1979, Genscher himself had delivered the speech in honour of Emilio Colombo who was awarded the Charlemagne prize. His intervention is of interest as a further confirmation of the admiration and respect he felt towards Emilio Colombo.

„[…] wir feiern heute einen bedeutenden Staatsmann Italiens und Europas. Wir ehren einen Mann, der Europa mitgestaltete, der dieses Europa immer zuerst als demokratische Gemeinschaft verstand [...]. Wir ehren den Menschen Emilio Colombo, den aufrechten Demokraten, den Humanisten in der besten Tradition Italiens und Europas. Es hat seine tiefe Rechtfertigung, daß das Europäische Parlament Emilio Colombo zu seinem Präsidenten wählte, daß in seiner Amtszeit ein

---

http://www.ilsole24ore.com/art/notizie/2013-06-25/morto-senatore-emilio-co-lombo-075503_PRN.shtml (last accessed 15.9.2016).

[136] See, in particular, Philip Bajon, Europapolitik am „Abgrund". Die Krise des „leeren Stuhls" 1956–66, Stuttgart 2012.

[137] See, in particular, Gian Enrico Rusconi, Germania Italia Europa. Dallo stato di potenza alla potenza civile, Torino 2003, p. 265.

[138] See Ibid., pp. 266–267.

[139] During his long political career, Genscher had the chance to cooperate with many Italian politicians. The ones who left him with the strongest impression were Giulio Andreotti and Emilio Colombo, to whom he devoted long passages of his Memoirs. However, he seemed to have also appreciated very much Aldo Moro, whom he described as a complex personality, clever and introvert, whose standpoints showed astonishing dignity and clarity of mind. He devoted limited but positive comments on Giovanni Spadolini and quoted Bettino Craxi as well, though underlining that he had not had the chance of developing any tight relationship with him. See Ibid., pp. 362–365. As for the relationship with Giulio Andreotti see, for example, Federico Scarano, Le Relazioni con la Repubblica Federale di Germania e la questione tedesca, p. 38. See also Ulrich Lappenküper, Hans-Dietrich Genscher-Emilio Colombo und der Kampf gegen die „Eurosklerose", p. 227.

> Fortschritt gelang, von dem wir hoffen, daß er als einer der entscheidenden
> Schritte in die Geschichte der europäischen Einigung eingehen wird: ich meine
> die Entscheidung für die direkte Wahl des Europäischen Parlaments. [...]."[140]

This speech is also of interest because of another usually neglected element. It is,
in fact, a confirmation of Genscher's desire that the Community could be a magnet for Eastern Europe, and this two years before the speech of Stuttgart.

> „Europa ist für uns nicht nur Westeuropa. Warschau, Prag und Budapest – um nur
> diese zu nennen – sind europäische Städte, wie Magdeburg und Dresden deutsche
> Städte sind. Wir sehen auch die Überwindung der deutschen Teilung nicht als ein
> europäisches Hindernis, sondern als eine europäische Aufgabe. Wir sind über-
> zeugt, daß die Geschichte mit der bestehenden Trennung unseres Volkes nicht das
> letzte Wort gesprochen hat."[141]

His main reference point in saying these words is more than evident: The German
division. That the choice to reaffirm that the division was not the final word of
History could be easily mistaken for either just a rhetorical pronouncement, or as
the result of Genscher's specific legacy. However, looking closer, a different explanation is possible. From the beginning of the Seventies, important aspects of
the Hallstein Doctrine had been abandoned in accordance with the new strategy
of Ostpolitik, which implied a policy of negotiating with the DDR government.
Such changes could let the Bundesrepublik's partners believe that the German
division had become, at least in the short and medium term, a condition set in
stone. The Ostpolitik was, however, also built on dynamic elements, which during the following decade would slowly define some of the preconditions for the
German re-unification. It was only during the Eighties, after the replacement of
the political combination Schmidt-Genscher was replaced by the couple Kohl-
Genscher, that these dynamic elements took a more defined shape.

    The boundaries of the German question kept, once again, moving. Those Eu-
ropean leaders able to understand or, at least, sense this transformation process
and to react accordingly would have, in comparison with other politicians, an
advantage in their relationship with Bonn during the re-unification process.

If we go back to discuss the relationship between Genscher and Colombo and
their joint project, on the basis of both their biographical profiles and archival
documents recently declassified, we must remark that the choice of Italy as a

---

[140] Text of this speech and its translation, in: http://www.karlspreis.de/de/preistraeger/emilio-co-
lombo-1979/rede-von-hans-dietrich-genscher-bundesministers-desauswaertigen-und-vize-
kanzler-der-bundesrepublik-deutschland (last accessed 15.9.2016).
[141] Ibid.

partner had not been the mere consequence of the inability to draw on the resources provided by a long-established partnership with Paris.[142] First and foremost, this was a choice made by Genscher for a specific interlocutor, Emilio Colombo[143], even if the path leading to a good understanding between them and a
sound agreement on the measures to be taken was not exactly strewn with roses.
Before embarking in such an ambitious project, it was, indeed, necessary to verify
the conditions for cooperation between the two countries. Their respective political aims and foreign policy guidelines had to be compared, the thorniest issues
discussed and, when necessary, clarified. The meeting between the Italian Foreign Minister and his German counterpart at the end of September 1980 provided
an opportunity to engage in preliminary discussions.[144]

After a short reference to their shared concern for the existing European integration stalemates[145], and to the risks related with the British budget issue, Emilio
Colombo proposed a "systematische Strukturierung" (systematic renovation) of
the Italian-German institutional bilateral framework. Turning to the main contents of this "systematic renovation", Colombo recommended to hold regular
consultations between Foreign Ministers, on at least a semi-annual basis, and to
sanction the participation of these consultations at high level meetings held between the heads of Government of the two states. These were to be realised in the
form of a preliminary four people-meeting followed by one-to-one meetings between Foreign Ministers, on the one side, and heads of Government on the
other.[146] It was the intention of Colombo that this renovation was not only meant
to ensure more frequent contacts, but also to set the conditions for a full and du-
rable involvement of Foreign Ministers in defining the guidelines of future developments in the relationship between Italy and Germany.

---

[142] Archival records show what a keen interest Germany took into Emilio Colombo's Foreign policy
action. See, for example, Politischer Halbjahresbericht ITALIEN II 1980, VS-NfD. PA AA, B26,
n. 123280.

[143] In addition to the description of Emilio Colombo provided by Hans-Dietrich Genscher in his
memoirs, see Doc. 253, Gespräch des Bundesministers Genscher mit dem italienischen Außenminister Colombo in Rom, VS-vertraulich, Rome, 11.9.1981, pp. 1340–1343, in: AAPD, 1981 Band
II, München 2012. See also Doc. 282, Gespräch des Bundesministers Genscher mit dem italienischen Außenminister Colombo in Rom, VS-vertraulich, Rome, 3 October 1981, p. 1492, in: AAPD,
1981 Band II, München 2012. For further information, see also the interview given by Bruno Bottai
to Maria Grazia Melchionni in Rome (17.2.1998), in: Voices on Europe, Oral History Collections,
Historical Archives of the European Union (http://www.eui/HAEU/OralHistory/, last accessed
1.2.2016).

[144] See Doc. 277, Gespräch des Bundesministers Genscher mit dem italienischen Außenminister
Colombo in New-York, VS-vertraulich, New-York, 22.9.1980, at 06.20 p.m. (until 07.15 p.m.), in:
AAPD, 1980 Band II, München 2011.

[145] See Ibid., p. 1428.

[146] See Ibid., pp. 1428–1429.

The meeting of 20/21 January 1981 was another equally important progress on the road on which Italy and Germany had to travel to become closer partners. Barely two weeks after the Stuttgart Appeal Foreign Minister Genscher travelled to Rome. During his stay, officially organized on the occasion of the "esposizione del nazzareno", he attended talks with the President of the Republic, Sandro Pertini, with the Italian Prime Minister, Arnaldo Forlani, and more widely with the Foreign Minister, Emilio Colombo.[147] Colombo intentionally left the choice of the issues to be discussed to his partner, provided that East-West relations and the European policy were addressed during their exchange of views.

The statement they issued the following day at the press conference was a further confirmation of their shared desire to promote a revival of the European integration process, and of the existence of strong and friendly bilateral bonds based on mutual respect and trust. Furthermore, Italy was considered by Genscher a partner which was fully aware of its security obligations and, like Germany, did not overlook the importance of a good transatlantic relationship.[148]

Nevertheless, this exchange of views had been far less straightforward than what the abovementioned press release suggests.[149] Before embarking into a joint initiative, it was of the utmost importance for Italy to have a full picture of the kind of commitment required by the German Ostpolitik, in order to be sure that it was not carried out at the expense of the relations with the American Superpower. Germany, in turn, was eager to present the specific features that its internal division imposed upon its foreign policy, thus affecting both its Eastern and its European engagement. It was also equally eager to take the opportunity to clarify that this engagement never had and never would have the potential to break the commitments which Bonn shared with Italy in NATO and in the EC.[150]

Once these potential reasons for mistrust were removed, the discussion focused on the main subjects addressed by Genscher in his Stuttgart declaration and, lastly, on the definition of a common strategy.[151] Within the long and detailed considerations of Colombo, three issues deserve special attention. Firstly, the

---

[147] See Visite de M. Genscher, télégramme n. 688, 23.1.1981, 23.1.1981, signed Puaux. AMAE 1930inva, Direction Europe, Série RFA, carton 4907, sous-série 11–6, période 1981–1985. See also Visita del ministro degli Esteri Hans-Dietrich Genscher, Rome, 21.1.1981, pp. 358–359. 1981, Testi e documenti sulla politica estera dell'Italia 1985.

[148] See Mitteilung für die Presse n. 2073 B/81, Rome, 22.1.1981. PA AA, B26, n. 124898.

[149] See Vermerk über Deutsch-Italienische Konsultationen in Rom am 21.1. Hier: Arbeitsgespräch AM Colombo und BM Genscher, VS-NfD, Rome, 21.1.1981. PA AA, B26, n. 124898.

[150] During these talks, as well as during the following meetings, there were also some discrepancies concerning the French stance. Genscher pointed out that France remained loyal to its international commitments, despite its rhetoric claiming a peculiar military role within the Alliance. Although Emilio Colombo agreed on that, he also emphasised how difficult, especially in recent times, its endless Anti-American rhetoric made it for Europe to reach common positions. Besides, this rhetoric could also have a negative impact on Italy. See Ibid.

[151] See Ibid., pp. 7–8.

Italian politician fully shared the judgment of the EPC that Genscher had expressed in Stuttgart; its thorough reform was deemed to be an unavoidable step. Secondly, the Italian Minister expressed his firm belief that a European Foreign policy could not exist if deprived of a security dimension. This was a strong *trait d'union* that linked the political analysis of Emilio Colombo to Genscher's political vision, but it was also an easy target for Member states who wished to reject their propositions. Last, but not least, between the lines Colombo also affirmed that he (and his Government with him) accepted the guidelines of Genscher's Epiphany Appeal, as he himself was fully aware of the extent of the difficulties the Community was facing and had, therefore, been wishing to favour its revival.

This statement shows that this initiative was taken on an equal footing, although the credit for having made the first move must be given to Genscher. In other words, Emilio Colombo did not, strictly speaking, join a German political initiative. Rather he agreed to share a negotiating track based on specific worries which he already harboured.[152]

This constitutes the general background to the declaration made by Colombo on 28 January 1981, delivered in Florence on the occasion of the inaugural session of the eighth National Congress of the "associazione italiana per il consiglio dei comuni d'Europa".[153]

As for the Stuttgart speech, the choice of this occasion for the launch of the appeal was not left to chance either. Colombo started, in fact, with a well chosen reference to Europe's ability to enhance local strengths, which was more than just

---

[152] Confirming this statement, see Ibid. See also Gespräch des Herrn Bundespräsidenten mit dem italienischen Botschafter, 30.11.1981: "[...] BM Genscher und der italienische Außenminister hätten den Vorschlag einer europäischen Aktion gemacht. [...]. Wichtig sei auch, daß dieser Vorschlag auf Italien und Deutschland gemeinsam zurückginge. [...]. (Foreign Ministers Genscher and Colombo put forward the proposal of a European action. [...]". It is also important that this proposal goes back to both Germany and Italy [...]). PA AA, B26, n. 123281. See, as well, Politischer Halbjahresbericht ITALIEN II 1980, VS-NfD. PA AA, B26, n. 123280. For additional proof, see Fernando Lay, L'iniziativa italo-tedesca per il rilancio dell'Unione europea. Origini sviluppi della Dichiarazione di Stoccarda, Padova 1983, pp. 2–3. During the negotiation of the plan Fernando Lay was the closest advisor of Bruno Bottai, Italian director for political Affairs. In his book he supports the hypothesis of a joint plan and identifies the origin of the Italian desire to support a political reform aiming at giving new momentum to the integration in the mid-1980 during the Italian rotating Presidency. See also Ulrich Lappenküper, Hans-Dietrich Genscher-Emilio Colombo und der Kampf gegen die „Eurosklerose", p. 229.

[153] A copy of the speech of Emilio Colombo is kept into the records of the archives of the French Foreign Ministry together with a translation in French. See Déclaration du ministre italien des affaires étrangères, Relance de la Construction européenne, Ministère des Affaires étrangères, Ambassade de France à Rome, Rome, 2.2.1981. AMAE 1930inva, Direction Europe, Série Italie, carton 5331, sous-série 11–1 11–6, période 1981–1985, See Discours d'Emilio Colombo, Agence Europe, 21.1.1981. Historical Archives of the European Union (hereafter HAEU), Box Emanuele Gazzo, quoted in Maria Eleonora Guasconi, L'Italia e la cooperazione politica europea, p. 65.

a tribute to the hosting institution. Thus, he showed a marked awareness that further European development needed a skilful combination of top-down and bottom-up strategies, namely an impetus from above associated with greater local sensibility enhancing the quality of the ongoing debate. According to Emilio Colombo, a reform process could not otherwise succeed.

This wish to enhance the "original ideals" on which Europe was based went hand in hand with a clear and realistic approach and it was fully aware of the obstacles that the majority of Member States would put on the way of a comprehensive reform process. It was probably the result of the expertise Colombo had accumulated as negotiator through his long-term involvement in European dynamics.[154]

The key-note of the Appeal by Genscher was its ideal dimension and its being drawn to Eastern Europe, whereas the key-note in the speech by Colombo was, mainly, its gradualism. The Italian politician shared, as the ultimate goal, the creation of a political union but, given the circumstances, he also believed that prudence and gradualism were required. Therefore, he favoured, as a first step, an approach which would take full advantage of the existing treaty provisions, before proposing the signing of a new legally binding text.

Certainly, this was no obstacle in his vision of implementing a set of three kinds of reforms, as proposed in the Stuttgart Appeal: the implementation of a common Foreign policy, of a Security policy and the definition of an institutional framework enabling Europe to appropriately react to new international challenges. In addition, Colombo also emphasized the importance of extending the powers of the Community to the cultural dimension, thus allowing a future harmonization of the different European legislations in the field of education.

By contrast, concerning the economic dimension, a comparison of the two speeches shows a greater divide in the approach taken by Hans-Dietrich Genscher and Emilio Colombo. Both of them agreed that market rules alone could not set the conditions for the economic development they called for. They also shared the belief that without adequate reforms, the EEC would run the serious risk of being lowered to a mere customs union. Nevertheless, Emilio Colombo placed more emphasis on economic aspects and argued for better coordination, investments and measures which would strengthen competitiveness and technological development.

---

[154] Domestic needs had had a certain influence on Genscher and Colombo in promoting a process of European reform. Italy wanted to avoid exclusion from mechanisms of coordination among other European states. See, in particular, Politischer Halbjahresbericht ITALIEN II 1980, VS-NfD. PA AA, B26, n. 123280. Throughout negotiations Germany was, therefore, always very careful about reassuring Italy that this was not its goal. See Deutsch-Italienische Konsultationen der Regierungschef am 07. März 1982 in Hamburg, Bonn, 29.4.1982. PA AA, B26, n. 124898.

As the speeches suggest, both Genscher and Colombo placed a strong focus on foreign policy, though with somewhat different nuances; and yet, their propositions were more than just a means of merely revitalising and boosting foreign policy coordination. They were a significant input towards far-reaching institutional changes, even though, at the beginning of 1981, neither Italy nor Germany had a well-structured plan, rather a clutch of ideas which would spark a debate on the objectives of a reform process.

Six months after the Stuttgart address, Giovanni Spadolini[155], leader of the small Republican Party, was appointed Italian Prime Minister. For once, the changing political balance of power in Italy provided the two countries with better tools to follow their path. A political duo between a Christian-Democratic Foreign Minister with long-term political expertise and with an undisputable European profile on the one side, and a resolute Prime Minister, head of a less influential party on the other side, arouse great curiosity and interest in Bonn.[156]

The German Foreign Ministry though was not unaware of the weaknesses affecting the executive led by Spadolini, of his reduced potential for manoeuvre and of the perception, widely spread in Italy, that it was just another transitional government. The period between 1979 and 1984 is not a monolithic bloc.

---

[155] Concerning Spadolini, see, for instance, Gespräch Bundeskanzler mit MP Spadolini am Rande des Wirtschaftsgipfels in Ottawa, Ottawa, no date (probably June 1981): "Spadolini hat als Generalsekretär der kleinen Republikanischen Partei eine politische Linie verfolgt, die den Republikanern eine Vermittlerrolle zwischen den wichtigsten Koalitionsparteien zuschreibt [...]. Spadolini zeichnen analytische Intelligenz, ausgleichendes Verhandlungsgeschick und eine Jovialität aus, die jedoch über die Härte und Durchsetzungswillen des Florentiners nicht hinwegtäuschen darf". (As secretary general of the small Republican Party, Spadolini has adopted a line that aims to ascribe the Republicans with a mediation role among the most important parties of the coalition [...] Spadolini distinguishes himself through his analytical intelligence, his negotiating skills and a bonhomie which should not disguise the strength and the determination of the Florentine). PA AA, B26, n. 123281.

[156] Loyalty to NATO, an overall good-relationship with the US and an enhanced European commitment were considered in Bonn the keynotes of Italian Foreign politics between 1981 and 1982. Still, the appointment of Spadolini was the sign of greater dynamism in the pursuit of these aims. Spadolini himself, despite the internal difficulties he had to face to ensure the survival of the government which he led, was by far more interested in the Italian international projection than his predecessor had been. Besides, the sense of a shared vision linking him to his Foreign Minister could be considered a guarantee for greater political coherency, being the approach to the Middle-East the only thorn in the good interaction established between Spadolini and Colombo. As for the European engagement, just a few differences in accents could be detected, being Colombo equally interested in the economic and in the political dimension of the European integration process, whereas Spadolini supported the necessity of economic reforms (hence, the Italian insistence during the Genscher-Colombo Plan negotiations on the economic component). See Deutsch-Italienische Konsultationen der Regierungschef am 7. März 1982 in Hamburg, Bonn, 29.4.1982. PA AA, B26, n. 124898.

Certainly, German concerns regarding the Italian political degeneration can be considered its common thread.[157] Still, between mid-1981 and 1982, the judgments were overall characterized by a less negative tone[158]:

> „Seit Ende Juni 1981 ist Spadolini Ministerpräsident, obwohl Parteivorsitzender einer Partei mit nur 3 % Stimmenanteil und einem noch geringeren Prozentualen Anteil von Abgeordneten […]. Seine Bilanz ist etwas besser als die seiner DC-Vorgänger. Außenpolitisch gewann die Regierung an Profil, ein Verdienst, das gleichermaßen Colombo zugutekommt. Innenpolitisch wurde die Regierung in keinen Skandal verwickelt […]. Spadolini, erster – laizistischer –Ministerpräsident nach 35 Jahren DC Herrschaft hatte einen relativ guten Start. Die fehlende Bindung zu einer großen Partei machte sich bei der Regierungsarbeit eher positiv bemerkbar […] Abstützten konnte er sich einerseits auf Pertini […] andererseits auf die Popularität bei dem italienischen Volk […]."[159]

At the same time, the election of François Mitterrand was the announcement of a more favourable wing in the relationship between France and Italy, the choice of Gilles Martinet for the post of French Ambassador to Rome being one of its most prominent signs. Compared to his predecessor, Gilles Martinet had a deeper knowledge of the country which he was sent to in 1981[160], and this mirrored the

---

[157] See Regierungskrise in Italien, Fernschreiben aus RomDiplo n. 485, 26.5.1981. PA AA, B26, n. 123280. See also Regierungskrise in Italien, Fernschreiben aus Rom n. 521, 4.6.1981. PA AA, B26, n. 123280.

[158] "Although the PSI, unlike the DC and the PCI, continued to lack control over the most prominent National associations, since the Congress of Palermo it had managed to achieve a certain maturity and its programme was more clearly defined, while its internal influence had also increased. Despite this more positive approach, opinions concerning its resilience over time diverged". See Von Nenni zu Craxi: Ein Kurzprofil der italienischen sozialistischen Partei (PSI) von Heinz Timmermann, no date. PA AA, B26, n. 123280.

[159] "Although Spadolini is leader of a party with 3% of total votes and even less MPs, since the end of June 1981 he is Prime Minister […] His balance sheet is a little better compared to his DC-predecessors. The Government has a more prominent profile in foreign politics. This is a merit which is beneficial for Colombo as well. Domestically the Government has been involved in no scandals. Spadolini, the first secular Prime Minister after a 35-yeard DC-rule, had a fairly good start. The lack of connection to a big political party has had a positive and visible impact. […] He can rest on the support of Pertini […] and on his popularity with the Italian people". See 6 Monate Regierung Spadolini, Fernschreiben aus Rom, 5.1.1982. PA AA, B26, n. 124897.

[160] Bruna Bagnato dealt with this sensitive issue thanks to the special authorisation to access to the section "Gilles Martinet" into the *archives d'Histoire Contemporaine* at the *Fondation Nationale de Science Politiques-Centre de l'histoire de l'Europe du vingtième Siècle*. See Bruna Bagnato, L'Italia vista da Palazzo Farnese: la missione di Gilles Martinet (1981–1984), in: Ennio di Nolfo (ed.), La politica estera italiana negli anni Ottanta, Bari – Roma 2003, pp. 225–283, 225.

interest of the new French Presidency for greater cooperation with its Southern neighbour.[161]

This ambition was, however, full of contradictions. In 1981, Italy was indeed courted by many suitors, but with different designs and in different contexts. Certainly, François Mitterrand was making overtures to the Italian establishment and he had very good relations with some of its members, such as Sandro Pertini. Nevertheless, when Gilles Martinet was appointed Ambassador to Rome, the overall French approach towards Italy still mirrored old patterns depicting the Mediterranean country as a state with limited sovereignty, overzealous whenever the USA was concerned. The close relationship between Bonn and Paris had put strain on Rome, but the link between Washington and Rome had caused in France the same reactions.

Even the Genscher-Colombo plan was, from the very beginning, the subject of mixed reactions in Paris. Sometimes the project was lowered to the level of a tactical move; Italy was allegedly pursuing it to gain a sort of moral advantage, which would buy the country more credibility.[162] Some other times Paris showed real concern that this project could pave the way for a closer cooperation between Rome and Bonn, regardless of its slim chances of success.[163]

Between winter and spring 1981, against a background of innovations and contradictions, of European ambitions and national concerns, of leaps forward and conflicting visions, the negotiations of the draft European Act were able to commence.

---

[161] See Georges Henri Soutou, L'Italie et le couple franco-allemand, in: Antonio Varsori/Piero Craveri (eds.), L'Italia nella costruzione europea: Un Bilancio Storico, Milano 2009, pp. 43–66, 57–58.

[162] Gilles Martinet informed his Government that Italy officially practiced its European "faith" with strong feelings and it shared with Germany the determination to support an institutional reform. The truth was, however, that Italy was well aware of the obstacles which this plan would face and therefore it aimed at gaining nothing else than a moral advantage. See Rapport de fin de mission. CHEVS, MR22, quoted in Bruna Bagnato, L'Italia vista da Palazzo Farnese, p. 247.

[163] At that time, France seemed to consider the European integration as if it were based on bilateral forms of cooperation. Traditionally, the Franco-German couple was the most influential among them, even if Paris feared that the combination of Rome with Bonn would slowly gain ground. At the beginning of the 1980s, this state of affairs strengthened the importance of the Bundesrepublik on the European stage, which was not necessarily a positive result for France. At first, Paris welcomed the joint Italo-German initiative with scepticism. Then, increasing worries concerning the closer cooperation between Rome and Bonn replaced such initial scepticism. See, for example, relance européenne, rencontre Genscher-Colombo, Ministère des relations extérieures, télégramme n. 607/télégramme n. 654, Jacques Senart, 1.10.1981. AMAE 1930inva, Direction Europe, Série RFA, carton 4907, sous-série 11–6, période 1981–1985. See also Ministère des relations extérieures, le conseiller technique du Ministre délégué chargé d'affaires européennes, M. André Chandernagor, 2.10.1982. ANF, série 5 AG 4, PM/8, dossier 2.

a)   From Stuttgart to Stuttgart (1981–1983): Ambitions and Constraints,
*   New Impetus and Old Obstacles standing in the Way*

After some not very encouraging talks that the German Foreign Minister had with both his London and Paris counterparts in February 1981[164], Italy and Germany started negotiations at a national and at a bilateral level to fill with specific contents the ideas sketched in Stuttgart and Florence.

Domestically, both Foreign Ministries were engaged in a debate, from which an Italian result was a programme-based document. It devoted equal attention to two sets of problems. On the one hand, there was the necessity to give birth to a common Foreign policy and to engage in consultations on issues of security. Besides, the objective of a political union was correlated with a set of specific economic provisions, this being the first step towards a future Economic and Monetary Union. On the other hand, Italian negotiators also wanted to use the opportunity to raise the question of eventually extending the EC competencies to higher education.[165]

These general aims were followed by a list of measures deemed necessary to transpose the set objectives into reality. The European Council would be the main body responsible for giving political direction, and its links with the Communities had to be deepened. The importance attached to both the General Affairs Council and the rotating presidency was stressed; the efficacy of the latter would be enhanced through the establishment of a permanent secretariat. The extension of the powers of the European Parliament in terms of enhanced cooperation with – and control over – the EPC was recommended. Moreover, the possibility of introducing a parliamentary vote of confidence on the appointment of the Commission President was also raised during preparatory work. Lastly, Italy deemed it advisable to suggest a substantial reduction of the unanimity requirement in the European decision-making process.

Paragraph 5 of the Italian proposal was fully devoted to the economic dimension. Further steps in the field of more economic and monetary integration were presented as the precondition for a future European Political Union. It was therefore proposed that Member States would from then on commit themselves to agree on binding targets in the fields of decisive anti-inflation strategies, common wage and employment policies, better deficit control, and effective growth policies.

The joint initiative would take the form of a declaration with a revision clause, namely a clause allowing, five years after its adoption, for an assessment of how

---

164 See Ulrich Lappenküper, Hans-Dietrich Genscher-Emilio Colombo und der Kampf gegen die „Eurosklerose", p. 230.
165 See Fernando Lay, L'Iniziativa italo-tedesca per il rilancio dell'Unione Europea, pp. 12–13.

much progress had been made and for the potential to draw up, in close cooperation with Parliament, a new treaty. Thus, the results achieved up to that point, both politically and economically, would be formalised.[166]

The German Foreign Ministry, for its part, also committed itself to drafting solid proposals, but, unlike Italy, three different documents were drawn up. The first, cherished by Hans-Dietrich Genscher, was an ambitious draft Treaty; the second consisted in a less ambitious set of measures for a draft declaration, very similar in content to the Italian project; whereas the last paper can be viewed as a document of minimums.

The draft Treaty proposed the creation of a European Government joined by a Parliament with co-decision rights, which would contain the seeds of a bicameral Parliamentary system.[167] It also reflected a keen interest, particularly by Werner Lautenschlager, the closest advisor of Foreign Minister Genscher, both for an enhanced cooperation in the field of justice, and for supporting further developments of the EMS with a view to the future establishment of an Economic and Monetary Union.

By contrast, the draft declaration was less ambitious, insofar as it only suggested better coordination and a more coherent institutional framework among the European Commission, the European Council and the European Parliament. The EPC would also be subjected to a reform process to provide it with a more efficient operational structure. The decision-making bodies of the EC and of the EPC would be brought under the responsibility of the European Council. Thus, German negotiators intended to ensure coherence and consistency between the objectives of the European Foreign and Economic policies. The European Council would be called upon to serve the European integration process functioning as a decision-making body of both the EC and the EPC. This would be done by providing general political direction and by taking binding decisions. The powers of Parliament would also be enhanced, even if the declaration proposed more limited innovations compared to the provisions of the draft Treaty. The European Parliament would be endowed with the right to discuss foreign policy issues, while the European Council would transmit a report to the Parliament soon after its appointment and at the end of its term. It was, however, unclear how security issues could be part of a future European Common Foreign policy.[168]

In summing up, the first German proposal, the draft Treaty, endorsed the economic dimension, cherished by the Italians, but it was so ambitious that it reached the point of worrying Rome, where the hypothesis of the immediate signature of a new Treaty was met with hostility. On the contrary, the second German proposal

---

[166] See Ibid., pp. 13–14.
[167] See Eckart Gaddum, Die deutsche Europapolitik in den 80er Jahren: Interessen, Konflikte und Entscheidungen, Lübeck 1994, pp. 213–215.
[168] See Ulrich Rosengarten, Die Genscher-Colombo-Initiative, pp. 35–42.

was more in tune with the programme-based document drawn up in Italy, but it was deprived of any significant reference to the economic dimension. It merely showed appreciation for the EMS as an area of stability. Specific proposals for its enhancement were, however, not provided.

In March 1981, Genscher and Colombo met once again, thus further reinforcing their mutual understanding.[169] To ensure better coordination, the decision was taken to set up a group of senior officials from both Foreign Ministries which would be under the guidance of their respective Directors-General, Bruno Bottai[170] for Italy and Franz Pfeffer for the Bundesrepublik. For Rome and Bonn, the ongoing negotiations provided the opportunity for socialisation, which, indirectly, favoured a closer cooperation and offered a solution to some points of contention, such as the so-called "Guadeloupe psychological complex".[171]

Also noteworthy was the active promotion "campaign" carried out in 1981 both at home and in other Member States. In March 1981, Emilio Colombo dealt with the "cultural dimension" of the joint initiative in an article published in the Italian newspaper *Corriere della Sera*.[172] One month later he accorded an interview to the French *Le Monde*, where he approached the problem of a European revival.[173] In May 1981, an article signed by Hans-Dietrich Genscher was published in the Belgian newspaper *Le Soir*.[174] The German Foreign Minister took advantage of this opportunity to warn against the risk of having Europe lowered to a tool of International politics, unless necessary reforms were implemented. Some months later, in August 1981, Italian Ambassador Ducci, former Director for Political Affairs, resorted to the prestigious Milanese newspaper *Corriere*

---

[169] See Doc.73, Gespräch des Bundesministers Genscher mit dem italienischen Außenminister Colombo, VS-vertraulich, Bonn, 17.3.1981, in: AAPD, 1981 Band 1, München, 2012. See also Incontro tra i ministri degli esteri Genscher e Colombo, Bonn, 17.3.1981, pp. 359–360. 1981, Testi e documenti sulla politica estera dell'Italia, Roma 1985.

[170] Bruno Bottai (Rome, 10.7.1930- 1.11.2014) was Director-General for Political Affairs from 1981 to 1985, and from 1987 to 1994 he was General-Secretary of the Foreign Ministry. Also noteworthy is the fact that he had already had, from 1970 to 1972, the opportunity to work closely with Emilio Colombo (back then Prime Minister) as his diplomatic counselor.

[171] This expression refers to worries Italians had of being excluded from the most important European and international summits. The Guadeloupe Summit of 1978 symbolically embodied these worries. See Politischer Halbjahresbericht ITALIEN II 1980, VS-NfD. PA AA, B26, n. 123280. For a similar conclusion see also Gespräch des Bundeskanzlers mit italienischen MP Spadolini am Rande des Wirtschaftsgipfels in Ottawa. PA AA, B26, n. 123281.

[172] See Politique extérieure de l'Italie : Déclaration de M. Colombo au Corriere della Sera, Ambassade de France en Italie, Dépêche d'actualité, 3.3.1981. AMAE 1930inva, Direction Europe, Série Italie, carton 5331, sous-série 11, période 1981–1985.

[173] See Interview de M. Colombo : politique étrangère italienne, Ambassade de France en Italie, Dépêche d'actualité, 7.4.1981. AMAE 1930inva, Direction Europe, Série Italie, carton 5331, sous-série 11, période 1981–1985.

[174] Hans-Dietrich Genscher, „Wohin geht Europa?", *Le Soir*, 19.5.1981.

della Sera, to make public the guidelines of the Farnesina, and to present the reasons for supporting the European integration process.[175]

It did not automatically follow though that Italy and Germany fully agreed on all aspects of the initiative.[176] Even if by July 1981 the two countries had achieved a general understanding on Foreign policy issues and had almost agreed on including security issues in the proposal, but with the exclusion of strictly militarily aspects, imbalances in the fields of culture, education, research, and above all, the economy, were far from being solved.[177]

The Roman proposals for binding principles in the field of economic policy coordination put, in fact, great strain on Hans-Dietrich Genscher. In all likelihood, the German Foreign Minister was receptive to the Italian reasoning. However, he was well aware of the tough opposition brought forward in the ranks of his own government.[178] This was confirmed by the reserved attitude which Chancellor Schmidt adopted, above all during the most critical time in the negotiations, between summer and autumn 1981.[179] The German Cabinet meeting called for 18 September 1981 was no exception to this picture. Genscher submitted both the draft Treaty and the draft declaration, strongly emphasising the utmost necessity of supporting the merging of the EC with the EPC mechanism. It was only after a long debate that Genscher received a mandate from his Government to negotiate

---

[175] See Rélance du projet européen, Ambassade de France en Italie, Dépêche d'actualité, 11.8.1981. AMAE 1930inva, Direction Europe, Série Italie, carton 5331, sous-série 11, période 1981–1985. The article published in *Corriere della Sera* offered a wider setting which included not only the Stuttgart and Florence speeches, but also Lord Carrington's proposal of a secretariat, the French proposal of a European research area and the creation of a committee to draft a new treaty based on Spinelli's approach. The article also suggests the idea that a great conference could be convened on the model of the conference Gaetano Martino had proposed in 1955.

[176] See also Deutsch-Itl. Gegensätze in der europäischen Gemeinschaft, Fernschreiben aus Bonn-Diplo, VS-NfD, 10.6.1981. PA AA, B26, n. 123282

[177] See Gespräch des Bundeskanzlers mit MP Spadolini am Rande des Wirtschaftsgipfels in Ottawa, Ottawa, no date (probably June 1981). PA AA, B26, n. 123281. On the sidelines of the summit, Schmidt had long talks with Spadolini (their Foreign Ministers were also present).

[178] See Vermerk Deutsch-italienische Außenminister Konsultationen, Bonn, 17.7.1981, and Vermerk Gespräch Staatssekretär mit dem italienischen Botschafter, Ferraris, Bonn, 13.7.1981. PA AA, B26, n. 123281.

[179] See Vermerk über das Gespräch des Bundeskanzlers mit dem italienischen Ministerpräsidenten Spadolini beim Frühstück in Montebello am 20 Juli. 1981, Montebello, 24.7.1981. PA AA, B26, n. 123282. See also Visite du Chancelier Schmidt à Rome, télégramme n. 609, 17.9.1981. AMAE 1930inva, Direction Europe, Série RFA, carton 4907, sous-série 11–6, période 1981–1985. Some days after the official submission of the European Act draft, in November 1981, the German Government displayed its unwillingness to provide more financial support for Europe, thus casting a shadow on the joint proposal. It was like putting a weapon in the hands of those European States which denounced the plan as a mere display of rhetoric.

with Italy, according to the guidelines of the draft declaration. The ambitious draft Treaty had been, for the present, put aside.[180]

In addition, during this ministerial gathering the proposed declaration also underwent another review process where further cuts were made. This particularly applied to security policy aspects. The idea of establishing a Council of Defence Ministers was definitively abandoned. Genscher and his supporters were though able to consistently and successfully forward the case for maintaining the principle of future cooperation on security issues, always with the exclusion of strictly military aspects.

Against this background Foreign Ministers Genscher and Colombo met in Rome on 11 September and on 3 October 1981 to finalise the details of their initiative before its official submission. The discussions mainly revolved around three matters: the implementation of new voting rules, the most relevant points concerning the interaction between Commission and Parliament, and how to deal with security issues. The essential need to overcome the practice of the "veto right", which the Luxembourg compromise of 1966 had adopted, was strongly supported by Emilio Colombo.

> „Colombo: Ich möchte nur noch ein anderes wichtiges Thema ansprechen. Wie drängen wir am besten den Luxemburger Kompromiß etwas zurück? Ich bin einer der Väter dieses Kompromisses. Es war damals nötig. Ich habe ihn zusammen mit Couve ausgearbeitet. Aber noch heute lassen mich die Skrupel nicht los. Können uns nicht näherer an eine Mehrheitsprozedur heranarbeiten? In Ihrem Text ist nur die Stimmenhaltung erwähnt."[181]

After some general remarks, the 3 October meeting focused, in fact, on specific issues, such as the contents of article 2 and of article 8 in the German proposal. In this regard, it was vital for Colombo to adopt measures to narrow down the field of the so called "vital interests", whereas Genscher was far more elusive. [182] He merely suggested making a distinction between the adoption of the European Act – where unanimity was the only possible way – and the day-to-day decision making-process – where alternative possibilities could be discussed –.

---

[180] Ulrich Lappenküper, Hans-Dietrich Genscher-Emilio Colombo und der Kampf gegen die „Eurosklerose", p. 233.

[181] "Colombo: I want to refer to another important issue: Which could be the best possible way to reduce a little the use of the Luxembourg compromise? I am one of the fathers of this compromise. At that time, it was indispensable. I drew it up with Couve. But even nowadays I still have a guilty conscience. Could we try to move towards a majority procedure? Your text merely refers to the abstention". See Doc. 282, Gespräch des Bundesministers Genscher mit dem italienischen Außenminister Colombo in Rom, VS-vertraulich, Rome, 3.10.1981, in: AAPD, 1981, Band II, München, 2012.

[182] Ibid., pp. 1492–1493.

Colombo's approach was far more innovative. He recommended indeed the adoption of more objective standards to define the notion of "vital interests". Finding an unambiguous definition was considered the first step to restricting recourse to them. Accordingly, each Member State could appeal to a "vital interest" to block the adoption of a certain measure only after submitting a detailed written explanation. Being this the case, the decision would be put on hold until the next session, giving the opponent state time to reconsider its attitude. This would also provide the opportunity for a wider discussion involving the European Parliament, thus the debate was likely to receive a great deal more media attention. In the end, Colombo aimed to enhance transparency and provide for more discipline on the part of Member States.

Here too, Hans-Dietrich Genscher seemed to share the approach his partner upheld, but German negotiators feared that this would lead to Parliament having the right to express a vote of no-confidence as a means of creating a new relationship between this assembly and the European Commission. Genscher was, therefore, forced to walk a tightrope over the divide between Italian demands, which in many ways mirrored his personal approach, and the lack of backing from his own government.

As for security issues, both Genscher and Colombo shared the idea of avoiding any possible reference to the failed European Defence Community (EDC), which could seriously undermine their chances of success. Nevertheless, there were several discrepancies both in the negotiations between Italy and Germany and, domestically, in Italy and Germany, as for example the October 1981 meeting between the diplomatic Counsellor of the French Embassy in Rome and Angelo Bernassola, the DC member in charge of international issues, remarked.

Speaking on behalf of its own party and not of the Italian Government nor of the Farnesina, Bernassola remarked that the EC needed a more efficient political and administrative structure with a secretariat as coordinating body. Bernassola also argued that security issues and defence issues could not be dealt with separately, even if the DC, unlike the PCI, did not consider it desirable to have a European defence policy to replace NATO. He showed appreciation for the German draft treaty, as in his opinion Colombo had also done; it was, however, not surprising that Colombo in his capacity as Foreign Minister had to be more cautious and find a balance in the midst of diverging "feelings and moods" both within the Government and the different ministries.[183]

---

[183] See Point de vue de la Démocratie-chrétienne sur les aspects politiques de la relance européenne, Ambassade de France en Italie, Dépêche d'actualité, Rome, 13.10.1981. AMAE 1930inva, Direction Europe, Série Italie, carton 5331, sous-série 11, période 1981–1985.

An overall agreement to include security issues in the initiative, with only the exclusion of militarily aspects, was not reached until the end of October 1981. It was supplemented by a more precise wording which was to be incorporated in the notes following the act.[184]

By contrast, controversial points concerning economic policy coordination, as had emerged during the meetings in Ottawa and Montebello in July 1981, had not been settled yet. Italian negotiators considered German proposals too general and vague to be acceptable and they had therefore made provision for stricter discipline by proposing penalties for "undisciplined Member States".[185] Even though Emilio Colombo probably sympathised with his German counterpart and the domestic difficulties he encountered, he could not contravene the instructions received by his own Government. After lengthy discussions, the only way out of this impasse was, therefore, found in a separate path, with Italy presenting its own economic document together with the joint Italo-German Draft European Act.

Certainly, by October there was a perfect understanding between Colombo and Genscher. Apparently though, this was not the case for their governments, economic policy coordination being just the most prominent sign of this disagreement.[186] It placed a large question mark over the chances of success of the common targets Genscher and Colombo were pursuing.

This unexpected "sodality" between the most prominent *Nettozahler* within the European Community and one of its main *Nettoempfänger* arouse curiosity in the press. This atmosphere of interest was a valuable source of help for promoting general acceptance of what Italy and Germany were planning, but it also uncovered the main imbalance within the Italo-German plan. Such imbalance was destined to give more weight to the oppositional stance adopted by other Member States.

On 12 November both proposals, the European Act and the economic declaration, were submitted to the Council, both officially presented as a joint Italo-German

---

[184] See Doc. 253, Gespräch des Bundesministers Genscher mit dem italienischen Außenminister Colombo in Rom, VS-vertraulich, Rome, 11.9.1981, in: AAPD, 1981, Band II, München, 2012.

[185] Colombo was ready to give specific examples to explain this idea, for instance referring to Great Britain and to his own country. It was not just his personal conviction that Europe needed a leap forward both in the realm of politics and in the realm of economics, but it also corresponded to what his government and the Ministry of Treasury kept asking.

[186] In September 1981 Italian negotiators still regretted the lack of mature German plans of action. See, in particular, Fernando Lay, L'Iniziativa italo-tedesca per il rilancio dell'Unione Europea, pp. 14–15.

proposal.[187] On the same day, Emilio Colombo wrote a letter to his fellow colleagues in other Member States:

> «Dopo i brillanti risultati raggiunti per un lungo periodo di anni dal processo unitario promosso dai Trattati di Parigi e di Roma [...] è subentrata, essenzialmente, ma non solo, per complessi motivi esteri di carattere internazionale, una fase di maggiore difficoltà. A queste difficoltà sarebbe inopportuno e dannoso per i nostri popoli se la Comunità reagisse con un arresto o un ripiegamento. Gli interessi, anche a volte legittimamente concorrenti, di ciascuno dei nostri diversi paesi si difendono meglio – ne siamo certi – collocando in prima fila tra essi lo sviluppo comune e il progresso della Comunità. Questo obiettivo non è sempre semplice da raggiungere, ma l'elaborazione tempestiva di una volontà politica comune rispetto ai grandi temi dell'integrazione economica e l'impegno politico di attenervisi [...] possono indubbiamente facilitarne il compito. [...] ».[188]

The European Act was a solemn commitment to move towards the European Union. One of its prime aims was to buttress the role of the European Council as the main source of political directions for both the EPC and the EC. Several points discussed throughout the previous months had been retained in the Act, such as the necessity of restricting the practise of the "veto right" and therefore extending the use of a qualified majority vote within the Council of Ministers. The proposals to extend the areas of coordination to security, justice, and culture had also been retained. The creation of new ministerial Councils in the abovementioned sectors was therefore recommended.

As for the European Parliament, it was recommended that the European Council should report to Parliament every six months, and also submit an annual report on the progress made towards the European Union. Henceforth, resolutions of the European Parliament would be notified to the Council for discussion. Before the appointment of the President of the Commission, the President of the Council was to consult the President of the European Parliament.

---

[187] See Fernando Lay, L'Iniziativa italo-tedesca per il rilancio dell'Unione Europea, part three: documents, «progetto italo-tedesco di Atto europeo», pp. 121–127, and «progetto italo-tedesco di temi di dichiarazione sull'integrazione economica», pp. 129–130. (copies of the original texts of both the draft European Act and the Italian declaration on economic integration).

[188] "After our many brilliant achievements following the signing of the Treaties of Paris and Rome [...] we have been going through difficult times, also, but not solely, as a result of complicated international dynamics. It would be both inappropriate and harmful for our people and for the Community to respond with a stop or a withdrawal. The interests of all our countries, though in competition, can be better protected – we are sure of that – if we give pride of place to a common development and to progress within the Community. This objective is hard to achieve. Still, if we are able to share a common political resolve concerning the main issues of economic and political integration and if we stick to it [...] this will facilitate our task". See Lettera di Emilio Colombo ai ministri degli Esteri, 12.11.1981. ILS, AGA, Section Europe, b.352.

Yet, after long discussions, Italy and Germany had agreed to give up the idea that the European Parliament could have the right to express a no-confidence vote on the choice of the Commission President. Lastly, special legitimacy was attached to the deliberations and decisions of the European Parliament in the further development of fundamental human rights.

The economic declaration was bound to look short and completely lacking in innovative contents by comparison. The paper merely called for a completion of the common market and for increasing convergence and closer coordination. An almost as general adjustment of the agricultural policy and an improvement in the budgetary structure were, moreover, deemed necessary.

It could be expected that the United Kingdom[189] and Ireland would oppose the proposal from its very infancy, the latter posing problems especially on security issues.[190] On the contrary, as far as France was concerned, the proposers of the draft Act harboured the hope that this influential Member State would demonstrate flexibility and willingness to negotiate. It was, however, a misplaced trust, especially on the Italian side, as examination of the extensive French diplomatic documentation confirms.

Fears and worries among German senior officials of the Foreign Ministry that France might be reticent about joining forces proved to be true. For instance, in the 13 October memorandum, the French Minister with responsibility for European Affairs, André Chandernagor (1981–1983), ruled out in advance any chance that his government would even consider "institutional proposals", i.e. a project trying to alter the institutional framework of the EC. What his country was pursuing was the realization of an "espace social européen". At the most, France could consider supporting a project which would boost the European economy.[191] Still, because Foreign Minister Genscher attached the utmost importance to this joint proposal, France had to at least to discuss it, even if nothing would change the strong determination of French Foreign Minister Claude Cheysson (1981–1985) to refuse binding commitments.

---

[189] "Ci fu un lungo negoziato dove partecipai come direttore generale degli Affari politici nel quale erano presenti [...] gli inglesi in una posizione [...] di grande freno". (Negotiations went on for a long time, I participated in my capacity of Director-General for Political Affairs. [...] British representatives were there [...] some of the most negative remarks came from them [...]). See the interview Bruno Bottai gave to Maria Grazia Melchionni in Rome (17.2.1998), in: Voices on Europe, Oral History Collections, Historical Archives of the European Union (http://www.eui/HAEU/OralHistory/, last accessed 1.2.2016).

[190] See Doc. 253, Gespräch des Bundesministers Genscher mit dem italienischen Außenminister Colombo in Rom, VS-vertraulich, Rom, 11.9.1981 and Doc. 282, Gespräch des Bundesministers Genscher mit dem italienischen Außenminister Colombo in Rom, VS-vertraulich, Rome, 3.10.1981, in: AAPD, 1981, Band II, München, 2012.

[191] See Ulrich Rosengarten, Die Genscher-Colombo-Initiative, p. 45.

The most innovative proposals of Genscher and Colombo had been, one after another, put aside with each passing month of negotiations.[192] Nevertheless, the draft was still too ambitious in the eyes of their European partners. France, for instance, feared its potential consequences. At a first glance, the draft Act put together cultural cooperation and cooperation on security issues in an intergovernmental framework. Still, on a closer look, this was not an obvious conclusion. Paris feared, therefore, the possibility of having to deal with a permanent secretariat that was "susceptible d'évolution" (capable of development): with time, it could expand its competencies.[193] France was also suspicious and distrustful of the German lack of financial and economic flexibility.

Fearing such a scenario, Genscher had made every possible effort to remove this obstacle, but the fact that Italy was left alone presenting its own declaration for economic policy coordination was a poor substitute for combined efforts. To make this picture worse, France seemed to look at the European Act draft through a sort of "deforming devise". In a note written by the Foreign Ministry two days after the official submission of the joint-proposal, it was claimed that the Act was almost exactly the same as the draft, which France had informally received from Germany at the end of September. This statement automatically led to the conclusion that Bonn had played the leading role, whereas Italy had just added some final touches.[194]

On 19 November, Emilio Colombo and Hans-Dietrich Genscher presented their proposal in front of the European Parliament and on 26 November they submitted it to the European Council of London. Aware of the difficulties which would be encountered, Colombo and Genscher had decided to travel to Strasbourg in order to vouch for their joint project.[195] This choice was seen as a minor revolution since, according to established practice, only the country holding the EC presidency had the right to address Parliament.[196]

---

[192] The French records also emphasize that, in the end, the innovations in the field of culture were not significant and that cooperation on security issues had been narrowed down in the official Act submitted by Italy and Germany. See La politique étrangère de l'Italie, note du Ministère des relations extérieures, direction d'Europe méridionale, 12.11.1981. AMAE 1930inva, Direction Europe, Série Italie, carton 5331, sous-série 11, période 1981–1985.

[193] See L'Union européenne, note du Ministère des relations extérieures, direction d'Europe occidentale, Paris, 14.11.1981. AMAE 1930inva, Direction Europe, Série Italie, carton 5331, sous-série 11, période 1981–1985.

[194] Ibid.

[195] For Colombo's speech see Fernando Lay, L'Iniziativa italo-tedesca per il rilancio dell'Unione Europea, part three: documents, «Intervento dell'On. Emilio Colombo al Parlamento europeo».

[196] See Ulrich Lappenküper, Hans-Dietrich Genscher-Emilio Colombo und der Kampf gegen die „Eurosklerose", pp. 234–235.

Socialist members of the Assembly were little convinced and all those who were in favour of Altiero Spinelli and the efforts for institutional reforms he supported with the *club du crocodile* were equally sceptical. The only remarkable exception to this atmosphere of general mistrust was the approach of the Liberal group. They were, indeed, in favour of what Genscher and Colombo recommended, even though they also called for coordination with Altiero Spinelli.[197] Even the Italian Ambassador to Bonn, Luigi Vittorio Ferraris (1980–1987), expressed his extreme surprise that Genscher and Colombo did not seek the assistance of the Italian Embassy to arrange a meeting with Spinelli.[198]

Was it an accident that this meeting never took place? Was it rather the result of Genscher's determination[199] (which Colombo fully shared and supported) to give priority to feasible targets without getting involved in grand designs for which it was too early?

The first hypothesis is utterly unconvincing, whereas the second one[200] might correspond to the perceptions of November 1981. Still, a third explanation is also possible.

> „Bundesminister: Wenn wir uns um die europäische Identität bemühen, produzieren wir gleichzeitig ein Serum gegen den Neutralismus.
> Colombo: Das ist richtig, aber einige sind gegen dieses Serum immun. Das sind diejenigen, die europäische Pläne machen, um den Neutralismus zu fördern.
> Bundesminister: Denken Sie an Spinelli?
> Colombo: Ja
> Genscher: Er wollte mich schon dreimal sprechen. Ich will aber nicht, daß dadurch, daß ich ihn empfange, unsere Initiative in ein falsches Licht gerät."[201]

---

[197] Report of Mechthild von Alemanns „Europäische Union und Krokodil" for FDP sitting (2–4 October 1981), quoted in Ibid, p. 233.

[198] See Luigi Vittorio Ferraris, Deutsch-italienische Beziehungen in den 1980er Jahren. Aufzeichnungen aus italienischen diplomatischen Akten, in: Michael Gehler/Maddalena Guiotto, Italien Österreich und die Bundesrepublik Deutschland, p. 250.

[199] See Genscher's address to Parliament in Europe Archive 37 (1982) D55–59.

[200] See the interview Bruno Bottai gave to Maria Grazia Melchionni in Rome (17.2.1998), in: Voices on Europe, Oral History Collections, Historical Archives of the European Union (http://www.eui/HAEU/OralHistory, last accessed 1.2.2016).

[201] "German Foreign Minister: While we are working for a European identity, we produce a serum against neutralism. Colombo: It is true, but there are some people who are immune against this serum. German Foreign Minister: Do you mean Spinelli? Colombo: I do. German Federal Minister: Three times did he want to talk to me, but I refused. I do not want that such a meeting cast a bad light on our initiative". See Doc. 253, Gespräch des Bundesministers Genscher mit dem italienischen Außenminister Colombo in Rom, VS-vertraulich, Rome, 11.9.1981, in: AAPD 1981, Band II, München, 2012, p. 1342.

Refusal to make contact with Altiero Spinelli to join efforts can be considered as the result of a specific fear related to this "neutralism" which dominated Spinelli's approach to reform. By contrast, Genscher and Colombo's ultimate goal was a more assertive Europe within the Western bloc. Working alongside the American behemoth, any diversion from this target was both dangerous and harmful.[202] This approach is another hallmark of both the agreement between Genscher and Colombo and, more generally speaking, of the Italian vision of the "deutsche Frage".

As a result of the 26 November London summit, Foreign Ministers were given a mandate for the examination of the submitted proposal. On this legal basis, Foreign Ministers meeting in Brussels on 4 January 1982 decided to set up a group of senior officials charged with the examination of the European Act draft. The senior official belonging to the country who had the rotating presidency, the Belgian Ambassador Philippe de Schoutheete, was selected to chair this group. Other members were mostly Ambassadors or Directors-General for Political Affairs, such as Bruno Bottai for Italy and Franz Pfeffer for Germany.[203]

During the first few months the proceedings were kept to a tight schedule, so that the first interim report was handed over on 23 February 1982. In the light of mounting economic and financial difficulties it was then agreed that proposals for both institutional and economic reform should be considered together. It was also agreed that senior officials would draw up a single document to submit to the next ministerial meeting. As for those aspects of the European Act draft concerning the powers of Parliament and of other EC bodies, it was decided to resort to the support of the Committee of Permanent Representatives.[204]

It looked as if the group had good chances of completing its work by June, in accordance with the directions of the Council. Nonetheless, against expectations the document submitted in May, containing the results of the examination carried out by both the group of senior officials and the COREPER, differed significantly from the initial joint Italo-German proposal, i.e. there was even less agreement about its contents than at the moment of the submission. This marked the beginning of a difficult negotiating phase corresponding to the Danish rotating presidency.

---

[202] Ibid., p. 1343.
[203] Members of this group were: Ambassador Gunnar Rieberhold (Denmark), Ambassador Paul Metz (Luxembourg), political directors Nicolas Katapodis (Greece), Padraic Mackernan (Ireland), Jakobovits de Szeged (Netherland), Sir Julian Bullard (United Kingdom), diplomatic counsellor Jacques Sénard (France). The Commission's legal Advisor Marchini-Camia was also a member of this group. Senior officials came accompanied by an assistant (being Fernando Lay for Italy and Werner Ungerer for the Bundesrepublik).
[204] Hereafter, also as COREPER.

After months of pointless discussions, Genscher and Colombo decided to hold a bilateral meeting in Bonn on 19 January 1983. They agreed that negotiations had to be brought to an end, but it was not until spring 1983, while the Bundesrepublik held the rotating presidency, that what remained of the project emerged from oblivion to be given the form of the "Solemn Declaration on the European Union".

4.4 Drawing Preliminary Conclusions

The contents of the "Solemn Declaration on the European Union", signed by the Ten on Sunday 19 June 1983, had been toned down compared with the compromise Italy and Germany had agreed on during November 1981. Compared with the original goals, these provisions were but a pale shadow of the targets which Genscher and Colombo had been pursuing.

An overall feeling of mistrust and a strong oppositional stance adopted by the majority of Members States had been a stumbling block. The United Kingdom, Ireland, Denmark and Greece had all rejected the initiative. Each one had opposed one or more of its proposals. They had nothing in common, the only exception being the determination they shared to prevent the plan from succeeding.

Denmark[205] had opposed every single aspect of the Italo-German joint plan, whereas, for instance, Ireland mainly feared the possibility to have a European Foreign policy that would include security issues.[206] Greece, the newest addition to the EC, had shunned every transformation of the EPC, i.e. the eventuality that a common European Foreign Policy could narrow down its freedom in pursuing its own international course.

British opposition to the plan had been broader and more complex. As a general rule, both the British Government and the Commonwealth and Foreign Office had endorsed from the 1970s the creation of foreign policy coordination mechanisms among Member States as if they were a sort of counterweight to a steady decline of His Majesty Government's international clout. As Foreign Minister Lord Carrington had pointed out in his Hamburg speech in November 1980, this substitute needed a subsequent structure in order to be effective. What the British Government actually had in mind was a quicker and more effective cooperation in an intergovernmental framework. Under no circumstances London would accept the establishment of a truly common European Foreign policy.[207]

---

[205] See Ulrich Rosengarten, Die Genscher-Colombo-Initiative, pp. 70–72.

[206] See Maria Eleonora Guasconi, L'Italia e la cooperazione politica europea, p. 68.

[207] Christopher Hill spoke of a "convenient British schizophrenia" to explain this contradiction within the approach of London to the EPC. He used this expression to indicate the combination of the search of a special relationship with Washington to discuss the most sensible issues and of a limited acceptance of the EPC, both overshadowed by a certain nostalgia for the imperial past. In

When Copenhagen took on the rotating presidency during the second half of 1982, an already precarious negotiation deteriorated further. For months the Danish Government had embraced a sceptical view of any step towards institutional reforms, and above all towards changes which could enhance the powers of the European Parliament. It had opposed with equal scepticism the establishment of a common European Foreign policy. Public opinion stance faithfully reflected this negative approach and the Folketing[208] fiercely opposed the plan in its entirety. The long list of saving clauses which Denmark demanded to be added even to the "Solemn Declaration" witnessed this state of affairs.[209]

A too ambitious plan for some, namely the majority of Member States, was a too timid approach for others looking for a decisive step in the direction of federalism. The initiative was, therefore, trapped in this net of contradictions, which slowly released it into oblivion. It was not until the first semester of 1983 that Genscher and Colombo were able to save some of its contents by giving them the form of a declaration of intent with no legal binding value.

Any reference to the signing of a future treaty, to the establishment of a European Union, to a partial revision of the Luxembourg compromise had been taken out. Even the very word "act" had disappeared. What was left of the original targets after two years of negotiations?

The Solemn declaration merely reiterated the need for closer Foreign policy coordination and institutional reforms. It also proposed to intensify cultural exchanges, encouraged to learn European languages and to deepen the knowledge of mutual history. Nevertheless, nothing altered the determination shared by Colombo and Genscher to refuse to settle for what had been achieved. More generally, they both had the merit of having contributed to an increased awareness of the need for reforms. This project had at least the merit of spotlighting on this thorny issue, whose solution had, however, to wait until better times.

What remained of the double dream of strengthening the Italo-German couple so that it could be one of the forces driving the revival of the European integration?

In the end this had also sunk into the quicksand of overall hostility. There are several reasons why this project failed. None of them, taken alone, can identify all the distinctive features of such a failure.

---

the eyes of many British officials, the EPC was a poor substitute for the lost British international influence. See Christopher Hill, National foreign policies and European political cooperation, London 1983, pp. 19–20. See also Christopher Hill/Reuben Wong (eds.), National Foreign Policies and European Political Cooperation, London 2011, ch. 5.

[208] Danish Parliament.

[209] See Rocco Antonio Cangelosi, "Dal Progetto di Trattato Spinelli all'Atto Unico Europeo: Cronaca di una riforma mancata", in: *Quaderni di Affari Sociali Internazionali*, Milano 1986, pp. 37–45.

At all stages of the negotiation process, France had tried to slow down the progress of the project. According to Paris, this initiative rested on a strong "institutional basis" and proposed three main kind of innovations: a renunciation to the compromise of Luxembourg, an overall merging of EC mechanisms and Foreign policy coordination, and an enhancement in the powers of the European Parliament, even if neither Italy nor Germany proposed to endow the assembly with legislative competences. The initiative, in its original form, also proposed the signing of a new treaty after a five-year transitional period.[210] Culture, security and justice were, according to French diplomats, the key words of this plan.[211]

The French diplomatic records present the EPC reform as one of the most controversial issues. France seemed to fear, in fact, that such a reform would imply the disappearance of all distinctions between Community method and Foreign policy coordination, which, associated with a stricter voting system, could result in a sort of "droit de regard" of the European Parliament on Foreign policy.[212] An alarming first step in this direction could be the allocation to the European Parliament of a no-confidence vote on the appointment of the President Commission. In the future it could lead to Parliament having a right of censure on Member States, a right of approving or refusing the signing of international agreements and even the right of passing resolutions on human rights.[213]

Another cause for concern was the proposed extension of the powers of the Community into new areas: defence and justice. To achieve this target, Italy and Germany had originally proposed hosting regular meetings of Defence Ministers, which constituted grounds for mistrust in Paris. The main bone of contention and subject of criticism was, indeed, the idea of establishing a common security policy.

Still, at a closer glance, we can notice that both the *Elysée Palace* and the *Quai d'Orsay*[214] not only mistrusted the set of reforms proposed by Genscher and Colombo, but they also feared the "side effects" of this path. Over time, the

---

[210] See Note du Ministère des affaires étrangères direction d'Europe sur le Projet Spinelli de Traité sur l'Union européenne, 2.2.1984. ANF, série 5 AG 4, PM/8, dossier 2.

[211] Jacques Senard (diplomatic counselor) represented France within the group of senior officials set up after the European Council of London. He was a leading figure of French diplomacy. He had been appointed Ambassador to Rome in February 1981. It had been, however, a short-term assignment. After national elections and the victory of François Mitterrand he had been replaced by Gilles Martinet in November 1981. Senard was appointed "conseiller diplomatique" on 4 November 1981 and he served his government in this capacity until November 1984, when he retired.

[212] See Note du comité interministériel sur le projet Genscher-Colombo, Ministère des relations extérieures, direction d'Europe, confidentiel, Paris, 14.5.1982. ANF, série 5 AG 4, PM/8, dossier 2.

[213] Ibid.

[214] Meaning the French Government and its Foreign Office.

secretariat for policy coordination could, for instance, replace the rotating presidency and the Commission was very likely to insist on being part of it. Eventually, this internal change could lead to an unwanted (from France) transfer of powers from Member States to the EC in the field of Foreign policy. Although France was sure that neither Genscher nor Colombo harboured such targets, the Court in Luxembourg might be tempted to use its increasing drive in this direction.[215] Furthermore, the Court could also take advantage of these reforms to exercise its jurisdiction over areas, such as the convention on the pollution of the Rhine, on which Paris fiercely refused to surrender sovereignty.[216] Even if the plan which Italy and Germany had submitted had no "federalist tones" – unlike the project supported by Spinelli and the crocodile club – federalist temptations could reappear in the future if the course set by Genscher and Colombo was followed.

In addition to this, Paris also feared that a successful initiative could contribute to a further rapprochement between Rome and Bonn.

Certainly, France alone cannot be considered responsible that the Genscher-Colombo plan failed, however, its negative stance weighed heavily on its inconclusive results. Rome lacked the capacity and, in all likelihood, the desire to compete with Paris for the role of Bonn's main partner.

This is not to suggest that Europe should be considered the sum of several different bilateral schemes of cooperation among Member States. It simply intends to points out that the EC was also the result of the Franco-German reconciliation and that the proper workings of this couple contributed to a successful integration process.[217] The Franco-German couple alone could not advance the European integration process, but its poor functioning could slow it down.

Another reason explaining the failure of the joint proposal was the necessity to fight on two fronts: against the mistrust of Member States and also against the project supported by Altiero Spinelli. The competition between the Italo-German joint initiative and the project by Altiero Spinelli had negative consequences for both of them.[218] This lack of coordination deprived the Italo-German initiative of an important institutional support and, probably, it was also partially responsible for the failure of Spinelli's proposal.

---

[215] See Problèmes européens, Ministère des affaires étrangères, le directeur des affaires politiques, Paris, 1.6.1984. ANF série 5 AG 4, PM/8, dossier 2.

[216] Ibid.

[217] As for the debate between a federalist approach and more gradual approaches, see, for example, Bini Olivi/Roberto Santaniello, Storia dell'integrazione europea, Bologna 2005, pp. 14–20.

[218] On 9 July 1981, the European Parliament had approved, under pressure of Spinelli, an act that created a Commission to discuss institutional problems. Spinelli considered this choice as the first necessary step to overcome the deadlock Europe was encountering. The debate within the newly founded Commission was heavily influenced by Spinelli's approach which had as ultimate goal the establishment of a European Union within a federal framework.

If we now move from the European to the national level, we have to recall that both Germany and Italy had embarked on the joint initiative not only on the basis of European considerations, but also in light of specific domestic needs. Italy wanted to avoid an over-close bond between France and Germany and also feared being left on the outside of coordination schemes between these two countries and London.

Italian domestic political instability and economic imbalances between Rome and Bonn may also have contributed to these poor results. However, their importance has too often been over-exaggerated. In the period considered in this sub-chapter, Italy had proved to be a reliable partner. Nobody in Bonn called into question Italy's Europeanism and the sound agreement which Genscher and Colombo had established could have been the first step towards improved coordination. Even economic imbalances would have not weighed so heavily, if the Bundesrepublik had taken a different approach regarding economic and monetary integration; such an approach might have resulted in France embracing a less negative stance.

On the contrary, a complete lack of "timing" resulted in a heavier burden. In 1981, it was as if Italy and Germany had changed trains: they had abandoned their regional train to get on a high-speed one. This high-speed train had two different engine drivers. Each driver gave the train a different speed.

At first, the tandem Colombo-Spadolini had laid sound foundations, whereas the government led by Helmut Schmidt had been reluctant to fully commit itself; in other words, this meant that the Italian engine driver wanted to go faster than his German colleague. This obstacle was suddenly removed in autumn 1982 after the German elections. On 12 October 1982, Helmut Kohl declared in his inaugural address[219] his support for the establishment of a European Political Union. Through Helmut Kohl and the new CDU/CSU-FDP coalition he led, Genscher finally gained the official backing his joint proposal had lacked.[220] It was, therefore, not a coincidence that in October 1982 Emilio Colombo was the first Foreign Minister to travel to Bonn.

Despite this positive change, the "timing" was once again not in favour of the joint proposal. In autumn 1982, the Italian engine driver was forced, in fact, to

---

[219] See Helmut Kohl, Bundeskanzler Reden 1982–1984, Bonn, Presse und Informationsamt der Bundesregierung, 1984, 9–48, in: http://www.helmut-kohl-kas.de and http://www.1000dokumente.de (last accessed 26.9.2016).

[220] Since 1982 the German Government offered an interesting combination between Foreign Minister Hans-Dietrich Genscher and the new Chancellor, Helmut Kohl, also a committed pro-European, but on a somewhat different basis. For Chancellor Kohl, Europe was more than the total amount of the GDP of its Member States or the sum of the directives adopted. It was a community of shared ideas and values. This was one of the leading features of his political course.

choose a slower speed than his German co-worker. The government of Spadolini was facing major difficulties. Even the regular Italo-German summit had been postponed. Helmut Kohl's first official visit therefore resulted in only a short trip.[221] Late in 1982, the Government led by Giovanni Spadolini was replaced by a *pentapartito* coalition under the guidance of Fanfani. It barely lasted eight months. Shortly after the adoption of the Solemn Declaration in Stuttgart, Emilio Colombo left his post. The Genscher-Colombo combination also ceased to exist.

The overall failure of the joint initiative did not imply a sort of black-out in the relationship between Rome and Bonn. The very nature of the international system and the commitments which the two countries shared made it a far-fetched possibility. It rather implied, in the immediate term, a certain slow down and loosening of the kind of interaction they shared.

After the appointment of Bettino Craxi as Prime Minister and of Giulio Andreotti as Foreign Minister, Rome remained faithful to the international course the country had followed until that moment. Its action became, however, more dynamic both in the Mediterranean and beyond the Iron Curtain. From 1984, an already complex Italian approach to the "German question" overlapped with a more assertive Ostpolitik, which enriched the relationship between Bonn and Rome with new nuances. Bilaterally, the high-speed train was replaced by a slower machine which allowed a modest, but steady improvement that culminated in 1988 with the establishment of the forum known as *Deutsch-Italienisches Gesprächsforum*.

At the European level, the partnership between Genscher and Colombo was the expression of a long-term path of strong cooperation.[222] From the Sixties, through the Seventies and up to the beginning of the Eighties, Italy and Germany had shared a very similar approach to European integration and had mostly

---

[221] See various documents, telegrams and notes in PA AA, B26, n. 124900. See also Sommet germano-italien commentaire général, Ministère des relations extérieures, télégramme n. 469, Rome, 2.5.1983. AMAE 1930inva, Direction Europe, Série RFA, carton 4907, sous-série 11, période 1981–1985. The Government in Rome feared that these difficulties could give a wrong impression to Kohl, jeopardising his positive attitude with regard to the joint-initiative. Therefore, the summit had been postponed. Although these internal difficulties had not been solved in April 1983, Rome had decided to host the bilateral summit anyway, under the impression that a further postponement might also give a negative impression. The last summit had taken place in Hamburg during spring 1982 when Helmut Schmidt was still German Chancellor. The summit was, however, transformed into a meeting organized in the spirit of "Christian-Democratic friendship".
[222] We must recall that, domestically, Italy and Germany had a lot in common at the end of the Second World War. It is, therefore, not surprising that their foreign policies shared from the 1950s several features, above all a similar approach to European integration. See, for example, the report of the conference (Rome, June 2010) where Italian Ambassador Fagiolo dealt with this subject in: "UniEuropa", June 2011, n. 10

worked side by side in an atmosphere of mutual trust.[223] The joint proposal could have crowned this cooperation path.

When referring to the Italian contribution to European integration in the 1980s, it is customary among diplomats and historians to focus on the dynamic and resolute course pursued by Prime Minister Bettino Craxi (1983–1987) and Foreign Minister Giulio Andreotti (1983–1989) at the Milan Council of June 1985.[224] This sub-chapter does not question such an approach. Generally speaking, it rather points out that the 1985 turning-point had its roots in the changes and innovations of the previous years. Dealing more specifically with the Italian-German relationship, it is, however, necessary to advance the so called phase of "European relaunch" by nearly four years.

The disappearance of the "Genscher-Colombo" political duo marked the failure of the double dream, namely the illusion that these two countries alone could provide Europe with the tools to overcome its deadlock. This did not, however, mean in any way the end of Italian-German cooperation at a European level. On the contrary, historical analysis proves that exactly the opposite occurred. Unlike the bilateral cooperation, which evolved over the following years at a slower pace, Italy and Germany continued to cooperate closely, making an important contribution to the process of European integration, for instance between 1984 and 1985 on the occasion of the Portuguese and Spanish negotiations for

---

[223] See author's interview with Ambassador Pietro Calamia (29.9.2016).

[224] See, in particolar, Marinella Neri Gualdesi, L'Italia e l'Europa negli anni Ottanta. Tra ambizione e marginalità, in: Piero Craveri/Antonio Varsori (eds.), L'Italia nella costruzione europea. Un bilancio storico (1957–2007), Milano 2009, pp. 78–108; Giuseppe Mammarella, Il Consiglio europeo di Milano del 1985, in: Ennio di Nolfo (ed.), La politica estera italiana negli anni Ottanta, Lacaita 2003, pp. 199–223; see also the previously mentioned interview with Ambassador Calamia and Pietro Calamia, "Il Consiglio europeo di Milano (28–29 giugno 1985)", in: *Rivista di Studi di politica internazionale* vol.79 n. 3 (2012), pp. 353–360.

accession[225] and also in laying the foundations of the Single European Act.[226] In this regard, Horst Teltschik did not hesitate in attaching a crucial importance to the regular meetings between himself and his French and Italian colleagues, namely Jacques Attali[227] and Renato Ruggiero[228], that provided the basis for the Single European Act.

In all likelihood, a dramatic change in French politics also had a significant influence on further developments of the Italian-German relationship.[229] The existing Franco-German bilateral instruments of cooperation made it easier for these two countries to cooperate closely both at a bilateral and at a European level. The good chemistry soon to be established between Chancellor Helmut Kohl and the French President François Mitterrand brought France and Germany even closer than before.

Historians should not indulge in wondering what "would have happened if". At the end of this chapter, however, it might be allowed to make the hypothesis that the history of the Italian-German relationship could have followed a different path after 1983, had the Colombo-Genscher couple been granted some additional time to take full advantage of the new conditions introduced by the election of Helmut Kohl.

---

[225] See Pietro Calamia, "La svolta europea del 1985. Il ruolo dell'Italia", in: *Rivista di studi politici internazionali*, vol.79 n. 1, 2012, pp. 18–20: "Tra martedì 19 e mercoledì 20 marzo 1985 il negoziato con la Spagna sembrava dovesse arenarsi. Stava svanendo l'ultima possibilità di mantenere l'obiettivo dell'entrata nella Comunità il 1° gennaio 1986 […]. La situazione era chiara. Sia pure con qualche esitazione nove delegazioni erano disposte ad accettare il compromesso, quella francese chiedeva tempo […] Riaprire il negoziato era il modo sicuro per far saltare il negoziato. […]. Non c'era più margine di manovra. Ricordo che il ministro Genscher, che aveva sentito dei contatti della Presidenza con gli Spagnoli venne personalmente da me a prendere notizie. Feci presente anche a lui il rischio che avrebbe corso il negoziato se gli Spagnoli avessero cercato di riaprire punti del compromesso. Era del tutto d'accordo e aggiunse dirò loro 'you must buy it!'. E si diresse, con la sua andatura caracollante, verso gli uffici della delegazione spagnola". (Ambassador Calamia affirmed: Between Tuesday 19 and Wednesday 2 March 1985 the Spanish negotiations seemed to be deadlocked. The last chance of maintaining the objective of accession by 1 January 1986 was quickly vanishing. The situation was clear. Nine delegations out of ten were ready to accept a compromise, though reluctantly, whereas the French delegation demanded more time […] Reopening negotiations was a sure way to torpedo them. […] There was no room for manoeuvre. I remember that Genscher, who had heard of our contacts with the Spanish Government, came to me to be updated. I also told him that negotiations would have been endangered if the Spanish Government tried to renegotiate. He fully agreed and he also added he would tell them 'you must buy it!'. Then he walked with his unsteady pace towards the Spanish delegation).

[226] See author's interview with Horst Teltschik (28.9.2017).

[227] Counsellor to President Mitterrand for a decade, form 1981 until 1991.

[228] Secretary-General at the Italian Foreign Ministry from February 1985 until July 1987.

[229] See Ulrich Lappenküper, Hans-Dietrich Genscher-Emilio Colombo und der Kampf gegen die „Eurosklerose", p. 242; see also Antonio Varsori, L'Italia e l'integrazione europea, l'occasione perduta?, in Simona Colarizi/Piero Craveri/Silvio Pons/Gaetano Quagliariello (eds.), Gli Anni Ottanta come Storia, Soveria Mannelli, 2004, pp. 155–184, 168.

5. Italy and Germany: The Second Stage (1984–1988) New Strains and Old Misunderstandings

Noi tutti siamo d' accordo sul fatto che debbano esistere buoni rapporti tra le due Germanie, [...] ma non bisogna esagerare in questa direzione. Il Pangermanesimo va superato: esistono due Stati germanici e due devono rimanere.[1]
(Giulio Andreotti)

Alle sind damit einverstanden, daß die beide Deutschlands gute Beziehungen zueinander haben. Es muss aber klar sein [...] daß der Panger-manismus eine Sache ist, die überwunden werden muß: Es gibt zwei deutsche Staaten, und zwei deutsche Staaten muß es auch weiterhin geben.[2]
(Giulio Andreotti)

On 13 September 1984, during the "Festa de l'Unità", the annual celebration organised by the Italian Communist Party for the anniversary of its newspaper, Foreign Minister Giulio Andreotti (1983–1989) uttered some comments (cited above), which caused a great deal of tension in Bonn.

The core questions of this chapter are twofold: More than thirty years later, under which specific circumstances can these statements be best explained? And what kind of connection was there between them and the Italian approach to the "German issue"?

Neither question would need an answer if we could simply explain the sentences quoted at the beginning of this chapter as an instance of Andreotti's sense of humour. His fondness for pungent quips was well known, both in Italy and abroad; even his closest advisors found it sometimes difficult to explain his

---

[1] "Everybody agrees that the two Germanies should have good relations. It should be clear, however, that Pangermanism is something that must be overcome. There are two German states and two German states must remain. A short quotation from the speech held by Foreign Minister Andreotti during the Festa de l'Unità". Radio Radicale recorded this speech and on 15 September 1984 sent a copy to the Farnesina and to the German Embassy in Rome. Another version was published in the Italian newspaper *Repubblica* with the title, "Queste le frasi all'origine del caso", 14. 9.1984.

[2] Upon German requests for clarification, on 15 September 1984, Italian Ambassador Luigi Vittorio Ferraris sent to the German Foreign Ministry a non-paper with an informal transcription and translation into German of Andreotti's speech. This non-paper was followed by further communications and somewhat different transcriptions and translations. See, for example, Hintergrundpapier Äußerungen Andreottis zur deutschen Frage (hier chronologische Entwicklung), Bonn, 28.9.1984. PA AA, B26, n. 140520. See also Italien/Bundesrepublik, Andreotti gegen Wiedervereinigung Deutschlands, dpa n. 107, 14.9.1984. PA AA B26, n. 140520.

"jokes"[3] out of context.[4] Still, several elements point in a different direction. For instance, the extensive diplomatic documentation kept in the German Foreign Ministry archives[5] offer ample evidence that a more balanced approach is required. Certainly, such an approach should not succumb to any bias in the opposite direction, i.e. over-exaggerating the importance and the consequences of this episode. Rather, it should provide the tools for placing these statements in their historical context in order to shed some light on the stage reached by the Italo-German relationship in the mid 1980s, thus removing the patina of bitter reactions on both sides of the Alps.

The next sub-chapter aims, therefore, at providing the reader with an overview of the specific historical context in which these words were uttered, and a more detailed picture of the reactions which followed. Thereafter, based on all the information gathered, some hypotheses will be formulated concerning the root causes of such an "event".

5.1 The 1984 Declarations: Just a Mistake, an Interlude or the Announcement of New Misunderstandings?[6]

In September 1984, when the Festa de l'Unità had been organised, a creeping feeling of insecurity permeated the international framework. It was due to the

---

[3] It has often been affirmed that Foreign Minister Andreotti also used to say he loved Germany so much that he even preferred to have two of them. In all likelihood Andreotti knew this sentence, even if he was not the one who had introduced it into the debate; all "the merit" can be taken by the French writer and journalist François Mauriac. See Dominique Vidal, "Faut-il avoir peur de l'Allemagne?", in: *Manière de voir*, n. 116, April 2011. See, as well, François Mitterrand, De l'Allemagne de la France, Paris 1996, p. 20. See also the interview Ambassador A. Indelicato gave to Federico Ferraù, in: https://www.ilsussidiario.net/news/cultura/2014/11/10/muro-di-berlino-dalle-due-germanie-di-andreotti-alla-guerra-di-kohl/552738/ "Andreotti era un gran plagiario. Quando sentiva qualcosa che gli sembrava interessante o spiritoso se lo annotava in un librettino che portava sempre con sé. Quella frase però non è di Andreotti, ma di François Mauriac, che la usò negli anni 50 scrivendo sul Figaro". (Andreotti was a real plagiarist. When he heard something interesting or witty he would jot it down in a notebook that he always carried with him. Still, he was not the one who came out with this specific sentence. François Mauriac was the one who used it for the first time in the 1950s for the newspaper *Figaro*). Last consulted 05.10.2016.

[4] Ambassador Luigi Guidobono Cavalchini, for instance, remarked that Andreotti was very clever, but that he also came out with these quips, which could hardly be explained, especially when they concerned touchy points, namely emotional issues, such as the German national division. See author's interview with Ambassador Cavalchini (05.2.2016).

[5] PA AA archival records concerning 1984 had not been declassified when these pages were written. A special authorisation issued by the Foreign Ministry granted, however, access to several documents concerning this "episode". This is, indeed, an extremely useful source of information, being access to Italian archival records still difficult.

[6] These sentences caused bitter controversies at both a political level and in the press of Italy and Germany. This sub-chapter mainly focuses on the political realm, whereas chapter six deals more accurately with the reactions of the press. This choice has been mainly motivated by the necessity

overlay of several trouble spots, such as the growing tensions in the Soviet-American relations, and a sense of uncertainty provoked by the postponement of the official state visit of Honecker to Bonn.

All these causes went hand in hand with the great difficulties to forecast the final outcome of the political transition that the Soviet Union was experiencing.[7] Barely one year after the appointment of Bettino Craxi and Giulio Andreotti, Italian foreign policy towards Eastern Europe had not stopped[8] as a consequence of mounting tensions between Moscow and Washington. It had nonetheless been negatively affected by this international atmosphere.[9] Relations with Poland were, for instance, burdened with the consequences of the economic sanctions imposed on that country, while Italian trade with Moscow and other satellites seemed to have no immediate prospects for growth.[10] In comparison, trade flows with the DDR were even lower, and commercial relations were stagnant.[11] Thanks to a stable exchange network, Hungary was the only significant exception in this gloomy picture.[12]

---

to have better clarity and structure in the narrative. To be sure, some paragraphs provide an overview of the complex interaction between these fields.

[7] See the author's interview with Ambassador Luigi Guidobono Cavalchini (05.2.2016). Ambassador Cavalchini drew similar conclusions in a non-paper which he wrote for an Italian Deputy. He very kindly accepted to provide a copy of the paper for this work.

[8] See Resoconto stenografico delle dichiarazioni programmatiche alla camera dei Deputati del presidente del Consiglio on. Bettino Craxi, Roma, 9.8.1983, p. 94, in: 1983, Testi e documenti sulla politica estera dell'Italia, Roma 1987.

[9] See Doc. 56, Gespräch des Bundeskanzlers Kohl mit Ministerpräsident Craxi, VS-vertraulich, Bonn, 23.2.1984, in: AAPD, 1984, Band I, München 2015.

[10] See Giorgio Petracchi, L'Italia e la Ostpolitik, in: Ennio Di Nolfo (ed.), La politica estera italiana negli anni Ottanta, Manduria 2003, pp. 293–318.

[11] See, for instance, Relations de l'Italie avec les pays de l'est, Ministère des relations extérieures, télégramme n. 335, confidentiel, Rome, 23. 3 1984. AMAE 1930inva, Direction Europe, Série Italie, carton 5331, sous-série 11, période 1981–1985. French records also point out that no Italian Cultural Institute existed in East Berlin. The DDR could exercise its cultural influence in Italy through the institute Thomas Mann (located in Rome), whereas Italy still had difficulties in the 1980s to reach an agreement on the opening of an Institute of Culture. See Alberto Indelicato, Memorie di uno stato fantasma: Berlino 1987–1990, Berlin 2004.

[12] See György Misur, Szarvasról Rómába. Diplomácia Küldetesbén, Budapest 2010, pp. 106–110. See also Riunione ministeriale di cooperazione politica europea, ministero affairi Esteri, riservato (restricted), Dublin, 11.9.1984. ILS, AGA, section Europa, b. 365. See Politique étrangère de l'Italie, note du Ministère des relations extérieures, Direction d'Europe, sous-direction d'Europe méridionale, Paris, 22.5.1984. AMAE 1930inva, Direction Europe, Série Italie, carton 5331, sous-série 11, période 1981–1985. See also Relations de l'Italie avec les pays de l'est, télégramme n. 335 au Ministère des relations extérieures, confidentiel, Rome, 23.3.1984. AMAE 1930inva, Direction Europe, Série Italie, carton 5331, sous-série 11, période 1981–1985. These documents create the impression that the importance of the interaction between Rome and Budapest might have been even greater than expected in light of official statements. This outward low profile seemed to be the aftermath of Italian longstanding concerns about jeopardising the Hungarian delicate transition, if its significant maturity, compared to other Eastern European countries, would be exposed.

Prime Minister Bettino Craxi (1983–1987), accompanied by Foreign Minister Giulio Andreotti, had paid a short official visit to Eastern Germany in July 1984. The meeting with President Honecker took place in a climate of apparent understanding, in which the Italian government, in the person of its Prime Minister, had expressed its satisfaction for what had been achieved until then and had reiterated its determination to increase bilateral trade and economic cooperation in sectors whose potential had not been fully exploited.[13]

A comparison between official statements and the data provided by the German archival records expose, however, a different situation. In economic terms, exchange and cooperation between these two countries were far from reaching the targets defined when Italy had officially recognized the DDR.[14] Italian business relations with Warsaw were, for instance, broader and deeper, the negative effects of the economic sanctions notwithstanding.[15]

Meanwhile, on the basis of the positive results achieved during previous years, Rome and Bonn had continued to enhance cooperation and to develop good neighbourly relations at a slow but steady pace. Positive developments were made possible by a well-established mechanism of regular bi-annual high-level meetings involving both Heads of Governments and Foreign Ministers. This scheme was strengthened by frequent meetings, which provided regular exchanges of views on specific issues, such as the visit of Hans-Dietrich Genscher to Rome in January 1984.[16]

At a first glance, the subjects discussed at Villa Madama with Foreign Minister Andreotti during this short visit, as well as during the regular Italo-German summit held in Bonn the following month, were basically the same as those that

---

[13] See Visita del presidente del Consiglio on. Craxi, Berlino, 9–11.7.1984, in: 1984, Testi e documenti sulla politica estera dell'Italia, Roma 1989.

[14] It was not until 1984 that Italy reported a surplus in trade goods with the DDR, even though bilateral exchanges still mainly concerned specific fields: the steel industry and chemicals. See Relations économiques entre l'Italie et la RDA, note du ministre conseiller pour les affaires économiques, ambassade de France en Italie, Rome, June 1985. Centre des Archives diplomatiques de Nantes (hereafter CADN), 579PO-4-39 Archives rapatriées de l'Ambassade de France à Rome 1981–1992.

[15] See Vermerk über ein Gespräch des Staatssekretärs und 1. Stellvertreter des Ministeriums für Auswärtige Angelegenheiten, Genossen Dr. Herbert Krolikowski, mit dem Staatssekretär im italienischen Außenministerium, Dr. Bruno Corti, 9.3.1984. PA AA, MfAA, ZR 183886. Economic data confirm the existence of a significant divide between commercial exchanges with Poland and Hungary on the one side (and also Czechoslovakia andmania in specific fields) and the DDR on the other, see Scambi commerciali dell'Italia con l'Est 1980–1983, 17.1.1984. PA AA, MfAA, ZR 184386.

[16] See Visita del ministro degli Esteri Hans-Dietrich Genscher, Rome, 24–25.1.1984, in: 1984, Testi e documenti sulla politica estera dell'Italia, Roma, Ufficio Studi Roma, Istituto Poligrafico, 1989.

Hans-Dietrich Genscher had already addressed in previous years with his former colleague Emilio Colombo.

At a closer glance, new trends were, however, slowly emerging[17] both bilaterally and within the European integration process. On the one hand, Germany noticed a more pragmatic approach[18] to European integration and its need for reforms[19] on part of Minister Andreotti, if compared to his predecessor. On the other hand, according to Bonn, an increased Italian emphasis on the Mediterranean, on the relations with Moscow, and more generally with Eastern Europe, was also a new trend to take note of.[20]

---

[17] See, in particular, Doc. 56 Gespräch des Bundeskanzlers Kohl mit Ministerpräsident Craxi, VS-vertraulich, Bonn, 24.2.1984, in: AAPD, 1984 Band 1, München, 2015.

[18] See Ibid. See also Apaisement de la polemique sur la politique étrangère, ambassade de France à Rome, télégramme n. 1256, Rome, 14.11.1983. AMAE 1930inva, Direction Europe, Série Italie, carton 5331, sous-série 11, période 1981–1985. Foreign observers had the impression that for Giulio Andreotti, unlike Emilio Colombo, European integration was not a target "in itself". They also noticed his more cautious approach concerning security and defence issues. See, in partiular, fiche d'entretien du Quai d'Orsay « Europe aspect institutionnel », Paris, 23.10.1984. AMAE 1930inva, Direction Europe, Série Italie, carton 5331, sous-série 11, période 1981–1985, Ministère des relations extérieures, Direction d'Europe, sous-direction d'Europe méridionale.

[19] Once again a comparison between Italian and foreign archival records uncovers a sort of "mirror trick", meaning the gap existing in 1984 between Italian intentions and how Paris and Bonn read them and vice versa. In other words, how Italy perceived German targets through the mirror of its Embassy in Bonn. The Italian Embassy suggested to keep a close watch on Kohl's dynamic approach, as it went hand in hand with increasingly high levels of cooperation with Paris. There was no denying that France had become a point of reference in the German approach to European integration. The traditional relationship between Bonn and Paris had evolved into a privileged partnership. To avoid any risk of being marginalised, it appeared necessary to take a more pragmatic approach, i.e. gaining recognition insofar as Italy could contribute to a rapid solution of some still pending sensible issues, for instance the common agricultural policy. In light of Italian records this more pragmatic approach seems to be the consequence of specific European trends, rather than an autonomous choice. In addition, Italy seemed to be also fully aware that the gap existing between its "heralded European faith" and its preference for US-sponsored projects (as in the Airbus case) had arisen suspicions concerning its reliability. At a time when France and Germany were determined to secure success in the integration process at any price, a more pragmatic, dynamic and coherent approach was the only viable way to dispel suspicion. See, among others, On ne veut pas parler d'airbus, télégramme ambassade de Rome n. 67, distribution strictement limitée, 20.2.1983.ANF, série 5 AG 4, archives d'Elisabeth Guigou (hereafter EG)/215, dossier 6 pays Italie. See also Voyage du Ministre De Michelis aux Etats-Unis, télégramme ambassade de Rome n. 1228, 16.11.1982.

[20] See Politique étrangère de l'Italie, note n. 602, Paris, 5.6.1985. AMAE 1930inva, Direction Europe, Série Italie, carton 5331, sous-série 11, période 1981–1985, Ministère des relations extérieures, Direction d'Europe, sous-direction d'Europe méridionale. In Moscow, Andreotti was a respected politician. According to Paris, this was, among other things, the result of Andreotti's greater sensitivity for political dynamics beyond the Iron Curtain. In addition, at the beginning of the 1980s a marked pro-American approach on the part of Emilio Colombo, and especially of Giovanni Spadolini had increased the prestige which Andreotti enjoyed in Moscow. See, for instance, Luca Ricciardi, Da Colombo ad Andreotti e Craxi: spinti di ricerca sulla politica medio-orientale

«Il merito di Craxi e di Andreotti fu quello di aver intuito, prima di altri membri della Comunità, l'emergere all'interno del blocco sovietico di forze e di interlocutori con cui poteva essere intessuto un dialogo impostato sul cambiamento e il rinnovamento. La percezione italiana di un possibile dialogo con i paesi dell'Europa orientale iniziò a manifestarsi nel 1983, all'apice della seconda guerra fredda, quando la tensione tra i due blocchi era arrivata alle stelle [...] ».[21]

Even if in 1983/84 the time had not yet come for a European policy of dialogue[22] with Moscow, Italy strongly advocated for at least a better coordination of Member States Foreign policies towards Eastern Europe. More specifically, it supported the idea of taking joint action towards politically mature satellites, starting from Poland.

Besides this, during previous years the lack of a favourable common European environment had not represented an obstacle for Italy to try and lay, at least bilaterally, the foundations for an enhanced policy of dialogue with Moscow. Although the first signs of a thaw can be traced back to 1983, officially it was not until the state visit of Foreign Minister Andreotti to the Kremlin in June 1984 that this political course acquired more defined features.[23]

Against this international background, the Italian Communist Party held its annual celebrations. On the evening of 13 September 1984, more than two thousand people were present at the debate on Foreign policy issues organised in

---

dell'Italia negli anni Ottanta, in: Gianvito Galasso/Federico Imperato/Rosario Milano/Luciano Monzali, Europa e Medio Oriente (1973–1993), Bari 2017, pp. 9–56. See also Riflessioni Ministero Affari Esteri, Rome, 11.9.1983. ILS, AGA, section URSS, b. 689. The governments led by Andreotti were considered in Moscow the best Italy had ever had. This could also have been the result of the clever strategic move of Andreotti, who back then was the leader of a centre-right coalition government, to travel to Moscow in 1973 with a delegation mainly composed by prominent economists, bankers and technocrats, all of them of course more interested in economics issues, rather than in political and ideological ones. See Giorgio Petracchi, L'Italia e la Ostpolitik, pp. 296–297.
[21] "Craxi and Andreotti had the merit of being among the first in the EC to sense the emergence of new forces and actors with whom a dialogue based on change and renewal was possible. This Italian perception began to appear in 1983, at the zenith of the second cold war, when tensions ran high". See Maria Eleonora Guasconi, L'Italia e la cooperazione politica europea, p. 72.
[22] At least four more years were necessary. See Marie-Pierre Rey, Gorbatchev et la « maison commune européenne » un retour à l'Europe ?, in: *La Revue Russe* 38 (2012), pp. 101–112. Concerning the Russian vision of Europe see also Marie-Pierre Rey, La Russie et l'Europe occidentale : le dilemme russe, in *Institut d'études européens, Université catholique de Louvain-documents* 32 (2013).
[23] Also, as a result of specific economic interests concerning Italian important investments, such as the Siberian pipeline. See, for instance, Relations de l'Italie avec les pays de l'est, télégramme n. 335, confidentiel, Rome, 23 Match 1984. AMAE 1930inva, Direction Europe, Série Italie, carton 5331, sous-série 11, période 1981–1985, ambassade de France à Rome au Ministère des relations extérieures.

connection with the celebrations for the "Festa de l'Unità". Paolo Bufalini, leading figure of the Italian Communist Party, and Foreign Minister Giulio Andreotti were its speakers.[24] Giulio Andreotti took the opportunity to express his personal belief that the existence of two German states was not to be questioned, while walking on the political path made possible by the Conference on Security and Cooperation in Europe.[25]

Surely, the audience welcomed these words with a big round of applause, but, within a few hours, a whirlwind of criticism exploded. The following day the German news agency, the *dpa*, published a short press release informing that during the 13 September celebration for the anniversary of the Italian newspaper "l'Unità", Foreign Minister Andreotti had commented on the German question.

To begin with, the abovementioned press release stressed the relevance of the critical remarks made by the Italian politician with respect to the international framework: „Wenn man das Abkommen von Jalta in Frage stellt, so ist dies eine weit größere Gefahr als die Atom-Arsenale es sind."[26] Although he had affirmed that nobody could deny the importance of the existence of good neighbourly relations between Western and Eastern Germany, he had also warned against the risk of "overdoing" it in this direction, according to dpa information.

Furthermore, he was alleged to have added that the "*Pangermanismus*" was an obstacle not yet fully overcome. Commenting on the failure of the DDR leader Honecker to visit Bonn, the Christian-Democratic Minister had excluded that Honecker might harbour the desire to modify the existing frontiers; however, he also believed that "angesichts dieser, wenn auch extrem entfernten 'pan-germanischen' Gefahr schadet eine Prise Vorsicht niemandem".[27]

In concluding, he had expressed his wish that two German states might continue to exist. The dpa also emphasised that Giulio Andreotti was the first Western politician[28] to comment with such harshness on the German question. In so doing the German media echoed what the leading Italian newspaper *Repubblica* had already brought to the attention of its readers.

---

[24] See Gian Enrico Rusconi, Germania Italia Europa: Dallo stato di potenza alla potenza civile, Torino 2003, pp. 268–269.

[25] Hereafter, also as CSCE.

[26] See Andreotti gegen Wiedervereinigung Deutschlands», dpa n. 107, 14.9.1984. PA AA B26, n. 140520, Italien/Bundesrepublik.

[27] Ibid.

[28] It is crucial to stress that Andreotti was depicted as the first *Western* politician to have spoken with such harshness. In the past, Soviet leaders and politicians belonging to its satellites had often expressed extremely negative judgments concerning the Bundesrepublik. See Pietro Calamia, Piccola cronaca di un viaggio a Mosca (gennaio-febbraio 1969), in *Rivista di Studi politici internazionali* 3 (2011), vol. 78, pp. 345–450, 348.

The immediate reactions coming from Bonn were extremely cautious, as no official transcription of this speech was available at first. For this reason, the German Government made contact with its own Embassy in Rome and with the Italian Embassy in Bonn to gather information. One of the first reports sent by the German Embassy in Rome merely summarized what had been published by the newspaper *Repubblica*. It briefly underlined the four main features of the speech held by the Italian Foreign Minister. Firstly, the report highlighted that a German re-unification was not perceived as an imminent event. Moreover, even if it was considered desirable to promote inter-German relations, it was also considered necessary to do everything possible to overcome the Pangermanism. Lastly, Andreotti had allegedly expressed the wish that two German states might continue to exist.[29]

Faced with a growing feeling of uncertainty about the real contents of Andreotti's declarations, it soon became crucial for Bonn to get a reliable transcription of the whole speech. By the next day, the reliability of the press statement released by the dpa was still questioned.[30] The German State Secretary, Meyer-Landrut, made contact with the Italian Embassy in Bonn to get an official transcription of the speech together with some explanations. Meyer-Landrut also emphasised that a confirmation of what had been published in the press would have caused *Befremden* (astonishment) and *Empörung* (indignation) in Bonn.[31] The issue was, in fact, a sensitive one in the Bundesrepublik. Even if in the mid-1980s re-unification was not considered a feasible target[32], and the Western German Government was capable of making a clear distinction between real politics on the one hand and ideals and aspirations on the other, the national unity had been and was still considered an aim to be defended and worth aspiring to. As a result, Bonn considered the attitude of Foreign Minister Andreotti and his suggestion of leaving the German situation as it was, as totally unacceptable. Above all, the use

---

[29] See Deutsch-Italienische Beziehungen, Äußerungen von AM Andreotti zur deutschen Frage am 13.9.1984 in Rom, Bonn, 14.9.1984. PA AA B26, n. 140520, Abteilung 2.

[30] See Ibid. See also Deutsch-Italienische Beziehungen, Äußerungen von AM Andreotti zur deutschen Frage am 13.9.1984 in Rom/Telefonat Schaad Kuhna, Fernschreiben 6192, 14.9.1984. PA AA B26, n. 140520. It is noteworthy that some terms used in the draft copy were changed in the last version. Faced with a growing uncertainty concerning the real contents of the speech held by Giulio Andreotti, the German word "protestieren" was replaced by a more neutral request for explanations.

[31] See also Deutsch-Italienische Beziehungen, Äußerungen von AM Andreotti zur deutschen Frage am 13.9.1984 in Rom/Telefonat Schaad Kuhna, Fernschreiben 6192, 14.9.1984. PA AA B26, n. 140520.

[32] See Ibid. It is also noteworthy that the German Government was extremely attentive to the terms used. In the draft, the word "unfeasible" was often used in connection with the term "reunification", whereas in the final versions it was considered better to define reunification as a target "still to be filled with contents".

of the term *"Pan-germanismus"* had had an extremely negative impact both within the Government and on German public opinion.

It was, therefore, not a coincidence that the Italian Ambassador to Bonn chose to mainly focus his first comments on this particular issue during his conversation with the German State Secretary. The Italian Ambassador stressed that he himself had been caught by surprise when he had learnt about the opinions expressed by Minister Andreotti.[33] The Ambassador believed nonetheless that Andreotti had not intended to question the well-balanced approach, which his country had kept on the German question so far. Although no official position by the Italian Government on this speech had been communicated to the Embassy until then, Ambassador Ferraris also made a few general remarks to try and explain the background of the matter at stake.[34] With particular reference to the term Pangermanism, he recommended considering the impact which the recent demonstrations in Innsbruck had had in Italy, especially on Foreign Minister Andreotti.[35] Besides, it is likely that, between the lines, Ambassador Ferraris also wanted to hint at the *Ereignisse von Innsbruck/Fatti di Innsbruck* (Events of Innsbruck) of 1904 while trying to explain the use of the word *"Pangermanismus"*.

---

[33] See Ibid. See also the account of events provided by Ambassador Luigi Vittorio Ferraris himself in Luigi Vittorio Ferraris, Una Germania due Germanie: fatti e delusioni, in: Enrico Serra (ed.), Professione diplomatico Vol.2, Milano 1990, pp. 106–107: "Ho poca simpatia per i rotoli del telex delle agenzie di stampa […] ma quando il 13 settembre 1985 [sic!] mi capitò sotto gli occhi una breve notizia di agenzia, della dpa, in cui si riportavano testuali dichiarazioni dell'allora ministro degli Esteri Giulio Andreotti sulla questione tedesca, saltai sulla seggiola". (I am no friend of press agencies telex scrolls […] still, when on 13 September 1985 [sic!] I got my hands on that short press release of the dpa, where the declarations of Andreotti were mentioned, I literally jumped out from my chair).

[34] See Deutsch-Italienische Beziehungen, Äußerungen von AM Andreotti zur deutschen Frage am 13.09.1984 in Rom/Telefonat Schaad Kuhna, Fernschreiben 6192, 14.9.1984. PA AA B26, n. 140520.

[35] On 3 November 1904, in a suburb of Innsbruck, the first Italian Law Faculty of the Austrian-Hungarian Empire had been officially inaugurated with a lesson held by its Dean, Andrea Galante. Many Italian-speaking students from Graz and Vienna had participated. Among them, as president of the "associazione universitaria cattolica trentina", a young Alcide De Gasperi. Everything had proceeded peacefully until the evening. At the end of the speech, several professors and students had gathered in the pub *Weißes Kreuz* to celebrate. Celebrations had, however, been brutally disrupted by fights and violent clashes between the participants and an angry mob. The level of violence had increased so quickly that the local police intervention had not succeeded in quieting things down. A military intervention had been necessary to restore order. This was the first and also the last attempt to give birth to an Italian-speaking faculty on Austrian soil. Italian students, including De Gasperi, were arrested, but eventually released for lack of evidence. See, in particular, Federico Scarano, Innsbruck e il conflitto per l'Università italiana nell'Impero asburgico agli albori del Novecento, in *Intra et Extra Moenia: Sguardi sulla città tra antico e moderno*, Napoli 2014, pp. 185–190. See also Michael Gehler/Günther Pallaver (eds.), Universität und Nationalismus: Innsbruck 1904 und der Sturm auf die italienische Rechtsfakultät, Trento 2004.

„Als 1984 – genau 80 Jahre nach den ‚fatti di Innsbruck' – deutschnationale Studenten im Innsbrucker Kongresshaus einen Freiheitskommers […] veranstalteten, warnte Andreotti als italienischer Ministerpräsident auch […] davor, dass der ‚Pangermanismus' wieder sein Haupt rühre. […] Die Teilung Deutschlands wurde als beste Lösung begriffen, kein europäischer Christdemokrat wagte dies aber so offen auszusprechen wie Andreotti, ehemaliger Sekretär De Gasperis, der 1984 in aller Hemmungslosigkeit artikulierte, dass es ein offenes Geheimnis sei, wonach die Wiedervereinigung Deutschlands von keinem europäischen Staat gewünscht werde […] Ein geteiltes und schwaches Deutschland sollte außerdem eine Garantie dafür sein, dass die Brennergrenze nicht wieder gefährdet werden würde"[36]

While waiting for an official governmental statement, the Italian Ambassador finally drew the attention of his interlocutor to the genuine difficulty which Italian politicians had in distinguishing between re-unification as a specific policy target, and the affirmation of the indivisible nature of the German nation.[37]

Eventually, soon after this meeting, the German Government received, through the Embassy in Bonn, the first official transcription of the declarations

---

[36] "In 1984 a group of German nationalist students organized at the congress centre in Innsbruck a *Freiheitskommers* (evening meeting of students) […]; soon after Andreotti, the Italian Prime Minister, warned that Pangermanismus was reemerging […]. The German division was considered the best solution; no Christian-Democrat had ever dared to say it out loud until in 1984 Andreotti, former secretary of De Gasperi, with no scruples at all, affirmed it was an open secret that a German reunification was not desired by any European State […]. Furthermore, a divided Germany should also be the guarantee that the Brenner boarding crossing was not jeopardised again". See Michael Gehler, Tirol im 20. Jahrhundert. Vom Kronland zur Europaregion, Innsbruck – Wien 2009, pp. 33–35. See also Günther Pallaver (ed.), Universität und Nationalismus. Innsbruck 1904 und der Sturm auf die italienische Rechtsfakultät, Trento 2013.

[37] Ambassador Ferraris also affirmed of having made contact, soon after this conversation, with the Head of Cabinet in order to receive a confirmation of what had actually happened during the *Festa de l'Unità*. According to Ambassador Ferraris, both agreed to prepare an official explanation in which the statements of the Italian Foreign Minister were not denied nor was the impression given that he had said something inappropriate. The reply had to simply stress that Andreotti had merely commented on a situation which existed and neither had he spoken as brutally as other politicians had in the past. It was supposed to also add that only History would have the last word on this issue and that the word "Pangermanismus" had been used in connection with the 9 September 1984 demonstrations of Innsbruck. This reply was, however, never written, allegedly as a result of contrasts within the Cabinet. Andreotti left therefore for an official state visit to Saudi Arabia, while the issue was still pending. See Luigi Vittorio Ferraris, Una Germania due Germanie: fatti e delusioni, p. 106. The use of the word "allegedly" highlights that, at present, no written evidence, other than the statements of Ambassador Ferraris himself, can confirm this report of events. The German documents merely provide information that no official explanation had been sent, whereas the Italian files already open for consultation are still too scanty to be able to reach clear conclusions.

uttered during the *Festa de l'Unità*.[38] Far from easing concerns, the transcription merely confirmed information that had already been reported by the media.

As if the atmosphere had not been tense enough, the official statement issued by the Farnesina[39], together with the interview given by Giulio Andreotti the next day (16 September 1984) to the Italian newspaper *Corriere della Sera* at the residence of the Italian Ambassador in Djibba[40], did nothing but add more fuel to the fire.[41]

---

[38] A copy of this reply is kept at the archive of the German Foreign Ministry in PA AA B26, n. 140520. At the beginning of the text a short handwritten note has been added: Vom ital. Botschafter Ferraris am 14/09 am StS als Hintergrundpapier, nicht als authentische Kopie.

[39] For a general overview of the events between 13 September 1984 and 16 September 1984, see Äußerungen von AM Andreotti zur deutschen Frage, Chronologische Entwicklung, Bonn, 18.9.1984. PA AA B26, n. 140520. See also Deutsch-Italienische Beziehungen: Äußerungen Andreottis, Fernschreiben aus RomDiplo, 15.9.1984, signed Schaad. PA AA B26, n. 140520. The official statement issued by the Farnesina provided no clarification or enlightening elements, rather it reaffirmed what Foreign Minister Andreotti had already expressed on 13 September. The statement affirmed that Italy had always taken a very positive view of the German Ostpolitik, as a guarantee of stability for Europe. The existence of two German states was nonetheless a fact. Moreover, calling into question territorial arrangements resulting from the Second World War would have meant uncertainty and the risk of creating a dangerous spiral of confrontation (these comments were underlined by the German recipient with a stroke of pen).

[40] See Äußerungen Andreottis zur Deutschland-Frage, innenpolitische Hintergründe, Fernschreiben aus RomDiplo, VS-NfD, Rom, 18.9.1984., PA AA B26, n. 140520.For the original text of this interview see, Tempesta in un bicchier d'acqua, *CdS*, 17.9.1984. The previous day the Italian Embassy had already sent to the German Government a short note highlighting the most relevant comments made by Andreotti in this interview: "Offen gesagt verstehe ich nicht diesen Lärm. Unter den vielen drängenden Problemen des Augenblicks meine ich, dass man nicht ein anderes hinzufügen sollte, wie das der Wiedervereinigung der beiden Deutschlands und der Revision der Grenzen in Europa. […] Was ich in Rom gesagt habe, habe ich in zahlreichen anderen Gelegenheiten bei internationalen Begebenheiten gesagt, und man hat mir nicht widersprochen. […] Das habe ich auch in Gegenwart von BM Genscher gesagt". (To be honest, I do not understand this reaction. I mean that we should not add this issue, the Reunification of Germany and the modification of the frontiers in Europe, to our numerous current problems […]. I had already said before what I affirmed in Rome and nobody did disagree with it. […] I said it even in the presence of Minister Genscher). See Vermutliche Übermittlung durch Botschaft Rom: Äußerungen des italienischen AM Andreotti vor italienischen Rundfunkjournalisten am 16. 9. 84 in Djibba, Bonn, 17.9.1984. PA AA B26, n. 140520.

[41] See, in particular, Erklärung des Regierungssprechers Peter Boenisch, Bonn, 15.9.1984. PA AA B26, n. 140520. Some aspects stressed by the German spokesman in this document must be carefully addressed. Peter Boenisch not only reiterated the negative impact that the declarations made by Foreign Minister Andreotti had had on his Government, but also reminded a few basic international commitments accepted by European states, including Italy, as, for instance, the Washington declaration of 31 May 1984. He also stressed another reason why Kohl had allegedly resented so much the declarations of Andreotti. Giulio Andreotti was not only the Foreign Minister of an important ally, but also a leading figure of the European Christian Democratic political "family". In light of the traditional importance of the "party pillar" in the relationship between Italy and the Bundesrepublik, these words gain significant importance. Besides, since 1983 Andreotti was

The interview given in Saudi Arabia deserves a closer look. It can be, in fact, a useful instrument to expand upon the Italian approach to the "deutsche Frage". Although this interview was not the opportunity for Andreotti to refute what he had previously affirmed, it adds some further remarks, which allow us to shed more light on the political background behind the reasoning of the Italian Foreign Minister. According to these remarks, it can be assumed that the 13 September declarations were rooted in a specific political tradition dating back to Aldo Moro. The Helsinki Final Act and the process set in motion by the CSCE were bound to slowly establish a sound basis for the accumulation of political progress, which, eventually, would make it possible for the division of the Continent to be overcome.[42] Despite their differences, Bettino Craxi and Giulio Andreotti shared a similar approach concerning the Helsinki Final Act, meaning that they both accepted the existence of a Community of Socialist countries as a precondition to establishing a dialogue with them.[43]

Assuming that in 1984 the time had not yet come for the German division to be peacefully removed, Andreotti was probably concerned about the risks posed by the accelerating pace in inter-German developments. This could challenge the principle of the inviolability of borders[44], thus jeopardising the whole process of European détente, whose milestone was the abovementioned Final Act of Helsinki.[45]

---

president of the Union of the European Christian-democratic parties. See Francesco Lefebvre D'Ovidio/Luca Micheletta (eds.), Giulio Andreotti e l'Europa, Rom 2017, p. 9.

[42] See interview with Ambassador Cavalchini (05.2.2016).

[43] See Giorgio Petracchi, L'Italia e la Ostpolitik, pp. 314–315. Giorgio Petracchi draws a fine distinction between the specific approach embraced by Giulio Andreotti, defined as "metternichiano" (informed on the approach to politics of Klemens von Metternich) and the political course of Bettino Craxi and his political party, described as more "irredentista" (irredentist).

[44] The word "inviolabilità" (inviolability) must be briefly analysed. The negotiations leading to the signature of the Helsinki Final Act involved complex discussions concerning the meaning associated with the term "inviolability "of borders. The question was whether it was a synonym of unchangeableness. A similar problem, at least in certain respects, had already affected, at the beginning of the Seventies, the German-Soviet negotiations for the Treaty of Moscow. The Soviets insisted on using the Russian term meaning "indestructible", whereas the Germans argued for the adjective, *unverletzlich*, meaning the prohibition to violate the existing borders, not their unchangeable nature. The Italian word "inviolabile" carries this fundamental ambiguity.

[45] "E'sotto questa luce, che tiene conto del contesto storico, che va letta l'affermazione di Andreotti sulle due Germanie: Nel 1984 non c'erano le condizioni per riunirle e la sortita dell'allora ministro degli Esteri alla Festa dell'Unità va letta tenendo presente il fondato timore che il 'bruciare i tempi' avrebbe significato la fine della cooperazione tra Est e Ovest contemplata dall'Atto di Helsinki e, in ultima analisi, della distensione. [...] Questa era la sua vera preoccupazione". (I think we should consider the words uttered by Andreotti in 1984 in this perspective. In 1984 the time had not yet come for a reunification. The quip of Andreotti during the Festa de l'Unità was the expression of this concern. "To do things in record time" was the best way to torpedo the progresses ensured by

Giulio Andreotti and the German government spoke, therefore, two different languages, both literally and metaphorically. In September 1984, Bonn used the term "German question" with the meaning *Deutschlandfrage*[46] and, as a result, considered the statements uttered by the Italian Foreign Minister unacceptable. In turn, Giulio Andreotti made reference to the *deutsche Frage*. In other words, for Andreotti the issue of Germany had to be read and understood in the broader context of East-West relations.[47] In chapter two, this unique Italian approach to the "German issue" has been explained on grounds of specific geographical and historical conditions. First and foremost, Italy did not share a common border with Germany, unlike for instance France and Poland, but with the "German speaking area". In 1984, the needs of an Italian Ostpolitik, whose framework was becoming more coherent and dynamic, further reinforced this traditional propensity of Rome to read the "German question" in the broader context of Central-Eastern European issues. If we consider things from this specific point of view, it was understandable for Giulio Andreotti, even if not exactly rightful, to show concern and wonder whether an increased speed in the internal German dynamics might be a disruptive factor for Europe in its entirety.

In those days, a huge amount of letters of protest were sent by ordinary people, groups, lobbies and even magazines to the Italian Embassy in Bonn, to the German Embassy in Rome, and to the German Foreign Ministry as well.[48] Access to the extensive documentation provided by the PA AA allows us to glance at the contents of some of these letters and their answers.[49] The issue would certainly

---

the Final Act of Helsinki and eventually détente itself. [...] This was his great concern [...]). See author's interview with Ambassador Cavalchini (05.2.2016).

[46] See chapter 2.1.

[47] Concerning the specific approach to the German question of Prime Minister Bettino Craxi (which Giorgio Petracchi describes as irredentist) see also author's interview with Ambassador Visconti di Modrone (12.5.2016). According to the Italian Prime Minister, a German re-unification was bound to happen in the long-term, not as a consequence of a militarily show of force, but, rather, as a result of a slow process of rapprochement, meaning that Western European countries could be a magnet for reform in Eastern Europe. In such a context, the German division was also bound to disappear in the end.

[48] Ambassador Ferraris affirmed he had received about six hundred letters of protest or request for information sent by ordinary people, without considering open letters sent to the newspapers. See Luigi Vittorio Ferraris, Una Germania due Germanie: fatti e delusioni, pp. 110–111. Information so far available at the PA AA does not allow us to estimate the exact number of letters sent. To be sure, they were very numerous, especially if we consider not only the letters sent to the Italian Embassy, but also the writings sent to both the German Foreign Ministry and the German Embassy in Rome.

[49] See PA AA B26, n. 140520. On 16 September, the *Konservative Aktion* of Hamburg also addressed a letter to the Embassy, as well as, soon after, the Italian-German magazine *Incontri* of Berlin: only a very small number of letters have been here quoted, amongst them the most

deserve extensive attention; here, it is, however, particularly important to stress the fact that ideas and emotions expressed in these letters can be divided into three main groups.

Letters belonging to the first group merely expressed harsh criticism and the threat of never again going on holiday in Italy[50], whereas letters included into the second group were usually written by older people, who resorted to traditional stereotypes associated with the "Mediterranean Country", such as its not being reliable as an ally and as an enemy, with reference to the First and the Second World War.[51]

More interesting, both for their somewhat unusual contents and their volume, are the writings of the third and last group. There is, in fact, a connection between these letters and the feelings expressed by the German Government, that is great astonishment (Befremden) and an overall inability to understand the reasons lying behind the September 1984 statements. Many letters written by Germans were, in fact, well-balanced, and their authors seemed to have had no great difficulty in drawing the line between Italy as an economic, cultural and also political partner on the one hand, and the approach of its Foreign Minister on the other.

To this group also belong the majority of the letters sent by Italian *Gastarbeiter* and even by ordinary Italian citizens, either to distance themselves from the unfortunate quip of Andreotti, or to vouch for good bilateral relations, by providing sometimes personal examples of their good time in Germany. The words uttered by Andreotti were, in fact, at the origin of a wave of reactions both from home and abroad. Not only did ordinary citizens wish to express their opinion, but even Italian-German associations in the Bundesrepublik took action to try and limit potential negative effects and to foster a climate of discussion on thorny issues such as the notorious "Pangermanism". In this respect, the Italian-German magazine *Incontri* addressed a petition to Hans-Dietrich Genscher to ask German politicians to accept to fill out a questionnaire, being this an instrument to foster a climate of better bilateral understanding, and, in so doing, to leave behind this regrettable incident.[52]

---

interesting. Some of them are typewritten, whereas other letters are handwritten, which makes it sometimes more difficult to decipher them.

[50] See, for example, letter on "Pangermanismus" sent to the Italian Ambassador on 17.9.1984. PA AA B26, n. 140520.

[51] See, for example, letter sent to the German Foreign Ministry on 14.9.1984. PA AA B26, n. 140520.

[52] See PA AA B26, n. 140520. The German magazine *Incontri* sent a questionnaire to the German Foreign Minister. German politicians and MPs were invited to answer a list of questions. They were asked how they judged the comments of Giulio Andreotti and the German reactions. Secondly, they were asked whether the issue of Reunification looked realistic and whether they saw evidence of a "Pangermanismus". Furthermore, they were also asked to give their opinion on whether the

This incident, though regrettable, was, however, also a precious opportunity for the German Government to take note of a phenomenon which until that moment had been neglected. For the very first time Bonn noticed how sensitive Italian public opinion had actually become on the German division.

> „[…] Wenn man den Vorgängen um Andreotti einen für uns positiven Aspekt abgewinnen will, so den, dass sie in einem langen nicht gekannten Masse das Interesse der italienischen Öffentlichkeit auf Fragen unserer Deutschlandpolitik gelenkt und uns dabei einen Sympathiebonus eingebracht haben. In der Botschaft gehen zahlreiche mündliche und schriftliche Bekundungen einzelner italienischer Bürger ein, die Verständnis für die durch die deutsche Teilung verursachten Probleme zum Ausdruck bringen. Wir werden uns auch im Rahmen der Öffentlichkeitsarbeit gezielt bemühen, dieses Interesse im Sinne unserer deutschlandpolitischen Belange zu nutzen."[53]

Certainly, it is not an easy task for historians to draw a clear line between politics *stricto senso* and reactions coming from public opinion. Old German stereotypes concerning, for instance, Italian unreliability went hand in hand, both in public opinion and among politicians, with a much more modern approach, critical of a traditional representation and less vulnerable to easy associations between a politician and the country he represented. Contrary to the Federal Government, German public opinion lacked the ability, and perhaps the willingness, for in-depth analysis of the reasoning behind the stance adopted by Giulio Andreotti. September 1984 left deep negative traces on the reputation of Giulio Andreotti among ordinary German citizens.[54]

As the next chapter deals more accurately with the press and the reaction of the public opinion, we can now continue to discuss the developments of politics after the interview of Djebba.

---

comments of foreign politicians on the German division were to be considered an interference in internal affairs. Lastly, they had to express their opinion on the possible long-term effects of the 1984 comments on the Italian-German relationship.

[53] "[…] If in all these vicissitudes we can find a positive aspect, it concerns the fact that they have drawn the attention of the Italian public opinion to the issues of our German politics as never before. This has allowed us to gain a sympathy bonus. The Embassy has been receiving from Italian citizens numerous oral and written expressions of support and understanding regarding the problems caused by the national division. We shall have to focus on the public opinion to use this interest in the spirit of our political interests". See Äußerungen Andreottis zur Deutschland-Frage, innenpolitische Hintergründe, Fernschreiben aus RomDiplo, VS-NfD, Rome, 18.9.1984. PA AA B26, n. 140520.

[54] See author's interview with Alfredo Venturi (3.2.2016). Alfredo Venturi, a keen observer of Germany, worked as correspondent in the Federal Republic approximately for ten years (from the mid-980s until the mid-1990s): First for the Italian Newspaper *La Stampa*, and from spring 1990 for the Milanese newspaper *Corriere della Sera*.

Faced with growing tensions, on 16 September at 8.00 in the morning the Italian Ambassador was called for an urgent meeting with Hans-Dietrich Genscher on the premises of the Foreign Ministry.[55] This was the opportunity for Genscher to express his disbelief and also his disappointment, both as a politician and as a German citizen, that the Foreign Minister of an allied country with good relations with Bonn had spoken as Andreotti had.

It is also interesting to consider some specific language aspects. In the translation of the 13 September statements provided by the Italian Embassy, the German verb "*müssen*" had been selected to express the Italian word "*dovere*", whereas German translations, both issued by the Foreign Ministry and published by the press, often preferred the German term "*sollen*". Compared to Italian, the German language is very specific, and this can also be a source of misunderstandings. In this case, for instance, a single Italian word could be translated by two different German verbs. The German verb "*sollen*" has different shades of meaning. It can be used as a synonym of "it is said, it is supposed", which would have toned down the polemic, but it is also used to express a moral obligation.

During the meeting, which took place on 16 September, it was, therefore, of the utmost importance to make it absolutely clear that Andreotti's statements did not want to hint, in any possible way, at a sort of moral duty to keep the German situation as it was. In other words, it was important for Italian diplomats to show beyond any doubt that Foreign Minister Andreotti had merely commented on something that existed on the ground. Still, despite this occasion for clarification, once again the issue had not been resolved definitively.

Not only was the German Foreign Ministry very attentive to evaluate the consequences of these declarations, but it was also extremely careful to try and understand the origins of this "incident", and whether it was a view shared by other Italian politicians. Andreotti was considered a "klug berechnender und taktisch äußert versierter Politiker, der seine Bemerkungen gerade von der Öffentlichkeit genau abwägt".[56] Therefore, it seemed far-fetched in Bonn that he had uttered such words without giving any thought to their consequences. This being the case, which were, then, the origins of this stance?

Bonn could only vaguely sense and understand the scope of an Italian line of thinking dating back to Aldo Moro and to the political inheritance he had left to his successors. In other words, on the northern side of the Alps this complex approach was like a fuzzy image. One and only aspect came out of all this

---

[55] This was an exceptional procedure both regarding the urgency of the meeting, and the early hour chosen. In addition, it was extremely unusual to organise a meeting with a foreign diplomat on Sunday morning.

[56] See Äußerungen Andreottis zur Deutschlandfrage: Motive und Innenpolitische Hintergründe, Fernschreiben aus RomDiplo, VS-NfD, Rom, 18.9.1984. PA AA B26, n. 140520.

complicated stance: the desire of the Italian Foreign Minister to send out a message to Moscow expressing his willingness to strengthen the ties between his country and the Soviet Union.[57] The forthcoming visit of Andreotti to Moscow provided further elements to support this explanation.

By contrast, there was a certain tendency in Bonn either to exclude as unfounded, or to express reservations, on the hypothesis that Andreotti had chosen his words merely in light of the internal political situation.[58] Even if there had been some truth in this last hypothesis, it was clear, however, that both the members of the Italian Government and of the Christian-Democratic party had reacted negatively to the approach[59] embraced by Foreign Minister Andreotti:

> „Vor allem auch im Lager der Christdemokraten hat der Vorfall Verwirrung hervorgerufen. Während der außenpolitisch wenig erfahrene Parteisekretär De Mita [...] Andreotti in Schutz nahm, indem er ein Missverständnis unterstellte, fand Parteipräsident Piccoli deutliche Worte der Kritik. Dies spiegelt auch die innerhalb der DC verlaufenden Fronten [...]. Allgemein neigt man hier auch in Kreisen der Christdemokraten persönliche Motive für die Äußerungen Andreottis zu vermuten. Ihre politische Wirkung ist von Andreotti eindeutig unterschätzt worden."[60]

---

[57] On 19 September 1984, the Head of Cabinet of the Italian Embassy in Rome had a private meeting with Bonvecchio, the new correspondent of the DC newspaper, *il Popolo*. This specific explanation of the approach of Andreotti was discussed during the meeting and short afterwords communicated to the German Government in a short note (in the meeting Bonvecchio affirmed being a keen expert of Andreotti and his political line). See Andreottis Ausserungen [sic!], Rom, 19.9.1984. PA AA B26, n. 140520. Besides, this is the only hypothesis, among the many speculations discussed in the 19 September meeting, to be also discussed in Bonn during the following days.

[58] "It happened during the Festa de l'Unità. At that time, Andreotti often attended these kind of celebrations. He wanted to be President of the Republic, but he needed the support of the Communists to succeed...and that sentence mobilised the enthusiasm of the PCI. It was a serious problem. Not only did those words legitimise the existence of the DDR, but they also endorsed its eternal nature". See the text of the interview Ambassador Alberto Indelicato gave to Federico Ferraù, in: https://www.ilsussidiario.net/news/cultura/2014/11/10/muro-di-berlino-dalle-due-germanie-di-andreotti-alla-guerra-di-kohl/552738/ (last consulted 05.10.2016). In the light of the documentation accessed, I can refute the statement that these words mobilised the enthusiasm of the PCI in its entirety. See, in particular, Äußerungen des italienischen Außenministers Andreotti zur Deutschland-Politik: Innenpolitische Auswirkungen, Anmerkung des Staatssekretärs, Bonn, 24.9.1984. PA AA B26, n. 140520. See also Äußerungen Andreottis zur Deutschlandfrage: Motive und Innenpolitische Hintergründe, Fernschreiben aus RomDiplo, VS-NfD, Rome, 18.9.1984. PA AA B26, n. 140520.

[59] See Äußerungen Andreottis zur Deutschlandfrage: Motive und Innenpolitische Hintergründe, Fernschreiben aus RomDiplo, VS-NfD, Rome, 18.9.1984. PA AA B26, n. 140520.

[60] "These events have caused confusion especially within the camp of the Christian-Democrats. The Party Secretary De Mita, little experienced in foreign policy issues, [...] has defended Andreotti by suggesting that it had been a misunderstanding, whereas the Party President Piccoli has expressed unmistakable words of criticism. This mirrors the DC inner division [...] Generally, the Christian-Democrats tend to suspect that Andreotti had personal reasons to say what he said. Andreotti had

Despite frequent subsequent meetings, the diplomatic and political issue at stake was not properly resolved until Bettino Craxi sent a letter of explanation to the German Government[61] and until Foreign Minister Andreotti had a personal exchange of views[62] with his German counterpart, which took place on 17 September 1984 on the sidelines of the Council of Ministers in Brussels.[63] It does not follow, however, that the reasons behind Andreotti's statement were then fully understandable.[64]

On 28 September 1984, Chancellor Kohl eventually answered the letter received from his Italian counterpart, Bettino Craxi. Not only did this long and articulated reply offer the opportunity to definitely put an end to this unfortunate issue, but it was also a precious account concerning the level of development and

---

clearly underestimated their political impact". See PA AA B26, n. 140520, Anmerkung des Staatssekretärs „Äußerungen des italienischen Außenministers Andreotti zur Deutschland-Politik: Innenpolitische Auswirkungen", Bonn, 24 September 1984.

[61] See PA AA B26, n. 140520, the original Italian letter sent by Prime Minister Bettino Craxi and its translation into German, together with the press release given by the official spokesman of the Government, Peter Boenisch, are all kept in this box. In the letter, Bettino Craxi did not, strictly speaking, refuse the statements that Foreign Minister Andreotti had uttered. He also very skilfully avoided any use of the terms unity and reunification. The Italian Prime Minister tried to tone down the level of tension, insofar as he expressed great moderation, admiration for the German contribution to peace and détente and respect towards the principles enshrined in the German *Grundgesetz*, above all the "Selbstbestimmungsrecht". Bettino Craxi also expressed similar thoughts in the speech which he held in Cremona on 23 September 1984. On that occasion, he added that Germany, like Italy, had the right to preserve its identity, to strengthen and to reaffirm it. See also Äußerungen Andreottis: Replik Craxis in einer Rede am 23.9.1984, Fernschreiben aus RomDiplo, Rom, 25.9.1984. PA AA B26, n. 140520.

[62] No official records with a transcription of this meeting are kept in the archives; we can merely rely on some papers kept at the PA AA, which summarise its contents. Giulio Andreotti is alleged to have expressed regret at the inconvenience which had arisen from his words. Moreover, he also remarked that the word "Pangermanismo" had not been referred to the Bundesrepublik, rather to the demonstrations in Innsbruck. He had only depicted what existed, but in no way he wanted to express a moral judgment or an opposition to the re-unification as a long-term target. See PA AA B26, n. 140520, neither the object of the document, nor its level of secrecy or the date are indicated. See also Äußerungen von AM Andreotti zur deutschen Frage, Fernschreiben aus RomDiplo, 17.9.1984. PA AA B26, n. 140520.

[63] Further information is provided by the interview with Ambassador Cavalchini (who participated in the meeting). He remembered that some days after the Festa de l'Unità a meeting of the European Council took place in Brussels. Towards the end Genscher demanded to speak with Andreotti. Genscher had come with his closet advisor, Michael Jansen, whom Ambassador Cavalchini knew very well. Thy all went into a room of the Council and Genscher launched a long tirade to Andreotti. He resented the speech as it was like an open wound; besides, he himself was born in Eastern Germany. See the author's interview with Ambassador Cavalchini (05.2.2016). In its guidelines the interview is coherent with the information provided by the German diplomatic records.

[64] See Äußerungen Andreottis zur Deutschlandfrage: Motive und Innenpolitische Hintergründe, Fernschreiben aus RomDiplo, VS-NfD, Rom, 18.9.1984. PA AA B26, n. 140520.

maturity that the vision of the Federal Government on the national division and on the "German issue" had reached in 1984.

> « Je comprends et j'apprécie votre lettre [...] comme expression du souhait du gouvernement italien de ne pas exposer les relations d'amitié entre la République fédérale d'Allemagne et l'Italie à d'inutiles tensions. [...] j'ai à cœur que nos amis italiens connaissent et comprennent bien notre point de vue et notre attitude. La division de l'Allemagne [...] que nous voulons rendre plus supportable [...] ne repose sur aucun fondement juridique. Cette division n'a pas été réalisée ou confirmée par un instrument de droit international et le peuple allemand n'y a jamais souscrit. Les documents de la guerre et de l'après guerre prennent pour point de départ l'unité de l'Allemagne et le rétablissement d'une autorité étatique allemande unique. [...] Mais la question allemande ne se limite pas à ses aspects juridiques, elle touche profondément les sentiments nationaux des allemands. Nous savons bien que les causes de la division de notre pays sont liées à l'horrible guerre que le Troisième Reich a fait subir aux peuples d'Europe [...]. Mais il ne saurait en résulter quelque motif de nature à dénier aux Allemands le droit élémentaire à l'autodétermination. [...] Il ne fait aucun doute pour moi que le peuple italien, et lui tout particulièrement, comprendra ce qui signifie pour d'autres peuples aussi le désir d'unité. Nous les Allemands, nous ne nourrisson pas de chimères. Nous comprenons parfaitement la différence qu'il y a entre ce qu'il est possible de réaliser aujourd'hui et l'évolution à long terme. [...] Nous avons donné la priorité à la liberté avant l'unité. [...] La République fédérale d'Allemagne a lié son destin de façon irrévocable à la communauté des peuples libres. Nous sommes, au même titre que nos amis italiens, des Européens convaincus. En beaucoup d'occasions, notamment par exemple lors de l'initiative germano-italienne pour l'Acte européen, nous avons fourni des exemples de notre attachement à la cause européenne. Nous savons que la question allemande ne peut pas être résolue que dans le tout européen. [...] ».[65]

---

[65] "I understand and appreciate your letter [...] as an expression of the wish of the Italian government to keep the friendly relations between the Federal Republic of Germany and Italy free from any unnecessary strain. [...] it is important to me that our Italian friends should know and properly understand our point of view and our position. The division of Germany [...] which we hope to make more bearable [...] has no legal basis whatever. The division has neither been effected or confirmed by an International instrument, nor has it ever been approved by the German people. The war-time and post-war documents start from the assumption of the unity of Germany and the restoration of a single German state authority. [...] However, the German problem is not confined to its legal aspects. It affects the National feelings of the Germans. We are well aware that the causes of the division of our country are connected with the terror with which the Third Reich enveloped the nations of Europe [...]. But it cannot give forth any reason for depriving the Germans of the fundamental right of self-determination. [...] I have no doubt that especially the Italian people will appreciate what the desire for unity means for other nations as well. We Germans are no dreamers. We know quite well the difference between what can be achieved today and long-term developments. [...] We have given freedom priority over unity. [...] The Federal Republic of Germany has formed an irrevocable bond with the community of free nations. We, like our Italian friends, are

The letter of Helmut Kohl is a precious account not only in light of the current difficulties in which the relationship between Italy and Germany was bogged down, but also as concerns the transformation of German politics in those years.

The German Ostpolitik was based on the recognition of the existence of two German States; thus, it had provided the first instruments to ease the most negative social and economic consequences of the national division. This did not mean though that the Bundesrepublik had recognised the existing division as having a valid legal basis. The division had neither been created nor confirmed by an international legal body, nor had it ever been approved by the German people, according to Chancellor Kohl. Helmut Kohl also strongly reaffirmed the choice made some decades back by his prominent predecessor: Freedom over unity, and European integration over neutralism. Was this approach still valid in the Eighties?

We cannot doubt that the bond with the Western World and with the European integration process had been a milestone for Konrad Adenauer and still was for Helmut Kohl, which none had the right to question. The German problem itself could only be resolved under a European roof.[66] It does not follow though that the political reasoning of Helmut Kohl was identical to the approach of the first Bundesrepublik Chancellor. On the contrary, the vision proposed by Kohl differed from the approach of Adenauer on politics in general and on the German problem in particular, also because of their different personal experience and educational background.

Helmut Kohl was born in Ludwigshafen am Rhein, belonging to the *Bundesland* Rheinland-Palatinate, and was married to a woman whose family came from Eastern Germany. In addition, he had a PhD in History; thus, it is not surprising that his approach to politics had been deeply influenced by his training as a historian. Both his personal background and his educational training resulted in him considering Germany as a whole and also in his not sharing many of the prejudices, which his well-known predecessor had harboured against "Prussia".

Certainly, in 1984 it would have been premature to speak of a German reunification and it would be incorrect to affirm that Kohl had a sort of programme

---

European by conviction. On many occasions, as for instance in connection with the German-Italian initiative for a European Act, we have demonstrated our commitment to the construction of Europe. We realize that the German problem can only be resolved under a European roof". See Le 28 septembre le chancelier Kohl a adressé la lettre suivante au Premier Ministre italien, Bettino Craxi. PA AA B26, n. 140520. The version written in French was the one sent to the Italian Government and has been, therefore, quoted into the text. The abovementioned English version is also kept in the same box at the PA AA.

[66] See also the speech held by Helmut Kohl on European issues as the heart of the German Foreign policy: Rede Kohls auf der Interparlamentarischen KSZE-Konferenz, 26.5.1986, in: Bulletin 1986, Bonn 1987, pp. 498–501.

to follow once the conditions for a re-unification came about. The records show nonetheless that, unlike Adenauer, he no longer considered the division as the precondition for the link between Germany and the Western world. On the contrary, throughout the years in which he led the Bundesrepublik, Kohl developed a vision where the bond with Western Europe went hand in hand with the perception that the internal division could be overcome. German politics was experiencing a sort of transitional stage intertwined with a certain natural ability of Helmut Kohl to improvise, to take risks and to engage in policy experimentation.[67]

Apparently, Andreotti owed to the political experience of his mentor, Alcide De Gasperi, more than what Kohl owed to the inheritance left to the CDU and to German politics by Adenauer.[68] It is very likely that, besides the abovementioned reasons, the 13 September speech had also been affected by the negative experience that the political mentor of Andreotti, Alcide De Gasperi, had had in Innsbruck in 1904.[69] On 18 September 1984, during the meeting with Genscher, Andreotti himself had confirmed that he was referring to the demonstrations of Innsbruck while using the word "Pangermanismus". It is rather difficult to state with absolute certainty whether Andreotti also feared the emergence of a wave of Pangermanism in the relations between the Bundesrepublik and the DDR, and, therefore, called for a cautious approach.[70]

After the letter written by Kohl on 28 September, both countries left behind this unfortunate "incident". The relationship between the Bundesrepublik and Italy evolved positively during the following years, as did the political relations between Giulio Andreotti on the one hand and Helmut Kohl and Hans-Dietrich

---

[67] See Michael Gehler, Le tre Germanie: Germania Est, Germania Ovest e Repubblica di Berlino, (translation by Sara Quarantani), Bologna 2011, pp. 280–281.
[68] For the key role which Alcide de Gasperi had on the approach to politics of Giulio Andreotti, see, for example, Francesco Lefebvre D'Ovidio/Luca Micheletta (eds.), Giulio Andreotti e l'Europa, Roma 2017, p. XII and p. 1.
[69] The importance of the demonstrations of Innsbruck of September 1984 has been highlighted in all the interviews I have gathered. Besides, the importance of this event can be also perceived between the lines of the diplomatic records. See, for instance, the interview with Ambassador Quaroni (12.2.2016). To confirm the importance of the events of Innsbruck and the impression that Andreotti did fear and personally dislike the idea of a single German state see also Federico Scarano, Le Relazioni con la Repubblica Federale di Germania e la questione tedesca, in: Francesco Lefebvre D'Ovidio/Luca Micheletta (eds.), Giulio Andreotti e l'Europa, pp. 38–40.
[70] The declarations of Andreotti had negative consequences in Austria as well. Although Austrian politicians believed that Andreotti had used the demonstrations of Innsbruck as an excuse to conceal what he really thought, they preferred not to speculate about them and to wonder whether the explanations provided by Andreotti in Brussels revealed the Italian determination to leave behind the dispute with Bonn, even if it had a negative impact on the interaction with Vienna. See Dpa Meldung n. 172. PA AA B26, n. 140520.

Genscher on the other.[71] Still, this case had uncovered a major disagreement on the nature and the possibilities of development of the "German problem". This divide was bound to surface again, nearly unchanged, at the end of 1989.

In conclusion, it is now possible to give an answer to the question raised at the beginning of this chapter. The declarations uttered on 13 September by Giulio Andreotti were neither a mistake nor an interlude. They were rather the sign of differences in the interpretation of the German question. The *Festa de l'U*nità had allowed them to violently come to the surface.

5.2 Looking beyond the Iron Curtain

> *Il nostro ministro degli Esteri ha ribadito le posizioni del governo di Roma, che poi sono la base dell'interessante – e, sotto qualche aspetto, anche ammirevole – "piccola Ostpolitik" italiana.*[72]
> (Sandro Viola)

---

[71] According to the German archival records, Andreotti was, before and after 1984, appreciated for his political skills and remained a reference while dealing with Italy for both Helmut Kohl and Hans-Dietrich Genscher. Such sources allow, however, to mainly analyse the political cooperation. They give scanty information on the personal relations between Andreotti and the leading German figures. In this regard, we can resort to interviews for further elements. All Italian diplomats interviewed underlined with great emphasis the overall good relation that Andreotti had with prominent German politicians, including Helmut Kohl. See, for instance the author's interview with Ambassador Roberto Nigido (2.3.2016): "Il rapporto tra Andreotti e Kohl…certo, ci fu la battuta del 1984 […] in realtà era una posizione largamente condivisa che in fondo all'Europa facesse bene avere una Germania divisa […]. Però poi i rapporti tra Andreotti e Kohl erano buoni, quelli che erano pessimi erano i rapporti con la Signora Thatcher, anche sul piano personale, mentre c'erano ottimi rapporti sul piano personale tra Cossiga e la Thatcher. Quindi, come vede, è anche un problema di personalità, insomma, la componente umana è fondamentale! Andreotti incontrava spesso Kohl […] ci fu una forte reazione in Germania, questo è vero, ma dopo il rapporto tra Andreotti e Kohl è rimasto ottimo". (The relationship Andreotti-Kohl…it is true that Andreotti had said that quip in 1984 […] it was, however, a shared feeling in Europe that it was a positive thing to have a divided Germany […]. The relationship with Kohl was nonetheless good, whereas Andreotti had a strained relationship with Mrs.Thatcher, personally and at a political level. As you see, it is also a problem of personalities, the human factor is essential! Andreotti often visited Kohl […] well, there was a strong negative reaction in Germany, that is true, but afterwards Kohl and Andreotti maintained good relations). Looking at the memoirs and the interviews with German politicians the issue appears more complicated, at least as far as Kohl is concerned. Rudolf Seiters, for instance, was very cautious in commenting on this episode. He confirmed that at a political level Andreotti and Kohl maintained good relations, but he also commented that Helmut had "ein Elephantengedächtniss" (a memory like an elephant) and cast a shadow on their personal relations. Horst Teltschik, one of Kohl's closest advisors, came to the same conclusion, that quip had had a rather negative effect on Kohl, who in 1989 still remembered it all too well.

[72] See Sandro Viola, *Varsavia torna in Europa*, *Repubblica*, 21 December 1984.

On the occasion of the state visit of Giulio Andreotti to Poland, in December 1984, the journalist of the *Repubblica* Sandro Viola wrote that Rome was pursuing a "small", but admirable, Ostpolitik. The previous day he had expressed similar thoughts:

> «La "piccola Ostpolitik italiana" continua la sua strada e ormai va iscritta nella colonna dei ricavi del governo Craxi. Nel mondo comunista si riconosce ormai un ruolo italiano nella politica europea, un ruolo di dimensioni limitate, beninteso, ma comunque non più circoscritto al "business" dei paesi socialisti».[73]

Between the lines of these articles, we can perceive the importance the government led by Bettino Craxi attached to the need of expressing a more dynamic approach towards the Soviet Union and Eastern Europe. This new political course is indicated in this sub-chapter with the expression *Italian Ostpolitik*.

Starting from 1983, the first aim of this Ostpolitik consisted in boosting trade relations with the Socialist countries.[74] Proof of this interest is the participation of the Italian Ambassador (as the only Western diplomat) in the military parade of Moscow on 7 November 1983[75], and the increasing exchange of views with the Polish and the Hungarian governments in 1984. However, it was not until 1985, when Michail Sergeevič Gorbačëv took the lead in Moscow, that the Italian Ostpolitik found a framework which could truly serve its ambitions.

On 28 May 1985, the Italian Prime Minister travelled to Moscow[76] for a two-days comprehensive exchange of views. By the end of this official visit, Italian diplomats and politicians were satisfied with the results achieved. They also discerned that Gorbačëv could be a leader truly capable of breathing new life into the stagnant Eastern European situation.[77] The Soviet leader seemed to offer the conditions that Italy had long awaited for its Ostpolitik to meet its full potential,

---

[73] "The 'small Italian Ostpolitik' continues on its path and it can be considered part of the income of the government led by Craxi. The Communist world already assumes that Italy has a role to play in European politics, no doubt a small one; still, it goes beyond simply doing business with the Socialist countries". See Sandro Viola, Andreotti a Varsavia continua la piccola Ostpolitik italiana, *Repubblica*, 20 December 1984.

[74] See Giorgio Petracchi, L'Italia e la Ostpolitik, pp. 293–294. Concerning the interest for greater cooperation with Moscow in the field of industry, see, for example, Travel to Moscow 22–24 April 1984 and the reports of the meeting between Andreotti and Gromyko, and between Andreotti and Cernenko on 23–24 April 1984. ILS, AGA, section URSS, b.708.

[75] See Maria Eleonora Guasconi, L'Italia e la cooperazione politica europea, p. 70.

[76] See Telegramma n. 1587 signed Migliuolo, confidential. ILS, AGA, section URSS, b.709, travel to Moscow on 28–30 May 1985. In the same period Hans-Dietrich Genscher too traveled to Moscow to have exchange of views with the new Soviet leadership.

[77] Concerning this visit see Bruna Bagnato, L'Italia vista da Palazzo Farnese: la missione di Gilles Martinet (1981–1984), in Ennio di Nolfo (ed.), La politica estera italiana negli anni Ottanta, Bari – Roma 2003, pp. 260–261.

with the ultimate goal to curve out for itself a leading role both economically and politically beyond the Curtain.

Many observers believed that it was, therefore, increasingly inappropriate to qualify the Italian Ostpolitik as "small", since it had developed such a coherent and ambitious design[78], and since it was supported by an enhanced capacity to quickly understand the potential of the ongoing transition beyond the Iron Curtain and to react to it appropriately:

> « [...] au cours de ces dernières années, les Italiens ont suivi avec la plus grande attention l'évolution de l'Europe de l'Est et, il faut l'admettre, ont perçu souvent avant nous les craquements annonciateurs de la débâcle d'aujourd'hui. Dès 1986, la Farnesina nous affirmait que des changements irréversibles allaient se produire auxquels il fallait se préparer en rectifiant les schémas hérités de la guerre froide et non seulement sur le plan de la sécurité, ce qui était le plus discernable, mais aussi dans les domaines économiques, financiers, sociaux…
> Les milieux politiques mais aussi ceux des affaires ont vite tourné leurs regards vers les pays proches, Yougoslavie, Hongrie, Pologne, [...]. Ils ont très rapidement senti, dès 1987, qu'un cas d'effondrement des structures communistes l'Europe occidentale et l'Italie [...] seraient sollicitées [...] ».[79]

If we carefully observe the previous quotation from the telegram the French Embassy in Rome sent to the Quay d'Orsay (French Foreign Ministry), we can notice that the DDR was not one of the countries which the telegram considered as being the most important, both politically and economically, in the Italian design.

An in-depth analysis of the relationship between Italy and the DDR in the 1980s and, undoubtedly, a thorough discussion of the multiple implications of the Italian Ostpolitik cannot be summarised in one brief sub-chapter. This would be neither feasible not desirable in light of the objectives discussed in the introduction.

By contrast, it is desirable to try and discuss whether the relationship between Italy and the DDR had implications on the Italian vision of the "German problem"

---

[78] See Giorgio Petracchi, L'Italia e la Ostpolitik, pp. 312–313.

[79] "[...] Throughout these last few years, the Italians have showed great interest for the evolution in Eastern Europe and, we must admit it, they have often heard before us the crunch announcing the current breakdown. As early as 1986 the Farnesina had told us that irreversible changes would happen. In order to be prepared for change, it would have been necessary to adapt the schemes, which the Cold War had left us, not only in the field of security, the most logical one, but also in the economic and social realms [...]. Italian politics and also its business communities have quickly turned their attention to their neighbours, to Yugoslavia, to Hungary, and to Poland [...]. Since 1987, they have quickly sensed that Italy and Western Europe would be challenged in case the Communist structures crumbled [...]". See Télégramme Ambassade de Rome n. 1377, Rencontre quadrilatérale de Budapest, 19 novembre 1989, Rome, 9 November 1989. AMAE 1935inva, Direction Europe, Série Hongrie, carton 6333, sous-série 11, dossier 1 période 1986–1990.

and on the nature of its interaction with Bonn, and, if so, to what extent. It is equally interesting to address, albeit briefly, the differences between the Italian and the German Ostpolitik.

a) Italy and Eastern Germany: The Pre-History of a Complex Deal
The diplomatic recognition of the Eastern German Government by Italian authorities in 1973 and the beginning of diplomatic relations with it had been preceded by a complex network of economic and cultural exchanges which had been developing in the shadow of the international ideological conflict.

From the very beginning of the Fifties, the choice made by Rome of "zero-relations" with East Berlin – the so called "Nullbeziehungen" – had been slowly eroded by the gradual establishment of what has been often referred to as "kryptodiplomatische Beziehungen". Through this expression, renowned experts in the field, such as Charis Pöthig, pointed to the set of bilateral linkages between Italy and Eastern Germany beyond the scheme of official governmental exchanges.[80] The peculiar nature of these linkages, within which – it goes without saying – the PCI had, especially in the beginning, the lion's share, raises several questions regarding the critical role played in their emergence by political parties other than the PCI, trade unions, associations, cultural foundations, as well as MPs and group of deputies. The answer to such delicate questions affects both the distinctive features of the bond between Italy and East Berlin and the kind of influence which it had on the path leading in 1973 to an official recognition of Pankow.

Furthermore, we should not omit to recall that the Italian Government, as we have so far discussed, did officially support the principle of the Unity of the German Nation.[81] In practice, this did not, however, always form part of a coherent approach toward the "German speaking world".

Last, but not least, the ups and downs of the abovementioned linkages cannot be considered regardless of two main trends, namely the transformation of the kind of confrontation opposing the super-powers and the progressive change of the Italian inner political scenario.

Certainly, an analysis of the Italian-Eastern German relations between 1949 and 1973 is inseparable from a thorough study of the interaction between the Italian Communist Party, one of the most prominent and influential in Western Europe, and the DDR one-party, the SED. This applies not only to the political sphere, but also to the economic and cultural arenas through the mediation of groups and associations – officially or unofficially – attached to both parties. Still, from the second half of the Fifties, neither the evolution which characterized the socialist realm, nor its determination to progressively free itself from the Soviet

---

[80] See Charis Pöthig, Italien und die DDR, Frankfurt am Main 2000, pp. 18–19.
[81] See, for example, Altiero Spinelli, Das deutsche Problem von Italien gesehen, in: *Frankfurter Hefte 25* (1970), n. 3, p. 238.

influence or its slow involvement in governmental responsibilities, should be fully overlooked.

Traditionally, the study of the relations between the DDR and Western European countries has been neglected or undervalued in favour of a research which mainly, if not exclusively, deals with its Western counterpart: The Bundesrepublik.[82] Throughout the last few years, as far as various Western European countries are concerned, this disparity has been, however, increasingly rectified by new prominent academic publications, such as the works by the Austrian Historian Maximilian Graf. [83] By contrast, the lack of publications regarding the Italian-Eastern German relations remains a "sore point". The possibility to get access to both the archival sources concerning the DDR and the documents collected in the Gramsci archive regarding the PCI has undoubtedly allowed young scholars to broaden their horizon to this in many ways unchartered field, thus providing food for further reflection.[84] It should be, therefore, possible to draw upon this literature that, despite its quantitative limitations, is certainly not lacking in contests or depth, in order to focus on a closely specific set of issues related to our subject of interest. Still, at a closer look, what is striking is the almost total lack of specific contributions concerning the influence that the peculiar vision of the so-called "deutsche Frage" developed by left-oriented parties and intellectuals had on the dyad Rome-Bonn. A comprehensive comparative regard on the features and implications of the approach to the "German question" developed both in the conservative realm, close to government circles, among the liberals, the socialists, and lastly the communists, at different levels among 1949 and 1973, has not been

---

[82] See Charis Pöthig, Italien und die DDR, p. 20.

[83] See, in particular, Maximilian Graf, Österreich und die DDR 1949–1990. Politik und Wirtschaft im Schatten der deutschen Teilung, Vienna, 2016. See also The Rise and Fall of "Austro-Eurocommunism". On the "Crisis" within the KPÖ and the Significance of Eastern German Influence in the 1960s, in: *Journal of European Integration History* 20 (2014) 2, pp. 203–218. See, as well, Maximilian Graf, Österreich und das Ende der DDR, in: Michael Gehler/Maximilian Graf (eds.), Europa und die deutsche Einheit, pp. 259–294.

[84] See, among others, Fiammetta Balestracci, Zwischen ideologischer Diversifikation und politisch-kulturellem Pragmatismus. Die Beziehungen zwischen der Partito Comunista italiano und der SED (1968–1989), in: Arnd Bauerkämper/Francesco Di Palma (eds.), Bruderparteien jenseits des Eisernen Vorhangs. Die Beziehungen der SED zu den kommunistischen Parteien West- und Südeuropas (1968–1989), Berlin 2011, pp. 167–185. See also Francesco di Palma, Der Eurokommunismus und seine Rezeption durch die SED (1968–1976). Einige theoretische Bemerkungen, in: *Jahrbuch für Kommunismusforschung* (2012), Berlin, pp. 233–248. See of the same author, Liberaler Sozialismus in Deutschland und in Italien im Vergleich. Das Beispiel Sopade und Giustizia & Libertà, Berlin 2010. See also Francesco di Palma, West European Communists reject Moscow – Die SED, die kommunistische Partei Frankreichs (PCF) und die kommunistische Partei Italiens (PCI) von 1968 bis 1989/90. Beziehungen, Verflechtungen, Policy-Making, (forthcoming). See, as well, Wolfgang Mueller/Francesco Di Palma, Kommunismus und Europa. Europapolitik und Vorstellungen europäischer kommunistischer Parteien, Paderborn, 2016.

provided yet.[85] One of the reasons behind this lack of contributions can be explained through the protracted and almost complete lack of access to the diplomatic files of the Italian Foreign Ministry. Furthermore, it has often been claimed, as further limitation, the fact that past scientific studies on the "deutsche Frage" have often been affected by a reasoning under ideological direct or indirect influence.

Here, it is of central importance to briefly mention one specific issue which cannot be neglected in any study dealing with the Italian-German relations: the so-called "Resistance-myth". As it has already been explained in the introductory chapter, this work has no pretention to deal in a comprehensive way with the relationship established between Italy and the DDR, neither before 1973 nor after the official recognition. On the contrary, it is our prime goal to deal solely with those specific matters which affect the analysis of the goals listened in the first pages of this contribution, among them the comprehension of the distinctive hallmarks of the "German question" in the Italian collective perception. In order to do so, a discussion, however brief, of the role played by the "founding myths" underpinning for – nearly – the entire national political spectrum the birth of the post-war Italian national identity is indispensable.

The resistance against Fascism and the occupying German forces between September 1943 and April 1945, the so-called "*Resistenza*"[86], was in fact an essential component of the national post-war (re)building process and one of the cornerstones on which the new Constitutional text was drawn up.[87] Besides, this was one of the few cross-items which, in spite of the different interpretations and uses it was subjected to, had an influence on both the "German vision" developed by the Conservative parties, and by the progressive and left-oriented political forces. This was the cradle for the slow emergence of a "una certa idea della Germania" (a certain idea of Germany), whose main features and borders were still partially undefined in the political magma which united all anti-fascists forces participating in the drawing of the new Constitution.

Throughout the years, the influence of this founding myth has more and more often been quantitatively and qualitatively relativised by scientific studies, in favour of more pressing economic and strategic objectives. In other words, as the years went by, it was allegedly often used for propaganda effect either to cover

---

[85] See, as one of the few exceptions, Jens Petersen, Eigentümliche italienischen Deutschlandperzeption nach 1945, in: Josef Becker, Wiedervereinigung in Mitteleuropa. Außen- und Innenansichten zur staatlichen Einheit Deutschlands, München, 1992.
[86] See Renzo de Felice, Fascismo, antifascismo e nazione. Note e ricerche, Roma 1996. See also Enzo Collotti/Lutz Klinkhammer, Il Fascismo e l'Italia in Guerra, Roma 1996. Enzo Collotti (ed.), Fascismo e antifascismo. Rimozione, revisioni, negazioni, Roma 2000.
[87] See Charis Pöthig, Italien und die DDR, pp. 31–34.

more pressing needs, on both sides of the political spectrum, or to strengthen its own profile, as the Communists did.[88] In a "neo-revisionist" approach, the influence of the abovementioned founding-myth, which had an undoubtedly force of attraction on large sections of the Italian public opinion, can be combined with strictly political and tactical needs. To provide just one example, the DDR could be a practical and successful instrument in the hand of the Communist Party to criticise the Bundesrepublik and, indirectly, the Italian government which was one of its main political and trading partners. For the DDR-leadership, Italy could, in turn, be considered as a sort of Troy horse in the Western Bloc, being the country where the Communists had the strongest influence.

The redefinition of any kind of cooperation with the German-speaking world required, as an inescapable precondition, to lay as much distance as possible between the "German-speaking state" chosen as potential interlocutor, and the recent Nazi-past. More generally speaking, any kind of interaction with the German-speaking area should be placed (at least officially) in a background coherent with the founding-myths of the new-born Italian Republic. Economic and strategic advantages were therefore placed, both by conservative and by progressive political forces, in the frame of an ideological and cultural discourse within which, by extreme simplification, the recent social-nationalist past was presented as the "natural" consequence of the militarist Prussian tradition. For both German states breaking points with such a past had to be found as precondition to the establishment of both official or sub-diplomatic relations.

It is now possible to better frame some statements of chapter three. Until the end of the Sixties, the vision of Germany was held hostage to a strong political polarisation. Conservative parties supported the image of the Bundesrepublik as a Catholic Republic, a "Latin" country, a sort of enlarged "Rhineland/Bavaria". Left-wing parties opposed to this the image of the DDR as a Socialist, Democratic and proletarian Republic. Both images were presented as the antithesis of the Prussian military legacy, the first one in light of its different geographic and cultural-religious dimension, the latter thanks to the positive influence of the Marxist/Leninist ideology. In both cases, an external element ensured the reliability of the new state. The same tools were used to deepen the ties between Italy and the chosen German state: a party pillar together with an economic/ cultural one.

In this regard, it is not without importance to remark that from the very beginning the DDR leadership could benefit of a slight "positional advantage", by which I mean that during war years, Socialist and Communist Italian politicians in exile had often had opportunities to bond with prominent DDR political figures. It should, therefore, be no surprise that ever since the 1950s, the Goethe Institutes of the Bundesrepublik were in competition with the activities promoted

---

[88] Ibid., p. 32.

by the Thomas Mann Centre. Economic exchanges with the Bundesrepublik were in competition with the creation of *de facto* relations with the DDR thanks to the support of the *Handelskammern*, which worked closely with the DIA compensation system. This does not mean thought that Italian-DDR relations were based on "equal terms" and took fool advantage of the available resources. Even after the official recognition, Italy had difficulties to develop a full cultural projection within the DDR.

At present, due to the lack of access to the files of the Foreign Ministry, it is, however, impossible to identify the exact degree of influence which this complex network of linkages between Italian and the DDR left on the Italian foreign political choices.

The most sensitive issues regarding the perception of Germany were never raised in the Italian debate, at least until the beginning of the 1980s. What has so far emerged is that fundamental unresolved contradictions lay at the very foundation of the (re)definition of the relationship between Italy and the two German states. A debate on the past had been skillfully avoided, the continued existence of a single German nation had been uncritically accepted. In practice, however, Italy had easily adjusted to a protracted state of division. It was on this basic misconception that the process of official recognition of the DDR unfurled.

This was a slow moving-process whose first hints date back to the second half of the Sixties. In January 1967, in parallel with the first signs of a new orientation in Western German foreign policy, the PCI had started organizing a political campaign to propagate in the then public opinion the idea of the necessity to officially recognize the existence of the DDR. This initiative also developed in parallel with a new approach promoted by the Farnesina[89], which can, in all likelihood, be considered, at least partially, as a reflexion of the new approach taken towards the Communist realm. Besides, a recognition of the DDR, in the context of a different inter-German interaction, could be considered as a guarantee of European stability and as a favourable move in order to both limit the influence of the PCI as the main, if not the sole, interlocutor of East-Berlin. It could also be regarded as a first step towards taking full advantage of the changed international conditions by broadening and strengthening the Italian influence beyond the Iron Curtain.

On 15 January 1969, the first Standing Committee in Western Europe to support the recognition of the DDR was established in Rome under the chairmanship of the Italian Socialist Benianimo Finocchiao. The fact that soon 115 MPs of both Chambers joined it and that it also progressively gained recognition in the DC-circles close to Amintore Fanfani and Aldo Moro is a clue that time were

---

[89] See Ibid, pp. 331–335.

changing. It was, though, not until spring 1970 that the issue finally became a matter of public interest through a congress organized in Florence.

A little over a year later, the signing of the *Ost-Verträge* laid another stepping stone. Soon after, 40 deputies belonging to all the main parties of the political spectrum – the DC, the PSI, the PCI and the PSIUP – signed an official declaration in favour of a quick recognition of the existence of Pankow. In 1972, the conditions were finally ripe, and one year later, on 18 January 1973, Rome was ready for a diplomatic recognition of the Eastern German Government.

From the very beginning, the DDR seemed willing to strengthen its ties with Western countries, above all with both France and Italy. It was certainly not a chance that the former Minister of Culture, Klaus Gysi, a prominent member of the Eastern German establishment, was chosen as the first Ambassador to Rome. Still, more than ten years elapsed before Rome seemed ready to take full advantage of the recognition of the DDR and strengthen its ties with its Eastern neighbour.

Nearly one year after the official state visit of Bettino Craxi to East Berlin, on 23 April 1985, the DDR leader, Erich Honecker, travelled to Rome. Italy was the first member state of NATO which he visited.[90] Apparently, the visit was, once again, the expression of the Italian ambition not only to strengthen the independence and flexibility of its Ostpolitik, but also to extend its geographical reach.[91] Did this state visit have, at a closer look, a significant impact on the Italian-German relations?

Archival files already declassified provide at times contradictory information. Unmistakably, a certain feeling of nervousness hovered over the meeting of Stresa of November 1984, as Bettino Craxi had accepted to host a DDR official delegation led by Honecker after the DDR leader had failed to visit Bonn.[92] Still, despite this visit, relations with East Berlin remained, unlike the contacts with Warsaw or Budapest, a political conundrum for Rome.[93]

---

[90] Honecker had already travelled to Western Europe. In 1980 he had, in fact, officially visited Austria, but Austria was no NATO member.

[91] See Télégramme n. 558 Visite de M. Honecker à Rome : aspects politiques, Rome, 30 April 1985. CADN, 579PO-4-39 Archives rapatriées de l'Ambassade de France à Rome 1981–1992, ambassade de France en Italie.

[92] See AAPD, 1984, Band II, München, 2015, Doc. 301 Gespräch des Bundeskanzlers Kohl mit Ministerpräsident Craxi, VS-NfD, Stresa, 14 November 1984, from 11.00 a.m. to 12.30 a.m., pp. 1400–1408.

[93] Pankow was officially the capital of the DDR. Being Pankow a suburb of East Berlin, both the term Pankow and the term East Berlin are used in the text as synonyms of the word DDR.

«Precedentemente c'era stata la visita del presidente del Consiglio Craxi a Berlino-Est (nel luglio 1984) e poi la restituzione del presidente Honecker a Roma (nell'aprile 1985). Tutto ciò non era servito molto per riscaldare i rapporti, ma soltanto per dare l'impressione ai tedeschi orientali di essere usciti dal ghetto in cui erano tenuti dagli Occidentali, malgrado la firma dell'Atto Finale di Helsinki. Da parte italiana le visite facevano parte di un programma di Ostpolitik che tendeva ad equilibrare quella tedesca-occidentale».[94]

«[...] Un fatto è predicare la Perestroika nei paesi satelliti, altro è farlo nella DDR che in qualche maniera non era né carne né pesce, nel senso che era difficile applicarle... l'Italia porta avanti una politica di apertura verso l'Est nel suo complesso, ma più forti sono assolutamente i rapporti con la Polonia e l'Ungheria. Era più difficile con la DDR....ricordiamo che ci furono varie visite di capi del governo, di ministri degli Esteri in Polonia e Ungheria [...]. Era più facile per la Polonia, date le aperture di Gorbačëv, proclamare che la SED non era più il solo partito rispetto a una DDR che non era una nazione. C'era un problema identitario che creava delle difficoltà [...]».[95]

«Craxi pose subito il problema dell'avvicinamento delle due Germanie e questo è qualcosa che da la misura della visione che aveva dell'Europa. La vedeva come un tutt'uno che inevitabilmente si sarebbe riunito. La Germania era una componente fondamentale dell'Europa che non poteva rimanere com'era [...] Quando noi andammo a Berlino, se ben ricordo l'invito avvenne dopo una visita...ma il primo paese che visitammo fu l'Ungheria che sembrava il più aperto e il più economicamente pronto a contatti con l'Occidente. Arriva l'invito di Honecker e fu sorprendente, però fu accettato, ma dopo una consultazione con Kohl. [...] La visita ad Honecker fu fatta in intesa con Kohl e sicuramente non in contrapposizione. Uno dei temi discussi nel corso della visita fu proprio quello del riavvicinamento delle famiglie che erano divise e che era un argomento umanitario rispetto al quale era difficile dire di no. L'allora consigliere diplomatico, l'ambasciatore Badini, andò a Bonn a parlarne alla cancelleria e per fissare l'agenda e io mi occupai degli aspetti formali. Honecker non era una persona facile, era piuttosto duro di

---

[94] "Some time ago Prime Minister Craxi had visited East Berlin (in July 1984) and later on Honecker had returned this visit (in April 1985). However, it had not been much use in warming up bilateral relations. It had merely given to Eastern Germans the impression to have found a way out of the ghetto, where Western countries had left them, even after the signing of the Helsinki Final Act. The visit of Bettino Craxi was part of a strategy aiming at balancing the successes of the German Ostpolitik". See the remarks that Ambassador Indelicato sent to the author.

[95] "[...] it is one thing to preach Perestroika in Eastern European countries, but it is a completely different thing to preach it in the DDR, which in a certain way was neither fish nor fowl, meaning that it was difficult to know where to have it...Italy pursued a policy of dialogue all over Eastern Europe, but its relations with Poland and Hungary were stronger. It was difficult with the DDR...let's remember that there were many official visits of Head of Governments and Foreign Ministries in Poland and Hungary [...] it was easier in Poland, on grounds of the opening of Gorbačëv, to affirm that it was no longer a one-party regime, than in the DDR which was not a nation. There was an identity issue, which caused problems". See author's interview with Ambassador Cavalchini, 05.2.2016.

carattere, alla fine credo si giunse ad un modo di capirsi, dimostrato dal fatto che l'anno dopo Honecker restituì la visita a Roma [...]».[96]

Information provided by the interviews with Ambassadors Indelicato and Cavalchini stress that the relations with the DDR were not part of an autonomous framework but, rather, served the overall design of the Italian Ostpolitik. In other words, such a policy could benefit from an extension of its geographical reach. Still, this did not significantly affect the fundamental features of the Italian vision of – and its approach to – the "deutsche Frage".

Besides, Italian diplomats seemed fully aware that relations with the DDR were also an endless source of troubles and contradictions. The opening promised by the new Soviet leader was an essential precondition for the success of the Italian Ostpolitik, but it was extremely difficult[97] to apply in a country as the DDR which lacked a true national identity, the only cohesive force therefore left in Eastern Germany was the power of the one-party.[98]

Equally interesting are the remarks offered by Ambassador Visconti di Modrone concerning the approach of Bettino Craxi to the European division. Moreover, both these remarks and the archival records have showed that the visit of Honecker had been planned in agreement with Bonn, not as opposed to the Bundesrepublik.

«Caro cancelliere e amico,
Desidero rivolgerle alcune considerazioni sulla visita che il presidente Honecker effettuerà in Italia per conoscere il suo pensiero a riguardo. La visita è inquadrata nella politica, che entrambi i nostri governi concordemente promuovono, di attivi

---

[96] "Craxi immediately raised the problem of the rapprochement between the German states, an element which is also a clue of the vision he had of Europe. Europe was a whole for him, its reunification was unavoidable. Germany was an essential part of Europe and it could not remain as it was [...] when we went to Berlin, if I remember well the invitation came after a visit...still, the first country we visited was Hungary. It seemed, indeed, the most open and economically ready for contacts with the Western world. The invitation of Honecker arrived and it was a surprise. It was only accepted after consultation with Kohl. [...] Honecker's visit took place in agreement with Kohl and certainly not as opposed to him. One of the issues discussed during the visit was the rapprochement of divided families, which was a humanitarian problem. It was difficult to say no. The Italian diplomatic counsellor, Ambassador Badini, went to Bonn to discuss with the chancellery and to set the agenda. I took care of procedural questions. Honecker was not an easy person, he had a sturdy temperament. In the end, I think we found an understanding, as confirmed by the visit Honecker returned to Rome the following year [...]". See the author's interview with Ambassador Visconti di Modrone, 12.5.2016.
[97] See Alberto Indelicato, *Martello e Compasso: Vita agonia e morte della Germania comunista*, Milano 1999, pp. 96–97.
[98] See, in particular, Alberto Indelicato, *Memorie di uno stato fantasma: Berlino 1987–1990*, Berlin 2004. The DDR was defined as a tree without roots, a "phantom state", meaning a country without history.

contatti politici con i paesi dell'Europa orientale [...]. Penso che la visita di Honecker potrebbe servire a mettere a fuoco alcuni specifici temi che interessano più direttamente il suo governo. Le sarei pertanto grato per ogni opinione e suggerimento [...]».[99]

In addition to the issues discussed in previous chapters, in the mid-1980s the approach to the "deutsche Frage" was also under the influence of an Italian Ostpolitik with a different background and a different nature compared with its German counterpart.

The very first steps of the German Ostpolitik were rooted in the period between the mid-1950s and the mid-1960s. Under the veil of a strongly pro-Western political course, an intense political debate was slowly flourishing together with several economic and cultural initiatives towards the Soviet Union.[100] This context was a sort of "political workshop" for the making of the first season of the German Ostpolitik after 1945, the years of the Brandt Chancellorship. This Ostpolitik was not a monolithic bloc, but, rather, the combination of three different elements: a *Deutschlandpolitik*, a *Rußlandpolitik* and an *Osteuropapolitik*.[101]

---

[99] "Dear Friend and Chancellor: I would like to discuss with you some matters concerning the visit to Italy of president Honecker, in order to know your opinion on this subject. This visit is part of the policy that both our governments pursue to increase contacts with Eastern Europe [...]. I believe that the visit of Honecker could be a useful opportunity to bring into focus some interesting elements for your government. Therefore, I would be very grateful for your opinion and suggestion". See ILS, AGA, section Europe, b.367, ministero affari Esteri, rapporti est-ovest (Diplomatic counsellor asks to send to the Italian Embassy in Bonn the letter addressed by Bettino Craxi to Chancellor Kohl on 23 January 1985), Rome, 9 February 1985.

[100] This, after the visit to Moscow of Konrad Adenauer in 1955. Besides, Richard Meyer von Achenbach (born in Kassel in 1833, expert on Foreign policy issues, a diplomat and director of the Eastern department in the Foreign Ministry, he had to leave his post as a result of the implementation of the racist law. In 1939 he emigrated to Swiss and only after the War came back to Germany) wrote a very critical report on the political course pursued by Konrad Adenauer. The Chancellor received this report in 1954. Still, it did not circulate within the government and it was published only years after. See Richard Meyer von Achenbach, Gedanken über eine konstruktive deutsche Ostpolitik: eine unterdrückte Denkschrift aus dem Jahr 1953, Frankfurt am Main 1986.

[101] See La politique à l'Est de la RFA, note, Paris, 4.11.1987. AMAE 1935inva, Direction Europe, Série RFA, carton 6772, sous-série 11, dossier 5 période 1986–1990, Ministère des affaires étrangères, direction d'Europe. The German Ostpolitik was based on three elements: the internal division, the wish to overcome this division and the desire to have better relations with the Soviet Union and its satellites. The document also expresses the worry that such a German dynamism towards Eastern Europe (and the equal dynamic approach of Italy and Austria, according to other records of the same box) could give the impression that the French approach was stagnant. Here I prefer to use the German word for "Russian policy" than the word for "Soviet policy", as this component of the German Ostpolitik was in many ways the continuation of the traditional German approach to Russia.

As a result, the German Ostpolitik had two different souls: Foreign policy targets, on the one hand, and a dimension corresponding to the history of the German nation and the consequences of its partition, on the other.[102]

Even if the Italian Ostpolitik also happened to be rooted in economic and cultural exchanges developed at the end of the Fifties in the context of the political course known as "neo-atlantismo" and promoted by Amintore Fanfani, Giovanni Gronchi, and Enrico Mattei[103], its essential cornerstones were the political breakthrough promoted by Aldo Moro and the consequences of the Conference held in Helsinki.[104]

This Ostpolitik was, in all respects, an expression of the Italian Foreign policy, which comprised a Soviet component and an Easter-European component. It had seen the light of day within the international order designed by the victorious powers of the Second World War. In other words, Italy was trying to find its place in the context of given conditions, whereas the Bundesrepublik moved from the necessity to ease some of the consequences of an order which at that moment could not be modified. Both countries had developed two extremely dynamic policies; still, their origins and, therefore, also their dynamism, were of a rather different nature.

Lastly, the Italian Ostpolitik also had a third component, which is one of the elements usually neglected in the literature of those years, despite its relevant consequences: The Mitteleuropean dimension. From the Seventies, this third dimension was implemented in the form of programmes of local and regional cooperation.

b) The Third Pillar of the Italian Ostpolitik: Arge Alp and Alpe Adria

> « Dès 1979, l'Italie a cherché de se rapprocher de l'URSS et de pays de l'Est. Ce rééquilibrage de l'action extérieure s'expliquait en partie par des raisons de politique intérieure […]. **Les changements apparus dans la politique extérieure** de M. Gorbatchev ont été accueillis avec enthousiasme à Rome […] Mais l'Ostpolitik

---

[102] Ambassador Ferraris affirmed that the German Ostpolitik was above all a "Deutschlandpolitik". See Luigi Vittorio Ferraris, La Ostpolitik italiana e tedesca, in Renato Cristin (ed.), Vie Parallele/Parallele Wege [Italien in Geschichte und Gegenwart Band 23], Frankfurt am Main 2005, p. 98.

[103] See, in particular, Bruna Bagnato, Prove di Ostpolitik. Politica ed economia nella strategia italiana verso l'Unione Sovietica 1958–1963, Firenze 2003.

[104] See Sara Tavani, L'Italia e la CSCE un negoziato a più livelli (1969–1985), in: Luciano Tosi (ed.), La diplomazia multilaterale italiana negli anni della guerra fredda, Padova 2013, pp. 373–426. See also Sara Tavani, Alle origini dell'Ostpolitik italiana: L'evoluzione della politica orientale dell'Italia negli anni del "centro-sinistra organico" di Aldo Moro, in: Renato Moro/Daniela Mezzana (eds.), Una vita un Paese: Aldo Moro e l'Italia del Novecento, Soveria-Mannelli 2014, pp. 467–488.

pour l'Italie revêt une importance toute spécifique lorsque elle concerne les relations avec la **MittelEuropa** : Hongrie, Yougoslavie et même l'Autriche [...] ».[105]

Germany and France were intrigued by this Mitteleuropean component of the Italian Ostpolitik, whose origins are rather complex.

On the one hand, it can be considered as a sort of "simulacro" (similacrum) of a comprehensive Ostpolitik, namely an attempt to use broad Italian local resources in order to pursue a low profile policy on the fringe of the Soviet area of influence. In doing so, Italy intended to avoid tensions with both superpowers.[106]

On the other hand, this Mitteleuropean action was also the answer to demands beyond the realm of Foreign policy *stricto senso*. The regions involved, both in Italy and in its neighbouring countries, were all newly industrialised areas with common needs. Even if after 1973 a deindustrialisation process had started to take its first steps in Western Europe, by the mid-1980s, the number of people employed in industry in Friuli-Venezia Giulia, in Venetia, in Bavaria, and in Carinthia was still above the National average.

In addition, even though this area was divided in opposite blocs, its regions shared a traditional high level of interaction among small and medium-sized enterprises. To be truly competitive, these enterprises had basically two alternatives: either they widened the range of products they offered to retain control over the local market through their high level of specialisation, or they could expand their geographical reach. It they opted for the second of these possibilities, they needed more local coordination.[107]

Starting from the late 1960s, local cooperation was at first tested in the Alpine region. On 2 October 1972, the agreement establishing the Association of the Alpine States (in German *Arbeitsgemeinschaft Alpenländer*, shortly *Arge Alp*) was signed in the Tyrolean village Mösern. The association grouped together, by means of a very flexible cooperation structure, the Italian regions of Trentino-Alto Adige and Lombardy, the Austrian Länder Salzburg, Tyrol and Voralberg, the German Bundesland Bavaria, and the Swiss canton Graubünden.[108]

---

[105] "Since 1979 Italy has tried to get closer to the Soviet Union and to Eastern-European countries. This rebalancing the Italian Foreign policy was, partly, the result of internal dynamics. [...]. **The changes in the foreign policy** of Gorbačëv have been welcomed with enthusiasm in Rome [...] but the Ostpolitik is of particular importance where it concerns the **Mitteleuropa**: Hungary, Yugoslavia and even Austria [...]". See La politique étrangère de l'Italie, note, Paris, 8.9.1989, signed Lamentini (in bold as in the original text). CADN, 579PO-4–5 Archives rapatriées de l'Ambassade de France à Rome 1981–1992, ministère des affaires étrangères, direction d'Europe, sous-direction d'Europe méridionale.

[106] See Giorgio Petracchi, L'Italia e la Ostpolitik, pp. 317–318.

[107] See Riccardo Cappellin, Alpe Adria: Opportunità e prospettive, in: *Relazioni Internazionali* n. 5 (1989), pp. 59–66.

[108] For further information on the Arge Alp and similar initiatives see, in particular, Bruna De Marchi/Giovanni Delli Zotti, Cooperazione regionale nell'area alpina, Milano 1985, pp. 82–86.

The Arge Alp had a flexible structure based on a small secretariat in Tyrol, as at first it was only an experiment of temporary nature. Its field of action included non-political issues such as economic exchanges, transports and culture. Its agreement was also flexible and short, so that the organisation could be easily adapted to the results achieved.

Not only was the Arge Alp the first important step to ensure a framework for flexible but stable cooperation at a sub-national level between Italian and German speaking regions, but it was also a test for this specific kind of cooperation. Through the implementation of technical commissions, the admission of new members, the institutionalisation of the secretariat together with the progressive extension of its powers, and, in 1981, the establishment of a documentation centre, the Arge Alp quickly became a model of success and the blueprint for further, more sophisticated, local experiments[109], such as the *Alpe Adria*.[110]

When it was created, in 1978, the *Alpe Adria* (short for *Alps-Adriatic Working Group*) was a framework to promote cooperation in the field of tourism, environmental protection, culture, science and economy among the regions of a small section within the Mitteleuropa: between the Eastern Alps and the Northern Adriatic area. At a first glance the Alpe Adria was just one more example of local cooperation in border areas created on the model of the Arge Alp.[111] At a closer look its establishment meant, however, a leap in quality in the targets until then pursued in the context of local cooperation.[112] The Alpe Adria had, in fact, been created not only to tackle local problems such as the ones that the Arge Alp had encountered, but also to try and erode, of course at a local level, the ideological frontiers between the blocs.

On a small scale the Alpe Adria was, therefore, an experiment to verify whether a more active approach towards Central-Eastern Europe was feasible. Austria, Germany and Yugoslavia were all involved in this experiment. Members of the organisation were, in fact, the Italian regions Friuli-Venezia Giulia and Venetia, the Austrian Carinthia, Upper Austria, and Styria, and the socialist republics of Slovenia and Croatia. Some years later Lombardy and Trentino also applied for membership. Salzburg and Bavaria participated only as observers until 1988.

---

[109] See Liviana Poropat, Alpe Adria e iniziativa centro-europea: Cooperazione nell'Alpe Adria e nell'area danubiana, Napoli 1993, p. 22.
[110] Created on 20 November 1978 in Venice with the signature of the Joint declaration of Prime Ministers.
[111] See Bruna De Marchi/Giovanni Delli Zotti, Cooperazione regionale nell'area alpina, pp. 27–35.
[112] See Communauté de travail Alpe-Adria, télégramme de l'ambassade de Rome n. 146, Belgrad, 20.2.1990. AMAE 1935inva, Direction Europe, Série Autriche, carton 6176, sous-série 13, dossier 7 période 1986–1990.

In order to rise to the challenge to deal with more complex issues, in 1978 a procedural regulation was defined in Venice which – compared to the Arge Alp – endowed the newly established organisation with a greater degree of institutionalisation. It possessed permanent commissions from the very beginning and a clearer delineation of internal roles. Moreover, not only could the Alpe Adria benefit from the successful experience of the Arge Alp[113], but it could also draw on bilateral schemes of sectoral cooperation, for instance between Carinthia and Friuli-Venezia Giulia, between Carinthia and Slovenia, or between Slovenia and Friuli Venezia Giulia.[114]

From the Fifties, and hardly noticed by high politics, some efforts to cooperate more closely had, in fact, been carried out at the Italian-Austrian border, such as exhibitions and joint ventures between local enterprises. After the signature of the Treaty of Osimo, further economic and cultural efforts could also be carried out at the border between Italy and Yugoslavia. Such were the agreements between the Italian RAI and the Slovenian Telecapodistria in order to broadcast Slovenian and German programmes in the Italian Friuli Venezia Giulia, and Italian programmes in Slovenia. On the basis of the good results achieved, in 1969 new structures of cooperation had been created such as *Quadrigon*, formed by Friuli-Venezia Giulia, Carinthia, Slovenia and Croatia.

The success in the early Seventies of the Arge Alp provided local cooperation in the area of *Quadrigon* with new and more effective legal tools. Besides, the regions participating in the Arge Alp, such as Bavaria, turned their attention towards this area, thus enhancing its importance. For Bavaria, this was indeed an excellent opportunity to have a flexible and effective structure to rely on when local problems had to be solved.[115] It was also a good chance to be involved in the transformations within the Mitteleuropa, thus expanding the reach of its "foreign" policy.[116] The use of local resources to enhance cooperation was also a way around the many obstacles which national states faced until the 1980s in their activities beyond the Iron Curtain.

Starting from 1985, the Alpe Adria enjoyed both the benefits of better relations between the EC and the COMECON, and of a climate of great movement

---

[113] See Communauté de travail Alpe-Adria, télégramme de l'ambassade de Vienne n. 92, Vienne, 19.2.1990. AMAE 1935inva, Direction Europe, Série Autriche, carton 6176, sous-série 13, dossier 7 période 1986–1990.

[114] Ibid.

[115] See Consul général à Venice à M. Gilles Martinet Ambassadeur de France en Italie. CADN, 579PO-4–39 Archives rapatriées de l'Ambassade de France à Rome 1981–1992.

[116] See Communauté de travail Alpe-Adria, télégramme de l'ambassade de Rome n. 175, Rome, 21.2.1990. AMAE 1935inva, Direction Europe, Série Autriche, carton 6176, sous-série 13, dossier 7 période 1986–1990.

all over the Mitteleuropa.[117] It was in the context of this arousal that Hungary applied for membership to the Alpe Adria.[118]

On 4 June 1988, the Italian, Austrian, Yugoslavian, and Hungarian governments signed the declaration of Millstadt, which provided the Alpe Adria with an enhanced legitimacy and visibility, hence raising its international profile. In so doing, the declaration of Millstadt laid sound foundations for the Alpe Adria to be an effective instrument to resort to in the 1989–1990 transformation process.

5.3 From the Visit of Cossiga to the *Gesprächsforum* (1986–1988)

> *Im deutsch-italienischen Verhältnis sollten wir dem hohen Grad an Übereinstimmung an bilateralen und internationalen Fragen durch eine weitere Verbesserung der gegenseiteigenen Konsultations-mechanismen und durch vermehrten Besuchsaustausch Rechnung tragen. Unsere Europa- und Bündnispolitik würde dadurch auf eine breitere Grundlage gestellt werden.[119]*

In view of the 1987 governmental declaration on the targets of the new German legislature, the first months of 1987 were marked by constant debates on Foreign policy issues, the aim of which was the identification of those aspects eligible because of their importance to be included into the text of the declaration. Starting from January 1987, the elements concerning the Italian-German relationship which were considered as the most relevant are:

> „Die bilateralen Beziehungen zwischen der Bundesrepublik Deutschland und Italien sind vertrauensvoll und freundschaftlich. Das traditionelle Einvernehmen findet eine solide Stütze in parallelen Interessen [...] insbesondere im EG und NATO-Bereich. Italien hat sich auf beiden Gebieten über lange Jahre und unabhängig von der Zusammensetzung der jeweiligen Regierungen als besonders zuverlässiger Partner erwiesen. Unsere Zielvorstellungen über eine europäische

---

[117] See Maria Enrica d'Agostini/Marino Freschi (eds.), Mitteleuropa storiografia e scrittura, Pavia, 1985.

[118] See Communauté de travail Alpe-Adria, télégramme de l'ambassade de Belgrade n. 588, Belgrade, 21.2.1990. AMAE 1935inva, Direction Europe, Série Autriche, carton 6176, sous-série 13, dossier 7 période 1986–1990.

[119] "In the Italian-German relationship we should take account of the high degree of consensus about bilateral and international issues through a further improvement of the consultation mechanisms and an increased number of exchanges. Our European- and Atlantic politics would be based on a more solid basis". See Außenpolitische Schwerpunkte der kommenden Legislaturperiode: deutsch-italienische Beziehungen für Regierungserklärung, Bonn, 14.1.1987. PA AA B26, n. 140520.

Union sind mit den italienischen weitgehend deckungsgleich. [...] Die italienische Regierung hat mehrmals den Wunsch geäußert, die politische Abstimmung mit der Bundesregierung noch auszuweiten. Auch [...] Staatspräsident Cossiga trug den Wunsch nach einer Intensivierung der deutsch-italienischen Zusammenarbeit nach dem Muster der deutsch-französischen und deutsch-britischen Beziehungen vor. Dies liegt auch in unserem Interesse, um namentlich unserer europäischer und Bündnispolitik eine möglichst breite Grundlage zu sichern [...] wobei allerdings ein gewisser Abstand zur Intensität der deutsch-französischen Konsultationen gewährt sollte."[120]

It seemed as if the time had come to reflect and take stock of the results achieved to date through the Italian-German cooperation. There was in fact the necessity to meet the needs connected to the European integration process, and, since the spring of the previous year, one occasion had been granted by the official state visit to the Bundesrepublik of the Italian President of the Republic, Francesco Cossiga, which had been planned on the occasion of the annual celebrations for the Anniversary of the Liberation.[121]

The state visit to Germany of the newly appointed President of the Republic took place on 21 to 25 April 1986. The choice of dates for the travel and places to be visited by the President was not a random one. Certainly, it was an instance of the peculiar sensibility Cossiga had until then showed towards Germany; still, it was also the proof of the Italian determination to give new impetus to bilateral relations. It was hoped that the choice of such a symbolic date for the recent Italian history would remove all remaining traces of unease and doubt, both in the

---

[120] "The bilateral relations between Italy and Germany are based on trust and friendship. Their traditional understanding is firmly rooted in common interests in the EC and NATO. In both areas, regardless of the ruling government, Italy has proved to be a reliable partner for many years. Our visions for the European Union are substantially consistent with each other. More than once has Italy expressed the wish to expand the common work. President Cossiga too has expressed the desire to intensify the cooperation in accordance with the model of the Franco-German and Anglo-German cooperation. It would be in our interest, notably to secure a wider basis for our European and Atlantic politics. [...] still, a certain distance from the intensity of the Franco-German consultations should be granted". See Außenpolitische Aufgaben der kommenden Legislaturperiode (1987–1991): Stärkung der deutsch-italienischen Zusammenarbeit, Bonn, 7.1.1987. PA AA B26, n. 140521. See also Außenpolitische Aufgaben der kommenden Legislaturperiode (1987–1991): Beziehungen zu Frankreich, Italien und Großbritannien, Bonn, 8.1.1987. PA AA B26, n. 140521.
[121] See Die deutsch-italienischen Beziehungen heute und morgen, Bonn, 5.6.1987. PA AA B26, n. 140521. See also Anmerkung: Gespräch BM mit dem italienischen Botschafter Prof. Luigi Vittorio Ferraris, Bonn, 29.1.1987, from 12 a.m. PA AA B26, n. 140521. See, also, also the author's interview with Ambassador Pietro Calamia (29.9.2016). Some months later, in September 1987, the meeting between the State Secretary Sudhoff and the Italian Ambassador Ferraris showed that Italy was considered by the Bundesrepublik as a reliable partner and that Germany was also eager to further enhance cooperation.

German press and in local public opinion, which the comments of Andreotti of September 1984 had left.[122]

Moreover, it was the first visit to a foreign country of the new Head of State[123], which also aimed at further stressing the utmost importance attached to the Bundesrepublik as a partner:[124]

> «Il 21 aprile si parte molto presto per la Germania, i giornalisti al seguito, circa cinquanta, sono già a Bonn da ieri sera. Vedo il Presidente nel pomeriggio e mi faccio dire alcune cose, in particolare come comportarmi se dovessero insistere per captare una linea comune italo-tedesca contro gli Stati Uniti. Mi sforzo di presentare la visita come la ricerca di sempre maggiori consultazioni con gli americani. Il 22 aprile il Presidente fa una prolusione in tedesco all'università di Bonn che riscuote molto successo. La copertura giornalistica è ottima. Dino Frescobaldi, che scriveva per il Corriere, parla di affinità elettive tra Cossiga e Von Weizsäcker. Una colazione è offerta da Kohl, è presente il meglio del mondo tedesco: politici, mondo dell'economia e intellettuali. Cossiga procede in modo piuttosto intenso con colloqui con Helmut Kohl, i ministri dell'Economia e dell'Interno».[125]

---

[122] The remarks on the state visit of Francesco Cossiga are mainly based on the documents kept at the Archive Francesco Cossiga and on the interview given by one of his closest advisors, namely Ambassador Ludovico Ortona. They are also based on the diaries which Ambassador Ortona was going to publish when the interview he gave me took place. Ambassador Ortona very kindly accepted to share with me some of the contents of his diaries before their publication.

[123] Cossiga had very good personal relations with his German counterpart, Richard Von Weizsäcker, as confirmed by their exchange of letters. See ASCD, Fondo Francesco Cossiga, archivio con titolario 1944–2010, Presidenza della Repubblica-Settennato 1985–1992, b.184, fascicolo Germania, several documents and letters. Concerning the personal and political background of President Von Weizsäcker, see, in particular, Günther Scholz/Martin Süsskind, Die Bundespräsidenten. Von Theodor Heuss bis Johannes Rau, Stuttgart 2003. At present there exists no literature on the relationship between these two politicians. It is, therefore, necessary to gather information through a thorough analysis of memoirs and biographies. It is noteworthy that the background of the Italian and the German Presidents shared many similarities. They were both the offspring of noble families and, even more relevant, they had grown up in a Christian-liberal milieu. In addition, both politicians had a legal training and had got involved in politics at a young age. Last, but not least, they both had held a certain critical distance towards the political parties they belonged to. See Günther Scholz/Martin Süsskind, Die Bundespräsidenten, p. 349.

[124] Soon after his appointment as Head of State Francesco Cossiga had shortly visited Brussels. It was not, strictly speaking, an official state visit to Belgium, rather the result of some delicate issues connected with the Integration process. The Bundesrepublik was, therefore, the first ally he visited. After 1986, Cossiga often met with the German Chancellor. During a private face-to-face meeting on 12 May 1988 Kohl and Cossiga talked about the changes in Eastern Europe. Kohl seemed to be aware that the innovations introduced by Gorbačëv had caused a political earthquake in the Soviet bloc. They also allegedly commented that the German division had already *de facto* disappeared. President Cossiga spoke about this exchange of views with Ambassador Ortona who then mentioned this event in his diary. See author's interview with Ambassador Ortona (22.3.2016).

[125] "On 21 April we left very early for Germany. The journalists chosen to follow the event had arrived in Bonn the previous day. I saw the President in the afternoon and I asked him a few things.

Undoubtedly, it was a novelty for an Italian President of the Republic to celebrate the 25 April Anniversary abroad, but it was even more astonishing that Germany had been chosen to commemorate "Liberation Day".

> «Il 25 aprile è l'ultimo giorno in Germania. Andiamo a Berlino con volo di linea Air France, subito a Plötzensee, dove c'è il sacrario delle vittime della resistenza tedesca e dove il Presidente insieme a Von Weizsäcker presenzia a una cerimonia celebrativa per 25 aprile».[126]

During the State visit, Cossiga often commented on the bilateral ties between his country and Germany:

> «[…] Io parlerei piuttosto della realtà italo-tedesca che delle prospettive italo-te-desche. Tale realtà si compone di una consonanza di ideali e di interessi. […] Non credo che esistano ancora risentimenti nel vero senso della parola. Che ci possano essere momenti in cui non solo i popoli e i Governi, ma anche singole persone o singoli esponenti della vita pubblica […] possano confrontarsi con ricordi storici in grado di appesantire il giudizio dell'uno o dell'altro, ciò è possibile. Io non ho tuttavia ancora incontrato un Tedesco che si senta a disagio nel nostro Paese, come nessun Italiano che si senta a disagio in Germania […]».[127]

In particular, I wanted to know how I was to behave if the journalists insisted on stressing the Anti-American approach shared by Italy and Germany. I did my best to present the visit as the search for more contacts with the Americans. On 22 April, the President held a speech at the University of Bonn, which was very much appreciated. The media coverage was excellent. Dino Frescobaldi wrote in the *Corriere della Sera* about the 'Wahlverwandtschaften' between Cossiga and Von Weizsäcker. Prominent German politicians, economists, and intellectuals participated in the breakfast bestowed by Helmut Kohl. Cossiga had intense discussions with Helmut Kohl and with both the Minister of Economy and the Interior Minister". Quotation from the diaries of Ambassador Ortona. For the meeting at the University of Bonn, see ASCD, Fondo Francesco Cossiga, archivio con titolario 1944–2010, Presidenza della Repubblica-Settennato 1985–1992, b.184 (translation into Italian of the speech held by Francesco Cossiga at the University of Bonn in April 1986). As for the breakfast bestowed by Chancellor Kohl, see Brindisi del Presidente della Repubblica in occasione della colazione offerta dal Cancelliere Federale, Bonn, 22.4.1986. ASCD, Fondo Francesco Cossiga, Presidenza della Repubblica-Settennato 1985–1992, b.184, fascicolo Germania.

[126] "25 April was the last day we spent in Germany. We travelled to East Berlin with Air France. Soon after we went to Plötzensee, to the shrine for the victims of the German resistance. There, the President and Von Weizsäcker attended the ceremony for the 25 April Anniversary". See the author's interview with Ambassador Ortona (22.3.2016). See, also, See Discorso al sacrario di Plötzensee [sic!], Plötzensee, 25.4.1986. ASCD, Fondo Francesco Cossiga, archivio con titolario 1944–2010, Presidenza della Repubblica-Settennato 1985–1992, b.184, fascicolo Germania. In his speech Cossiga made specific reference to the German resistance, referring, for instance, to the "Weiße Rose" and to the "Verein von Kreisau".

[127] "[…] I would speak of the real situation of the Italian-German relationship, rather than of its future perspectives. This situation is based on common ideals and interests. […] I do not believe that there still is a grudge in the proper sense of the word. To be sure, there are moments when not

The contents of the interviews given by Francesco Cossiga to the German press further illustrate the level of knowledge and understanding of Germany which he had acquired. He further increased and deepened this knowledge in the seven-year period when he was Italian Head of State. Two years after the visit of 1986, he also commented on the historical and legal inheritance, which the past had bequeathed to modern Germany:

> «Guardi, la struttura della Repubblica Federale Tedesca è profondamente diversa dalla struttura, diciamo dalla nostra struttura culturale e sociologica. [...] Non è che la Germania sia una Repubblica Federale per l'invenzione di ingegneri costi-tuzionali. La Repubblica di Bonn è una Repubblica Federale, è uno stato federale, lo è sempre stata, salvo la parentesi del nazismo, perché la storia della Nazione tedesca è la storia di tanti paesi diversi. Il termine "Land" in italiano è intraduci-bile, è assolutamente intraducibile. Perché? Perché esprime tutta la storia. Non dobbiamo dimenticarci che c'è un nesso, vi è un filo dal Sacro Romano Impero di Nazione germanica alla Repubblica Federale di Germania. [...] Le città anseatiche erano profondamente diverse dalla Baviera. La Renania, nonostante fosse soggetta al dominio della Prussia, è totalmente diversa dalla Prussia orientale o anche solo dal Brandeburgo. Mentre noi siamo una Repubblica unitaria. [...]».[128]

---

only the people and the Governments, but also single men and politicians [...] are faced with his-torical reminiscences which can burden the assessment we have of one another. However, I have never met neither a German who feels uncomfortable in Italy nor an Italian who is uncomfortable in Germany [...]". See Intervista del presidente Cossiga al quotidiano tedesco *die Welt*, Roma, 17.4.1986. ASCD, Fondo Francesco Cossiga, Presidenza della Repubblica-Settennato 1985–1992, b.192, fascicolo 4. Full German text of the interview in the archives of the German newspaper *die Welt*. In 1989, soon after the Fall of the Berlin Wall, when the declarations uttered by Giulio An-dreotti in 1984 were still quoted and criticised, Cossiga took the following stance on the "Panger-manismus": "Io vorrei dire questo, che la Germania non ha inventato il fascismo. Questo è stato importato in Germania. La Germania non ha inventato l'antisemitismo. La Germania ha concorso ad inventare il liberalismo [...] bisognerebbe chiedersi quanto siano colpevoli le potenze vincitrici di Versailles dopo la prima guerra mondiale nel creare condizioni che non aiutarono i democratici tedeschi [...]. Io non temo il pangermanesimo, salvo che noi siamo così schiocchi, noi Europei dico, da voler noi creare condizioni perché sorga [...]". (I would like to say that Germany did not invent Fascism. It was imported into Germany. Germany did not invent anti-Semitism. On the contrary, Germany contributed to the birth of liberalism [...] we should wonder how guilty the victorious powers of Versailles were after the First World War in imposing conditions which did not support the Germans. [...] I do not fear *pangermanism*, unless we are so foolish, we European people I mean, to create the conditions for its emergence [...]). See Intervista del presidente Cossiga con il signor Andreas Srenk e la signora Rose Marie Borngasserper per il quotidiano tedesco Die Welt, Roma, 10.12.1990. ASCD, Fondo Francesco Cossiga, Presidenza della Repubblica-Settennato 1985–1992, b.192, fascicolo 40.
[128] "Look, the internal organisation of the Bundesrepublik is different compared to our cultural and sociological framework. [...] Germany is not a Federal Republic as a result of just a constitutional engineering work. The Republic of Bonn is a Federal Republic, it is a Federal State, and it always was so, with the only exception of the period of Nazism, because the history of the German Nation is the history of many different states. We cannot translate the word 'Land' into Italian. It is really

Undoubtedly, this interest for Germany and its historical inheritance was not widespread among Italian politicians. There was nonetheless a general agreement as to the necessity of removing any remaining reason for mistrust, to have a better chance to enhance cooperation.

Such a strong determination to boost cooperation was mirrored not only in official state visits and press releases, but also in the choice of the issues to be discussed during regular summits, as, for instance, the 1987 meeting held in the German city of Trier.[129] In preparation for this summit, frequent exchanges had been organised between the speaker of the Farnesina and the people responsible in the German Foreign Office. The cornerstone of the meeting was the discussion of the respective approaches to East-West cooperation in Europe.

The decision of the German Chancellor to spend not even a single word on the bilateral cooperation with Italy in the March 1987 governmental address came, therefore, completely unexpected for Rome, and it arouse both deep concern and significant astonishment. To make the situation even worse, not only had Helmut Kohl dedicated a significant amount of attention to the traditional ties with Paris, but he had also deemed it necessary to focus on the relationship with the United Kingdom, whereas any mention of Italy had been considered neither necessary nor desirable. A short phase of diplomatic tensions followed the announcement.[130]

Even if such tensions did not last for a long time and they had no significant impact on the level of cooperation by then achieved, the constant resurgence of such unpleasant issues, which could trigger misunderstandings, encouraged politicians to consider the strengthening of bilateral ties as useless without a clear political signal of change.[131] A common declaration could serve this purpose,

---

impossible. Why? Because it summarises all history. We should not forget that there is a link, a thread from the Holy Roman Empire of German Nation to the Bundesrepublik. The Hanseatic cities differed substantially from Bavaria. The Rhineland, even though it was under the control of Prussia, was not the same as Eastern Prussia or Brandenburg, whereas we Italians have a Unitary State". See Intervista del presidente Cossiga con il signor Horst Schlitter del quotidiano tedesco Frankfurter Rundschau, Roma, 1.8.1988. ASCD, Fondo Francesco Cossiga, Presidenza della Repubblica-Settennato 1985–1992, b.192, fascicolo 23.

[129] See Vorbereitung des Treffens von BM AM Andreotti am 16/17.03.1987 in Trier, Bonn, 25.2.1987. PA AA B26, n. 140521. Back then in 1984, during the meeting held in Stresa, Helmut Kohl had shown great interest in the Italian-German relationship, and he had also supported the necessity to further enhance cooperation. See also Entretien Craxi-Kohl Stresa, au Ministère des relations extérieures, télégramme 1296, Rome, 20.11.1984. AMAE 1930inva, Direction Europe, Série RFA, carton 4907, sous-série 11, période 1981–1985.

[130] See PA AA B26, n. 140521, exchanges of letters between Ambassador Ferraris and Horst Teltschik, March 1987.

[131] See Intervention BM in der Debatte über die Regierungserklärung, Bonn, 19.3.1987. PA AA B26, n. 140521. See also Koalitionsgespräch am 29.Mai 1987: Stärkung der deutsch-italienischen Zusammenarbeit, Bonn, 13.5.1987. PA AA B26, n. 140521.

provided that a genuine wish for change could be discerned even by other countries.[132]

This was the background of the 12 May 1988 joint declaration signed by Chancellor Helmut Kohl and the Italian Prime Minister Ciriaco de Mita at Villa Dora Pamphili.[133] The declaration can be considered both the culmination of a process of rapprochement launched in 1979, and as a stepping stone for the new dynamics starting from 1989.

From a short time perspective the joint declaration was the crowning achievement of a two-year effort to establish a forum for dialogue modeled on the *Königswinter Gespräch*, the framework facilitating wide-ranging contacts between London and Bonn.[134] Ever since the summer of 1987, i.e. nearly one year before the signature of the joint declaration, the German Foreign Office had carried out preparatory works to hold a test-session of the soon to be established forum for dialogue. The chosen venue was the newborn institute *Villa Vigoni*.[135] MPs of both countries would participate in the meeting to address both prominent bilateral and European issues and to speak about the possibilities for boosting the Italian-German cooperation beyond the strict realm of high-politics, in order to include, for instance, also trade and new technologies.[136]

In its early stages, the Forum was supposed to be composed by no more than fifteen members among leading figures from both countries and from the field of politics, economics, and information. At a later point of development it was, however, considered possible to increase the number of participants up to fifty people[137], to also include representative figures in the field of culture, science and

---

[132] According to Maurizio Ferrera and Elfriede Regelsberger, in the context of the relations among the four most influential European countries – Italy, France, the Bundesrepublik and the United Kingdom – the relationship between Rome and Bonn was the most fragile. However, the authors also notice that in 1987 a new wind of change was blowing between Rome and Bonn. See Maurizio Ferrera/Elfriede Regelsberger, Il foro di dialogo italo-tedesco, in: *Relazioni Internazionali* 7 (1989), pp. 61–69, 61.

[133] See Sommet italo-allemand du 12 mai, télégramme n. 500, Rome, 14.5.1988. CADN, 579PO-4–39 Archives rapatriées de l'Ambassade de France à Rome 1981–1992, ambassade de France en Italie. A copy of the Italian declaration is attached to the document.

[134] See Anmerkung Verbesserung der deutsch-italienischen Zusammenarbeit: Veranstaltung eines Gesprächskreises nach dem Vorbild des deutsch-britischen Königswinterer Gesprächs, Bonn, 8.7.1987. PA AA B26, n. 140521.

[135] For further information on Villa Vigoni see chapter 6.2.

[136] See Anmerkung Verbesserung der deutsch-italienischen Zusammenarbeit: Veranstaltung eines Gesprächskreises nach dem Vorbild des deutsch-britischen Königswinterer Gesprächs, Bonn, 8.7.1987. PA AA B26, n. 140521. Attached to the document we can also find a first rough cost estimation of the project.

[137] See Deutsch-italienisches Gesprächsforum/foro di dialogo italo-tedesco, Bonn, 25.2.1988. PA AA B26, n. 140521.

public administration.[138] The forum would not take place in a fixed location, but rather in a different place, either in Italy or in Germany, and it would take place once a year. Regarding the costs of the project and the organisation of it, it was deemed appropriate by both Foreign ministries to select two major "sponsors", the *Institut für Europäische Politik* in Germany and the *ISPI* in Italy.[139]

Based on what had been achieved until then, the Forum would establish a platform for continuous and comprehensive dialogue among the different sources of the Italian-German relations: the political, economic, and cultural centres and the field of the media, which until that moment had operated in isolation, but needed to be linked up in order to ensure a leap forward in the quality of relations.

The significance of the joint declaration cannot nevertheless be limited to the establishment of this bilateral forum of discussion, no matter how important it may be.[140] The declaration was, in fact, also a first step to reinforce cooperation between the Italian *CNR* and the *Deutsche Forschungsgemeinschaft* in the field of scientific research. New initiatives to improve language learning were also considered necessary.

Support facilities were essential to the success of the abovementioned targets. In other words, a better and more efficient cooperation between the Italian and German public administrations[141] was to be achieved by means of personnel exchanges for alternative periods of six months, as it was customary between France and Germany.[142] The possibility to appoint a jointly figure (Beauftragte) for bilateral relations was also discussed, but, in the end, both countries preferred to

---

[138] See Deutsch-italienisches Gesprächsforum/foro di dialogo italo-tedesco, Bonn, 9.12.1987. PA AA B26, n. 140521.

[139] See Ibid. At the beginning of December 1987, the *Institut für Europäische Politik* had already given its consent, whereas the discussion between the Farnesina and the ISPI had not achieved a satisfactory outcome yet.

[140] See PA AA B26 boxes 140524 and 140525. The first box provides documents concerning the first preliminary phase of preparation, between 1987 and 1988, whereas the second box offers information on the first steps after the signature of the declaration, between 1988 and 1989.

[141] Concerning cooperation in the field of public administration see PA AA B26, n. 173559, note on the Italian-German cooperation, Bonn, 15 August 1989.

[142] The level of cooperation between Italy and Germany had been significantly enhanced and its nature had been improved, even though this relation was still far from reaching the kind of cooperation which Bonn shared with Paris. It is debatable if Germany harboured the intention to also establish a cooperation with Italy in the military field, on the model of the Franco-German Brigade. See, for instance, Luigi Vittorio Ferraris, Il rilancio delle relazioni italo-tedesche a villa Dora-Pamphili (12 maggio 1988), in: *Affari Esteri* 80 (1988), pp. 539–555, 549. See also Anmerkung Erste Konsultationen der Direktoren für deutsch-italienische Beziehungen: Dg 20-Stellvertretender Politischer Direktor Negrotto, Bonn, 21.12.1988. PA AA B26, n. 140521. According to this document, in 1988 negotiations were ongoing to establish a closer cooperation between the Italian and the German Navy, whereas the German Defense Ministry was more cautious.

resort to a more traditional approach, meaning that each state would appoint a "director", a senior official of the Foreign Ministry, to monitor the developments.

One year after the signature of the joint declaration, on the 21 May 1989 meeting, the Italian and German Foreign ministries noted that the cooperation established between the Institut für Europäische Politik and the Italian ISPI in view of the forthcoming inauguration of the *Gesprächsform* (scheduled for October 1989) proceeded as originally planned. Meanwhile, the desire for enhanced ties had been extended to further fields. For instance, such ties were to be created among Italian and German diplomatic missions to third countries. During the regular meetings between the two "directors", the possibility of Foreign Ministries personnel exchanges had also been discussed.[143]

From a medium term perspective, the 12 May 1988 bilateral summit, and the signature of the joint declaration, embodied the culmination of a ten-year period effort. It hinted at the possibility that the declaration might also lay the foundations for Italy and Germany to work even more closely for further integration among Member States. It was no chance that both Foreign ministries had decided to devote the first session of the forum of dialogue to the contribution provided by their two countries, both separately and jointly, to the European integration process.

5.4 Drawing Preliminary Conclusions on the Verge of 1989

Should we ascribe the objectives established by the joint declaration, as have been mentioned at the end of the last sub-chapter, to the realm of rhetoric devices only?

It is hard to deny that it is customary in diplomatic agreements and official declarations to set ambitious targets which may then slide in the direction of purely declaratory exercises of an artificial nature. Still, in the specific context of the Italian-German relationship these targets, however ambitious, had deep roots. In a medium and long term perspective the joint declaration can be considered part of a wide range of initiatives among which the Genscher-Colombo Plan is one of the most interesting and, despite its failure, challenging.

Maurizio Ferrera and Elfride Regelsberger considered such a declaration as one of the most prominent examples of the "attivismo bilaterale" (bilateral activism) pursued by Rome and Bonn in the 1980s. To better explain their reasoning the authors coined the expression "neo-bilateralismo" (neo-bilateralism).[144] The term "neo-bilateralism" is extremely appropriate to summarise the results of a ten-year cooperation and the framework in which they had been achieved. This cooperation was born both in the spirit of reinforcing bilateral ties and with the

---

[143] See Ministero Affari Esteri, nota del 21 maggio 1989 (working paper of the Italian Foreign Ministry). PA AA B26, n. 140521.

[144] See Maurizio Ferrera/Elfriede Regelsberger, Il foro di dialogo italo-tedesco, pp. 61–64.

aim of strengthening the "House of the Twelve". It can also be considered another way of expressing the core concept discussed in the first introductory chapter: the necessity to embrace a "flexible bilateral approach" to study the ties between Italy and Germany in the Eighties.

It is equally important to bear in mind that the joint declaration was signed on the eve of the European Council of Hannover (June 1988) on whose success the German presidency harboured high expectations. During the first half of 1988, the support provided to – and the faith put into – the reform process pursued by the European Commission under the guidance of Jacques Delors, had been reflected in the unprecedented decision of the German Chancellor to allow Delors the possibility to participate in the ministerial meetings in preparation for the Council.[145] In this period, the internal difficulties of the EMS and the possibility to give practical effect to the objective of the Economic and Monetary Union were at the heart of the European debate.

The first coherent attempt of setting out a conceptual framework to overcome the deficiencies affecting the EMS, the Padoa-Schioppa report[146], had been required by the European Commission. Although the report emphasised the necessity of institutional changes to ensure an effective monetary coordination, it did not advocate for immediate far-reaching reforms. It rather pointed at the contradictions between formally independent monetary policies and a shared agreement for stable exchange rates. Helmut Schmidt and Valery Giscard d'Estaing, former Heads of Government and founding fathers of the EMS, supported the establishment of a Committee for the European Union which in April 1988 drew up the proposal for a European bank.[147]

---

[145] See Jacques Delors, Mémoires, pp. 239–241.

[146] See Tommaso Padoa-Schioppa, Efficiency, Stability and Equità: a strategy for the evolution of the Economic System of the European Community, Oxford 1987.

[147] According to information provided by Ambassador Roberto Nigido, the idea to establish a Central European Bank was conceived some months before April 1988 against the background of a fruitful Italian-German cooperation which was not to be considered a substitute to the ties between Paris and Bonn, but rather as an element which naturally complemented them: "Il progetto della moneta unica, o meglio, della banca, lo lanciò Genscher non come ministro degli Esteri, ma come leader liberale nel febbraio del 1988. Lo ricordo molto bene […] Io ero all'aereoporto di Bruxelles insieme al mio ambasciatore, Piero Calamia, era lunedì, stavamo aspettando un ministro italiano, non ricordo chi, e Calamia mi disse, 'sai Roberto, ho saputo che Genscher ha lanciato l'idea di una banca europea'. […]". (The project of a common currency, or better the idea of a common bank, was launched by Genscher, not in his capacity of Foreign Minister, but as leader of the Liberal Party, in February 1988. I remember it well […] it was on Monday and I was at the Airport in Brussels with my Ambassador, Piero Calamia. We were waiting for an Italian minister, whom precisely I do not remember, when Calamia told me: 'Roberto, do you know that Genscher has launched the idea of a European bank' […]). See author's interview with Ambassador Nigido (02.3.2016).

Still, it was not until the end of the German rotating presidency, under the strong support of Helmut Kohl and Hans-Dietrich Genscher, that the idea to give birth to a monetary union assumed a more defined shape. Armed with the French and Italian negative remarks against the EMS, Germany supported the establishment of a panel under the leadership of Jacques Delors. It would be composed of central bank governors of Member States, a Commission member, and three independent members. Not only its targets, but also its composition was in itself a marked innovation compared to the traditional panel of experts. In light of the magnitude of the pursued objective, and also of the reluctance of the central bank governors – the Bundesbank governor above all others – to endorse it, Helmut Kohl had to improve the ties with his most important European partners if he wanted to have a real chance to succeed.

In conclusion, the Italo-German couple drew its strength primarily from a sound convergence both in the EC and in NATO, and from an in the making bilateral framework of cooperation. These pre-conditions alone had not made possible the progress achieved in the Eighties, to which the *Gesprächsform* had added greater European resonance and more efficient tools. These pre-conditions had, however, allowed to smooth away the rough edges in the dialogue and to push into the background some major discrepancies in the vision of the *deutsche Frage*.

The joint declaration had been conceived as a stepping stone to further successes on grounds of the existing "impalcatura di sistema" (international framework) and of the fruitful dialogue between the Italian DC and the German CDU.

1989 created new options, while the international framework fell apart. The scope and the very nature of the European integration process were subjected to dramatic changes. The division of Germany disappeared in less than one year, and this resulted in new responsibilities and demands, both politically, economically, and culturally. The main Italian interlocutor of Germany during the last forty years, namely the DC, also fell apart.

How did Italy perceive and react to the process leading to the German reunification? How did its vision of the *deutsche Frage* evolve? What kind of tools had the evolution of the Italian-German relationship in the 1980s provided Rome with in order to rise to the challenge issued by this "acceleration of history"?

All these questions can be summoned up by just one word: a test. The year 1989 was a test of the level of maturity attained by the Italo-German couple.

6. The Italo-German Relations, 1979–1988.
Beyond Politics: Economy, Culture and the Press

> *Souvent passionnées, voire polémiques, les rela-*
> *tions entre l'Italie et l'Allemagne n'en apparaissent*
> *pas moins fécondes et, en tout cas, inévitables. De*
> *fait, l'intensité des échanges peut surprendre,*
> *s'agissant de deux pays qui ne partagent pas de*
> *frontières.*[1]

The intensity of the relationship between Italy and Germany concerned the polit-ical-diplomatic realm but also, and foremost, the economic and cultural ones. During summer 1987, Jacques Andréani (1984–1988), the French Ambassador to Rome, wrote to his Ministry that Germany was the first economic partner of Italy and its second cultural partner, while among the partners of Germany, Italy held the third place at an economic level, and the first one, together with France, in the cultural realm.

In chapters four and five, our attention was mainly focused on the Italian-German relationship in political and diplomatic terms. To provide a complete a picture as possible, it is now necessary to focus on at least two further fields of cooperation: the economic and cultural exchanges.

During the Eighties, they played a very significant role in the ups and downs that by 1988 led to the signing of the joint statement for the revival of the Italian-German relations. They were both linked to the political and diplomatic trends of the Italo-German couple, but they were also prompted by different forces which sometimes allowed them to proceed according to divergent lines of development, and, at other times, even to precede the political developments.

In this chapter we will, therefore, recover the second of the two pillars ad-dressed in the historical introduction regarding the 1950s[2]; the trends and trans-formations of this pillar in the 1980s will be addressed. This will be followed by a discussion concerning the developments of the relations between the two coun-tries through the prism of the press.

Both the term economy and the word culture are concepts of a polysemic nature. They are multifactorial notions intrinsically linked to the controversy con-cerning the difficulties in defining the borders of the identity of a country, which

---

[1] "The relationship between Italy and Germany may often be passionate, and even polemic, but this does not mean that it is for that less productive; anyway it is inevitable. The intensity of the ex-changes between these two countries – which actually have no common border – may even sur-prise". The French Ambassador to Rome, Jacques Andréani, writes to his Foreign Ministry, 1 July 1987.

[2] See ch. 3.

is in itself a very elusive concept. In the economic field, it is, for instance, rather difficult to draw a clear line between what can be considered an instance of foreign policy and what, on the contrary, takes shape on the fringes of the activities of the public bodies in the strict sense of the term.

The cultural realm is an even more complicated conundrum. Firstly, we must bear in mind that the cultural projection, especially the dissemination of the historical, artistic and literary heritage, has traditionally been an important tool used by the Italian foreign policy through a network of embassies, consulates and cultural institutes. In a way, the Farnesina seemed eager to counterbalance its many weaknesses through the force of attraction which its cultural heritage had beyond the national frontiers. Secondly, since the beginning of the Fifties, the cultural relations were characterized by an inherent driving force which was beyond the control of the public bodies. This allowed, even before the signing of a cultural agreement in 1956 and the redefinition of an efficient network of cooperation, to breathe new life into cultural exchanges. The Goethe Institutes – which, unlike the Italian cultural institutes, enjoyed in the 1980s significant autonomy from the Ministry of Foreign Affairs – the foundations of the most influential political parties, the banking foundations, and many other private associations, all contributed to the deepening and the consolidation of cultural relations. In Italy, as well as in Germany, the 1980s marked the beginning of a process in which the so called "third sector" gradually curved out for itself a leading role. Associations, as *the museum friends*, but also banking foundations gave their contribution to the initiatives promoted by the state through fund raising and many other supporting activities.

Finally, while dealing with the Italian projection in Germany, we should not forget the utmost importance of the migration flows of the previous decades. They resulted in the multiplication of bilingual magazines and in the gradual increase of local Italian-German associations.[3] Surely, these associations were not in the position of carrying out – mainly for lack of adequate resources – a wide-ranging action. However, each one of them contributed to enrich, deepen and also modify the boundaries of the very notion of cultural relations.

---

[3] The cultural turmoil of the 1980s also resulted in an increase in the number of the Italo-German associations, both in the great cities and in smaller towns and villages. On 28 November 1991, the *Deutsch-italienische Gesellschaft* was created in Hildesheim. The idea was actually born in the context of a small group of people who had taken part in the Italian courses of the local Volkshochschule. To the present day, it includes more than three hundred and fifty members, among them forty Italians (the Italian Consul in Hannover as member of honour). See http://www.dig-hildesheim.de (last accessed 24.10.2016), and information kindly provided by its president, Dr. Christian Vogel.

6.1 The Realm of Economy

In order to understand the kind of interaction between the Italian and the German economies, we shall address the trends of the Italian Foreign Trade in the 1980s first, and then we shall pay particular attention to two specific phases[4] chosen as frame of reference: 1981–1982 and 1987–1988. Finally, we shall conclude this sub-chapter with some comments on the months which preceded the fall of the Berlin Wall.

The following table provides data regarding Italian imports and exports from 1970 until 1990. A sharp increase in imports and also in exports is evident. For both trade flows, until 1990 Europe as a whole was the main partner of Italy.

	1970	1975	1980	1985	1990
Imports	4832	13015	44190	89249	112434
Exports	4263	11809	34458	77326	105107

Fig. 2: Italian imports and exports (in euro/lire) Source: Istat, foreign trade statistics.

On the imports ranking list, as well as in the exports ranking list, the main commercial partners for Italy were always the same throughout the entire time-period: Germany and France.

IMPORTS	1970	1975	1980	1985	1990
Europe	61.6	56.7	59.2	61.9	73
France	13.2	13.3	13.9	12.5	14.2
Germany	20.1	17.4	16.8	16.8	21.3
United Kingdom	3.8	3.3	4.4	4.9	5.2

EXPORTS	1970	1975	1980	1985	1990
Europe	70,0	67.1	66.5	62.7	73.8
France	12.9	13.2	15.1	14,0	16.4
Germany	21.8	19,0	18.5	16.3	19.1
United Kingdom	3.8	4.6	6.1	7,0	7.1

Fig. 3: European Imports and Exports. Source: Istat, foreign trade statistics (in percentages)

---

[4] The source of the data used in this sub-chapter is the Italian ISTAT (National Institute of Statistics). This data was collected during archival research in the German, French and Italian archives. Later on, information collected has been personally verified in the ISTAT archive. Since 2006, ISTAT has been made available for all those interested in an on-line database (archivio storico) concerning trade for the time-period 1970–1990. See http://www.coeweb.istat.it (last accessed 25.10.2016). Charts and graphs have been personally made up to summarise information.

In chapter three, the discussion on the economic trends in bilateral relations had ended with an overall positive assessment on the results achieved, despite the gradual emergence after 1952 of a creeping layer of tensions. During the decades that followed, trade with Bonn was kept on a path of steady growth.

By 1982, the Federal Republic had taken over the role of first customer and of first supplier of Italy. In both areas, bilateral trade covered approximately 16 % of the total exports and imports of Rome. In this regard, it is also important to observe that the Italian trade balance with Germany had by then a record deficit of approximately 2500 billion lire for imports and slightly under 1930 billion lire for exports, which was the second most important for Rome. Still, straddling between 1981 and 1982, the aforementioned deficit was re-balanced by cross-border tourism revenues and by unilateral monetary transfers due to the strong presence of Italian immigrants in Germany.[5] As a result of the huge migration flows of the previous decades, the number of Italian residents in the main German cities was significant. The largest Italian community in Europe lived, in fact, in Germany. This had significant social consequences on cultural and also on economic exchanges.

German Cities	Italian Residents	% of the total Amount of Foreigners
MUNICH	21700	9.81 %
COLOGNE	20000	14.5 %
FRANKFURT	17800	12 %
STUTTGART	16400	16 %
DÜSSELDORF	8200	9.1 %

Fig. 4: Italian Communities in Germany. Source: Fischers Weltalmanach, 1988

In addition, during the Eighties Germany improved its position in the field of tourism in order to become, by the end of the decade and along with Great Britain, the main non-Mediterranean tourist destination for Italians (mostly young people). As for Germany, tourism to Italy covered in the same time-period up to 40 % of the overall touristic flows with peaks that exceeded 50 % in some regions. The revenues of tourism and unilateral money transfers allowed to rebalance the Italian trade deficit with Germany.

If we now compare data of 1981–1982 with those of twenty-five years before, we can notice that the total amount of imports of the Bundesrepublik from other states had been multiplied by eleven, whereas as far as Italy was concerned it had

---

[5] The second generation at that time.

been multiplied by seventeen.[6] If we look closer at the trade pattern, we will also notice the significant role that, between 1981 and 1982, a high percentage of finished products had in bilateral trade: they amounted to 52 % in 1981 and to 62 % in 1982.

If we look further into details, there was an increase both in absolute and in percentage terms in all sectors considered: 7.8 % in raw materials, 13.3 % in semi-products, 16.2 % in finished goods and 59.2 % in energy.[7] Only in the field of investments there was a certain in-balance between Italy and Germany, since by the end of 1981 German investments in Italy amounted to 704 billion lire, whereas Italian investments to Germany amounted to 226 billion lire. By contrast, German investments in France amounted to 565 billion and Italian investments in France to 479 billion.

Lastly, one further aspect must be briefly addressed before analysing the bilateral trade situation in 1987–1988:

> « Le parallèle est saisissant entre la similitude de la condition qui leur a été réservée […] et le développement de relations bilatérales privilégiées, dont l'importance n'exclut pas la discrétion ; la stratégie de présence allemande en Italie passe souvent par des canaux informels mais efficaces […] ».[8]

Compared to the Fifties, by 1982 the two countries could rely on a more efficient network to support economic exchanges. The Italo-German Chamber of Commerce in Milan was extremely active in fostering bilateral ties among Italian and German companies, and by then it could also rely on two branches located in Rome and Bari. Official channels usually intermingled and overlapped with informal channels and with the propensity of big companies to assert their own foreign projection.[9]

This combination of a high degree of flexibility and informality with an extremely efficient official network ensured a strong growth in all sectors

---

[6] See L'Influence de la R.F.A. en Italie, note de l'ambassade de France en Italie, Gilles Martinet à Claude Cheysson ministre des affaires étrangères, 27.12.1983. AMAE 1935inva, Direction Europe, Série RFA, carton 4907, sous-série 11, dossier 6 période 1986–1990.

[7] See Ibid.

[8] "There exists an astonishing parallel between the similarity of the conditions they were subjected to […] and the development of privileged bilateral relations, whose importance does not prevent them from pursuing a low profile course; in Italy, the German strategy proceeds through informal, but efficient channels". See Les relations italo-allemandes, note de l'ambassade de France en Italie, Jacques Andréani à Jean-Bernard Raimond ministre des affaires étrangères, 1.6.1987. AMAE 1935inva, Direction Europe, Série RFA, carton 4907, sous-série 11, dossier 6 période 1986–1990. The record refers to the similarities which Italy and the Bundesrepublik shared at the end of the Second World War, to the economic miracle in both countries by the end of the Fifties and to the wave of terrorism in Italy and Germany in the Seventies.

[9] Thyssen, Volkswagen and Ford were among the most active German companies. They also contributed to the financing of the Institute for Foreign affairs. See Ibid.

throughout the Eighties, and this can also help us understand the utmost importance which the German market had for Rome, and, some caveats notwithstanding, the importance the Italian market had for Bonn. By 1987, the Bundesrepublik had the capability to absorb 18 % of Italian exports, against 16 % of French exports, and 9.6 % of US exports. In turn, Italy had the capability to absorb more than 19 % of German exports, against 14 % of French exports, and 5.3 % of US exports.

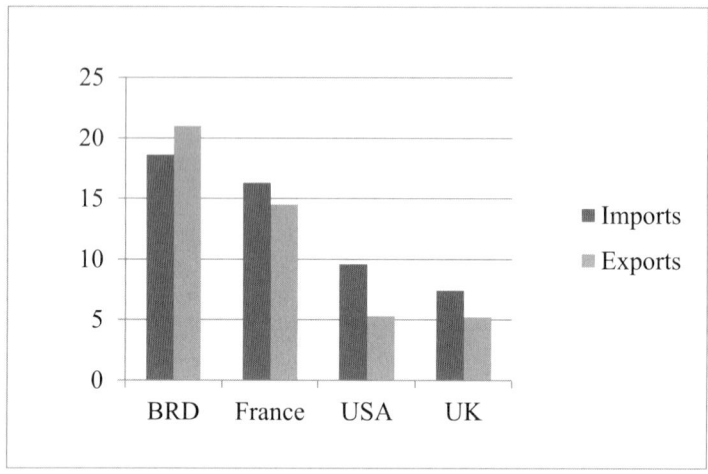

Fig. 5: The largest trading partner of Italy in 1987. Source: Istat.

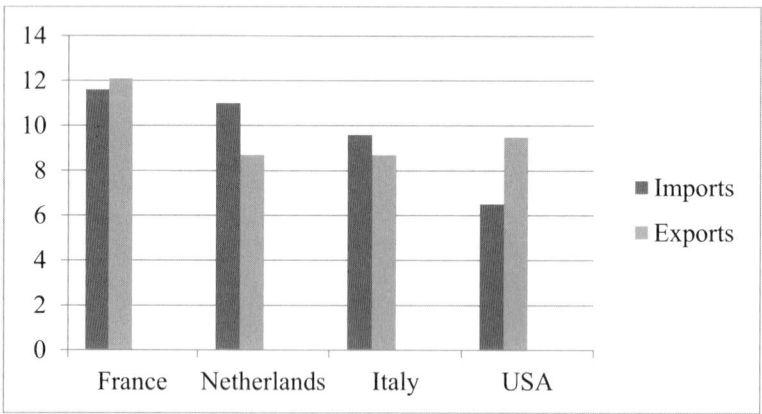

Fig. 6: The largest trading partner of Western Germany in 1987. Source: Istat

In the first half of 1987, approximately 21 % of Italian imports came from the Bundesrepublik, with peaks of 27 % in manufactured products. Compared to trade flows with other partners, the differences were quite considerable in textile, telecommunications, and high-precision instruments, whereas the gap was not so significant[10] in the agri-food sector and in leather articles.[11]

> « La présence allemande sur le marché italien est tout à fait impressionnante. Pour le premier semestre la RFA a représenté 21.1 % des importations italiennes et la France 14.6 %. Pour les produits manufacturés les pourcentages respectifs sont de 27.5 % et de 15.7 %. Au niveau de masses, au premier semestre 1987, les ventes allemandes en Italie ont dépassé les nôtres de 44 % et de 75 % pour ce qui est des produits manufacturés. [...] ».[12]

In spite of its internal difficulties, Italy had by then become one of the largest world producers of consumer goods. In the mid-1980s, up to 70 % of Italian exports were finished products, among them machines and means of transport amounted to approximately 34 %. In Europe, Italy and the Bundesrepublik had therefore secured big slices of the local market, which further increased the relevance of their bilateral ties.[13]

Last, but not least, the armaments sector is a topic requiring and deserving our attention, while dealing with the Italian-German economic ties in the Eighties. The Air Force was the first area to benefit from an increasingly close cooperation. For instance, benefits came in the shape of the trilateral project *Tornado*[14] and in the shape of the programme for the construction of the European fighter jet.[15] Both projects not only insured good revenues for all governments involved, but they also allowed Italy and Germany to gradually set up a network of contacts among major industrial companies and "experts in the field".[16]

---

[10] Only in the fragrance sector, Germany was not the largest partner of Italy.

[11] See Portions de nos principaux concurrents sur le marché italien, ambassade de France en Italie, Rome, 23.10.1987. AMAE 1935inva, Direction Europe, Série Italie, carton 6373, sous-série 8, dossier 5 période 1986–1990.

[12] "The German presence on the Italian market is quite impressive. In the first half of the year, the Bundesrepublik has provided 21.1% of Italian imports, whereas France has provided for 14.6%. For manufactured goods, the figures are 27.5% and 15.7%. At a global level, in the first half of 1987, German sales in Italy have exceeded our sales by 44%, and by 75% for manufactured goods [...]". See Ibid.

[13] France seemed to be aware of its relative weaknesses in the inter-European trade, but it explained it, and also its growing trade-deficit with Italy, merely as the result of its disadvantages with respect to the German production structure.

[14] Supported by the Italian, the French and the British governments.

[15] Supported by the Italian, the French, the British, and the Spanish governments.

[16] This also resulted in a remarkable transfer of Italian people, together with their expertise and their financial resources towards Munich. See Les relations italo-allemandes, note de l'ambassade de France en Italie, Jacques Andréani à Jean-Bernard Raimond ministre des affaires étrangères, 1.6.1987. AMAE 1935inva, Direction Europe, Série RFA, carton 4907, sous-série 11, dossier 6 période 1986–1990.

However, despite the favourable economic climate and a GDP growth up to 3 %, by 1988, Italy had not yet succeeded in curbing inflation risks.

> „Die Bundesrepublik Deutschland ist weltweit Italiens wichtigster Handels-partner, Italien ist der zweitwichtigste Handelspartner der Bundesrepublik. [...] Doch fast jedem einzelnen dieser Rekorde steht ein nicht minder wichtiger Nega-tivrekord gegenüber und zwar in den meisten Fällen bei der finanziellen Situation des Staates [...].“[17]

This had been at the beginning of the decade – and still was at its sunset – one of the major concerns of the Federal Government. This is something that emerges very clearly from the correspondence between the German Foreign Ministry and the Embassy in Rome.[18] According to this flow of information, it had become increasingly difficult in Italy to proceed as if this issue was a concern of no great significance. Quite the contrary, according to Bonn, the Italian press, the indus-trial sector and even the government[19] were becoming increasingly aware that their country could no longer follow a path of economic growth which would result in a further increase of inflation and of the already significant public debt. In other words, they were slowly becoming aware that the public debt „nicht von allein unter der Sonne einer strahlenden Konjunktur hinweg schmelzen wird, son-dern dass sie zwangsläufig verschlimmern muss.“[20]

The decade ended with quite contrasting opinions. Experts have often stressed the significance which the German market had for Italy. The last para-graphs have tried and demonstrate that the converse is equally correct. Despite its weaknesses, Rome had become by the end of the Eighties an important partner for Bonn as well.

> „Das gesamtwirtschaftliche Wachstum betrug 1988 2.9 % und wird 1989 voraus-sichtlich 3.5 % erreichen. Die Auslastung der industriellen Kapazität liegt derzeit

---

[17] "Worldwide the Federal Republic is Italy's most important trading partner, and Italy is the second most important trading partner of Germany [...]. However, nearly all these records are overshad-owed by approximately as many negative records, namely in most cases concerning the financial situation of the State". See Italienische Staatsschulden und den Haushalt, Vermerk deutsche Bot-schaft in Rom, 2.2.1989. PA AA B26, n. 173569.

[18] In addition to the abovementioned document, the box n. 173569 provides further interesting files on the Italian difficulties and weaknesses which cast a shadow on its good economic performance, in particular the notes of 1 June 1998 and of 5 September 1988.

[19] See, in particular, Wirtschaftliche Situation Italiens, deutsche Botschaft in Rom, 1.6.1989. PA AA B26, n. 173569. The record makes specific reference to the comments of the then Italian central bank governor, Carlo-Azeglio Ciampi, in his 31 May declaration, and also to the comments of Pininfarina at the 5 May meeting of the Italian *Confindustria*.

[20] See Italienische Staatsschulden und der Haushalt, Vermerk deutsche Botschaft in Rom, 2.2.1989. PA AA B26, n. 173569.

bei über 88 %. Die Konsum- und Investitionsgüter Nachfrage hat sich auf bisher unbekannter Höhe stabilisiert. Die Steuereinnahmen steigen und zugleich gehört die italienische Gesamt-Sparrate, trotz enormer Konsum-Ausweitung, unverändert zu den höchsten der Welt. Die Lira hat von lauter Kraft Mühe sich in den ihr von EWS vorgeschriebenen Bereich zu halten, aber Italien ist ein leistungsfähiger Partner […]. Italienische Unternehmen investieren in der ganzen Welt und sind auf allen wichtigen Finanzmarkten vertreten.“[21]

This was in part due to endemic reasons – among others the complementarity existing between Italian and German industries – in part to European specific conditions which made the exchanges among Member States extremely advantageous, and in part to bloc reasons too. As for the latter, the many hurdles which hindered the possibility of fully exploiting the advantages of doing business with Eastern European countries had a significant role. We must not forget that traditionally trade and business within the Mitteleuropean area had had a significant role for Germany. The division of the Continent had, however, reduced the benefits of this line of development. Against this uncertain environment, the 1989 events made their entrance on the international scene.

6.2 The Realm of Culture

„Die kulturellen Beziehungen zwischen Italien und Deutschland haben sich im vergangenen Jahr noch mehr intensiviert. Zahlreiche privat organisierte kulturelle Veranstaltungen fanden neben den mannigfaltigen Aktivitäten der staatlich von uns geförderten Institutionen statt. Der hohe Standard der deutsch-italienischen Kulturbeziehungen verpflichtet für die Zukunft.
Das italienische Publikum zeigt sich am Kulturaustausch mit der Bundesrepublik, insbesondere an der modernen Entwicklung in Kunst, Literatur und Musik immer mehr interessiert. Deutsche Kulturveranstaltungen sind in Rom auch ein gesellschaftliches Ereignis, und die Residenz des Botschafters wird im steigenden Maße zu ihrem Mittelpunkt.
Die Bundesrepublik Deutschlands steht mit Güte und Vielfalt ihres kulturellen Angebots in Italien wohl vor Frankreich, sicher aber vor Großbritannien, Österreich und anderen Staaten an erster Stelle. […] Die Villa Vigoni ist dabei, ihren

---

[21] "In 1988 the overall economic growth amounted to 2.9 % and by 1989 it will probably reach a rate of 3.5 %. The utilisation rate of the industrial complex accounts for more than 88 %. The demand of products and investment is stabilised at a so far unmatched level. Tax revenues are increasing and Italian savings rates are among the highest in the world, despite the increase in consumer demand. The Lira has difficulties to stay in the range prescribed by the EMS […] Italy is, nevertheless, a solvent partner. Italian companies invest all over the world and they are represented in the most important markets". See Italienische Wirtschaft, Vermerk deutsche Botschaft in Rom, 5.9.1989. PA AA B26, n. 173569.

festen Platz in den bilateralen kulturellen Beziehungen aufzubauen. Dabei sind wir allerdings zurzeit die treibende Kraft. [...].["22]

Why has such a long quotation been chosen to start this chapter?

This quotation was part of the annual report of the German Foreign Office on cultural exchanges with Italy in 1987. In the realm of culture, it summarises all the most significant aspects of the Italo-German couple in the mid-1980s, especially its strengths and weaknesses. It has been, therefore, selected as the main thread of this sub-chapter. We will follow this thread, in order to identify and discuss the main "cultural pieces" of the Italian-German puzzle[23], starting from the role of the *Goethe-Institut*.[24]

During the first two decades after the end of the Second World War, Italy had been under the strong influence of the US model. It was only later that cultural exchanges among European States started growing in importance. As for the Italian-German ties, experts in the field have consistently held that Italian literature, its historical and musical heritage, as well as its many artistic riches, have always enjoyed great standing and high praises in the German speaking area. Still, in spite of long-standing cultural exchanges, after the war Italy and Germany lacked a modern and efficient framework to cooperate. This was certainly due to the consequences of the conflict and also due to the fear shared by both countries that their European partners could react adversely to the emergence of an "axis" between Rome and Bonn so soon after the end of the war, even if it merely applied to cultural issues.

It was not until 1956 that a cultural agreement was eventually signed. Back then and for a long time to come, the activities of both the Goethe Institutes in

---

[22] "Last year cultural ties between Italy and Germany were further strengthened. Alongside all sort of initiatives carried out by institutions supported by the State, many private activities have been organised. The high standard of the Italo-German cultural relations commits to invest in the future. The Italian audience is more and more interested in cultural exchanges with the Federal Republic, especially in recent artistic developments, in literature, and in music. German gatherings are in Rome quite an event and the residence of the ambassador is becoming their central stage. The cultural offering of the Federal Republic in Italy is, for quality and variety, at the top of the list, probably compared to France, and certainly to Great Britain and Austria. [...] Villa Vigoni is curving out a role in cultural exchanges. But, in this respect, we are still the main driving force". See Kulturpolitischer Jahresbericht 1987, die deutsche Botschaft in Rom, Rom, 8.3.1988. PA AA B90, n. 1371.

[23] This sub-chapter mainly focuses on the German cultural projection in Italy, rather than on the Italian cultural projection in Germany. This appeared as the most reasonable choice since our ultimate goal consists in discussing how Italy reacted to the fall of the Berlin Wall, and more generally, how the vision of Germany changed in Italy throughout the 1980s.

[24] The main sources for this sub-chapter have been the records kept at the German Foreign Ministry archives (*Bestand* 90), the records of the archives of the French Foreign Ministry (boxes of the sections *inva1930* and *inva1935*), and last, but not least, the reports of the Goethe Institutes.

Italy and of the Italian cultural institutes in Germany were sporadic, and their influence was limited. In addition, it was only decades after 1945 that the development of tourism from élite domain to mass phenomenon allowed this interest in Italy to gain new dimension and importance.[25]

At the dawn of the 1980s, the background had substantially changed. Private initiatives still had a relevant importance, but meanwhile the framework for cooperation which reported – either directly or indirectly – to the German Foreign Ministry had been subjected to a major reorganization. By 1983, the "cultural" department of the German Embassy in Rome could rely on a first cultural Advisor, on a first Secretary, and also on two cultural attachés. Moreover, the German Foreign Ministry could also count on a highly efficient and closely connected framework of institutes. In France, and only in France, Bonn could rely on an equally efficient operational structure.

The Goethe Institutes[26] were the crown jewel in a network which could rely on several institutions widespread in the main Italian cities, such as Rome, Venice, and Florence.[27] In addition, four private German schools had been established in Rome and Milan.[28] Formally, the Goethe Institutes were part of a network which was tied to the Foreign Office, they could though enjoy a great level of autonomy.[29] Besides, they were not subjected to the control of the local Embassy.[30]

---

[25] See, in particular, Les relations italo-allemandes, note de l'ambassade de France en Italie Jacques Andréani à Jean-Bernard Raimond ministre des affaires étrangères, 1.6.1987. AMAE 1935inva, Direction Europe, Série RFA, carton 4907, sous-série 11, dossier 6 période 1986–1990.

[26] Goethe Institutes had been established in Rome, Milan, Turin, Naples, Trieste, Genova and Palermo.

[27] Among them the most influential were: The *German Archeological Institute in Rome*, the *Deutsche Akademie Rom* at Villa Massimo, the *Deutsches Historisches Institut in Rom* (which celebrated in 1988 its anniversary in the presence of the Italian and the German Presidents of the Republic, Cossiga and Von Weizsäcker), and the *Bibliotheca Hertziana*. In Florence, the Bundesrepublik could rely on the *Kulturhistorisches Institut*, and in Venice on a well-known centre for art studies. See PA AA B90, n. 1371, Aufnahme des Deutschen Studienzentrums in Venedig in die Liste der deutschen Kulturinstitute in Italien, Bonn, 1 February 1988.

[28] See Kulturpolitischer Jahresbericht 1987, die deutsche Botschaft in Rom, 8.3.1988. PA AA B90, n. 1371.

[29] See L'Influence de la R.F.A. en Italie, note de l'ambassade de France en Italie, Gilles Martinet à Claude Cheysson ministre des affaires étrangères, 29.11.1983. AMAE 1935inva, Direction Europe, Série RFA, carton 4907, sous-série 11, dossier 6 période 1986–1990.

[30] This process of growing independence of the activities of the Goethe Institutes did not start in the 1980s, but rather in the previous decade. In 1969, the *Kooperationsvertrag* with the Federal Government was signed, and in 1976 the *Rahmenvertrag*. According to Jörg Lau, the Seventies marked the beginning of a "double transition process" for the Goethe Institutes worldwide. They gradually increased their freedom both as regarded their cultural programme and their financial decisions. See Jörg Lau, Bildungsroman Bundesrepublik: Das *Goethe-Institut* und die Entwicklung

Italy, in turn, could rely on forty Italian lectors in the major German universities, on the Dante Alighieri Institutes for Italian language teaching, and on six cultural institutes which were located in Bonn, Wolfsburg, Hamburg, Cologne, Munich and Stuttgart.[31]

At a first glance, the German cultural network had more financial resources, and was more extensively disseminated in Italy than its Italian counterpart in the Federal Republic. Still, the Italian network in Germany should be considered in the context of the resources which Rome had devoted to culture, and also in comparison with the framework of cooperation which Italy had established in other countries. All things considered, the Italian effort was far from being negligible. Only in France had Italy opened the same number of cultural institutes.[32]

In the Fifties and in the Sixties, the Goethe Institutes had operated in adverse social conditions, as it has been already discussed in chapter three. The years 1976–1977 marked both the hardest time for the Institutes and also the opportunity to give to the German cultural projection in Italy a fresh start.[33] The hardest time for the activities of the Goethe Institutes corresponded to the explosion of the Kappler Affair.

Surely, we should eschew the establishment of a causal connection between the diatribe related to the Kappler Affair and the difficulties of the Goethe Institutes. It is, nonetheless, undeniable that this case violently brought to the surface the inherent contradictions of the approach to cultural exchanges embraced by the Institutes, and, more generally speaking, by the Federal Government. The literary and cultural legacy left by the past had not been enough, neither to support a leap in quality, nor to remove the negative associations attached to Germany. Even if the Goethe Institutes wanted to remain true to their mission of cultural circles, they had to modify, at least partially, their focus. History and sensitive political issues could no longer be left on the sidelines.

Starting from 1977–1978, seminars, exhibitions and reviews were no longer solely devoted to literature and philosophy, but also to artistic and cultural

---

der Bundesrepublik, in: http://www.dhm.de/archiv/ausstellungen/goethe/katalog/lau.htm (last accessed 17.6.2016).

[31] See L'Influence de la R.F.A. en Italie, note de l'ambassade de France en Italie, Gilles Martinet à Claude Cheysson ministre des affaires étrangères, 29.11.1983. AMAE 1935inva, Direction Europe, Série RFA, carton 4907, sous-série 11, dossier 6 période 1986–1990.

[32] Back then, Italy had established five cultural institutes in the USA, three in Switzerland, and two in the United Kingdom. See Les relations italo-allemandes, note de l'ambassade de France en Italie Jacques Andréani à Jean-Bernard Raimond ministre des affaires étrangères, 1.6.1987. AMAE 1935inva, Direction Europe, Série RFA, carton 4907, sous-série 11, dossier 6 période 1986–1990.

[33] Murnau - Manila - Minsk, 50 Jahre *Goethe-Institut,* München 2001.

developments in the Republic of Weimar.[34] This was a first step to lay the foundations for a far-reaching debate aimed at discussing historical sensitive issues in light of more recent social developments and difficulties. It was, therefore, not a chance that the first activities of this kind focused on Constitution, fundamental rights, freedom of the press, freedom of opinion, and last, but not least, on the European integration process. The latter subject was discussed both for its intrinsic importance and as an answer to national weaknesses. In 1976, the seminar *"Die italienische Krise aus der Sicht der deutschen Presse"* was organised in Milan, while in Rome the conference *"Verteidigung der Verfassung und der Grundrechte der Demokratie in der Bundesrepublik"* gave voice to prominent legal experts of both countries.[35]

Only some years later, the same approach was also applied to another issue of the past, perhaps the most sensitive of all questions which still burdened bilateral relations: the Nazi-past.[36] Surely, the choice of organising seminars and conferences regarding the Weimarer Republik and the National-Socialism in close connection with current social difficulties and based on the use of short films and documentary films is debatable, to put it mildly. The choice to deal with cultural and political aspects at the same time with no clear distinction between a critical historical evaluation of the past and an informal discussion of the present, is also questionable. Still, we should not forget that in that time the institutes had to face an atmosphere of strong social and political polarisation. Misunderstandings were rapidly increasing. What was needed were effective and simple strategies. The public had to be informed and historical sensitive issues had to be discussed in a way which had to be accessible to a wide audience.[37]

This experimental course of action delivered some relevant positive results. It was, nonetheless, only in the 1980s that the interest for the Bundesrepublik truly surged in Italy. In that decade, the Goethe Institutes not only carefully preserved a balance between the attention devoted to literature and philosophy and the interest for current issues, but they also fully exploited the opportunity to address political and historical subjects.

This resulted in an impressive number of debates, conferences, seminars, colloquiums, and other initiatives. In 1980, the *Goethe-Institut* in Rome organised

---

[34] In addition to activities with a focus on philosophy, such as the seminar *Heidegger und das Problem der Technik*, the *Goethe-Institut* in Naples organised a meeting: *Intellektuelle, Gesellschaft und Staat in der Weimarer Republik*. Well-known Italian and German experts in the field of arts, literature, cinema, but also history and politics were invited to participate.

[35] Information was gathered through the internet sites of the Goethe Institutes.

[36] From the mid-1970s, the *Goethe-Institut* in Turin was actively involved with the organisation of film festivals, seminars on Leni Riefensyahl, and the German cinema in the Nazi-period, as for instance the seminar on the new film by Hans-Jürgen Syberberg: Hitler, ein Film aus Deutschland.

[37] See Gian Enrico Rusconi, Cinquant'anni di successo. I *Goethe-Institut* in Italia, in: http://www.goethe.de/ins/it/it/lp/uun/102523.html (last accessed 11.8.2016).

two symposiums on Martin Heidegger and Max Weber and in 1987 a seminar on "*Der Widerstand in Deutschland*". Thanks to the support of distinguished political experts, the *Goethe-Institut* in Genova paid special attention to the relationship between modern state and democracy and also on finding a balance between economic growth and environmental protection. The latter issue was, for example, addressed in the colloquium: "*Durch Umweltschutz zu neuem Wirtschaftswunder?* ". Last, but not least, the *Goethe-Institut* in Turin opted for seminars mainly focused on terrorism and human rights, such as the three-day conference "*Menschenrechte und Bürgerrechte im 19. Jh. in Europa*".

These few examples also point at another interesting aspect of the new strategy chosen by the Goethe Institutes: From the end of the 1970s, they also started to define their cultural offer in light of the city and the region in which they had their premises. This meant that all Goethe Institutes in Italy followed the same path in order to strengthen the interest for the Bundesrepublik and its cultural projection, but it also meant that each one of them pursued this goal according to somewhat different means. The profile of the Italian city in which seminars and any other initiative were organized was by then carefully taken into account, and the target audience as well.

In addition, in the 1980s, the Goethe Institutes could develop their activities in a climate of better and more frequent cooperation with local institutions. In 1980–1982, the municipality of Rome financed the "Progetto Germania" (project Germany) whose ultimate goal consisted in strengthening and deepening the ties and the opportunities for cooperation among Italians and Germans in literature, in the arts, and in science. Italian experts started talking of a "boom della cultura tedesca" (German culture boom).[38] Even the press and the media coverage improved significantly compared to the previous decades.

In 1987, the exhibition "*Der Deutsche Widerstand*" was organized in Milan under the auspices of the Italian and the German presidencies of the Republic. Meanwhile, the Italian President of the Republic inaugurated in Rome the documentary exhibition on the *Third Reich,* and the lecture and film circuit which followed the exhibition. Just a month later, Nilde Jotti, president of the Italian *Camera dei Deputati*, was the guest of honour at a symposium of Italian and German Costitutional law experts. The symposium was the opportunity to discuss the principles, the foundations, and the last forty years of history of the Constitutions adopted after the war both in Italy and in Germany. Last, but not least, on

---

[38] See Ibid.

Christmas 1987, the Italian Foreign Minister Andreotti, together with his German counterpart Genscher, inaugurated the new premises of the Goethe Institute in Rome.[39]

In the 1980s, the Goethe Institutes did stand out not merely in light of their new strategy, but also on grounds of the rapid changes in the contents of their cultural offer, and because of the accuracy with which these contents were tackled. Compared to the previous decade, National-Socialism was for instance no more generically addressed, but rather discussed in its different aspects. Furthermore, highly topical issues were also, and for the first time, addressed. An example is the idea of fatherland, Heimat, and that of historical revisionism. Until then, these subjects had either been left on the sidelines of the debate or addressed partially and with extreme caution. The Goethe Institute in Turin was a precursor of this course, and it showed both flexibility and originality in dealing with an "uncharted territory". In 1985, the institute hosted the meeting *"Auf der Suche nach 'Heimat'. Nationalismus, Regionalismus und Identität in der zeitgenössischen italienischen und deutschen Literatur"*, and soon after it hosted the film cycle *Heimat im Neuen Deutschen Film*. The latter was followed by the debate *"Wie viel 'Heimat' braucht der Mensch? Nationalismus und Identität in Italien und Deutschland"* with the participation of historians and political experts coming from Italy and Germany. Two years later, in 1987, the Goethe Institute in Turin gathered Italian and German prominent experts in Contemporary History to address the question: *"Welche Vergangenheit hat unsere Zukunft? Ein Kolloquium zwischen italienischen und deutschen Zeithistorikern"*. Ernst Nolte, Renzo De Felice, Wolfgang Mommsen, and Karl Dietrich Bracher were among the participants.

The Italian audience reacted to this new course with a mixture of curiosity, admiration, and fear which had a deep influence on its vision of the "deutsche Frage". For the first time after the war, the Italian audience could approach in a whole new light the Bundesrepublik. This brought a new gateway to modern German cultural closer to Italian observers: its dithering between compulsion towards modernity and "rootedness" in traditions.

The Goethe Institutes were not alone in supporting the external projection of the Bundesrepublik. The *Stiftungen* (foundations) of the then main political parties also had an impact on this cultural turmoil. The Konrad Adenauer Stiftung of the CDU (KAS), the Friedrich Ebert Stiftung of the SPD (FES), the Friedrich

---

[39] See Andreotti e Genscher inaugurano la nuova sede del Goethe Institut, Agenzia giornalistica italiana, 7.12.1987, in:
http://archivio.agi.it/articolo/342394aa1a0b0928c8a147c4c5149729_19871207_andreotti-e-genscher-inaugurano-nuova-sede-goethe-institut/ (last accessed 13.8.2015).

Naumann Stiftung of the FDP (FNS), and the Hanns-Seidel Stiftung of the CSU (HSS) all[40] had a role to play; still, the Konrad Adenauer Stiftung was by far the most influential thanks to its wider availability of resources and staff.[41] Based on its head office in Rome, not only did it promote an intensive lobbying among DC members and within the Catholic associations, but it also encouraged contacts among conservative MPs, politicians, intellectuals, and journalists on both sides of the Alps.[42] The Foundation was also very generous in granting scholarships for Italian students to complete their studies in social sciences, economy and history in the Bundesrepublik.[43]

Against this background, the German-Italian centre *Villa Vigoni* was established in 1986. On grounds of its peculiar features, its somewhat different profile compared to other centres for cooperation, and also in light of its growing importance, its history and its scope must be carefully addressed.

Villa Vigoni is located in Menaggio, on the shore of the Como Lake. Since he had no heirs, Ignazio Vigoni had passed on the property of Villa Vigoni to the Federal Government in 1983, provided that the estate would be turned into a scientific and cultural circle, in order to bring closer Italian and German scholars.[44]

> «Nasce dalla volontà di Ignazio Vigoni, amico dei miei genitori, che non aveva eredi, era benestante e culturalmente riuniva un filone di origine milanese e un filone tedesco, quello dei Mylius, discendenti da banchieri di Francoforte. Era una famiglia colta, con antenati che erano stati amici di Goethe, di Manzoni…e quando morì Ignazio Vigoni lasciò la villa e tutto il parco al governo tedesco a patto che

---

[40] In the mid-1980s a new Bavarian foundation, Rotonda Romana, was also established in Rome. Its focus was on politics and religion. An Italian-German institute on contemporary history was established in Rome under the auspices of this foundation, and a music academy as well. See, in particular, Römische Aktivitäten der deutschen Stiftung Rotonda Romana, 8.3.1988. PA AA B90, n. 1371.

[41] In Rom, the *Stiftung* could rely on a secretary and on a broadcast manager. In 1983, the latter office was held by a personality of known repute and professional competence, the former Chief of Staff of the CDU president and future president of the European People's Party (hereafter, also EPP). Its annual budget amounted to approximately 250000 deutsche Marks. See L'Influence de la R.F.A. en Italie, note de l'ambassade de France en Italie, Gilles Martinet à Claude Cheysson ministre des affaires étrangères, 29.11.1983. AMAE 1935inva, Direction Europe, Série RFA, carton 4907, sous-série 11, dossier 6 période 1986–1990.

[42] To support these activities, twice a year, seminars and conferences were organized in Berlin.

[43] The Friedrich Ebert Stiftung carried out the same activities within the left-wing Italian circles, but it could rely on fewer resources. Back then, its activities were usually channeled towards the countries of the so-called "Third-World". It is, therefore, not in the least surprising that its influence in Italy, and in other European countries as well, was not comparable with that of the Konrad Adenauer Stiftung.

[44] See Kulturpolitischer Jahresbericht 1987, German Embassy in Rom, 8.3.1988. PA AA B90, n. 1371.

ne facesse un centro di studi italo-tedesco. Il governo tedesco era molto incerto se accettare questo lascito, era piuttosto impegnativo e…fu Andreotti che negoziò una formula accettata dai tedeschi per la creazione di un'associazione italo-tedesca. In altre parole la proprietà della villa è tedesca, ma l'associazione è paritaria italo-tedesca, il bilancio di Villa Vigoni è diviso in due, un bilancio della proprietà a carico del governo tedesco e un bilancio dell'attività dell'associazione, diviso al 50 % tra i due partner».[45]

Fig. 7: Villa Vigoni, view on the lake. Foto Deborah Cuccia

---

[45] "The cultural centre Villa Vigoni was born from the determination of Ignazio Vigoni who was in friendly terms with my parents. He had no heirs. He was a wealthy man and he combined two different cultural strands: A Milan strand and a German one. The latter was the legacy of a family of bankers of Frankfurt: The Mylius. It was a really cultured family, whose ancestors had been friends of Goethe, of Manzoni…when he died, Ignazio Vigoni passed on the estate and its garden to the German Government, under the condition that it would become an Italian-German cultural centre. The German Government hesitated before accepting the legacy. It was demanding, and…it was Andreotti the one who negotiated a compromise to establish an Italian-German association which was acceptable for both Italy and Germany. In other words, the German Government has got the ownership of Villa Vigoni, whereas the cultural association was created on an equal footing. The budget is divided into two halves: the estate is at the expense of the Federal Government, whereas the association is paid by both countries". See author's interview with Ambassador Visconti di Modrone who has been president of the association Villa Vigoni until 2017.

The history of Villa Vigoni is closely linked to the life and deeds of Heinrich Mylius. Mylius was the offspring of a wealthy family of Frankfurt bankers who moved to Milan. In a few years, he managed to make an immense fortune. Still, he was more than a businessman who profited from clever investments in the modernisation of the local silk industry to establish a new bank. He was also very active in supporting the modernisation of local transports, and throughout his entire life he maintained close ties with major personalities at the Weimar's Court, as, for instance, with Goethe. Besides, he was also fully involved in the Italian cultural arousal of the first decades of the 19th century. The Estate, which he bought in 1829, quickly became one of the most popular cultural venues for both Italian and German intellectuals. His contribution to the promotion of cultural exchanges between Germany and Italy is invaluable.

Fig. 8: Villa Vigoni. Foto Deborah Cuccia

The vicissitudes surrounding the estate cannot be addressed in details; here, it is, however, particularly important to signal that the old Mylius passed the estate on to the young widow of his only son, Luigia Vitali. Some years later, the new owner remarried to Ignazio Vigoni.[46] His grandson died in 1983 without an heir. The estate was therefore passed on to the German Government in the wish that it could once again be restored to its original role of a Italian-German meeting place for major cultural exchange projects. Back then, there were talks of a "poisoned gift", as significant financial support was needed to restore the estate to its original role, and the German Government was also forced to face major legal hurdles to succeed in the operation.[47]

It was not until 21 April 1986 that Giulio Andreotti and Hans-Dietrich Genscher signed a joint intergovernmental agreement for the mutual promotion and usage of the estate. Thus Villa Vigoni was born. The ultimate scope was to support and strengthen Italian-German ties in the field of science, culture and education.[48] The cultural centre was born in a new climate in which it was considered necessary to broaden and strengthen the existing framework in order to rise to the challenge of the 1980s cultural turmoil.

Despite the aforementioned positive changes, language skills were still a thorny issue. Surely, the sole knowledge of the language spoken by one's partner cannot succeed in supporting a process of cultural rapprochement. Still, this lack of knowledge was an obstacle in establishing ties that could go beyond the strict institutional sphere. By the mid-1980s, less than 10 % of Italian citizens were proficient in more than one foreign language. In spite of the activism of the cultural institutes, even fewer people were proficient in German. As far as public schools were concerned, less than 5 % of scholars were taught German.[49] German was no more the domain of an élite, but it was still the domain of a minority.[50] In

---

[46] For further information, see Villa Vigoni 1986–2016 Rassegna Stampa Speciale per il trentennale-Sonderpressespiegel zum dreißigjährigen Jubiläum 2–3 maggio 2016.

[47] The main hurdles concerned the consequences of the Distomo Massacre, a Nazi-crime perpetrated by members of the SS in the Greek village of Distomo. Four relatives of victims had brought legal proceedings against the Federal Government. After having failed in claiming ownership of the premises of the Goethe Institute in Athen as part of the restitution, they had turned their attention to Villa Vigoni. In 2008, an Italian Court had ruled that the plaintiffs could take German property in Italy as a compensation, but, four years later, the International Court of Justice rejected the claims of the plaintiffs.

[48] See, in particular, Sachstand: Intensivierung der deutsch-italienischen Beziehungen, Bonn, 4.12.1987. PA AA B90, n. 1371.

[49] See L'Influence de la R.F.A. en Italie, note de l'ambassade de France en Italie, Gilles Martinet à Claude Cheysson ministre des affaires étrangères, 29.11.1983. AMAE 1935inva, Direction Europe, Série RFA, carton 4907, sous-série 11, dossier 6 période 1986–1990.

[50] The same also applied to the knowledge of Italian in the Bundesrepublik. Even if the knowledge of the Italian language was more widespread in the Bundesrepublik, compared to the knowledge of German in Italy, the teaching of these two languages was no common choice neither in the Italian nor in the majority of the German public schools.

the 1980s, in public schools the teaching of French and English had the lion's share, even if German had slightly improved its position.

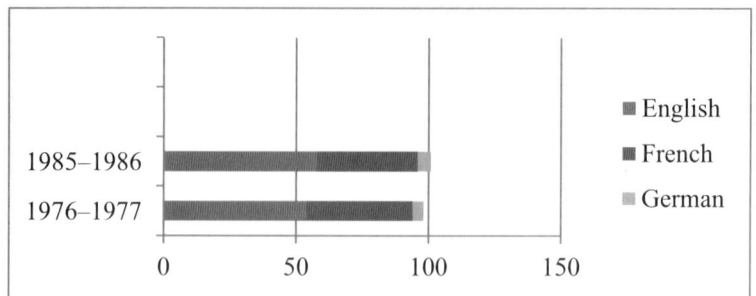

Fig. 9: Italian Ministry of Education, language learning in secondary public schools[51]

This was a clear concern both in the 1986 protocol and in the 1988 joint declaration. The protocol would apply for three years, and it was organized along three main axis. One of them was closely linked to the utmost importance of boosting language teaching. The Bundesrepublik committed itself to select twenty more language lectors to be send to Italian universities, while the Italian government accepted to raise the number of its lectors in the Bundesrepublik from thirty up to forty people. Lastly, the Federal Government also expressed the wish that the initiatives promoted by the autonomous region *Alto Adige-Süd Tirol* could be extended to other Italian regions. Alto Adige-Süd Tirol had successfully supported and implemented regular programmes of six-month and one-year exchanges between Italian and German secondary school pupils.

In conclusion, this declaration showed a higher level of awareness around the fundamental issues of cultural exchanges. As the Austrian philosopher, Ludwig Josef Johann Wittgenstein, affirmed "die Grenzen meiner Sprache, sind auch die Grenzen meiner Welt".[52]

---

[51] See Maurizio Ferrera/Elfriede Regelsberger, Il foro di dialogo italo-tedesco, pp. 66–67.
[52] "The borders of my language are also the borders of my world". Tractatus logico-philosophicus, 1918.

6.3 The Press: From the Kappler Affair to Andreotti's Comments.
A Slow Process of Change

> *Plonger dans l'histoire, les mots, les traditions, les représentations, les stéréotypes des uns et des autres, afin de se connaître et de se tolérer, car tel est le défi principal.*[53]

This text by Eva Sabine Kuntz on the perception of Germany in the Italian press opens with these words by the French journalist Dominique Wolton.[54]

There exists a vast body of scientific texts on the images and the stereotypes relating to a country which are provided by the press, and more generally speaking, by the media of another country. Still, the body of literature on the vision of Germany provided by the French, the British, and also the American media – and vice-versa – is more extensive that its Italian counterpart.

Among the most significant works on the latter subject, the texts by Susanne Wilking and by Eva Sabine Kuntz deserve, therefore, special attention. In her research, Susanne Wilking mainly focused on the German perception of Italy in the 1970s and in the 1980s through in-depth analysis of a wide range of German newspapers and magazines, such as *Frankfurter Allgemeine Zeitung*, *Süddeutsche Zeitung*, *die Welt*, *Frankfurter Rundschau*, *Stuttgarter Zeitung*, *Rheinische Merkur*, *die Zeit*, and last, but not least, *der Spiegel*.[55]

By contrast, the abovementioned text by Eva Sabine Kuntz mainly examines the perception of Germany by the Italian press. The author opted for a long-term analysis, as she focused her attention on the entire time-frame between the end of the Second World War and the last decade of the 20th century. As for the newspapers, the author mainly used the two national newspapers with the most significant print-run: The *Corriere della Sera* and *La Stampa*.

These two texts and their conclusions will be our reference point in this subchapter, in order to try and understand how the image of Germany in the Italian press changed throughout the Eighties. Our analysis will be based on a limited number of the most influential and best selling national newspapers of that time: mainly the *Corriere della Sera*, *La Stampa* and *Repubblica*.

---

[53] "Delving into history for words, traditions, images, mutual stereotypes, in order to know and tolerate each other, because that is our ultimate goal". Quotation from Dominique Wolton, *Le Monde*, 6.4.1994.

[54] See Eva Sabine Kuntz, Konstanz und Wandel von Stereotypen: Deutschlandbilder in der italienischen Presse nach dem Zweiten Weltkrieg, Frankfurt am Main 1997.

[55] Susanne Wilking, Das Italienbild in der bundesdeutschen Presse der 70er und 80er Jahre, in: Susanne Wilking (ed.), Deutsche und italienische Europapolitik-historische Grundlagen und aktuelle Fragen, Ergebnisse des deutsch-italienischen Gesprächsforums, Bonn, pp. 39–70.

Politics, diplomacy, economy, and also cultural relations have already been addressed in the previous chapters. The press is, therefore, the only element still missing. This is, indeed, an essential contribution to provide a picture as complete as possible of the different aspects which had an influence on the transformation of the Italian-German relationship from the late Seventies until the fall of the Berlin Wall.

In addition to the abovementioned books, there exists a significant number of short essays and articles which are also a precious source of information. Among them, the contribution of the Italian journalist Roberto Giardina stands out both for its overall clarity, for its depth of analysis, and for its foresight in covering all the essential guidelines that had an influence on mutual perceptions and descriptions.[56]

The analysis will also be supplemented by additional data gathered through interviews with journalists who worked in Germany, and by the use of their memoirs and essays.[57]

As Dominique Wolton stressed, the ultimate goal of research consists in delving into history not merely to describe the events, but rather to unearth new material, that is words, stereotypes and prejudices which have a significant influence on mutual perceptions. Before going into further details, it is therefore indispensable to briefly clarify the main differences between the notions of "stereotype" and of "prejudice".

Firstly, the notions "stereotype" and "prejudice" are to be understood as related, but different. Although closely related, the two concepts can, in fact, exist independently of each other. An affective feeling towards a person or a group prior to – or not based – on actual experience is designated by the lexeme

---

[56] Born in Palermo in 1940, Roberto Giardina is one of the keenest Italian observers of Germany. He spent there most of his working life. Before the election of Willy Brandt, he worked for different Italian news media, as for the newspaper *il Giorno*. From 1986, he was correspondent in Germany of the Florentine newspapers *la Nazione*. After having spent half of his life in Hamburg and Bonn, he retired to Berlin. Among his many contributions, see, for example, Roberto Giardina, Stampa e mezzi di informazione nella Germania occidentale, Milano 1976; Roberto Giardina, Guida per amare i tedeschi. Come abbattere il Muro dei pregiudizi e scoprire la verità su un popolo simpaticamente imperfetto, Milano 1995; Roberto Giardina, Un amore ambiguo, in: Secondo Congresso di Bolzano sul management, Bolzano, accademia europea di Bolzano, 1999, pp. 37–43.

[57] Interviews with journalists, as well as interviews with politicians and diplomats, must always be used critically in light of the hidden risk that the interviewee tries to emphasise, consciously or subconsciously, certain actions and to conceal others. Still, recent developments in historical research have shown that a concomitant recourse to different sources can prove extremely useful in expanding the analysis by emphasizing some points which both the diplomatic records and the articles printed in the press might sometimes leave in the shade.

"prejudice".[58] The term "stereotype"[59] refers, in turn, to a set and to a strict idea widespread in society about a thing, a person or a group. The stereotype has a cognitive component in which a set of features is attached to a single object, to a person, or, in our specific case study, to a group of people: The Germans. Social stereotypes are based on both a cognitive and an affective component. As for the cognitive component, stereotypes are a form of categorization which helps to simplify and systematize information. Certain specific characteristics are gradually attached to a certain social group, whereas others are left out.[60] This process is the result of social interaction and social learning; as for the latter, the images offered on a daily basis by the media play a significant role. Here, an example of a stereotype about European people:

> "Heaven is where: The police are British, the cooks are French, the mechanics are German, the lovers are Italian, and everything is organized by the Swiss.
> Hell is where: The police are Germans, the cooks are British, the mechanics are French, the lovers are Swiss, and everything is organized by the Italians". [61]

The affective component allows, in turn, to attach to the simplified and strict idea a value judgment, either positive or negative.[62]

Each social stereotype possesses both a descriptive and a prescriptive function. Through the first function the in-group can define things around it through a process of simplification, and it can also strengthen its internal cohesion, insofar as the stereotype identifies all what differentiates it from the out-group.[63] The latter function can, in turn, guide the behaviour of the in-group according to the characteristics which the stereotype has defined as its own.

All these things considered, the question remains as to whether stereotypes can change. According to the famous American journalist Walter Lippmann[64], stereotypes are like "military fortresses" which are the guardians of traditions;

---

[58] See Gordon Allport, La natura del pregiudizio, Firenze 1974 (the original text was published in 1954 by Cambridge University Press).

[59] The term "stereotype" derives from the Greek words στερέος (firm, solid) and τύπος (sign, example, impression), and it was not until 1922 that it was used for the first time in its modern sense by the American journalist and scholar Walter Lippmann.

[60] See Hermann Bausinger, Stereotype und Wirklichkeit, Jahrbuch Deutsch als Fremdsprache, 1988, p. 160. According to the author, stereotypes are uncritical representations which are resistant to change. "Stereotype" is the scientific term for a non-scientific concept.

[61] See Jens Petersen, Deutschland-Italien. Eine furchtbar spannungsreiche Nachbarschaft, in: *Zibaldone* 16 (1993), pp. 5–6.

[62] In this context, I share the approach to stereotypes of Eva Sabine Kuntz. See Eva Sabine Kuntz, Konstanz und Wandel von Stereotypen, pp. 27–30.

[63] Ibd., pp. 34–35.

[64] See Walter Lippmann, Public Opinion, New York 1950.

hence, they are impervious to change. Certainly, this does not preclude the possibility that certain specific events may have an influence on stereotypes associated to a single person or to a group. Only spectacular events can though set in motion a process of change.[65] Stereotypes are the ultimate result of a long and gradual formation process. As far as national stereotypes are concerned, the oldest are the ties between two countries, the largest is the number of stereotypes.

In this respect, Roberto Giardina has often remarked that the ties between "Italy" and "Germany" are rooted in the ancient past, being the text by the Roman writer Tacito the first picture of "Germany" offered to "Latin" observers. Particular attention is, however, attached to modern history, especially to the period straddling between the end of the 18th century and the first decades of the 19th century. The painting by Friedrich Overbeck "Italia und Germania" has been considered by several scholars of the Romantic period as the emblem of the strong ties between the two countries. [66]

Fig. 10: Italia und Germania, Friedrich Overbeck, 1828 (Munich Neue Pinakothek)

Roberto Giardina stressed how ambiguous this canvas actually is. The author painted two female allegorical figures, two young women looking at each other with affection. The painter hinted at a caress between them. But who is Germany and who is Italy? According to Roberto Giardina, the sibling-like connection is so strong that, at a first glance, it is rather difficult to answer this question.

In light of these ideas and preconditions, the next paragraphs will analyse a short time-frame: The Eighties. At first, the results of the most significant studies on the approach of the Italian press to Germany during the previous decades will

---

[65] See Eva Sabine Kuntz, Konstanz und Wandel von Stereotypen, p. 38.
[66] See Roberto Giardina, Un amore ambiguo, in: Secondo Congresso di Bolzano sul management, Bolzano, accademia europea di Bolzano, 1999, pp. 37–38.

be addressed. The aim consists in identifying the main stereotypes which in Italy were attached to Germany at the end of the 1970s. Then, two spectacular events will be selected, one at the beginning of the time-frame chosen and one in the middle with the ultimate goal to verify the abovementioned hypothesis: Had the 1980s the potential to favour a process of change in the set of stereotypes attached to the German neighbour?

According to the conclusions drawn by Eva Sabine Kuntz and Susanne Wilking, after the end of the Second World War two different "categories" had a significant influence in the process of creation of stereotypes associated to Germany. The first one corresponded to the "German past", by which the writers refer to the romantic period, to the era of Bismarck, to the Republic of Weimar, and especially to the Nazi-period and the Italian resistance movement.[67] The second one corresponded to the so called "Sekundärtugend".[68] In addition, from the mid-1950s, the European integration process and the approach of the Bundesrepublik to it also had an increasing importance on the stereotypes associated to Germany.[69]

A posteriori, we could be tempted to depict the process of post-war transformation of the perception of Germany as if it had been a linear process from the very beginning until its end. This, however, was not the case. The process was rather characterised by constant fluctuations due to the alternation of surges of interest followed by phases of disaffection.

The beginning of the 1950s offers a good example of a marked surge of interest towards the Bundesrepublik. Still, we have also discussed how unfulfilled and fragile the roots of this interest were. It did not go so deep to modify the stereotypes associated to Germany. Another good example of a marked surge of interest towards Germany is the chancellorship of Willy Brandt. The Chancellor was depicted in the Italian newspapers as a true democrat who could face with political courage the challenge of wiping out the German atmosphere of intolerance and short-sighted provincialism, in order to support a genuine democratisation process of his country.[70] Five years after his election, in 1974, the stereotypes attached to Germany were still unchanged. The most frequent stereotypes were associated with the allegations of authoritarianism and illiberalism. The Italian press usually made a clear distinction between the "bad German" who was

---

[67] The importance of this first category has also been stressed in the author's interview with Alfredo Venturi, 3.2.2016. See also Alfredo Venturi, Noi Tedeschi vittime della stampa, *CdS*, 27.11.1992.
[68] See footnote 18 in the preface.
[69] See Eva Sabine Kuntz, Konstanz und Wandel von Stereotypen, p. 6.
[70] Ibid.

trapped in the past, and the "good German" who merely enjoyed economic advantages without second thoughts.

In turn, in the German press of the 1970s, the most recurrent terms in association with Italy were still "unpredictability" and "unreliability".[71] The tensions, related to the wave of terrorist attacks in both countries and emphasised by the disinformation of the German public opinion concerning the Italian social situation and the resulting reaction of the Italian press, had lead to a spiral of misunderstandings. In addition, an important role was played by the fact that the Italian public opinion was prone to explain the anti-communist approach of the Federal Republic as nothing else than a reactionary feeling.[72] Different economic conditions and equally different definitions of the notion of the rule of law and individual liberty also deepened the divide and strengthened traditional stereotypes.

The lowest point came in 1977 with the Kappler affair. Herbert Kappler had been the Head of the German security services in Rome during the Second World War. In 1944, he had been ordered to serve as Chief for all SS and policy units deployed in the Italian capital. In 1948, he had been tried by an Italian military tribunal for war crimes – included the organisation of the Ardeatine massacre – and sentenced to life imprisonment in the Gaeta military prison. By 1975, due to severe health conditions, he had been moved to a military hospital in Rome. On 15 August 1977, a public holiday, his second wife organised his escape. In the following days, the major Italian newspapers expressed feelings of anger, humiliation, and insult both regarding what had happened and also at being depicted by the European media as an "inefficient country". The escape of Kappler had been allegedly made possible because almost unlimited access had been granted to his wife Annelise during his time in hospital.[73]

Herbert Kappler quickly became the emblem of all stereotypes which until then had been associated to the Germans. The German man was depicted as the soldier-man type, he epitomised discipline, order and blind obedience.[74] On the latter point, the press seemed ready to accept the defence of Kappler, that he had

---

[71] Susanne Wilking, Das Italienbild in der bundesdeutschen Presse, p. 39.

[72] See Hansjacob Stehle, Das italienische Experiment und die Kommunisten, in: *Europa Archiv* 23 (1976), pp. 732–742.

[73] See, in particular, Carlo Casalegno, Uno scandalo umiliante, *La Stampa*, 17.8.1977; Come non credere ai complotti, *Repubblica*, 17.8.1977; Un insulto e una grave sfida, *L'Unità*, 17.8.1977; Luigi Bianchi, Ricorderemo a lungo questo amaro Ferragosto, *CdS*, 17.8.1977. As for the use of the term "humiliation", see, for example, Gaetano Scardocchia, Forlani spiega perché fu deciso di sospendere la pena a Kappler, *CdS*, 20.8.1977; see also Mistero nella fuga-beffa del SS Kappler, *La Stampa*, 17.8.1977.

[74] See Guido Guidi, E poi le Fosse Ardeatine, *La Stampa*, 17.8.1977. Guido Guidi had been the first Italian journalist to interview Kappler after his imprisonment.

merely carried out orders.[75] This image of the German soldier was closely linked to both the abovementioned categories of the "German past" and of the "Sekundärtugend". In Germany, the benefits of the "middle-class" virtues were – and never had been – balanced by an equal respect for the so called cardinal-virtues.

Surely, it was not the first time that the Italian press launched such a bitter diatribe on this issue. Still, in 1977, it had greater emphasis since it also became an occasion for harsh criticism against a German unfinished democratisation process.[76] In turn, Annelise – a nurse of Soltau whom Kappler had married in prison in 1974 after a long correspondence – also fulfilled all the stereotypes traditionally associated to the "donna germanica" (Germanic female), both physically – blond hair, blue eyes, strong and with a willful nose – and psychologically: a fanatic.[77]

With each passing day, the dispute further degenerated. According to the allegations of the major Italian newspapers, at the end of August 1977, Kappler could not only rely on the help of his wife and of a group of former soldiers who had supported him throughout the years of imprisonment, but he could also rely on that of the German Red Cross[78], of the Federal Government[79], and, in all likelihood, on the sympathy of the entire German people[80]:

> «L'Europa intera applaudì Brandt quando in Polonia si inginocchiò davanti al monumento dei caduti nel ghetto di Varsavia e in quel gesto di umiltà vide il significato di una vittoria. Il silenzio di Bonn cancella quel gesto».[81]

All things considered, the main question is whether the 1980s marked the beginning of a process of genuine improvement of the image of Germany in the Italian press. In other words, two issues are now to be addressed.

---

[75] See, in particular, Ulderico Munzi, Hai solo obbedito a un ordine, *CdS*, 17.8.1977.

[76] See Galante Garrone, Serietà, *La Stampa*, 19.8.1977. See also Leo Valiani, I Tedeschi, *CdS*, 20.8.1977. See Anche Brecht era Nazista? *CdS*, 23.8.1977. And see Giorgio Signorini, Un cattivo servizio alla democrazia tedesca, *Repubblica*, 20.8.1977.

[77] La crocerossina nazista fanatica e intrigante, *La Stampa*, 17.8.1977. See also Lidia Storoni, Lo ha rapito per assolverlo, *La Stampa*, 19.8.1977.

[78] See Ettore Petta, Manifestazione contro l'ex. SS a Soltau. La Croce Rossa tedesca finanziò la fuga? *CdS*, 20.8.1977.

[79] See Tito Sansa, In Germania la polizia conosce il luogo segreto dov'è nascosto, *La Stampa*, 17.8.1977.

[80] See, in particular, Luca Goldoni, I turisti tedeschi in Italia, ormai è ora di dimenticare, *CdS*, 17.8.1977. See also Tito Sansa, Il mancato gesto da parte di Schmidt, *La Stampa*, 21.8.1977.

[81] "The whole of Europe welcomed with a big round of applause the decision of Brandt to kneel in front of the shrine of the victims in Warsaw, in such humility it saw the meaning of the victory. The silence of the Federal Government has deleted the symbolic meaning of his behaviour". See Giovanni Trovati, Il silenzio di Bonn, *La Stampa*, 24.8.1977.

Firstly, it is necessary to wonder whether in the 1980s the media echoed the political improvement in bilateral relations and the new cultural strategy pursued by the Goethe Institutes.

Secondly, it is equally important to wonder whether the changes in the 1980s were so spectacular to start a process of transformation – even if a partial one – of the stereotypes until then attached to Germany.

Following the Kappler affair and the end of the wave of political terrorism, some signs of improvement in mutual images depicted by the Italian and the German press timidly emerged. The German press expressed positive judgements about Sandro Pertini – President of the Republic from 1978 until 1985 – and Francesco Cossiga – both as Prime Minister and President of the Republic from 1985–1992.

Surely, these comments did not modify the entirety of the stereotypes attached to Italy, but they did lessen some of their most negative aspects. This also had positive side-effects in Italy.[82] In order to verify if the 1980s marked a significant change, a specific event has been selected among the most spectacular of that decade. This event has already been addressed at a political level: the 1984 declarations of Andreotti.

On the evening of 13 September 1984, the dpa was one of the first media to comment on the statements by Andreotti. The *Repubblica* was the one and only Italian newspaper to react nearly as quickly.[83] As regards the contents of Andreotti's declarations, both the Italian and the foreign newspapers expressed disbelief and astonishment.[84] These feelings were followed by attempts to comprehend the reasons behind the comments of Andreotti, both in Italy and in Germany.[85]

> „Giulio Andreotti wusste natürlich was er tat, als er auf die Crescendo-Walze der Deutschlandfrage trat. Der Politiker war fünfmal Regierungschef seines Landes, er unterhielt enge Beziehungen zur Kurie […] Er kennt alle Gassen, Winkel und

---

[82] See, in particular, Heinz-Joachim Fischer, Der Sarde mit den traurigen Augen, *Frankfurter Allgemeine Zeitung*, 10.8.1979. See also Horst Stankowski, Der neue Mann in Rom, in: dpa, 8.10.1979. See Herzlich und tiefgreifend: Cossiga in Bonn/Schmidt hat von Italien gelernt, *Frankfurter Allgemeine Zeitung*, 10.10.1979, in: ACDP, Abteilung Pressedokumentation, Francesco Cossiga.

[83] Queste le frasi all'origine del caso, *Repubblica*, 14.9.1984. See also Non riunire le Germanie, *Repubblica*, 14.9.1984.

[84] See, in particular, Mario Ciriello, Bonn all'ambasciatore: Roma si spieghi, *La Stampa*, 15.9.1984, p. 2. See also Vanna Vannuccini, Lo schiaffo italiano ai tedeschi, *Repubblica*, 15.9.1984.

[85] See, for example, Mario Ciriello, Kohl aspro con Andreotti non capisco le sue parole, *La Stampa*, 16.9.1984. See also Herbert Kremp, Andreotti und sein Fall, *Die Welt*, 17.9.1984; Karl Feldmeyer, Dem Herrn Andreotti ist es halt passiert: Wer denkt was über den Wunsch der Deutschen nach Einheit, *Frankfurter Allgemeine Zeitung*, 29.9.1984, in: ACDP, Abteilung Pressedokumentation, Italien 1984.

Tapetentüren der italienischen Innenpolitik, bewegt sich mit gleicher Sicherheit aber auch auf den Boulevards der internationalen Politik. Er zeigt Ehrgeiz, nach zahllosen Ämtern auch den Mantel des Staatspräsidenten überzustreifen. Die Aussichten sind zwar minimal, aber er bedarf auf jedem Fall des Zuspruchs der Kommunisten [...] Ist es der ganze Grund für seinen Tritt? Wir können diese Frage auf sich beruhen lassen. [...] da er in klassischen Disziplinen gebildet ist, weiß er den Unsinn-Begriff von Pangermanismus richtig einzuschätzen [...]."[86]

Rather than focusing on the search for the reasons behind these comments, it is more interesting to delve deeper into the strategies used by the press to address this event.

It appears that these strategies were rather different from those used some years before after the Kappler affair. Both issues, the Kappler affair and the declarations of Andreotti, were spectacular enough to hide the potential to influence the image of a nation. Still, the latter was not solely the opportunity for the German and the Italian press to reaffirm traditional stereotypes, as it had happened after the escape of Herbert Kappler. Quite the contrary, a more constructive approach – which drew a clear line between the declarations of the Italian Foreign Minister and the country which he led – had replaced criticism for criticism's sake.[87]

«Un intervento dall'esterno sul tema dell'unificazione che suoni eterna condanna è la via per far rinascere [...] qualche ventata di nazionalismo; è il modo per fiaccare la resistenza ideale e morale delle forze democratiche tedesche [...]».[88]

The Roman newspaper *Repubblica* openly criticised the lack of sensitivity displayed by Giulio Andreotti in such a delicate transitional phase both for the Bundesrepublik, the DDR, and the balance within Europe:

---

[86] "Andreotti knew what he was doing when he danced the waltz of the German question. He has been five times Head of Government of his country, he maintains close links with the Vatican [...] he knows every single aspect, every corner, every closed door of Italian politics, but he can also act with equal confidence on the international stage. He covets countless offices, included the Presidency of the Republic. His odds may be minimal, but he needs, anyway, the support of the Communists [...]. Is this the whole explanation behind his behaviour? We can leave this question unanswered [...] as he is trained in classical disciplines, he can properly understand the meaningless of the expression Pangermanism". Herbert Kremp, Andreotti und sein Fall, *Die Welt*, 17.9.1984.

[87] See, for example, Craxi distanziert sich offensichtlich vom Außenminister Andreotti: Auch Deutschland hat ein Recht auf Wiederherstellung seiner nationalen Einheit, *Die Welt*, 26.9.1984, in: ACDP, Abteilung Pressedokumentation, Italien 1984.

[88] "Interventions from the outside on the issue of the German unity, which would sound like an everlasting condemnation [...], would pave the way for the resurgence of nationalism; in this way the ideal and moral resistance of the democratic forces in Germany is undermined". See Andrea Purgatori, Piccoli: con le sue parole Andreotti ha colpito i democratici tedeschi, *CdS*, 16.9.1984.

«Cosa c'entra infatti il "pangermanesimo" con la "Deutschlandpolitik" della coppia Kohl-Honecker? Cosa c'entra la manifestazione dei sud-tirolesi nostalgici dell'Austria, svoltasi qualche giorno fa a Innsbruck, con lo sfortunato tentativo di Eric [sic!] Honecker di muoversi sulla linea di una qualche autonomia, fuori dagli schemi rigidissimi della politica dell'Urss verso l'Occidente? Che cosa intende il ministro degli Esteri quando sostiene che "non bisogna esagerare in questa direzione", vale a dire nel dialogo tra tedeschi dell'Est e dell'Ovest? Intende dire che per questa strada si va al Quarto Reich? […] Dopo che i sovietici avevano martellato per varie settimane sul 'revanscismo' di Bonn, il ministro degli Esteri di un paese alleato della Repubblica Federale doveva sapere che c'era un termine da non usare: appunto il termine e il concetto di pangermanesimo […]».[89]

Should we ascribe the abovementioned comments as a good opportunity to criticise an Italian politician?

An accurate analysis of the articles published in September 1984 leads to the conclusion that this was not the unique reason behind the statements of the press. It looked as if the Italian press was developing a deeper approach to the German issue.[90] An accurate analysis also allows to identify some terms which were more often used in association with the word Germany, namely "Europe" and "understanding", whereas the use of negative terms still popular in 1977 dropped dramatically. In *La Stampa*, the Italian journalist Aldo Rizzo, tackled the root of the problem, insofar as he affirmed that the division of Germany was the result of the crimes commited during the Second World War. Nobody had the right to modify this division by the use of the force. Still, given the transformations of the previous years both in the Federal Government and in Germany society, he also added that one had to be more flexible in case the Bundesrepublik tried to modify the status quo by means other than military force.[91]

Vanna Vannuccini, journalist of *Repubblica*, did not only reaffirm this vision, but she also expressed the belief that the Federal Republic had demonstrated of having the capacity to draw a clear line between theory and reality. For a while already, Bonn had embraced a more mature approach to the divison of Germany.

---

[89] "Which is the link between the 'Pangermanism' and the 'German policy' of the team Kohl-Honecker? Which is the link between the demonstrations of the South Tyroleans nostalgic for Austria – which took place in Innsbruck some days ago – and the luckless experiment of Erich Honecker to act with a sort of greater autonomy outside the extremely rigid pattern of the Soviet world politics? What did the Foreign Minister want to say when he affirmed that we should not exaggerate in the dialogue between Eastern and Western Europe? Did he want to say that this could lead to a Fourth Reich? The Foreign Minister of a country allied to the Federal Republic had to know, after weeks of relentless Soviet propaganda on the revanchism of Bonn, that there was one word which should not be used: the word Pangermanism". See Sandro Viola, Sarebbe meglio chiedere scusa, *Repubblica*, 16.9.1984.
[90] See, for example, Alberto Ronchey, Un Muro per i secoli? *CdS*, 18.9.1984.
[91] See also Aldo Rizzo, La bugia vitale del popolo tedesco, *La Stampa*, 17.9.1984.

«Dopo le schizofrenie dell'era adenaueriana, parlare sempre di riunificazione e non pensarci mai, la maggioranza dei tedeschi si è identificata in questa politica ma non a tutti i prezzi. Non ad esempio al prezzo della propria libertà né a quello di rompere i legami con l'Occidente».[92]

This new vision expressed in the Italian press was no unconditional acceptance of the German goals, but rather an approach which critically analysed and discussed the different aspects of the course pursued in Bonn, expressing both positive and negative judgements.

On 18 September 1984, Vanna Vannuccini commented once again on the declarations of Andreotti and on the political rhetoric of Helmut Kohl[93], while Piero Sormani wondered whether some aspects of the political rhetoric of the German Chancellor had rightly given rise to the doubts of Andreotti:

«Kohl, sebbene non lo ammetta apertamente, si è sentito chiamato direttamente in causa dall'accenno di Andreotti al pangermanesimo; dopotutto, da quando è al potere, egli non fa che insistere sulla necessità della riunificazione della Germania, sia pure in modo pacifico e in tempi lontani, e alcuni suoi ministri sono giunti ad auspicare il ripristino dell'unità nazionale entro i confini del 1937».[94]

This picture, albeit brief, of the reactions to the 1984 declarations allows us to draw some useful conclusions for the next chapters.

Firstly, so far it has been found that in the Eighties traditional prejudices and stereotypes had neither been completely deleted nor fully replaced by new representations. Still, it has also been found that the Eighties set the stage for a riper approach. The Italian vision of Germany no longer dithered between recycling old stereotypes and merely lavishing words of praise on a single man, be it Konrad Adenauer or Willy Brandt. The Italian press was not indifferent to the Europeanization policy promoted by Chancellor Kohl, but it was also attentive to the existence of divergent views within the Federal Government, and to the

---

[92] "After the schizophrenia of the era of Adenauer, when everyone always spoke of reunification and never actually thought about it, the majority of the Germans have embraced this political approach, but not at any price. Not at the price of giving up their freedom, nor at the price of breaking the bonds with the Western World". See Vanna Vannuccini, Lo schiaffo italiano ai tedeschi, *Repubblica*, 15.9.1984.

[93] See Vanna Vannuccini, Pangermanesimo e riunificazione. Produce sospetti la retorica di Kohl, *Repubblica*, 19.9.1984.

[94] "Kohl does not admit it openly, but he had the impression of been called into question when Andreotti hinted at Pangermanism. After all, since his accession to power, he has placed constant emphasis on the reunification of Germany, even if by peaceful means and in a distant future. Some of his ministers have even called for the restoration of the national unity within the 1937 frontiers". See Pietro Sormani, A Bonn tutti si dicono soddisfatti, ma ognuno con una propria posizione, *CdS*, 18.9.1984.

contradictions introduced into the debate by the 1973 ruling of the German Constitutional Court.[95]

Secondly, it is undeniable that during the 1980s the category "past" applied to Germany had been weakened. The recurrence of the stereotypes attached to the category "past", and especially to National-Socialism, decreased significantly. In September 1984, it was used only twice in *La Stampa* and in the *Repubblica*, and only once in the Milan newspaper *Corriere della Sera*. The recurrence of stereotypes based on the category "Sekundärtugend" carried to their extreme, and the destructive consequences of the Second World War, were also dropped, whereas the use of the word Europe associated to Germany gained in importance both quantitatively and qualitatively. As every simplified image of Germany, the description of its participation to the European integration process as well was the result of a process of categorization which helped to simplify and systematize information. It was based on both a cognitive and an affective component, in this specific case a positive value judgment.

The Eighties set the stage for the year 1989, that is for a wide debate on the grounding of the abstractions and generalisations on which the stereotypes attached to Germany were based.[96] Therefore, they meant change, also in the realm of the press.[97] Positive results may had been achieved; it is though undeniable that the relationship between Italy and Germany was going through a delicate transitional stage. By 1989, the new associations had only partially been internalized and stabilized.

What impact did the 1989 earthquake have on this scenario?

---

[95] See chapter 2.2.

[96] See, for example, Leo Valiani, Le regole della democrazia, *CdS*, 18.9.1984.

[97] According to the scientific literature in this field, the same happened in Germany concerning the stereotypes attached to Italy. The articles written on some Italian politicians are a good example of this climate of change. See, in particular, Heinz-Joachim Fischer, Der Mutigste der Gemäßigten, *Frankfurter Allgemeine Zeitung*, 25.6.1985; Hansjakob Stehle, Ein Moralist der die Ohnmacht kennt, *Die Zeit*, 28.6.1985; Cossiga liest an der Bonner Universität, *Frankfurter Allgemeine Zeitung*, 23.4.1986; Friedrich Meichsner, Aus dem sonnigen Süden kommt Cossiga in die Wärme am Rhein, *Die Welt*, 23.4.1986, in: ACDP, Abteilung Pressedokumentation.

III. ITALY BETWEEN *DEUTSCHE FRAGE* AND RE-UNIFICATION

1989–1990

7. Autumn 1989: The Unbelievable becomes Possible
From Disbelief to the Quest for a Strategy

М.С. Горбачев:
Если мы начнем пересматривать итги войны, то сразу встанет вопрос как быть с границами? Ето очень опасный путь. Пусть Европа расвиваеться, пусть мир джижется вперед и будуший мир даст ответ нам етот вопрос. Я прямо сказал что воссоединение ФРГ и ГДР не актуальный вопрос». ДЖ. Андреотти: «Ето абсолютно верно.[1]
(M.S. Gorbačëv to G. Andreotti)

On which specific issues did Giulio Andreotti agree with his Soviet interlocutor?

How did he react to the "German events", also in light of his comments of 1984?

And, last but not least, what kind of approach did he develop towards the earthquake in Eastern Germany?

The abovementioned Russian quotation is part of a rich collection of Soviet records released by the Gorbačëv foundation approximately a decade ago. It refers to the 29 November meeting of Rome between Prime Minister Giulio Andreotti and the Soviet leader Michael Sergeevič Gorbačëv. The summit had been planned long before the fall of the Berlin Wall; under the new circumstances it became, however, an occasion for a first significant exchange of views on the facts that had unfolded in November. As a result, it has been selected to be the end point of this first chapter of Part Three. The main focus of this chapter is, in fact, on the transformations which preceded the 9 November watershed, and then on the Italian reactions to such an event during the whole month of November.

The main challenge faced in the following pages consists in the attempt to place the Italian actions and reactions to the fall of the Berlin Wall in a broader European context of changes, in order to have the best conditions possible to

---

[1] See Doc. 54, *Из беседы Горбачевас Дж. Андреотти, Rome*, 29.11.1989, in: Alexander Galkin (ed.), *Михаил Горбачев и гирманский вопрос, сборник документов* 1986–1991, Moskva 1996. In the following pages the German translation of this collection of documents will be used, unless the original version is preferred to the translation proposed of a specific document. For the German translation see Andreas Hilger (ed.)/Joachim Glaubitz (translator), Michail Gorbatschow und die deutsche Frage: Sowjetische Dokumente 1986–1991, München 2011. "Gorbačëv: if we start overturning the final decisions of the war, one question is bound to be raised: What about the frontiers? It is a dangerous path. Let Europe and the world further develop, and the future will provide an answer to this question. I have said it outright: the reunification of the Bundesrepublik and the DDR is not a topical issue. Andreotti: I absolutely agree with you".

discuss a comment constantly repeated in the scientific literature: Italy was completely taken by surprise and was totally unprepared to face the events.

Fig. 11: Gorbačëv official State-Visit to Rome (November 1989). Istituto Sturzo, Archive Andreotti (copyright AGI)

The issues addressed in section two concerning the Italian vision of the *deutsche Frage* with its inherent contradictions, and the new trends that emerged in the relationship between Rome and Bonn, are now to be used to support the analysis of the Italian stance, and to try and comprehend the politics behind-the-scenes which are implied by the affirmation that Italy was fully unprepared. The obstacles on the road to the quest for an effective strategy will be discussed together with the specific elements which could give to European partners the impression that the Italian strategy was weak and contradictory.

In sum, section three in its entirety – chapters seven, eight and nine – makes extensive use of the stock of knowledge gathered so far to address the events which unfolded from November 1989 until October 1990. In this section, as anticipated in the first introductory chapter[2], the events are divided into three different groups according to the main turning points of the Italian stance. Chapter seven covers the time-period up to November 1989, whereas chapter Eight deals

---

[2] See footnote 46, ch. 1.2.

with the events taking place from November 1989 until February-March 1990. Chapter nine outlines the developments from spring 1990.

Chapter seven is based on an approach from the general to the particular as if the events were part of a system of Chinese boxes or better, a Russian nesting doll, a *Matryoshka*, as an homage to the importance of the Soviet Union in this initial phase of the Italian strategy. The Matryoshka is a traditional Russian set of wooden dolls of decreasing size placed one inside the other. Each figure has its own "identity", but it also forms part of a whole. This chapter deals at first with the biggest Matryoshka doll: the distinctive features of the international context. Then, it moves to details of the dynamics in Eastern Europe and in the DDR – above all in light of the perception which Italy had of them – to finally look inside the smallest nesting doll, the Italian political and social picture and its most prominent actors. Not only is the stance of the Italian *presidente del Consiglio* Giulio Andreotti to be accurately discussed, but also the perception of the Italian Head of State Francesco Cossiga – whose vision of the German issue has already been the object of a thorough reconstruction – and of the newly appointed Foreign Minister Gianni de Michelis, is to be considered. The contribution of the Italian Ambassador to Bonn, Marcello Guidi, will be also an object of discussion, albeit more briefly.

In summer 1989, Marcello Guidi had been selected to replace Raniero Vanni D'Archirafi as head of the Italian Embassy in Bonn. At a time when new means of transport and communication had made it easier and quicker for political leaders to have direct exchanges of views, diplomacy – and not only the Italian one – was subjected to a process of transformation of its role, and of progressive adaptation to new environmental conditions. It does not follow though that the mediating role played by diplomats had fully lost its original *raison d'être*. Quite the contrary, this role of intermediation between the country which the Ambassador represented and the country where he had been sent to was still of importance in the late 1980s, with regard to the Italian-German relationship too.

In conclusion, the aim pursued in this last section does not consist in merely providing a clear and detailed as possible description of the events. The aim pursued rather consists in identifying and attentively discussing their main turning points as a test case for the level of maturity attained by the Italian vision of the "German issue". This long path will finally allow to provide an answer to the question proposed in the very title of this work, as to whether Germany must have continued to be a divided country.

7.1 Reaching to 9 November 1989 through a Mastryoshke System

"Am Anfang war Gorbatschow. Seine Politik setzte einen ungeplanten Prozess im Gang, der […] die deutsche Wiedervereinigung erst möglich machte".[3]

With these words the historian Andreas Rödder opened the book which he devoted to the road of German re-unification. Michail Sergeevič Gorbačëv, the fifty-four years old *sorcerer's apprentice,* – as Andreas Rödder himself qualified him at the beginning of the abovementioned text[4] – seemed to combine his approach to politics with a constant struggle to reconcile the irreconcilable: Marxism with market economy and Leninism with democracy.

Political openings and an unmistakable aversion to dogmatic positions were just one side of his complex personality. The other side consisted in a combination of unresolved contradictions, indecision and discontinuity. In 1985 very few Western politicians believed that his appointment was the sign of a radical shift in Soviet politics. After years of tensions and uncertainties in East-West relations – as a result of events such as the invasion of Afghanistan, the euromissiles issue and the upheavals in Poland – the peculiar profile of the Soviet leader gave, however, the hope that a new détente and a climate of cooperation could blossom again *vis-à-vis* the Soviet Union.

Bettino Craxi, François Mitterrand and Margaret Thatcher were some among the European leaders who from the very beginning sensed this approaching change and therefore expressed both curiosity for – and interest in – the approach of their recently appointed Soviet interlocutor. During a meeting in December 1984, some months before the official appointment of Gorbačëv, the British Prime Minister had allegedly commented: "I like Mr. Gorbachev […] We can do business together".[5] By contrast, German Chancellor Helmut Kohl had initially opted for a more cautious and guarded approach.[6]

---

[3] "In the beginning was Gorbačëv. His politics set in motion an unplanned process which in a few years led to the collapse of the Soviet empire and made even the German reunification possible". See Andreas Rödder, Deutschland einig Vaterland. Die Geschichte der Wiedervereinigung, München 2009, p. 15.

[4] See Ibid.

[5] See James Sheehan, The Transformation of Europe and the End of the Cold War, in: Jeffrey A. Engel (ed.), The Fall of the Berlin Wall, Oxford, Oxford University Press, 2009, pp. 36–68, 46–48.

[6] Even after the first months, following the appointment of the new Soviet leader, relations between Moscow and Bonn did not proceed without difficulties. It was in fact a complex period also in light of the Soviet fears that under the pressure of mounting economic difficulties, the DDR could slip into the embrace of Western Germany. See Doc. 1, Protokoll der Sitzung des Politbüros vom 27. März 1986, Moscow 1986, in: Michail Gorbatschow und die deutsche Frage: Sowjetische Dokumente 1986–1991, München 2011, (Archiv der Gorbačëv-Stiftung Фонд [Bestand] № 2, опись [Verzeichnis] № 2). Besides, on 27 October 1986, in an interview given to the magazine *Newsweek*, Helmut Kohl allegedly made an unfortunate comparison between the secretary of the Soviet Communist Party and Joseph Goebbels, namely Minister of Propaganda in Nazi Germany. Although the

From the moment when the fifty-four-year-old Gorbačëv took the lead of power in the Kremlin, in March 1985, he strongly advocated for a reform process. This process certainly accelerated, but did not cause the upheavals in Eastern Europe which finally led to the demise of the Warsaw Pact and of the Soviet behemoth with it.

Certainly, the Sorcerer's Apprentice was back then in March 1985 a reformer, perhaps also a visionary[7], but he was neither an outsider nor a revolutionary man.[8] In 1985, the "transfer of power" had, in fact, been carefully organized at the highest level, while throughout the previous years Gorbačëv had constantly strengthened his position and his influence within the Politburo where from 1984, due to the delicate health conditions of his predecessor Černenko, he had practically chaired every significant meeting. During the first phase of his leadership, Gorbačëv was in all respects an instance of a long-term Soviet archetype, even though

---

episode resulted in a bit of coldness in the months to come, it did not have such a significant impact on the medium-term relationship between Moscow and Bonn. The wide documentation kept at the Gorbačëv foundation shows that ever since 1986, the Bundesrepublik was considered in Moscow a "gewaltige Macht" (big power) which could not be ignored. In the short term, this Soviet coldness was, therefore, the result of the determination to "teach Bonn a lesson" and, perhaps, to also safeguard relations with the SPD, which in 1986 was in the opposition. To attain this target, Moscow had defined a dual strategy: a cautious approach to keep good relations with the German Left, together with the search for a *modus vivendi* with the new German leadership guided by Helmut Kohl. According to Soviet records, a good understanding with Kohl could also have positive secondary effects on the interaction between the Kremlin and the German SPD, insofar as it would demonstrate to the SPD that it had no more the monopoly of contacts with the Socialist countries. See Doc. 6, Protokoll der Sitzung des Politbüros des ZK der KPdSU 24. Juli 1986 über die Ergebnisse der Genscher-Reise Aufzeichnung A. S. Cernajev, in: Michail Gorbatschow und die deutsche Frage: Sowjetische Dokumente 1986–1991, München 2011. Despite the wave of sympathy showed by Western German citizens towards the Soviet leader between 1988–1989, and the good understanding which eventually developed between Kohl and Gorbačëv, the ties between the two leaders never had the warmth of the relations which Helmut Kohl had with other European leaders or that other European leaders had with Gorbačëv. Kohl himself revealed to harbour mixed feelings towards the Secretary of the Soviet Communist Party, meaning that he believed him to be a reformer, but not a true democrat. See Hanns Jürgen Küsters/Daniel Hofmann (eds.), Deutsche Einheit: Sonderedition aus den Akten des Bundeskanzleramtes 1989/1990, München 1998, introduction. See also Svetlana Savranskaya, Masterpieces of History: The Peaceful End of the Cold War in Europe 1989, New York – Budapest 2010.

[7] When M.S. Gorbačëv took the lead in the Kremlin, he embodied a new generation compared to the leaders who had come before him. The novelty of the situation was evident in the approach to international politics of the "new guard" which the Soviet leader had chosen displayed and even in their physical appearance. Ambassador Visconti di Modrone remembered in the interview given on 12.05.2016 that the decline of the Soviet Union was more and more evident, also in the person of its last leaders, whose faces were impenetrable and awful, whereas Gorbačëv looked like a normal man.

[8] See, in particular, Jens Hacker, Michail Gorbatschow und die engere »sozialistische Gemeinschaft«, in: *Aus Politik und Zeitgeschichte* 19–20 (1990), pp. 30–39. See also Gabriel Gorodetsky (ed.), Soviet Foreign Policy 1917–1991, Tel Aviv University 1994.

he applied to such a tradition a different tone. Neither the perestrojka nor the "new thinking", which are the two main axes of his policy course at internal and international level, were completely new proposals. On the contrary, in the first stages of application, from 1986 until 1987, the perestrojka shared, for instance, many similarities with the project for political and economic reform introduced by Andropov between 1982 and 1984.[9]

The "new thinking", as well as rediscovered ideas and practices, had been discussed for at least a decade within the Academy of Sciences and the army. As far as, for instance, Germany was concerned, the idea supported by Falin and by members of the KGB in 1969 had been retrived to the ongoing debate, meaning that it was desirable for the Soviet Union to avoid a climate of tension with Bonn and to leave the Bundesrepublik to expand its economic influence beyond the Iron Curtain.[10]

The "new thinking" had been discussed ever since March 1985 in the inner circle of Gorbačëv's closest advisors: Eduard Shevardnadze – appointed Foreign Minister in July 1985 – Aleksandr Yakovlev and Anatoly Chernyaev. But it was not until the 26th Congress of the Central Committee in February 1986 that the "new thinking" was officially launched. At its initial level of development, it merely proposed to resort to new practices and diplomatic concepts in dealing with the Americans.[11] Moscow needed vast resources to implement the necessary economic and political internal reforms, but it was also forced to shift its priorities from military expenditures to productive expenditures to have a chance of success. This would only be possible in a climate of détente and better understanding with Washington. In 1986, all other international objectives were, therefore, in a position subordinated to this key target, including the concept of the "European Common House".[12] Back then, it was still a vague and undetermined programme launched for the first time by Gorbačëv himself in 1984 while he was on a diplomatic mission in London.[13]

Furthermore, this "new thinking" was born in an atmosphere of growing rivalry among three different schools of thought: a progressive approach to far-

---

[9] See Georges-Henri Soutou, La guerre de Cinquante Ans. Les relations Est-Ouest 1943–1990, Paris 2001, p. 664.

[10] See Doc. 3, Protokoll der Sitzung des Politbüros vom 13. Juni 1986, in: Michail Gorbatschow und die deutsche Frage: Sowjetische Dokumente 1986–1991, München 2011 (in the Soviet edition the document belongs to Bestand 2, Verzeichnis 2).

[11] See Marie-Pierre Rey, La Russie dans les représentations politiques et mentales, pp. 23–25.

[12] The importance of this idea was stressed two years later, in October 1986, during a State visit to France.

[13] See Georges-Henri Soutou, La maison commune européenne : Tactique et stratégie, in: "Géopolitique" n. 36, hivers 1991–1992. See also Marie-Pierre Rey, La Russie dans les représentations politiques et mentales, p. 25. According to Marie-Pierre Rey, in this first phase the Soviet leadership applied a strategy of *divide et impera* in its relations with Western Europe. The same conclusion has been drawn by Anatoly Chernyaev in his memoirs.

reaching projects, a more gradual and tactical approach proposing the implementation of reforms which in the end would not alter the very foundations of the Soviet economic and political structure, and a traditional orthodox vision, which rejected every change. The first approach was supported in the mid-1980s by Eduard Shevardnadze and Aleksandr Yakovlev, the first in his capacity of Foreign Minister and the second as director of the Institute for International Relations. The second approach corresponded to the stance of influential circles within the KGB and of prominent politicians such as Falin, the person in charge of the relations with Germany. Gorbačëv had to try and act to maintain a balance in this unsteady situation, at first by means of an overall tactical approach towards Western Europe, which, however, changed significantly between 1987–1988. His declarations[14] of 1987 in the Politburo confirm this change: "Europe is our business. There our interests are enormous [...] you have to understand that Western Europe is our essential partner".[15] The new direction embraced by the Soviet leader became even more evident on the occasion of the July 1988 conference organized on the premises of the Soviet Foreign Ministry with the participation of both the most prominent personalities involved in Foreign policy and the second most important figure in the KGB.[16]

The conclusions reached at the end of the conference were further extended in the speech given by the Soviet leader in the UN on 7 December 1988. Gorbačëv called for a significant reduction of the burden of ideologies on international relations.[17] Internal changes in the Soviet Union, and above all the so called "historical debate"[18], stressed that the words uttered in December 1988 went beyond the usual rhetoric statements. Through the official acknowledgement in 1988 of the existence of the protocol annexed to the Molotov-Ribbentrop Pact (23 August 1939) – which until then the Soviet Propaganda had always denied – the historical debate had stepped over the line of solely cosmetic changes to get to the heart of the Soviet ideology.[19]

The issues presented in the previous paragraphs are a general framework in which more detailed information concerning the origins and the significance of the "European Common House" are to be added in the next sub-chapter. This is

---

[14] His exchange of views with Foreign Minister Hans-Dietrich Genscher on the occasion of his visit to the Bundesrepublik, and also the contents of his meeting with the German Head of State Richard von Weizsäcker in Moscow in July 1987, are part of this new atmosphere.

[15] See Marie-Pierre Rey, La Russie dans les représentations politiques et mentales, p. 26.

[16] See Georges-Henri Soutou, La maison commune européenne, p. 687.

[17] See Andreas Rödder, Deutschland einig Vaterland, p. 18.

[18] See Joachim Hösler, Perestroika und Historie. Zur Erosion des sowjetischen Geschichtsbildes, in: Helmut Altrichter (ed.), Gegen Erinnerung, Geschichte als politisches Argument im Transformationsprozeß Ostmittel- und Südeuropas, München 2006, pp. 1–27.

[19] See Andreas Rödder, Deutschland einig Vaterland, p. 17.

a necessary step in light of both the choice to analyse the Italian reaction to the fall of the Wall in connection with its vision of the "German question", and of the differences between the Italian and the German Ostpolitik.

On the one hand, it has been affirmed in chapter two[20] that together with a number of common features, each European country had at the end of the Second World War its own set of critical elements vis-à-vis the *deutsche Frage*. These elements resulted from its geographical and political specific conditions as well as from its historical inheritance. It can now be added that the vision which each country had of the *deutsche Frage* did not stand forever still, but rather had a dynamic and unstable nature. In other words, the gradual evolution of the new concept of the European Common House further enriched the "German issue", and above all the vision which Italy had of it, with new reference points.

On the other hand, chapter five[21] has remarked that the Italian Ostpolitik, unlike its German counterpart, was in all respects an expression of the Italian Foreign policy. The gradual evolution of the European Common House project further accentuated the discrepancies between the *Deutschlandfrage* of Bonn and the *deutsche Frage* of Rome.

a) European Common House versus deutsche Frage
Throughout the second half of the Eighties, the relations with the Bundesrepublik – which reached their peak in June 1989 on the occasion of the official visit to Bonn of the Soviet leader – were always a key element in the overall reform project promoted by Gorbačëv. As troubles in Berlin after the Second World War had been a sort of "litmus paper" of the Cold War, so relations with Bonn or, to be even more precise, the *Deutschlandfrage*, seemed to be the "litmus paper" of the level of development reached by the European Common House.

At the beginning of 1985, the possibility of a German re-unification was not even addressed in Moscow, even though the reformers were aware that some changes were unavoidable and that an enhanced flexibility in the approach of Pankow was also necessary. In all likelihood, Gorbačëv had sufficient information at his disposal on the economic and political difficulties of the DDR; still, the DDR conundrum, though vexing, did not alter the Soviet determination to confine itself to the implementation of cosmetic changes both in its relations with Germany, and more generally with Western States.[22]

---

[20] See ch. 2.1.
[21] See ch. 5.2.
[22] See Doc. 9, Gespräch Gorbačevs mit dem Staatsratsvorsitzenden Honecker, dem DKP-Vorsitzenden Mies und dem SEW-Vorsitzenden Schmitt am 3. Oktober 1986, in: Michail Gorbatschow und die deutsche Frage: Sowjetische Dokumente 1986–1991, München 2011 (Archiv der Gorbačëv-Stiftung, Bestand 1, Verzeichnis 1): "S. Gorbačev: In letzter Zeit hatten wir zahlreiche

The year 1987 marked, however, a watershed both in methods and scope of the relations with Germany, while the European Common House – which until then had been nothing more than a slogan – turned into a more efficient tactical instrument to ensure better European coordination between the blocs. This turning-point in the nature of the Soviet reform project deserves specific attention.

During the 29 January 1987 Politburo meeting, the tenor of the remarks concerning the DDR decay festered fears that a general process of reform could no longer be enough to mend social and political divisions. The eventuality of a *Führungswechsel* in the DDR was also timidly addressed.[23] One month after the meeting, Eduard Shevardnadze affirmed:

> „Ševardnadze: Die Idee einer geeinten deutschen Nation lebt in der Psychologie und im Denken sogar der Kommunisten. Sie beginnen mit den Westdeutschen anzubändeln. Sie kritisieren die BRD nicht. Und es geht nicht nur um wirtschaftliche Interessiertheit. Die Idee eines geeinten Deutschland ersucht eine ernsthafte, wissenschaftliche Untersuchung."[24]

Gespräche mit Vertretern Westdeutschlands. Hier in Moskau insbesondere mit Genscher und dann direkt in der Bundesrepublik, […]. Bei diesen Unterredungen verfolgen unsere Gesprächspartner beharrlich den Gedanken, dass die Entwicklung der Lage in Europa insgesamt in hohem Masse davon abhängt, wie sich die Beziehungen zwischen den Deutschen und Russland entwickeln. Natürlich muss man sich darüber klarwerden, was sie im Sinne haben, […]. Aber eines ist klar: Die Zusammenarbeit zwischen der UdSSR und der DDR hat eine gewaltige Bedeutung für die sozialistische Gemeinschaft, ja, auch für ganz Europa. […]". (Gorbačëv: We have recently had numerous talks with representatives of Western Germany. In Moscow with Genscher and then also in the Federal Republic, […]. In these talks our interlocutors persistently pursued the idea that the developments in Europe mainly depend from the development of the relations between Germans and Russians. To be sure, we must clearly figure out what they mean, […]. But one thing is clear: the cooperation between the Soviet Union and the DDR is of great significance for the socialist community, also for Europe as a whole. […]). This quotation forms part of the text concerning a high-level meeting between Soviet senior officials and DDR politicians. Moscow seemed very eager to reassure its Eastern German interlocutors concerning its increased number of contacts with the Bundesrepublik, above all with Foreign Minister Hans-Dietrich Genscher.

[23] "Gorbačëv: Wir haben Meinungsverschiedenheiten mit ihnen im Bereich des Überbaus. Honecker setzt unsere Selbstverwaltung mit der jugoslawischen gleich: So schlecht kennen wir einander!". (Gorbačëv: We disagree with them on almost everything. Honecker equate our administration with the Yugoslavian one. So badly do we know each other!). See Doc. 10, Protokoll der Sitzung des Politbüros, Aufzeichnung A. S. Cernjaev, 29.1.1987, in: Michail Gorbatschow und die deutsche Frage: Sowjetische Dokumente 1986–1991, München 2011 (Archiv der Gorbačëv-Stiftung, Bestand 2, Verzeichnis 2). See also Doc. 14 concerning the meeting between Gorbačëv and Honecker, 28.5.1987. New motives of tension emerged in this meeting, and, between the lines, we can also perceive the Soviet fears that Pankow's approach could have negative effects both on the Soviet-Western Germans relationship, and on the success which a sound development of the concept of the Common European House could provide.

[24] "The idea of a united German nation haunts even the psychology and the thinking of the Communists. They begin to fraternize with Western Germany. They no more criticize the

Certainly, Eduard Shevardnadze represented in 1987 the spearhead advocating for reforms in the USSR. This means that his perception was not widely shared; still, it was noteworthy that beyond the strict boundaries of academics, the subject of re-unification had been finally addressed, at first briefly in the aforementioned comments, and then in more depth in the meetings that did follow. In July 1987, the German issue was one again addressed, this time in connection with the broader issue of the relations with the Bundesrepublik and with Western Europe:

> „Dobrynin: Der Hauptgedanke von Michail Sergeevič ist, den gesamten Komplex der Beziehungen BRD-UdSSR neu zu interpretieren. Wir verwirklichen das und begeben uns in einen umfangreichen Dialog mit einem der bedeutendsten Länder. [...]
> Gorbačev: Eigentlich, Genossen, betrifft dieser Besuch eine der wichtigsten Ausrichtungen unserer Politik. Die BRD ist das bedeutendste Land Westeuropas.
> Wir haben ihnen zu verstehen gegeben, dass wir mit einer Revision der Ergebnisse des Krieges nicht einverstanden sind, aber dass wir bereit sind, ihnen weit entgegen zu kommen [...] Auf diese Weise haben wir den ersten Schritt getan. [...] Die BRD wird natürlich fürchten, sowohl Amerika als auch Frankreich durch ein neues Rapallo zu erschrecken. Deshalb dürfen wir sie auch nicht unter Druck setzen. Obwohl in Wirklichkeit von keinem Rapallo die Rede ist. Wir haben eine andere historische Zeit, andere Bedingungen.
> Ich denke, dass es sich lohnt, sich den Deutschen anzunähern, auch wenn es ein Risiko ist. Und, versteht sich, wir dürfen Frankreich und England nicht vergessen. Hier muss alles in der Norm bleiben. Weiter, weiterarbeiten. Ja, und es gibt Österreich und Finnland, mit denen wir eng verbunden sind. [...] Es gibt aber auch die BRD – das ist eine andere Sache. [...].“[25]

Bundesrepublik. And this is not just about economic interests. The idea of a united Germany requires a serious scientific investigation". See Doc. 12, Protokoll der Sitzung des Politbüros, Aufzeichnung A. S. Cernjaev 12.2.1987, in: Michail Gorbatschow und die deutsche Frage: Sowjetische Dokumente 1986–1991, München 2011 (Archiv der Gorbačëv-Stiftung, Bestand 2, Verzeichnis 2). The document should be read together with document 15 concerning the 4 June 1987 Politburo meeting, where the "attractiveness" of the Bundesrepublik was addressed.

[25] "Dobrynin: The main goal of Michail Sergeevič consists in rethinking the entire complex of the relations between the Bundesrepublik and the USSR. We will carry it into effect and we will get into a comprehensive engagement with one of the most important countries. [...] Gorbačëv: Actually, comrades, this meeting concerns one of the most important guidelines of our politics. The Bundesrepublik is the most influential country in Western Europe. We have made them know that we would not agree with a revision of War decisions, but we have also made them know that we are ready to be flexible [...] We have thus taken the first step. [...] The Bundesrepublik will certainly be afraid of scaring both America and France with a new Rapallo. That is why we must not put pressure on them. Even if actually there is no talks of a Rapallo. We are currently living in different historic times, under different conditions. I think that a rapprochement to the Germans is worth a try, even though it is a risk. And, it goes without saying, we must not forget France and England. In the latter case, nothing should change. Keep on working and working. To be sure, there are also Austria and Finland, we are closely connected to them. [...] There is also the

Since 1987, the Soviet Union also showed the determination to leave behind old fixed ideological schemes in order to try to understand the mechanisms that were at work within the European integration process.[26] Aleksandr Yakovlev had until then strongly advocated for the creation of an Institute for Western Europe which was established in 1988 under the direction of Vitali Zhurkin[27]. Its objective was not to attack the European Community, but rather to conduct an in-depth study of its functioning to verify whether it could be a useful model to reform the COM-ECON.

In February 1989, the Institute finally delivered its report to the Academy of Sciences and it proposed the establishment of a Pan-European system to operate within the broader framework of a Pan-European security system which would be based on structures connecting NATO to the Warsaw Pact. The report was also the crowning of a process which had lead the European Common House from the level of a slogan to the higher level of a tactical instrument. It had then turned it into a political course whose aim was the promotion of a rapprochement between Communism and Western social-democracies as a precondition to the end of East-West confrontation. In May 1988, Gorbačëv commented to SPD member Vogel:

> „Gorbačev: Ich möchte noch einen Gedanken über Europa äußern. Es ist notwendig, dass wir ein einheitliches Verständnis hinsichtlich eines bestimmten Problems herstellen. Wir hören: ‚Wir müssen die Spaltung Europas überwinden'. [...] Wir sagen: Lasst uns ein gemeinsames europäisches Haus bauen unter Respektierung der Souveränität, der Wahl der Gesellschaftsform und der territorialen Realitäten. Aber einige Forderungen nach der Überwindung der Spaltung Europas zielen

---

Bundesrepublik – that's another matter. [...]". See Doc. 17, Protokoll der Sitzung des Politbüros, Aufzeichnung A. S. Cernjaev 16.7.1987, in: Michail Gorbatschow und die deutsche Frage: Sowjetische Dokumente 1986–1991, München 2011 (Archiv der Gorbačëv-Stiftung, Bestand 2, Verzeichnis 2). It relates to the meeting between Gorbačëv and Strauss in December 1987 and it stresses the desire to improve relations with the Bundesrepublik, but also with its most prominent Länder, such as Bavaria.

[26] The approach to European Integration proposed in summer 1957 by the Soviet Institute for World Economy and International Relations stressed that it was an alliance between the Vatican and reactionary forces subordinated to NATO. European integration was therefore considered the economic arm of NATO, namely a tactical attempt to strengthen the position of imperialism against the Soviet Union. Five years later, the Academy did recognize that the Common Market was in all respects an economic entity with its own identity, even though contrary to the kind of development promoted by Moscow, and therefore reprehensible. In spite of some attempts to improve relations with the EC, the USSR never altered the approach officially taken in 1957 up to the coming to power of M.S. Gorbačëv.

[27] See Maria Eleonora Gusconi, L'Italia e la cooperazione politica europea nella prima metà degli anni Ottanta, pp. 57–82.

darauf, dass einige Staaten verschwinden. Das ist unannehmbar und unrealistisch. Man muss auch in dieser Frage Realist sein."[28]

The core of the European Common House lied in the possibility of reconciling two different targets. It was in fact supposed to provide a "common roof" where a peaceful coexistence and cooperation between Western and Eastern Europe would be possible by means of political and economic transformations. Western and Eastern Germany were to draw substantial benefits from such new environmental conditions. Still, it was also a means to not put at stake the existing territorial realities.[29]

The DDR was, therefore, the main obstacle and risk to the implementation and success of the European Common House. It was an obstacle because the failure to apply an effective plan for reforms would have made it incompatible with the new framework of coexistence. And it was also a risk because its demise would have thrown open the door to dangerous territorial changes which would have jeopardized the European Common House itself.

The core question was, therefore, whether the first scenario, the implementation of far-reaching reforms in the DDR, was feasible, and also whether it was possible to hold the reins of such a process, thus avoiding the second scenario: the demise of the DDR and its slipping into the Bundesrepublik embrace.

Archival records provide evidence to support the theory that in 1987, two years before the fall of the Berlin Wall, Gorbačëv still believed that a process of reform in the DDR was feasible as a precondition to the success of his European Common House:

> „Gorbačëv: Vom politischen Standpunkt aus ist die Lage klar, aber rein menschlich ist sie dramatisch. Ich habe mir deswegen auch Sorgen gemacht. Ich hatte im Großen und Ganzen kein schlechtes Verhältnis zu Honecker, aber in letzter Zeit schien es, als sei er blind. Denn wenn er sich vor zwei, drei Jahren aus eigener

---

[28] "Gorbačëv: I wish to express an idea about Europe. It is necessary to reach a consistent agreement regarding a certain issue. We hear: 'We must overcome the division of Europe'. [...] We say: Let build a Common European House while respecting sovereignty, the choice of the social organisation and territorial integrity. But certain demands as regards the overcoming of the European division aim at the disappearance of certain states. That's unacceptable and unrealistic. Also on this matter we must be realistic". See Doc. 22, Gespräch Gorbačevs mit dem SPD-Vorsitzenden Vogel, 11.5.1988, in: Michail Gorbatschow und die deutsche Frage: Sowjetische Dokumente 1986–1991, München 2011 (Archiv der Gorbačëv-Stiftung, Bestand 1, Verzeichnis 1).

[29] One year later, Gorbačëv showed more flexibility in speaking of the existing territorial realities, even though he did not envisage the hypothesis of a German re-unification in the short and medium term. See Doc. 42, Gespräch Gorbačevs mit Bundeskanzler Kohl, 14.7.1989, and Doc. 44, Pressekonferenz Gorbačevs in Bonn, 15.7.1989, both in: Michail Gorbatschow und die deutsche Frage: Sowjetische Dokumente 1986–1991, München 2011 (Archiv der Gorbačëv-Stiftung, Bestand 1, Verzeichnis 1).

Initiative auf die unerlässlichen Veränderungen in der Politik eingelassen hätte, wäre alles in vielerlei Hinsicht anders. [...] Aber [...] er hörte auf, die realen Prozesse in der Welt und im eigenen Land zu sehen. Das ist ein menschliches Drama, aber da Honecker eine sehr hohe Position bekleidete, hat es sich in ein politisches Drama entwickelt.
[...]
Krenz: Als Motto unseres Plenums haben wir gewählt: ,Der Wahrheit direkt ins Auge sehen'. Aber wenn man die ganze Wahrheit so darlegen würde, wie sie ist, dann wäre das ein Schock."[30]

In sum, the *Deutschlandfrage* was both at the core of the European Common House and its testing ground. This does not imply though that the European Common House had an interesting profile for the sole *Bundesrepublik*. On the contrary, it was an object of fascination in several European governments, starting from Rome. It exerted its influence on the Italian Foreign policy through two separate but related channels of transmission. The first one consisted in the bilateral ties between Rome and Moscow and its results on the Italian vision of the "German question", whereas the second one was related to the approach taken vis-à-vis the European Common House within the EPC, as a forum for coordination among Member States.[31]

As for the first channel of transmission, Rome had developed a marked interest for stronger ties with the world beyond the Iron Curtain[32] long before the

---

[30] "Gorbačëv: From a political point of view, the situation is pretty clear, but in strictly human terms it is a drama. That is why I am worried. Overall, I had no bad relations to Honecker, but recently he seems to be blind. Had he engaged two or three years ago on his own initiative in the inevitable transformations of politics, everything would in many respects be different. [...] But [...] he shut up about seeing the real processes in the world and in his own country. This is a human drama, but, as Honecker had a very high position, it has become a political drama as well. [...] Krenz: The slogan we chose for our plenum is, 'to look the truth in the eye'. But if we described reality just as it is, this would be a shock". See Doc. 52, Gespräch M.S. Gorbačevs mit E. Krenz, 1.11.1989, in: Michail Gorbatschow und die deutsche Frage: Sowjetische Dokumente 1986–1991, München 2011 (Archiv der Gorbačëv-Stiftung, Bestand 1, Verzeichnis 2).

[31] Regarding the EPC see, in particular, Frank R. Pfetsch, Die Entwicklung der Europäischen Politischen Zusammenarbeit. Zwischen Identität und Handlungsfähigkeit, in: Franz Knipping/Matthias Schönwald (eds.), Aufbruch zum Europa der zweiten Generation. Die europäische Einigung 1969–1984, Trier 2004, pp. 115–130.

[32] According to ISTAT data, trading with Eastern European countries improved between 1988–1989 also as a result of the great activism carried out by Italy in the previous years. Both in absolute and percentage terms, trading with Bulgaria and the DDR had increased (respectively by 41% and 32%). This data is, however, to be considered in comparison with date of the previous years. This comparison points out that previous levels of exchanges with Bulgaria and the DDR were particularly low, as a result the increase in trading with Poland and Hungary was far more relevant. See ILS, AGA, section URSS, b.695, ISTAT data until May 1989.

appointment of M.S. Gorbačëv.[33] Still, since his appointment, the Soviet Foreign policy seemed to be prompted by an enhanced dynamism, with greater interest for Western European partners[34], together with a desire for renewal and political updating, which at the beginning of 1987 had already spread to Soviet diplomacy in its entirety.[35]

> «[…] Si osserva che è la prima volta che i Sovietici hanno voluto discutere con noi a livello alti funzionari temi economici di carattere generale [...] se ne trae una conferma del nuovo orientamento sovietico emerso dopo l'avvento di Gorbaciov. [...] La Piristroika [sic!] (trasformazione) è un processo complesso che dovrà investire tutti i settori della vita nazionale. Non si tratta solo di un problema di efficienza economica, poiché mutamenti profondi sono necessari anche nel settore culturale, politico, sociale e amministrativo».[36]

Italian observers were fully aware that in the beginning all this desire for change was mainly the expression of the imperative need to break the state of

---

[33]See also Michail Sergeevič Gorbačëv, Erinnerungen, translated from Russian into German by Petrowitsch Gorodestki, Berlin, 1996, pp. 656.

[34] Since 1985, bilateral relations between Rome and Moscow were enhanced both politically and economically. Still, economic results did not always meet the Italian expectations. In 1988–1989, bilateral trading was on a path of decline. According to Soviet data, in 1989 trade had dropped by 13% compared with 1988, and exports had decreased by nearly 20%. Despite some differences in the methods for calculating, Italian data confirms this negative trend, whereas exchanges with Bonn had undergone a genuine improvement. Trading with Paris had also increased, though not so significantly. At the beginning of 1989 Rome had, therefore, lost its third place among the main trading partners of the Soviet Union. The only relevant exception to this gloomy picture concerned "mixed companies" which had nearly doubled. See, in particular, Telegramma sugli incontri tra Ruggiero e Katuchev, Italian Embassy to Moscow, 18.10.1988, signed Sergio Romano. ILS, AGA, section URSS, b.689. Good political relations were also a stepping stone to improve exchanges between the two countries. See also Telegramma dall'ambasciata italiana a Mosca, Appunto per l'on. Ministro, 5 aprile 1989, sulla visita a Mosca del ministro Ruggiero, Italian Embassy in Rome, riservato (restricted), signed Salleo, and Visita del ministro per le relazioni economiche esterne dell'URSS Konstantin Katuchev, 9–12.10.1989. ILS, AGA, section URSS, b.689.

[35] See, for example, Appunto del MAE sulla politica estera sovietica, November 1989. ILS, AGA, section URSS, b. 695.

[36] "[…] For the first time the Soviets are ready to deal with us on economic issues at an official senior level [...] this is a further confirmation of the new course introduced by Gorbačëv. [...] The Piristroika [sic!] (transformation) is a complex process which will have to affect every sector of National life. It is not solely a problem of economic efficiency, because deep cultural, political, social, and administrative changes are also indispensable". See Appunto MAE per la missione a Mosca dell'on. Ministro, Roma, 9.5.1987. ILS, AGA, section URSS, b.689. Other records in the same box show that according to Rome the perestrojka offered interesting opportunities for dialogue and change and that, therefore, was bound to have an increasing influence on East-West dynamics. Two years later, observers also added that the reform which Gorbačëv was carrying out would soon attain a point of no return. See, in particular, Nota del MAE relativa agli sviluppi nell'Unione Sovietica, not dated (approximately written in March 1989). ILS, AGA, section URSS, b.703.

international isolation in which the USSR had slipped in the last years of Breznev, and to re-energize its external projection to face American dynamism.[37] But behind a set of sometimes non converging initiatives – whose interpretation was a rather difficult task – they also saw the seeds of a completely new approach towards Western Europe[38] and its integration process[39]:

> «La visita del Presidente del Consiglio e dell'on. Ministro si è svolta a Mosca in un clima di grande cordialità che ha pienamente riflesso il positivo andamento dei rapporti bilaterali. [...] Il colloquio allargato che è stato incentrato soprattutto sulle tematiche europee, ha dato modo al segretario del PCUS di illustrare l'importanza che l'Europa riveste nella politica estera dell'URSS. [...] Gorbaciov l'ha fatto con notevole impegno diffondendosi soprattutto sul concetto di "casa comune europea", di cui ha indicato tra le finalità di fondo quella di non accrescere le divaricazioni esistenti. Egli ha sottolineato l'importanza del progetto per la promozione di nuove relazioni tra le due Europe in particolare nel campo della sicurezza e in quelli economico e culturale [...]».[40]

The many caveats affecting this new approach of the Kremlin notwithstanding, the possibility was beginning to emerge, according to Rome, of creating a dialogue based on the Soviet acceptance of the EC as an entity in its own right.[41]

---

[37] See Nota del MAE del 19 febbraio 1987 inerente l'Unione Sovietica, February 1987. ILS, AGA, b.709.

[38] See Gerhard Simon, Der Umbruch des politischen Systems in der Sowjetunion, in: *Aus Politik und Zeitgeschichte* n. 19–20 (1990), pp. 3–15.

[39] See Nota del MAE sui rapporti CEE-Unione Sovietica (concerning the meeting between EC experts and Soviet representatives in Brussels on 15–16 January 1987. ILS, AGA, section URSS, b. 709. See also Appunto MAE dialogo politico tra i dodici e l'Unione Sovietica (no date). ILS, AGA, section URSS, b.695.

[40] "The official State visit of the *presidente del Consiglio* and of the honourable Minister took place in Moscow in an atmosphere of warmth and great personal trust. [...] The enlarged exchange of views, which was mainly focused on European issues, has allowed the President of the Central Committee to explain the importance of Europe in the Soviet Foreign policy. [...] In doing so, Gorbačëv showed great commitment and he spent many words on the 'European Common House'. Among its many purposes, he stressed the desire to avoid increasing the already existing disparities. He also stressed the importance of this project in the promotion of new European relations between the blocs, above all in the fields of security, economy, and culture". See Telegramma dall'ambasciata italiana a Roma, visita in URSS del presidente del Consiglio e dell'on. Ministro, Moscow, 13–16.10.1988, riservato (restricted), signed Bottai. ILS, AGA, section URSS, b.710.

[41] This greater Soviet flexibility could also be the result of the fears harboured by Gorbačëv that Western Europe could turn into a "fortress", which would have been dangerous in light of its attractiveness for Eastern European countries. On several occasions, Gorbačëv expressed this fear, for instance during his meetings with the German Chancellor Helmut Kohl, the French President François Mitterrand and the Italian Head of Government Ciriaco De Mita. See, in particular, Rapporto del ministro degli Esteri italiano sulla casa comune europea, 24.3.1989. ILS, AGA, section Europe, b.404.

In 1988, the EC adopted a package of economic support measures for Eastern European countries that were more advanced on the path to reforms: Poland and Hungary. They were not only supposed to facilitate economic transformations, but also to encourage these states to proceed on the road of far-reaching political reforms.[42]

On the European side, these rapid transformations behind the Iron Curtain also retained the attention of the Working Group on Eastern Europe created in the EPC. Even though in October 1988, on the occasion of the meeting of Joannina[43], the Belgian Foreign Minister Leo Tindemans, supported by his German colleague Hans-Dietrich Genscher[44], had drawn the attention of fellow Members on the opportunity to engage on a comprehensive dialogue that would also include the Soviet Union, it was not until December 1988 that the aforesaid Working Group addressed for the first time the notion of the "European Common House".[45] Within the Working Group, two competing approaches prompted the debate. They mirrored the discrepancies existing among Member States on the Soviet issue.

In December 1988, the first school of thought still considered the European Common House as a pure propaganda proposal without noteworthy contents whose sole aim consisted in persuading Western public opinions to trust the new Soviet course. As a result, Members States that supported this reasoning firmly believed that the pre-conditions for the Twelve to alter their approach had not been met yet.

By contrast, the second school of thought considered the new Soviet course as an early sign of a renewed Russian awareness which Western Europe had the duty to support through the promotion of the European Common House.

Great Britain belonged to the first school of thought and was decidedly in favour of a wait-and-see approach, whereas Italy and Germany, together with France and Belgium, were the main supporters of the second school of thought. They advocated for the immediate establishment of a broader platform for dialogue with Moscow. Although in mid-1989 the European Common House was

---

[42] See Maria Eleonora Gusconi, L'Italia e la cooperazione politica europea nella prima metà degli anni Ottanta, pp. 57–82.

[43] See Rapporto dell'ambasciatore Jannuzzi a Giulio Andreotti sull'incontro dei ministri degli Esteri a Joannina, 15–16.10.1988, riservatissimo (confidential). ILS, AGA, section Europa, b.381.

[44] Hans-Dietrich Genscher had already expressed his wish that Eastern Europe would be a magnet for countries beyond the Iron Curtain, namely in his Stuttgart speech of January 1981, and on the occasion of the award of the Charlemagne Prize to Emilio Colombo in 1979.

[45] See Michael Gehler, Mehr Europäisierung in Umbruchzeiten? Die europäische politische Zusammenarbeit (EPZ) und die revolutionären Ereignisse in Mittel-, Ost- und Südosteuropa Ende der 1980er Jahre, in: Gabriele Clemens (ed.), Limits of Europeanization (Studien zur modernen Geschichte), Stuttgart, 2017, pp. 77–106, 90.

still a general target, a framework for the discussion of different issues rather than a genuine political programme[46], Italy and the Bundesrepublik were persuaded that it had the potential to accelerate the process inaugurated by the signature of the Helsinki Final Act and thereby to also foster the specific Italian and German interests beyond the Iron Curtain.

Despite some differences in tones, all countries belonging to this second group were favourable to an "explorative approach", and shared the common perception that the world beyond the Iron Curtain could no more be considered and dealt with as if it was a monolithic bloc. They believed that something had to be undertaken. The question as to what concretely could be done to fill the European Common House with specific contents was, however, still vague and undefined.[47]

The openings promoted by the new Soviet leadership provided both Bonn and Rome with greater room for manoeuvre in Eastern Europe[48]; still, this did not delete the discrepancies existing in their respective approaches to the world beyond the Curtain. In this way Rome perceived things, the maintenance of territorial integrity and the protection of frontiers as defined at the end of the Second World War would guarantee in the short and medium term the stability needed to consolidate results and to develop a more dynamic approach. In due course, the German issue itself would find a solution within this general roof of peaceful coexistence.

After the conclusion of the Second World War, the German issue had been given a solution – which in the beginning was considered of temporary nature – in the partition of the Reich. As the decades went by, the "box" *Deutschlandfrage*, which in the aftermath of the War was rather empty for Italy, had been gradually filled with contents: the existing status quo based on territorial division. In time, this partition had become one of the pillars of the Italian-German relationship, of the balance existing between the Italian and German Ostpolitik, and even of the cooperation that the two countries shared within the European integration process. The European Common House did not question this assumption, but rather provided a framework to update the status quo without losing its meaning.

In conclusion, the choice of embracing a "flexible bilateral approach" of analysis has proven once again extremely useful. In section two, this approach had been an instrument to stress the specific weight that Paris had had in the interaction between Rome and Bonn. In this third section it has been a tool to shed some

---

[46] See Telegramma dall'ambasciata italiana a Mosca, rapporti italo-sovietici, colloqui con esponenti del MID, Moscow, 7.7.1989, signed Salleo. ILS, AGA, section URSS, b.689.

[47] Michael Gehler, Mehr Europäisierung in Umbruchzeiten?, p. 91 and p. 105.

[48] As far as Bonn is concerned, the process allowed it both to strengthen the Ostpolitik, and to favour its "Europeanisation" within the framework of the EPC. See, in particular, Hanns Jürgen Küsters, Die Entstehung und Entwicklung der Europäischen Politischen Zusammenarbeit aus deutscher Perspektive, pp. 148–150.

light on the significance of the Soviet Union and its proposal for a European Common House as an essential piece of the Italian vision of the "German puzzle".

Until mid-1989, Bonn and Rome had had similar reactions to the input of the Kremlin. As long as stability in Eastern Europe was not endangered, the discrepancies in the Italian and German vision of the "deutsche Frage" would remain under control. Within the EPC, both Rome and Bonn represented the Member States which had more to lose if the effort Gorbačëv made for reform failed. In other words, both of them shared the determination to do their utmost to support the new Soviet course.

November 1989 brought to the surface, quickly and also dramatically, the specific sensitivity of the German élite towards the issue of the national division, which, of course, did not exist in Italy. Nearly a week after the fall of the Wall, on the occasion of the 18 November Elysée summit, Helmut Kohl commented that, although he was fully aware of the delicate situation of the Soviet leader, priority had to be given to the respect of the will of the German people. The Ten-Point Plan presented to the Bundestag one week after the Summit removed any trace of doubt still lingering on the intentions of the German Chancellery.

The declarations of Helmut Kohl were not unanimously upheld even within the political spectrum of the Bundesrepublik. It is, therefore, not in the least surprising that they were the source of huge stress in the Italian Government and in the Foreign Ministry. How could Italy succeed in supporting the struggle to success of Gorbačëv without causing major damage to relations with Bonn?

In the previous pages, the "international pieces" of the German-Italian puzzle have been discussed; still, it is also indispensable to look at the smallest Russian nesting doll, the "Italian internal pieces" in 1989, to formulate hypotheses to answer this question.

b) Looking within the Italian Borders

In July 1989, after marked disagreements between the DC and the PSI which corresponded to a ministerial crisis that had been affecting the executive led by Ciriaco De Mita for some months, an agreement was eventually reached among Socialists and Christian-Democrats close to Andreotti and Forlani. Andreotti himself was handed by the Italian Head of State, Francesco Cossiga, the task of creating a new government.[49] This government, the sixth led by Andreotti, was, as the previous ones, based on the *pentapartito* (a recurring political formula in

---

[49] Giulio Andreotti led Italy as President of the Council of Ministers until 1992. Due to internal tensions, he had to tender his resignation in spring 1991, but he was soon after once again appointed Head of Government. Both coalition governments were composed by the same political parties (with the only exception of the Republicans). See Antonio Varsori, L'Italia e la fine della guerra fredda. La politica estera dei governi Andreotti 1989–1992, Bologna 2013, pp. 7–10.

the 1980s). Gianni de Michelis, a prominent member of the PSI and former vice-president of De Mita's Cabinet, was appointed Foreign Minister.

So far, the German vision of both Andreotti and Cossiga has been attentively analysed. It is now necessary to also address the personality and the perceptions of Gianni de Michelis.

Kenneth Dyson and Keith Featherstone, well-known British political scientists, have described the Italian Foreign Minister as follows: "De Michelis [...] was an intelligent loquacious bon vivant, liable to pursue grand political gestures [...]".[50]

The German magazine *Der Spiegel* rather stressed the contrast between Henry Kissinger's words of praise for the intellectual capacities of the newly appointed Minister, and the criticism leveled by the New York Times defining him "scharfzüngig, sinnenfroh und nonkonformistisch" (sharp-tongued, enjoying the pleasures of life and unorthodox).[51] The German magazine carefully draws attention to the contradictions of his personality. On the one hand, his "modernity" – compared with the then Italian political élite – was praised. On the other hand, the magazine also pointed at his fickleness and at his lack of knowledge of – and interest for – the internal workings of the Minister which he led. According to the German magazine, several Italian officials had complained about this lack of knowledge.[52]

Born in Venice in a prominent local family, Gianni de Michelis had chosen at first an academic career, which he later abandoned to devote himself to politics. Before being appointed Foreign Minister, he had been an important figure in the PSI at first at a regional level, and later on in national politics[53], as Minister for State's participation from 1980 to 1983 and as Minister of Work and Social Protection from 1986. These posts had provided him with an overall good knowledge of the Italian working framework, and had also allowed him to develop strong relations with the industrial environment of the Northern-Eastern Italian regions. A natural proclivity for grand political gestures completed his profile.

According to de Michelis the Soviet political course seemed to offer to Italy new opportunities beyond the Iron Curtain and above all more favourable conditions for an enhanced cooperation in the Danube-Balkan area. From the very beginning of his mandate as Foreign Minister, de Michelis showed an unmistakable

---

[50] See Kenneth Dyson and Keith Featherstone, The Road to Maastricht, negotiating Economic and Monetary Union, Oxford 1999, p. 494.

[51] See Valeska von Roques, Ich bin fett, na und?, in: *Der Spiegel* n. 46 (1990), pp. 199–204.

[52] In the author's interview on 02.3.2016, Ambassador Nigido affirmed: "He let me think to a nobleman of the 15th century, with all their virtues and vices".

[53] For further information on de Michelis see also his autobiographical text: La lunga ombra di Yalta: la specificità della politica italiana, Venezia 2003.

interest in strengthening the ties with the most prominent states of the Danube-Balkan area, with Yugoslavia, Austria and Hungary.[54] He himself confirmed that this was one of his main targets in his first inaugural address to the Chamber of Deputies on 20 September 1989.[55]

Foreign Minister de Michelis was not alone in advocating for greater dynamism in Eastern Europe. The Italian Minister for Foreign Trade, Renato Ruggiero, was equally enthusiastic about these new opportunities, especially as far as Poland and Hungary were concerned. In June 1989, Italy had become the third most important Western trade partner of Hungary, only preceded by Austria and the Bundesrepublik.[56] In 1989, Italian imports from Hungary, which were already remarkable, had further surged by 22 %, while Italian exports had also increased, by 23 %. Italy had also a leading role in providing Hungary with the necessary credit lines to support and complement local initiatives.[57] The main difference between economic relations with Hungary and contacts with Poland concerned the methods used, rather than their scope. In dealing with Poland, Italy made extensive use of national channels, whereas as far as Hungary was concerned, local resources and the role of regions were equally important.

In October 1989, an Italian-French summit was held in Venice. During this meeting, the project for an Economic and Monetary Union supported by the Delors Commission was subjected to a thorough discussion. The situation in Poland and Hungary was also widely debated, but not a single word was spent on the DDR.[58]

---

[54] See Gespräch Staatssekretär Dr. Sudhoff mit dem Generalsekretär des italienischen AM, Bottai, am 9.Oktobre 1989, Bonn, 9.10.1989. PA AA B26, n. 140725

[55] See Atti Parlamentari (parliamentary proceedings), Camera dei Deputati, X legislatura, terza commissione, 20 settembre 1989 (the transcriptions are available on the internet site of the Italian Camera dei Deputati). According to Emil Brix, Gianni de Michelis had already expressed his ambitions before this inaugural address, on 7 August 1989, in an impromptu European speech at Bassano del Grappa on the occasion of a boy scout meeting. See Emil Brix, Die Mitteleuropapolitik von Österreich und Italien im Revolutionsjahr 1989, in: Michael Gehler/Maddalena Guiotto, Italien Österreich und die Bundesrepublik Deutschland in Europa/Italy Austria and the Federal Republic of Germany. Ein Dreiecksverhältnis in seinen wechselseitigen Beziehungen und Wahrnehmungen von 1945/49 bis zur Gegenwart/A Triangle Relationship: Mutual Relations and Perceptions from 1945/49 to the Present, Wien – Köln – Weimar 2012, pp. 455–468, 456.

[56] See Ambassade de France en Italie, le ministre conseiller pour les affaires économiques et commerciales, note sur les relations de l'Italie avec la Hongrie et la Pologne : une "Ostpolitik" économique offensive, Rome, January 1990. AMAE 1935inva, Direction Europe, Série Italie, carton 6378, sous-série 11, période 1986–1990.

[57] See Ibid. Minister Ruggiero paid frequent official and non-official visits to Hungary, as it is also confirmed by the French archival records. The available French documents also refer to the comments of the then Hungarian Minister of Commerce. According to him, in 1989 Italy was one of the most prominent partners of his country in all respects.

[58] In light of the records already declassified, it is extremely difficult to accurately reconstruct the vision which Gianni de Michelis had concerning the "German issue". The bulk of diplomatic files

Can the conclusion be drawn that Italy was really so unprepared to face the November 1989 events?

Even in light of a combined analysis of Italian and foreign records, it is a rather difficult task to provide a single response, either positive or negative, to the question raised. Firstly, we must bear in mind that the perceptions and suggestions formulated by the Italian Embassy in Bonn were not always – and often only partially – shared and accepted by the Farnesina, which had to take into account a bigger picture than solely the relations with Bonn. In December 1987, Ambassador Luigi Vittorio Ferraris had been replaced, after seven years of Service in Bonn, by Raniero Vanni d'Archirafi. Nearly one and a half year later, a new Italian Ambassador arrived to Bonn, Marcello Guidi. Although in Italy Marcello Guidi is certainly not as widely known as some of his predecessors, he has a special place in German records, both qualitatively and quantitatively. This can be a surprise for a researcher, considering the traditional Italian scientific literature in which his role has often been nearly ignored.[59] The newly appointed Ambassador not only confirmed the expertise of the Italian diplomatic corps, but he also embodied a leap in quality. Certainly, he lacked the media resonance attained by some of his predecessors, but, in exchange, he had a deeper feeling for all that was German.[60] He did not simply read and speak German, but he was bilingual, as a result of having a German-speaking parent. As he had attended the German school in Rome, he was also in possession of bi-national educational training:

> „Er besuchte längere Zeit die deutsche Schule in Rom. [...] Er leitete mit bemerkenswertem Geschick und großer Geduld wichtige Ausschüsse [...]. Mehrfach hat

---

concerning the 1980s at the Italian Foreign Ministry archives have not been opened for consultation yet, whereas other archives, both in Italy and abroad, provide interesting but insufficient information. Besides, in quantitative terms the amount of German records concerning Francesco Cossiga, and, above all, Giulio Andreotti with respect to the "deutsche Frage" is wider than the documents concerning Foreign Minister de Michelis. Information gathered suggests that de Michelis did not share some of the prejudices against Germany of his Italian colleagues, also because of him being younger than the majority of them; however, it also suggests that he was more at ease in dealing with Great Britain, both bilaterally and within the European integration process, and that he was neither particularly interested nor drawn to Germany. In Bonn he was believed to be an intelligent politician, whose innovations arouse curiosity, but his approach to Foreign politics – often perceived as lacking in consistency – and his natural proclivity for great designs in such a delicate transitional phase made the dialogue with Bonn and with Foreign Minister Genscher more difficult.

[59] Many clues gathered both through personal interviews with Italian diplomats and journalists and through an analysis of the German archival records, clearly point in this direction. See, in particular, PA AA B26, n. 140535 (box concerning Italian ambassadors in Germany from 1985 to 1990) and PA AA B26, n. 173581 (box reserved to Ambassador Guidi).

[60] See in PA AA B26, n. 140535 the "Persönlichkeitsbild" of Ambassadors Luigi Vittorio Ferraris and Raniero Vanni d'Archirafi.

er uns gegenüber in Brüssel als hilfreich erwiesen. […] Er ist mit den Problemen der Bundesrepublik vertraut und auch freundschaftlich verbunden. Die Verwendung in Rom entspricht seinem Wunsch […]. Er spricht fließend Deutsch."[61]

In summer 1989, news arrived to Rome from the Italian Embassy in Bonn concerning the ongoing transformations. Within the two previous years, the Bundesrepublik had allegedly moved from a stable political equilibrium to the resurgence of old fundamental questions. This had upset expectations of political stability and predictability which in Germany were supposed to be stronger than elsewhere. Changes in the balance of power among the most prominent Western German parties could, therefore, not be excluded.[62] Several endogenous factors had prompted this change of atmosphere, whereas in Foreign policy – which had a far greater impact in political debate and public opinion than in Italy – the consensus on the traditional International guidelines had not been shaken. Still, it was considered inevitable that forasmuch as the changes beyond the Iron Curtain were concerned, the Bundesrepublik would enhance its European profile in East-West relations.[63]

At the end of the 1980s, the Bundesrepublik appeared in the eyes of Italian observers as a cradle of two different trends: A strong and deep rooted commitment – both in the political spectrum and in the public opinion stance – to European integration and a renewed discussion about the wounds caused by the amputation of the Eastern territories which had not completely healed. Germany, just like Italy, though for different reasons, was a border country between the blocs filled with a "physiological" need to be fully integrated in the Western world to pursue a dynamic eastward action. For the Italian Embassy, this was the appropriate gateway to interpret the different aspects which had prompted the German rotating presidency in 1988. Foreign Minister Genscher epitomized this combination both in his personality and in his political course. He was in fact a crusader for deeper European integration and, at the same time, he was also the spearhead for a policy of dialogue with Moscow. When the Eastern tide was out, new opportunities appeared on the strand and it was only logical that Italy and Germany were the first countries in the EC to sense it and to try and take advantage of the situation. The final question raised at the Italian Embassy in Bonn was as to whether an even lower tide could also leave the possibility of a re-

---

[61] "He attended for a rather long time the German school in Rome. […] He led important committees with remarkable ability and great patience […]. More than once he was very helpful in Brussels. […] He is not only familiar with the problems of the Federal Republic, but he is also in friendly terms with Germany. The relocation to Bonn corresponded to his own wish […]. He is fluent in German". See Persönlichkeitsbild Botschafter Marcello Guidi, Bonn, 16.6.1989. PA AA B26, n. 17358.
[62] See Lettera dall'ambasciata d'Italia al ministro Andreotti, Bonn, 3.7.1989.
[63] See Ibid.

unification open. The Embassy echoed what the President of the Deutsche Bank, an influential figure in Germany and a personal friend of Helmut Kohl, had allegedly remarked some months before. Although Italy had strong ties with Bonn, it was more than evident that in 1989 the ties with France were considered more valuable in Germany. The best answer to this rapidly changing international framework lied for the Embassy in the acceleration of the integration process in which Italy and Germany could, once again, find the tools to try and establish a closer cooperation, as close to the German-French partnership as possible. If changes in Eastern Europe proceeded at that speed, it was considered reasonable that, soon, the bells of a German re-unification would chime. By then, it was necessary to have established a European Political Union, but, meanwhile, the possibility was envisaged to grant the DDR the status of associated member.

The Italian Embassy in Bonn was not alone in sensing the approaching of a phase marked by great changes. The correspondents in Bonn of the most influential Italian newspapers were also becoming increasingly aware of the risk that the process of change could soon achieve a breaking point.[64] Those who worked in Germany and therefore had a daily contact with its changing dynamics, being both diplomats and journalists, were, in fact, more sensitive than the officials in the Italian Foreign Ministry.

One month before the fall of the Wall, on 9 October 1989, the German Secretary of State met in Bonn with the Italian Secretary-General of the Foreign Ministry, Bruno Bottai[65], to discuss both the targets of the approaching Italian rotating presidency of the EC, and the organisation of the regular Italian-German summit. During the meeting, the changes in Hungary and Poland were, however, also addressed, and the DDR issue was as well.[66]

> „StS Sudhoff erläuterte sodann auf ital. Wunsch ausführlich die Einschätzung der Bundesregierung zu den jüngsten Entwicklungen in der DDR [...]. Botschafter Bottai stimmte seiner Bewertung der Lage vorbehaltlos zu. Er unterstrich das Interesse Italiens, in enger Abstimmung mit der Bundesrepublik, nach Mitteln und

---

[64] The Italian journalist Alfredo Venturi, correspondent of *La Stampa*, noticed that between 1987 and 1988 those who lived in Germany could sense that something was rapidly changing in the German-German relations and that on both sides of Curtain there was a creeping feeling that after all the Berlin Wall was not so necessary. Still, it was not until October 1989 that the perception that everything was changing or would soon to change was strengthened. See author's interview with Alfredo Venturi (3.2.2016).

[65] Italian Ambassador Marcello Guidi and Vittorio Surdo (diplomatic counsellor in Bonn until July 1989. From November 1989 he worked with the Director-general for political Affairs in the Farnesina).

[66] See Anmerkung Gespräch Staatssekretär Dr. Sudhoff mit dem Generalsekretär des italienischen AM, Bottai, am 9.Oktober 1989, Bonn, 9.10.1989. PA AA B26, n. 140725.

Wegen zu suchen [...] um namentlich in der DDR zu einer Lockerung der ver-
krusteten Strukturen beizutragen.
Bottai betonte, die italienische Öffentlichkeit reagiere weniger empfindlich auf die
Frage einer möglichen Wiedervereinigung beider Teile Deutschlands [...]. Sicher
werde es eines Tages zu einer Wiedervereinigung kommen. Wenn und in welcher
Form, müsse z.Zt. offenbleiben. [...] Nur im Rahmen der EG werde eines Tages
eine friedliche Wiedervereinigung möglich sein. Er glaube persönlich, jetzt könne
man die Frage von außen nicht beschleunigen."[67]

The meeting confirmed that Italy followed with great and constant interest the
changes beyond the Iron Curtain and also in the DDR, although this country was
neither its first nor its main target.

Contrary to what has been traditionally affirmed, in 1989 Italy was not unaware of the growing internal difficulties affecting the DDR. The possibility of a
re-unification was also slowly becoming a subject for analysis and discussion.
Still, based on a dual reasoning – both deductive and inductive – and contrary to
what the Italian Embassy suggested, the majority of the Italian élite did believe
that this possibility would become reality, but only in a distant future. On the one
hand, Italian observers estimated that the Eastern German social and economic
difficulties were not of such a dangerous nature to infer from them that radical
political changes were a short term real possibility. On the other hand, they also
believed that Moscow was not ready to consent to a re-unification, from which it
could be deduced that for the present, the overcoming of the territorial division
was a far-fetched possibility. Besides, Europe was back then in a delicate phase
of its development, and therefore it was not yet considered ready to face the challenges which a re-unification would have unleashed.

The thought of a re-unification as a short term target appeared in Rome not
only unrealistic, but also not desirable. Dealing with the approach of Rome to the
re-unification process, some further remarks can also be useful.

Firstly, by 1989, in Italy, just like in Germany, an overall consensus was predominant on Foreign policy issues and, more generally, on international issues as
well. Still, unlike its northern ally, in Italy Foreign policy was rarely a crucial

---

[67] "Then, at the Italian Request, State Secretary Sudhoff explained in detail the view of the Federal
Government concerning the recent transformations in the DDR [...]. Ambassador Bottai agreed
unreservedly with this assessment of the situation. He also stressed the Italian interest in a closer
cooperation with the Federal Republic to find ways and means [...] to contribute to an easing of
encrusted frames, specifically in the DDR. Bottai affirmed that the Italian public opinion was not
particularly worried about the possibility of a reunification [...]. To be sure, he knew that it would
happen one day, the when and the how this would happen, had though to remain for the time being
an open question. [...] Only within the framework of the EC, would one day a peaceful reunification
be possible. Personally, he believed that one should not accelerate the issue from the outside". See
Ibid.

issue in the internal debate. Besides, until then the Farnesina had exercised a *de facto* monopoly over Foreign policy.[68] The management of economic and financial issues was allocated in Italy among three different ministries, which, despite being from time to time led by prominent personalities, often lacked both the necessary internal cohesion and the resources – compared to the expertise provided by the diplomatic corps – for entering into competition with the Foreign Office in strictly international issues.[69]

This does not mean that the significance of the Treasury Department, or of the Ministry of Foreign Trade, was negligible. It rather means that the Treasury Department, for instance, dealt with issues related to the re-unification, such as the European Economic and Monetary Union, which, however, could not be purely confined to the context and the outcomes of such a process.

Secondly, in 1989 not only had the newly appointed Prime Minister, Giulio Andreotti, a wide stock of knowledge and expertise dealing with international issues, but he also had been for nearly a decade Foreign Minister. Therefore, he still had strong ties with the ministry which he had led and, particularly, with its Secretary-General, Bruno Bottai. This added a new element to the overall picture. In 1989, the Foreign Office and the Government were both actively involved into the management of Foreign policy.

While dealing with the Italian reaction to the re-unification process, any kind of competition among different ministries can be detected as a consequence of both the existence of an overall consensus on the most relevant international questions, and of the abovementioned limitations. What can be observed is not a conflict between the Farnesina and Palazzo Chigi[70], but rather a dialectic approach between different nuances whose background was a set of shared principles and traditional guidelines.

This dialectic between the Italian Foreign Office and the Government often mirrored the divergent personalities and approaches to politics of their respective guides, Giulio Andreotti at Palazzo Chigi and Gianni de Michelis at the Farnesina. This dialectic was also flanked by the role played by the Head of State, Francesco Cossiga. In theory, he should have had a minor influence because of the limitations of his post, which, however, was no stumbling block for him to follow the events with constant and great attention and to express his comments

---

[68] See Ambassade de France en Italie, note sur la Farnesina 1981–1988, Rome, no date. CADN, 579PO-4–15 Archives rapatriées de l'Ambassade de France à Rome 1981–1992. The Presidency of the Republic usually had a feeble influence over this monopoly and the executive, though far more influential, was often hampered by frequent changes of governments.

[69] The Ministry for Foreign Trade had limited resources at its disposal and had to often resort to the assistance of the direction for economic affairs of the Farnesina. Some improvements were, however, introduced in 1987 when Renato Ruggero was headed with the task of leading this ministry.

[70] Official residence of the Prime Minister, used in the text as a synonym of executive or government.

– sometimes diplomatically and sometimes more loudly – whenever he deemed it necessary.

Lastly, one further issue must be addressed, namely the short comment uttered in October 1989 by Bruno Bottai concerning the Italian public opinion, which was allegedly favourable to the possibility of a German re-unification. The question is therefore: what data can confirm or refute such an affirmation?

Among the records recently released by the PA AA[71], a report based on the USIA-commissioned surveys in the Bundesrepublik, France, Great Britain, and also Italy on 5–17 October 1989, can provide valuable data to deal with the afore-mentioned issue.[72] The first question asked in the interviews was a yes or no question: whether the interviewees were favourable or not to the eventuality of a German re-unification. Next table shows that, in defiance of what was considered conventional wisdom, large majorities of Western Europeans, especially Italians, supported the idea of a re-unification.[73]

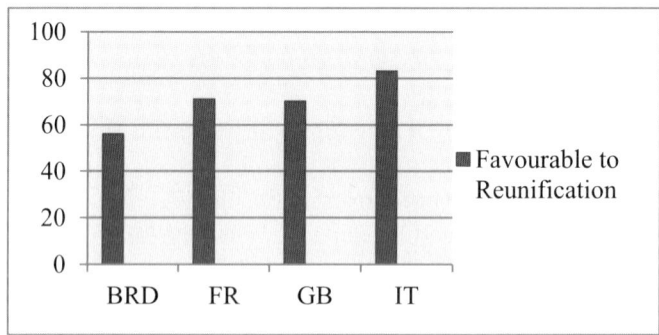

Fig. 12: Favourable to Reunification. Source: USIA Survey

---

[71] As anticipated in the preface, starting from 2009 the archives of the German Foreign Ministry have begun to release records concerning 1989. At first, such records mainly related to the role of the Superpowers, whereas more recently diplomatic documents concerning the approach of other countries, such as France, Great Britain, Austria, and even former members of the Warsaw pact, have been declassified.

[72] See West Europeans broadly favour a single German State but not at the cost of the NATO. PA AA Zwischenarchiv 140.729E. The report was based on approximately 1000 face-to-face interviews in a nationally representative sample of adults, meaning 18 years old or older, and included cities of all sizes and rural areas. The questions were written by the USIA office of research, whereas the polls on the ground were conducted by SOFRES in Paris, EMNID-Institut of Bielefeld in Germany, PRAGMA in Rome, and SOCIAL SURVEYS in London.

[73] The USIA estimated that the data collected in the Bundesrepublik could be not entirely reliable, because the West German institute which had conducted the poll had not asked a yes-no question, but rather hard and specific questions concerning what a reunified Germany would have looked like.

Fig. 13 presents data concerning the Bundesrepublik on the question whether German citizens were in favour of a reunification, and it was coupled with a set of conditions.

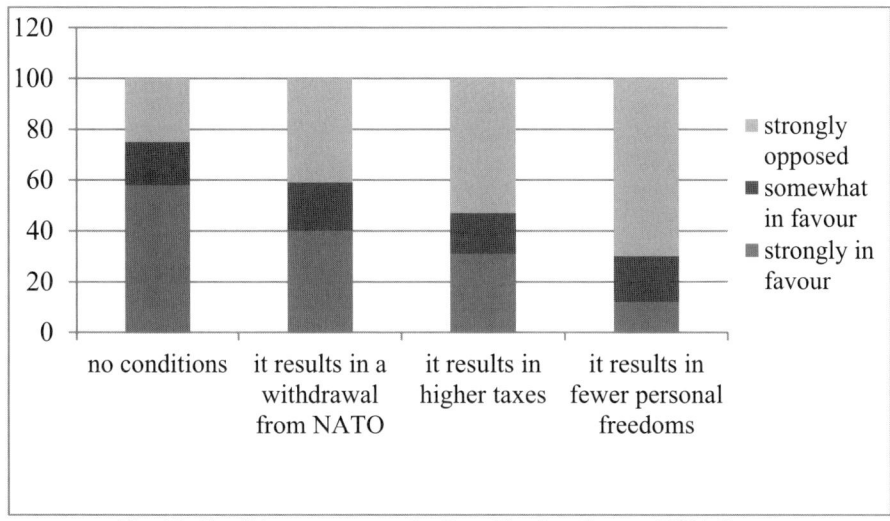

Fig. 13: Conditions to support the Reunification. Source: USIA Survey

According to the survey, support for a single German state fell dramatically in the Bundesrepublik if the reunification was seen to imply changes in critical national policies.

The last table (Fig. 14) stresses that the majority of citizens in the countries selected for the survey did not consider a reunified Germany as a military threat. Somewhat more, but still far less than a majority, expected a unified Germany to pose an economic threat.

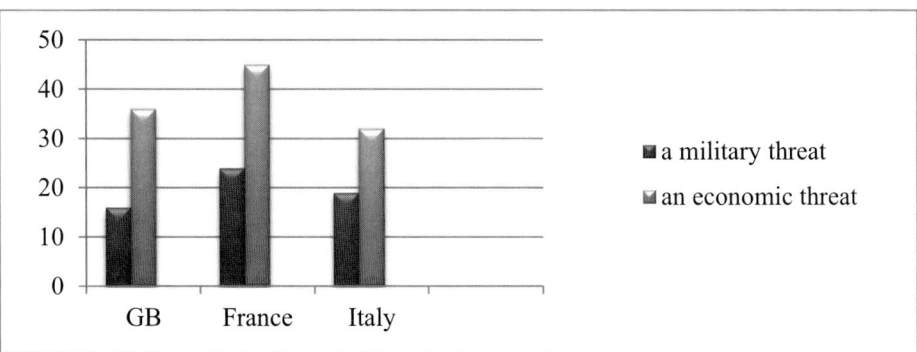

Fig. 14: Germany reunified: Perceptions abroad. Source: USIA Survey

From these results, USIA drew the final conclusion that the data reflected the trust and the "socialising effect" that had developed from nearly four decades of German cooperation within NATO and the EC.

It seems that the comments briefly expressed by Bruno Bottai in October 1989 mirrored a significant change in the perceptions of the Italian public opinion, which could reasonably be the result of both the previously mentioned "socialising effect", and also of the positive and profitable economic ties established between Bonn and Rome.

In conclusion, the affirmation that Italy was unprepared for the approaching earthquake cannot be entirely refuted, but its extent can be significantly reduced.

One final piece of the Italian-German puzzle, which is rather difficult to fully frame either in the "official Italy" or in the box "non-official Italy", is still to be considered: the approach and the perception of the Italian Communist Party.

c) A New Player walks in: The Italian Communist Party
Both the history of the interaction between the Italian Communist party (PCI) and the German SED, and the approach of the Italian Communists to the German issue from the creation of the DDR until 1973, has already been the object of several Italian and foreign major studies.[74] On the contrary, as far as the Seventies and, above all, the Eighties, are concerned, only more recently has the release of further archival records allowed new approaches and contributions to research to see the light of day.[75] Based on these new studies and with the support of the archival material kept at the Gramsci Foundation, this sub-chapter briefly deals with a few key-elements to better frame in a broader context the Italian reaction to the fall of the Berlin Wall and the process towards re-unification.

Until the beginning of the 1970s, the Italian Communist Party had written another "story" of the Italian perception of the "German issue". In doing so, it could rely on a comprehensive and complex framework of relations with the DDR. This different perception of the German issue was, in fact, sustained by a

---

[74] See, in particular, Charis Pöthig, Italien und die DDR. See also Johannes Lill, Die Beziehungen zwischen der DDR und Italien in den fünfziger Jahren, in: Villa Vigoni (ed.), Italia-Germania. Deutschland-Italien 1948–1958. Riavvicinamenti-Wiederannäherungen, in: *Studi Italo Tedeschi* vol. 6 (1997), pp. 161–210.

[75] See, for example, Francesco Di Palma, Die SED die Partito Comunista Italiano und der Eurokommunismus (1968–1989). Akteure, Netzwerke und Deutungen, in: Arnd Bauerkämper/Francesco Di Palma (eds.), Bruderparteien jenseits des Eisernen Vorhangs. Die Beziehungen der SED zu den kommunistischen Parteien West- und Südeuropas (1968–1989), Berlin 2011, pp. 149–166. See also Fiammetta Balestracci, Zwischen ideologischer Diversifikation und politisch-kulturellem Pragmatismus. Die Beziehungen zwischen der Partito Comunista italiano und der SED (1968–1989), pp. 167–185. See, as well, Wolfgang Müller/Francesco Di Palma (eds.), Kommunismus und Europa. Europapolitik und Vorstellungen bei den europäischen kommunistischen Parteien (1945–1989), Paderborn 2016.

network of asymmetric relations between a one-party based system and a Western party, whose participation in government, in spite of its growing influence and its remarkable poll results, was excluded *a priori*. It was as if the official "story" and the "story" of the Communist approach to the *deutsche Frage* had been two parallel lines which could never meet.[76]

However, starting from 1968, under the impact of the new concept of *Eurocommunism*, relations between the SED and the PCI started to change. This was the beginning of a road which allowed to narrow the ideological gap between the Italian official approach to the *deutsche Frage* and the perception which the Communists had of it, thus allowing the two parallel lines to get closer.

Firstly, the Italian official recognition of the DDR in 1973 had a certain impact on the aforementioned relations, insofar as from that moment the DDR sole-party seemed eager to engage into a strategy focused on the improvement of official contacts with the Italian government as part of an overall course aimed at gaining greater international visibility.[77]

Moreover, a recent study of Francesco Di Palma has also stressed that in the mid-Seventies, when the concept of *Eurocommunism* attained its peak in popularity, the discrepancies within the family of Western and Eastern communist parties surged.[78] Above all, this meant the divergences between the new approach supported by the Italian Communist Party, and the line followed by the DDR.[79] But which can be considered the main features of *Eurocommunism*?

It was not a traditional point-by-point programme, but rather a set of values and propositions which could achieve credibility in light of both the significant electoral gains of the Italian Communist party, and of the stronger ties established with the French and the Spanish Communist fellow parties.[80]

---

[76] In addition to its comprehensive network of relations with the SED, the Italian Communist Party had played a significant role of mediation in 1966–1969 between the German SPD and the DDR sole-party, which had at first expressed harsh criticism on the choice of the Western German Socialists to engage into a coalition government with the CDU. See Fiammetta Balestracci, Zwischen ideologischer Diversifikation und politisch-kulturellem Pragmatismus, p. 170.

[77] According to Fiammetta Balestracci, Eurocommunism was not the cause of radical transformations in the relationship between the PCI and the SED, but it rather laid the foundations for a process of diversification in the choices of both parties. See Fiammetta Balestracci, Zwischen ideologischer Diversifikation und politisch-kulturellem Pragmatismus, p. 168.

[78] See Francesco di Palma, Die SED die Partito Comunista Italiano und der Eurokommunismus (1968–1989), p. 158. See also Silvio Pons, Berlinguer e la fine del comunismo, Torino 2006, and see Laura Fasanaro, L'Eurocomunismo nelle carte della SED, in: *Mondo Contemporaneo* 3 (2006).

[79] Fiammetta Balestracci also stressed that in the 1970s, the SED apparently still acted in tune with Moscow, whereas the PCI began to be more critical on the decisions and approaches taken by Moscow.

[80] See Duccio Basosi/Giovanni Bernardini, The Puerto Rico Summit of 1976 and the End of Eurocommunism, in: Leopoldo Nuti, The Crisis of the Détente in Europe from Helsinki to Gorbachev 1975–1985, Londra, Routledge, 2008, pp. 256–267, 257. Both authors of this essay stressed that

Still, several obstacles stood in the way of Eurocommunism. One of the most prominent was its inability to get the support of the relevant actors within the European Social Democracy, starting from its most influential member, the SPD, which led the third largest economy of the world.[81] Even though the "left" wing of the SPD, including former Chancellor Willy Brandt, did show a certain degree of interest for the new course embraced by the PCI, the party leadership, and Chancellor Helmut Schmidt more than any other of its members, both feared and disliked the PCI, Eurocommunism, and its implications.[82]

Certainly, the new message of the PCI did not always fall on death ears. Still, all interlocutors interested in this new course and eager to develop deeper relations with the Italian Communist Party either were not in power – French Socialists for example – or were at the head of less influential countries, as were the Scandinavian Social-Democrats.

In 1979, the PCI had to accept that few results had been attained thanks to its new course both in terms of material gains and in terms of a full national recognition. Eurocommunism was not formally abandoned, but the international framework and the PCI itself changed dramatically at the dawn of the new decade. According to Duccio Basosi and Giovanni Bernardini, this meant that by the end of the Seventies, Eurocommunism had been forgotten just as quickly as it had become popular.[83] The dramatic changes of the International system and the shift towards new economic models of growth meant that there would not be a second chance for the Italian Communists. Yet, as far as Eurocommunism is concerned, the documents of the Gramsci archives allow to nuance the abovementioned negative judgment. The ongoing international and national transformations notwithstanding, at the beginning of the Eighties, Eurocommunism had left a significant inheritance and a still unexplored potential to the approach of Botteghe Oscure[84] towards the German issue. Learning from the experience of the previous decade and also in light of an unstoppable deterioration in relations

---

the success of Eurocommunism in the Seventies paralleled the rise and fall of the PCI poll successes, whereas other researchers, such as Silvio Pons, ascribed the overall failure of Eurocommunism to its inability to rescind all link with the Soviets and to fully embrace social-democracy.
[81] See Ibid., p. 259.
[82] See Giovanni Bernardini, The SPD and the rising star of Bettino Craxi, in: Michael Gehler/Maddalena Guiotto (eds.), Italien Österreich und die Bundesrepublik Deutschland, pp. 209–224, p. 209 and 214. In 1976, Schmidt commented to the German press that he did not like the Communists in Italy or anywhere else.
[83] See Duccio Basosi/Giovanni Bernardini, The Puerto Rico Summit of 1976 and the End of Eurocommunism, p. 264.
[84] The PCI had its headquarters in a Roman street named *Botteghe Oscure*. The expression "Botteghe Oscure" is, therefore, used as a synonym of PCI.

with the SED[85], in the Eighties the PCI resolutely followed a path whose priority was the definition of a fruitful cooperation with the SPD.[86] Still, it was not until the mid-1980s that this strategy seemed to have a real chance of success.[87] This happened thanks to both a dramatic change in the course pursued by Moscow[88] and the gradual marginalisation within the SPD of Helmut Schmidt's approach, which went hand in hand with the failure of the Western German Social-Democrats to gain National elections.

The 9 November 1989 events happened while the Italian Communist Party was in the middle of this process of transformation aimed at defining the conditions for the party to be accepted within the European Social-Democratic family. This target, together with a steady deterioration of the relations with the SED, had in the Eighties a significant impact on the approach to the German issue, insofar as Botteghe Oscure gradually started to question the traditional image of the DDR as the model for a new Germany and, therefore, also its former rigid positions towards the Bundesrepublik.

---

[85] See Fiammetta Balestracci, Zwischen ideologischer Diversifikation und politisch-kulturellem Pragmatismus, p. 184. See also Nota sulla visita dell'ambasciatore della RDT Voos, 27.1.1981. Archivio del Partito Comunista Italiano (hereafter APCI) Mikrofilm 0488. During the meeting with Paolo Bufalini, DDR Ambassador Voos used harsh tones to criticise what was considered a lack of support on the part of the PCI, and an attempt to interfere in the DDR approach towards the Polish events. See Incontri con i partiti comunisti in occasione del Congresso del POUP, riservato (restricted), Warsaw, February 1980. APCI, Mikrofilm 0488, fascicolo 8102.

[86] See Intervista di Napolitano al quotidiano L 'Unità del 26 novembre 1980. APCI, Mikrofilm 0440, p. 2303. See also Appello di Schmidt al dialogo del 18 gennaio 1980. APCI, Mikrofilm 0440. This new strategy was at first heralded in 1980 in the newspaper of the Communist Party, but it was not until 1981 that it started getting more defined features. In 1981, a meeting between representatives of the PCI and Veronika Isenberg of the Foreign direction of the SPD was organised in Bonn, in which the PCI tried to identify a platform of common interests to deepen its ties with the SPD, for instance concerning the European Integration process. During the meeting, which lasted for two hours instead of the few minutes originally planned, Veronika Isenberg praised Eurocommunism also in light of the deterioration in East-West relations which left the door open to more concrete steps in the future.

[87] According to the records of the Italian Communist Party, after some initial hesitations, the SPD started looking more favourably to the possibility of strengthening its ties with the PCI. They could become part of a model of dialogue inspired to the relations between SPD and SED in its structures, and in its contents to the relations between SPD and French Socialists. SPD secretary, Peter Glotz, indicated in 1985 his willingness to travel to Rome to discuss the idea in more details. The occasion could be either a conference hosted by the Goethe-Institut, or a courtesy visit to the PSI. See Rapporto sulla visita a Bonn del febbraio 1985. APCI, Mikrofilm 0574, fascicolo 8505.

[88] See Incontro tra i dirigenti sovietici e le delegazioni straniere, 12/15 marzo 1985. APCI, Mikrofilm 0574, fascicolo 8505. The PCI had mixed feelings concerning the new course pursued in the Kremlin by Gorbaciov [sic!]. This means that the Communist Party, more than other Italian actors was aware, for obvious reasons, of the internal obstacles which the new Soviet leader would face.

„Trotz der zunehmenden Meinungsverschiedenheiten zwischen beiden Parteien erlebten ein erheblicher Teil der italienischen Kommunisten […] den Fall der Mauer als vollkommen unerwartetes und traumatisches Ereignis. […] Viele Intellektuelle hatten bis zu diesem Zeitpunkt an eine Selbsterneuerung des Sozialismus geglaubt und waren noch immer überzeugt, dass die DDR das bessere Deutschland sei. Demgegenüber waren viele Intellektuelle seit dem Ende der siebziger Jahre auf Distanz zur sowjetischen Propaganda und zur ostdeutschen Staatspartei gegangen. Auch Mitglieder der PCI-Führung, allen voran Berlinguer, tendierten stark dazu, sich von dem östlichen Partner auf ideologischer und kultureller Ebene abzuwenden. Es darf daher nicht verwundern, dass die *l'Unità*, das Parteiorgan der PCI, […] voller Zuversicht und Hoffnung auf die Zukunft eines wiedervereinigten Deutschlands nach dem Mauerfall blickte."[89]

On the 10 October 1989 symposium organised by the CESPI (the PCI centre of studies), in cooperation with the Friedrich Ebert Foundation, PCI member and Shadow Foreign Minister Giorgio Napolitano commented in detail on the mounting difficulties within the DDR. He also advocated for a process of far-reaching reforms[90] coupled with a comprehensive dialogue between Eastern and Western Germany, which he thought that in the very short term did not necessarily require the disappearance of Eastern Germany.[91]

The fall of the Wall sharply accelerated the need for reforms within the PCI. A long lasting debate had started on its targets and its identity.[92] Part of the Italian link intellectuals, the majority of the Communist Party, and its newspaper *L'Unità* all looked with both interest and hope to the events of November 1989. They believed that these could be the long waited opportunity for the SPD to consolidate its national and international position as a force capable of leading the transformation towards a path of cooperation between Bonn and Pankow, which, eventually, would have been beneficial for the PCI project as well.

---

[89] "Despite increasing divergences of opinion between both parties, a relevant segment of the Italian Communists […] perceived the fall of the Wall as an unexpected and dramatic event. […] Many intellectuals had believed until them in the possibility of a self-renewal of Socialism and that the DDR was the "best Germany". On the contrary, since the end of the 1970s, many other intellectuals had distanced themselves from Soviet propaganda and the Eastern sole-party. Even members of the PCI-élite, none more so than Berlinguer, definitely tended to turn their back to their Eastern partner both ideologically and culturally. It should, therefore, not be a surprise that *L'Unità*, the newspapers of the PCI, […] looked at the possibility of a reunified Germany after the fall of the Wall with great confidence and expectations". See Fiammetta Balestracci, Zwischen ideologischer Diversifikation und politisch-kulturellem Pragmatismus, pp. 183–184.
[90] See also Fernschreiben Gespräch Occhetto/Napolitano mit dem hiesigen Botschafter am 12.10, Rome, 17.10.1989. PA AA B38, n. 140704.
[91] See Entwicklung in der DDR und West-Ost Beziehungen in Europa: Kolloquium in Rom, Fernschreiben aus RomDiplo, Rome, 11.10.1989. PA AA B38, n. 140704. Far-reaching reforms in the DDR were considered an unavoidable step to preserve the very existence of the DDR as a state.
[92] See Le PCI et les changements à l'Est, télégramme ambassade de Rome n. 1394, Rome, 20.11.1989. AMAE 1935inva, Direction Europe, Série Italie, carton 6378, sous-série 11, période 1986–1990.

7.2 *Eppur si muove*! The Arduous Task of defining a Strategy

"*Eppur si muove!*" (And yet, it moves!) is a phrase attributed to the Italian mathematician and philosopher Galileo Galilei by Giuseppe Baretti in his collection *Italian Library* published in London in 1757. The *Italian Library* presents to an English-speaking public the life and deeds of Galileo Galilei up to the trial of the Inquisition.

The expression has in time entered into everyday Italian to explain a truth which no pressure from the outside can alter. Still, there exists also another, though less popular, meaning used to express astonishment or great surprise at an event, which occurs even if all circumstances worked against it.

The expression has been used at the beginning of this sub-chapter with the second meaning, as it perfectly embodies the first reactions to the fall of the Berlin Wall coming from the Italian press, from public opinion, and from the realm of politics as well. In the immediate aftermath of the 9 November events, Italy watched Berlin with both disbelief and astonishment. It soon followed with attempts to comprehend the case of such events and their potential in a broader international context whose accelerated path Rome tried to chase.

This sub-chapter will focus on the Italian action during the month of November 1989, mainly in the realm of politics[93], whereas the following chapter will broaden our view to also look at the reaction of public opinion and of the press.

In chronological order, the first Italian reaction came on 10 November 1989 through the sitting of the third Committee of the Chamber of Deputies.[94] Both Foreign Minister Gianni de Michelis and Renato Ruggiero, Minister of Foreign Trade, participated in a sitting, which had originally been organised with the aim

---

[93] Compared to the scientific literature dedicated to the transformation of the Italian-German relationship in the 1980s, the field of studies dealing with the Italian approach to the process of re-unification is even narrower. Antonio Varsori commented in his essay on Italy and the German re-unification that Hubert Védrine's volume on the Foreign policy of President Mitterrand in 1989/1990 only once quoted the name of Giulio Andreotti. See Antonio Varsori, Italy the East European Revolutions and the Reunification of Germany, p. 405. Similar comments also apply to the memoirs of French Foreign Minister Roland Dumas, to the memoirs of Helmut Kohl, and to the baseline study on the German re-unification published by Tilo Schabert, the latter quoted the name of Andreotti only three times in his text. Even rarer are the comments on other Italian politicians. See Helmut Kohl, Erinnerungen 1982–1990, München 2005. For Tilo Schabert see footnote 7, p. 14. Carrying out a study on Italy and the German re-unification is in many respects like writing on a white page, which requires to rely mainly on archival records as a guide.

[94] See Atti Parlamentari, Camera dei Deputati, X legislatura, terza commissione, seduta del 10 novembre. On 10 November, soon after the abovementioned parliamentary sitting, the Farnesina issued an official statement, which, however, expressed nothing more than an understanding and the wish that from then on the German people could have a leading role in all decisions regarding its future. See also Ereignisse in der DDR, Reaktionen Italiens, Fernschreiben aus RomDiplo, Rome, 11.11.1989. PA AA B26, n. 140725.

of collecting and discussing information related to the approaching state visit of Gorbačëv.

For the specific purpose of this research, the comments of the Italian Foreign Minister deserve particular attention, insofar as they anticipated some distinctive features of what was to become the Italian strategy to the German re-unification. Despite the political earthquake of the previous day, the sitting started with a general discussion of the situation beyond the Iron Curtain with specific reference to Poland. It was, in fact, assumed as necessary to start by discussing the ways in which Western Europe, the European Community, and Italy could effectively respond to the changes in Eastern Europe in its entirety. From the very beginning, Italy supported an approach which tried in every possible way to avoid for Europe and for itself to be forced to deal with the German problem as if it were an "isolated phenomenon". Although the DDR had overnight become the most "spectacular instance" of change, what had happened in Berlin, whose potential consequences were not in the least clear on 10 November, was not to be considered a unique case. It was rather an example of more general transformations[95] which de Michelis was tempted to read through the lens of his regional projects of co-operation.[96]

Initial statements given to the Italian press by de Michelis himself show that he wholeheartedly sympathised with the events of November 1989 and that, at the same time, he carefully wanted to distance himself from the cautious approach embraced by Prime Minister Andreotti.[97]

Still, soon enough other elements started pointing to a different direction.[98] These induced his German interlocutors to question the extent and the motives of

---

[95] See Haltung Italiens gegenüber Veränderungen in Mittel und Ost Europa, Fernschreiben aus RomDiplo, Rome, 13.11.1989. PA AA B38, n. 140705.

[96] During the parliamentary sitting Gianni de Michelis stressed that, unlike his colleagues both in Italy and in the Bundesrepublik, he was the only one who had understood that the process of transformation was bound to "essere accelerato al massimo" (to proceed at the maximum speed possible). Italian, German and also French archival records provide evidence that the Farnesina had sensed earlier than other Foreign Offices the existence of a growing pressure towards far-reaching changes in Eastern Europe in its entirety. The same, however, cannot be affirmed as far as the sole DDR is concerned. No evidence is provided to support the specific declaration of de Michelis. Quite the opposite, German diplomatic files seem to confute it. See Ibid.

[97] See Haltung Italiens zur deutschen Frage, Fernschreiben aus RomDiplo, vertraulich-NfD, Bonn, 13.11.1989. PA AA B26, n. 173561.

[98] Ever since November 1989, the Italy Embassy in Rome had sent several reports to its Foreign Ministry concerning declarations of –and meetings with– Foreign Minister de Michelis. Such reports provide a rather different picture of the position embraced by the Italian Foreign Minister when compared with both his first declarations of support printed by Italian and international media, and with the version of events, which he himself spread later on. See, in particular, Haltung Italiens gegenüber Veränderungen in Mittel und Ost Europa, Fernschreiben aus RomDiplo, Rome, 13.11.1990. PA AA B38, n. 140705.

this initial unreserved support.[99] It was the beginning of a road where misunderstandings accumulated one after another until reaching a climax in Ottawa during the conference Open Skies.[100]

It was for instance extremely hard for Bonn to justify or even simply understand the suggestion expressed by de Michelis to use the *Quadrangolare* (the four-cornered initiative) as a model for a similar endeavour in Northern-Central Europe. The suggestion was not only considered to be practically unachievable, but also completely out of context and useless to solve a problem which by then went far beyond the opportunity to strengthen ties between the two Germanies. The more DDR citizens suffered from a downward spiral in their social and living conditions, the more their pressure and demands increased. Even the idea to build a confederation seemed increasingly inappropriate to provide an answer to this problem.

> „[…] Ich habe Genscher vorgeschlagen etwas Ähnliches für Mittel und Nord-Europa ins Auge zu fassen. Das heißt wenn wirklich etwas mit Ost-Deutschland geschehen muss, dann sollte diese Gemeinschaft in einem größeren Kontext […] Warum man nicht etwas mit West und Ost-Deutschland, Polen, der Tschechoslowakei und z. B. Schweden? Das hätte den Vorteil, zu den gleichen Ergebnissen zu gelangen, die deutsch-deutschen Beziehungen zu vertiefen, und gleichzeitig das Problem der Grenzen zu lösen. Die alleinige innerdeutsche Vertragsgemeinschaft birgt in sich das Risiko destabilisierend und gefährlich zu sein."[101]

---

[99] On 15 November 1989, Ambassador Friedrich Ruth wrote to his Government about two interviews given by de Michelis to the Italian newspapers *La Stampa* and *Repubblica*, on 10 and on 12 November. They revealed a certain degree of unease and nervousness with regard to the German events. Just like Prime Minister Andreotti, de Michelis as well seemed to worry as to whether what was happening in Germany could have negative consequences for the integration process and also as to how Moscow would react.

[100] See Doc. 38, Ambassadeur de France à Ottawa à Roland Dumas Ministre des affaires étrangères, le 13 février, télégramme n. 112 François Bujon de l'Estang, in: Maurice Vaïsse/Christian Wenkel, La diplomatie française face à la réunification allemande, Paris 2012, pp. 218–221. See also Doc.50, NATO-Ministerratstagung in Ottawa, 13.2.1990, in: Heike Amos/Tim Geiger/Horst Möller/Ilse Dorothee Pautsch/Gregor Schöllgen/Hermann Wentker/Andreas Wirsching (eds.), Die Einheit. Das Auswärtige Amt, das DDR-Außenministerium und der Zwei-plus-Vier-Prozess (im Auftrag des Instituts für Zeitgeschichte München-Berlin), Göttingen 2015, pp. 260–261. For further information see chapter 8.

[101] "I have proposed to Genscher to consider something similar for Central and Northern Europe. It means that if something must really happen in Eastern-Germany, then why should not it be in a bigger framework? […] Why not something with Western and Eastern Germany, Poland, Czechoslovakia and for example Sweden? This would have the advantage of getting the same results, i.e. enhancing the inter-German relations, and also solving the border issue. A German contractual community would carry the risk of being destabilising and dangerous". See AM De Michelis zur deutschen Frage, Fernschreiben aus RomDiplo, Bonn, 19.1.1990. PA AA B26, n. 140725. The quotation was underlined with a marked stroke of pen and a big question mark was added. See also

On the one hand, it goes without saying that it was both reasonable and under-standable that Italy and its Foreign Minister framed the German events in a broader Europe context.

On the other hand, this approach collided firstly with the existence of specific German features and requirements and, from the end of November, also with the choice of the Chancellery to face the social and political decay of the DDR by speeding up the process of rapprochement between the two German states. Such an acceleration could hardly be compatible with the Italian need for a slow and gradual process of transformation in Eastern Europe. From the immediate after-math of the fall of the Berlin Wall, Italy and its Foreign Minister were concerned about unilateral modifications of the existing frontiers, which would adversely affect not only German-Polish relations, but also the Baltic delicate equilibrium and which eventually could also have knock-on-effects at the frontiers between Italy and Yugoslavia.

Still, this overall picture, even if correct up to a certain point, lacked one es-sential element: the Italian Foreign Minister failed to see the specific extent of the German problem, and the level of development which the inter-German rela-tions had so far already attained.[102]

The Italian political system was forced to face phenomena which were likely to present real risks for the main targets until then pursued. The use of the word "forced" deliberately stresses the fact that the aforementioned events happened in the worst possible moment for Italy. This was a moment when its Ostpolitik seemed to finally have the tools for a leap in quality. Western Europe was in a transitional stage in which neither the target of the Economic and Monetary Un-ion, nor that of the Political Union, had been achieved. Last but not least, in this period the relations that Italy held with Bonn were also in the infancy of the *Gesprächsforum*'s test phase.

Audience à Francesco Cossiga, Paris, 29.1.1990. ANF, série 5 AG 4, archives de la cellule diplo-matique de l'Elysée (hereafter CD)/304, dossier 11 et 12. This document briefly refers to the meet-ing between Genscher and de Michelis which had taken place during the previous week. That meet-ing had been the opportunity for de Michelis to propose to Genscher to replace the idea of "reuni-fication" with the establishment of a Northern-European confederation.

[102] See Italien und die deutsche Frage, Fernschreiben aus RomDiplo, Rome, 25.1.1990. PA AA B26, n. 140725. The comments of Foreign Minister de Michelis mirrored one distinctive feature associated in Germany with the approach of the Italian political élite: Support for the re-unification as a medium-term target, and worries about its potential side-effects in the short run. According to Bonn, this explained the Italian emphasis on the idea of quickly convening a conference on the model of the CSCE. Through such a conference, Italy had three objectives to achieve: To slow down the German internal developments, to reassure the Soviet Union by fully engaging it in ne-gotiations, and to prevent any Soviet drift towards the use of force.

Besides, these rapid and unexpected developments imposed the Federal Government to focus its attention on the inner dynamics, and this subsequently required it to prioritise the need for more frequent contacts with those countries that disposed of a greater leverage: The Superpowers, France and Great Britain.

This did not imply though that the Bundesrepublik fully neglected to take into account and analyse the reactions, feelings and moods coming from its traditional European partners, such as Italy. On the contrary, the daily flow of information exchanged between the German Foreign Ministry and its Embassy in Rome points at the degree of interest with which Bonn had followed the attitude taking shape southwards the Alps[103]:

> „Im Gegensatz zu MP Andreotti haben sich andere italienische Politiker, auch aus den Reihen der Democrazia Christiana [sic!], vor allem aber die Sozialisten, positiv über die deutsche Frage geäußert. Staatspräsident Cossiga, selbst Mitglied der DC, äußerte während seines Staatsbesuchs in Algerien am 12.11.1989 Verständnis für den «legitimen Wunsch der Deutschen nach Wiedervereinigung». [...] stv. MP Martelli, Parteichef Craxi als Vertreter des PSI, und sogar PCI-Chef Occhetto sprachen sich grundsätzlich für die Respektierung des Rechts auf Selbstbestimmung aus. [...]."[104]

Particular emphasis was placed in Bonn on the comments uttered by Francesco Cossiga on 12 November during his visit to Algeria. Francesco Cossiga had accepted the legitimacy of the aspiration towards re-unification, provided that it found its realisation in full respect of the right of people and in the context of an appropriate international security framework. German observers welcomed with

---

[103] German records stressed the overall positive comments of Forlani and Piccoli within the DC, and in the PSI the equally positive attitude embraced by vice-Prime Minister Martelli, whereas the silence of Giulio Andreotti puzzled German observers and was often seen with astonishment. See, in particular, Ereignisse in der DDR, Reaktionen Italiens, Fernschreiben aus RomDiplo, Rome, 11.11.1989. PA AA B26, n. 140725. For more information, see, also, Austrian archival records, in particular Doc. 85 Bericht: Haltung Italiens zu Kohls Zehn-Punkte-Programm, 30.11.1989, in: Michael Gehler/Maximilian Graf, Österreichs und die deutsche Frage 1987–1990. Von Honecker-Besuch in Bonn bis zur Einheit, Göttingen 2018, pp. 403–405.

[104] "Contrary to Andreotti, other Italian politicians – even from the ranks of the Christian-Democrats – but, above all, the Socialists, have taken a positive look at the German issue. President Cossiga, member of the DC, have showed during his State-visit to Algeria on 12 November 1989 understanding for the 'legitimate wish of the Germans for reunification'. [...] Vice-prime minister Martelli, party leader Craxi as representative of the PSI, and even PCI-leader Occhetto have spoken, in principle, in favour of the respect of the right to self-determination". See Doc. 32, Vorlage des Referatsleiters 203, Kuhna, für Staatssekretär Sudhoff. Italienische Haltung zur deutschen Frage nach den Deutschland-kritischen Äußerungen von MP Andreotti, 18.12.1989; in: Heike Amos/Tim Geiger/Horst Möller/Ilse Dorothee Pautsch/Gregor Schöllgen/Hermann Wentker/Andreas Wirsching (eds.), Die Einheit. Das Auswärtige Amt, das DDR-Außenministerium und der Zwei-plus-Vier-Prozess, p. 179.

satisfaction such an early expression of support coming from a man in a prominent political position.[105] The great emphasis placed by the Italian Head of State on the German events found a further confirmation during the state visit of Gorbačëv to Rome.

> «Il 1° dicembre 1989 è una giornata storica [...] Porto un giornalista americano del Washington Post da Cossiga. Si parla molto di Germania, questo è un tema a cui Cossiga dedica attenzione e passione. Avrebbe voluto dire qualcosa a Gorbačëv sul tipo di quello che aveva detto ad Algeri, ma sia Andreotti che de Michelis glielo hanno impedito. Lui sente che si deve fare qualcosa per aiutare Kohl che l'altro giorno ha promosso i Dieci Punti. Teme che se non li aiutiamo i Tedeschi scelgono la strada del neutralismo e che comunque la riunificazione sia nelle cose. Mi fa assistere a una sua telefonata a Forlani a cui dice queste cose. In effetti, siccome sa che Andreotti è su posizioni diverse e siccome i due (Andreotti e Forlani) andranno insieme nella Repubblica Federale per una riunione della DC chiede a Forlani di portare i suoi saluti a Kohl senza che l'altro sappia. La posizione di Cossiga era molto più spinta rispetto a quella degli altri. Lui addirittura si appoggiò a Forlani perché desse dei messaggi a Kohl all'insaputa di Andreotti».[106]

---

[105] See Haltung Italiens zur deutschen Frage, Fernschreiben aus RomDiplo, vertraulich-NfD, Bonn, 13.11.1989. PA AA B26, n. 173561. The German Head of State personally sent a message to Cossiga to thank him for his comments, and for being one of the first European politicians to have supported so clearly and without second thoughts the target of re-unification. See also the author's interview with Ambassador Ortona (22.3.2016): "Cossiga l'aveva eccome una consapevolezza di quello che stava accadendo in Germania! Il caso ha voluto che Cossiga il 10 fosse dovuto andare in visita ufficiale in Algeria. Le notizie erano sempre più incalzanti [...] si vedevano alla televisione migliaia di persone che scavalcavano il Muro e inneggiavano alla libertà. [...] La delegazione è ampia [...] ma l'attenzione è rivolta all'Est e a Berlino ed infatti di questo parla Cossiga appena sbarcato dall'aereo. Cossiga dice che è legittima l'aspirazione alla riunificazione, ma è necessario che si verifichino prima le condizioni di sicurezza". (Cossiga was definitely aware of the extent of what was going on in Germany! As it happened on 10 November, Cossiga had to travel to Algeria. News were more and more pressing [...] on television we could see thousands of people climbing over the Wall, celebrating liberty. [...] Quite a large delegation [...] the attention, however, went to the East, towards Berlin, and indeed Cossiga approached this issue as soon as he got off the plane. Cossiga said that the Germans had a legitimate aspiration to reunification, but he also added that the necessary securities guaranties should precede it).

[106] "1st December 1989 is an historic day [...] I accompanied an American journalist of the Washington Post to Cossiga. They spoke a lot about Germany, this was an issue on which Cossiga dedicated both attention and passion. He would have liked to say something to Gorbačëv as he had already done in Algeria, but Andreotti and de Michelis prevented him from doing so. He felt that it was his duty to undertake something to help Kohl, who the previous day had presented his Ten-Point Plan. He feared that if we did not help the Germans, they might choose the path of neutralism. Besides, the re-unification was in the air. I was present when he phoned Forlani to tell him such things. All right, he knew that Andreotti had a different approach and as the two of them (Andreotti and Forlani) would travel to the Bundesrepublik, he asked Forlani to greet Kohl from him without mentioning it to Andreotti. Cossiga had an extreme position compared to his fellow politicians. He even asked Forlani to pass personal messages to Kohl unbeknown to Andreotti". See author's

An overall interest in keeping a close eye on Italian perceptions and reactions went hand in hand with a more pressing need to shed some light on the path which Andreotti would choose. His decision to keep silent until 16 November was rather puzzling. Only then, in a parliamentary debate strictly focused on European questions[107], he openly and for the first time took a position on the events of Berlin.

> „Nach der plötzlichen Öffnung der Mauer am 09.11.1989 äußerte MP Andreotti sich nicht zu den Fragen der Zukunft beider deutschen Staaten[108], sondern mahnte »Nerven zu behalten«[109]. Ungeachtet der dramatischen Veränderung in der DDR blieb er in der Folgezeit in mehreren Interviews dabei, daß die Frage der Wiedervereinigung »nicht aktuell sei«. Aktuell in »absehbarer Zukunft sei vielmehr das Konzept: eine Nation-zwei Staaten«.[…].“[110]

The attention in Bonn was retained by two distinctive features in the comments uttered by Andreotti. Firstly, in mid-November, he still seemed to be faithful to the principle that Germany was a single nation composed of two states. Secondly, his words sounded even colder and more detached, as they were not matched by any single expression of understanding or solidarity with the difficult situation which Germany was facing.[111]

Two days later, on 18 November 1989, the Italian newspaper *Repubblica* published a cartoon signed by the popular cartoonist Forattini depicting Giulio Andreotti with a beer in front of him and an enormous sandwich in his hands.

---

interview with Ambassador Ortona (22.3.2016). German records stress both the interest showed in Germany for the comments uttered by Cossiga, and the awareness of his limited leverage on the Italian decision making process. It was therefore mainly a heuristic interest. On the contrary, diplomatic documents provide no evidence of Cossiga's attempts to develop a direct channel with Kohl. Admitting that these attempts actually took place, they either failed to reach the Chancellor, or they merely had no relevant consequences and therefore they left no trace in the documents.

[107] See Ausführungen von AM Andreotti, Fernschreiben aus RomDiplo, Rom, 16.11.1989. PA AA B38, n. 140705.

[108] As for the initial choice of Andreotti to keep silent see Doc. 102, Vorlage des Ministerialdirektors Teltschik an Bundeskanzler Kohl, Bonn, 30.11.1989, in: Hans Jürgen Küsters/Daniel Hofmann (eds.), Deutsche Einheit: Sonderedition aus den Akten des Bundeskanzleramtes 1989/1990, München 1998, p. 574.

[109] As for the necessity expressed by Andreotti to "keep calm", see Anmerkung aus RomDiplo: Medienecho Italien, Rom, 13.11.1989. PA AA B38, n. 140704.

[110] "After the sudden opening of the Wall on 9 November 1989, Prime Minister Andreotti did not say a word on the issue regarding the future of both German states, rather warned to 'keep calm'. Regardless of the dramatic changes in the DDR, in the aftermath he remained faithful in several interviews to the idea that the reunification issue was not 'on the agenda'; rather, it was topical the concept 'one nation two states'". See Doc. 32, Vorlage des Referatsleiters 203, Kuhna, für Staatssekretär Sudhoff. Italienische Haltung zur deutschen Frage nach den Deutschland-kritischen Äußerungen von MP Andreotti, 18.12.1989, in: Die Einheit. Das Auswärtige Amt, das DDR-Außenministerium und der Zwei-plus-Vier-Prozess.

[111] Ibid.

Fig. 15: Il Pan Germanesimo. Caricature by Forattini, published on Repubblica (18.11.89)

For Italian readers, the pun implied by the cartoon was all too clear. A sandwich is made of bread, whose translation in Italian is "pane". The Italian word for bread sounds very much like the first part of the expression *Pan*germanismus. Pangermanismus became "pane-germanico": German bread. It plainly hinted at the 1984 declarations.

In 1989, Andreotti was trying, not without great difficulties, to swallow a "pane germanico". He was trying to digest the idea of a possible German re-unification, which, as in 1984, was making him sweat.

Do all these different hints show that in speaking of "pangermanesimo", Andreotti was addressing, back in 1984, the two German states, and was not referring to the Innsbruck-events? Were his approach and his fears fundamentally unchanged in 1989? Did Giulio Andreotti and Margaret Thatcher share in essence a similar position?

We can start by assuming that in 1984, and in 1989, Andreotti did fear the consequences of a new wave of "pangermanesimo". He did therefore share the same concerns as the British Prime Minister. We should then try to verify if this hypothesis is supported by sufficient evidence.[112]

---

[112] See Antonio Varsori, Italy the East European Revolutions and the Reunification of Germany 1989–1992, in: Wolfgang Mueller/Michael Gehler/Arnold Suppan (eds.), The Revolutions of 1989. A Handbook, pp. 403–417, p. 408. In December 1989, Andreotti received a report of the CESIS (executive committee for information and security) where the existence of Pangermanic tendencies and of pro-Nazi elements both in Germany and in Central-Eastern Europe was well-documented. See Memorandum CESIS to Andreotti su prospettive di riunificazione delle due Germanie: eventuali ritorni nazionalistici e pangermanici, strettamente confidenziale (secret), 15.12.1989. ILS, AGA, section Germany, b.458, quoted in Antonio Varsori, Italy the East European Revolutions and the Reunification of Germany 1989–1992, p. 408. Antonio Varsori seems to support the hypothesis that at least at first, Andreotti did fear a wave of "Pangermanismus" in Germany, and therefore mistrusted the idea of a re-unification.

The collection of documents of the German Foreign Office edited by Heike Amos and Tim Geiger on behalf of the *Institut für Zeitgeschichte* in 2015 shows astonishment at the behaviour of Giulio Andreotti. He was one of the first European politicians to have sensed the approaching changes beyond the Iron Curtain and to have resolutely supported them, and he could be so cold and detached when referring to Germany. In the documents collected, this feeling of astonishment is quickly replaced by an explicit mention of the 1984 declarations, which Andreotti, so as to the records, had never officially denied.[113] This does not, however, provide an answer to the question on whether Andreotti and Thatcher shared similar worries.

Fig. 16: Drømmeland. Cartoonist: Bo Bojesen/Denmark 1990

In February 1990, the Danish newspaper *Politiken* also published a cartoon, called *Drømmeland*[114] (meaning dreamland) concerning the German re-unification. It depicted Helmut Kohl who, while looking at his image in the mirror, saw a new Bismarck in the reflection. His worried and astonished Foreign Minister Genscher quickly leaves the room. Behind a veil of irony, the picture pointed at a widespread concern, both in Denmark and in Great Britain, that the very essence of the German nature was impervious to change.[115] This made of the rebirth of a German single state in the heart of Europe a threatening perspective.

---

[113] See Doc. 32, Vorlage des Referatsleiters 203, Kuhna, für Staatssekretär Sudhoff. Italienische Haltung zur deutschen Frage nach den Deutschland-kritischen Äußerungen von MP Andreotti, In: Die Einheit: Das Auswärtige Amt, das DDR-Außenministerium und der Zwei-plus-Vier Prozess.

[114] See AHUE, EG-168, Réunification, coupures de presse, 1985 to 1991, in *Politiken*, 16.2.1990.

[115] See Thorsten Borring Olesen/Niels Wium Olesen, Denmark and German Reunification. Anxious Feelings and the Limits of Europeanization, in: Michael Gehler/Maximilian Graf, Europa und die deutsche Einheit. Beobachtungen, Entscheidungen und Folgen, pp. 439–466.

Still, German and French records, e.g. concerning the 18 November Elysée Summit, also stress that this fear of an unchangeable German nature represented only one side of the complex reasoning developed by the Italian Prime Minister soon after the fall of the Wall. In a note written on 12 November 1989, the French Foreign Minister Roland Dumas (1988–1993) remarked that the EC Presidency, back then held by France, had been submitted during the previous days to constant pressure from Member States, including Italy, to host an emergency meeting to discuss the transformations in Central-Eastern Europe.[116]

According to the memorandum issued by Jean-Luis Bianco, the Secretary-General of the French presidency, François Mitterrand, in his capacity of political leader who held the EC presidency, opened up the debate with three main questions. They mainly concerned the issue of the frontiers and the stance which Gorbačëv would assume.[117] As for the first question, François Mitterrand believed that for the moment it was desirable to not raise the problem of the existing frontiers, whereas as far as the second one was concerned he urged his colleagues to make every possible effort so as not to destabilise Gorbačëv and the fragile Soviet equilibrium. In the handwritten notes at the end of the memorandum some specific comments on the participants have been added.[118]

The Spanish Head of Government Felipe Gonzalez, who wholeheartedly and unreservedly supported the idea of a German re-unification[119], and Prime

---

[116] See Réunion de l'Elysée, note du 12 novembre, 12.11.1989. ANF, série 5 AG 4, archives de Françoise Carle (hereafter FC)/83. Roland Dumas himself, in a note written on 18 November 1989, stressed that the meeting had had its main focus on changes in Eastern Europe. Still, the German question had been, though not officially, at the very heart of the discussions. See Réunion de l'Elysée, note du 18 novembre, 18.11.1989. ANF, série 5 AG 4/FC/83.

[117] See note du 18 novembre de Jean-Luis Bianco : Réunion de l'Elysée, 18.11.1989. Archives Nationales de France, série 5 AG 4/FC/83.

[118] Ibid.

[119] Unlike other Member States, in modern history Spain had rarely had strong ties, or shared common interests, with Germany, with the exception only of the civil war period and the Second World War. Still, we also must bear in mind that recent studies have shed light on the key role played by the Bundesrepublik in the Spanish transition from the Franco dictatorship to democracy. German foundations, especially the Friedrich Ebert Stiftung, had indeed had a key role in helping Spanish political and social forces to tackle the challenge issued by this process of transformation. Moreover, in the early Eighties not only did Felipe Gonzalez and Helmut Kohl develop fruitful personal relations, but the Bundesrepublik also supported the accession of Spain to the EC and was one of its most important partners within NATO. According to Eduardo Foncillas, Spanish Ambassador to Bonn in 1989, the Bundesrepublik support during the negotiations for Spanish accession to the EC, and the good chemistry between Kohl and Gonzalez notwithstanding, Germany was a second-rate partner compared with the USA, France, and Great Britain. The German issue was therefore not a crucial question to Spain, and the words uttered by Gonzalez on 18 November 1989 were the expression of a general lack of interest rather than an enthusiastic acceptance of the changes which lied ahead. On the contrary, Fernando Perpiñá Robert, in 1989 Secretary-General, took the opposite view. He affirmed that the re-unification was a crucial issue for both the *Palacio de Santa Cruz* (the

Minister Margaret Thatcher, who, on the contrary, ceaselessly reminded the risk of a "balkanisation" of the Continent, embodied the two extremes of a range of positions in the debate.

As for Giulio Andreotti, no hints to an opposition in principle to the idea of a German re-unification were mentioned, but only the utmost importance to strengthen the existing alliances and the CSCE could be detected in the notes. The records of the French Foreign Ministry also confirm that, regardless of the tensions during the meeting, a general agreement – with the only exception of Great Britain – was eventually reached. The only way to face this challenge was with an acceleration of the European integration process.[120]

Still, certain crucial knotty issues, such as the inviolability of the existing frontiers and the notion of self-determination, remained unresolved for a long time to come. During the following month of December, the final declaration of the summit of Strasbourg stated the right of Eastern Germans to choose their economic and political system, including the possibility of a "reunited" Germany within Europe. It must be though reminded that "reunited" in this particular context was no clearance to go ahead with the re-unification.

On the contrary, the declassified archival records do not provide any evidence, neither directly nor indirectly, of the comments given to the Italian magazine "Limes" some years after 1989 by Gianni de Michelis concerning the Elysée summit. He affirmed that during the 18 November emergency summit the "scambio geopolitico" (geopolitical exchange) enshrined in the Maastricht Treaty was

---

premises of the Spanish Foreign Ministry) and above all for the *Moncloa* (the residence of the Prime Minister). Fernando Perpiñá Robert believed that Spain had developed a "sensibilidad distinta" (a different approach) precisely because, unlike other European states, it had little common history with Germany and no pending disputes. In addition, even though the re-unification was not a crucial issue in Spain, the Secretary-General also believed that it had a strong influence on the Spanish Foreign policy in light of its potential side-effects on the European integration process. Felipe Gonzalez himself affirmed: "No tenemos nada que perder y sí que ganar [con la unidad alemana] siempre que nuestra respuesta sea profundizar la construcción europea". (We have nothing to lose and so much to win thanks to German unity, provided that our answer aims at strengthening the integration process). In all likelihood, the Spanish government decided to bring its weight and influence to bear not by means of its diplomatic channels, the Embassy in Bonn, but rather within the EC. See Antonio Muñoz Sanchez, Von der Franco-Diktatur zur Demokratie: die Tätigkeit der Friedrich-Ebert-Stiftung in Spanien, Berlin 2013. See also Alonso Álvarez de Toledo, En el país que nunca existió. Diario del último embajador español en la RDA, Barcelona 1990; Florentino Portero, El nuevo orden europeo y la cuestión alemana, in *Política Exterior* n. 4/14 (1990), pp. 115–124. On the role of Felipe Gonzalez, see also the author's interview with Rudolf Seiters, 26.6.2016 (about the specific reasons why Gonzalez chose this positive stance, Seiters provides, however, no explication).

[120] See, in particular, Commentaires des autorités italiennes sur la réunion informelle des Douze, télégramme ambassade de Rome, Rome, 20.11.1989, signed Perol. AMAE 1935inva, Direction Europe, Série CE, carton 5910, période 1986–1990.

gradually emerging. This meant the surrender of the German currency in ex-change for the European green light to re-unification.[121] The former Italian Foreign Minister also added that the Europeans could have "stopped" the reunification, but they were clever enough to use their negotiating power in a constructive manner. In an informal meeting which took place on the same evening, Helmut Kohl allegedly presented the first steps of his Ten-Point Plan in an atmosphere of growing hostility: "Kohl diventava sempre più rosso di rabbia e quando toccava a lui sembrava quasi che stesse per piangere (Kohl's face was becoming bright red with anger and when it was his turn to speak it seemed as if he was about to cry)". Andreotti, on the advice of de Michelis himself, allegedly forgot his hostility and said a few words to support Kohl. These words, according to de Michelis, sealed a good relationship with the Germans for times to come.[122]

Some specific aspects of these comments can easily be discarded as contrary to the information provided by every existing source, including all the diplomatic records declassified in the last thirty years, in particular the affirmation that Kohl had discussed some elements of his Ten-Point Plan.[123] Some others aspects, such as the hypothesis of the "geopolitical exchange", have also been refuted throughout the years by scientists and diplomats. At present, no evidence has been found in the records to support them.[124] As for the sentence which Andreotti allegedly uttered during the 18 November informal supper, no evidence to either support or refute it can be found in the records. According to Gian Enrico Rusconi, as time passed the Italian Foreign Minister probably started to rationalise a situation which in November 1989 was still uncertain and was in no way as clear as he had depicted it.[125] Concerning the sentence uttered by Andreotti, and more generally

---

[121] See Gianni de Michelis, La vera storia di Maastricht, in: *Limes* n. 3 (1996), pp. 137–144.

[122] Ibid.

[123] All collections of diplomatic documentation mentioned in the first introductory chapter confirm this feeling of astonishment which followed the announcement of the Ten-Point Plan. Nearly all experts are inclined to believe that not even Foreign Minister Genscher had been previously informed of the proceeding of the Chancellor. It is still a matter of discussion, whether the US President had been informed soon before the official announcement. See, in particular, Andreas Rödder, Deutschland einig Vaterland. Die Geschichte der Wiedervereinigung, München 2009, pp. 139–140.

[124] Giulio Andreotti always denied that a "marchandage" (exchange) between the re-unification and the German currency ever took place, for instance in the interview he gave to Aspenia in 2002, published with the title "Mezzo Secolo di Germania". See also the personal interview with Ambassador Roberto Nigido (2.3.2016). Ambassador Nigido as well denied the existence of such a "marchandage". Other interviews, in particular with Ambassador Cavalchini and with Ambassador Calamia, stressed that in all likelihood the process of re-unification had accelerated the German choice to give up the mark, which, however, was a process already in the air.

[125] See Gian Enrico Rusconi, Germania Italia Europa: Dallo stato di potenza alla potenza civile, Torino 2003, p. 278.

the 18 November meeting, it is equally interesting to consider the words of one eye-witness of the events, Ambassador Cavalchini:

> «Il 18 novembre 1989 si svolse la riunione dell'Eliseo...per la verità c'erano tre tavoli, quello presieduto da Mitterrand dei capi di Stato, quello presieduto da Dumas dei ministri degli Esteri e quello degli sherpa presieduto da Attali. [...] Quando de Michelis sostiene che la grossa mano al processo di riunificazione venne data da Andreotti proprio in quell'occasione dicendo che l'Italia auspicava la riunificazione, in definitiva interpretava una situazione di fatto che non poteva consentire di andare molto al di là. Entro questa cornice si collocava quella parte dell'intervista rilasciata a Limes da Gianni de Michelis, all'epoca dei fatti nostro ministro degli Esteri. A dire di de Michelis, Kohl doveva essere grato all'Italia e, in particolare, ad Andreotti se molte cose erano andate nel verso giusto».[126]

Even admitting that Andreotti did say something to support Kohl, which was in contrast with his usual extremely cautious approach, this sentence did neither change nor ease the fears and worries which Andreotti still harboured in mid-November 1989. On 22 November, the German Embassy in Rome once again stressed that for Andreotti, a re-unification was not an issue on the agenda. Furthermore, the Italian Prime Minister also believed that it was necessary to face more urgent problems, rather than meddling with things which could only become pressing in a longer time frame. The Embassy also highlighted that the background of each of his declarations always was the integration process as a stabilizing factor for the Continent.[127]

Similar considerations were provided by the Embassy on 27 November, the day before the announcement in the Bundestag of the Ten-Point Plan. Still, on this occasion, rather than merely presenting matters and statements, a thorough discussion of their roots and implications was also provided.[128] The Embassy was in fact aware of the tendency of both the German and the Italian media to simplify reality, even in the choice of the titles of their articles. In other words, the media

---

[126] "On 18 November 1989, the meeting of the Elysée took place...to tell the truth there were three tables: The table of the Heads of State was chaired by Mitterrand, then the table of Foreign Ministers chaired by Dumas, and lastly there also was the table of the sherpa coordinated by Attali [...] When de Michelis affirms that it was Andreotti who really lent a hand to Kohl as he said that Italy wished a reunification, well, he gave voice to an actual situation. I mean that this situation was not allowed to go further. Within such context, we must consider the interview given to Limes by Gianni de Michelis, by then our Foreign Minister. According to him, Kohl shoul be grateful to Italy and, above all, to Andreotti, if things had turned out as they had". See author's interview with Ambassador Luigi Guidobono Cavalchini, 5.2.2016.

[127] See Haltung Italiens zu den Veränderungen in Mittel- und Osteuropa, Fernschreiben aus RomDiplo Rome, Rom, 22.11.1989. PA AA B26, n. 140725.

[128] See Äußerungen von AM Andreotti zur deutschen Frage, Fernschreiben aus RomDiplo, Rom, 27.11.1989. PA AA B26, n. 140725.

usually explained to readers the approach of Andreotti solely as an instance of what he had already affirmed in 1984.[129] The German diplomats feared this equivalence between the stance of Andreotti and a refusal in principle of a re-unification.[130] Moreover, it was also noticed that the advocacy of the "*Endgültigkeit*" (finality) and "*Unberührbarkeit*" (untouchability) of frontiers, in light of the Helsinki Final Act, was applied by Andreotti to Eastern Europe in its entirety, and not merely towards Germany.[131] In addition, Andreotti had also affirmed, this time making specific reference to the events of Berlin, that a freer movement of goods, ideas and people in a finally homogeneous Europe would end up in nullifying the effects of borders.

At a first glance, his coldness of the previous weeks and his usual detached tone might accentuate the distinction between him and his colleagues, in particular with Francesco Cossiga. Yet, at a closer glance this stance fully neglects Andreotti's many correct references to the preamble of the German Fundamental Law and his expressions of support and appreciation towards the Europeanization policy promoted by Kohl. This is why the conclusion was drawn that „es wäre nicht richtig seine Äußerungen immer im Licht seiner Bemerkungen von 1984 zu interpretieren."[132]

The approach to the German problem backed by Andreotti, with its richness of different nuances, which so far have been briefly depicted, cannot be considered the exact equivalent to the stance of Margaret Thatcher. In his recently published essay, Dominik Geppert has remarked that only Margaret Thatcher tried by any possible means to prevent Germany from reunifying.[133] As for the motives

---

[129] See Ibid. The record makes specific reference to the interview given by Andreotti to the Italian newspaper *Corriere della Sera* and published on 26 November with the title: "I confini con l'Est non si toccano". The comments uttered by Andreotti concerning the German issue were just one aspect of his approach to the changes in Central-Eastern Europe, which was not so static as the title given by the author suggests.

[130] See Ibid.

[131] See Ibd. Although once again the comments of Andreotti were understandable, the German Foreign Ministry discussed the possibility to send a note to Italy to clarify that an interpretation of the Final Act of Helsinki, such as the words pronounced by Andreotti seemed to imply, was not shared by Bonn. A note signed by Kuhna on 1 December 1989 did provide more information on this German approach. Firstly, the possibility of a peaceful transformation to be carried out by mutual consent was recalled. Secondly, the note stressed that for Bonn the Final Act had not sanctioned the "Unantastbarkeit" (immutability) of frontiers, but rather their "Unverletzlichkeit" (inviolability), meaning that frontiers could be modified by peaceful means. See Äußerungen vom MP Andreotti zur deutschen Frage, Bonn, 1.12.1989. PA AA B26, n. 173561.

[132] "It would be a mistake to read his declarations always in light of what he said in 1984". See Äußerungen von AM Andreotti zur deutschen Frage, Fernschreiben aus RomDiplo, Rom, 27.11.1989. PA AA B26, n. 140725.

[133] See Dominik Geppert, Isolation oder Einvernehmen? Großbritannien und die deutsche Einheit 1989–1990, in: *Geschichte und Wissenschaft in Unterricht* 67 (2016), n. 1/2, pp. 5–22. As for the

behind such a stance, it is highly possible that not only the worries of destabilising Gorbačëv, but also the concern that Europe as a whole could be weakened, had an impact. Even more important for its influence on the stance of the British Prime Minister was, however, an old British perception of the German nature as a force destined to try and conquer the Continent.[134]

In other terms, the German issue was considered as an instance of the unchangeable German nature, an uncertain identity which had and still dithered between aggressive policies and a continuous questioning of its very essence, which in turn was the result of its being a late-born state.[135] It was for Margaret Thatcher a problem which more European integration could not solve, but rather worsen, by providing a unified Germany with a framework to impose its hegemony on the Continent. The American guarantee associated with a French-British entente was considered the only effective barrier to prevent this risk from becoming a reality. A deeper European integration was considered the best way to prevent or nullify this guarantee.[136]

By contrast, what Prime Minister Andreotti actually feared was a certain process of re-unification, which would question the German support to the European integration process.[137] He was, therefore, in favour of a pragmatic and of a wait-and-see approach.[138] His unfortunate reference to Pangermanism notwithstanding, in 1989 he was not interested in chasing the ghosts of the past, but rather in defining instruments in such a way as to support Italy in achieving sensible present targets.[139] Andreotti intimately mistrusted uncontrolled changes liable to

---

British approach see Yvonne Klein, Obstructive or promoting? British Views on German Unification 1989/1990, in: *German Politics* n. 5 (1996), pp. 404–43. See also Norman Himmler, Zwischen Macht und Mittelmaß: Großbritanniens Außenpolitik und das Ende des Kalten Krieges. Akteure, Interesse und Entscheidungsprozesse der britischen Regierung 1989–1990, Berlin 2001.

[134] See, in particular, Margaret Thatcher, Statecraft: Strategies for a changing world, Londra, Harper Perennial, 2002, pp. 2–5.

[135] See Dominik Geppert, Thatcher's konservative Revolution. Der Richtungswandel der britischen Tories (1975–1979), München 2002, pp. 140–142.

[136] See Doc.1, Sir C. Mallaby to Sir G. Howe, WGR 020/3, Confidential, Bonn, 10.4.1989, in: Patrick Salmon (ed.), Documents on British Policy Overseas: German Unification 1989–1990, Series III Volume VII, London 2010. Concerning the attempts of the British Prime Minister to reach un entente with France see Dominik Geppert, Isolation oder Einvernehmen? Großbritannien und die deutsche Einheit 1989–1990, p. 12. See Letter from Mr. Powell to Mr. Wall, Secret and strictly personal, 8.12.1989, in: Documents on British Policy Overseas: German Unification 1989–1990, p. 162.

[137] See Audience à Giulio Andreotti, Paris, 13.2.1990. Archives Nationales de France, série 5 AG 4, CD/304, dossier 11 e 12.

[138] See Gabriele D'Ottavio, 1989 oder das Ende der "parallelen Geschichte" Deutschlands und Italiens? in: *Geschichte und Wissenschaft in Unterricht* 67 (2016), n. 1/2, pp. 39–57, 49.

[139] A further element did differentiate the Italian and the British stance. Although the DDR was never a priority for Italian policy, the Italian Foreign Ministry did sense, at least up to a certain degree, the extent of the ongoing transformation in the DDR. In all likelihood, this was probably

interrupt and jeopardise the patient work of politics and diplomacy which provide order.[140]

This fear was also mirrored, though at different degrees and with different intensity, both within the Government and the Italian Foreign Office in a general concern that the German Chancellery could lose control over the re-unification process, which could as a result be achieved outside the three main Western "protective structures": the EC, NATO and the CSCE.

> „Wenngleich auch die italienische Regierung in den Wochen nach dem Mauerfall Zweifel und Sorgen bezüglich einer voreiligen deutschen Wiedervereinigung hatte, begriffen die italienischen Führungskräfte schon bald, im Gegensatz zu Margaret Thatchers Großbritannien und auf einer ähnlichen Wellenlage wie Mitterrands Frankreich, dass die Bonner Regierung imstande war, das Ziel eines vereinten Deutschlands in relativ kurzer Zeit zu erreichen."[141]

In conclusion, I cannot but agree with the remarks proposed by Gabriele d'Ottavio. In spite of initial uncertainties, in Italy by the end of November the perception of the importance of what was actually at stake, and that the German process could not be stopped, was slowly but gradually gaining acceptance. On this basis, the attempt to define a three-pillar strategy to cope with the events took shape. The 29 November-1 December 1989 official State visit of Gorbačëv to Rome strongly stimulated this creative process.[142]

7.3 Drawing Preliminary Conclusions

> „Umso mehr Aufsehen haben dafür die wiederholten Äußerungen von MP Andreotti, die in erster Linie von der Besorgnis über eine Gefährdung des delikaten Gleichgewichts in Europa und um die politische Zukunft des sowjetischen Staats-

---

not the case in Britain. In mid-1989, the Ambassador to the DDR, Nigel Broomfield, stressed, for instance, that the Politburo still strongly supported Honecker, and that immediate changes were a far-fetched possibility. See http://www.margaretthatcher.org/documents/111018 (lastly consulted on 1.12.2016), also quoted in Dominik Geppert, Thatcher's konservative Revolution, p. 8.

[140] See Gabriele D'Ottavio, 1989 oder das Ende der "parallelen Geschichte", p. 48: "[…] auch ein gemäßigter Führer wie Giulio Andretti konnte den Fall der Berliner Mauer aus der Sicht der innenpolitischen Auseinandersetzung positiv betrachten; andererseits zeigte sich der damalige italienische Ministerpräsident sehr besorgt über die internationalen Auswirkungen des 9. November. […]". (Even a cautious leader as Andreotti could take a positive view in light of the inner German development. He was, nonetheless, seriously worried about the international implications).

[141] "Even though, in the weeks following the fall of the Wall, the Italian government was also worried about a hasty German reunification, its élite quickly understood – unlike Margaret Thatcher and similarly to Mitterrand and the country he led – that the government in Bonn was capable of reaching the target of a reunified Germany within a relatively short time". See Ibid., p. 51.

[142] See, in particular, Telegramma urgentissimo sui colloqui tra Gorbaciov e Cossiga, signed Perlot, riservato (restricted), 29.11.1989, ILS, AGA, section URSS, b.695.

und Parteichefs Gorbatschows geprägt waren, dessen Schicksal Andreotti mit einer ausgewogenen und schrittweisen Lösung der deutschen Frage im gesamteuropäischen Rahmen verbunden sieht. Hierbei wurden Divergenzen zu der allgemein positiveren Einschätzung des PSI, aber auch der DC selbst deutlich."[143]

In light of what has been so far presented, we can finally turn our attention to the 29 November meeting between Andreotti and Gorbačëv, and to the sentences quoted at the beginning of this chapter.

The German, Soviet, and Italian[144] records all confirm that at the end of November 1989, Andreotti still kept faithful to the stance "one Nation-two States" and that, as a result, he estimated that the German re-unification was not for the present an issue to be put on the agenda.

> „Andreotti: Jetzt zu Deutschland. Ich habe wiederholt gesagt [...] dies ist eine Nation, aber es sind zwei Staaten. Das ist unsere feste, sogar sehr feste Haltung. Ich stimme völlig mit Ihrer berechtigten Bemerkung überein, dass niemand von uns voraussehen kann, was letztlich in der Zukunft geschehen wird. Ende dieser Woche werden sich die Regierungschefs und Führer der christdemokratischen Parteien aus jenen der zwölf europäischen Länder in denen sie an der Macht sind

---

[143] "All the more astonishing were the reiterated comments of Prime Minister Andreotti. They were primarily affected by concerns about the delicate balance in Europe and about the political future of the Soviet party, and of Gorbačëv, whose destiny, according to Andreotti, was inseparably associated with a well-balanced and step-by-step solution of the German issue in a Pan-European framework. In this regard, differences between him and the more positive assessments of the PSI – but also of the DC – are undeniable". See Doc. 32, Vorlage des Referatsleiters 203, Kuhna, für Staatssekretär Sudhoff. Italienische Haltung zur deutschen Frage nach den Deutschland-kritischen Äußerungen von MP Andreotti, 18.12.1989, in: Die Einheit. Das Auswärtige Amt, das DDR-Außenministerium und der Zwei-plus-Vier-Prozess, p. 175.

[144] In 2016, the section "Soviet Union" of the Archives Andreotti was eventually officially opened to consultation. Box 695 contains several documents concerning Gorbačëv's state visit to Rome at the end of November 1989, among them an interesting handwritten note: "Circa la Germania l'ho detto in Parlamento: una nazione, due stati; è una posizione molto ferma. Come dice lei non si può sapere quello che sarà in futuro. Con dodici paesi europei avremo un incontro per parlare con chiarezza con Kohl. Nell'incontro con Mitterrand [probabile riferimento al vertice dell'Eliseo n.d.r.] nessuno parlò di unificazione per essere esatti, ma ci può essere il calcolo elettorale (per me sbagliato), per non aiutare i Republikaner si usa questa idea di ieri del cancelliere un po' improvvisata. Nulla vieta che essi abbiano, come già detto, maggiori rapporti economici. Una cosa non ho capito, perché la situazione è precipitata così velocemente? ...ci ha presi tutti molto impreparati con il crollo del Muro. [...]". (As for Germany, I have already said it in Parliament: one nation, but two states: this is indeed a firm position, a very firm one. As you say, we cannot know what the future will bring. In the meeting with Mitterrand [Andreotti probably hints at the Elysée meeting] nobody spoke of re-unification, to be honest... but it was perhaps a matter of the election approaching (a miscalculation if you ask me). The Chancellor introduced this improvised idea, so as not to help the Republikaner. As I have already said, nothing prevents the two states from having more economic bonds. One thing I did not understand; why did the situation fall apart so quickly?... it caught us all off guard with the fall of the Wall [...]).

treffen. Und wir haben vor, sehr offen mit Kohl in dieser Hinsicht zu sprechen. Wenn man ganz genau ist hat auch Mitterrand niemals direkt über eine Wiedervereinigung Deutschlands gesprochen.
In der BRD gibt es jetzt Wahlkalküle. Die Regierung befürchtet eine Stärkung der Republikaner […] daher auch die verschiedensten Improvisationen in der Art der gestrigen Kohl-Rede im Bundestag. Aber wir werden natürlich nicht der Entwicklung der Beziehungen, auch nicht der Wirtschaftsbeziehungen, zwischen den beiden deutschen Staaten im Wege stehen. Sie existieren übrigens schon seit langem. Ich möchte Ihnen eine Frage stellen. Wo liegt die Ursache für eine so rasche Entwicklung der Ereignisse in der DDR? Zuerst die Demonstrationen in Leipzig und Dresden und dann plötzlich diese schnelle Veränderung mit der Mauer."[145]

Still, his fears and worries notwithstanding, he was also increasingly aware of the actual impossibility to stop the ongoing rapprochement between Eastern and Western Germany. This provides a first answer to the key question of this research. Andreotti did not rank amongst those leaders busy writing a plot able to block the German changing process. His political experience and his personal intuition probably showed him how such an attempt would have been doomed to failure. The formula "one Nation-two States" was rather a temporary strategy to try and slow down its speed for as long as necessary.[146]

---

[145] "Andreotti: And now about Germany. I have already said it […]: one nation, but two states. This is indeed a firm position, a very firm one. I fully agree with your legitimate assessment that we cannot know what the future will bring. At the end of this week, all leaders belonging to those European Member States where the Christian-democrats are in power will meet together. And we have the intention to speak very frankly to Kohl about this issue. To be more precise, Mitterrand too has never directly addressed the reunification issue. The Federal Republic is swept by calculations concerning the approaching elections. The government fears a stronger Republican party […] which would explain the many improvisations such as the speech which Kohl held yesterday in front of the Bundestag. But, of course, we will not stand in the way of a further development of relations – also at an economic level – between the two German states. By the way, they have existed for a long time. I wish to ask you a question. What was the main cause of such a rush development in the DDR? At first the demonstrations in Leipzig and Dresden, later on, out of the blue, this rapid change with the Wall". See Doc. 57 Gespräch Gorbačevs mit dem italienischen Ministerpräsidenten Andreotti am 29. November 1989, Rom, 29.11.1989, in: Michail Gorbatschow und die deutsche Frage: Sowjetische Dokumente 1986–1991, München 2011. This text and the abovementioned handwritten note follow the same guidelines with only one relevant exception, namely the reference to Mitterrand. The Italian note affirms that nobody spoke of re-unification during the meeting with Mitterrand, whereas the Soviet text affirms that Mitterrand himself did not address the issue of re-unification.

[146] See the interview with Ambassador Cavalchini (5.2.2016). According to this interview Margaret Thatcher was the leader one mostly feared a reunified Germany. The great ability of the Chancellor lied in understanding that a closer European link was the precondition of the reunification, which was reassuring for the Italian government. The Chancellor seemed to be aware that a re-unification could not proceed separated from the process of European integration. Nobody could question the principle of re-unification, what was, however, originally questioned in Italy was the idea of Kohl of attaining the reunification in record time.

Two more specific elements in the previous quotation are worthy of attention: the perception of Andreotti vis-à-vis the Ten-Point Plan, and the questions concerning the fall of the Wall which he had addressed to the Soviet leader.

Andreotti was not alone in having expressed negative judgments and harsh criticism against Kohl's choice to present the Ten-Point Plan. French President Mitterrand had, for instance, also been highly critical of some specific points of the Plan. Still, not only had the Italian leader criticised the contents of the Plan, but he had also brought attention to a further element, namely one of the reasons why it had been so quickly and unexpectedly presented. It was considered an improvisation conceived in light of the approaching elections.[147]

As had already happened in the past, Italian and German politicians had often a distorted picture of their objectives and of the motives behind their actions. In 1984, the possibility that Andreotti had spoken of pangermanism in light of internal political needs had been discussed even in Bonn, while just five years later, in 1989, it was the turn of Italy and its leader to simplify the roots and implications of the Ten-Point Plan by reducing it to an electoral issue. As for the questions Andreotti addressed to Gorbačëv, no answer was at first provided. So Andreotti had to repeat once again his doubts:

> „Gorbačev: Möglicherweise existiert ein solcher Grund. Die Führung der DDR hat aufgrund der Konfrontation mit der BRD die Gesellschaft über viele Jahre im Zustand der Mobilmachung gehalten. Und das funktionierte auch. Als bei uns die Veränderungen begannen, hätten sie genau dasselbe tun müssen: Möglichkeiten eröffnen, damit die Menschen sich verwirklichen können und der Zeit entsprechende Formen finden: auch was die Kontakte mit der BRD betrifft. Aber Honecker hielt sich für den Hüter des heiligen Feuers. Und das, was die anderen taten, betrachtete er beinahe als Verrat […]. Das gesellschaftliche Bewusstsein verlangte nach Veränderungen, aber die politische Führung hat nicht reagiert.
> Andreotti: Ich habe Honecker nicht gut gekannt, kannte aber einige Mitglieder der DDR-Führung. So mancher von ihnen hielt sich für einen modernen denkenden Funktionär, aber das war nur der äußere Schein. Ein Beispiel dafür ist Axen.
> Gorbačev: Sie alle waren Funktionäre von gestern […]."[148]

---

[147] See also interview with Ambassador Cavalchini (05.2.2016). Kohl was allegedly worried about the risk of jeopardising the support to his re-election of millions of electors who either came from the Eastern territories or descended from people forced to abandon those territories at the end of the Second World War.

[148] "Gorbačëv: Maybe there exists such a reason. In light of the confrontation with the Bundesrepublik, the DDR leadership has kept society in a state of permanent mobilisation. And it has worked. But when the changes began for us, they should have done the same: to offer opportunities, in order to allow men and women to express themselves in shapes coherent with the time we live in (also concerning the exchanges with the Bundesrepublik). But Honecker thought that he was the guardian of the holy fire. He considered what we all did a betrayal […]. The social conscience urged for

Gorbačëv was for Andreotti the only man who had the potential to fulfill a genuine process of reform not only in the USSR, but also in the entirety of the Eastern bloc. To achieve this goal he had to maintain an unstable balance between those who wanted to accelerate the process or even question the existing framework – which would result in unforeseeable consequences – and those supporting reactionary proposals.[149]

In conclusion, the Italian stance was like a pendulum swinging from one target to the opposite one. The first target was the willingness to maintain good relations with Bonn, hence working to avoid a detachment of Germany from the EC in chasing the re-unification. The second one corresponded to the desire to also maintain good relations with Moscow and to promote its stability. For Italy, this was the extent of the challenge and the conundrum it would face in the following months. The question was, therefore, how Italy could keep its balance on the edge of the blade.

A great deal of support towards Germany had been voiced during the month of November within the Italian Socialist Party, whereas the Christian Democratic area was rather split in different approaches and views. Still, it was the DC which, throughout the decades, had been the most relevant Italian interlocutor with German governments. If we combine this last consideration with the importance of the party pillar in the Italian-German relationship, it cannot be in the least surprising that both politicians who developed the more nuanced and complex approaches to the aforementioned conundrum belonged to the Christian Democratic Party: Giulio Andreotti and Francesco Cossiga.[150] They were the only personalities, with major institutional roles, to have developed over time a vivid and systematic view of both the German and the Soviet situation. At a first glance they were at opposite ends of an imaginary line; at a closer glance they, however, simply provided different answers to the same central question. Their main concerns were basically the same: the risk of a German neutralisation on the one side, and a Soviet coup d'état on the other. The choice to give priority either to providing support to Kohl and his policy towards re-unification announced in his Ten-Point Plan, or to safeguard the position of Gorbačëv and his reform course, was the combined result of political considerations regarding the future of Europe, of emotional reactions to the German issue, and also of a bet about the credibility and the chances of success of the Soviet leader.

This allows us to finally provide an answer to the question raised at the end of the sub-chapter concerning the German issue and the European Common

---

changes, but the leadership did not react. Andreotti: I do not know Honecker very well, but I know some members of the DDR-élite. Some of them thought that they were modern officers, but it was just appearance. An example is Axen. Gorbačëv: They were all officers of the past". See Ibid.

[149] See author's interview with Ambassador Cavalchini (5.2.2016).

[150] With the exception of part of the élite of the Communist party (see ch. 7.1.3).

House: how could Italy support the struggle towards reform undertaken by Gorbačëv without damaging its relations with Bonn. If the support to the Soviet new course was the top priority, as Andreotti seemed to believe, it was necessary to slow down the speed of the German rapprochement, even though by the end of 1989 the re-unification appeared less like a hypothesis like many others and more like the main German target. If, on the contrary, the support to Helmut Kohl and his political action was the top priority to secure the future of Europe, it had to be taken into account that the new Soviet course could suffer some setbacks. It was then difficult to affirm to what extent.[151]

Fig. 17: Gorbačëv official State-Visit to Rome (November 1989).
Istituto Sturzo, Archive Andreotti (copyright AGI)

Italy did not rank among the winning powers of the Second World War. Therefore, it had not been involved in the decisions taken at the end of the conflict, and neither would be engaged in 1990 in the 2+4 negotiations. From this it follows

---

[151] See, in particular, Telegramma urgentissimo sui colloqui tra Gorbaciov e Cossiga, riservato, 29.11.1989. ILS, AGA, section URSS, b.695. Cossiga had a rather cautious approach towards the European Common House. He certainly reaffirmed that Italy appreciated its roots and motivations, but he also stressed that it required long-term close scrutiny and some interim-steps to be translated into actual initiatives. See also author's interview with Ambassador Ludovico Ortona, 22.03.2016: "4 dicembre: al Presidente continua a preoccupare la Germania e soprattutto il rischio che l'Occidente si faccia scappare la Repubblica Federale Tedesca mettendola nella condizione di chiedere aiuto all'Unione Sovietica che non chiederebbe di meglio che vedere una Germania neutrale". (On 4 December: The President was always worried about Germany and about the risk that the West would let Germany slip away by forcing it to ask the Soviet Union for help. The Soviet Union would like nothing more than a neutral Germany).

that in chapter eight it will not be possible to discuss how these perceptions evolved through the analysis of relevant international conferences and negotiating mechanisms. We will rather find ourselves on the margins of such conferences and looking at the edges of the main negotiations, which is an interesting place to be to analyse the Italian stance and the perceptions which its European partners had of it.

8. The Making of a Triple Strategy: December 1989–February 1990

The former chapter ended with some comments on the contrast within Italian politics at the end of November 1989, between the demands linked to the internal German developments, and those linked to the political developments in Moscow. This chapter instead will begin with some remarks on German internal dynamics, especially those concerning the genesis of the Ten-Point Plan, its contents, and the reactions which it unleashed in Italy.

Just as the state visit to Rome of M.S. Gorbačëv symbolically represented the conclusion of the first phase of the Italian reaction to the German events, so also the Ten-Point Plan – presented by Helmut Kohl on 28 November 1989 to the German Parliament – epitomised the conclusion of this first stage, but it also acted as springboard for the launching of the next phase of the Italian strategy. After weeks of high uncertainty in the European capitals and in Germany itself, the 28 November Plan was in fact a document which left enough leeway for the Government in Bonn to undertake political action. At the same time, it also provided a set of guidelines which shed some light on the objectives that the Chancellor intended to pursue in the coming months.

In which political context was this statement prepared and then made public? And how many different interpretations could it lend itself to? Which were its internal and external implications?

First of all, it is necessary not only to recall that the first reactions of the partners of Germany to the 9 November events had been very cautious, but it is also essential to remark that both the German Chancellor and his Foreign Minister had kept a rather low profile in the days which followed this spectacular event and which resulted in the growing exodus of DDR citizens towards Western Germany. On 16 November 1989, nearly a week from the statements of Günther Schabowski[1], Helmut Kohl was still extremely cautious in addressing the political developments. He merely affirmed that his government would respect the decisions freely taken by Eastern German citizens.[2]

The Ten-Point Plan was the final outcome of different trends at odds with each other, both at an internal and at an external level.[3] At a national level, both the rapidly deteriorating social conditions in Eastern Germany, and the increasing tensions within the Bundesrepublik, are to be taken into account. The latter were

---

[1] See Michael Gehler, Deutschland: Von der Teilung zur Einigung 1945 bis heute, Wien – Köln – Weimar 2010, pp. 321–322.

[2] See Andreas Rödder, Deutschland einig Vaterland: Die Geschichte der Wiedervereinigung, München 2009, p. 137.

[3] See Michael Mertens, Die Entstehung des Zehn-Punkte-Programms vom 28. November 1989, in: Heiner Timmermann, Die DDR in Deutschland. Ein Rückblick auf 50 Jahre, Berlin 2001, pp. 17–35.

the result of the inputs coming from East Berlin, and of the contrasts within the Federal political spectrum. The day after the 16 November official declarations, that is on 17 November 1989, the new DDR Head of Government, Hans Modrow, launched the proposal of a "Vertragsgemeinschaft" between the two German States[4], while on 27 November Franz Schönhuber, leader of the *Republikaner*, declared that both the re-unification and the reaffirmation of the 1937 borders were to be regarded as the primary goals to achieve in Bonn. In so doing, the Republikaner leader inflamed the current debate by raising issues which could bring it into a direction rather difficult for the central Government to keep under control.

The same feeling of general confusion seemed to prevail among the leading German newspapers, like the conservative *die Welt* or the prestigious *Frankfurter Allgemeine Zeitung*.[5] Since mid-November there were, however, some isolated calls for a re-unification, such as the voice of the Chief Editor of the magazine *Der Spiegel*, Alfred Herrhausen, who also criticised the lack of dynamism of the Federal Government.[6] On 20 November 1989, Horst Teltschik wrote in his memories:

> „Die internationale wie die innenpolitische Diskussion über die Chancen einer Wiedervereinigung Deutschlands ist voll entbrannt und nicht mehr aufzuhalten [...]. Mehr und mehr sind wir dessen bewußt, doch die Weisung des Bundeskanzlers bleibt, in der öffentlichen Diskussion Zurückhaltung zu üben. Weder innerhalb der Koalition, und damit innenpolitisch, noch außenpolitisch will er Angriffsflächen bieten."[7]

---

[4] See, for example, Gian Enrico Rusconi, Capire la Germania: Un diario ragionato sulla questione tedesca, Bologna 1990, pp. 115–118.

[5] See, in particular, the Frankfurter Allgemeine Zeitung editorials from 11 up to 27 November 1989. As for the debate in the German press, see, in particular, Herbert Kremp, Lassen wir uns die Wiedervereinigung von anderen formulieren? *Welt am Sonntag*, 19.11.1989, and Hanns Hermann Tiedje, Wiedervereinigung: die deutsch-deutsche Tonart ändert sich, *Tageszeitung*, 23.11.1989.

[6] In the editorial published by the German newspaper *die Welt* on the second Sunday after the fall of the Berlin Wall, the German Government was criticised as it was considered unprepared to develop ideas going beyond the existence of a Western German State. The newspaper ironically remarked that the Government seemed to act as if an annoying wind had swept some documents off its desk. Quoted in Andreas Rödder, Deutschland einig Vaterland, p. 138.

[7] "A heated debate on the opportunities of a German reunification has arisen both domestically and internationally and it cannot be stopped [...]. We are increasingly aware of that, but the instructions given by the Chancellor are unchanged: we must exercise restraint in the public debate. He does not want to provide arguments to be challenged, neither within the ruling coalition, i.e. in domestic policy, nor in foreign policy". See Horst Teltschik, 329 Tage. Innenansichten der Einigung, Berlin 1991, p. 41.

For the Federal Government, to follow a strategy which aimed at the immediate implementation of a State reunification of Eastern and Western Germany would have been like jumping into the unknown. Even though during the previous years the issue of re-unification had been slowly coming through the folds of the national political debate, no concept or operational programme had been until then drawn to face the occurrence of events like the fall of the Berlin Wall.

Ex post, we could be tempted to depict the path towards re-unification as if it had been a linear process following an inherent logic from the very beginning until its end. This, however, was not the case. The first reactions were the palpable expression of a high degree of hesitation. This was not only the result of events which took the Federal Republic by surprise, but it was also the result of a creeping fear of endangering the relations with Western European partners by erroneous actions.

At the same time, an excessively cautious approach also presented for Helmut Kohl and his government the risk of being more and more criticised at home, of eventually losing the capacity for initiative and, if the worst came to the worst, even the control over the situation.[8] Besides, with his proposal of a contractual community, Hans Modrow had given a significant input to the ongoing debate. Bonn had to provide a viable alternative.[9]

At an international level, the information which came from the most influential European capitals, and especially from Moscow, was equally contradictory. On the one hand, the Soviet leader had repeated on 15 November, while talking in front of a group of students in Moscow, that a German re-unification was not a question on the agenda.[10] On the other hand, however, on 21 November 1989 in a private meeting in Bonn, Nikolaj Portugalow – Counsellor to the International Relations Section of the Soviet Central Committee – handed to Horst Teltschik a short piece of paper with a list of thorny issues to which a re-unification could allegedly have given an answer. The sole existence of such a document seemed to represent a green light to the target of re-unification, meaning that it led Teltschik to believe that the Soviet Union was ready to accommodate the

---

[8] The risk of losing the capacity of initiative refers to both the relations with the DDR and to those with the main Western German parties, meaning the SPD and the FDP. See Ibid., pp. 42–44.

[9] Andreas Rödder analysed the reasons behind the proposal of Hans Modrow of a "Vertragsgemeinschaft". If Modrow aimed at calming social tensions in the DDR and at proposing an alternative to avoid the possibility of a reunification, he did not, according to Rödder, succeed in his goals. The debate concerning the search of a viable political solution did rather accelerate in the following months. See Andreas Rödder, Deutschland einig Vaterland, p. 137.

[10] See Doc. 23, Vorlage des Referatsleiters 213, Neubert, für Bundesminister Genscher. Äußerungen Gorbatschows zur Wiedervereinigung vor Studenten in Moskau (15.11.1989), 17.11.1989, in: Die Einheit. Das Auswärtige Amt, das DDR-Außenministerium und der Zwei-plus-Vier-Prozess.

implementation of this political target.[11] Against the advice of the then major experts of German politics within the Central Government, Kohl decided, for both contingent domestic needs and Foreign policy demands, to pursue an initiative that led him and his closest collaborators to formulate within a few days – mainly by working in the Chancellor's private residence in Ludwigshafen, in order to guarantee the maximum degree of secrecy – the 28 November programme.

This is one possible explanation to the approach taken by the German Chancellor at the end of November 1989. Its basic elements are those items which were the most visible to the Western European partners of the Bundesrepublik, including Italy, i.e. the worries related to the mounting social, economic and political difficulties of the DDR, coupled with the opportunity for Kohl to gain an electoral advantage from this turmoil.[12]

It is, however, possible to enrich this basic interpretation with a more in-depth analysis of the personality, the educational path, the political career, and the style of government of Chancellor Kohl.[13] As regards his education, his political career, and their effects on his approach to the "German question", the hallmarks which had emerged after the September 1984 comments of Giulio Andreotti, were far more pronounced and visible to foreign observes by the end of 1989. Kohl's stance remarkably differed from the political orientation embraced by his predecessor and former German Chancellor, Konrad Adenauer.[14] In other words, Helmut Kohl did not share the very essence of Adenauer's approach to the German question, embodied by his well-known dictum "keine Experimente".[15] He rather supported the perception that Germany was an economic, cultural and political "unicum" that, for contingent historical reasons, found itself in a provisional state of territorial division.[16] Kohl's personal experience, as much as his academic education, had brought him to look at Germany as a unity. He did not share most of the prejudices expressed by his famous predecessor towards

---

[11] See Doc. 112, SU und die deutsche Frage. Vorlage Teltschiks an Kohl, Bonn, 6.12.1989, pp. 616–618, in: Einheit: Sonderedition aus den Akten des Bundeskanzleramtes 1989/1990, München 1998.

[12] See Doc 57, Gespräch Gorbačevs mit dem italienischen Ministerpräsidenten Andreotti am 29. November 1989, Rom, 29.11.1989 (Archiv der Gorbačëv Stiftung, Bestand 1, Verzeichnis 1), in: Michail Gorbatschow und die deutsche Frage: Sowjetische Dokumente 1986–1991, München 2011.

[13] See, in particular, Karl-Rudolf Korte, Deutschlandpolitik in Helmut Kohls Kanzlerschaft. Entscheidungsprozeß und Regierungsstil 1981–1989, Geschichte der deutschen Einheit Band I, Stuttgart 1998.

[14] See ch. 5.1.

[15] This slogan was successfully used in the election campaign in the Federal Republic in 1957 and it granted to the conservative forces the absolute majority.

[16] See Michael Gehler, Deutschland: Von der Teilung zur Einigung 1945 bis heute, ch.11, p. 352.

"Prussia".[17] In 1984, it would have been premature to even think of a re-unification, whereas 1989 provided the Chancellor with a real opportunity to launch an active policy in favour of German unity.[18]

For Kohl this issue was, therefore, both a political chance to be handled carefully in order to avoid negative internal and external side-effects, and a "Herzensanliegen", a highly emotional question. In the absence of specific programmes and concepts to help implement this objective, the capability of Helmut Kohl to combine toughness with tenacity in the pursuit of set targets, together with his inborn ability for political experimentation and his remarkable disposition to accept risks, had a paramount role in the re-unification process.[19] The first two qualities might have been a heritage of his well-known predecessor, Konrad Adenauer, but the particular disposition of Helmut Kohl was certainly a personal addition to German politics.

> „In Bonn war Deutschlandpolitik 'Chefsache', und im Kanzleramt regierte Kohl auf einer ganz persönlichen Weise: nicht aus der spezifischen Rationalität des bürokratischen Apparats heraus […] sondern spontan, situationsbezogen und ungezwungen und vor allem mit dem Mittel des direkten persönlichen Gesprächs und

---

[17] It is important to stress once again that Helmut Kohl had an academic background in history, which also meant that he had in-depth knowledge of the history of the Holy Roman Empire, successively known as the Holy Roman Empire of German Nation. In the interview with the author (28.10.2016), Ambassador Ferdinando Salleo described Kohl as the typical representative, both emotionally and in his approach to politics, of Western Germany, who had very little in common with the "Prussians". A more emotional approach to politics was considered in Italy a hallmark of Southern and Western Germans compared to politicians from the Northern and the Eastern regions of the country, by which "Prussia" was usually meant. Kohl had, however, a peculiar stance compared to other Christian Democrats from the West, Konrad Adenauer included. Certainly, at the beginning of the 1950s, many hurdles stood on the way of a German re-unification. Still, Adenauer himself did not seem to feel very "deeply" the importance of pursuing the goal of re-unification. After the First World War, he allegedly considered, as mayor of Cologne, the idea of an autonomous role for the area of Rhineland, which his opponents then used to accuse him of separatism.

[18] As discussed in the introductory chapter, the collection of diplomatic documents of the German Chancellory were the first to be published. They provided for a greater understanding of the contribution made by the Chancellor, along with his closest advisors, to the chain of events which paved the way for the establishment of a German unified state between 1989 and 1990. On the contrary, the contribution of other German players, such as the Federal Ministries – the Foreign Office, but also the Treasury Department, the Ministry for Economic Affairs, the Ministry of Justice and that of Defence – became relegated to a second place. Only in 2009 hundreds of diplomatic records of the German Foreign Ministry covering the two-year period 1989–1990 were declassified. They shed new light on the importance of the role played by Hans-Dietrich Genscher and of the Foreign Ministry which he led. Still, it is rather difficult to deny that it was Helmut Kohl who took the initiative by launching the Ten-Point Plan, and that he shaped the process towards re-unification with his skills and determination.

[19] See Michael Gehler, Le tre Germanie: Germania Est, Germania Ovest e Repubblica di Berlino, (translation from the German of Sara Quarantani), Bologna 2011, pp. 280–281.

des persönlichen Vertrauensverhältnisses, auch und gerade auf internationaler Ebene. Auf dieser Weise wirkte der Politiker Kohl [...] durch seine persönlichen Eigenschaften: [...] Bodenständigkeit, unerschöpfliche Aktionspotentiale und hohe Willenskraft, verbunden mit – bei aller Sensibilität – hartnäckiger Selbstsicherheit. [...] An der Spitze der Regierungszentrale stand [...] Rudolf Seiters als Chef des Bundeskanzleramtes: ein umsichtiger, nüchtern-analytischer Koordinator und Mann der effizienten Administration. Von ganz anderem Schlage war sein Stellvertreter Horst Teltschik, der Leiter der außenpolitischen Abteilung und Kohls engster politischer Berater. Wie Kohls engste Umgebung entstammte er nicht dem Apparat der Karrierebeamten, sondern dem parteipolitischen Umfeld, aus dem Kohl den inneren Zirkel der Macht im Kanzleramt rekrutierte [...]. Strategisch und leidenschaftlich [...] optimistischer und unbefangener als die Vertreter von Bürokratie und Diplomatie, trieb Teltschik die im Vergleich zum Auswärtigen Amt [...] offensivere Politik der Regierungszentrale voran."[20]

This picture, which is drawn by the German historian Andreas Rödder, sums up some of Kohl's major features in approaching public affairs, both domestically and internationally, and thus they provide the last pieces to complete the discussion of the magma in which the idea and the implementation of the Ten-Point Plan took its shape.

On the basis of the issues so far discussed, the contents of the Plan and the reaction which it unleashed in the Bundesrepublik and, above all, abroad, may now be addressed.

---

[20] "In Bonn the German politics was '*Chefsache*', namely an issue under the sole responsibility of the Chancellor. And Helmut Kohl ruled over the Chancellery in a rather personal way, not according to the inner logic of the bureaucratic apparatus [...] but on impulse, according to the current situation and, above all, by means of personal exchanges of views and relationships of trust, also and especially on the international stage. In this way Helmut Kohl acted [...] through his personal qualities [...] his practicality, his inexhaustible potential for action and through his strong determination, coupled with – his political sensitivity taken into account – a tenacious sense of self-confidence. [...] In charge of the administration [...] Rudolf Seiters as Chief of the Chancellery: a prudent, unemotional coordinator and an example of an efficient administration. By contrast, his deputy, Horst Teltschik (the Head of the Department for Foreign issues and the closest advisor of Kohl), was made of a quite different matter. Like Kohl's closest entourage, he did not belong to the civil servants by career, but rather to the political realm, from which Kohl had recruited his inner circle [...]. Strategic and passionate [...] more optimistic and unbiased than the bureaucrats, Teltschik supported the more proactive –compared to the Foreign Office – politics of the Government". See Andreas Rödder, Deutschland einig Vaterland, pp. 130–131.

8.1 The Quick and Bristling Path to Re-unification

> *Bundeskanzler Helmut Kohl hatte [...] später ge-*
> *schrieben: Nie habe er einen europäischen Gipfel*
> *in eisiger Atmosphäre, wie den am 8. und 9. Dezem-*
> *ber 1989 in Strasbourg, beinahe tribunalhaft, emp-*
> *funden. Unsere Freunde und Partner wurden über*
> *den 10-Punkte Plan nicht informiert.*
> *Und es hielt sich ohnehin die Begeisterung über*
> *eine mögliche Wiedervereinigung in Grenzen.[21]*
> (Rudolf Seiters)

The quotation, albeit brief, can help us stress one relevant point: On the eve of the announcement of the Ten-Point Plan, just a handful of people in Bonn had been informed about the move which Kohl intended to make. Abroad, the Plan came like a thunderbolt. A copy of the document was handed out to the Soviet Ambassador only when Helmut Kohl was already presenting it to the Bundestag, and while M.S. Gorbačëv was travelling to Rome. None of the European partners of Germany had received prior notice, not even the French President François Mitterrand, with whom Kohl had developed a close and friendly relationship. To date, scholars still discuss as to whether at least the US President had been informed about the political card that Kohl intended to play.[22]

Firstly, it is worthy to remark that none of the Ten Points addressed by Helmut Kohl were, apparently, completely new, nor did they hide a revolutionary content for the balance within Europe.

---

[21] "The German Chancellor Helmut Kohl later [...] wrote: I had never experienced a European Summit in such a cold atmosphere, as the Summit of 8 and 9 December 1989, it looked almost like a tribunal. Our friends and partners had not been informed about the 10-Point Plan. And, anyway, the enthusiasm for a potential reunification was limited". Interview with Dr. Rudolf Seiters (30.6.2016).

[22] "Der viel zitierte Zehn-Punkte Plan [...] erreicht den US Präsident zur gleichen Zeit als ihn Kohl im Parlament verkündete. Kanzlerberater Teltschik ließ wissen, dass man mit dem Fax nach Washington bewusst so lange gewartet habe. Es war kein kommunikatives Missgeschick, sondern politische Absicht. (The much quoted Ten-Point Plan [...] reached the US President when Hohl was announcing it in Parliament. The Counsellor of the Chancellor, Teltschik, let it be known that it had deliberately taken a while before the fax was sent. It was no accident, it was rather political intention). See Michael Gehler, Von der Teilung zur Einigung 1945 bis heute, ch.5, p. 324. For a partly different opinion see Andreas Rödder, Deutschland einig Vaterland, p. 140: „[...] die West-mächte, die entgegen diplomatischen Gepflogenheiten nicht unterrichtet worden waren: allein im Weißen Haus war der Text vor Beginn der Bundestagssitzung eingegangen, wo es zu diesem Zeit-punkt Nacht war". (The Western Powers, against every diplomatic custom, had not been informed: The White House had just received the text before the beginning of the parliamentary meeting. There it was nighttime).

The first five points referred to domestic measures which had to be taken to ease the negative effects triggered by the turmoil going on in Eastern Germany. The fifth point concluded the list of domestic issues by proposing a transition leading from a contractual community to a confederative community, with a view to the establishment of a German federation.[23]

Going further into details, the first two points of the programme proposed the implementation of a set of measures, defined as "emergency measures", to regulate the increasing flow of people across the boundaries, to provide rules regarding the freedom of movement and of migration and, just as important, to tackle currency problems and their economic and social side-effects. Health assistance was also foreseen, together with the possibility to pursue cooperation initiatives not only in the field of economics, but also in scientific and telecommunication areas. Starting from the contractual community proposed by Hans Modrow, it appeared possible to create joint committees for the solution of urgent problems in the above mentioned fields. Compared with these points, the third paragraph dealt with more sensitive political issues, since the Federal Government was willing to commit itself to further deepen and develop the existing cooperation framework, provided that the DDR adopted incisive reform measures of its political system.

The formulation of – and, above all, the conclusions drawn in – the fifth point of the Plan raised even more sensitive issues.[24] This is why it appears preferable to add some further remarks before embarking in the discussion of the other points of the programme.

Even the most critical observers seemed to have been favourably impressed by the contents of the Plan. Nobody could either deny the need to implement immediate measures to face the burden of managing the existing emergency situation, or question the appropriateness of the sequence of steps proposed by Kohl: "contractual community – confederation – federation". These steps appeared both well-thought out and in line with the complex historical heritage of the German speaking area. The latter element is not surprising given the academic background of the Chancellor.

Despite some initial reluctance, the Plan was therefore generally well accepted within the entire German political spectrum, with the sole exception of the *Grünen*, and it quickly became an inescapable reference for debate. Vis-à-vis national public opinion, Helmut Kohl gave the impression of being in full control

---

[23] For the full text of Kohl's address before Parliament see the internet site: http://webarchiv.bundestag.de/archive/2009/0109/geschichte/parlhist/dokumente/dok09.html (last accessed 5.1.2017).

[24] See Ibid.

of the developments. Besides, thanks to the success of the Plan, he also achieved a second target, i.e. he regained the power of initiative over the DDR leadership and the Social-Democrats[25] in Bonn. Since the announcement of the Plan, the idea of a confederation, which had been circulating among Western Social-Democrats for years, became in fact monopoly of the Chancellor.[26]

In turn, the DDR government did not only loose the benefits of the initiative, but it also found itself confronted with an even more complex conundrum. In principle, the Ten-Point Proposal seemed to respect and guarantee both the management of the independence of Pankow, and the free expression of the will of its citizens. Still, mounting social difficulties in the East were producing a sort of self-nourishing spiral between growing local expectations and the measures which Bonn was ready to implement. Its first consequence was an increasing reduction of the operational space of the new DDR political class which was hardly making its way in the corridors of power.

Reactions abroad were by far more "virulent" compared to those at home, as they usually dithered between harsh criticism and total rejection.[27] What was causing major tensions and worries in the most important European capitals, Rome included, were not the contents of the first part of the Plan, but rather the following five Points. In the note sent to the *Farnesina* soon after the announcement of the 28 November Programme, the Italian Ambassador to Bonn, Marcello Guidi, stressed in fact that, domestically, the Plan was a political response suitable to face the first outcomes resulting from the fall of the Wall in Berlin.

Still, only some of the reasons behind the proposal clearly emerged for Italian observers, as, for instance, the need for Kohl to respond promptly and effectively to the allegations of political deadlock, and lack of ideas issued by the opposition parties and even by members of his own ruling coalition. In other words, the programme was considered an organic and gradual proposal in its domestic

---

[25] See Gian Enrico Rusconi, Capire la Germania: Un diario ragionato sulla questione tedesca, p. 121.

[26] It was only in mid-December 1989 that the SPD, on the occasion of the annual Social-Democratic Congress, which should have taken place in Bremen, but was moved to Berlin in light of the ongoing events, proposed its own programme to tackle the German developments. Unlike the Ten-Point Plan of Helmut Kohl, it had no elaborate structure organised into different points, and it was also less attentive to institutional issues, insofar as it solely stated that whatever political kind of state would take shape on German territory, it would not question the existing frontiers.

[27] See Doc. 25, Vorlage des Referatsleiters 210, Lambach, für Staatssekretär Sudhoff. Ämtliche Äußerungen des Auslandes zu dem 10-Punkte-Plan des Bundeskanzlers, 1.12.1989, in: Die Einheit. Das Auswärtige Amt, das DDR-Außenministerium und der Zwei-plus-Vier-Prozess, p. 147. This document mainly focuses on the reactions of those countries which by 1 December had already taken an official position: the United States, France, and the Soviet Union. The "virulent" reaction of Moscow was matched by the worries and the sceptical stance of France and the United States respectively.

recommendations, whereas the same could not been affirmed for its international aspects.

One of the first reasons behind the negative stance of Italy was in all likelihood related to the way in which the Plan had been drawn and presented. This process had not been carried out through the normal diplomatic channels, and this was highly irritating for all the European partners of the Bundesrepublik.[28]

Fig. 18: Caricature: Goodbye Genschman: Hanels Porträt einer Ära, Walter Hanel 1992, Düsseldorf/Wien/New York/Moskau, Econ Verlag GmbH

This general feeling of irritation was also motivated by the perception that it was no coincidence that the Chancellor had decided to present his project on 28 November 1989, on the eve of important international and European summits, and without even involving his Foreign Minister. Could observers draw from this the conclusion that the German Chancellor not only harboured a strong determination to provide an answer to the DDR internal degeneration, but also wanted to make use of this opportunity to strengthen his own political clout, in order to negotiate from a better position?

---

[28] See the author's interview with Ambassador Cavalchini (5.2.2016). According to the interview, it was not only Prime Minister Margaret Thatcher to be deeply disappointed, Mitterrand was also both disappointed and vexed as Kohl had never hinted to his decision to present this statement and everything had been carried out very discreetly. Ambassador Cavalchini also remarked that, in all likelihood, Horst Teltschik was one of the few advisors of Kohl to be fully informed about – and involved in – the drawing of the document.

Allegations expressed in such a clear manner do not appear in any declassified document, but the tone and the contents of the declarations after the announcement point in this direction.

The peculiar arrangements chosen for drawing up the proposal were not the sole source of concern. Rather, the contents of its second part, or more correctly the lack of certain contents, both irritated and worried foreign observers. The second part of this programmatic statement concerned the international and the European context in which the "new Germany" should be placed. Points seven and eight hint at the role of the European Community and of the CSCE. Both the EC and the CSCE are presented as essential points of reference for the future architecture of Europe. Point nine refers to the progress made in the field of arms control and disarmament as a precondition to overcome the division of the Continent, whereas the last Point of the Plan concludes by expressing the hope that peace could be preserved on a Continent where Germany would regain its unity.

Kohl was therefore openly and for the first time affirming that re-unification was the political goal of the Federal Government, even if in so doing he neither set a precise timetable nor fixed detailed procedures for its implementation. To be more correct, even before the last paragraph, that is the second part of the Plan all along, Kohl had broken a traditional taboo. I do not mean the fact of openly talking of the German Unity – the issue had formally remained part of the debate since the Second World War – but rather of his clearly putting it on the agenda of Bonn.[29]

Although the Chancellor had made specific reference to the EC, the CSCE and NATO, by affirming the utmost importance of the German question for Europe in its entirety, his remarks appeared to European partners too vague to be reassuring. At a closer glance, it emerges that no specific reference either to the Atlantic solidarity or to the role of NATO concerning security issues had been deemed necessary, which meant that there was a risk that in the near future the inter-German joint committees could also deal with foreign and security issues. Moreover, the fact that Helmut Kohl had said nothing about the thorny question of the position of the future Confederation with respect to the two blocs, as the two German States were actually member of different military alliances, also raised fears and doubts.

During the Malta Summit on 2–3 December 1989, the Plan was addressed more than once by its participants, even though it did not officially form part of the agenda. Since, at the beginning of December, support to the liberalisation process of Eastern Europe was regarded as the key target to pursue, the demands of Helmut Kohl were not rejected, but they were certainly considered with strong reserve. Especially since there was no satisfying reference to NATO, and more

---

[29] See Michael Gehler, Deutschland: Von der Teilung zur Einigung 1945 bis heute, ch. 5.

generally to security and defence issues, the contents of the Plan needed to be thoroughly analysed.

Besides, the short reference to the EC was far from being satisfying, and this also raised concerns and worries about the degree of loyalty Germany presented to the whole integration process.

Finally, in light of the declarations of the Republikaner leader, the absence in the Plan of a reference to Poland and to the German-Polish border was equally puzzling and worrying.

A posteriori, the records show beyond any possible doubt that Helmut Kohl was a convinced European. Even though he did not always share the approach of Konrad Adenauer, he would have never sacrificed the integration process on the altar of a re-unification or accepted the neutralisation of his country to get the support of Moscow. Quite the reverse, a major political achievement of Helmut Kohl consisted in his capacity to indissolubly link the "nationaldeutsche Lösung" (the solution of the German issue) with the further development of the European construction.[30] However, at the beginning of December, before the Council of Strasbourg, the approach of Kohl was for contemporaries still lingering in a sort of grey area.

Italian worries concerning the Ten-Point Plan were no isolated reaction[31], but rather part of a more general European feeling of apprehension that a reunified Germany could modify the course of Foreign policy embraced and pursued from 1949 by the Bundesrepublik:

> „Sie wissen, dass Minister Andreotti, mit dem ich mich früher auch mehrfach zu-sammentraf, meinte wir lieben Deutschland so sehr, dass wir am liebsten zwei davon haben. Das war die Stimmung! Dieselbe Stimmung gab es aber nicht nur in Italien, sondern auch in den Niederlanden und natürlich auch in Großbritannien [...]. Mitterrand war im Jahr 1989 nicht der Mitterrand aus dem Jahr 1990. Italien war 1989 genau so besorgt wie andere europäischen Länder auch. Was passiert, wenn plötzlich diese starke Bundesrepublik Deutschland mit der DDR

---

[30] Ibid., p. 356.

[31] See the author's interview with Ambassador Cavalchini (5.2.2016). According to this interview, there were several difficult moments. Even French politicians did not go easy on the Germans, Mitterrand was very strict as regards the Ten Points, because the general concern was that a reuni-fied Germany would go off at a tangent towards Eastern Europe. The declassified records, both in Italy and abroad, confirm this creeping feeling of worry, which of course each Italian politician expressed in a different away according to his personal background and to his approach to politics. In other words, part of the Italian political élite suspected that Bonn, once freed of the ties imposed by the Second World War, would once again pursue a "seesaw policy" between East and West, whereas other politicians, traditionally more in tune with Bonn, feared that the inherent ambiguities in the approach of Bonn combined with the indecision of its Western partners would force Kohl to make a choice between German re-unification and European integration. Francesco Cossiga, for instance, belonged to this second group of politicians.

wiedervereinigt wird? Wird dann Deutschland wie früher den Kurs ändern […]? Wie wird sich Deutschland mit Russland arrangieren? Trotz allen Vereinbarungen und Dokumente, wobei sich Italien und andere Länder zur Wiedervereinigung Deutschlands bekannt hatten, als der Gedanke der Wiedervereinigung näher kam, war man besorgt."[32]

Even though the previous quotation of Rudolf Seiters has confirmed that the reaction of Andreotti was on the same line of other European leaders, the German politician also used a sentence to describe it, which has often been improperly attributed to the then Italian Prime Minister. As this issue has been already accurately discussed in chapter five[33], it will be sufficient to add some short details to complete the picture.

After the unfortunate events of September 1984, the Italian-German bilateral relationship had not been permanently affected, but it had rather been further developed in a positive atmosphere of cooperation. This does not mean though that the comments uttered by Andreotti had not left some traces in both the perception of the Federal Government and in that of the German press. In 1989, the initial reluctance of the Italian Government led by Andreotti did not exactly annoy Bonn, but it certainly raised a certain feeling of anxiety in a moment in which Helmut Kohl needed every possible European support for the difficult course he was on the verge of pursuing.[34]

The wave of enthusiasm and support expressed by the Italians soon after the fall of the Berlin Wall and which were echoed in the national press notwithstanding, the marked sympathy which not only Andreotti but also his country showed for the new orientations followed by the Soviet Union, was often seen in the German press as a clear indication of an overall lack of true interest in the German re-unification. Besides, the prejudices against Andreotti were in 1989 still deeply rooted in many prominent German newspapers.[35]

---

[32] "Do you know that Minister Andreotti, whom I had previously met very often, said he loved Germany so much that he would rather have two of them. That was the mood! Not only in Italy, but also in the Netherlands, and, of course, in Great Britain as well […]. In 1989 Mitterrand was not the man he was in 1990. Italy was as concerned as other European countries. What would happen, if out of the blue a strong Federal Republic was reunited with the DDR? Would Germany change course as it had done in the past […]? What kind of deal would be stroke with Russia? Despite all agreements and documents, in which Italy and other countries had committed themselves with the goal of the German reunification, as the very thought of it approached, they were worried". See author's interview with Rudolf Seiters (26.6.2016).

[33] See ch.5.1.

[34] See Franz Smets/Laszlo Trankovits, dpa, 30 November 1989, in: ACDP, "Abteilung Pressedokumentation: Giulio Andreotti".

[35] The interviews with Italian journalists who worked in Germany in 1989 also confirm this general prejudice. Alfredo Venturi, who worked for approximately a decade in Bonn, at first as a correspondent of the Italian Newspaper *La Stampa*, and then of the *Corriere della Sera*, addressed the

„[…] die offizielle Haltung der verbündeten Regierungen sollte dem Grundgesetz der Bundesrepublik entsprechen: so ist es Brauch unter befremdeten Staaten. Schon als Außenminister hatte Andreotti diesen Grundsatz verletzt, als er im September 1984 erklärte: ‚Es gibt zwei deutsche Staaten, und zwei sollen es bleiben'. Obwohl Andreotti wusste, daß er damit die Beziehungen zur Bundesregierung vor allem zum Bundeskanzler, erheblich belastete, nahm er davon nichts zurück, eben weil es seine persönliche Meinung war. […]. Mehr deutet darauf hin, daß dem italienischen Ministerpräsidenten der Status quo ante Murum, lieb geworden war. Die Völker Mitteleuropas, die Deutschen eingeschlossen, sollten ruhig bleiben, damit nichts die Stabilität gefährde. Für den Freiheitswillen der Tschechen, Slowaken und Ungarn, der Balten und Ostdeutschen scheint Andreotti kein Sensorium zu besitzen. […] Warum Andreotti so denkt? Der Christliche Demokrat ist 70 Jahre alt. Der Schüler des europäischen Gründungsvaters De Gasperi ist auf Westeuropa ausgerichtet: da ist der Osten ausgeblendet. […].“[36]

It was extremely difficult for the German press to fully comprehend the concerns of the Italian political élite regarding a possible destabilisation of the Continent, and above all the distinction Rome made between a "question of Germany" and a "German question".[37]

---

issue with a touch of irony, as he affirmed that in the German press and in the local public opinion the Italian Prime Minister was often considered a sort of "diavoletto con strani poteri" (a little devil with strange powers). See the author's interview with Alfredo Venturi (2.2.2016).

[36] "Officially, the allied governments should have conformed to the Fundamental Law of the Federal Republic. In his capacity as Italian Foreign Minister, Andreotti had already come in conflict with the Fundamental Law. In 1984, he had affirmed: 'Es gibt zwei deutsche Staaten, und zwei sollen es bleiben'. Even though Andreotti knew that this would put a significant strain on the relations with the German Chancellor and the German Government, he did not rectify his remarks, because he believed what he had said. […] There are even more signs to indicate that the Italian Prime Minister appreciated the Status quo ante Murum. The people in Mitteleuropa, the Germans included, had better keep calm, to avoid jeopardising the stability achieved. Apparently, he was not in the least sensitive to the desire for freedom of the Czechs, the Slovaks, the Hungarians, the Baltic people and the Eastern Germans. […] Why? The Christian-Democratic politician is 70 years old. The pupil of De Gasperi is focused on Western Europe, Eastern Europe is invisible by comparison". See Hans-Joachim Fischer, Ambivalenz der Vergangenheit, *Frankfurter Allgemeine Zeitung*, 9.12.1989, in: ACDP, Abteilung Pressedokumentation: Giulio Andreotti. The article chosen belongs to the group of documents written by German journalists, which more clearly point at the prejudice against Andreotti. See also Bedenken Andreottis gegen deutsche Wiedervereinigung, *Frankfurter Allgemeine Zeitung*, 27.11.1989; Differenzen in Rom zur deutschen Frage: Polemik Martellis gegen Andreotti, *Neue Zürcher Zeitung*, 10.12.1989; Andreotti verstehe die Deutschen nicht, *dpa*, 12.12.1989, all in: ACDP, Abteilung Pressedokumentation: Giulio Andreotti.

[37] German diplomatic records usually consider the reluctance of Giulio Andreotti as an isolated phenomenon. Still, they do not rule out a priori the possibility that he was more vocal about what other politicians intimately felt. See, in particular, Italien und die deutsche Frage, Fernschreiben aus RomDiplo, Rom, 7.12.1989. PA AA B26, n. 173561. See also Doc. 32, Vorlage des Referatsleiters 203, Kuhna, für Staatssekretär Sudhoff. Italienische Haltung zur deutschen Frage, 1.12.1989, in: *Die Einheit. Das Auswärtige Amt, das DDR-Außenministerium und der Zwei-plus-Vier-Prozess.* What did not emerge in the comments of the German press was that Andreotti was primarily

At first, the complete lack of access to the Italian primary sources and, later on, their very limited availability in comparison with all what has been so far declassified in other European countries, has contributed to the persistence of this prejudice. It has also made it difficult to develop a historical analysis able to offer a more accurate framework of interpretation.

Less than a week after the announcement of the Ten-Point Plan, on 4 December 1984, the Heads of State and Government of NATO Member States gathered for a meeting in Brussels. Once again, the guidelines conveyed by Ambassador Cavalchini are a useful starting point to address the fundamental issues raised during this meeting.

> «Due giorni dopo Malta, al vertice NATO ci fu un vivace scambio di vedute tra Kohl e Andreotti perché i Dieci Punti facevano riferimento alla nozione di auto-determinazione e in particolare c'erano alcuni punti, come quello in cui si parlava di comunità contrattuale (l'idea di un processo a diversi stadi che cominciava con la messa in piedi di una confederazione che doveva sfociare in istituzioni comuni per arrivare ad un governo comune). [...] dopo l'illustrazione da parte di Kohl si chiese ai presenti quali reazioni avessero e Andreotti disse che il principio di au-todeterminazione andava bene, ma si doveva andare con i piedi di piombo (ricordando anche quello che aveva sentito dire a Gorbačëv quando era venuto a Roma il 30 novembre), dove lui non era contrario a questo processo di apertura, però metteva diversi caveat. [...] Andreotti promuove una linea di cautela e da qui le grosse ire di Kohl al vertice atlantico, quando dice ad Andreotti tu non parleresti così se il Muro fosse il Tevere. [...]».[38]

At the opening of the meeting, US President Bush presented his "four principles" which from that moment on became the reference point of the American

---

worried by uncontrolled developments which could escape the control of politics and diplomacy. Even though he had been deeply influenced by the approach to politics of his mentor, Alcide De Gasperi, it would be going too far to argue that he was solely interested in Western Europe. It is, however, reasonable to make the hypothesis that the nature of his interest for Eastern Europe had more in common with the stance of De Gasperi than with the approach of Kohl compared with that of Adenauer.

[38] "Two days after Malta, at the NATO summit, there was a squabble between Kohl and Andreotti about the fact that the Ten Points referred to the concept of self-determination and, more specifically, some paragraphs also dealt with the issue of a contractual community (meaning a stepwise process starting with the establishment of a confederation leading to common institutions and finally to a common government). [...] After further comments made by Kohl, the participants were asked to express their opinion, and Andreotti said that he agreed with the principle of self-determination, but that it was important to tread gingerly with it. This also recalls what he had heard from Gorbačëv on 30 November during his visit to Rome; that he was not against such an opening-up process, but he did raise several *caveats*. [...] Andreotti was promoting a prudential approach which unleashed the anger of Kohl at the Atlantic summit, who said to Andreotti: 'You wouldn't talk like this if the Wall was the Tiber'. [...]". See the author's interview with Ambassador Cavalchini (5.2.2016).

government in dealing with the German problem.[39] To summarize, the "four principles" accepted the right of self-determination of the German people and, implicitly, they also presented the process leading to re-unification, under the non-
negotiable conditions that the change would be completed peacefully, within
NATO and the EC, and with no prejudice for the commitments assumed by the
Bundesrepublik at the international level, thus also reiterating the respect of the
principles enshrined in the Helsinki Final Act as regards the question of national
borders. The US statement was rather flexible as far as forms and contents of the
German re-unification were concerned, provided that it would not imply a neutralisation of Germany. President Bush and Chancellor Kohl fully agreed on this.

As for the development of the second part of the summit, opinions differ.
According to Horst Teltschik, Helmut Kohl was satisfied with the words uttered
by the US President and therefore wanted to conclude the proceeding as soon as
possible in order to prevent the expression of dissent or to avoid that less favourable interpretations about the contents of the Ten-Point Plan would find fertile
soil. His fears were soon confirmed by the perplexities expressed by the Italian
Prime Minister.[40]

This second part of the summit has been usually briefly addressed in the texts
published in the following years. Mainly, reference has been made to the annoyed
reply uttered by Kohl, summarized in the sentence regarding the Tiber. This has
indirectly led to draw the conclusion that Andreotti and his government were in
principle opposed to the very idea of re-unification.[41] The only notable exception
to this approach is the Italian political scientist, Gian Enrico Rusconi. Basing
himself mostly on journals, such as those written by Horst Teltschik, he investigated the matter more attentively.[42] His analysis confirms what later emerged
from the analysis of the first declassified diplomatic sources.

Giulio Andreotti was puzzled and worried by the use of the word "self-determination". He wondered whether, once accepted in the time and way suggested
by the Chancellor, it would also apply to other contexts, such as the Baltic Republics of Estonia, Latvia and Lithuania, which would thus quickly raise to the
status of independent states. Furthermore, he was also worried that the precarious
political situation in which the issue of the German re-unification had been raised

---

[39] See, in particular, Philip Zelikow/Condoleza Rice, Germany unified and Europe transformed,
Massachusetts – London 1996.
[40] See Horst Teltschik, 329 Tage. Innenansichten der Einigung, pp. 65–66. See also Philip Zeli-
kow/Condoleza Rice, Germany unified and Europe transformed, p. 133.
[41] See, for example, Werner Weidenfeld, Geschichte der deutschen Einheit. Außenpolitik für die
deutsche Einheit: die Entscheidungsjahre 1989/1990, Stuttgart 1999, p. 177.
[42] See Gian Enrico Rusconi, Germania Italia Europa: Dallo stato di potenza alla potenza civile,
Torino 2003, pp. 280–281.

would let people believe that "barriers" could more easily and profitably be over-thrown through popular uprisings than with the support of a patient diplomacy. In other words, Andreotti advocated for a more cautious approach because he feared the risk that European leaders could lose control over events.

The reply of Helmut Kohl, though unmistakably angry in its tones, was much more complex and multifaceted than the brief quotation regarding the Tiber would suggest.[43] At first, Kohl ensured his interlocutor that the Ten-Point Plan had no intention to hurry things up; indeed it had fixed no tight deadline. Still, he also considered to be of the utmost importance not to lose sight of the emotional climate that dominated in Germany and of the expectations which its people had every right to. Re-unification remained therefore the objective to be pursued, not as an undue acceleration but as an expression of respect for the expectations of an entire people, who, in the words of Helmut Kohl, since the Second World War had given ample proof of sense of responsibility and self-restrain.

The two approaches were not fully incompatible, but they were profoundly different both as regards their premises and their conclusions. The reaction of Andreotti had been until then, and still was in Brussels, the result of the fears of a cautious leader who had a broad knowledge of international issues and, no less important, had a legal training. From a strictly legal point of view the principle of self-determination, once accepted, could not be limited in its application to the German case. Andreotti seemed to think of the Baltic Republics as not merely "Satellite States", but rather as part of the Soviet territory. The application of this principle could reasonably trigger reactions which would have been difficult to keep under control, and the consequences of which would have also endangered the internal stability of the Soviet Superpower.[44]

The concerns expressed by Giulio Andreotti, even though not entirely under-standable and not quite acceptable in Bonn, fully emerge in their inherent com-plexity through the German archival records. The question as to whether the con-cerns expressed by the Italian Prime Minister during the NATO Summit were also the instance of his intimate fear of side-effects on territorial realities much closer to Italy than the Baltic Republics – the South Tyrol and the Brenner frontier – remains at present unanswered.[45]

---

[43] The comments of Andreotti paved the way for further criticism, especially from the British Prime Minister, whose tones and arguments were far less balanced than those of the Italian politician. See Werner Weidenfeld, Geschichte der deutschen Einheit, Stuttgart 1999, p. 177.

[44] See Italien und die deutsche Frage, Fernschreiben aus RomDiplo, Rom, 7.12.1989. PA AA B26, n. 173561.

[45] Concerning the approach of Giulio Andreotti to the principle of self-determination, see Andreotti zur deutschen Frage, Fernschreiben aus RomDiplo, Rom, 11.12.1989. PA AA B26, n. 173561. At present, the already declassified Italian records are too meager to allow scholars to provide an an-swer to the question as to whether Andreotti really feared side-effects in South Tyrol, or if it was

„So sieht Andreotti auch die Gefahr Infragestellung der Einheit der SU mit entsprechenden politischen Rückwirkungen auf den Entspannungsprozess […]. Die
von ihm geäußerte Sorge von einer Störung des ‚Ausgewogenheit' der KSZE-
Schlussakte muss so verstanden werden, dass er die KSZE-Schlussakte als eine
Art Gleichgewicht zwischen Anerkennung einer Permanenz der Grenzen gegen
die sowjetische Bereitschaft, durch Fortschritte im Bereich der Menschenrechte
und menschlichen Kontakte […]. Und nicht zuletzt ist Andreotti in erster Linie ein
gouvernamental denkender Politiker, dem spontane und unkontrollierte Volksbe-
wegungen zutiefst verdächtig sind. […]."[46]

The concerns expressed during the 8/9 December 1989 European Summit in
Strasbourg were not in their essence fundamentally different. The real problem
was not so much the application of self-determination to Germany, but rather the
imitation effects which such a decision could trigger. [47]

The Strasbourg Council did start in an "icy climate", but through it the participants could come to an arrangement, and hence achieve some significant results. Here, its most significant aspects concerning the transformation of the Italian stance will be addressed, whereas other issues more generally related to the
history of the European integration process that did not directly affect the position
of Rome will be left aside.

«Naturalmente la nostra preoccupazione molto viva, e presente a Kohl, era il timore che una Germania unita facesse paura e questo era soprattutto il pensiero
della Thatcher. Quello che ci tranquillizzava era l'atteggiamento del Cancelliere
che si era reso conto che la riunificazione non poteva non passare attraverso il
processo di integrazione europea […]. L'abilità del Cancelliere fu quella di aver
capito che la riunificazione tedesca doveva passare attraverso un rafforzamento
del vincolo europeo. È un elemento fondamentale che troviamo già nei Dieci Punti

---

merely a German suspicion. As far as concerns the importance of the "vertenza altoatesina" in the
then Italian Foreign politics, see Luciano Monzali, Giulio Andreotti e le relazioni italo-austriache
1972–1992, Merano 2016, pp. 23–25.

[46] "This is how Andreotti also sees the danger of questioning the unity of the URSS with its inherent
political implications for the process of détente […]. The worries which he expressed regarding the
interference with the 'balance' of the CSCE Final Act must be understood in this way: he considers
the CSCE Final Act as some sort of bargain between the recognition of the unchanging nature of
the frontiers and the Soviet willingness to progress in the domains of human rights and human
contacts […]. Lastly, Andreotti is, first and foremost, a traditionalist who deeply distrusts spontaneous and uncontrolled popular movements […]". See Andreotti zur deutschen Frage, Fernschreiben aus RomDiplo, Rom, 11.12.1989. PA AA B26, n. 173561.

[47] See Gian Enrico Rusconi, Capire la Germania: Un diario ragionato sulla questione tedesca, pp.
282–283.

e nessuno all'epoca lo contestava, si contestava l'idea di Kohl di bruciare i tempi, di restringere le tappe per arrivare all'obiettivo finale della riunificazione. [...]».[48]

Firstly, Helmut Kohl's ability to persuade the participants of the summit of his determination to incorporate the process of re-unification in a European framework did help to ease concerns, if not to wholly remove all fears and worries.

Only from that moment on did several European leaders and Foreign ministries, the *Farnesina* included, start to regard the Ten-Point Plan as an overall balanced text. From a strictly legal point of view and in the absence of a peace treaty, it could be claimed that the frontiers of the Bundesrepublik and those of the Reich in 1937 should have been the same. The refusal of Chancellor Kohl to provide a formal guarantee concerning the intangibility of the Eastern German frontier was therefore unquestionable. Still, Chancellor Kohl was ready to ensure his partners that his country had no intention to question what had been agreed on in the Helsinki Final Act by putting forward territorial claims.

Shortly afterwards, a private meeting between the French and the Italian Foreign Ministers was held at *Palazzo Farnese* (on the premises of the French Embassy in Rome) to discuss the results of the Strasbourg summit. Baldocci, the Director of Cabinet of Gianni de Michelis, and Bottai, the Secretary-General of the Italian Foreign Ministry, were also among the participants to this meeting. Some issues discussed at *Palazzo Farnese* deserve close attention.

> « M. De Michelis a affirmé d'emblée qu'il s'agissait d'un grand succès. Le climat psychologique avait été exceptionnellement favorable et se distinguait, de l'aveu même de M. Andreotti, de tous les précédents, y compris le conseil de Milan qui, pour avoir fait progresser l'Europe, avait été cependant marqué de tensions [...]. Elle avait pris un bon départ, le chancelier Kohl avait été des plus clairs dans son engagement sur la conférence intergouvernementale et avait tracé les grandes lignes de ses échéances et de ses délais d'une manière qui correspondait tout à fait à l'analyse italienne. [...] Il faillait maintenant entrer dans la phase préparatoire et bien en baliser le chemin. [...] La formule élaborée par le Conseil au sujet de l'Allemagne n'était pas quelconque compromis. C'était une prise de position, réfléchie, claire et équilibrée. Elle avait affirmé le droit du peuple allemand à l'autodétermination car il n'y avait pas d'autre solution possible. M. De Michelis a démenti qu'il y avait eu une volonté d'italienne d'esquiver ce concept, ce que M. Andreotti avait voulu faire comprendre [...] c'était que l'autodétermination ne pouvait valoir

---

[48] "Naturally, our real concern was – and Kohl was well aware of it – that a unified Germany would be frightening, which was certainly Mrs. Thatcher's thought. What was reassuring for us was the attitude of the Chancellor. He had realized that the reunification would have never taken place without the framework of European integration [...]. The ability of the Chancellor consisted in having understood that the German reunification had to go through a process of strengthening of the European bond. It is a cornerstone expressed in the Ten Points and nobody challenged it; what we contested was Kohl's idea of forcing the timing, of cutting corners in order to achieve the final aim of reunification. [...]". See the author's interview with Ambassador Cavalchini (5.2.2016).

en soi. Ainsi avait-il toujours refusé l'autodétermination pure et simple pour les populations germanophones du Haut-Adige. En revanche il avait accepté de s'y référer à condition qu'elle fut restituée précisément dans le contexte d'Helsinki, c'est-à-dire en relation avec d'autres principes comme l'inviolabilité des frontières et l'existence des traités et des accords concernant l'OTAN et le Pacte de Varsovie. Il y avait eu, a-t-il reconnu, une discussion sur les notions de "peuple", "nation" et de "d'état" et M. Andreotti avait clairement indiqué les dangers qu'il y avait à se référer à la première de celles-ci. […] A propos du poids futur de l'Allemagne dans la communauté le ministre a répondu en se tournant vers mon collègue allemand par une formule qu'il voulait plaisante "nous avons mis sur la table la réunification et l'U.E.M. c'est à vous maintenant de nous donner le mark" ».[49]

First of all, from mid-December 1989 onwards, the French – as well as the German – attention began to focus more on the position of the Italian Government and of the Ministry of Foreign Affairs and less on the Italian political spectrum in its entirety.

There still remained some traces of a heuristic interest in the analysis of the reactions to the German events within the Italian political spectrum, but, as significant European deadlines approached, priority was to be given to those figures and bodies which would define the guidelines of the Italian stance on the international stage. Even though several Foreign observers sensed that the vision of Andreotti was not necessarily representative of Italy in its entirety, at the end of 1989 the greatest part of interest was to be accorded to his stance. Not only was

---

[49] "Gianni de Michelis has immediately affirmed that it [meaning the European Council of Strasbourg] had been a great success. The psychological climate had been really positive and, on the admission of Andreotti himself, so different from all previous summits, including the Summit of Milan. Even though the latter had advanced the European integration process, it had also been marked by tensions. […]. It had got a good start, Chancellor Kohl had been crystal clear in his commitment to the Intergovernmental Conference, and he had also outlined its deadlines and its time frame in a manner consistent with the Italian stance. […] We must enter the preparatory phase and mark its trail. […] The agreement we reached concerning Germany is not a compromise. It is a mature, clear, and balanced stance. The right to self-determination of the German people has been asserted as there was no other possible solution. Gianni de Michelis denied that his country wanted to avoid this notion. What Andreotti actually wanted to explain […] was that self-determination could not be worth in itself. Therefore, he refused a plain and simple self-determination of the German-speaking people of South Tyrol. On the contrary, he had accepted to use it, as long as it is used within the agreement of Helsinki. It must be related to other notions, such as the inviolability of frontiers and the respect of the existing treaties and alliances: NATO and the Warsaw Pact. He has admitted that there had been a discussion about the terms 'people', 'nation' and 'state'. Andreotti had clearly pointed at the risks of using them. […] Concerning the future clout of Germany within the Community, the Minister has turned to my colleague and used a deliberately pleasant expression 'we have put on the table the reunification and the EMU. It is your turn to give us the mark'". See Réflexions de M. De Michelis après Strasbourg, télégramme de l'Ambassade de Rome, Rome, 12.12.1989, signed Perol. AMAE 1935inva, Direction Europe, Série Italie, carton 6377, période 1986–1990.

Andreotti the Head of the Italian Government, but he also had a significant influence on the Farnesina, hence on the making of the Italian Foreign policy.

Secondly, the "psychological climate" of the European Council in Strasbourg has been described in the quotation as extremely positive.[50] This could appear surprising if we consider the tensions before the opening of the Summit and also the atmosphere prevailing during the informal dinner held in Paris on 18 November 1989. On that occasion, the manifest objections of the British and the Dutch Prime Ministers, M. Thatcher and R. Lubbers, not merely to the possibility of a re-unification but even to a discussion about the events of Berlin, had reached alarming dimensions. Still, the Strasbourg summit paved the way for an overall agreement.

Surely, this agreement did not consist in an unconditional acceptance of the German aspiration to unity. The 9 December final declaration reaffirmed the determination of the "Twelve" to reinforce peace in Europe where the German people could regain political unity through an auto-determination process. This statement was the result of delicate discussions that had lasted the whole night between 8 and 9 December, and had been marked by concerns regarding the terms to be used.[51] It was not until the Dublin Summit, four months later, that the European Council gave its full support to the re-unification process.[52]

Finally, it is also noteworthy to focus on the sentence used by Foreign Minister de Michelis regarding the conclusions reached in Strasbourg, where he affirmed that "car il n'y avait pas d'autre solution possible" (there was no other way). In other words, the abovementioned sentence, together with many clues to be found in the diplomatic documentation, suggests that the Italian acceptance of the conclusions of the Summit did not result from Rome definitively overcoming its doubt and worries, but rather from the perception that, given the circumstances, it was the only reasonable choice. A stance based on tough resistance, as the British Prime Minister proposed, was rightly considered in Rome as counterproductive.

Several different reasons contributed to this more flexible Italian approach towards re-unification. In addition to an increasing awareness of the real social and economic conditions in the DDR – which could in no possible way be

---

[50] See Conseil européen de Strasbourg, Paris, no date. ANF, série 5 AG 4, CDM/12, dossier 2.
[51] See Conseil européen de Strasbourg, Paris, 11 December 1989. ANF, série 5 AG 4, EG/59, dossier 1.
[52] See Préparation du Conseil européen, confidentiel, Brussels, April 1990. HAEU, UEF-450 Documents de la Commission et du Conseil CE. See also AMAE 1935inva, Direction Europe, Série CE, carton 5912, période 1986–1990, several documents on the Summit.

considered as an alternative interlocutor to Bonn[53] – the new attitude of the French and the American Presidents also had an impact on the Italian stance. The principles stated by the US President at the NATO Summit of December 1989 had left no room for doubt: the US leadership did not intend to hinder or slow down the path traced by Kohl, provided that some basic commitments were fulfilled. It was therefore highly unlikely that Washington would support Rome in a firm oppositional stance. For all these different reasons Rome decided to accept the course of events.

Still, by mid-December 1989 it was not at all clear whether Italy still secretly wanted to slow down the speed of re-unification for as long as possible, or whether it would be content with having a voice in the re-unification process. The Italian strategy[54] to cope with the German events took shape on the basis of such fundamental ambiguity. After the Ministerial Council of 15 December, the Italian Presidency of the Council of Ministries published a press release concerning the formal position of the Italian Government as regards the transformations in Central-Eastern Europe. Four points of the Italian governmental statement specifically related to the German question.[55] According to the German Foreign Ministry, they showed the desire of Rome to overcome the tensions that had characterized the previous weeks.[56] In light of the Helsinki Final Act, it was considered possible to allow a "rightful achievement" of the German people's desire to a State re-unification within the existing borders.

This reunification process [sic!] would be submitted to free elections in order to respect the will of the German people. Point one and two regarding the German question in the Italian statement provided further details on this process, whereas the third point stressed the necessity to both safeguard the achievements of the European integration path and to proceed gradually towards re-unification. Finally, the fourth point expressed the desire that the process of re-unification could be incorporated into the framework of a second Helsinki Conference. All this reinforced in Bonn the feeling that Italy had not yet fully given up the hope to slow down the course of events. What was being fashioned in the shadow of the

---

[53] See interview with Ambassador Cavalchini (5.2.2016): «Quanto alla RDT, che non aveva sviluppato né con Ulbricht né con Honecker una propria identità, la sola strada ragionevolmente percorribile non poteva che essere quella della riunificazione» (As for the DDR, it had not developed its own identity neither under the guidance of Ulbricht nor of Honecker. The only viable way was, therefore, the path of a reunification).
[54] For more information on the Italian strategy developed at the end of 1989 see Doc. 96 Bericht. Haltung Italiens zur Wiedervereinigung 18.12.1989, in: Michael Gehler/Maximilian Graf, Österreich und die deutsche Frage 1987–1990, Göttingen 2018, p. 436.
[55] See Italienische Haltung zum Selbstbestimmungsrecht, Fernschreiben aus RomDiplo, Rom, 16.12.1989. PA AA B26, n. 173561. The box also contains a copy of the original Italian text.
[56] Ibid.

16 December declaration was the frame of a three-pillar strategy: EC, NATO and the CSCE.[57]

Even though some original elements could be detected in this Italian approach, on 20 December the French presidency still hesitated to accept the document as proof of a mature "Italian stance". The Italian approach was considered in Paris very similar to the French vision, but some new items[58] had been introduced. These, according to France, were to be analysed and handled carefully to avoid unpleasant consequences.

> « Sur le problème allemand l'Italie apparait comme l'une des plus vigilants parmi les Douze, qu'il s'agisse de la conception de l'autodétermination ou du problème des frontières. M. Andreotti l'a dit avec une fermeté que sa conduite habituelle ne fait que renforcer et M. De Michelis s'en est fait écho dans son style plus flamboyant.[59] On peut regretter à cet égard que la presse française n'ait vu dans l'attitude italienne que de rodomontades […]. Il est très clair que l'Italie voudra non seulement être informée, mais aussi avoir voix au chapitre. Elle l'a déjà manifesté à Bruxelles et nous devons y être plus attentifs qu'elle dit sans doute tout haut ce que les autres pensent tout bas ».[60]

---

[57] It is widely debated whether the CSCE can be rightly considered a "third pillar", as the interviews with leading Italian diplomats confirmed. Ambassador Nigido for instance affirmed: "È vero che l'Italia sviluppò una politica su tre pilastri: CEE, NATO e CSCE…in realtà i pilastri sono stati due da sempre! Certo abbiamo creduto nella CSCE, era un modo per coinvolgere la Russia e i paesi dell'Est in un disegno di pacificazione europea e questo ha funzionato. La CSCE nasce nel 1980, invece la politica dei due pilastri, europeo e atlantico, nasce nel 1950 […]". (It is correct that Italy developed a three-pillar strategy: EEC, NATO and CSCE…well, to be correct there have always been just two pillars! To be sure, we believed in the CSCE, it was a way to involve the Russians and the Eastern European countries in a peace-making plan, and it has worked well. The CSCE exists since 1980, whereas the two-pillar policy, that is the European one and the Atlantic one, were conceived in 1950). See author's interview with Ambassador Nigido (2.3.2016). I do not intend to question the assumption that the Italian Foreign policy was based on two pillars. The expression "three pillars" solely refers to the Italian strategy to cope with the German events and from this perspective the CSCE had, at least at first, a significant role in the Italian vision.

[58] See L'Italie dans le nouveau contexte européen, Paris et Rome, 20.12.1989, signed Perol. ANF, série 5 AG 4, EG/11, dossier 11. The document summarizes the comments sent to Paris by ambassador Perol and also added some further remarks.

[59] Concerning the approach of a prominent figure of the Italian Socialist Party, Bettino Craxi, see Michael Gehler/Andrea Brait, Am Ort des Geschehens in Zeiten des Umbruchs, Hildesheim – Zürich – New York, 2018, p. 351. See also, among Austrian Archival Records, Doc. 96 Bericht. Haltung Italiens zur Wiedervereinigung 18.12.1989, in: Michael Gehler/Maximilian Graf, Österreich und die deutsche Frage 1987–1990. Von Honecker Besuch in Bonn bis zur Einheit, Göttingen 2018, pp. 434–435.

[60] "On the German problem, Italy appears to be one of the most watchful countries among the Twelve, be it regarding the concept of self-determination or the border problems. The firmness of Minister Andreotti on these issues is emphasized by the contrast with his usual behaviour, and Minister de Michelis has echoed it in his more blazing style. One could regret that the French press

By the end of December, it appeared evident for Paris that the priorities in Rome were shifting. Rome's first and principle aim would be soon identified in the attempt to gain – unlike what had happened at the end of the Second World War – a place at the negotiating table where the conditions for a new Germany would be discussed. Italy believed that negotiations would be conducted either within NATO, in the EC, or in the CSCE. Besides, nothing excluded that more than one of these organisations could be involved. The main point of contention between Rome and Paris mainly concerned NATO and the CSCE.

> « [...] l'Italie est fidèle à elle-même autant en se ralliant sans hésiter à la proposition d'un Helsinki II de M. Gorbatchev qu'un applaudissant au plan Baker pour un nouvel atlantisme. Dans les deux cas elle retrouve sa préoccupation d'une part d'une Europe unie ouvrant la voie jusqu'à l'Oural, et d'autre d'un ensemble englobant [...]. La formule lancée par M. De Michelis "l'Europe de San Francisco à Vladivostok" est comme j'ai déjà souligné beaucoup plus d'une boutade. Elle traduit le même état d'esprit qui fait que le mauvais procès fait à la CEE sur le thème de la forteresse européenne est ici sans cesse renaissant, entretenu par tous ceux qui [...] redoutent d'instinct une Europe à la française bien bâtie et organisée. Plus que française une construction franco-allemande qu'[...] on craint ici trop rigide et trop contraignante. Quand [...] on se félicite de voir disparaître, sous le choc des événements, l'axe Paris-Bonn, c'est moins par satisfaction d'amour propre que parce-que l'architecture européenne s'en trouve remise en question et que dans le chantier nouveau l'Italie sera mieux placée pour jouer son jeu [...]. En réalité deux courantes se mêlent et parfois se contredisent : [...] il y a d'un côté l'indiscutable attachement au processus déclenché par le traité de Rome, le sentiment qu'on peut dire unanime du peuple italien de "faire l'Europe" le souci enfin qui inspire particulièrement le gouvernement de M. Andreotti de faire en sorte que l'Italie assume pleinement sa place et ses responsabilités dans la communauté de 1993. D'un autre côté la tentation toujours renaissante de jouer un jeu à part et de trouver dans un ensemble flou et instructuré, "l'Europe est une conception politique et non pas géographique" déclare M. De Michelis, l'occasion de mieux utiliser ses qualités de souplesse et d'adaptation. La relance pour M. Gorbatchev de l'architecture de Helsinki autant que l'idée de M. Baker de donner à l'OTAN un contenu nouveau sont porteuses à cet égard d'autant de tentations dangereuses pour l'Italie. Le Péril n'est pas imminent, mais nous devons y prendre garde. Pour l'heure, le gouvernement de M. Andreotti a autant que nous-mêmes le souci de garder la tête froide et

---

has only seen empty boasts in the Italian stance [...]. It is very clear that Italy does not only want to be informed, but also to have a say in the matter. It has already indicated it in Brussels, and we should pay more attention as it probably says out loud and clear what others are thinking for themselves". See Ibid. For another copy (without the remarks added by the French presidency) of the telegram, see AMAE 1935inva, Direction Europe, Série Italie, carton 6377, période 1986–1990. This quotation only refers to the comments of the French Embassy in Rome.

d'éviter les dérapages [...] nous pouvons compter sur lui pour poursuivre avec intelligence et réalisme l'œuvre amorcée ».[61]

According to Paris, both the NATO pillar and the CSCE pillar, respectively under the influence of the Soviet proposal for a new Conference of Helsinki and of the American Secretary of State's project to reform NATO, were hiding dangerous temptations for Italy, which could induce Rome to loosen its European engagement.

In Paris, it was considered a bit simplistic and, at the same time, dangerous, to set aside expressions, like those formulated in his "flamboyant" style by Minister de Michelis, as sheer blusters. The German events seemed in fact to have thrown open the door to risky "subversive" trends not only in Germany, but also in other European countries, Italy included. In Italy, the existing climate of uncertainty was giving new impetus to some undertones critical toward a certain kind of European construction.

On this point, it is necessary to point out that Italy, just like France and the Bundesrepublik, had fully contributed to lay, at the beginning of the Fifties, the foundations of the European integration process. Otherwise, we could run the risk of assimilating the Italian approach to that of London. On the contrary, Rome had traditionally supported the European construction and it had traditionally been focused on its institutional aspects. Besides, it was undeniable that the country

---

[61] "[...] Italy sticks to its principles both in rallying without hesitation to the Gorbačёv's proposal of a Helsinki II, and in applauding Baker's plan for a new Atlantism. In both cases, it expresses its concern for a united Europe opened up to the Ural, on the one hand, and for a comprehensive body, on the other [...]. The expression launched by Minister de Michelis 'Europe from San Francisco to Vladivostok' is, as I have already stressed, much more than a witty remark. It conveys the same state of mind that makes the groundless accusations against the EEC on the subject of the 'European Fortress' to surface again, kept alive by all those who [...] instinctively fear a Europe built on the French model, well structured and organized. More than French, a Franco-German construction that [...] it is feared to be too strict and compelling. When [...] under the shock of events [...] some are pleased to see the Paris-Bonn axis disappear, it is less for self-satisfaction than because of the challenge to the European construction, and because in this new construction site Italy will be better placed to play its own game [...]. There are indeed two trends, sometimes intertwined, sometimes contradicting each another [...] on the one hand, there is the unquestionable commitment to the process started with the Treaties of Rome, the feeling of unanimous consent of the Italian people that it is necessary 'to make Europe', and the real concern which guided Andreotti's government especially, that of making sure that Italy will fully assume its role and its responsibilities in the 1993 Community. On the other hand, there is always a tendency for Italy to play its own game and to find in a loose and unstructured gathering the opportunity to make better use of its flexibility and adaptability skills. 'Europe is a political not a geographical concept' declares de Michelis. The revival of the Helsinki architecture by Gorbačёv, as well as Baker's idea to give NATO a new content, are offering, from this point of view, dangerous temptations for Italy. The Peril is not impending, but we should be careful. For the moment, Andreotti's government is, as much as we are, concerned about keeping a cool head and avoiding lapses [...] we may count on him to pursue with realism and understanding the task just started". See Ibid.

had been and still was in 1989 permeated with an extremely positive attitude towards Europe.

Paris feared, however, that new trends, that until then had remained silent,
could make their way through the political uncertainty which the fall of the Wall
had triggered, and advocate for a looser European bond. Even Foreign Minister
de Michelis was alleged not to be indifferent to such temptations. On the contrary,
France believed that Andreotti's realism and intelligence could be relied upon to
guide Italy on the path of confirming its European commitments and of further
supporting the European integration process. Hence, the French records provide
another interpretation of the political approach to politics of the Italian Christian-
Democratic politician. His "conservatism", so often presented in German records
as a mere defence of the existing *status quo*, appeared in French eyes as a guarantee of continuity and stability.

In conclusion, by the month of December Italy had developed a three-pillar
strategy, supported by both the Italian Government and by the Foreign Office.
This strategy had different nuances which corresponded to the approach of a
Prime Minister much more attentive to the European integration framework and
that of a Foreign Minister inclined towards a more flexible vision of Europe.

In light of all that has been so far discussed, I can now offer an answer to the
question mark added to the title of this work. There existed two German states
and this was a fact. On this "reality", Italy had built its network of relations with
Germany. In 1989, two German states could, however, no longer continue to exist. And this was also a fact, which by the end of the year, Italy itself had to
acknowledge.

By the end of the Second World War, the lack in Italian politics of a *Deutschlandfrage* had guaranteed a certain degree of flexibility in swiftly establishing a
fruitful network of relations with Bonn. However, in the following years it would
have been necessary to capitalize on such results in order to develop a comprehensive and well-structured vision of the *Deutschlandfrage*. This never happened, and it was therefore one of the big weaknesses of the Italian strategy.

Surely, Italy was not the only Western European State to have encountered
difficulties in taking leave of the past, but unlike France it had some heavy Achilles' heels that in the following months would impair its capacity of influence.
These Achilles' heels will be discussed in chapter nine, whereas the next sub-
chapter will look further into the second phase of the Italian reaction from a different point of view. The perspective will shift from politics and from diplomatic
relations to the level of regional cooperation, to the press, and finally also to the
view of public opinion.

8.2 From the Alpe Adria to the Quadrangolare

> «La sostanza di quest'iniziativa […] è che nasce da un'esperienza di collabora-
> zione tra le regioni dell'Austria del sud, Stiria e Carinzia, la Slovenia […] e il
> nostro Friuli Venezia-Giulia che già da molto tempo avevano sviluppato delle ini-
> ziative di collaborazione che poi si sono espanse con questo meccanismo […].
> Rimangono fuori Germania e Francia, ma questa non è un'iniziativa contro di loro,
> è un'iniziativa che nasce da un'idea italo-austriaca poi sviluppatasi attraverso la
> collaborazione tra le regioni scaturite dalla dissoluzione del blocco orientale. […].
> Non ho mai avuto l'impressione che la quadrangolare avesse un carattere anti-
> tedesco. E'chiaro che tedeschi e francesi erano perplessi di fronte a quest'iniziativa
> non capendo quali limiti avesse […]. Che ci sia stata una volontà di costruire un
> edificio anti-tedesco è una teoria che non potrei mai accettare».[62]

This entire sub-chapter is built around the abovementioned quotation of the former Ambassador to Vienna Alessandro Quaroni (1987–1992).
Firstly, the origins of the *Quadrangolare* shall be presented, then its developments in 1989–1990[63] shall be analysed. The target is the discussion of its role in
– and its impact on – the Italian strategy in front of the German events, in order
to verify the nature of the initiative.

During these last few years the Quadrangolare has been the centre of increasing attention and curiosity. This does not mean though that a huge number of
records are available to delve deeper into it. Access to Italian archival sources
concerning the Eighties is at present difficult; information provided by those records which are already accessible is meager. Nor is the archival situation in Germany any better. The Quadrangolare did not exactly raise enthusiastic reactions
north of the Alps. Still, the attitudes of different countries produced rather different results in the diplomatic records which could be accessed.

---

[62] "The essence of this initiative […] stems from an experience of cooperation between the regions
of South Austria, Styria and Carinthia, Slovenia […] and our Friuli Venezia-Giulia, which had
been developing for a long time forms of cooperation that merged into this mechanism […]. Germany and France remained outside it, but it was not an initiative against them, it was an initiative
coming out from an Italo-Austrian idea, which was implemented through a cooperation among
regions born from the demise of the Eastern bloc. […]. I have never had the impression that this
Quadrangolare had an anti-German character. To be sure, the Germans and the French were puzzled by this initiative, as they did not understand its limits […]. Still, I could never accept the
theory that the intention was harboured to create an anti-German body". See author's interview
with Ambassador Alessandro Quaroni (12.2.2016).
[63] The *Quadrangolare* evolved into a five-cornered initiative (Pentagonale) in summer 1990, with
the accession of Czechoslovakia. One year later, after the accession of Poland, it once again
changed its name: it became the six-cornered initiative (Esagonale). This sub-chapter mainly focuses on the first steps of this regional project of cooperation, the *Quadrangolare,* and on the
premises leading to the creation of the *Pentagonale*.

When the Quadrangolare was created, in November 1989, Germany was going through a delicate moment. Besides, it appeared rather difficult in Bonn to
understand the motives that lay behind it. It is therefore not in the least surprising
that Germany paid little attention to it. Although France shared the same worries
of Germany as to the aims and limits of this four-cornered initiative, this did not
result in an overall lack of interest. Quite the contrary, a huge number of files
were devoted to its analyses both in the central body of the French Foreign Ministry and in the French embassies abroad, for instance in Rome, Budapest and
Vienna.

Three different pre-conditions – which can be compared to three boxes – had
laid the foundations[64] for the establishment of the Quadrangolare.

The first box encompassed a diverse range of local cooperation initiatives,
especially the Alpe Adria. Born in 1978 within the framework of the Italian Ostpolitik, the Alpe Adria had reached its peak of development in 1988 with the
signature of the Millstadt declaration by the representatives of the Italian, Austrian, German, Yugoslav, and Hungarian Governments. This declaration had
guaranteed not only full legitimacy and a better international exposure[65] in regional cooperation among the regions of the Danube basin, but also a clearer position of the Alpe Adria in the framework of international relations.

Some scholars also add to this first box the 1986 signature in Budapest of a
triangular arrangement between the Hungarian Communist Party, the Finnish Social-Democratic Party, and the Italian Socialist Party.[66] In dealing with the latter
initiative, Giorgio Petracchi has, for instance, stressed its importance in not considering it only as a mere step in a process of transformation of the political parties involved, but rather as an occurrence which anticipated the climate of 1989.[67]
It may appear somewhat disproportionate to give such importance to an initiative
which produced limited results compared to other frameworks of local cooperation. Still, I agree with the necessity to mention it as a testimony of the growing
interest shown by Italy for the dynamics beyond the Iron Curtain. Such an interest

---

[64] See, in particular, Dusan Necak, Die Alpen-Adria-Region 1945 bis 1991, in: Andreas Moritsch
(ed.), Alpe Adria: Zur Geschichte einer Region, Klagenfurt 2001; Liviana Poropat, Alpe Adria e
iniziativa centro-europea: Cooperazione nell'Alpe Adria e nell'area danubiana, Napoli 1993. See
also Andrzej Marcin Suszycki, Italienische Osteuropapolitik 1989–2000, Münster–Hamburg–London 2003; Rudolf Stamm, Die Pentagonale als Beitrag zur Annäherung in Europa, in: *Europäische
Rundschau* Bd.19 (1991), n. 2, pp. 35–41.
[65] For further details, see ch. 5.
[66] See Giorgio Petracchi, L'Italia e la Ostpolitik, in: Ennio di Nolfo (ed.), La politica estera italiana
negli anni Ottanta, Manduria 2003, pp. 293–318, 317.
[67] See Ibid., p. 318.

was reflected in high politics, in diplomatic relations, in local activities, and even in the cooperation found among political parties.[68]

All initiatives belonging to the first box shared the same vision of Mitteleuropa. This notion of Mitteleuropa can be thought of as the second box. The debate concerning the meaning and the significance of Mitteleuropa has traditionally revolved around two opposing approaches: a *"Mitteleuropa mit Deutschland"* (a comprehensive vision of Mitteleuropa including Germany) versus a *"Mitteleuropa ohne Deutschland"* (Mitteleuropa without Germany). Still, this notion is more complex than what such a polarisation would let us believe.

To broaden and deepen the significance of Mitteleuropa in Italy, it is of interest to follow the lead of Ennio Di Nolfo, and to use a double interpretative framework: to consider Mitteleuropa both as a tool of national politics, and as a European project.[69] If we focus on the latter dimension, it is noteworthy to remark that Mitteleuropa is located at the intersection of three different cultural areas, each with its own historical heritage: The Latin area, the Germanic area and the Slavic area. Furthermore, it is equally important to also remember that these three cultural areas had been united under the Habsburg hegemony. In Italy the word "Habsburg" was used in the 1980s to indicate the synthesis of these three cultural experiences. As already anticipated in chapter two, from the second half of the Eighties, Italy had been a fertile soil for inputs coming from Eastern Europe[70], where the notion Mitteleuropa recalled memories of time past, and also hinted at the elaboration of new political strategies which would provide the countries entrenched between Russia on the East, and Germany on the West, with a new identity. At that stage Mitteleuropa was for Italy a geographic, economic and cultural area which almost exclusively corresponded to the territories of the former Austrian-Hungarian Empire. Its main reference points were the cities of Trieste, Venice, Budapest, Ljubljana, and Zagreb. Its fringes extended to Cracow in the East and to Munich in the West. This second geographical and historical box was supposed to encompass and harmonise both the political aspirations and economic interests on which regional initiatives like the Alpe Adria were based, on the one

---

[68] In light of what has been discussed, I somewhat disagree with the theory that Italy was mainly concerned with the future of Yugoslavia, whereas Austria followed with great attention the developments in Poland, Hungary and Czechoslovakia. See Emil Brix, Die Mitteleuropapolitik von Österreich und Italien im Revolutionsjahr 1989, in: Michael Gehler/Maddalena Guiotto, Italien Österreich und die Bundesrepublik Deutschland in Europa/Italy Austria and the Federal Republic of Germany. Ein Dreiecksverhältnis in seinen wechselseitigen Beziehungen und Wahrnehmungen von 1945/49 bis zur Gegenwart/A Triangle Relationship: Mutual Relations and Perceptions from 1945/49 to the Present, Wien–Köln–Weimar 2012, pp. 455–468, 459.

[69] See Ennio di Nolfo, Il quadrangolare Mitteleuropeo, pp. 93–99.

[70] See Emil Brix, Die Mitteleuropapolitik von Österreich und Italien im Revolutionsjahr 1989, p. 456.

hand, and the intellectual and political flowering beyond the Iron Curtain, on the other. In conclusion, the Italian notion of Mitteleuropa in the mid-1980s was not anti-German by nature, it simply connected to a different vision than the Mitteleuropa conceived in Germany.

The third and last box refers to the South-Tyrolean dispute and its gradual solution that was found right in this period. It was, in fact, during the summer of 1987, under the Government led by Giovanni Goria, that Italy showed a strong activism in promoting the implementation of the measures of the so called "pacchetto" which had been discussed and agreed on throughout the two previous decades. The intention was to finally put an end to the South-Tyrolean dispute, and so to improve the relationship with Vienna.[71]The choice of Alessandro Quaroni as new Ambassador to Vienna was also a testimony of such course of action.

Former Vice-Consul in Innsbruck at the beginning of the 1960s, Alessandro Quaroni seemed to represent an excellent choice to improve bilateral contacts with Vienna and to build a relationship based on mutual trust with Alois Mock (1987–1995), the Austrian Minister of Foreign Affairs. Not only had the new Ambassador a thorough knowledge of Austriac politics and traditions, but he had also played a significant intermediary role between Rome and Vienna in the South Tyrolean issue. Hence, he was already known and appreciated in Vienna for having given his personal contribution to the settlement of a long-lasting burden.

Once freed of this heavy burden, both countries were eager to use their energy to improve and strengthen bilateral ties.[72] Documents and interviews of that time point at the significant negative impact which the South-Tyrolean dispute had had on the Italian-Austrian relationship. The comments of Alessandro Quaroni are, among others, of particular relevance.

> «Quindi il negoziato sul problema dell'Alto Adige è stato condotto su un piano bilaterale Italia-Austria, e da parte italiana anche molto attivamente a livello Roma-Bolzano [...] Tutto questo portò gradualmente alla misura che chiuse la controversia nel giugno del 1992, in base al calendario [...] che si chiamava calendario operativo già nel 1979 su cui erano stati concordati una serie di adempimenti da una parte e dall'altra per arrivare a chiudere la controversia con reciproche garanzie [...] il nuovo atteggiamento italiano rispetto a una possibile adesione dell'Austria alla CE contribuì a rendere più positivo il clima dei rapporti con l'Austria. Tutto questo per dire che il miglioramento definitivo dei rapporti con l'Austria, che oggi sono ottimi, è stato favorito dall'assunzione di questa serie di decisioni che riguardava i rapporti bilaterali, ma anche l'atmosfera. Nel periodo nel

---

[71] See Luciano Monzali, Giulio Andreotti e le relazioni italo-austriache 1972–1992, pp. 28–30.
[72] See Emil Brix, Die Mitteleuropapolitik von Österreich und Italien im Revolutionsjahr 1989, p. 455.

quale ero a Vienna, mi sono occupato principalmente di questa trattativa, si sentiva a Vienna un clima particolare anche per la composizione della popolazione della capitale che rimane quella dell'impero asburgico. Nell'elenco telefonico due terzi dei cognomi sono ungheresi, cecoslovacchi, polacchi, e questo vuol dire che a Vienna c'è un polso particolare per sentire in anticipo gli sviluppi. Questo è confermato fin dall'inizio del 1989, a Vienna si percepiva che l'URSS di Gorbačëv e gli sviluppi distensivi avrebbero mutato radicalmente il volto del centro Europa. [...]. Alla luce di questi sviluppi possiamo situare il progetto italo-austriaco di cooperazione quadrangolare che nacque proprio nel periodo 1989–1990 con un'iniziativa soprattutto del nostro ministro degli Esteri de Michelis e di quello austriaco. [...]».[73]

Opinions differ as for the identity of the "architect" who designed and promoted the *Quadrangolare*. Some experts argue that Italy was the architect of the initiative, whereas some other scholars rather lean towards Hungary and Austria.[74] Based on a thorough analysis of interviews, memoirs and, above all, of Italian diplomatic records, the historian Luciano Monzali has come to the conclusion that the initial idea had been formulated in Budapest, but the "architects" who supported the drawing of the initiative and its implementation were no other than

---

[73] "Negotiations on the South-Tyrolean issue were pursued bilaterally, between Austria and Italy, and at home between Rome and Bolzano [...] All this gradually favoured the adoption of the measure that settled the dispute in June 1992, following an agenda [...] already called operational agenda in 1979. According to it, the parties had agreed to a series of conditions to put an end to the dispute through the exchange of mutual guarantees [...] The new Italian attitude towards the accession of Austria to the EC helped in creating a more positive atmosphere in the relationship with Austria. All this to say that the significant improvement in the relationship with Austria, which today is excellent, has been favoured by the decisions taken at a bilateral level and also by this new atmosphere. At that time, I was in Vienna working on these negotiations. One could sense in Vienna a unique atmosphere, which was the direct consequence of the composition of the local population, which was the same as that of the Habsburg empire. If you take a look at the phonebook, two thirds of the family names are Hungarian, Czechoslovak and Polish names, which means that Vienna has a special pulse to feel and anticipate certain developments. From the beginning of 1989, in Vienna one could clearly sense that the URSS of Gorbačëv and his new policy course would radically alter the face of Central Europe. [...]. It is in light of such developments that we can understand the Italian-Austrian framework of cooperation named *Quadrangolare*, which was conceived in the period 1989–1990 on the basis of an initiative taken by our Foreign Minister de Michelis and the Austrian Foreign Minister. [...]". See the author's interview with Ambassador Quaroni, 12.2.2016. See also Luciano Monzali, Giulio Andreotti e le relazioni italo-austriache 1972–1992, p. 27. On the basis of the records concerning Europe and South Tyrol kept at Andreotti archives in Rome, Monzali reaches the same conclusions as Ambassador Quaroni.

[74] For the first theory see, in particular, Gianni de Michelis, La lunga ombra di Yalta: La specificità della politica italiana, Venezia 2003, and by the same author see also Le priorità italiane sulla scena internazionale, in: *Relazioni Internazionali* n. 8 (1989), pp. 81–90. For the contribution of the Hungarian Government see György Misur, Szarvasról Rómába. Diplomácia Küldetesbén, Budapest 2010. Concerning the Italian role see also Nota del ministero degli Affari Esteri sull'iniziativa esagonale, Rome, October 1991. ILS, AGA, section Trentino-Alto Adige, b.21.

Austria and Italy.[75] In light of what has been so far discussed, I am also inclined to support this last theory.

On 11–12 November 1989, the then Italian Foreign Minister and his colleagues in Austria, Hungary and Yugoslavia – together with the Vice-Ministers of the same countries – met in Budapest to sign the act which would establish the Quadrangolare. During preliminary discussions, the Italian speakers had placed much emphasis on the multiplier effect which a multilateral cooperation would have as compared to bilateral initiatives. By the expression multiplier effect, the Italian speakers meant both an exponential increase in the speed of economic development of all participating countries on the one side, and the balancing role that a multilateral cooperation could have in reducing the risk that Eastern Europe would fall apart, on the other.[76]

In the meeting of Budapest, it was evident that the new organisation was prompted by two distinct kinds of ambitions: the first one was of economic and technical nature, the second one was of a more political nature. It was precisely this political vocation that from the very beginning was supported by Rome more than by other participants. This caused tensions within the organisation itself, and misunderstandings with other European states.

At a technical level, the founding document of the *Quadrangolare*[77] advocated for greater cooperation in the economic, scientific and cultural fields based on a flexible and lightweight apparatus. This choice in favour of a limited degree of institutionalisation had in fact given good results in the local forms of coordination which had preceded the Quadrangolare. Regular meetings among the Prime Ministers and the Foreign Ministers would increase the efficiency of the organisation compared to previous experiments. In other words, the initiative was created in order to have a certain political clout without losing the advantage of the positive results achieved to date through local cooperation. Based on a six-month rotating presidency, each participating state – starting from Hungary – would alternatively play a coordinating role to ensure the smooth functioning of the mechanism. Italy would assume this coordinating role since 1 July 1990. Therefore, it was agreed that Italy would organise the first official meeting in summer. Back then, Venice appeared as the most suitable location to hold it.[78]

---

[75] See Luciano Monzali, Giulio Andreotti e le relazioni italo-austriache 1972–1992, p. 35.
[76] See Collaborazione quadrangolare, telegramma, Roma, 16.11.1989, signed the Secretary-General. ILS, AGA, section Europe, b.382.
[77] See Liviana Poropat, Alpe Adria e iniziativa centro-europea: Cooperazione nell'Alpe Adria e nell'area danubiana. In the Appendix of this book there are collected all the founding acts of the most significant regional forms of cooperation which preceded the *Quadrangolare*, together with the document establishing the *Quadrangolare* itself.
[78] See telegramma su collaborazione quadrangolare, Roma, 16.11.1989, signed by the Secretary-General. ILS, AGA, section Europe, b.382.

Specific issues would be discussed by regular meetings of technical Ministers and they would be supported by experts in the field.[79] Priority was given to five areas of cooperation: transport, environmental protection, telecommunications, small and medium enterprises, and culture. Each state would take responsibility for one specific area.[80]

In January 1990, an informal meeting involving both the Foreign Ministers and the Vice-Prime Ministers was held in Budapest. In May 1990, it was followed by another informal gathering in Vienna, just a few months before the summit of summer 1990. Both meetings were organised to verify the good functioning of the mechanism in the international arena during its first steps. In the Budapest meeting of January 1990, participants not only addressed technical issues and good practices of cooperation, but also focused on relevant political issues.[81]

Firstly, the opportunity to engage regional financial institutions and other financial institutions as well, like the ECB and the EBRD, in order to support far-reaching projects, was discussed.

Secondly, the advantages of accepting new members, like Czechoslovakia, were also examined, together with the possibility to use the Quadrangolare to overcome the existing ideological barriers. This would also support the implementation of the principles enshrined in the Helsinki Final Act. The Italian Foreign Minister was very active in advocating for the opportunity to use the Quadrangolare in the spirit of the CSCE as a bridge to bring closer countries belonging to different military blocs. Italy seemed to aspire, by means of the newly established Quadrangolare, to a leading role within the EC, the Council of Europe and NATO. The Quadrangolare was, therefore, conceived as a sort of antechamber to enable gradual adaptation of Hungary and Yugoslavia, and partially also of Austria, towards Western European practices.[82] In due time, other Eastern European countries could join in the mechanism.

Still, it was not until the Summit of Venice in July 1990 that such ambitions took a more defined shape. On that occasion Italy – which by then had both the presidency of the EC and that of the *Quadrangolare* – promoted a major updating of the essence of the kind of cooperation established nine months earlier. According to the Italian Foreign Minister, the time had come for the four-cornered initiative to not only promote economic and technical cooperation, like the Alpe

---

[79] See Liviana Poropat, Alpe Adria e iniziativa centro-europea: Cooperazione nell'Alpe Adria e nell'area danubiana, p. 61.
[80] Italy was responsible for transports, Austria for environmental protection, Yugoslavia for telecommunications and Hungary for culture and small and medium enterprises.
[81] See Liviana Poropat, Alpe Adria e iniziativa centro-europea: Cooperazione nell'Alpe Adria e nell'area danubiana, pp. 62–64.
[82] Ibid.

Adria had done before it, but also to fully engage in shaping a new model of economic, social and cultural cooperation for Eastern Europe.[83] In other words, the Quadrangolare would bring Hungary, Yugoslavia, Czechoslovakia – which by then had joined the four-cornered venture – and any other Eastern European country which would accept to join it, closer to the European Community. In summer 1990, a quick enlargement of the EC towards the East was considered in Italy both unlikely and dangerous, while the approaching German re-unification was alleged as able to arise a wave of fear in Eastern Europe.[84]

So far, nothing indicated that the Quadrangolare was anti-German in its essence. As it has been already discussed, the Quadrangolare, together with other local cooperation initiatives which preceded it, had been built on a specific notion of Mitteleuropa which did not include Germany. By the end of 1989, the Quadrangolare had not become a tool to cope with the German events *stricto senso*, but rather to cope with the worries and all kind of potential consequences which the fall of the Wall could arise beyond the Iron Curtain. According to both primary and secondary sources, this should be considered the link between the Italian three-pillar strategy and the Quadrangolare.

In other words, the Quadrangolare had been originally conceived on the basis of the experience collected through local cooperation experiences of a technical nature. The interest of the regions which had participated in such ventures was first and foremost prompted by economic issues, to which the liberalisation of the Eastern European markets offered new opportunities of growth.

Still, in 1989 Rome slowly transformed its original approach to go beyond the sole economic dimension in its proposals, and to fully embrace the sphere of political ambitions. The 1989 earthquake seemed in fact to offer to Italy the chance to capitalise on the results so far achieved at a local level and to create a framework which would give Rome greater influence in Central-Eastern Europe, and a significant intermediary role between the former Communist countries and Western Europe. Could these intentions be ascribed to the Ministry of Foreign Affairs, or to the ambitions of the then Italian Foreign Minister, Gianni de Michelis?

This question has indeed a paramount role in the analysis of the motives behind the Quadrangolare. Unfortunately, the available records do not allow us to provide a clear answer to it. It is, however, possible to make some hypotheses by looking at the records available.

On the one hand, it is once again necessary to reaffirm that the Quadrangolare had its roots in previous local frameworks of cooperation whose implementation

---

[83] See Appunto MAE sulla cooperazione regionale, Roma, July 1990. ILS AGA, section URSS, b.711.
[84] Ibid.

preceded the rise to power of Gianni de Michelis. In addition, in the mid-1980s there was a general consensus in the then Italian political spectrum concerning the necessity to both improve relations with Austria and to develop a more-dynamic approach towards Eastern Europe. This interest was a transversal element which underpinned the vision of both Gianni de Michelis, of the Socialists, and of the majority of the Christian-Democrats, Giulio Andreotti and Francesco Cossiga included.[85]

On the other hand, the specific design behind the Quadrangolare was closely linked to the great visions and the ambitions of Foreign Minister de Michelis.[86]

> „Tatsächlich verknüpften sich in dem italienischen Interesse an Mitteleuropa die Suche nach einer neuen Dimension italienischer Außenpolitik, (Italien müsse [...] ‚one of the leaders of the EC in the 1990s werden') mit der Überzeugung, den Transformationsstaaten helfen zu müssen (‚We are moving to fill a vacuum'). Diese Zitate von de Michelis stammen aus einem Artikel in der Financial Times vom 10.11.1989, der mit einem Hinweis auf die messianische Persönlichkeit von De Michelis schließt: ‚He might also add that it takes a Venetian with a sense of history like himself to see the opportunities'. Explaining his view of the world, he says, only half in jest: ‚There is the world, there is the centre of the world, which is Europe, and at the centre of Europe, there is Venice'."[87]

In 1989, on being appointed Head of Government, Giulio Andreotti had vacated the post of Foreign Minister, whereas Gianni de Michelis, a Venetian politician rather unscrupulous in his political ascent[88], had taken his place at the Farnesina.

---

[85] See Luciano Monzali, Giulio Andreotti e le relazioni italo-austriache 1972–1992, pp. 34–35 for the South-Tyrolean issue. Concerning Italy and Mitteleuropa, see, in particular, Note pour le président de la République : Visite d'état du président Cossiga, Paris, 29.1.1990. ANF, série 5 CD/304, dossier 11.

[86] According to Ambassador Quaroni, the launching of the initiative was a dream of de Michelis which harboured such great designs for the Italian role. See the author's interview with Ambassador Alessandro Quaroni (12.2.2016). Concerning the role of de Michelis in the designing of the Quadrangolare, see also Rencontre Quadrangulaire de Budapest, télégramme 1377, Rome, 9.11.1989, signed Perol. AMAE 1935inva, Direction Europe, Série Hongrie, carton 6333, période 1986–1990, dossier 11.1.

[87] "Actually, the Italian interest in Mitteleuropa is connected with the search for a new dimension in the Italian Foreign Policy (Italy must be [...] 'one of the leaders of the EC in the 1990s'), and with the conviction to have the resources to support the process of transformation ('We are moving to fill a vacuum'). This quotation by de Michelis is from an article published on the Financial Times (10.11.1989), which ends up by a reference to the messianic personality of De Michelis: 'He might also add that it takes a Venetian with a sense of history like himself to see the opportunities'. Explaining his view of the world, he says, only half in jest: 'There is the world, there is the centre of the world, which is Europe, and at the centre of Europe, there is Venice'". See Emil Brix, Die Mitteleuropapolitik von Österreich und Italien im Revolutionsjahr 1989, p. 456. Brix refers to the article of John Wyles, Italy aspires to a bigger regional role, *Financial Times*, 10.11.1989.

[88] See Luciano Monzali, Giulio Andreotti e le relazioni italo-austriache 1972–1992, pp. 32–33.

Luciano Monzali has signalled that the political designs and ambitions of the latter were not always and not necessarily in tune with the political course traced by Giulio Andreotti. In addition, Andreotti also continued to keep a certain influence on the making of the Italian Foreign policy.[89]

By the end of 1989, it was the purpose and the desire of Gianni de Michelis that the four-cornered initiative would take a proactive role in the transformation process of Central-Eastern Europe and in the making of a new European framework. In accordance with this ambition, between the end of 1989 and the mid-1990, the Quadrangolare underwent a far-reaching process of progressive extension of its boundaries and of its goals. This implied a partial, though significant, loss of its original scope. Until then, local initiatives of cooperation had been indeed created within a limited local area, the Danube basin, and on the basis of a specific notion of Mitteleuropa. Starting from 1990, the boundaries of the Quadrangolare extended steadily with the alleged aim of embracing the entirety of Central-Eastern Europe.

A correct understanding of the reactions to the Quadrangolare of the European partners of Italy is equally important as is the comprehension of the Italian ambitions and goals. Vienna, for instance, attached a certain importance to this venture as an unbureaucratic and flexible enough tool to further foster local cooperation and to handle it in a more pragmatic and effective way. Still, the Italian and the Austrian approaches differed widely when it came to the political ambitions associated by Foreign Minister de Michelis to the initiative.

Firstly, differences existed within the Austrian government regarding the notion of Mitteleuropa itself and the significance of local initiatives of cooperation. Chancellor Franz Vranitzky was, for instance, more sceptic about ventures such as the Quadrangolare than was the Conservative Foreign Minister Mock and vice-Chancellor Erhard Busek. At a broader level, Austria seemed to prefer to proceed according to the model of local initiatives of a technical or economic nature.

> „In Österreich war das Interesse an gemeinsamen mitteleuropäischen Initiativen deutlich geringer, weil die Österreichische Außenpolitik an ihrem Konzept der bilateralen, guten Nachbarschaftspolitik festhalten wollte und fürchtete, dass eine zu enge Partnerschaft mit Italien den vor 1989 erarbeiteten eigenen Gestaltungsraum einengen würde. Außerdem unterstützte Außenminister Alois Mock nicht die italienische Position, dass eine gemeinsame Mitteleuropastrategie ein Gegengewicht gegen deutsche Ambitionen in diesem Raum darstellen sollte."[90]

---

[89] See Ibid.

[90] "In Austria, the interest for common Mitteleuropean initiatives was substantially less relevant, because the Austrian Foreign Policy wanted to hold on the principle of the bilateral, "good

The abovementioned quotation introduces the suspicion that, for Italy, this Mitteleuropean cooperation initiative should be a sort of "counterweight" to German ambitions. Was this a widespread suspicion?

In France, the issue of the Quadrangolare stirred up contradictory reactions which were the ground for different answers. During the first months which followed the establishment of the four-cornered initiative, France looked at the emergence of a network of new regional forms of cooperation, epitomised by the Quadrangolare, with both scepticism and concern. According to Paris, the resurgence of old bonds of solidarity in Mitteleuropa also meant the re-emergence of old problems. The notion *Mitteleuropa* had quickly regained in importance, and with it so had the borders of the former Austrian-Hungarian Empire. The inherent contradictions which had brought about the demise of the Empire had, however, not been definitively solved.[91] Certainly, an enhanced interest for regional forms of cooperation had its own internal logic in a country like Italy in which regions had a deeply rooted identity up to the point of being able to sometimes carry out a sort of "Foreign policy" of their own, especially in the economic field. Still, such developments raised growing concerns in Paris in light of its "jacobinical" model of centralisation of power.[92] These fears and concerns did, however, not get to the point of suspecting the Quadrangolare either of having an anti-German character, or of being a tool to oppose the German re-unification. During the preparatory stage of the four-cornered initiative, nobody could have anticipated that the German re-unification would soon become a short term feasible target, whereas in the mid-1990, when the Quadrangolare was at its peak, Rome itself had to acknowledge that the re-unification process could neither be stopped nor indefinitely delayed. What the Quadrangolare actually lacked was the desire to fully involve Germany. As a result, it could be assumed for France that Rome had an underlying goal in promoting this venture other than its oft-stated desire to support regional integration: Rome wanted to strengthen its position against the German Ostpolitik which was its main competitor beyond the Iron Curtain.

---

neighbouring policy" and, therefore, it also feared that a too close partnership with Italy would reduce the freedom acquired before 1989. Besides, Foreign Minister Alois Mock does not support the Italian stance that a common Mitteleuropean strategy should be a counter-weight to the German ambitions in this area". See Emil Brix, Die Mitteleuropapolitik von Österreich und Italien im Revolutionsjahr 1989, p. 459.

[91] See Doc.16, Note de Jacques Blot, directeur d'Europe, Le réveil d'Europe, secret, Paris, 16.11.1989, in: Maurice Vaïsse/Christian Wenkel (eds.), La diplomatie française face à la réunification allemande.

[92] See AMAE 1935inva, Direction Europe, Série Hongrie, carton 6333, période 1986–1990, sous-série 11, several documents.

« Il est clair qu'à ce stade préliminaire les Italiens souhaitent conserver une cer-
taine prééminence vis à vis surtout de l'Allemagne à propos de laquelle M. de
Michelis [...] "la reconstruction d'une Europe centre-méridionale sans la participation de la RFA pourrait apparaitre insuffisante, mais la RFA est actuellement
projetée vers une autre direction [...]". Autant dire, et M. Borga l'admet, que l'Italie a actuellement un premier rôle à jouer pour être le canalisateur de cette zone
[...] et il précise que pourrait ultérieurement s'y agréger la Suisse et…la Bavière ».[93]

Therefore, the Quadrangolare was neither considered anti-German by nature, nor
was it considered as aiming at opposing the re-unification process. The *Quai
d'Orsay* was rather inclined to believe that, given the circumstances, the Quadrangolare had, over time, added to its original targets the goal of acting as a counterweight to possible German ambitions in Central-Eastern Europe. Even if Paris
acknowledged that the scope and the potential of the four-cornered initiative was
much more than a mere *foucade* (whim) or a personal ambition of Minister de
Michelis, by the mid-1990s the French government still signalled its vague
(*fumeux*) formulation and its "clumsy" (*cahotant*) implementation.[94]

By contrast, Vienna was usually far more critical of the anti-German scope
allegedly associated by Italy to the four-cornered initiative. In this regard, the
comments developed by Emil Brix on the basis of Austrian primary sources deserve special attention. Italian efforts to strengthen its influence in Central-Eastern Europe were alleged to suffer prejudicial effects as a result of the contrast
opposing Andreotti to de Michelis as regarding the scope of the Quadrangolare,
whether it should be used as a tool to curb the German influence in the area.

„Der Österreichische Generalkonsul in Triest berichtet dazu Anfang März 1990:
‚Über die Beherrschung des Apparates der Farnesina durch de Michelis prävaliere
nun wohl dessen Auffassung, doch bleibe Andreotti bemüht, über die ihm zur Ver-
fügung stehenden Möglichkeiten die antideutsche Spitze abzustumpfen'. Der auf

---

[93] "It is clear that in this preliminary phase the Italians want to retain a certain pre-eminence especially towards Germany. In this regard, M. de Michelis [...] 'the reconstruction of a South-Central
Europe without the participation of the Bundesrepublik could appear inadequate, but the Bundesrepublik is presently projected in another direction [...]'. All this to say, and M. Borga recognizes it,
that Italy has actually a primary role to play in order to be the channel to cluster this geographical
zone [...] And he specifies that later on Switzerland and … Bavaria could also aggregate to it". See
Rencontre Quadrangulaire de Budapest, télégramme 1377, Rome, 9.11.1989, signed Perol. AMAE
1935inva, Direction Europe, Série Hongrie, carton 6333, période 1986–1990, sous-série, 11, dossier 1. The last sentence of the quotation regarding a possible accession of Switzerland and Bavaria
had been confuted in the interviews with Italian diplomats. Ambassador Quaroni remarked, for
instance, that to consider Switzerland, Bavaria or Germany engaged in the Quadrangolare would
have be unrealistic.
[94] See Pentagonale, télégramme 1484, Rome, 12.12.1990, signed Perol. AMAE 1935inva, Direction
Europe, Série Hongrie, carton 6333, période 1986–1990, sous-série, 11, dossier 1.

ein gutes Verhältnis mit der Bundesrepublik Deutschland bedachte Österreichische Außenminister Mock lässt einer Weiterleitung dieser Nachricht an die Österreichische Botschaft in Bonn hinzufügen, dass er bei seinen Kontakten und Gesprächen mit De Michelis solche Intentionen nie registrieren konnte."[95]

It might seem somewhat paradoxical that it was Andreotti who would try to "blunt the anti-German edge of the Quadrangolare". Still, this confirms what has been so far discussed and allows us to better contextualise the approach of Andreotti to the German question. It also allows us to put aside the myths about Andreotti, and to draw the attention instead to the reasons and the context in which he opposed the German re-unification.

What final conclusions can be drawn from this presentation revolving around the initiatives of local cooperation which Italy supported?

We can draw the conclusion that the four-cornered initiative did not have its roots in an anti-German atmosphere. More generally, we can also come to the conclusion that the Mitteleuropean policy pursued by Italy, in spite of its not having an anti-German nature, was prompted by fears and concerns regarding the destabilising effects which the fall of the Wall could trigger beyond the Iron Curtain.

It is however impossible, based on the records so far available, to rule out the possibility that the specific concept of the Quadrangolare, as Gianni de Michelis understood it, had some anti-German roots. When more Italian diplomatic files are eventually accessible for researchers, it will probably be possible to look further in the subject and to provide a clear answer to this thorny question. So far, it is at least possible to make some hypotheses. If in the vision of de Michelis, the Quadrangolare concealed some anti-German elements, the ambitions of Minister de Michelis were heavily frustrated by the reactions of his European partners and also by his interlocutors within the Quadrangolare itself. If, on the contrary, this suspicion was unsubstantiated and merely mirrored the concerns widespread in the partners, the behaviour and the statements of de Michelis were not clear enough to cut it off at the source. In any case, this kind of allegations had a rather negative effect on the four-cornered initiative devaluing its scope to a mere instrument used to face the ambitions of Bonn.

---

[95] "At the beginning of March 1990, the Austrian Consul General in Trieste had informed that de Michelis controls the apparatus of the Farnesina; however, Andreotti continues to work, with the means at his disposal, to smooth its Anti-German edge. When this message was forwarded to the Austrian Embassy in Bonn, the Austrian Foreign Minister Mock – who is interested in good relations with the Federal Republic – added that in his contacts with de Michelis, such intentions had not been recorded". See Emil Brix, Die Mitteleuropapolitik von Österreich und Italien im Revolutionsjahr 1989, p. 462. Based on the report of the Austrian General-Consul in Trieste, Zl. 29-RES/90, 3 March 1990.

Whatever hypothesis one decides to support, it is undeniable that, beyond the strictly technical and economic level, the Quadrangolare proved to be too vague and fragmentary to be truly effective. Moreover, the Quadrangolare was based on an assumption which historical developments would soon contradict: The conviction that an enlargement of the EC to Eastern European countries was for the moment unfeasible and that, as a result, European countries would be ready to accept the Quadrangolare as a framework to cross this transitional phase. Austria was worried about its anti-German edge, while Germany found it extremely hard to understand its scope, and the local press considered it with amused scepticism.

To conclude, Bonn recognised that the *Quadrangolare* presented an ambitious bottom line. It reflected the resourcefulness of the Italian Foreign Minister, who seemed to constantly come up with new ideas. If these could be accomplished, and if they would be effective, was though a constant object of doubt.

An initiative born on the sturdy base of efficient cooperation and which had produced practical results at a local level seemed to feed the suspicion towards Rome right when the 2+4 mechanism was taking shape.

8.3 And now to the Italian Public Opinion and the Press

The fall of the Berlin Wall came for the Italian public opinion as unexpected and surprising as it did for the public opinion of other European states. Still, unlike reactions in other countries, Italy was the stage of a wave of enthusiasm and support.[96] According to data provided by the German opinion poll institute Allensbach, in September 1989, 66 % of Italian people had answered positively to the question of whether a re-unified Germany would favour world peace.[97] Two months later, the fall of the Wall did not produce, as anticipated by several opinion poll institutes, a drastic drop in these figures, but rather a surge: 80 % of the Italian interviewees declared themselves in favour of a German re-unification.[98] These figures remained steady until the official birth-date of the re-unified Germany, apart from some slight variations at the beginning of spring 1990. The Italian enthusiasm seemed to confirm the existence of a positive trend which united the citizens of the Northern Mediterranean countries, i.e. these countries

---

[96] See the author's interview with Ezio Mauro, chief editor of the newspaper *Repubblica*, (17.3.2016). Ezio Mauro stressed the positive reaction of the Italian public opinion not only towards the German events, but also, more generally, towards the turmoil beyond the Curtain.

[97] See Michael Wolffsohn, Keine Angst vor Deutschland, Erlangen – Bonn – Wien 1990, pp. 190–191.

[98] See Ibid. Despite different approaches in gathering data, all polls of 1989/1990 confirm these positive results. See PA AA B26, n. 173561. See also Gabriele d'Ottavio, 1989 oder das Ende der "parallelen Geschichte", p. 45. See, in particular, Eurobarometer n. 32, early release flash November 1989, 14 December 1989; Eurobarometer n. 34, December 1989; Eurobarometer flash n. 3, October 1990. Lastly, see also the study commissioned by *Corriere delle Sera* to the Institute Makno and published on the Milan newspaper on 17 December 1989.

figured the highest degree of support of the target of re-unification. According to the Eurobarometer surveys concerning the reactions of Member States public opinions to a possible re-unification, only Portugal and Greece, with 83 % of interviewees in favour of re-unification, and Spain, with 85 % (the highest percentage in the survey), ranked better than Italy. Italy also ranked high as regards the figures of those who opposed re-unification, with a high of barely 10 %. Once again, only Spain and Portugal (7 %) and Greece (3 %) ranked better. The remaining 10 % of Italian interviewees declared being indifferent to the fate of the two German States.

> „Die Fernsehaufnahmen von Volksfest lösten Anteilnahme und Begeisterung aus. Zum ersten Mal vielleicht nach 1945 kam es […] auch in Italien zu einer Sympathiewelle für die Deutschen. Die Schlagzeilen der Tageszeitungen vermitteln etwas von jener Atmosphäre: Elezioni libere in Germania Est (La Stampa); Il trionfo della Libertà (la Repubblica); Oltre il Muro verso la Democrazia (il Corriere della Sera); il Giorno più bello per la Democrazia (l'Unità); […] Le due Berlino si abbracciano (il Tempo)."[99]

This brief quotation of Jens Petersen, a well-known expert in the field, not only confirms what national and European polls affirmed, but it also expands upon the approach of the Italian press.

Soon after the 9 November events, two among the major Italian newspapers, namely the *Corriere della Sera* and *La Stampa*, both devoted a significant number of articles to Germany, namely 99 in the first and 117 in the latter. As many as 81 articles in the conservative newspaper *Corriere della Sera* and 98 in the liberal *La Stampa* had a special focus on the fall of the Wall and on its potential consequences.[100] Similar figures can be found in other major Italian newspapers, such as *Repubblica* and *L'Unità*.

Differences did not concern the interest showed towards the German events, but rather the way to deal with this issue. The Turin newspaper *La Stampa* gave, for instance, more attention to the "potential international consequences" of the fall of the Wall. Its Milan opponent *Corriere della Sera* was more interested in its socio-cultural aspects and in the Italian public perception, whereas the Roman

---

[99] "The television pictures of popular celebrations generated interest and enthusiasm. Probably for the first time after 1945, […] Italy too was the stage of a wave of sympathy towards the Germans. The headlines of the daily newspapers gave a sense of this atmosphere: Elezioni libere in Germania Est (La Stampa); Il trionfo della Libertà (la Repubblica); Oltre il Muro verso la Democrazia (il Corriere della Sera); il Giorno più bello per la Democrazia (l'Unità); […] Le due Berlino si abbracciano (il Tempo)". See Jens Petersen, L'Unificazione tedesca del 1989–1990 vista dall'Italia, in: *Storia contemporanea* n. XXIII (1992), pp. 1087–1124, quoted in Gabriele D'Ottavio, 1989 oder das Ende der "parallelen Geschichte", p. 45.

[100] See Eva Sabine Kuntz, Konstanz und Wandel von Stereotypen: Deutschlandbilder in der italienischen Presse nach dem Zweiten Weltkrieg, Frankfurt am Main 1997, p. 361.

Repubblica was the most attentive of the three to Italian politics and to the course of action which it would choose.

The kind of articles published in each one of the abovementioned newspapers mirrored these different editorial choices. In addition to articles written by its correspondents in Germany, Alfredo Venturi and Tito Sansa, *La Stampa* often gave voice to correspondents in the most important European and World capitals to inform its readers about the German events. By contrast, the *Corriere della Sera* rather leaned towards a combination of articles written by its journalists in Germany, Ettore Petta and Massimo Nava, and commentaries of Italian "experts" with an established reputation, as, for instance, Gian-Enrico Rusconi and the former Italian Ambassador to Moscow, Sergio Romano.

These different editorial choices notwithstanding, in the first days which followed the fall of the Wall, all published articles shared the same enthusiasm and referred mostly to the same set of images and metaphors[101] to express it. On 12 November 1989, the journalist Biagio di Giovanni wrote in the newspaper *L'Unità* about a "riapertura della storia" (re-opening of History), while the previous day another journalist of the same newspaper had described 9 November 1989 as "il giorno più bello per tutta l'Europa" (the most beautiful day for Europe).[102] In Milan, Franco Venturini proposed in the *Corriere della Sera* a comparison between the fall of the Wall and the storming of the Bastille exactly two hundred years before, while Massimo Nava offered to his readers an article with the ironic title "Vieni, ti porto a ballare a Ovest" (Come with me, let's go dancing in the West).[103] Tito Sansa and Alfredo Venturi used very similar tones in *La Stampa*.[104] Regardless of different titles and editorial choices, in those first days all the major newspapers shared the same feeling, a sort of "union of hearts"[105], a "kollektive Umarmung" (collective embrace) that could join together the Italians and the Germans.[106]

---

[101] For instance, the metaphor of Odysseus from ancient Greek mythology, or that of Fidelio from German opera were very popular in those days

[102] See Biagio di Giovanni, La storia di riapre, *L'Unità*, 12.11.1989, p. 1. See also Paolo Soldini, Il giorno più bello per l'Europa, *L'Unità*, 11.11.1989, p. 1.

[103] See Franco Venturini, Cade la Bastiglia dell'Est, *Cds*, 10.11.1989, p. 1. See also Massimo Nava, Vieni ti porto a ballare a Ovest, *Cds*, 11.11.1989, p. 1.

[104] See, for example, Tito Sansa, La notte del Muro: 28 anni dopo, *La Stampa*, 11.11.1989, p. 3 See also Alfredo Venturi, Kohl: Unità per la nazione tedesca, *La Stampa*, 11.11.1989, p. 2. See, as well, Alfredo Venturi, Il futuro tedesco è cosa nostra, *La Stampa*, 17.11.1989, p. 5.

[105] See Massimo Nava, Un popolo diviso è tornato ad abbracciarsi, *Cds*, 12.11.1989, p. 1.

[106] The first metaphor has been used by Alida Koch in Alida Koch, Italiens Rolle beim Prozess der deutschen Wiedervereinigung, Grin Verlag 2007, p. 12. As for the second, see Deborah Cuccia, Italien und die deutsche Einigung 1989–1990, in: Michael Gehler/Maximilian Graf (eds.), Europa und die deutsche Einheit: Beobachtungen, Entscheidungen, und Folgen, pp. 677–699, 683.

Things became, however, more complicated, once this initial wave of enthusiasm faded away.[107] From the end of November, and especially since December 1989, the articles published in the abovementioned newspapers started to be less sensational and more thoughtful in the tones used. In *La Stampa* Enzo Bettiza wrote, for instance, that the re-unification of Germany should not be considered *a priori* a positive or negative event, but it should be rather regarded as a problem to be quickly handled as it was unquestionably on the agenda, even though the Italian political élite found it hard to acknowledge that.[108] However, both the "Italia ufficiale" and the "Italia non ufficiale", press included, agreed on at least one single aspect: the day of change had arrived too soon for Italy.

As the specific issue of the approach adopted by the Italian press towards the so-called "German events" has been throughout the years the subject of a significant number of essays and publications, there exists a rich scientific literature to refer to. Among other works, the volume by Eva Sabine Kuntz – to which I have already made specific reference in chapter six –, and the text of Ines Lehmann, which devotes some interesting chapters to Italy, are both worthy to be mentioned.[109] Rather than retracing all the most relevant issues discussed in the articles published between 1989 and 1990, it appears therefore more challenging to build on the results so far achieved in the aforementioned scientific literature and to focus on the recurrence of specific words and stereotypes. Thus, it will be possible to formulate some hypotheses to answer one of the key questions formulated at the beginning of this work: Did old stereotypes associated with the Germans survive 1989?

So far it has been found that in the 1980s traditional prejudices and stereotypes had neither been deleted nor fully replaced by new representations. Still, it has also been found that the Eighties had set the stage for a wide debate on the grounding of the abstractions and generalizations on which such stereotypes were based. Within the huge number of articles published in Italy between November 1989 and October 1990, a significant amount of different judgments and images related to the character of the German people, to its past, especially to National-Socialism, its political views and tendencies, as well as its level of democratic maturity, were offered to Italian readers. A thorough analysis allows, however, to identify two terms which were more often used in association with the word Germany, namely *Europe* and *Reich*. It is also possible to detect two distinct trends:

---

[107] Italy had been looking with enthusiasm at the turmoil beyond the Curtain even before the Fall of the Wall. See, for example, Alberto Ronchey, La grande evasione del popolo di Prussia, *Repubblica*, 3.10.1989.

[108] See Enzo Bettiza, Convulsioni nel cuore dell'Europa, *La Stampa*, 21.11.1989, p. 1.

[109] See Ines Lehmann, Die deutsche Vereinigung von außen gesehen: Angst Bedenken und Erwartungen in der ausländischen Presse (BAND II: Die Presse Dänemarks, der Niederlande, Belgiens, Italiens, Portugals und Spaniens und jüdische Reaktionen), Frankfurt am Main 1997.

the first one unconditionally in favour of this process, the second one instead raised doubts and suspicions in light of specific conditions.

The second of these trends gave expression to a certain Germanophobia, which seemed to lie dormant in some sections of the Italian population. One of its most important channels of expression was the criticism against the refusal of Helmut Kohl to provide an early guarantee of the Polish-German border. In mid-November 1989, the left-wing newspaper *L'Unità* published on its second page a caricature of two men in front of a globe, where the first man was asking to the second to guess what he loved most of Germany. The second man answered if it was Poland that he loved most of Germany.[110] Shortly afterwards, *Repubblica* published on the pages of its popular insert *Satyricon* a short comic strip with an imagined dialogue between Chancellor Kohl and the phantom of Hitler. After a brief crosstalk, Kohl concluded by affirming that the idea of Poland could have been designed by Hitler, but, after sixty years, its copyright was over, hence Kohl could claim it as its own.

Even though such criticism was a cross-cutting element in the majority of the Italian newspapers[111], it was usually more easily noticeable in the conservative *Corriere della Sera*, not through articles signed by its journalists, but rather through its editorial choice to give space to the opinion of "experts" in the field or to prominent figures of the Italian cultural and social landscape of that time, by means of interviews or comments.[112]

The second trend focused essentially on the question of borders, whereas the strong points of the first trend were the issue of the level of democratic maturity attained in Germany and the benefits associated with the kind of growth pursued by Bonn. The latter was not hegemonic in the traditional sense of the word, rather economic. A high level of democratic awareness and social maturity was attributed to both Western and Eastern Germany, though with some differences.

---

[110] See the second page in *L'Unità*, 11.11.1989.
[111] See, for example, Ernesto Galli della Loggia, La "pallida madre" ora guida l'Europa, *La Stampa*, 12.11.1989, p. 1.
[112] See, in particular, the articles published in *Corriere della Sera* in summer 1990 under the title "Chi ha paura della Grande Germania" (Who fears the Big Germany). More generally, left-wing "old" intellectuals were usually critical towards the re-unification process, as for instance Enzo Collotti. By the term "old", I don't only mean the average age of these intellectuals. Throughout the previous years, people belonging to this category had made extremely harsh comments on the Bundesrepublik and its political system. Besides, they had often given voice to the fear that the "democratisation" of Western Germany was but a cover to conceal continuity with the Reich. To be more precise, these intellectuals belonged to the group of those people who regardless the transformation of the PCI in the 1980s, had remained tied to a Manichaean view of the relationship between Eastern and Western Germany. This small group of intellectuals often had more echo abroad than others. For instance, Jens Petersen considered Collotti as one of the best experts on Germany. See Eva Sabine Kuntz, p. 363.

Besides, both strong points were always presented in close association with the "fattore Europa" (factor Europe).[113] The interdependency within the EC was indeed converting the aforementioned achievements into an irreversible path.[114]

For reasons of clarity, the ideas so far developed are based on an oversimplification of an extremely complex background in which the two trends usually intermingled and overlapped. The aforementioned recurrent terms "Europe" and especially "Reich" are an excellent example of this problematic issue. The use of the latter was in fact crucial both to support and to oppose the possibility of a German re-unification. This makes it extremely difficult to attribute the articles written between 1989 and 1990 to one or the other trend.

To further explore the subject, it can be helpful to pay attention to the article written by Mario Pirani: "Chi ha paura del Quarto Reich?" (Who is afraid of the IV Reich?).[115] Pirani did not hide the motives for doubting whether the future of Germany could be secured by re-unification, but he also gave special attention to the reasons for being optimistic, also on ground of the nature of the popular uprising in Eastern Germany. In the words of the journalist himself, this did not mean that one should forget the past, National-Socialism included. It only meant

---

[113] See Alberto Cavallari, Se l'oro del Reno sconfigge il Reich, *Repubblica*, 07.7.1990. See also Bernard Henri-Lévy, Quanti pregiudizi negli occhi degli Occidentali. L'Est e il futuro della Germania, *La Stampa*, 21.11.1989. In the second article, the author stressed that the reunification [sic!] was the obsession of the Europeans, not of the Germans. He also pointed that one had to know German history to comprehend it and avoid alarmism. Above all, it was considered necessary to deepen on the relations between the notion of state and that of nation at the heart of Europe, as in that specific geographical area the latter had traditionally had precedence over the first.

[114] See, for example, Mario Deaglio, Anche ai tedeschi fa bene l'Europa, *La Stampa*, 16.11.1989, p. 1. According to Deaglio, Germany had neither the potential nor the intention to decide alone about the future of Europe; still, nothing could be agreed upon without its consent. Germany could reasonably assume a role of leadership in the future, but not a hegemonic role. Similar issues also emerged in the interview with Ezio Mauro. Many journalists were in fact persuaded that Germany had the potential to assume in the 1990s a more assertive political role and a greater cultural influence. See also Eva Sabine Kuntz, Konstanz und wandel von Stereotypen, pp. 364–367. The "factor Europe" was, throughout the all process of re-unification, a point of reference in the debate, both for those who considered it an element which had contributed to a sound transformation of the Bundesrepublik, and for those who considered it the necessary "cage" to keep a more powerful Germany under control. See Barbara Spinelli, Prima l'Europa e poi la Germania, *La Stampa*, 10.11.1989. Spinelli adopted in her article the dictum of Adenauer "Keine Experimente" to advocate caution until Western Europe (and not the European Common House dreamed by the Soviets) would be ready to host a bigger German state. Europe was more frequently considered an element which had had a positive influence in supporting the democratic transformation of Germany, rather than a "cage". Still, there existed some voices "out of the choir". Indro Montanelli, for instance, wondered whether a reunified Germany would continue to work in the service of Europe or if it would be Europe the one to work, more or less freely, in the service of Germany. See Indro Montanelli, Ein Volk, ein Reich, ein Kohl, *il Giornale*, 3.10.1990.

[115] See Mario Pirani, Chi ha paura del Quarto Reich?, *Repubblica*, 15.11.1989.

that it was important to avoid making a drama of the ongoing process. Developments had to be put in the right context and analysed rationally.

This constant attempt of contextualization and rationalization is what best characterized the approach of the Italian press in its entirety. In other words, in the eyes of the press, the Italian political class appeared both disoriented and undecided, whereas public opinion was persistently – and for some intellectuals inexplicably – optimist on a future re-unification. For this reason, the major newspapers deemed it necessary to debate with a critical eye both euphoric frenzies and stiff refusals. This "operation" carried out by the most influential Italian newspapers to assume the role of national "critical conscience" can be considered a *trait-d'union* of the reaction of the press to the German events. Its results were divergent.

All things considered, the one and only constant element in this complicated approach by the Italian press to the changes in Germany was a specific trend, which has already been addressed in chapter three: A Manichean way of depicting Germany. Its South-Western part, Catholic and peaceful, was presented as opposed to "Prussia", that is its Northern and Eastern area, Protestant and militarist. Since the 1950s, this association had found in the conservative newspapers a fertile soil, for instance, in the *Corriere della Sera*. The year 1989 showed that not only had it survived, but also that it had extended its sphere of influence. The liberal newspaper *La Stampa* affirmed that the word *Reich* should not be feared anymore, because the re-unification process was not bound to be achieved by way of a military conquest – as it had happened under pressure from Evangelic Berlin – but under the auspices of the Catholic Bonn.[116] The same newspaper also brought to the attention of its readers that modern Berlin had symbolically broken its past bond with Prussia.[117]

In the short term, this oversimplified association had a positive effect as it seemed to be able to weaken the bond between the German recent past and its future. In the medium term, however, this was a stumbling block in terms of the capacity to produce a more comprehensive and structured vision, also in tune with the reality of a reunified Germany. After 1990, Germany encompassed six new Eastern *Länder* which were miles away both from the old stereotype of Protestant militarist Prussia and also from the stereotype of the "better Germany" that left-wing Italian intellectuals had perpetuated for decades.

Which conclusions can be drawn at the end of this sub-chapter?

According to Eva Sabine Kuntz, the fall of the Berlin Wall and the re-unification process had contributed in a significant way to promote the emergence of

---

[116] See Alberto Cavallari, Chi ha paura del quarto Reich?, *La Stampa*, 1–2.7.1990.
[117] See Alberto Cavallari, Due capitali per la nuova Germania, *La Stampa*, 3.7.1990.

a *neues Bild* (a new image) of Germany. This, however, had not cancelled, but rather supplemented former images.[118] A key question immediately follows the abovementioned comments: whether the fall of the Wall belonged to that category of rare events which have the potential not only to affect the history of a nation, but also to cancel "vererbte Ängste" (inherited fears). In other words, did the fall of the Wall have the potential to modify the image of a nation or had it merely had a temporary positive effect?

Based on what has been so far discussed, it is undeniable that during the 1980s the category "past" applied to Germany had been weakened. Some of its most popular representations, for instance the image of the Nazi soldier as the embodiment of the average German, seemed to have disappeared by the end of 1990. Other representations, though still present, were constantly contested by new associations in which the weight of Europe had a paramount importance.

In conclusion, 1989 played a catalytic role in the process which had been developing since 1977. This meant calling into question a set of old stereotypes, the abandonment of some of them, but also the resurgence of a creeping Germanophobia, significantly less important and influential compared to previous decades, but still existent. From this point of view, 1989 means change. It was no end point, but rather the culmination of some dynamics and the starting point for a set of new dynamics which would develop during the following decade. Some among them will be the object of the conclusions of this research.

8.4 Drawing Preliminary Conclusions

> *Die Haltung [...] ist von zwei Elementen geprägt: Grundsätzlich dominiert eine aufgeschlossene und freundliche Einstellung gegenüber dem – langfristigen – Ziel der Wiederherstellung der deutschen Einheit. Andererseits besteht Übereinstimmung, dass dieser Prozess nicht autonom und daher potentiell unkontrollierbar ablaufen darf, sondern nur unter bestimmten Bedingungen [...].[119]*

The end of the year 1989 marked the conclusion of a period clouded with high uncertainty and doubts. The Italian strategy had finally taken shape. It was a

---

[118] See Eva Sabine Kuntz, Konstanz und Wandel von Stereotypen, pp. 368–369.

[119] "The attitude [...] is characterised by two different elements: in principle an open-minded and friendly attitude predominates regarding the long-term goal of re-establishment of the German unity. There is, nonetheless, a broad consensus in favour of a process which should not proceed unassisted, i.e. with potential uncontrollable developments, rather under certain conditions". See Italien und die deutsche Frage, Fernschreiben aus RomDiplo, Rome, 25.1.1990. PA AA B26, n. 173561.

three-pillar approach based on the following reasoning: by the end of the year it was undeniable that the re-unification process could neither be stopped nor be indefinitely delayed. Even the stance of the Soviet Union had gradually shifted from stiff opposition to greater flexibility.

It was therefore important to bind the re-unification process tightly to the European integration so that, in the future, Germany would no more represent a destabilizing factor for the balance of the Continent.[120] In the short run, the target was to have a voice in the decisions concerning re-unification which, according to Italy, would be taken by NATO.

> « L'OTAN est le lieu où doivent être discutés les aspects externes de la réunification allemande. Aucun pays, mêmes les quatre vainqueurs, ne peut intervenir sur les questions internes à la réunification, mais sur les conséquences extérieures [...] nous ne pouvons tolérer qu'il existe des raccourcies [...] ».[121]

Theoretically, the CSCE could actually also be a forum for the discussion of the conditions for re-unification; still, as the weeks passed, it became increasingly evident that its dimensions and its own nature did not make it exactly fit for the purpose.

Thus, a complex "diplomatic ballet" began between Rome, Bonn, Paris, Washington and Moscow.[122] Meanwhile, the German Foreign Minister was patiently spinning his web in order to both calm down worries and fears and to reconcile the German needs with those of the Superpowers, and more generally with those of the winning powers.[123]

On this canvas, the conference "Open Skies" was organised by mid-February in Ottawa. For the first time, representatives of both NATO and of the Warsaw

---

[120] See Antonio Varsori, Italy the East European Revolutions and the Reunification of Germany, in: Wolfgang Mueller/Michael Gehler/Arnold Suppan (eds.), The Revolutions of 1989. A Handbook, p. 409.

[121] "The NATO is the place where the external aspects of the German reunification have to be discussed. No country, even the four winning powers, may intervene on the internal questions of the reunification, but concerning its external consequences [...] we will not tolerate shortcuts [...]". See M. de Michelis et la situation en Europe, télégramme de l'ambassade de Rome, Rome, 21.3.1990. AMAE 1935inva, Direction Europe, Série Italie, carton 6377, sous-série 11, période 1986–1990. Foreign Minister de Michelis still used similar tones one month after the summit of Ottawa.

[122] Bonn attached a certain importance to the 13 February state visit of Andreotti in France. The Italian Prime Minister was alleged to have travelled to France in order to slow down the re-unification process and to link it to the speed of development of the European integration. See Fernschreiben aus RomDiplo, signed Ruth, Rome, 12.2.1990. See PA AA B26, n. 173561.

[123] See Gian Enrico Rusconi, Le perplessità italiane nel corso della riunificazione tedesca e i rapporti italo-tedeschi negli anni seguenti, in: Renato Cristin (ed.), Vie Parallele/Parallele Wege, Italien in Geschichte und Gegenwart Band 23, Frankfurt am Main 2005, p. 84.

Pact sat at the same table. On the fringe of this conference, the winning powers of the Second World War reached an agreement on the establishment of a 4+2, or, according to the German definition, a 2+4 mechanism. The mechanism would provide the conditions for the United States of America, the Soviet Union, France, the United Kingdom and the two German States to discuss the preliminary conditions to overcome the division of Germany. According to Gian Enrico Rusconi, all other states had little or no influence at all.[124] Based on records so far declassified, historians have generally agreed with this comment. Beside Washington and Moscow, Paris was the only actor which succeeded in curving itself a major, although not decisive, role in the negotiations. In comparison, it is more complicated to assess the performance of London. The uncompromising stance taken by its Prime Minister put Britain in an uneasy position to participate into negotiations.

However historically correct these statements may be, they require further comments as regards the process which, by the end of February 1990, led Italy into a dead end. Given the traditional French role as a point of reference for the Italian-German relationship, it will be useful for us to start with a few points concerning the ties between Rome and Paris at the beginning of 1990.

Straddling between the end of January 1990 and the beginning of the new month, two State visits were organized to France. On 29 January 1990, the Italian President of the Republic, Francesco Cossiga, travelled to Paris to meet with the French President, while two weeks later, on 13 February, it was Prime Minister Andreotti who had private exchanges of views with François Mitterrand.[125]

Francesco Cossiga was accompanied in his travel by a strong delegation which featured, among others, Foreign Minister Gianni de Michelis, Undersecretary for Foreign Affairs Claudio Vitalone, Secretary-General of the Foreign Office Bruno Bottai, the Italian Ambassador to Paris Giacomo Attolico, the Diplomatic Counselor of President Cossiga and the Head of his Press Service Ludovico Ortona. A private meeting between the two Presidents was planned for 06.00 p.m. It ended several hours later. Little has been written so far about it, as there are few records and no eyewitness accounts at all on its contents. Therefore, the comments of Ambassador Ortona, who collected the impressions of Francesco Cossiga soon after the end of the meeting, are highly relevant:

> «Il 29 e 30 gennaio abbiamo la visita in Francia nella quale Cossiga si incontra con Mitterrand e inizia a capire come in Europa si stava percependo il fenomeno tedesco, un fenomeno complesso e difficile che andava affrontato e risolto, mentre

---

[124] Ibid.

[125] Concerning these meetings, Italian records do not provide much information, whereas far more valuable is the contribution of the files of the ANF, even though for reasons of National security not all boxes are accessible.

questo in Italia non avveniva. Lì Cossiga ha la svolta, inizia a picconare, in Italia si continua a stare legati al passato, non ci si rende conto che il mondo sta cambiando, che tutto sta cambiando [...]. Nel mio diario riferisco dei briefing avvenuti [...] ma hanno parlato di un solo argomento, la Germania. Cossiga mi riferisce che Mitterrand è molto preoccupato, quasi ossessionato [...] Mitterrand dette una grande pompa a queste visite di stato proprio perché cercava di avvicinare noi a loro per affrontare il problema tedesco, che era la sua principale preoccupazione. Il rapporto Cossiga-Mitterrand è un rapporto di grande rispetto, ma non di amicizia, intanto perché Mitterrand non è il tipo amicone, mentre Cossiga è più caloroso, e soprattutto perché Cossiga non ha mai avuto una grande [...] sintonia con i francesi. La sintonia era con tedeschi e inglesi [...] però rispettava Mitterrand che l'aveva colpito moltissimo».[126]

After this visit, Cossiga did continue to follow his lonely path which gradually transformed his early support of the legitimacy of the re-unification target into an overall criticism of Italian political immobilism. Its slowness in understanding the scope of the German events, its huge difficulties in accepting and supporting the road to re-unification, and, finally, its choice to adopt a low profile, if not a passive attitude, were perceived by Cossiga as the tangible sign of the inability to renew the Italian political system. In a recently published work, it has been argued that this state visit to France marked the beginning of the "picconate al sistema" (pickaxes to the system). This expresses the harsh criticism uttered by Cossiga vis-à-vis the Italian political system.[127] In other words, through the meeting of Paris, the German events are alleged to have assumed paramount importance in the eyes of Francesco Cossiga, as the first step towards the demise of the existing international framework in its entirety, which risked to catch Italy fully unprepared and off guard.

---

[126] "On 29–30 January we have the visit in France where Cossiga met Mitterrand, and Cossiga began to understand how the German phenomenon was being perceived in Europe; it was a complex and difficult phenomenon that had to be handled and solved, something which did not happen in Italy. This marked a turning-point for Cossiga. After it, he began to "picconare" (pickaxe). Italy was still tied to the past, nobody was fully aware that the world was changing, that everything was changing [...]. In my diaries I refer to the briefings [...] but, actually, they talked only about one single issue: Germany. Cossiga told me that Mitterrand was very worried, almost obsessed [...] Mitterrand celebrated these visits with great pomp precisely because he wanted to bring us closer to them in order to handle the German problem, which was his main concern. Relations between Cossiga and Mitterrand were based upon mutual respect, but they were not very friendly. First of all, Mitterrand did not have a very friendly nature, whereas Cossiga was more affectionate. Besides, Cossiga was not really in tune [...] with the French. He was more in tune with the Germans and with the British [...] but he held Mitterrand in high esteem. Mitterrand had really impressed him". See the author's interview with Ambassador Ortona, 22.3.2016. Ambassador Ortona quoted both some paragraphs from his diaries concerning the impressions of Cossiga and, he later added his own personal comments.
[127] See Clio Pedone, Cossiga: L'uomo che guardò oltre il Muro, Soveria Mannelli 2013.

If we now leave aside the visit of Cossiga – whose peculiar link with Germany will be once again addressed in the next chapter[128] – to focus on the state visit of Giulio Andreotti, some further elements are to be discussed. While accepting the idea of the German re-unification, Andreotti warned once again, during his exchanges of views with the French leader, that the existing boundaries had to be respected and also that a cautious attitude was more than ever suitable.[129] Was it possible that Andreotti still mistrusted the very hypothesis of a re-unification in spite of the changes of the previous months?

The information provided by different diplomatic sources about the specific contents of the meeting diverge significantly. Whereas some documents merely stress the desire of the Italian Prime Minister to secure that France would give its full support to the acceleration of the European integration process[130], so that it could match the speed of the re-unification process, others suggest that Andreotti still feared a "wild re-unification". According to the latter, he had travelled to Paris to agree on a reasonable timetable for completing the re-unification process. He is also alleged to have proposed three different alternatives: either two years or eighteen months or, at least, a whole year, until spring 1991.[131] Meanwhile, Rome was also multiplying its contacts with Washington to get its support in order to secure a role for itself in the forthcoming negotiations.

While Prime Minister Andreotti still proposed to his partners timetables spread over time, and the Atlantic tropism of Foreign Minister de Michelis was increasingly evident, as his growing attention for – and emphasis on – the possibilities of using "his" Quadrangolare to steer the ongoing transformation process, Italy was unexpectedly hit by the tornado of the decisions taken during the conference "Open skies". It was an éclat, which arouse a great deal of interest both in the national press and in the media in general. The sentence which Hans-Dietrich-Genscher had addressed to his Italian colleague to close the proceedings, "You are not part of the game", was repeated over and over again as some sort of reminder of the demise of the Italian targets. The Italian strategy did indeed fall apart after the establishment of the 2+4 mechanism.

The next chapter will deal more accurately with the reasons of such demise through in-depth analysis of both the development of the conference of Ottawa

---

[128] See Note pour le président de la République : Visite d'état du président Cossiga, Paris, 29.1.1990. ANF, série 5 cellule diplomatique (herafter CD)/304, dossier 11.

[129] See Note pour le président de la République : Entretien avec Andreotti, Paris, 13.2.1990. ANF, série 5 AG 4, CD/304, dossier 12.

[130] See Note pour le président de la République : Votre entretien avec Andreotti, Paris, 12.2.1990, signed chargé de mission du président. ANF, série 5 EG/215, dossier 6. During an exchange of views between the diplomatic Counsellor of Andreotti, Vattani, and Elisabéth Guigou, this issue was carefully addressed.

[131] See Note pour le président de la République : Entretien avec Andreotti, Paris, 13.2.1990. ANF, série 5 AG 4, CD/304, dossier 12.

and of the meeting of Pisa, which both took place in February 1990. Its first part will offer a "bridge" to lead us from the second to the third and last phase of the Italian strategy, whereas the second part will mainly focus on the third phase of the Italian reaction to the "German events", in order to allow us to draw some necessary historical conclusions.

9. A Necessary Conclusion

> *An beide Kollegen sagte ich deshalb: „Gehören Sie zu den vier für Deutschland verantwortlichen Mächten? Sind Sie einer der beiden deutschen Staaten? Sie sind keines von beiden.“ Und [...] schloß ich meine ebenso drastische wie kurze Intervention mit den Worten: „You are not part of the game!“[1]* (Hans-Dietrich Genscher)

Hans-Dietrich Genscher used in his memoirs the abovementioned words to depict the key moment of the Summit of Ottawa. Throughout the summit, the features of a mechanism to guide the process of re-unification, namely the 2+4 mechanism, took their definite shape. Italy had been neither consulted nor invited to participate. To close the proceedings, Genscher addressed a reply to the Italian Foreign Minister and to his Dutch colleague which he himself, *a posteriori*, defined both brief and sharp.

Commenting on the opinions expressed by eyewitnesses, Gian Enrico Rusconi has remarked that the atmosphere in the conference room was extremely tense. The choices taken in Ottawa were, in fact, of crucial importance both for the Germans and for the allies of the Bundesrepublik.[2] Still, the episode has been usually depicted as if de Michelis and his advisors were some actors of a *commedia dell'arte*.[3] In other words, throughout the years, instead of analysing its motives, observers have either considered the verbal confrontation opposing Genscher to de Michelis of secondary importance in the process leading to the German re-unification, or have turned it into an object of ridicule.

---

[1] "I said, therefore, to both my colleagues: 'Are you one of the four powers responsible for Germany? Are you one of the German States? You are neither of them'. And [...] I put an end to my sharp and brief intervention with these words: 'You are not part of the game'". See Hans-Dietrich Genscher, Erinnerungen, Berlin 1995, p. 729.

[2] See Gian Enrico Rusconi, Germania Italia Europa: Dallo stato di potenza alla potenza civile, Torino, Einaudi 2003, pp. 285–288.

[3] "Die Atmosphäre im Konferenzraum war aufgeladen. Gianni de Michelis stand in seiner beträchtlichen Leibesfülle erregt gestikulierend an seinem Delegationsplatz. Hinter ihm wirbelten seine beflissenen Berater, alle von ungleich kleinerer Statur. Es war wie eine Szene aus der Commedia dell'Arte". (The atmosphere in the conference room was tense. Gianni de Michelis was there at his place and he made nervous gestures with his fat body. His efficient advisers whirled behind him, and they were all so small. It was like a Commedia dell'arte). Ibid., p. 286. Rusconi makes specific reference to the report of events provided by Richard Kiessler and Frank Elbe in: Ein Runder Tisch mit scharfen Ecken. Der Diplomatische Weg zur deutschen Einheit, Baden-Baden 1993, pp. 103–104.

Certainly, the considerations uttered by de Michelis were inappropriate and misplaced, but the reasoning in itself could be considered sensible.[4] Which elements composed this reasoning which Genscher himself considered understandable, given the circumstances, but out of place? Why had Genscher reacted with such a harsh tone?

9.1 The Italian Strategy crumbles away

Genscher's memoirs provide several further elements on the summit, and none of them can be considered ironic.

> „Die Open-Skies-Konferenz wurde zu dem nächsten entscheidenden Schritt auf dem Weg zur deutschen Einheit. […] Ich hatte mir fest vorgenommen, nicht aus Ottawa abzureisen, ohne eine abschießende Verständigung erreicht zu haben. […] Nach der Pressekonferenz ging ich zu dem Sitzungsraum, in dem die NATO-Kollegen tagten. Jim Baker kam aus dem Saal auf mich zu. ‚Da drin ist einiges los‘, sagte er. ‚Die Kollegen sind verärgert darüber, daß die Vereinbarung […] ohne Absprache mit ihnen getroffen worden sei. Sie verlangen eine Neueröffnung der Gespräche. Wir haben die Stellung gehalten; jetzt mußt du ran.‘ Ich war auf das höchste alarmiert. Mit welchem Ziel sollten die Verhandlungen neu eröffnet werden? Schewardnadse hatte nach meinem Gefühl das Äußerste zugestanden, später hörten wir […] er habe sogar mehr als das getan. An beide Kollegen gerichtet, sagte ich […] ‚You are not part of the game!‘ Es fiel mir nicht leicht, so zu reden, und doch gab es keine andere Wahl. […].“[5]

First and foremost, it was of the utmost importance to find, as quickly as possible, a mechanism which had to be broad enough to cope with the needs expressed by the Superpowers, and, more generally, by the winning powers of the Second World War, and yet small enough to allow for speedy and fruitful negotiations.[6] This was the challenge faced by Foreign Minister Genscher at the beginning of the Open Skies Conference in Ottawa.

---

[4] See the author's interview with Ambassador Nigido (2.3.2016): "La richiesta di de Michelis era tutto sommato ragionevole, ma, a mio giudizio, sbagliata".

[5] "The Open-Skies-Conference represented one of the next most important steps on the path to the German unity. […] I was determined not to leave Ottawa before reaching a final agreement on the establishment and the contents of the Two-Plus-Four mechanism. […] After the press conference I went to the meeting room, where the Nato-colleagues were speaking. Jim Baker left the room and came to me. He told me: 'Something is wrong in there. Our colleagues are angered that the decision has been reached [...] without their agreement. They insist on reopening negotiations. We held down the fort, now it's up to you.' I was extremely worried. For what purpose should we reopen negotiations? My feeling was that Shevardnadze had conceded the outmost, later we heard […] he had done more than that. I told both my colleagues […] 'You are not part of the game!' It was not easy for me to talk like this, but I had no other choice. […]". See Hans-Dietrich Genscher, Erinnerungen, Berlin 1995, pp. 724–729.

[6] In addition to the memoirs of Hans-Dietrich Genscher, see also James Baker, Drei Jahre, die die Welt veränderten: Erinnerungen, Berlin 1996.

In addition, Genscher had also to keep a close eye on the mounting difficulties in the DDR and on the changing moods in the Kremlin. The latter element was also linked to a growing feeling of insecurity concerning the resilience of the Soviet leader and consequently the range of political concessions which he would be ready to grant or would be in the position to grant. Throughout the conference, the Soviet Foreign Minister was continuously interrupting the debate. Genscher remembers in his memoirs of never having asked Shevardnadze whether his behaviour was motivated by the necessity to take instructions from Moscow. He also remembers having wondered to what extent the approach of his Soviet counterpart mirrored the position of the Kremlin.

After a long debate, right when a compromise had been hard-won, the Dutch Foreign Minister, Hans Van den Broek, expressed his total disagreement.

> « Au cours de la réunion à 16 de cet après-midi, M. Clark a présenté aux alliés le texte de la formule qui avait été agrée entre les six ministres pour traiter de la question de l'unification allemande. Sa lecture a déclenché une réaction de la part du ministre néerlandais des Affaires étrangères, qui a déclaré s'opposer à la formule du communiqué concernant les questions de sécurité des états voisins. […] Il s'interrogeait aussi sur le fondement juridique de cette démarche des Six ».[7]

It was not de Michelis the one who opened "hostilities"; still, he rapidly took the opportunity offered by his colleague to vehemently argue that the diverse aspects of the re-unification process affected all members of NATO. This was, therefore, the sole acceptable arena to discuss them.[8]

This paved the way for further criticism on the part of the Belgian representative, Marc Eyskens, the Luxembourg representative, Jacques Poos, and their Danish colleague, Uffe Ellemann-Jensen:

> « Les ministres belge, danois et luxembourgeois ont exprimé leur accord avec les interventions italienne et néerlandaise en soulignant notamment qu'il serait difficile d'expliquer un tel communiqué à leur Parlement et à leur opinion publique. Le Belge a ajouté qu'il souhaitait être en mesure de dire à l'opinion que l'Alliance

---

[7] "During the meeting of the sixteen (NATO members) of this afternoon, Minister Clark has presented to the allies the text of the agreement reached by the six Ministers that deals with the German unification. It has triggered in the Dutch Foreign Minister, who has declared his opposition to the point of the declaration concerning security of the neighbouring states […] He has also wondered about the legal basis of the decision taken by the Six". See Doc. 38, Unité allemande, réactions des Alliés au communiqué des Six, télégramme de François Bujon d'Estang ambassadeur de France à Ottawa à Roland Dumas ministre des affaires étrangères, Ottawa, 13.2.1990, in: Maurice Vaïsse/Christian Wenkel (eds.), La diplomatie française face à la réunification allemande.

[8] See Doc. 50, NATO-Ministerratstagung in Ottawa, 13.2.1990, in: Heike Amos/Tim Geiger/Horst Möller/Ilse Dorothee Pautsch/Gregor Schöllgen/Hermann Wentker/Andreas Wirsching (eds.), Die Einheit: Das Auswärtige Amt, das DDR-Außenministerium und der Zwei-plus-Vier Prozess.

Atlantique avait pris sa part dans les décisions concernant le processus de réunification ».[9]

It was the beginning of a heated argument in which the Dutch Minister did not hesitate to qualify the communiqué establishing the so called 2+4 mechanism as a "patronizing statement".[10] In the middle of this argument, Foreign Minister Genscher returned into the conference room – as both his memoirs and the diplomatic records confirm – and he was swiftly updated by the Bundesrepublik representative to NATO, Graf zu Rantzau, on the latest developments. To call into question the result so hardly won appeared both unacceptable and dangerous for Bonn.[11] Besides, several participants, including the French Foreign Minister, Roland Dumas, had already left. The Italian and Dutch grievances had been, therefore, raised in the worst possible moment. Despite having sympathy or at least understanding some of the complaints raised, the German Foreign Minister saw no other way out of that impasse than to rapidly close the proceedings, even though this required such harshness of tones which was in sharp contrast with his usual proclivity to discuss and compromise whenever possible.

In the following weeks Bonn and Rome had two relevant occasions for clarification. The first occasion was provided by the Congress of the European Heads of State and Government belonging to the Christian-Democratic family[12], which took place in Pisa on Saturday 17 February 1990, whereas the second one was represented by the official state visit of Genscher to Rome on 21 February.

In Pisa, three main items were on the agenda.[13] The first one concerned the reforms and further development of the European People's Party[14], the second

---

[9] "The Belgian, Danish and Luxembourg Ministers have expressed their agreement as regards the Italian and Dutch interventions. They have also stressed how difficult it would be to explain such a communiqué to Parliament and public opinion. The Belgian Minister has added that he hoped he could say to the public opinion that the Atlantic Alliance had assumed its share in the decisions concerning the reunification process". See Maurice Vaïsse/Christian Wenkel (eds.), La diplomatie française face à la réunification allemande, pp. 218–221, 219.

[10] See Heike Amos/Tim Geiger/Horst Möller/Ilse Dorothee Pautsch/Gregor Schöllgen/Hermann Wentker/Andreas Wirsching (eds.), Die Einheit. Das Auswärtige Amt, das DDR-Außenministerium und der Zwei-plus-Vier-Prozess, p. 261.

[11] See Hans-Dietrich Genscher, Erinnerungen, pp. 724–729, in particular, p. 729.

[12] Among the participants: German Chancellor Helmut Kohl, and the Prime Ministers of Italy, Giulio Andreotti, of the Netherlands, Ruud Lubbers, of Belgium, Wilfried Martens, of Luxembourg, Jacques Santer, of Irland, Garret Fitzgerald, and of Greece, Konstantinos Mitsotakis.

[13] In addition to these three key points, legal and political issues related to the establishment of a European Monetary Union, of a more active environmental policy also involving Eastern European states, and of European social policies, were also discussed. Finally, the issues of the powers of the European Parliament and the difficulties in persuading member states to give up further slices of their sovereignty were also addressed.

[14] Hereafter also EPP.

one related to the challenge issued by the changes in Central-Eastern Europe, whereas the third and last item dealt with the potential effects of the ongoing transformations on the European integration and its priorities for the years to come.[15] Still, after a brief discussion concerning the first item on the agenda, the meeting mainly focused on the fall of the Berlin Wall and its effects.[16] The core of the meeting corresponded to the confrontation between Helmut Kohl and Giulio Andreotti, who after the summit of Strasbourg had practically kept silent on the German issue.[17]

> „[...] Der italienische Ministerpräsident Giulio Andreotti demonstrierte zur Ent-täuschung Kohls alles andere als christdemokratische Solidarität. Er sprach sich für zwei deutsche Staaten in Europa, also gegen deren Einigung, aus. Auf der Konferenz der Europäischen Volkspartei (EVP) in Pisa am 17. Februar 1990 konnte Kohl Fehldeutungen seiner Politik richtigstellen, Missverständnisse auf der Seite seiner Parteifreunde aus den letzten Wochen klären und dabei auch Andreotti in die Schranken verweisen [...] Kohl ergriff [...] auch in Pisa als erster das Wort und gab die Richtung klar vor [...], dass mit der Frage der Einheit Deutschlands für die europäische Einigung keine Gefahren, aber viele Chancen verbunden seien. [...] Kohl versicherte, dass die Einheit nur gelingen könne, wenn sie in den politisch-institutionellen Rahmen des atlantischen Bündnisses und der Europäischen Gemeinschaft eingebettet bleibe [...]."[18]

During the press conference which followed the meeting[19], the correspondent of the German newspaper *Frankfurter Allgemeine Zeitung*, Heinz Joachim Fischer, asked the Italian President of the Council of Ministries whether he still believed that the existence of two German states was a guarantee for stability in Europe.

---

[15] See, in particular, Aide memoire für die EVP-Konferenz der Regierungs- und Parteichefs, Pisa, 17.2.1990. ACDP, Archiv der EVP, Signatur 09-007, Karton 043/2.

[16] See, in particular, Thomas Jansen, Die Entstehung einer europäischen Partei: Vorgeschichte, Gründung und Entwicklung, Bonn, 1996, pp. 136–137.

[17] See Andreotti, l'Allemagne et l'Europe, télégramme de l'ambassade de Rome n. 167, Rome, 19.2.1990. AMAE, Direction Europe, Série Italie, carton 6377, sous-série 11 dossier 3/2, période 1986–1990.

[18] "[...] At Kohl's disappointment, the Italian Prime-Minister Giulio Andreotti showed no Christian-Democratic solidarity at all. He spoke in favour of two German states, namely against their unity. At the conference of the European People's Party (EPP) in Pisa on 17 February 1990 Kohl set the record straight, he cleared up misunderstandings which during the previous weeks had being spreading among his party colleagues, and in so doing he also put Andreotti in his place. [...] Kohl was the first to speak [...] also in Pisa, and he showed clearly the direction to be taken [...], the issue of the German unity was not a threat to the European unity, rather a chance. [...] Kohl guaranteed that the unity could only be possible if it was embedded in the broader framework of the Atlantic Alliance and of the European Community. [...]". See Michael Gehler, Deutschland. Von der Teilung zur Einigung 1945 bis heute, pp. 340–341.

[19] Even before the press conference, Forlani had unequivocally expressed his view in favour of the German reunion.

In response, not only did Andreotti plainly affirm that he had no reason to doubt of the guarantees provided by his German counterpart, but he also remarked that the international context had changed and that therefore what was necessary in the past could not have the same meaning in the present, i.e. he openly and for the first time declared being in favour of a German re-unification. The German press stressed the following elements of his comments:

> „Niemand hat jemals daran gezweifelt, dass der Wunsch der Deutschen nach Einheit sich verwirklichen würde. Was bis vor einiger Zeit Schwierigkeiten verursachte, war der internationale politische Rahmen. Persönlich bin ich dafür all das zu intensivieren, was bisher Deutschland und die anderen europäischen Länder gemeinsam an gutem [sic!] gemacht haben.“[20]

According to the analysis provided by the German Embassy in Rome, the declarations of Andreotti were the sign that he was finally ready to give up a sceptical, if not openly critical, attitude, which he had maintained towards the German problem ever since 1984.

> „MP Andreotti gibt öffentlich seine bisherige Zurückhaltung auf und unterstützt im Lichte der Darlegungen des Bundeskanzlers eindeutig die Politik der Bundesrepublik zur Herstellung der deutschen Einheit. MP Andreotti reflektiere damit die starke Unterstützung, die die Wiedervereinigung Deutschlands in der italienischen Öffentlichkeit genießt. Die Klarstellung hat große Bedeutung und ist wichtig für die in dieser Woche bevorstehenden Gespräche zwischen Andreotti und MP Thatcher in London. Als Ergebnis des Treffens von Pisa […] ist davon auszugehen, dass die von den Äußerungen vom September 1984 potentiellen Irritationen als überwunden betrachten werden können.“[21]

Foreign observers, both in France and in Germany, paid particular attention to the comments of Andreotti at the press conference, especially to those concerning the newly established 2+4 mechanism. While German records merely stressed that

---

[20] "Nobody has ever doubted that the wish of the Germans for unity would be fulfilled. It was the international framework that until very recently caused difficulties. Personally, I support a strengthening of all that Germany and other European countries have achieved so far". See Haltung MP Andreotti nach dem Gipfeltreffen der EVP-Politiker in Pisa, Fernschreiben aus RomDiplo, Rom, 19.2.1990, signed Ambassador Ruth. PA AA B26, n. 173561.

[21] "Prime Minister Andreotti has relinquished his previous reluctant approach and now he supports the policy for unity of the Federal Republic. In doing so, Andreotti mirrors the strong support that the German reunification enjoys from the Italian public opinion. This clarification is of great significance and it is important for the imminent talks between Andreotti and Prime Minister Thatcher. We can assume that […] the irritation provoked by the sentences of September 1984 has been overcome as an outcome of the meeting of Pisa". Ibid.

the Italian Prime Minister had not opposed it[22], the French diplomatic documents also remarked that with his unexpected declarations, Andreotti had wrong-footed his Foreign Minister. He had not in fact opposed the legitimacy of the 2+4 framework, but he had rather accepted it, even though in doing so he had tried to confine its duties to Berlin and to all those questions strictly related to the responsibilities of the winning powers.[23]

This choice must be read and understood in light of other references made by the Italian politician during the press conference, especially concerning the European integration process and its achievements. The meeting of Pisa had, in fact, confirmed the reliability of Kohl as a fully committed partner on the path of the European integration. It cannot be ruled out the possibility that Andreotti's change of attitude vis-à-vis the re-unification target was the result of the desire to strengthen the German commitment to Europe. On grounds of this objective it appeared for Andreotti increasingly counterproductive to further persevere in an attitude of "loud" opposition, of whose poor results the approach of de Michelis in Ottawa was an excellent instance.

Soon after the summit of Pisa, Andreotti himself affirmed in a letter addressed to Cossiga that before the Pisa meeting a re-unification would have been an "avventura sconvolgente" (appalling adventure).[24] The guarantees offered by the Chancellor that the ruling given by the German Constitutional Law in 1973 would have no consequences, meaning that his country would not put forward territorial claims, had persuaded Andreotti to temper his worries. The summit had also showed beyond any possible doubt that the process towards re-unification was of an irreversible nature. In Ottawa, the Soviet Union itself, regardless of the many caveats still harboured, had accepted its inevitability.

If we combine these elements with the issues discussed in the 23 February Downing Street private talk between the British Prime Minister and her Italian counterpart, the picture becomes even clearer.

In referring to the meeting of Pisa, Andreotti firstly shared with Margaret Thatcher his fears concerning the speed with which Kohl was pursuing the realisation of his targets. For Italy, it was no more a question of potential territorial claims. The summit of Pisa had, in fact, persuaded Andreotti that the Bundesrepublik did not harbour such aspirations.[25] Still, he agreed with the British

---

[22] See Ibid.

[23] See Andreotti, l'Allemagne et l'Europe, télégramme de l'ambassade de Rome n. 167, Rome, 19.2.1990. AMAE, Direction Europe, Série Italie, carton 6377, sous-série 11 dossier 3/2, période 1986–1990.

[24] See Andreotti a Cossiga, Roma, 19.2.1990. ILS, AGA, section Germany, b.458. The document is quoted in Antonio Varsori, Italy the East European Revolutions and the Reunification of Germany, p. 409.

[25] See Colloqui tra il presidente del Consiglio e la signora Thatcher, riservato, 23 February 1990.

politician regarding the risk that the pace at which the negotiations were advancing could introduce the ferment of new nationalistic trends.

Secondly, he also affirmed of being worried about the potential side-effects on the NATO consistency of the decisions taken in Ottawa: that the 2+4 mechanism could be perceived as some sort of directorate of large countries. This being the case, and in the absence of a new strategic concept in line with the current changes, NATO could run the risk of entering into an irreversible crisis. This was the main reason why he firmly insisted on clearly confining the 2+4 mechanism to the problem of Berlin and to the responsibilities of the winning powers, whereas more general external aspects of the re-unification were considered suitable to be discussed in a broader forum. Besides, the mechanism had to be presented as nothing else that the ultimate instance of the decisions still to be taken as a result of the Second World War, and not as the gateway to future developments. The items discussed in London were, therefore, not purely and simply prestige issues, but rather real security concerns.

The views of the Italian and of the British Heads of Government seriously diverged on the potential consequences for the European integration process.[26] The British Prime Minister believed that the EC would be negatively affected by the ongoing transformations, and she also feared that more integration would but provide Germany with a framework to exercise its influence in Europe, whereas her Italian colleague was in favour of more integration and supported the process of establishment of an Economic and Monetary Union.

In conclusion, the summit of Pisa had been the scene of a relevant improvement, but not of a comprehensive clarification, and nor would such be the official visit of the German Foreign Minister to Rome during the following week. In other words, the worries of Andreotti had been significantly tempered, but not fully deleted.

Barely one week after the Conference Open-Skies and the summit of Pisa, on 21 February 1990, Genscher travelled to Rome for urgent exchanges of views with Giulio Andreotti and Gianni de Michelis.[27] The allies of Italy, starting from the Bundesrepublik, were in fact worried about Italy's reactions in Ottawa. Through this visit to Rome, the German Foreign Minister wanted to show that he was willing to mend fences, even though it was difficult for him, as he later revealed, to fully comprehend the motives behind the intense reaction of his Italian counterpart.

---

[26] See Visite de M. Andreotti à Londres, télégramme de l'ambassade de Rome n. 201, Rome, 23.2.1990. AMAE, Direction Europe, Série Grande Bretagne, carton 6283, sous-série 11 dossier 6, période 1986–1990.

[27] See Doc. 128 Bericht. Besuch Genschers in Rom 21.2.1990, in Michael Gehler/Maximilian Graf, Österreich und die deutsche Frage 1987–1990, pp. 529–530.

„Am 21. Februar flog ich nach Rom um mich mit Ministerpräsident Andreotti und Außenminister de Michelis zu treffen. Bei den Italienern, zu denen ich stets ein besonders gutes Verhältnis unterhielt, sollte nach den Ereignissen in Ottawa keine Mißstimmung aufkommen, schon gar nicht bei Andreotti, mit dem ich lange und eng zusammengearbeitet hatte. Er war für mich ein Beispiel eines Politikers, der sich mit großem Engagement für die europäische Einigung einsetzte. […] er hatte mich auch häufig unterstützt […]. […] Ohne Zweifel ist Andreotti ein ebenso erfahrener wie geschickter Politiker; stets habe ich mit ihm die Erfahrung verläßlicher Zusammenarbeit gemacht, die mich ihm damals wie heute vertrauen läßt. […] Zu Gianni de Michelis war über die Jahre ebenfalls ein gutes Verhältnis entstanden. Bis heute bin ich mir nicht im Klaren darüber, warum er in Ottawa so heftig reagierte."[28]

These motives notwithstanding, misunderstandings with Italy had to be avoided especially in light of its prominent role in the European integration process and of the approaching of its six-month rotating presidency of the EC. Even though throughout the previous year Genscher had developed an overall good working relationship with Gianni de Michelis, the Italian politician on whom he mainly relied as the most dependable partner to steer Italy out of the storm caused by the decisions taken in Ottawa was Giulio Andreotti.

Besides, not only was the meeting a convenient opportunity to mend fences, but it was also a propitious time to table and discuss issues concerning the latest developments in Moscow.[29] Based on information collected during the meetings of the previous weeks – both with Schewardnadze and with Gorbačëv – Genscher

---

[28] "On 21 February I flied to Rome to meet Prime Minister Andreotti and Foreign Minister de Michelis. I had always had very good relations with Rome. After the outcomes of Ottawa, we had to avoid frictions with our Italian partners, above all with Andreotti, with whom I had been working on very good terms for a long time. For me he was the model of a politician who devoted great efforts to European unification. […] He had often supported me […]. […] Andreotti is unquestionably an experienced and skilful politician; I have always worked with him on term of a reliable cooperation. I, therefore, have trusted and still trust him. […] Over the years, I have also developed a good relation with Gianni de Michelis. Even today, I still don't fully understand why he reacted so violently". See, in particular, Werner Schwan/Heribert Filmer, Hans-Dietrich Genscher, Düsseldorf 1988, pp. 736–737. See also Ibid., pp. 425–427. The "Unterstützung" (support) provided by Giulio Andreotti had been highly appreciated by Hans-Dietrich Genscher in light of a creeping feeling of mistrust among European, and above all, American politicians. Many among them had qualified Genscher's political course towards Eastern Europe and Moscow in negative terms as "Genscherism". See, in particular, Lettera dell'ambasciatore d'Italia a Washington al ministro degli affari Esteri, Giulio Andreotti, riservato (restricted), 16.8.1988. ILS, AGA, section Europe, b.408. The above-mentioned document refers to a private conversation between the Italian Ambassador to Washington and the President of the US Congress Foreign Committee, Dante Fascell. In the conversation the American politician addressed the many worries which Genscher's policy arouse in the US government by using the abovementioned expression "Genscherism".
[29] See Lettera del consigliere diplomatico del presidente del Consiglio dei Ministri all'ambasciatore Bruno Bottai, Rome, 24.2.1990. ILS, AGA, section Europe, b. 382.

was under the impression that Moscow had no specific and effective guidelines on how to approach the ongoing transformations in Europe.

This can be subjected to different interpretations. On the one hand, this could be considered a clue to the new flexible course embraced by the Kremlin, which, unlike what happened in the past, was no more based on dogmatic assumptions. On the other hand, this lead to uncertainty as to the ways and the time which the Kremlin would consider suitable for the implementation of the re-unification target.[30]

The records do not go any further; still, it is reasonable to assume that Foreign Minister Genscher was fully aware of the extent to which Rome was influenced in its approach by elements not merely related to a *Deutschlandfrage*, but rather connected with a wider picture, which included both the tribulations within the Soviet Union and the increasingly precarious situation of the project for a European Common House. It is, therefore, equally reasonable to assume that Genscher was trying to convey a message to his Italian interlocutors concerning the situation in Moscow and its fast political decaying.[31]

This being the case, the answer given by Andreotti was probably not the one expected by the German Foreign Minister. Although Andreotti affirmed that he did understand and share Genscher's worries, he also pointed out that it was necessary to avoid putting too much pressure on Moscow in pursuing the target of the German re-unification. The new Soviet flexibility could have been, in fact, easily mistaken in Eastern Europe for a sign of weakness, which could result in Eastern European countries taking a misstep. In addition, Andreotti also believed that the decline of both the Warsaw Pact and the COMECON could encourage the Kremlin to look towards Western Europe and the CSCE to find a solution to its stability problems. Even when faced with information provided by Genscher on the Soviet demise, the Italian Prime Minister remained confident in February 1990 that his political bet of the previous year had been the right course to take.[32]

In dealing with the origins of the 2+4 mechanism, Genscher paid particular attention in presenting to his interlocutors all the urgent internal difficulties, above all the social and economic demise of the DDR, which in Ottawa had made it unavoidable to opt for the only way which could allow a speedy path towards re-unification. The social and economic demise of the DDR required in fact to shorten the time of negotiations. Genscher brought to the attention of the Italian politicians that the German Central Bank had no appropriate statistic data to make

---

[30] During his meetings with Italian prominent politicians, Genscher was always extremely careful to avoid the term "reunification". He rather used the expression "unification".
[31] German historian Andreas Rödder used the expression "surrealistischer Wust von Ideen" (a surreal jumble of ideas).
[32] See ch.7.3.

a precise assessment of both the amount of cash issued and the volume of deposits in the DDR.[33] Economic decline, a creeping feeling of monetary uncertainty, both being combined with rising unemployment, especially in East Berlin, resulted in the impoverishment of the Eastern German regions and in very large migration flows, while social discontent in both German states surged. The German Foreign Minister was very attentive in pointing to his personal contribution in defining the mechanism established in Ottawa, meaning the contribution of a German politician who had always been very keen on the Italian-German relationship.

Hans-Dietrich Genscher also drew discreetly the attention of his interlocutors on one further issue. Throughout the years, the Allies had always reaffirmed their prerogatives and responsibilities towards Germany. The Conference of Ottawa had been, however, the first occasion in which Germany itself had been involved in defining its own future. The Bundesrepublik politician also remembered having warned the Foreign Ministers of the winning powers – James Baker, Roland Dumas, Douglas Hurd and Eduard Shevardnadze – against repeating the errors of the past, as Germany would not accept to be relegated once again to a *Katzentisch*. Germany relied on Italy's understanding that the 2+4 mechanism was the only formula able to be accepted by both the Allies and the two German states. This did not mean though that Bonn intended to neglect the importance of NATO. Finally, Foreign Minister Genscher deemed it necessary to also explain that Bonn did not harbour the ambition to expand eastwards the frontiers of NATO. As far as the DDR was concerned, a special regulation could be agreed on. Was this information enough to reassure the Italian government?

It was enough to temper some worries, but not sufficient to solve the tangle of problems concerning the external aspects of re-unification. An overall understanding had been reached concerning the European integration process, whereas many unresolved issues still lingered on the Atlantic Alliance. Whenever Italy proposed to engage in a redefinition of the NATO strategic concept, once it had accepted the 2+4 negotiations, Genscher answered prudently and in vague terms that such a proposition went far beyond the limits of the German issue.

Washington and Paris were not less worried than Bonn about the Italian reaction in Ottawa.[34] At the beginning of March, Andreotti travelled to the USA for a ten-day official visit:

---

[33] See Lettera del consigliere diplomatico del presidente del Consiglio dei Ministri all'ambasciatore Bruno Bottai, Rome, 24.2.1990. ILS, AGA, section Europe, b. 382.
[34] See, in particular, White House Background briefing: The Visit of Prime Minister Andreotti, Washington, 5.3.1990. ILS, AGA, section USA, b.637. See also Baker to De Michelis, 20 February 1990; De Michelis to Baker, 25 February 1990 and the secret note of the Italian Foreign Ministry

"[…] There were a number of meetings between Italian diplomats and US representatives, whereby the latter appeared eager to reassure the Italian government
concerning Italy's role in the new balance emerging in Europe, especially through
Rome's role in the Atlantic Alliance".[35]

Concerned about the impact which the decisions of Ottawa could have in Rome,
Washington seemed eager to find some fora where Italy could be, at least partially, involved in the decisions to be taken.

"The Italian Prime Minister is a frequent visitor in this city. And […] it is not
related to a particular problem or set of problems, but just rather to the general
desire to keep in touch, to have a close exchange of views, which is something
particularly important in these times when events are moving very fast in Europe.
[…] Italy is a very key player in European events. We have made clear that while
we think the two-plus-four mechanism is a very important mechanism, it is only a
first step in this large process of German unification […]. We have never regarded
the two-plus-four mechanism, useful as it is, as something that runs contrary to
consultations in the Alliance, or in any way precludes them. As to the modalities
of such consultations, these are under discussion now […]. To give a sense of what
sorts of consultations are going on […] Foreign Minister Genscher has been in
Italy and in The Hague recently […]".[36]

A comparison between Italian and non-Italian diplomatic records provides an
overall impression of the extent to which the Italian stance appeared both complex and ambiguous in the eyes of foreign observers. In Paris for instance, the
Italian stance seemed to dangerously dither between a sheer defence of its
wounded pride and related prestige issues on the one side, and a more substantial
desire to be involved in defining the new European order on the other.

« Aux Etats-Unis […] le premier Ministre a redit sur ce sujet, de manière nette, la
position de l'Italie : "Les deux Allemagnes ne doivent pas avoir le dernier mot sur
leur réunification et sur les frontières de la nation allemande unie" et la discussion
sur les problèmes posés par la réunification "doit être la plus large et la plus internationale possible". Ce qui dans l'esprit italien signifie […] l'OTAN pour sa part
devant également être consulté sur les conséquences à tirer de la réunification pour
le système de sécurité occidentale. Ainsi que l'exposait à mon collaborateur le
responsable OTAN de la Farnesina, l'enceinte "2+4" ne pose pas seulement pour
l'Italie une question de prestige qui pourrait se régler par un élargissement à "2+5

---

of the meetings that took place on 3 March. ILS, AGA, section Germany, b.458. All are quoted in
Antonio Varsori, Italy the East European Revolutions and the German Reunification, p. 409.
[35] Ibid., p. 409.
[36] See White House Background briefing: The Visit of Prime Minister Andreotti, Washington,
5.3.1990. ILS, AGA, section USA, b.637.

ou 6", mais aussi un problème de principe : l'unification aura des conséquences sur le système de sécurité de l'Europe et l'OTAN [...] doit avoir son mot à dire ».[37]

The ambition to be invited to participate in the most relevant negotiations – regardless of the nature and the specific implications of the issues discussed – as a mark of acceptance in the club of the big powers, was usually considered a distinctive feature of the Italian post-war politics. According to Paris, the inherent ambiguity of such a policy course had emerged both in Ottawa and in Pisa.

> « Tirant les leçons de l'histoire qui se fait sous nos yeux, il reconnaît l'évidence, admet qu'il s'agit d'une question qui 'concerne principalement les allemands eux-mêmes'. Quant à lui, quelle qu'ait été sa préférence, il sait s'adapter aux circonstances car la politique de l'Italie dès l'Unité a toujours été marquée par le transformisme ».[38]

Theoretically, a solution to the Italian feeling of wounded pride could have been easily found in transforming the 2+4 mechanism into a 2+5 or 2+6 framework for negotiations. Still, it was difficult to anticipate the extent of requests and consequences to which such a choice would pave the way. Other regional powers could require equal treatment, hence harming the efficiency and effectiveness of the framework established. This is why Bonn decisively rejected such an option. What both France and the United States had in mind was a partial involvement on specific issues pursuant an arrangement to be made with all those involved.

By insisting on an enlargement of the mechanism established in Ottawa, Rome would have automatically discredited its requests and lowered them to the level of mere prestige issues. Pushing for the re-unification issue to be discussed within NATO could, on the contrary, be perceived as the sign of more mature worries; still, such a request also encountered remarkable hurdles. None of the

---

[37] "In the United States [...] the president of the Council of Ministries has said it once again that the Italian position is plainly that the two German states should not be allowed to have the last word on their reunification and on the frontiers of a united Germany. The debate on the problems related to a reunification must be as large and international as possible, which in the Italian reasoning means that [...] NATO must be involved concerning the effects on the Western security framework. As the Italian representative in NATO has explained to my aide, the 2+4 club does not merely raise prestige issues for Italy – which could be solved by its extension to 5 or 6, but also a problem of principle: the re-unification will affect the Western security system and NATO [...] must have a say in it". See Visite de M. Andreotti aux Etats-Unis, télégramme de l'ambassade de Rome, Rome, 6.3.1990, signed Perol. AMAE 1935inva, Direction Europe, Série Italie, carton 6377, sous-série 11, dossier 1, période 1986–1990.

[38] "Learning from the history taking shape under our eyes, he (Andreotti) acknowledges the evidence. He concedes that this issue primarily regards the Germans. For his part, whatever his preference might have been, he knows how to adapt to changing circumstances, as transformism has always been a distinctive feature of Italian politics since National Unity". See Andreotti, l'Allemagne et l'Europe, télégramme de l'ambassade de Rome n. 167, Rome, 19.2.1990. AMAE, Direction Europe, Série Italie, carton 6377, sous-série 11 dossier 3/2, période 1986–1990.

traditional Italian interlocutors was eager to support this request. For Moscow, NATO could not be considered an acceptable arena for discussion, while the CSCE was for both the Kremlin and the Western winning powers, namely Washington, Paris and London, a too plethoric forum to be efficient. Bonn was even more worried about reopening the debate, thus running the risk of either being once again relegated to a "Katzentisch" or to have to negotiate with a further weakened Gorbačëv.

In conclusion, Italian worries cannot be merely explained as an instance of the national wounded pride in not being invited to participate in the 2+4 negotiations. Rather, Rome was attracted by the project of a new Helsinki: a security framework which could also involve the Soviet Union. Still, such a project had to face increasing hurdles, the most important among them was the unsteady context in which the government led by Gorbačëv and the political forces supporting reforms were acting.

The Italian strategy smashed against this unsolved and apparently unsolvable conundrum. The exclusion of Italy from the 2+4 mechanism was not the reason why its strategy fell apart, but rather the occasion for its fragile and ambiguous roots to be unveiled. Italy had remained trapped in the net of its own contradictions.

9.2 New Points of Reference for the *deutsche Frage*

A thorough study of the declassified files has led to the conclusion that the Italian strategy shattered into pieces at the beginning of spring 1990. It is, however, more difficult to comprehend the reasons why this happened.

In order to make some hypotheses on this issue, information collected so far on the Italian vision of the "deutsche Frage" will be valuable, but not sufficient. It will be in fact necessary to also find a frame of reference. Comparing different actors on the international stage is always a rather risky *modus operandi* in any historical work. This is not just about carefully selecting the items to be compared and the chronological time-frame of the comparison, it is also about being attentive on how we investigate and on the kind of conclusions which we draw from the established comparison. Still, having a frame of reference is indispensible to try and make some final hypothesis on the third and last phase of the Italian strategy. This frame of comparison can be none other than Paris.

After the Second World War France had always been a fundamental point of reference for the Italian-German relationship. In addition, France and Italy, despite their differences in domestic policy as well as in Foreign policy, were both founding members of the EC, and the two Western States had developed deeper and more articulated relations with Bonn.

The first question to be answered before making hypotheses relates as to whether the different "weight" of Rome and Paris in the "operational phase" of re-unification, from February up to October 1990, can be solely explained through their different international status.

If Italy intimately harboured the ambition to play a role as significant as that of the Superpowers or of the winning states of the Second World War, it was only logical that its hopes were disappointed. Although Italy was not, as it has already been often remarked, a negligible actor on the international stage, it was pointless – and probably also far beyond its resources – to hope to have a part to play as significant as that of Paris. It does not follow though that Italy could not have played a much more active role. But on which tools could Rome rely on for this purpose?

Firstly, Italy could have tried and curve out its own spot through strong bilateral contacts with Bonn, provided that the legitimacy of the re-unification target was soon and unambiguously accepted. The legitimacy of this target was, however, accepted late and with ambiguity. In addition, further difficulties were related to the phase of development attained by the Italian-German bilateral framework. The bilateral dialogue structures, such as the *deutsch-italienisches Gesprächsforum*, by the end of the 1980s were still in an embryonic phase, quite fragile compared to the Franco-German machinery. The 1980s had given a strong boost to such dialogue structures, but there had not been sufficient time for the necessary running-in period.

According to the three-pillar framework of interpretation proposed in chapter three, Italy could have relied on two further alternatives to play a more active role, either the economic/cultural pillar or the party pillar. However, neither of them in 1990 could offer all the instruments needed to rise to the challenge. Even though in certain respects economic and cultural exchanges between Italy and Germany were more relevant than the exchanges with France, they were an added value rather than a substitute for the lack of adequate political contacts.

As for the party pillar, though it was a sine qua non condition for cooperation in the 1950s, its significance had been gradually decreasing during the following decades and especially in the 1980s both a result of the DC internal decay and of the transformations of the CDU under the guidance of Helmut Kohl. The DC politicians were still the main interlocutors of Bonn, but in many respects the two parties had driven apart. All that was left was the "Männerfreundschaft", the personal relations among political leaders.

While we should eschew from explaining historical events solely with biographical and behavioural criteria, it is though necessary to also consider this aspect when dealing with the re-unification process. Given both the high speed of developments in 1990 and the personal approach to politics of Helmut Kohl, the significance of the so-called "human factors" had increased exponentially.

„[…] im Kanzleramt regierte Kohl auf einer ganz persönlichen Weise: nicht aus der spezifischen Rationalität des bürokratischen Apparats heraus […] sondern spontan, situationsbezogen und ungezwungen und vor allem mit dem Mittel des direkten persönlichen Gesprächs und des persönlichen Vertrauensverhältnisses, auch und gerade auf internationaler Ebene […].“[39]

The relationship forged between Helmut Kohl and François Mitterrand provides ample evidence of this. Jacques Attali has, for instance, stressed the many fears and worries harboured by Mitterrand vis-à-vis a re-unification. By contrast, based on new primary sources, Tilo Schabert has showed the other side of the coin, meaning the *confiance mutuelle élémentaire* (fundamental mutual trust) between Kohl and Mitterrand as the driving force behind the Franco-German relationship. Fears and worries notwithstanding, according to Tilo Schabert "François Mitterrand a fait reposer toute sa politique à propos de l'unification allemande sur sa confiance dans l'homme Helmut Kohl" (François Mitterrand based its entire policy towards the German unification on his trust in Helmut Kohl as a man).[40] In the heart of François Mitterrand two rather different souls coexisted, of which the first represented his love for France, for its past and its prestige as a great Nation, whereas the second soul was the reflection of his admiration for the revolutionary potential of the 1989 events and of an irresistible drive to support the right to self-determination of all people, Germans included.[41]

It was precisely this second soul which Giulio Andreotti did not possess. Not unlike Andreotti, Mitterrand as well had at first expressed negative comments and from time to time even harsh criticism against the first moves of Kohl. Still, through the 6 January 1990 meeting in Latche, Kohl and Mitterrand had left behind previous misunderstandings and they had reached a lasting agreement.[42] Kohl and Andreotti also shared good relations, but they had never attained the same level of friendship and mutual trust as between Kohl and Mitterrand. Andreotti and Mitterrand had often shared the same worries, but there was no Latche between the Italian Prime Minister and his German counterpart. The meeting of Pisa came in fact too late, and besides, it was only a partial clarification.

The human pillar alone cannot account for the weaknesses of the Italian stance, but it can help in understanding some of its reasons. Surely, a different

---

[39] "[…] in the Chancellery Kohl ruled in a very personal way: not according the inner logic of the bureaucratic apparatus […] he was rather impulsive, he acted according to the situation and informally. Besides, he often used the personal contacts and relationships of mutual trust, also and especially on the international arena". See Andreas Rödder, Deutschland einig Vaterland, pp. 130–131.
[40] Tilo Schabert, Mitterrand et la réunification allemande: Une histoire secrète (1981–1995), Paris 2005, pp. 507–508.
[41] Ibid., p. 438. Very similar comments have been also expressed in Andreas Rödder, Deutschland einig Vaterland, pp. 161–162.
[42] See the author's interview with Rudolf Seiters (26.6.2016).

human component would not have solved all the existing problems, but it would have probably mitigated some of their negative effects. Giulio Andreotti was, especially for Hans-Dietrich Genscher, an esteemed partner, whom the German politician appreciated for his capacity of political critical analysis and for his clarity of purpose. Still, in that specific moment the extreme cautious stance of Andreotti was not the strongest card to play to avoid misunderstandings with Kohl.

It is unquestionable that at first the political course pursued by Kohl was not unanimously accepted in Bonn and that Hans-Dietrich Genscher, though no less determined than the Chancellor, acted in a more prudent manner. Still, Helmut Kohl and Hans-Dietrich Genscher had forged throughout the years an excellent working partnership in which in 1989/1990 the impatience of the first was balanced by the prudence of the latter. Italy instead lacked such a lucky combination. The cautious and reflective approach of Andreotti, which was held in high esteem by several European governments, and his priority of not weakening the position of Gorbačëv, should have been balanced by a Foreign Minister more flexible and sympathetic with the feelings and moods in Bonn and Paris.

«È stato il mio ministro degli Esteri in quegli anni, ma non aveva capito che i rapporti andavano stretti con i Tedeschi, i Francesi e gli Olandesi. E invece che faceva? Inseguiva gli Inglesi!
Nel luglio del 1991 presero la presidenza gli Olandesi e presentarono un documento certamente ambizioso, ma non rivoluzionario in materia di Unione Politica. Venne a Roma a presentarmelo il mio omologo olandese. Io dissi: "Questo è un piano bellissimo! Dobbiamo sponsorizzarlo". Non ho mai saputo se de Michelis lo abbia letto; quando fu presentato alla prima riunione informale dei ministri degli Esteri in Olanda, non disse una parola per difenderlo e il piano affondò. Certo se si potessero leggere i verbali di quella riunione, si vedrebbe che de Michelis andava dietro agli Inglesi. Ma torniamo all'Unione politica. Gli Olandesi [...] erano convinti che gli Italiani li avrebbero appoggiati, se l'avessimo fatto le cose sarebbero forse andate in modo diverso [...].
Con de Michelis i Tedeschi non si capivano [...] perché Genscher era una persona molto concreta e de Michelis non lo era. Pensi al progetto quadrangolare! Era percepito male in Germania, perché ai Tedeschi piacciono le cose chiare, concrete, non vogliono vivere di illusioni, mentre de Michelis girava sulla Quadrangolare, l'Adriatica...»[43]

---

[43] "He was my Foreign Minister in those years, but he had not understood that we had to strengthen our relations with the Germans, the French and the Dutsch people. What did he do instead? He went after the British! In July 1991, the Netherlands had the rotating presidency and they presented a proposal regarding the Political Union, certainly an ambitious attempt, but not a revolutionary one. My Dutch counterpart came to Rome to present the draft. I said: 'This is a wonderful project. We must support it!' I never knew whether de Michelis read it, when it was submitted at the informal gathering of Foreign Ministers in Holland he did not say a word to defend it and the project sank.

Gianni de Michelis was not the right person, at the right moment or in the right position. His political approach seemed to be designed to enhance the contradictions which Bonn sensed in the stance of Andreotti. Andreotti was a statesman who had lucidly and realistically perceived what was at stake in 1989: the opportunities related to a German substantial transformation, but also the risks which it would pose to Gorbačëv. Still, he had eventually lost his bet.

Italy was striving to be admitted to the club of the big powers summoned to define the future of Germany, but without having a clear vision of the *Deutschlandfrage*. Meanwhile, the ongoing transformations were eroding the foundations on which its vision of the *deutsche Frage* had relied for nearly half a century. This was in sum the major contradiction underlying the strategy of Italy from November 1989 until the spring of the following year.

In mid-March 1990, the demise of the Italian approach was increasingly palpable. It was by then officially a twin-track strategy, based on both the EC and NATO as its reference points.[44] Still, with every passing week the possibility that NATO could be involved in the definition of the preconditions to re-unification was ever more remote. The decision to first accept the 2+4 mechanism and then to try and limit its responsibilities and duties had turned into a failure.

> « Notre collègue reconnait aujourd'hui volontiers que l'interprétation excessivement restrictive que M. Andreotti avait voulu donner à la formule 2+4, en la limitant aux aspects strictement quadripartites et au statut de Berlin, ne tenait pas. La raison et l'expérience montraient qu'elle allait embrasser l'ensemble du problème de sécurité posé par l'Allemagne réunifiée ».[45]

Certainly, if we could read the meeting's minutes, we would see that de Michelis run after the British. Still, let's go back to the Political Union. The Dutch people [...] were persuaded that the Italians would have supported them; if we had done it, the issue would have been different. De Michelis and the Germans did not understand each other [...] because Genscher was a very realistic man, whereas de Michelis was it not. Let's think to the Quadrangolare! The Germans had negative reactions, because the Germans like realistic things, they refuse to live on illusions. De Micheils, on the contrary, revolved around the Quadrangolare, the Adriatica". See the author's interview with Ambassador Roberto Nigido (2.3.2016).

[44] See L'Italie et la situation en Europe, télégramme de l'ambassade de Rome n. 276, Rome, 16.3.1990. AMAE, Direction Europe, Série Italie, carton 6377, sous-série 11 dossier 1, période 1986–1990. The document concerns the 16 March meeting between the Italian *direttore generale aggiunto* Borga and the French *ministre-conseiller*.

[45]"Our colleague [Borga] is now willing to acknowledge that the excessively restricted notion applied by Giulio Andreotti to the 2+4 mechanism – insofar as he limited it to the definition of the status of Berlin and the strict responsibilities of the winning powers – does not hold up. Reason and experience showed that it was going to have to deal with the tangle of security issues raised by the German re-unification". See Ibid.

By the end of March, there was no longer an Italian strategy, all that was left was its European component. It is, therefore, not in the least surprising that the few scholars who wrote about the Italian reaction to the re-unification process concluded their essays with an analysis of the Italian contribution to the European integration process up to the end of autumn 1990 and, more frequently, until the signing of the Maastricht Treaty.[46] As Gabriele d'Ottavio has stressed, from March 1990, the achievement of the Monetary Union, the creation of the European Union and the strengthening of Parliament were the main pillars of the Italian political agenda.[47]

Still, on the basis of information so far presented and discussed, it is also evident that these goals pre-existed the fall of the Berlin Wall and the re-unification process. In affirming this, I implicitly refute the hypothesis of the "scambio geopolitico" supported by Foreign Minister de Michelis, meaning an European green light to re-unification in exchange for the German acceptance of the establishment of the European Economic and Monetary Union.[48] The German events had accelerated the desire to attain the goal of an Economic and Monetary Union,

---

[46] See, in particular, Antonio Varsori, Italy, The East European Revolutions and the German Reunification, pp. 404–417. See Gabriele D'Ottavio, 1989 oder das Ende der "parallelen Geschichte", p. 49. See also Gian Enrico Rusconi, Le perplessità italiane nel corso della riunificazione tedesca e i rapporti italo-tedeschi negli anni seguenti, pp. 81–96.

[47] See Gabriele d'Ottavio, 1989 oder das Ende der "parallelen Geschichte", p. 51.

[48] In this respect Ambassador Nigido affirmed: "Il crollo del Muro di Berlino l'ho appreso proprio a Bonn durante una visita ufficiale di Andreotti in Germania […]. […] la moneta unica non è stata una conseguenza della riunificazione, perché il progetto della moneta unica, o meglio della banca centrale, lo lanciò Genscher […] come leader del partito liberale nel febbraio 1988. […] era fallito negli anni Settanta a causa delle turbolenze finanziarie e dei mercati. Fu ripreso dal 1984 anche sulla scia del progetto sponsorizzato da Spinelli […] nel 1987 l'Atto Unico Europeo era entrato in funzione […] quindi era necessaria una moneta unica per gestire il mercato interno. […]. L'unificazione tedesca ne ha accelerato la realizzazione, ma l'idea l'hanno lanciata i tedeschi prima. Si vive di stereotipi, ma chi ha vissuto le cose le ricorda bene. […]. L'accelerazione dunque […] viene da Strasburgo, ma quel Consiglio europeo del dicembre 1989 […] non fu l'origine della moneta unica. Il disegno della moneta unica è partito nel giugno del 1988 ad Hannover, quando il consiglio europeo presieduto da Kohl dette incarico a Delors e ai governatori delle banche centrali europee di preparare un progetto sull'unione economica e monetaria. Il progetto fu poi presentato ad aprile del 1989 […]". (I learnt about the fall of the Wall during an official visit to Germany of Andreotti […]. […] the common currency was not the consequence of the German reunification, it was rather Genscher, as leader of the liberal party, who launched this project, or better the project of a European Central Bank, in February 1988. […] it had failed in the Seventies as a result of financial international turbulences. The idea was regained in 1984 on the wave of the project supported by Spinelli, […] by 1987, the Unique Act had entered into force, a unique currency was therefore necessary to run the single market […]. The reunification gave it a boost, but the idea had been launched by the Germans before those events. We live a life of stereotypes, but those who were there remember it well. […] This acceleration came from Strasbourg, but that European Council of December 1989 was not the origin of the common currency. The project for a common currency started in June1988 at Hannover, in the moment when the European Council chaired by Kohl gave to Delors and the Governors of the Central Banks the charge to draw proposals for the European Economic and Monetary Union).

but had not given birth to this project. The re-unification process, on the one hand, and the process towards more European integration, on the other, are therefore to be considered two intertwined but different paths. An acceptable analysis of the road leading to the signing of the Maastricht Treaty would require some interpretative tools which a study of the Italian stance to the German events has only partially offered.

Furthermore, being the object of this book the analysis and the discussion of the Italian vision of the *deutsche Frage* and its reaction to the 1989/1990 events, it appears as the most coherent and appropriate choice to put an end to this study in the moment when the Italian strategy crumbled. By March 1990, there was no more denying that Italy had been excluded from the main tables exactly when the future of Germany would take its definite shape, meaning above all the 2+4 mechanism.

Rather than walking on the uncertain territory which led to the signing of the Maastricht Treaty, I prefer to conclude this third and last section with a little known fact concerning Francesco Cossiga and his relations with Germany. In his capacity of President of the Republic, he had had few opportunities to influence the making of the Italian strategy towards re-unification. In addition, he was a constitutional expert, who knew and until then had generally respected the limitations of his political office. Still, his relations with Germany left a small trace in the celebrations for the rebirth of a united German state. Francesco Cossiga was in fact the only Foreign Head of State to be invited to participate in the first session of the new German Parliament.

> «19 dicembre 1990: Partiamo prestissimo per Berlino…la giornata scorre pienissima di eventi. Andiamo a Bellevue per l'incontro con von Weizsäcker, un incontro che si è svolto a quattr'occhi e poi a Charlottenburg. Dopo colazione passiamo a Plötzensee per un omaggio ai caduti e il 20 dicembre, dopo una visita a Sanssouci a Potsdam, andiamo al Reichstag dove si tiene la prima seduta del Parlamento riunito. Questa è un'enorme impressione, vedere i comunisti ridotti ad un gruppetto sparuto sedere di fronte al bisonte Helmut Kohl, che è forte, ricco, sicuro e potente. […] Il presidente è raggiante, ha lunghi colloqui separati con Kohl, con Hans-Dietrich Genscher e con Otto von Lambsdorff. È l'unico capo di stato presente e il suo discorso riceve lunghi applausi […]. Dopo, von Weizsäcker ci accompagna a fare un giro turistico, attraversiamo il check Point Charlie, che effetto quel Muro che non c'è più».[49]

---

[49] "19 December 1990: We left very early for Berlin…the day was full of events. We went to Bellevue for the meeting with von Weizsäcker, which was a face-to-face meeting, and later we went to Charlottenburg. After eating breakfast, we travelled to Plötzensee to pay a tribute to fallen soldiers and on 20 December, after a visit to Sanssouci in Potsdam, we went to the Reichstag for the first

On the same day, on the occasion of the conference "vecchia e nuova Europa alle soglie del terzo millennio" (Old and New Europe on the threshold of the third millenium) Cossiga gave to a great crowd of people a speech of more than thirty pages. Some sentences from this speech in which Cossiga quoted one of the major Italian experts on German philosophy and thinking, Benedetto Croce, provide the ideal conclusion for this book.

> «[…] Il Muro è caduto…già in ogni parte dell'Europa si assiste al germinare di una nuova coscienza, di una nuova nazionalità; e così francesi e tedeschi e italiani e tutti gli altri s'innalzeranno ad europei e i loro pensieri indirizzeranno all'Europa e i loro cuori batteranno per lei come prima per le patrie più piccole, non dimenticate già, ma meglio amate […]».[50]

---

session of the united Parliament. It made a very strong impression to see the Communists reduced to a very small fringe in front of the bison Kohl, who was rich, powerful and confident […]. The Italian President seemed to glow, he had separate meetings with Kohl, with Hans-Dietrich Genscher and with Otto von Lambsdorff. He was the only Foreign Head of State to be there and his speech was followed by a big round of applause. Later on, von Weizsäcker accompanied us on a tour of Berlin; we also crossed the check Point Charlie: what an emotion that the Wall no more existed!". See the author's interview with Ambassador Ortona (22.3.2016), where he also quoted his soon to be published diaries.

[50] "The Wall has fallen…all over Europe we can already see the traces of a budding new conscience, of the creation of a new nationality. The French and Germans and the Italian people will rise up as Europeans, and their thoughts will be for Europe. Their hearts will beat as it once did for their smaller lands, not forgotten, but better loved […]". See Discorso di Cossiga al Parlamento tedesco, 20.12.1990. ASCD, Fondo Francesco Cossiga, archivio con titolario 1944–2010, b.184, fascicolo Unione Sovietica/Russia. The day after the speech of 20 December, Cossiga sent a letter of thanks to Ambassador Marcello Guidi for his great support in October 1990 on the occasion of the re-unification, which Cossiga had also celebrated in Germany.

> *Zu den treuesten Weggefährten der Deutschen zählten, in Bonn nicht immer gewürdigt, die oft wechselnden, aber im ganzen erstaunlich erfolgreichen Repräsentanten der italienischen Politik: De Gasperi und Pietro Nenni, Aldo Moro, Andreotti und Craxi-auch Enrico Berlinguer. [...] Die Deutschen hatten mehr Freunde, als sie wahrnehmen oder wahrhaben wollten.[1]*
> (Willy Brandt)

Postface

As I had started this research with a brief quotation of the First Chancellor of the Bundesrepublik, Konrad Adenauer, it seems appropriate to conclude it with a short quotation uttered by another well-known Chancellor, Willy Brandt. His sentences are undoubtedly significant, even though relatively brief. They highlight the keen interest and respect harboured towards Italy and many of its politicians northwards of the Alps. It was during one of the interviews which I was given that Ambassador Pietro Calamia drew my attention to the words expressed by Willy Brandt in his memoirs.[2]

Despite their different approaches and tones, all interviewees made specific reference to the long and fruitful relationship established between Rome and Bonn. This perception is also confirmed by the evidence provided from in-depth analysis of the available diplomatic records, including the French ones. France looked at the Italo-German couple with mixed feelings. It merged worries about its potential with pure astonishment and admiration that two not technically neighbouring countries had managed to establish such a close network of cooperation.

It is equally significant that these words were uttered by Willy Brandt, a Socialist and a Northerner. The previous chapters have often showed, both explicitly and between the lines, that the Italian-German relationship was under the best conditions when a Christian-Democratic Chancellor held the reins of the Federal government. The conditions were even more fruitful if this Chancellor came from South-Western Germany. Certainly, the interaction between the DC and the CDU had an important impact on bilateral relations. Besides, for obvious geographical reasons, both the cultural and the economic exchanges were bound to be more

---

[1] See Willy Brandt, Erinnerungen, Frankfurt am Main 1989, p. 491.
[2] See the author's interview with Ambassador Pietro Calamia (29.9.2016).

intense between the Northern Italian regions and the Southern German *Länder*, especially Bavaria.[3]

It does not follow though that the ties with Rome were the exclusive domain of a specific political group, namely the CDU. In chapter four, for instance, the close, even though problematic, relationship established with his Italian counterparts by another Socialist and Northern Chancellor, Helmut Schmidt, has been discussed.

The interviews collected also point at the great relevance of the link between Italy and Germany at the European level. Within the European integration process, Rome and Bonn learned to cooperate even more closely than at a strictly bilateral level, and on several occasions their cooperation was more coherent and effective. Unfortunately, the literature concerning this issue is scanty, mainly as a consequence of the choice made by both the Italian and the German academic community to focus either on the role of Paris within the integration process, or on the bilateral relationship of their country with France.

If we now compare the words of Willy Brandt with the comments of Gian Enrico Rusconi about the Italian-German interaction after the re-unification, the contrast is striking:

«Può un paese apparire simpatico, economicamente interessante, culturalmente affascinante e nello stesso tempo essere considerato scarsamente rilevante dal punto di vista politico? E quindi essere trattato in modo un po' opportunistico, anche perché sospettato di essere scarsamente affidabile? Sì. E il caso dell'Italia di oggi agli occhi di gran parte della classe politica tedesca. Naturalmente queste affermazioni non si leggono nelle dichiarazioni ufficiali degli organi di governo e di partito. Ma si possono tranquillamente trovare (non sempre tra le righe) nei commenti giornalistici e pubblicitari. Viceversa: può un paese coltivare ammirazione per un'altra nazione; possono i suoi rappresentanti proclamare continuamente di avere identità di vedute e assicurare la volontà di una stretta collaborazione senza che tali volenterose parole abbiano conseguenze politiche davvero rilevanti? Sì. E il caso del governo italiano, e, più in generale, del ceto politico italiano, nei confronti della Germania di oggi. [...]. E in questo quadro che va collocata quella che con intenzionale provocazione chiamo "estraniazione strisciante"».[4]

---

[3] See, in particular, Thomas Schlemmer, Una fitta rete. Università e istituti di ricerca – l'esempio di Monaco, in: Gian Enrico Rusconi/Hans Woller/Thomas Schlemmer, Estraniazione strisciante tra Italia e Germania?, Bologna 2008, pp. 147–156.

[4] "May a country look nice, can it be economically attractive, culturally charming, and, at the same time, can it be also considered politically insignificant? And, therefore, can it be treated with a bit of opportunism (also because it is suspected of being hardly reliable)? Yes, this is perfectly possible. Nowadays, this is the case with Italy and the majority of the German political élite. Of course, nothing of it can be read in public addresses. But we can found traces of it in newspapers and

Throughout the years, Gian Enrico Rusconi, professor of Political Science at the Turin University, and from 2005 to 2010 director of the *Italienisch-Deutsches Historisches Institut* in Trento, has often warned against the risks of an unnoticed deterioration of the Italian-German relations. To draw the attention of the academic community to this issue, he coined the provocative definition of "estraniazione strisciante/schleichende Entfremdung" (creeping estrangement).[5]

In Germany, this approach has been discussed by two prominent historians, Hans Woller and Thomas Schlemmer. This approach has also caused much controversy in recent years in both countries and, therefore, cannot be ignored. On the contrary, it seems appropriate to focus the postface of this book on the discussion of the implications of the abovementioned theory.

Each chapter of this research ends with a brief sub-chapter named "preliminary conclusions", so as to draw some comments on the issues discussed in the previous pages of each specific section. These "conclusions" do not intend to reiterate what has already been discussed; rather, they intend to take account of all the main subjects analysed, and to use this stock of knowledge in order to conduct a critical examination of the framework of interpretation known as "creeping estrangement".

This popular framework of interpretation has often been "rehashed" and adapted to the changing conditions of the Italo-German couple. Our reference point is the formulation proposed at the conference organised in May 2007 by the *Italienisch-Deutsches Historisches Institut* and the *Institut für Zeitgeschichte*.[6] A significant number of historians, experts on contemporary history, experts of German studies, but also economists, journalists, and cultural agents were invited to participate.

Firstly, we should wonder what specific field Rusconi referred to in the conference and in his essays. Even if the Italian social scientist has made general mention of the Italian-German relationship, what he seems to have in mind when

---

advertising (not always between the lines). And, the other way round, may a country admire another Nation, may the representatives of this country constantly reaffirm their identity of views and their determination to cooperate more closely, and, yet, may these words have no practical consequences? Yes, this is also perfectly possible. Nowadays, this is the case of Italy, and, more generally, of its political élite, with Germany. [...] In this broad framework, I think we should read and understand what I call, in a deliberately provocative manner, the 'creeping estrangement'". See Gian Enrico Rusconi, Le radici politiche dell'estraniazione strisciante tra Italia e Germania, in: Hans Woller/Gian Enrico Rusconi/Thomas Schlemmer, Estraniazione strisciante, pp. 11–18

[5] See Friederike Hausmann, Die Deutschen und ihre Nachbarn: Italien, München 2009, p. 217.

[6] The results of this conference were published in: Gian Enrico Rusconi/Hans Woller/Thomas Schlemmer, Estraniazione strisciante tra Italia e Germania?, and in the German edition: Hans Woller/Gian Enrico Rusconi/Thomas Schlemmer, Schleichende Entfremdung? Deutschland und Italien nach dem Mauerfall, München 2009.

speaking of an unmistakable imbalance between Rome and Bonn is the field of politics (in this research defined as official Italy). It is, therefore, hardly surprising that renowned economists, cultural experts and diplomats in both countries have rejected his approach.

As far as the economic and cultural "pillar" is concerned, evidence does not actually point at any sharp deterioration after the re-unification. Rather, it allows experts to identify a preservation of what has been achieved to date and, in some specific cases, to notice even some improvements.[7]

Looking more closely at the cultural exchange, we should bear in mind that, even though the knowledge of the German language is still not widespread in Italy, German is no longer the domain of an élite, meaning of the experts on German literature and of those people with a legal training, as was the case in the years following the end of the Second World War. The results achieved in the Eighties were maintained and strengthened in the three following decades. Not only is the contribution provided by the Goethe Institutes and the cultural institutes noteworthy, but it is also equally noteworthy that between 2004 and 2007, data concerning the teaching of German in secondary schools show a slight improvement.[8]

The changes at university level are even more striking.[9] After 1989, the two countries have continued to follow the path outlined in 1956 by the first cultural agreement signed after the Second World War. Just like in the economic field, so also in cultural exchanges, the results achieved in the Eighties have been preserved and extended. In 2005, according to data provided by the German *Hochschulrektorenkonferenz* (the conference of German university deans), 1.293 German students were in Italy, while Germany had welcomed nearly 6.700 Italian students, that is to say twice as many students as compared to 1995.[10]

This trend is even more impressive if we consider the situation in Southern Germany, for instance in the Bavarian city of Munich. The Ludwig Maximilian Universität in Munich houses an institute for Italian Philology which cooperates closely with both the *Historisches Seminar* of the same University, and with the local Italian Cultural Institute. The *Historisches Seminar* reserves a great deal of attention to Italian history, not only Ancient and Medieval History, as one might

---

[7] See Marco Mutinelli, Rapporto sugli investimenti diretti tedeschi in Italia e italiani in Germania, Milano 2011.

[8] See Deborah Cuccia, Italien und die deutsche Einigung 1989–1990, in: Michael Gehler/Maximilian Graf (eds.), Europa und die deutsche Einheit: Beobachtungen, Entscheidungen, und Folgen, 2017.

[9] See Ulrike Stepp, Nel segno di Erasmo. Scambi universitari tra Italia e Germania e integrazione europea, in: Gian Enrico Rusconi/Hans Woller/Thomas Schlemmer, Estraniazione strisciante, pp. 109–120.

[10] See the internet site of the *Hochschulrektorenkonferenz*: http://wwww.hrk.de (accessed 10.10.2016)

guess, but also Modern and Contemporary History. A Chair of Modern and Contemporary History with a specific focus on Italy and Spain is also provided at the Ludwig Maximilian Universität. Certainly, it could be argued that there is nothing extraordinary in the interest showed by the university and the cultural institutes of the city of Munich towards Mediterranean countries. Still, if we carefully consider Germany in its entirety, where can we find a Chair with a specific focus on one or two countries which are neither superpowers nor economic giants?

We have, therefore, to agree with the comments formulated by German historian Thomas Schlemmer, insofar as he rejects the interpretative framework of the creeping estrangement in the cultural field. Rather, he proposes to adopt the "kommunikative Verdichtung" (communicative densification) as a more appropriate scheme for analysis.[11]

Certainly, Rusconi is not wrong when he calls for an improvement in the relationship. Neither are cultural experts when they regret the limited use Italy made of Villa Vigoni, and nor are Italian ambassadors in suggesting to focus on cultural exchanges as a stepping stone to further improvements into the Italian-German cooperation.[12] Cultural exchange has always been a heartstring in post-War Germany, especially in its relationship with Italy.

Still, it cannot be necessarily concluded that the relationship is affected by a creeping estrangement. The comments uttered by the diplomats interviewed are the expression of the high expectations between Rome and Bonn. The difficulties on the path to improvement cannot be merely traced back to the weaknesses of this relationship in itself. They are rather the consequence of administrative hurdles impeding the realization of common projects, of the fact that in the "humanities", many researchers publish their works in Italian – thus confining their results within the national borders – and also of the lack of Italian resources to support junior scientists.[13]

Dealing more specially with politics, some preliminary remarks are necessary before analysing the framework of the "creeping estrangement". In his essays, the Turin professor takes into account a specific field of politics, while other

---

[11] See Thomas Schlemmer, Una fitta rete. Università e istituti di ricerca – l'esempio di Monaco, in: Gian Enrico Rusconi/Hans Woller/Thomas Schlemmer, Estraniazione strisciante, pp. 147–156.

[12] See the author's interviews with ambassadors Leonardo Visconti di Modrone (12.5.2016), and Ferdinando Salleo (28.10.2016).

[13] See Elena Agazzi, La germanistica in Italia dopo il 1989, in: Gian Enrico Rusconi/Hans Woller/Thomas Schlemmer, Estraniazione strisciante, pp. 85–98. The author remarks that after the German re-unification, the increase in the number of chairs for German language, literature and history went unnoticed because of the more relevant increase of interest in learning and teaching English. It was not until the so called "Berlusconi phase" that a national plan solely focused on the teaching of English and computer resources was carried out at the expense of other school subjects, such as the German language.

arenas of cooperation are left on the sidelines. I am referring to the many improvements achieved through regional cooperation on grounds of a German federal structure, and a gradual decentralization of powers from the Italian central
state to regional authorities. This trend has had a significant positive impact not
only in economic and cultural exchanges, but also in a gradual improvement of
political contacts at a local level, and in the image that the local media offers of
the two countries. The framework proposed by Rusconi must be once again refo-
cused. In the end, it solely refers to high-politics. In this specific field, it is comparatively a far more difficult task to try and confute the "creeping estrangement".

In the early Nineties, most of the time of Italian politics was absorbed by the
scandals which marked the symbolic end of the so called First Republic.[14] What
remained of the attention of the political élite was focused on the difficult course
towards political reforms that would allow Italy to meet the strict requirements to
be eligible for the common currency. The election of Silvio Berlusconi[15] cast a
dark shadow on bilateral relations and on cooperation at the European level.

A recently reunified Germany had in turn its own urgent needs to meet concerning both a process of gradual harmonisation after nearly half a century of
division, and the necessity of redefining its role in European and world politics.
There was not much space left to focus on the Italian-German relationship.

Should we, therefore, surrender and admit that in the field of high-politics the
framework for interpretation known as "creeping estrangement" is "bulletproof"?
Or should we rather try and identify some weak points?

The first weak element has been suggested by German historian Hans Woller.
According to the "creeping estrangement" in the aftermath of the re-unification,
the "agents" appointed for the promotion of closer bilateral ties have acted in a
very precise niche. Hans Woller has underlined that this has always been the case
in the Italian-German relationship.[16] In the previous chapters it has, for instance,
been often brought to the attention of the readers that the knowledge of the German language and culture was not widespread, neither among politicians nor
among ordinary citizens. There is no evidence to allow experts to state beyond
doubt that such a significant deterioration is underway, that the expression
"schleichende Entfremdung" can be justified.

Secondly, there is a very fine line between alarm and alarmism. Even if we
accept that the "creeping estrangement" was a cry of alarm, this framework remains a risky journey, as each warning, once repeated too often, can easily turn

---

[14] See footnote 20 in the preface.
[15] See Giovanni Orsina, Berlusconi as Circumstantial Populist, in Günther Pallaver/Michael Geh-
ler/Maurizio Cau (eds.), Populism, Populists and the Crisis of Political Parties. A Comparison of
Italy, Austria and Germany 1990–2015, Berlin – Bologna 2018, pp. 157–180.
[16] See Hans Woller, Sul mito dell'estraniazione strisciante, in: Gian Enrico Rusconi/Hans Wol-
ler/Thomas Schlemmer, Estraniazione strisciante, pp. 19–30.

into a *self-fulfilling prophecy*. In other words, by using the theory of the "creeping estrangement", there is a risk of applying to reality a model which does not fully take into account its multiple dimensions.

Thirdly, it is useful to wonder which specific frame of reference Rusconi had in mind when he coined the expression "strisciante alienazione". Was he perhaps referring to the Fifties?

The significant achievements of that decade have already been discussed in chapter three, but in doing so, its many limitations have also come to the surface. Back then, the relationship was mainly based on the good chemistry between De Gasperi and Adenauer, and on a "transmission belt", namely the party pillar, which did not succeed in translating what had been achieved into a strong institutional Italo-German umbrella. As far as the press[17] is concerned, the association established between Adenauer and the country he led was a fragile one. Besides, this association was only partially accepted in an ideologically polarised country as Italy was. Deep rooted prejudices still affected the cooperation.

Are the Sixties or rather the Seventies the correct frame of reference? It has been written that the frequent changes of governments in Italy were "compensated" by the political dominance of the DC, which provided both flexibility and continuity, regardless of the chronic governmental instability. New diplomatic files show, however, how this picture can be misleading. In 1978, Italy and Germany had agreed to a marriage of convenience which had been made possible, despite huge discrepancies, by the existing international conditions, namely the cage in which both countries lived. The convergence of interests between Italy and Germany, which the 1989 earthquake had allegedly smashed, has also been mentioned. But there is no denying that this was a hard-fought convergence built on the slopes of an active volcano, the degeneration of the DC.

Should we accept the "creeping estrangement" on ground of the overall good relations established between Emilio Colombo or Giulio Andreotti and the leading politicians of the Bundesrepublik? Although the "Männerfreundschaft" is not unimportant in international relations, if we justify a specific approach based on a single pillar, in this case the "personal pillar", we are also bound to face the inherent difficulties provided by it. In the Sixties and Seventies, as well as after the German re-unification, an equal number of examples of good and difficult personal relations can in fact be provided. A rather contentious relationship between Berlusconi and the Germans was matched by a sound understanding between German politicians and, for instance, Susanna Agnelli, in her capacity of

---

[17] It is essential to also consider the press, as Professor Rusconi has often used the articles published in the press to substantiate his analysis.

Foreign Minister, Romano Prodi[18], Carlo Azeglio Ciampi, and Giorgio Napolitano, both Italian Heads of State.[19] As for the Italian press, the image of Germany
depicted in the mid 1990s was, undoubtedly, not always positive, and from time
to time old stereotypes which had supposedly disappeared, surfaced again; still,
hardly ever have Italian journalists expressed such harsh criticism towards Germany as in the 1970s. The so called "Kappler Affair" has already been compre-
hensively covered in chapter six; here it is, however, interesting to recall a less-
known episode connected with this affair. On 19 August 1977 Eugenio Scalfari,
editor in chief of *Repubblica*, wrote that he was not always satisfied with being
born Italian, but with every passing day he was more thankful to fate for not being
a German.[20]

May the Eighties be our frame of reference? Certainly, the 1980s, namely the
focus of this research, potentially led to substantial improvements in all respects.
This was, however, a slow and slippery path which cannot be taken for granted.
Besides, this process of gradual improvement developed in the shadow of two
mighty uncertainties. The first source of uncertainty concerned the time and the
way in which the demise of the DC and of the Italian political system would happen. The second source of uncertainty can be traced back to the contrast between
a *deutsche Frage* and a *Deutschlandfrage*, which the Fall of the Wall unveiled.

Only for the Eighties it is advisable to replace the theory of the creeping estrangement with a more flexible approach, the "verpasste Chance" (missed opportunity), as Thomas Schlemmer suggested in the cultural field to replace the
"schleichende Entfremdung" by the "kommunikative Verdichtung". Embracing
the theory of the "creeping estrangement" requires in fact forcing the Italian-German interaction before 1989 into a model whose main features are agreement and
harmony.

Many frameworks for interpretation have explained the 1949–1989 phase of
the bilateral relations in the light of an overall conformity of interests and of the
"twin nations" *topos*[21], meaning that both countries had affirmed their national
unity relatively late. By contrast, after 1989 the main trend had consisted in

---

[18] See, in particular, Manfred Görtemaker, Angela Merkel und Romano Prodi: Antithesis of Populism? in: Günther Pallaver/Michael Gehler/Maurizio Cau, Populism, Populistis and the Crisis of
Political Parties, pp. 217–236, 229–234.

[19] See the author's interviews with Ambassador Roberto Nigido (2.3.2016), and with Ambassador
Pietro Calamia (29.9.2016). Throughout his long political career, Carlo Azeglio Ciampi always had
good relations with Germany, where he had attended the University of Leipzig. See Paolo Peluffo,
Carlo Azeglio Ciampi l'uomo e il presidente, Milano 2007.

[20] See Eva Sabine Kuntz, Konstanz und Wandel von Stereotypen, p. 302.

[21]See Christoph Cornelißen/Lutz Klinkhammer/Wolfgang Schwentker, Erinnerungskulturen:
Deutschland Italien und Japan seit 1945, Frankfurt 2004. See also Christof Dipper, Deutschland
und Italien 1860–1960: Politische und kulturelle Aspekte im Vergleich, München 2005.

proposing models based either on the *topos* "ferner Nachbarn" (faraway neigh-bours) or on the "schleichende Entfremdung".[22]

A historical approach can, therefore, be extremely useful to uncover the risks of applying too strict a framework for interpretation. Excessively optimist ap-proaches to the study of the Italian-German rapprochement after the Second World War, which inevitably left undiscussed the still existing sources of tension, have been replaced in the last decades by rather pessimistic assessments. Both approaches can be dangerous. Too optimistic interpretations are vulnerable to lose touch with reality by trying to see in the evolving relations what the model suggests should happen, whereas the new trend offers interpretations which can too easily turn into a *self-fulfilling prophecy*.

Why a "missed chance"? Because the German re-unification and the trans-formations which it unleashed came too soon for Italy. At the end of 1989, the process of rapprochement between Rome and Bonn was still in the making, and the two abovementioned sources of uncertainty lingered on still unresolved.

In 1994, from the ashes of two years of scandals, a new picture arose in Italy. Berlin had not the instruments necessary to quickly comprehend the changes that had affected the Italian political system. It was not a "Schuss Opportunismus" which led the German reactions to the Italian internal changes, but rather a gen-uine difficulty in redefining bilateral relations. All interviewees, both journalists and diplomats, though opposed to the theory of the "schleichende Entfremdung", noticed, sometimes smoothly and some other times reluctantly, that a certain cli-mate of tension has indeed affected bilateral relations after 1996/1998. Far from being random tensions, the choice of 1996/1998 as a reference point is highly significant. Between the beginning of the 1990s and 1998, the main partners of Italy during the previous years left the German political scene. These were poli-ticians who had both the expertise and the sensibility to sense the Italian political feelings and moods. First Hans-Dietrich Genscher left his post, then Helmut Kohl was replaced in 1998 by Gerhard Schröder.

After 1998, the "verpasste Chance" must be replaced by a different approach, as relations, figuratively speaking, slipped into some sort of "Dornröschenschlaf" (Sleeping Beauty's Slumber). This image wants to be as evocative as that of the "creeping estrangement". If historians could, just like natural scientists, draw a graph of bilateral relations, we would not see a downward parabolic curve after 1989, but rather constant fluctuations due to the alternation of surges of interest followed by phases of disaffection.

Since 1990, Italy and Germany have slipped into a restless sleep, often haunted by nightmares, such as Berlusconi's political course. Berlusconi

---

[22] See Gabriele D'Ottavio, 1989 oder das Ende der "parallelen Geschichte" Deutschlands und Ita-liens?, pp. 39–57, 40.

contributed to rock the boat of many German prejudices and old representations of Italy, such as opportunisms, shallowness, superficiality and amateurism, which had not been completely removed in the 1980s. The Eighties had in fact provided both countries with the opportunity to question several old *topoi* and stereotypes; however, there was not sufficient time for new associations to fully replace the old ones. In this perspective, the Fall of the Berlin Wall left a sort of vacuum to be filled. Economic and cultural exchanges were from the Nineties deprived of the political superstructure which had until then worked as a glasshouse that sheltered them from adverse weather conditions. Political contacts remained trapped in a net of unresolved contradictions. The party pillar was swept away, while the "Männerfreundschaft" has been subjected to the ups and downs typical of human relations.

I must nonetheless fully agree with the theory proposed by Gian Enrico Rusconi on one specific aspect: his theory can be applied to the Italian-German cooperation in the field of European integration. In this specific field, Italy and Germany had shared for nearly half a century much more than a good cooperation or a sound agreement; they had rather developed a community of interests. For both countries, the European integration had become an objective and a pillar of their Foreign policy.

Not only did the European framework for cooperation change after the signature of the Treaty of Maastricht, but also the very nature of integration was altered. On December 1990, on the occasion of the conference "vecchia e nuova Europa alle soglie del terzo millennio", the Italian Head of State Cossiga had prophesied that "tutti gli altri s'innalzeranno ad europei […] e i loro cuori batteranno per lei come prima per le patrie più piccole, non dimenticate già, ma meglio amate". [23] This prophesy has not been fulfilled.

Under today's new international conditions Europe can no more embody the same ideals which had animated it in the Fifties. This creates the questions: Nowadays, what is Europe's specific weight in the Foreign policy of Member States? Which are the main characteristics of its specific identity, and which is its specific role?

What actually lacked both in Germany and in Italy was a process of re-thinking based on such core questions.[24] This is a delicate issue not only for Italy and

---

[23] See ch.9.2.

[24] This problem actually affects several European member states such as Italy, Germany, as well as France, and it is not limited to the Italian-German cooperation. After the end of the presidency of François Mitterrand, France has, for instance, shown a growing uncertainty in defining and successfully implementing a coherent "German politics". Likewise, Germany seems to be unable to embrace its new role in a European process, which faces new challenges, and to consequently redefine its network of interactions with Italy, France, and, more generally, with Southern Europe.

Germany but also for the European Union. Rome and Bonn are deprived of a fundamental area for dialogue, where they would have had good tools to redefine their relations, while Europe can no more depend on one of the engines which had guaranteed its sound development. By stating this, the central role held by the French-German couple is not undermined. Rather, attention is shifted towards the complex nature of the European Union.

Europe is like an orchestra, which features different instruments. The violin will always have more bars – and more notes – to play than a triangle. Each instrument though is essential and has its own part to play, even if some have a longer, and some a shorter, score.

Surely, France and Germany were the first violins in this "European orchestra". However, Italy was no triangle; it was rather a second violin, meaning that it was often called to play long and difficult "pieces of music". An orchestra without its first violins would not be an orchestra, but even all other instruments are necessary. Whenever the first violins do not play in tune and the second violins do not play at all, the concert is a debacle. Reason itself suggests that all instruments must play in tune to have a successful concert because, quoting the famous Spanish painter Francisco Goya, "the sleep of reason produces monsters" (el sueño de la razón produce monstruos).

See, for example, Beligh Nabli, L'Union pour la Méditerranée : Le boulet diplomatique de Sarkozy, *Iris Tribune* (avril 2012). As for Germany, see, in particular, the recent contribution of Prof. Dr. Michael Gehler in the Italian Magazine Limes. Michael Gelher, Da Bonn a Berlino, La Transizione incompiuta, in: *Limes* (12) 2018.

Bibliography

ITALIAN ARCHIVAL SOURCES:

Istituto Luigi Sturzo (ILS), Archivio Giulio Andreotti (AGA), Roma
Europa, Questioni comuni e Vertici (1957–2004):
    Buste 360, 361, 365, 367, 368, 378, 382, 383, 404
Stati Uniti d'America (1937 -2007):
    Buste 591, 637, 647
Unione Sovietica:
    Buste 685, 691, 692, 694, 695, 696, 703, 710, 712
Trentino:
    Busta 21

Archivio Storico Camera dei Deputati (ASCD), Fondo Francesco Cossiga, Roma
Archivio 1965–1985
Presidenza del Consiglio dei Ministri/Governi Cossiga I e Cossiga II (1979–
1980):
    Buste 4, 5, 6, 8, 10
Ricordi (1983–2010):
    Buste 18, 20
Archivio con titolario 1944–2010
Affari internazionali (1984 -2010):
    Buste 24, 62
Convegni-incontri-commemorazioni-viaggi (1992–2009):
    Buste 60, 78, 82
Fondazioni e enti morali:
    Busta 108
Presidenza Repubblica-Settennato (1985–1992):
    Buste 183, 184, 187, 192

Istituto Luigi Sturzo (ILS), Fondo Democrazia Cristiana, Roma
Serie Segreteria politica (1944–1992), sottoserie Corrispondenza Estera:
    Flaminio Piccoli 1980–1982
    Ciriaco de Mita 1982–1989
    Arnaldo Forlani 1989–1992

Fondazione Gramsci, Archivio del Partito Comunista, Roma
Carte del PCI (Partito Comunista italiano)

1979	MF0411	FASC1403	
	MF0411	FASC 1405	
	MF0411	FASC1435	
	MF0400	FASC1313	
	MF0400	FASC1319	
1980	MF0440	FASC0052	
	MF0440	FASC0058	
	MF0440	FASC1669	
	MF0440	FASC2298	
	MF0466	FASC8003	PAGG.283/282
	MF0466	FASC8003	PAGG.348/351
1981	MF0488	FASC8107	PAGG.33/74
	MF0507	FASC3254	
	MF0507	FASC8201	PAGG.30/32
	MF0559	FASC0401	PAGG.25/27
	MF0559		PAGG.96
	MF0559		PAGG.99
	MF0555		PAGG.1330
	MF0507	FASC8202	PAGG.29/32
1983	MF0559	FASC8401	PAGG.25/27
	MF0559		PAGG.96
	MF0559		PAGG.99
	MF0555		PAGG.1330
1984	MF0561	FASC8403	PAGG.262/263
	MF0561	FASC8403	PAGG.262
	MF0561	FASC2204	
	MF0561	FASC2243	
	MF0561	FASC2242	
1985	MF0574	FASC8506	PAGG.40/149
	MF0574	FASC8505	PAGG.151/173
	MF0574	FASC8505	
1988	MF0574	FASC8806	PAGG.1/16
	MF0574	FASC8806	
	MF0574	FASC8806	PAGG.17/61
	MF0574	FASC8803	PAGG.123/130
	MF0574	FASC8810	
1989	MF8912		PAGG.30/98
	MF8912	FASC0100	
	MF8912	FASC0110	

MF8912   PAGG.99/108

MF8902   FASC0041

MF8904   PAGG.241/249

Atti parlamentari delle Commissioni affari esteri della Camera dei deputati e del Senato
November 1989-October 1990

OTHER ARCHIVAL SOURCES[1]:

European Union

Historical Archives of the European Union (AHUE), Florence
CPPE-1156, Intégration européenne, 1987
CPPE-1338, Sommet du Conseil européen, 1988–1989
CPPE-1219, Commission politique : Relations est-ouest, 1989–1990
CCRE-146, Section allemande, 1989–1990
EG-168, Réunification, coupures de presse, 1985 to 1991
CPPE-1345, Allemagne: Dossier Allemagne, réunification et frontières, 1990
GSPE-80, Documents officiels du Groupe socialiste au Parlement européen, 1990
UEF-344, Congrès de Cologne, 1984
UEF-450, Documents de la Commission et du Conseil CEE, 1986 to 1990

France

Archives diplomatiques, Ministère des Affaires étrangères (AMAE), Paris La Courneuve
Bureau d'ordre Europe 1986–1990 :

1935inva carton 6125	Allemagne Statut	1935inva carton 6156	Autriche
1935inva carton 6719	RDA	1935inva carton 6333	Hongrie
1935inva carton 6734	RFA	1935inva carton 6742	RFA
1935inva carton 6750	RFA	1935inva carton 6754	RFA
1935inva carton 6764	RFA	1935inva carton 6769	RFA
1935inva carton 6771	RFA	1935inva carton 6772	RFA
1935inva carton 6805	RFA	1935inva carton 6283	GB
1935inva carton 6357	Italie	1935inva carton 6373	Italie
1935inva carton 6377	Italie	1935inva carton 6378	Italie
1935inva carton 6384	Italie	1935inva carton 6385	Italie
1935inva carton 6716	Italie	1935inva carton 5875	Europe
1935inva carton 5876	Europe	1935inva carton 5877	Europe

---

[1]In strict chronological order of consultation.

1935inva carton 5910	CEE	1935inva carton 5911	CEE
1935inva carton 5912	CEE	1935inva carton 5913	CEE
1935inva carton 5914	CEE	1935inva carton 6003	COE
1935inva carton 6004	COE		

Bureau d'ordre Europe 1981–1985 :

1931inva carton 4907	Allemagne	1931inva carton 4934	Autriche
1931inva carton 5266	Hongrie	1931inva carton 5308	Italie
1931inva carton 5309	Italie	1931inva carton 5331	Italie

Centre des Archives diplomatiques (CADN), Ministère des Affaires étrangères, Nantes

579PO/4/39	Ambassade Rome	579PO/4/5	Ambassade Rome
579PO/4/9	Ambassade Rome	579PO/4/10	Ambassade Rome
579PO/4/11	Ambassade Rome	579PO/4/12	Ambassade Rome
579PO/4/15	Ambassade Rome	579PO/4/230	Ambassade Rome
579PO/4/231	Ambassade Rome	579PO/4/237	Ambassade Rome
579PO/4/260	Ambassade Rome	579PO/4/33	Ambassade Rome
579PO/4/35	Ambassade Rome	105PO/1/224	Ambassade Bonn
1130PO/1/214	Ambassade Budapest	130PO/1/265	Ambassade Budapest
130PO/1/264	Ambassade Budapest		
101PO/1999038/270	Ambassade Bonn	105PO/1999038/8	Ambassade Bonn

Archives Nationales de France (ANF), Pierrefitte-sur-Seine, Paris
Série Présidents de la République, 5-AG-4 Mitterrand
Archives du président de la République et de son secrétariat particulier
AG/5(4)/580, extrait :
Projet de discours du président de la République pour le dîner d'Etat en l'honneur du président de la République italienne Francesco Cossiga (29 janvier 1990).
Archives d'Alain Holleville
AG/5(4)/AH/14 :
Préparation, déroulement et bilan du Conseil européen de Strasbourg les 8 et 9 décembre 1989.
AG/5(4)/AH/15 :
Préparation et déroulement du Conseil européen de Dublin les 25 et 26 juin 1990 et du Conseil européen extraordinaire de Dublin le 28 avril 1990.
Archives de la cellule diplomatique
AG/5(4)/CD/52, dossier 10 :
Communauté économique européenne et Union européenne. - Préparation du dîner du 18 novembre 1989 au palais de l'Élysée.

AG/5(4)/CD/304, dossier 11 :
Dossier pays-Italie. Préparation de l'audience accordée par François Mitterrand à Francesco Cossiga, Président de la République d'Italie, le 29 janvier 1990.
AG/5(4)/CD/304 Dossier 12 :
Dossier pays-Italie. Préparation de l'audience accordée par François Mitterrand à Giulio Andreotti, Président du Conseil de la République d'Italie, le 13 février 1990.
Archives de Caroline de la Margerie
AG/5(4)/CDM/13 Dossier 2 :
Conseil européen de Strasbourg (Bas-Rhin) des 8 et 9 décembre 1989.
Archives d'Elisabeth Guigou
AG/5(4)/EG 11, dossier 1 :
Préparation des assises de Prague tenues du 12 au 14 juin 1991, dans le cadre du projet de confédération européenne, 1989–1991
AG/5(4)/EG/59, dossier 1 :
Préparation et suites du Conseil européen de Strasbourg (Bas-Rhin) des 8 et 9 décembre 1989
AG/5(4)/EG/60, dossier 1 :
Préparation et conclusions du Conseil européen de Strasbourg (Bas-Rhin) des 8 et 9 décembre 1989. - Informations transmises à François Mitterrand.
AG/5(4)/EG/60, dossier 2 :
Préparation et conclusions du Conseil européen de Strasbourg (Bas-Rhin) des 8 et 9 décembre 1989. - Informations rassemblées par Élisabeth Guigou.
AG/5(4)/EG/63, dossier 1 :
Préparation et conclusions du Conseil européen de Dublin les 25 et 26 juin 1990.
AG/5(4)/EG/63, dossier 2 :
Conseil européen de Dublin des 25 et 26 juin 1990. - Informations transmises à François Mitterrand.
AG/5(4)/EG 215 Dossier 6 :
Italie. Dossier pays. 1981–1990
Archives de Françoise Carle
AG/5(4)/FC/83 Dossier 2 :
Politique étrangère. Pays d'Europe centrale et orientale, Union soviétique et Communauté des états indépendants. Le « dîner des douze » : réunion des chefs d'État et de gouvernement européens au Palais de l'Élysée le 18 novembre 1989, pour évoquer notamment les bouleversements en Europe de l'Est (A-06–36). - Chronologie. 1989–1993

Archives de Pierre Morel
  AG/5(4)/PM 8, dossier 2 :
  Réformes des institutions européennes. Préparation, présentation et conclusions du plan Genscher-Colombo, du projet Spinelli et des comités ad hoc,
  1982–1984

Germany

Politisches Archiv des Auswärtigen Amtes (PA AA), Berlin
ZA 140.730E   Haltung der USA zur deutschen Frage   1989–1990
ZA 140.729E   Haltung Ungarns zur deutschen Frage   1989–1990
ZA 140.723E   Haltung Frankreichs zur deutschen Frage   1989–1990
ZA 140.701E   Gespräche mit der ständigen Vertretungen   1989–1990
ZA 140.724E   Haltung Großbritanniens zur dt. Frage   1989–1990
B130 13503E   Politische Bz. der BRD zu fremden Staaten 1989–1990
B130 13523E   Deutschlandpolitik   1989–1990
B26 ZA 320.02 Regierung   1980–1984
B26 ZA 320.03
B26 ZA 320.40 Presse   1980–1984
B26 ZA 321.00 Politische Beziehungen   1980–1984
B26 ZA 321.10 Deutsch-Italienische Konsultationen   1980–1984
B26 ZA 321.11 Bilaterale Konsultationen   1980–1984
B26 ZA 321.20 Vertretung der BRD   1980–1984
B26 ZA 321.00 Dt.-Ital. Beziehungen*   1984–1986
B26 ZA 321.00 Dt.-Ital. Beziehungen*   1987–1989
B26 ZA 321.00 Dt.-Ital. Gesprächsforum*   1987–1988
B26 ZA 321.00 Dt.-Ital. Gesprächsforum*   1988–1989
B26 ZA 321.00 Deutsch-Italienische Beziehungen*   1988–1992
B26 ZA 321.21 Ital. Vertret. in der BRD*   1985–1990
B26 ZA 321.00 Italien und die dt. Frage*   1989–1990
B26 ZA 322.00 Italiens Haltung zu Ost-Europa*   1989–1991
        und der dt. Frage
B26 ZA 400.00 Wirtschaftspolitik*   1989–1992
B26 ZA 321.21 ITA. Botschafter Marcello Guidi*   1989–1992
B26 ZA 600–650 Kulturbeziehungen*
B38 322.00 Bez. DDR-Italien*   1989–1990
B38 330.29 Haltung zur dt. Frage: Italien*   1989–1990
B90 600.51Kulturbeziehungen Italien*   1988–1989
M44 ZR 1838/86
M44 ZR 1842/86
M44 ZR 1843/86

M44 ZR 1496/83
M44 ZR 1517/83
M44 ZR 1662/84
M44 ZR 2516/82
M44 ZR 3018/81

M44 ZR88/10	Außenpolitik Italiens*	1988–1990
M44 ZR101/10	Chronik der Beziehungen	1973–1989
M44 ZR75/10	Außenminister Meckel in Italien*	1990
M44 ZR78/10	Italienischer Außenminister in der DDR*	1990
M44 ZR70/10	Noten der italienischen Botschaft*	1990
M44 ZR56/10	Italienische Sozialistische Partei*	1979–1989
M44 ZR48/10	Christdemokratische Partei*	1982–1989
M44 ZR104/10	Konsultationen zur KSZE-Fragen*	1990

Records with this sign * refer to boxes not declassified yet. A special authorisation in spring 2016 granted me access.

Archiv für Christlich-Demokratische Politik (ACDP), Konrad Adenauer Stiftung, Sankt Augustin, Bonn
ACDP, Präsidium 1986–1991 Sitzungen in Pisa, 09-007
ACDP, Korrespondenz mit Parteimitgliedern: Korrespondenz mit DC und PPI (1988–1994), 09-007
ACDP, Corrispondenza Jansen auf italienisch, 09-007
ACDP, Abteilung Presse Dokumentation (1979–1990)

EDITED DOCUMENTARY SOURCES:

Germany
Buchstab Günter/Kleinmann Hans-Otto (eds.), Helmut Kohl: Berichte zur Lage 1982–1989, Reihe Forschungen und Quellen zur Geschichte KAS, Düsseldorf 2012.
Buchstab Günter/Kleinmann Hans-Otto (eds.), Helmut Kohl: Berichte zur Lage 1989–1990, Reihe Forschungen und Quellen zur Geschichte KAS, Düsseldorf 2013.

Genscher Hans-Dietrich, Deutsche Außenpolitik. Ausgewählte Reden und Aufsätze 1974–1985, Stuttgart 1985.
Küsters Hanns Jürgen/Hofmann Daniel (eds.), Deutsche Einheit: Sonderedition aus den Akten des Bundeskanzleramtes 1989/1990, München 1998.

Möller Horst (ed.), Akten zur Auswärtigen Politik der Bundesrepublik Deutschland, in particular:

Ploetz Michael/Szatkowski Tim (eds.), Akten zur Auswärtigen Politik der Bundesrepublik Deutschland 1979, München 2010.

Geiger Tim/Amit das Gupta (eds.), Akten zur Auswärtigen Politik der Bundesrepublik Deutschland 1980, München 2011.

Taschler Daniela/Matthias Peter (eds.), Akten zur Auswärtigen Politik der Bundesrepublik Deutschland 1981, München 2012.

Ploetz Michael/Szatkowski Tim (eds.), Akten zur Auswärtigen Politik der Bundesrepublik Deutschland 1982, München 2013.

Geiger Tim/Matthias Peter (eds.), Akten zur Auswärtigen Politik der Bundesrepublik Deutschland 1983, München 2014.

Taschler Daniela/Szatkowski Tim (eds.), Akten zur Auswärtigen Politik der Bundesrepublik Deutschland 1984, München 2015.

Ploetz Michael /Mechthild Lindemann/Franzen Christoph Johannes (eds.), Akten zur Auswärtigen Politik der Bundesrepublik Deutschland 1985, Berlin 2016.

Hilger Andreas (ed.), Diplomatie für die deutsche Einheit, Dokumente des Auswärtigen Amts zu den deutsch-sowjetischen Beziehungen 1989–1990, Hamburg 2011.

Geiger Tim/Amos Heike (eds.), Die Einheit: das Auswärtige Amt, das DDR-Außenministerium und der Zwei-plus-Vier-Prozess, Göttingen, München 2015.

Italy

Serneri Simone Neri/Casali Antonio/Errera Giovanni (eds.), Scritti e discorsi di Sandro Pertini vol. II 1964–1985, Roma, Giovanni Errera direzione scientifica Fondazione di studi storici "Filippo Turati, Presidenza del Consiglio dei ministri dipartimento per l'informazione e l'editoria, Roma 1992.

Ministero degli Affari Esteri, Servizio Storico e Documentazione, Testi e documenti sulla politica estera dell'Italia, in particular:

1979, Testi e documenti sulla politica estera dell'Italia, Roma, Ufficio Studi Roma, Istituto Poligrafico, 1981.

1980, Testi e documenti sulla politica estera dell'Italia, Roma, Ufficio Studi Roma, Istituto Poligrafico, 1983.

1981, Testi e documenti sulla politica estera dell'Italia, Roma, Ufficio Studi Roma, Istituto Poligrafico, 1985.

1982, Testi e documenti sulla politica estera dell'Italia, Roma, Ufficio Studi Roma, Istituto Poligrafico, 1985.

1983, Testi e documenti sulla politica estera dell'Italia, Roma, Ufficio Studi Roma, Istituto Poligrafico, 1987.

1984, Testi e documenti sulla politica estera dell'Italia, Roma, Ufficio Studi Roma, Istituto Poligrafico, 1989.

1985, Testi e documenti sulla politica estera dell'Italia, Roma, Ufficio Studi Roma, Istituto Poligrafico, 1990.

1986, Testi e documenti sulla politica estera dell'Italia, Roma, Ufficio Studi Roma, Istituto Poligrafico, 1990.

1987, Testi e documenti sulla politica estera dell'Italia, Roma, Ufficio Studi Roma, Istituto Poligrafico, 1992.

1988, Testi e documenti sulla politica estera dell'Italia, Roma, Ufficio Studi Roma, Istituto Poligrafico, 1993.

France

Vaïsse Maurice/Wenkel Christian (eds.), La diplomatie française face à la réunification allemande (d'après des archives inédits), Paris 2012.

Former Soviet Union

Galkin Alexander (ed.), Михаил Горбачев и гурманский вопрос, сборник документов 1986–1991, Moskva 1999.

Hilger Andreas/Glaubitz Joachim, Michail Gorbatschow und die deutsche Frage: Sowjetische Dokumente 1986–1991, München 2011.

United Kingdom

Salmon Patrick (ed.), Documents on British Policy Overseas: German Unification 1989–1990, Series III Volume VII, London 2010.

Austria

Gehler Michael/Graf Maximilian, Österreich und die deutsche Frage 1987–1990: Vom Honecker-Besuch in Bonn bis zur Einheit, Göttingen 2018.

MEMOIRES AND BIOGRAPHIES:

Adamishin Anatolij, Tramonto e declino di una grande potenza: Diario politico dell'ultimo ambasciatore dell'URSS e del primo della Federazione russa a Roma (con una prefazione di Francesco Cossiga), Milano 1995.

Adenauer Konrad, Erinnerungen 1955–1959, Stuttgart 1967.

Andreotti Giulio, De Gasperi visto da vicino, Milano 1985.

Andreotti Giulio, L'URSS vista da vicino, Milano 1989.

Andreotti Giulio, 1947. L'anno delle grandi svolte nel diario di un protagonista, Milano 2005.

Barone Mario/Di Nolfo Ennio (a cura di), Giulio Andreotti l'uomo, il cattolico, lo statista, Soveria Mannelli 2010.

Bayer Alfred/Baumgärtel Manfred (eds.), Weltanschauung und politisches Handeln. Hanns Seidel zum 100. Geburtstag (Sonderausgabe der Politischen Studien), München 2001.

Carli Guido, Cinquant'anni di vita italiana, Roma – Bari 1993.

Cherniaev Anatolij, Gorbachev and the Reunification of Germany. Personal recollections, in: Gabriel Gorodetsky (ed.), Soviet Foreign Policy 1917–1991, Tel-Aviv 1994.

Colombo Emilio, Per l'Italia per l'Europa, Bologna 2013.

Cossiga Francesco, La passione e la politica, Torino 2010.

De Maizière Lothar, Ich will, dass meine Kinder nicht mehr lügen müssen: Meine Geschichte der deutschen Einheit (mit einem Vorwort von Michail Gorbatschow), Wien 2010.

De Michelis Gianni, La lunga ombra di Yalta. La specificità della politica italiana, Venezia 2003.

Dumas Roland, Affaires étrangères I : 1981–1988, Paris 2007.

Ferraris Luigi Vittorio, Wenn schon denn schon, aber ohne Hysterie: An meine deutschen Freunde, München 1998.

Gardner Newton Richard, Mission Italy. Gli anni di piombo raccontati dall'ambasciatore americano a Roma 1977–1981, Milano 2004.

Genscher Hans-Dietrich, Erinnerungen, Berlin 1995.

Gorbachev Foundation, Михаил Горбачев и гурманский вопрос, Moskva, Ves Mir Publishers, 2006 [tr. td. Igor Petrowitsch Gorodestki, Erinnerungen] Berlin 1996.

Groß Hans Ferdinand, Hanns Seidel 1901 bis 1961. Eine politische Biographie, München 1992.

Indelicato Alberto, Memorie di uno stato fantasma: Berlino 1987–1990, Berlin 2004.

Kohl Helmut, Ich wollte Deutschlands Einheit, dargestellt von Kai Dieckmann und Ralf Georg Reuth, Berlin 2010.

Kohl Helmut, Erinnerungen 1982–1990, München 2005.

Konrad Adenauer Stiftung (ed.), Ein Leben für Deutschland und für Europa: Stationen eines politischen Lebens, Düsseldorf 2008.

König Ewald, Menschen Mauer Mythen, Halle 2014.

Lay Fernando, L'Iniziativa italo-tedesca per il rilancio dell'Unione Europea. Origini e Sviluppo della Dichiarazione di Stoccarda (pubblicazioni della società italiana per l'organizzazione internazionale), Padova 1983.

Ortona Ludovico, La svolta di Cossiga. Diario del Settennato (1985–1992), Firenze 2016.

Massimo Franco, Andreotti. La vita di un uomo politico, la storia di un'epoca, Milano 2010.

Mitterrand François, De l'Allemagne de la France, Paris 1996.

Musella Luigi, Craxi: Biografia, Salerno 2007.

Misur György, Szarvasról Rómába. Diplomácia Küldetesbén, Budapest 2010.

Padoa Schioppa Tommaso, La lunga via per l'euro, Bologna 2004.

Pedone Clio, Cossiga: L'uomo che guardò oltre il Muro, Soveria Mannelli 2013

Peluffo Paolo, Carlo Azeglio Ciampi l'uomo e il presidente, Milano 2007.

Pruys Karl Hugo, Helmut Kohl: die Biographie, Berlin 1995.

Schäuble Wolfgang, Der Vertrag. Was ich über die deutsche Einheit verhandelte, Stuttgart 1991.

Schmidt Helmut, Menschen und Mächte, Berlin 1999.

Schwarz Hans-Peter, Konrad Adenauer der Aufstieg 1876–1952, Stuttgart 1986.

Seidel Hanns Stiftung (ed.), Josef Müller: Der erste Vorsitzende der CSU, München 1988.

Steinberg Jonathan, Bismarck: A Life, New York 2011.

Tchernaiev Anatolij, Die letzten Jahre einer Weltmacht: Der Kreml von innen, Stuttgart 1993.

Thatcher Margaret, The Downing Street Years 1979–1990, London 1993.

Thatcher Margaret, Statecraft: Strategies for a changing world, Londra 2002.

Védrine Hubert, Les mondes de François Mitterrand à l'Elysée 1981–1995, Paris 1996.

Zeno Livio, Il Conte Sforza ritratto di un grande diplomatico, Milano (ristampa) 2000.

BOOKS:

Alistair Cole, Franco-German relations, Essex 2001.

Álvarez de Toledo Alonso, En el país que nunca existió. Diario del último embajador español en la RDA, Barcelona, 1990.

Garton Ash Timothy, Ein Jahrhundert wird abgewählt: Aus den Zentren Mitteleuropas 1980–1990, München 1990.

Ash Garton Timothy, In Europe's name: German and the divided Continent, London 1993.

Bagnato Bruna/Guderzo Massimiliano/Nuti Leopoldo (eds.), Nuove questioni di Storia delle relazioni internazionali, Roma – Bari 2015.

Bajon Philip, Europapolitik „am Abgrund". Die Krise des „leeren Stuhls" 1956–66, Stuttgart 2012.

Bauer Friedrich, Botschafter in zwei deutschen Staaten: Die DDR zwischen Anerkennung und Auflösung (1973–1990): Die aktive Österreichische Neutralitätspolitik, Wien 2006.

Bauerkämper Arnd/Di Palma Francesco (eds.), Bruderparteien jenseits des Eisernen Vorhangs. Die Beziehungen der SED zu den kommunistischen Parteien West- und Südeuropas (1968–1989), Berlin 2011.

Bély Lucien, Les relations internationales en Europe XVII-XVIII siècles, Paris 1992.

Berger Hilge/Ritschl Albrecht, Die Rekonstruktion der Arbeitsabteilung in Europa: Eine neue Sicht des Marshallplans in Deutschland 1947–1951, Berlin – München 1995.

Bernardini Giovanni, Nuova Germania, antichi timori: Stati Uniti, Ostpolitik e sicurezza europea, Bologna 2013.

Bienert C. Michael/Creuzberger Stefan/Hübener Christa/Oppermann Matthias (eds.), Die Berliner Republik: Beiträge zur deutschen Geschichte seit 1990, Berlin 2013.

Bolaffi Angelo, Il sogno tedesco – la nuova Germania e la coscienza europea, Roma 1993.

Bosco Elia, La nuova Germania: Società, istituzioni, cultura politica dopo la riunificazione, Milano 2001.

Bozo Frédéric, Mitterrand, la fin de la guerre froide et la réunification allemande, Paris 2005.

Bozo Frédéric (ed.), Europe and the End of the Cold War: A Reappraisal, London 2008.

Brait Andrea/Gehler Michael, Am Ort des Geschehens in Zeiten des Umbruchs: Lebensgeschichtliche Erinnerungen aus Politik und Ballhausplatzdiplomatie vor und nach 1989 (Reihe Historische Europa-Studien Band 17), Hildesheim 2018.

Busek Erhard/Brix Emil, Mitteleuropa revisited. Warum Europas Zukunft in Mitteleuropa entschieden wird, Wien 2018.

Bussière Eric/Schirmann Sylvain, Economies nationales et intégration européenne, Stuttgart 2014.

Burkhardt Armini/Fritzsche K. Peter (eds), Sprache im Umbruch: Politischer Sprachwandel von "Wende" und "Vereinigung", Berlin 1995.

Craveri Piero, La Repubblica dal 1958 al 1992, Milano 1996.

Craveri Piero/Varsori Antonio (eds.), L'Italia nella costruzione europea. Un bilancio storico (1957–2007), Milano 2009.

Cristin Renato (ed.), Vie Parallele/Parallele Wege, Italien in Geschichte und Gegenwart Band 23, Frankfurt am Main 2005.

Colarizi Simona/Craveri Paolo/Pons Simone (eds.), Gli Anni Ottanta come Storia, Soveria Mannelli 2004.

Comi Anna/Pontzen Alexandra, Italien in Deutschland/Deutschland in Italien. Die deutsch-italienischen Wechselbeziehungen in der Belletristik des 20. Jahrhunderts, Berlin 1999.

D'Agostini M.E. Tullio, Mitteleuropa storiografia e scrittura (atti del convegno di studi- Parma 18–20 aprile 1985), Parma 1987.

De Marchi Bruna/Delli Zotti Giovanni, Cooperazione regionale nell'area alpina, Milano 1985.

Di Maio Tiziana, Alcide de Gasperi e Konrad Adenauer. Tra superamento del passato e integrazione europea (1945–1954), Torino 2004.

Di Nolfo Ennio, La politica estera italiana negli anni di Craxi, Milano 2007.

Di Nolfo Ennio, La politica estera italiana negli anni Ottanta, Manduria 2003.

D'Ovidio Francesco Lefebvre/Micheletta Luca (eds.), Giulio Andreotti e l'Europa, Roma 2017.

Dürkop Olivier/Gehler Michael, In Verantwortung: Hans Modrow und der deutsche Umbruch 1989/1990, Innsbruck – Wien – Bozen 2018.

Elvert Jürgen, Mitteleuropa! Deutsche Pläne zur europäischen Neuordnung (1918–1945), Stuttgart 1999.

Engel A. Jeffrey, The Fall of the Berlin Wall, Oxford 2009.

Favier Pierre/Martin Roland Michel, La décennie Mitterrand vol I: «Les ruptures» (1981–1984), Paris 1990.

Favier Pierre/Martin Roland Michel, La décennie Mitterrand vol II: «Les épreuves» (1984–1988), Paris 1991.

Favier Pierre/Martin Roland Michel, La décennie Mitterrand vol III: «Les défis» (1988–1991), Paris 1999.

Gorodetsky Gabriel, Soviet Foreign Policy 1917–1991, Tel-Aviv University 1994.

Garton Ash Timothy, Ein Jahrhundert wird abgewählt: Aus den Zentren Mitteleuropas 1980–1990, München – Wien 1990.

Garton Ash Timothy, We are the People: The Revolutions of '89 witnessed in Warsaw, Budapest, Berlin and Prague, Cambridge 1990.

Gehler Michael, Österreichs Außenpolitik der Zweiten Republik Band 1 und 2, Innsbruck 2005.

Gehler Michael, Modellfall für Deutschland? Die Österreichlösung mit Staatsvertrag und Neutralität 1945–1955, Innsbruck 2007.

Gehler Michael, Tirol im 20. Jahrhundert: Vom Kronland zum Europaregion, Innsbruck 2009.

Gehler Michael, Deutschland: Von der Teilung zur Einigung 1945 bis heute, Wien – Köln – Weimar 2010.

Gehler Michael, Le tre Germanie: Germania Est, Germania Ovest e Repubblica di Berlino (traduzione Sara Quarantani), Bologna 2011.

Gehler Michael/Guiotto Maddalena, Italien Österreich und die Bundesrepublik Deutschland in Europa/Italy Austria and the Federal Republic of Germany. Ein Dreiecksverhältnis in seinen wechselseitigen Beziehungen und Wahrnehmungen von 1945/49 bis zur Gegenwart/A Triangle Relationship: Mutual Relations and Perceptions from 1945/49 to the Present, (Institut für Geschichte der Universität Hildesheim, Arbeitskreis Europäische Integration, Historische Forschungen, Veröffentlichungen 8), Wien – Köln – Weimar 2012.

Gehler Michael/Luif Paul/Vyslonzil Elisabeth, Die Dimensionen Mitteleuropa in der Europäischen Union: Geschichte und Gegenwart (Reihe Europa Studien), Hildesheim 2015.

Gehler Michael/Gonschor Markus/Meyer Hinnerk/Schönner Johannes, Mitgestalter Europas. Transnationalismus und Parteiennetzwerke europäischer Christdemokraten und Konservativer in historischer Erfahrung, St. Augustin – Berlin 2013.

Geppert Dominik, Thatchers konservative Revolution. Der Richtungswandel der britischen Tories (1975–1979), München 2002.

Guasconi Maria Eleonora, L'Europa tra continuità e cambiamento. Il vertice dell'Aja del 1969 e il rilancio della costruzione europea, Firenze 2004.

Guérin Sendelbach Valérie, Frankreich und das vereinigte Deutschland: Interessen und Perzeptionen im Spannungsfeld, Berlin 1999.

Ginsborg Paul, L'Italia del tempo presente. Famiglia, società civile, Stato 1980–1996, Torino 1998.

Golfari Cesare, Cossiga due Forlani uno. Gli anni del preambolo, Varese 1982.

Gonschor Markus, Politik der Feder. Die Vereinigten Staaten und die Bundesrepublik Deutschland 1945/1949 bis 1990 in Spiegel der Erinnerungen von US-Präsidenten und Bundeskanzlern (Reihe Historische Europa Studien Band 19), Hildesheim 2017.

Grosser Pierre, L'année où le monde a basculé, Paris 2009.

Gruner Wolf, Die deutsche Frage in Europa 1800–1990, München 1993.

Haftendorn Helga, Sicherheit und Stabilität: Außenbeziehungen der Bundesrepublik zwischen Ölkrise und NATO-Doppelbeschluss, München 1986.

Hancock M. Donald/Welsh Helga A. (eds.), German Unification: Process and Outcomes, San Francisco 1994.

Hausmann Friederike/Schmidt Helmut, Die Deutschen und ihre Nachbarn: Italien, München 1999.

Herberg Dieter/Steffens Doris/Tellenbach Elke, Schlüsselwörter der Wendezeit: Wörterbuch zum öffentlichen Sprachgebrauch 1989/1990 (Schriften des Instituts für deutsche Sprache), Berlin 1997.

Hill Christopher, National foreign policies and European political cooperation, London 1983.

Hill Christopher/Wong Reuben (eds.), National Foreign Policies and European Political Cooperation, London 2011.

Himmler Normann, Zwischen Macht und Mittelmaß: Großbritanniens Außenpolitik und das Ende des Kalten Krieges. Akteure, Interesse und Entscheidungsprozesse der britischen Regierung 1989–1990, Berlin 2001.

Indelicato Alberto, Martello e compasso. Vita, agonia e morte della Germania comunista, Milano – Trento 1999.

Jansen Thomas, Die Entstehung einer europäischen Partei: Vorgeschichte, Gründung und Entwicklung, Bonn 1996.

Johnson R. Lonnie, Central Europe. Enemies, Neighbors, Friends, Oxford – New York 1996.

Kaiser Wolfram/Gehler Michael/Wohnout Helmut (eds.), Christdemokratie in Europa, Wien 2001.

Katzenstein Peter, Mitteleuropa between Europe and Germany, Oxford 1997.

Kinkel Klaus, (ed.), In der Verantwortung: Hans-Dietrich Genscher zum Siebzigsten, Berlin 1997.

Korte Karl-Rudolf, Deutschlandpolitik in Helmut Kohls Kanzlerschaft. Entscheidungsprozeß und Regierungsstil 1981–1989, Geschichte der deutschen Einheit Band I, Stuttgart 1998.

Knipping Franz/Schönwald Matthias, Aufbruch zum Europa der zweiten Generation. Die europäische Einigung 1969–1984, Trier 2004.

Kuntz Eva Sabine, Konstanz und Wandel von Stereotypen: Deutschlandbilder in der italienischen Presse nach dem Zweiten Weltkrieg, Frankfurt am Main 1997.

Küsters Hanns Jürgen (ed.), Deutsche Europapolitik Christlicher Demokraten: Von Konrad Adenauer bis Angela Merkel (1945–2013), Düsseldorf 2013.

Lappenküper Ulrich, Mitterrand und Deutschland. Die enträtselte Sphinx, München 2011.

Laursen Johnny (ed.), The Institutions and Dynamics of the European Community 1973–1983, Baden-Baden 2014.

Lehmann Ines, Die deutsche Vereinigung von außen gesehen: Angst Bedenken und Erwartungen in der ausländischen Presse (BAND II: Die Presse Dänemarks, der Niederlande, Belgiens, Italiens, Portugals uns Spaniens und jüdische Reaktionen), Frankfurt am Main 1997.

Libardi Massimo/Fernandi Orlando, Le definizioni storiografiche della Mitteleuropa, Levico Terme 2000.

Longerich Peter, Was ist des Deutschen Vaterland?, München 1990.

Lundestad Geir, The United States and Western Europe since 1945: From "Empire" by invitation to Transatlantic Drift, Oxford 2003.

Lunzer Renate, Triest. Eine italienisch-österreichische Dialektik, Klagenfurt 2002.

Luks Leonid, Katholizismus und politische Macht im kommunistischen Polen 1945–1989. Die Anatomie einer Befreiung, Köln – Weimar – Wien 1993.

Martens Stephan, La politique à l'est de la République d'Allemagne depuis 1949 entre mythe et réalité, Paris 1998.

Mayeur Jean-Marie, Pio XII e i movimenti cattolici in Europa, Bari – Roma 1984.

McCarthy Patrick (ed.), France-Germany 1983–1993: The Struggle to cooperate, London 1993.

Menyesch Dieter/Manac'h Bérénice, France-Allemagne Deutschland-Frankreich Rélations internationales et interdépendence bilatérale 1963–1982, Münich 1980.

Ménudier Henri, Le couple franco-allemand en Europe, Paris 1993.

Ménudier Henri, Das Deutschlandbild der Franzosen in den siebziger Jahren. Gesammelte Aufsätze, Bonn 1981.

Merkl Peter, German Unification in the European context, Pennsylvania 1993.

Monzali Luciano, Giulio Andreotti e le relazioni italo-austriache 1972–1992, Merano 2016.

Morgan Roger/Bray Caroline, Partners and Rivals in Western Europe: Britain, France and Germany, Dorset 1996.

Moritsch Andreas, Alpe Adria: Zur Geschichte einer Region, Klagenfurt 2001.

Mueller Wolfgang/Gehler Michael/Suppan Arnold (eds.), *The Revolutions of 1989. A Handbook (*Österreichische Akademie der Wissenschaften/Philosophische Historische Klasse/Institut für Neuzeit- und Zeitgeschichtsforschung), Wien 2015.

Müller Wolfgang/Di Palma Francesco, Kommunismus und Europa. Europapolitik und –vorstellungen bei den europäischen kommunistischen Parteien, Paderborn 2016.

Oplatka Andreas, Der erste Riss in der Mauer. September 1989: Ungarn öffnet die Grenze, Wien 2009.

Pallaver Günther/Gehler Michael (eds.), Universität Innsbruck und Nationalismus: Innsbruck 1904 und der Sturm auf die italienische Rechtsfakultät (Fondazione Museo Storico del Trentino), Trento 2013.

Pfetsch R. Frank, Die Außenpolitik der Bundesrepublik 1949–1992, Frankfurt am Main 1993.

Pfeil Ulrich (ed.), Allemagne 1974–1990 : De l'Ostpolitik à la Réunification, Lille 2009.

Picq Jean, Une histoire de l'Etat en Europe : Pouvoir, justice et droit du Moyen Age à nos jours, Paris 2009.

Pöthig Charis, Italien und die DDR: Die politischen ökonomischen und kulturellen Beziehungen von 1949 bis 1980, Frankfurt am Main 2000.

Pons Silvio, Berlinguer e la fine del comunismo, Torino 2006.

Poropat Liviana, Alpe Adria e iniziativa centro-europea: Cooperazione nell'Alpe Adria e nell'area danubiana, Napoli 1993.

Rey Marie-Pierre, Le dilemme russe, la Russie et l'Europe occidentale d'Ivan le Terrible à Boris Eltsine, Paris 2002.

Rieder Maximiliane, Deutsch-italienische Wirtschaftsbeziehungen. Kontinuitäten und Brüche 1936–1957, Frankfurt am Main 2003.

Rödder Andreas, Deutschland einig Vaterland: Die Geschichte der Wiedervereinigung, München 2009.

Rödder Andreas, Geschichte der deutschen Wiedervereinigung, München 2011.

Röhrlich Elisabeth, Kreiskys Außenpolitik: Zwischen österreichischer Identität und internationalem Programm, Wien 2008.

Romano Angela, From Détente in Europe to European Détente: How the West shaped the Helsinki CSCE, Frankfurt am Main 2009.

Romeo Giuseppe, La politica estera italiana nell'era Andreotti (1972–1992), Soveria Mannelli 2000.

Romero Federico, Emigrazione e Integrazione 1945–1973, Roma – Bari 1991.

Rosengarten Ulrich, Die Genscher-Colombo Initiative: Baustein für die Europäische Union, Baden-Baden 2008.

Rouger Werner, Schwierige Nachbarschaft am Rhein, Bonn 1998.

Rusconi Gian Enrico, Capire la Germania: Un diario ragionato sulla questione tedesca, Bologna 1990.

Rusconi Gian Enrico, Germania Italia Europa: Dallo stato di potenza alla potenza civile, Torino 2003.

Rusconi Gian Enrico/Woller Hans, Italia e Germania 1945–2000: la costruzione dell'Europa, Bologna 2005.

Sanchez Muñoz Antonio, Von der Franco-Diktatur zur Demokratie: die Tätigkeit der Friedrich-Ebert-Stiftung in Spanien, Berlin 2013.

Saxonberg Steven, The Fall. A comparative Study of the End of Communism in Czechoslovachia, East Germany, Ungary and Poland, Amsterdam 2001.

Schabert Tilo, Mitterrand et la réunification allemande : Une histoire secrète (1981–1995), Paris 2005.

Schabert Tilo, Wie Weltgeschichte gemacht wird: Frankreich und die Deutsche Einheit, Stuttgart 2002.

Schlemmer Thomas, Aufbruch Krise und Erneuerung. Die Christlich-Soziale Union 1945 bis 1955, Stuttgart 1998.

Schönner Johannes/Meyer Hinnerk/Gonschor Marcus/Gehler Michael (eds.), Mitgestalter Europas: Transnationalismus und Parteinetzwerke europäischer Christdemokraten und Konservativer in historischer Erfahrung, Sankt Augustin 2013.

Schmidt-Bergmann Hans-Georg, Zwischen Kontinuität und Rekonstruktion. Kulturtransfer zwischen Deutschland und Italien nach 1945 (Reihe der Villa Vigoni), Tübingen 1998.

Scholz Günther/Süsskind Martin, Die Bundespräsidenten. Von Theodor Heuss bis Johannes Rau, Stuttgart – München 2003.

Schotters Frederike, Frankreich und das Ende des Kalten Krieges: Gefühlsstrategien der équipe Mitterrand 1981–1990 (Studien zur Internationalen Geschichte 44), Berlin – München 2019.

Schroeter Sabina, Die Sprache der DDR im Spiegel der Literatur: Studien zum DDR-typischen Wortschatz, Berlin 1994.

Schwabe Klaus, Weltmacht und Weltordnung. Amerikanische Außenpolitik von 1989 bis zur Gegenwart. Eine Jahrhundertgeschichte, Paderborn 2007.

Sebestyen Victor, Revolutions 1989. The Fall of the Soviet Empire, London 1999.

Service Robert, The End of the Cold War: 1985–1991, London 2015.

Sodaro Michael, Moscow, Germany and the West from Khrushchev to Gorbachev, London 1991.

Soutou Georges-Henri, L'alliance incertaine : les rapports politico-stratégiques franco-allemands 1954–1996, Paris 1996.

Staniszkis Jadwiga, Poland's Self-Limiting Revolution, Princeton 1984.

Steininger Rolf, Der Kalte Krieg, Frankfurt am Main 2006.

Steininger Rolf, Deutschland und die USA. Vom Zweiten Weltkrieg bis zur Gegenwart, Reinbeck – München 2014.

Suszycki Andrzej Marcin, Italienische Osteuropapolitik 1989–2000, Münster – Hamburg – London 2003.

Tacito Cornelio, La Germania, Palermo 1993.

Tavani Sara, Non dovrà essere un'altra Yalta. L'Ostpolitik italiana degli anni Sessanta e la ricerca di un nuovo ordine europeo, Padova 2017.

Tismăneanu Vladimir, The Revolutions of 1989 (Re-writing Histories), London 1999.

Tosi Luciano, Politica ed Economia nelle Relazioni Internazionali dell'Italia del Secondo Dopoguerra, Roma 2002.

Varsori Antonio, L'Italia e la fine della guerra fredda: La politica estera dei governi Andreotti (1989–1992), Bologna 2013.

Venturi Alfredo, Il Novecento visto da Berlino: Il futuro è passato di qui, Milano 2004.

Von Achenbach Richard Meyer, Gedanken über eine konstruktive deutsche Ostpolitik: Eine unterdrückte Denkschrift aus dem Jahr 1953, Frankfurt am Main 1986.

Von Plato Alexander, Die Vereinigung Deutschland. Ein weltpolitisches Machtspiel: Bush, Kohl, Gorbatschow und die geheimen Moskauer Protokolle, Bonn 2003.

Vordermann Christian, Deutschland-Italien 1949–1961: Die diplomatischen Beziehungen, Geschichte und Gegenwart III, Frankfurt am Main 1994.

Wallander Celeste A., Mortal friends, Best enemies: German-Russian, Cooperation after the Cold War, London 1999.

Weinachter Michèle, Valéry Giscard d'Estaing et l'Allemagne. Le double rêve inachevé, Paris 2004.

Weinachter Michèle, L'Est et l'Ouest face à la chute du Mur. Questions de perspectives, Cergy Pontoise 2013.

Weidenfeld Werner/Wagner M. Peter/Bruck Elke, Geschichte der deutschen Einheit. Außenpolitik für die deutsche Einheit: die Entscheidungsjahre 1989/1990, Stuttgart 1999.

Weidenfeld Werner/Wessels Wolfgang (eds.), Europa von A-Z. Taschenbuch der europäischen Integration, Bonn 2000.

Weisenfeld Ernst, Welches Deutschland soll es sein? Frankreich und die deutsche Einheit, München 1986.

Woller Hans/Rusconi Gian Enrico/Schlemmer Thomas (eds.), Schleichende Entfremdung? Deutschland und Italien nach dem Mauerfall, München 2009.

Zamperini Valentina, Uno più due può fare tre se il partito lo vuole! La Repubblica Democratica tedesca tra Mosca e Bonn 1971–1985, Firenze 2014.

Zelikow Philip/Rice Condoleezza, Germany unified and Europe transformed, Massachusetts – London – Cambridge 1996.

ARTICLES, ESSAYS AND CONFERENCE PAPERS:

Arnold Hans, I rapporti italo-tedeschi dopo la svolta europea, in: *Affari esteri* (rivista trimestrale) n. 91 (1991), pp. 429–437.

Aschmann Birgit, Mein Freund Felipe – Spanien und die deutsche Einheit, in: Michael Gehler/Maximilian Graf, Europa und die deutsche Einheit. Beobachtungen, Entscheidungen und Folgen, Göttingen 2017, pp. 639–662.

Bachetti Fausto, Considerazioni sulla politica estera italiana, in: *Affari esteri* (rivista trimestrale) n. 100 (1993), pp. 747–761.

Baiocchi Giovanni, L'opzione danubiana, in: *"30 giorni" mensile internazionale diretto da Giulio Andreotti 1993–2012* n. 6 (2000), sezione approfondimenti.

Bolaffi Angelo, Eine besondere Beziehung, in: *Zeitschrift für Kulturaustausch* 2/2000, IFA Institut für Auslandbeziehungen, pp. 20–22.

Bozo Frédéric, Trois Allemagne deux Europe et la France, in: *Politique étrangère* n. 55–1 (1990), pp. 119–138.

Bozo Frédéric, Mitterrand's France the end of the Cold War and German unification: A Reappraisal, in: *Cold War History* 7:4 (2007), pp. 455–478.

Bozo Frédéric, The failure of a Grand Design: Mitterand's European Confederation 1989–1991, in: *Contemporary European History*, vol. 17 special issue 03 (2008), pp. 391–412.

Braithwaite Rodric, Gorbachev and Thatcher, in: *Journal of European Integration History* vol.16 (2010), pp. 31–44.

Brandt Harm-Hinrich, Von Bruck zu Naumann: „Mitteleuropa" in der Zeit der Pauluskirche und des Ersten Weltkrieges, in: Michael Gehler/F. Rainer Schmidt/Harm-Heinrich Brandt/Rolf Steininger (eds.), Ungleiche Partner?

Österreich und Deutschland im 19. und 20. Jahrhundert, Stuttgart 1996, pp. 315–352.

Brechenmacher Thomas, „Österreich steht außer Deutschland, aber es gehört zu Deutschland." Aspekte der Bewertung des Faktors Österreichs in der deutschen Historiographie, in Michael Gehler/F. Rainer Schmidt/Harm-Heinrich Brandt/Rolf Steininger (eds.), Ungleiche Partner? Österreich und Deutschland im 19. und 20. Jahrhundert, Stuttgart 1996, pp. 31–53.

Brown Archie, Margaret Thatcher and the End of the Cold War, in: *Journal of European Integration History*, vol.16 (2010), pp.17–30.

Bongiovanni Bruno, Gli intellettuali, la cultura i miti del dopoguerra, in: Giovanni Sabbatucci/Vittorio Vidotto (eds.), Storia d'Italia, Bari 2004.

Busek Erhard, Besinnung auf Mitteleuropa, in: *Europäische Rundschau* 2 (1985), pp. 3–13.

Calamia Pietro, Il Consiglio europeo di Milano (28–29 giugno 1985), in: *Rivista di Studi di politica internazionale* vol.79 n.3 (2012), pp. 353–360.

Calamia Pietro, La svolta europea del 1985. Il ruolo dell'Italia, in: *Rivista di studi politici internazionali* vol.79 n.1 (2012), pp. 18–20.

Calamia Pietro, Piccola cronaca di un viaggio a Mosca (gennaio-febbraio 1969), in: *Rivista di Studi politici internazionali* vol. 78 n.3 (2011), p. 345–350.

Cangelosi Rocco Antonio, Dal Progetto di Trattato Spinelli all'Atto Unico Europeo. Cronaca di una riforma mancata, in: *Quaderni di Affari Sociali Internazionali*, Milano 1986.

Cappellin Riccardo, Alpe Adria: Opportunità e prospettive, in: *Relazioni Internazionali* n.5 (1989), pp. 59–66.

Cuccia Deborah, Italien und die deutsche Einigung 1989–1990, in: Michael Gehler/Maximilian Graf, Europa und die deutsche Einheit. Beobachtungen, Entscheidungen und Folgen, Göttingen 2017, pp. 677–700.

Cuccia Deborah, The Genscher-Colombo Plan: A forgotten page in the European Integration History, in: *Journal of European Integration History* vol. 24 (2018), pp. 59–78.

De Michelis Gianni, Le priorità italiane sulla scena internazionale, in: *Relazioni Internazionali*, n.8 (1989), pp. 81–90.

De Michelis Gianni, La vera storia di Maastricht, in: *Limes* n.3 (1996), pp. 137–144.

Di Nolfo Ennio, Il quadrangolare Mitteleuropeo, in: *Relazioni internazionali* (1990), pp. 93–99.

Di Palma Francesco, Eurocommunism and the SED: A contradictory relationship, in: *Journal of European Integration History* vol. 20 (2014), pp. 219–232.

Deutinger Stephan, Hanns Seidel (1901–1961), in: *Zeitgeschichte in Lebensbildern. Aus dem deutschen Katholizismus des 19. und 20. Jahrhunderts*, Bd.11 (2004), pp. 160–174.

D'Ottavio Gabriele, 1989 oder das Ende der "parallelen Geschichte" Deutschlands und Italiens? in: *Geschichte und Wissenschaft in Unterricht* 67 n.1/2 (2016), pp. 39–57.

Fagiolo Silvio, L'Europa di Adenauer, in: *Ventunesimo Secolo* vol.6 n.14 (2007), pp. 83–102.

Ferraris Luigi Vittorio, Il rilancio delle relazioni italo-tedesche a villa Dora-Pamphili (12 maggio 1988), in: *Affari esteri rivista trimestrale* n.80 (1988), pp. 539–556.

Ferraris Luigi Vittorio, Kultur und Politik in den deutsch-italienischen Beziehungen, in: *Aus Politik und Zeitgeschichte* B.39, 1998, pp. 24–30.

Ferraris Luigi Vittorio, L'unità della Germania e l'unità dell'Europa, in: *Affari esteri rivista trimestrale* n.85 (1990), pp. 19–31.

Ferraris Luigi Vittorio, L'unificazione della Germania, in: *Affari esteri rivista trimestrale* n.91 (1991), pp. 438–450.

Ferraris Luigi Vittorio, Un'opzione russa per la Germania?, in: *Affari esteri rivista trimestrale* n.107 (1995), pp. 504–520.

Ferraris Luigi Vittorio, Le relazioni tra Italia e Germania: eredità e prospettive, in: *EUROPA EUROPAE/Cespeco* 2–3 (1995), pp. 73–90.

Ferraris Luigi Vittorio, Un'associazione utile: l'iniziativa centro-europea, in: *Affari esteri rivista trimestrale* n.132 (2001), pp. 751–758.

Ferrera Maurizio/Regelsberger Elfriede, Il foro di dialogo italo-tedesco, in: *Relazioni internazionali* n.7 (1989), pp. 61–70.

Gehler Michael, Österreich, die Bundesrepublik und die deutsche Frage 1945/49–1955. Zur Geschichte der gegenseitigen Wahrnehmungen zwischen Abhängigkeit und gemeinsamen Interessen, in: Michael Gehler/F. Rainer Schmidt/Harm-Heinrich Brandt/Rolf Steininger (eds.), Ungleiche Partner? Österreich und Deutschland im 19. und 20. Jahrhundert, Stuttgart 1996, pp. 535–580.

Gehler Michael, Die Umsturzbewegungen 1989 in Mittel und Osteuropa, in: *Aus Politik und Zeitgeschichte* B 41–42 (2004), pp. 36–46.

Gehler Michael, Il contesto politico della monarchia asburgica del 1904, in: *Archivio Trentino* rivista di studi sull'età moderna e contemporanea del museo storico di Trento (2009), pp. 13–45.

Gehler Michael, Paving Austria's Way to Brussels: Chancellor Vranitzky (1986–1997) a Banker, Social Democrat, and Pragmatic European Leader, in: *Journal of European Integration History* vol.18 (2012), pp. 159–182.

Gehler Michael, »Zentralmacht Europas«? Die Berliner Republik außer- und innerhalb der Europäischen Union, in: Michael C. Bienert/Stefan

Creuzberger/Kristina Hübener/Matthias Oppermann (eds.), Die Berliner Republik. Beiträge zur deutschen Zeitgeschichte seit 1990, Berlin – Brandenburg 2013, pp. 91–122.

Gehler Michael, Bonn – Budapest – Wien: Das deutsch-österreichisch-ungarische Zusammenspiel als Katalysator für die Erosion des SED-Regimes 1989–
1990, in: Andrea Brait/Michael Gehler (eds.), Grenzöffnung 1989: Innen und
Außenperspektiven und die Folgen für Österreich [Schriftenreihe des Forschungsinstituts für politisch-historische Studien der Dr.-Wilfried-Haslauer-
Bibliothek Salzburg], Wien – Köln – Weimar 2014, pp. 135–162.

Gehler Michael, „Friedliche Revolutionen" und die Vereinigung Deutschlands:
Interne und externe Faktoren im Zusammenspiel 1989/90, in: Hans-Joachim
Veen/Franz-Josef Schlichting/Manuel Leppert (eds.), Von der Urkatastrophe
Europas bis zur Wiedervereinigung Deutschlands: Etappen deutscher Ge-
schichte 1914 bis 1990, Weimar 2014, pp.111–144.

Gehler Michael, The Revolutions in Central and South Eastern Europe. Austrian
Perceptions and International Reactions 1989–90, in: Wilfried Loth /Nicolae
Paun (eds.), Disintegration and Integration in East-Central Europe 1919-post
1989 [publications of the European Union Liaison Committee of Historians
16], Baden-Baden 2014, pp. 186–204.

Gehler Michael, 1989 Ambivalent Revolutions with different Backgrounds and
Consequences, in: Wolfgang Mueller/Michael Gehler/Arnold Suppan (eds.),
The Revolutions of 1989. A Handbook [Österreichische Akademie der Wis-
senschaften/Philosophische Historische Klasse/Institut für Neuzeit- und Zeit-
geschichtsforschung], Wien 2015, pp. 587–603.

Gehler Michael, Austria the Revolutions and the Unification of Germany, in:
Wolfgang Mueller/Michael Gehler/Arnold Suppan (eds.), The Revolutions of
1989. A Handbook [Österreichische Akademie der Wissenschaften/Philoso-
phische Historische Klasse/Institut für Neuzeit- und Zeitgeschichtsfor-
schung], Wien 2015, pp. 437–466.

Gehler Michael, "Europe", Europeanizations and their Meaning for European Integration History, in: Journal of European Integration History vol. 22 (2016),
pp. 141–174.

Gehler Michael, Mehr Europäisierung in Umbruchzeiten? Die europäische politische Zusammenarbeit (EPZ) und die revolutionären Ereignisse in Mittel-,
Ost- und Südosteuropa Ende der 1980er Jahre, in: Gabriele Clemens (ed.),
Limits of Europeanization [Studien zur modernen Geschichte], Stuttgart
2017, pp. 77–106.

Gehler Michael, Different Paths towards Europe? Germany, Italy and Austria
1945–2009, in: Günther Pallaver/Michael Gehler/Maurizio Cau (eds.), Populism, Populists and the Crisis of Political Parties. A Comparison of Italy, Austria and Germany 1990–2015, Berlin – Bologna 2017, pp. 17–44.

Gehler Michael, Da Bonn a Berlino, la transizione incompiuta, in: *Limes* (12) 2018.

Gehler Michael, The Fall of the Iron Curtain. Causes, Structures, Timelines and Effects, in: Heinz Fischer/Andreas Huber/Stephan Neuhäuser, The Republic of Austria 1918–2018. Milestones and Turning Points, Wien 2018, pp. 185–200.

Geppert Dominik, Isolation oder Einvernehmen? Großbritannien und die deutsche Einheit 1989–1990, in: *Geschichte und Wissenschaft in Unterricht* 67 n.1/2 (2016), pp. 5–22.

Graf Maximilian, Österreich und das Ende der DDR, in: Michael Gehler/Maximilian Graf, Europa und die deutsche Einheit. Beobachtungen, Entscheidungen und Folgen, Göttingen 2017, pp. 259–294.

Görtemaker Manfred, Angela Merkel und Romano Prodi: Antithesis of Populism?, in: Günther Pallaver/Michael Gehler/Maurizio Cau, Populism, Populists and the Crisis of Political Parties. A Comparison of Italy, Austria and Germany 1990–2015, Berlin – Bologna 2017, pp. 229–234.

Guasconi Maria Eleonora, Il Piano Genscher-Colombo, in: Lara Piccardo (ed.), L'Italia e l'Europa negli anni Ottanta. Storia, politica, cultura, Milano 2015, pp. 33–46.

Guidi Marcello, Una consonanza esemplare, in: *Relazioni internazionali* n.7 (1989), pp. 71–74.

Guiotto Maddalena/Lill Johannes, Italia-Germania Deutschland-Italien 1948–1958. Riavvicinamenti-Wiederannährungen, Annali dell'Istituto di Storia italo-tedesca Villa Vigoni, Firenze 1997.

Günther Pallaver, Populism in the Mainstream Media. Germany, Austria and Italy in comparison, in: Günther Pallaver/Michael Gehler/Maurizio Cau, Populism, Populists and the Crisis of Political Parties. A Comparison of Italy, Austria and Germany 1990–2015, Berlin – Bologna 2017, pp. 99–122.

Hacker Jens, Michail Gorbatschow und die engere »sozialistische Gemeinschaft«, in: *Aus Politik und Zeitgeschichte* n.19–20 (1990), pp. 30–39.

Hanak Peter, Gab es mitteleuropäische Identität in der Geschichte? in: *Europäische Rundschau* 1986/2.

Hilger Andreas, Die getriebene Großmacht – Moskau und die deutsche Einheit 1989–1990, in: Michael Gehler/Maximilian Graf, Europa und die deutsche Einheit. Beobachtungen, Entscheidungen und Folgen, Göttingen 2017, pp. 117–140.

Hofmann Gunter, Willy Brandt und die europäische Revolution, in: *Blätter für deutsche und internationale Politik* (2001).

Hürter Johannes, Anti-Terrorismus Politik. Ein deutsch-italienischer Vergleich 1969–1982, in: *Vierteljahrshefte für Zeitgeschichte* n. 57, Heft 3 (2009), pp. 329–348.

Klein Yvonne, Obstructive or promoting? British Views on German Unification 1989/1990, in: *German Politics* n. 5 (1996), pp. 404–431.

Kohl Christiane, Rücksicht auf Italien, in: *Zeitschrift für Kulturaustausch* 2 (2000), IFA Institut für Auslandbeziehungen.

Küsters Hanns Jürgen, Helmut Kohl, die CDU und die Wiederherstellung der deutschen Einheit, in: Michael Gehler/Maximilian Graf, Europa und die deutsche Einheit. Beobachtungen, Entscheidungen und Folgen, Göttingen 2017, pp. 27–42.

Lappenküper Ulrich, Prekäres Vertrauen. François Mitterrand und Deutschland seit 1971, in: Reinhild Kreis (ed.), Diplomatie mit Gefühl. Vertrauen, Misstrauen und die Außenpolitik der Bundesrepublik Deutschland (Zeitgeschichte im Gespräch 21), Berlin – München – Boston 2015, pp. 83–96.

Lill Johannes, Die Beziehungen zwischen der DDR und Italien in den fünfziger Jahren, in: Maddalena Guiotto/Johannes Lill, Italia-Germania. Deutschland-Italien 1948–1958. Riavvicinamenti-Wiederannäherungen (Studi Italo Tedeschi), Firenze 1997, pp. 161–210

Ludlow Piers, European Integration in the 1980s: on the Way to Maastricht? in: *Journal of European Integration History* vol. 19 (2013), pp. 11–22.

Maćków Jeryz, Polen im Umbruch: Die Wahlen 1989. Politische Hintergründe, Verlauf, Analyse, in: *Zeitschrift für Parlamentsfragen* 20/4 (1989), pp. 561–580.

Mertens Michael, Die Entstehung des Zehn-Punkte-Programms vom 28. November 1989, in: Heiner Timmermann, Die DDR in Deutschland. Ein Rückblick auf 50 Jahre, Berlin 2001, pp. 17–35.

Missiroli Antonio, La questione tedesca tra storiografia e politica, in: *"Passato e Presente" Rivista di Storia contemporanea* n. 5 (1984), pp. 223–235.

Missiroli Antonio, Italia-Germania: le affinità selettive, in: *Il Mulino Europa* n.2 (1995), pp. 26–40.

Möllemann W. Jürgen, Le basi della politica estera tedesca, in: *Affari esteri rivista trimestrale* n.72 (1986), pp. 433–443.

Nigido Roberto e altri, Italia e Unione Europea e le loro relazioni con la Russia, in: *Dialoghi Diplomatici* n.217 (2015).

Ostermann Christian F., The United States and German Unification, in: Michael Gehler/Maximilian Graf, Europa und die deutsche Einheit. Beobachtungen, Entscheidungen und Folgen, Göttingen 2017, pp.93–116.

Olesen Thorsten Borring/Olesen Niels Wium, Denmark and the German Reunification. Anxious Feelings and the Limitations of Europeanization, in: Michael Gehler/Maximilian Graf, Europa und die deutsche Einheit. Beobachtungen, Entscheidungen und Folgen, Göttingen 2017, pp. 439–466.

Orsina Giovanni, Berlusconi as a Circumstatial Populist, in: Günther Pallaver/Michael Gehler/Maurizio Cau, Populism, Populists and the Crisis of

Political Parties. A Comparison of Italy, Austria and Germany 1990–2015, Berlin – Bologna 2017, pp. 157–180.

Pahl Franz, Die deutsche Frage aus der heutigen italienischen Sicht, in: Hannelore Horn/Siegried Mampel (eds.), Die deutsche Frage aus der heutigen Sicht des Auslandes, Berlin 1997.

Portero Florentino, El nuevo orden europeo y la cuestión alemana, in: *Política Exterior* n.4/14 (1990), pp. 115–124.

Quagliarino Alain, La question allemande dans les relations franco-italiennes au cours de l'année 1955, in: *Storia delle relazioni internazionali* 1–2 (1992), pp. 135–165.

Quagliarino Alain, La question allemande dans les relations franco-italiennes de 1951 à 1954, in: *Mélanges de l'Ecole Française de Rome Italie et Méditerranée* 104 (1992/2), pp. 871–897.

Quagliarino Alain, Les relations italo-allemandes en 1956: Le triomphe des Intérêts, in: *Mélanges de l'Ecole Française de Rome Italie et Méditerranée* 105 (1995), pp. 177–205.

Quagliarino Alain, La nouvelle donne allemande dans les relations franco-italiennes 1949–1951, in: *Revue d'histoire contemporaine* 42–4 (1995), pp. 622–657.

Rau Johannes/Ciampi Carlo Azeglio, L'amicizia italo-tedesca al servizio dell'integrazione europea/Deutschland Italien und die europäische Integration, in: *Humboldt Reden zu Europa*, Deutsche Nationalstiftung, Juni 2003.

Rey Marie-Pierre, L'Europe occidentale dans les représentations politiques et mentales des décideurs soviétiques, in: *Matériaux pour l'histoire de notre temps* n.3 (1993).

Rey Marie-Pierre, L'URSS et l'Europe communautaire, représentations et pratiques, 1957–1991, in: Anne Deighton/Gérard Bossuat (eds.), L'Union européenne, acteur de la sécurité mondiale, Paris 2007, pp. 52–69.

Rey Marie-Pierre, Chancellor Brandt's Ostpolitik, France and the Soviet Union, in: Carol Fink/Berndt Schaefer (eds.), Ostpolitik, 1969–1974, European and Global Responses, Cambridge 2009.

Rey Marie-Pierre, Gorbatchev et la «Maison commune européenne» un retour à l'Europe ?, in: *La Revue Russe* n.38 (2012), pp. 101–111.

Rey Marie-Pierre, La Russie et l'Europe occidentale : Le dilemme russe, in: *Institut d'étude européens - Université catholique de Louvain-documents*n.32 (2013)

Ricciardi Luca, Da Colombo ad Andreotti e Craxi: Spunti di ricerca sulla politica medio-orientale dell'Italia negli anni Ottanta, in: Gianvito Galasso/Federico Imperato/Rosario Milano/Luciano Monzali, Europa e Medio Oriente (1973–1993), Bari 2017.

Ritter Harry, Austria and the Struggle for German Identity, in: *German Studies Review*, Special Issue, 1992, pp. 111–129.

Ruth Friedrich, Legati da comuni interessi, in: *Relazioni internazionali* n.7 (1989), pp. 75–80.

Scarano Federico, Innsbruck e il conflitto per l'università italiana nell'impero asburgico agli albori del Novecento, in: *Intra et Extra Moenia: Sguardi sulla città fra antico e moderno* [a cura di Rossana Cioffi e Giuseppe Pignatelli], Seconda Università di Napoli Dipartimento di Lettere e Beni Culturali (2014), pp. 185–190.

Schmidt-Schweizer Andreas, Die Offnung der ungarischen Westgrenze für die DDR-Bürger im Sommer 1989. Vorgeschichte, Hintergründe und Schlussfolgerungen, in: *Südosteuropa Mitteilungen* 37 (1987) Heft 1, pp. 33–53.

Schotters Frederike, 1984 - François Mitterrand und die Suche nach Auswegen aus dem Kalten Krieg, in: Markus Berhardt/Wolfgang Blösel/Stefan Brakensiek/Benjamin Scheller, Möglichkeitshorizonte. Zur Pluralität von Zukunftserwartungen und Handlungsoptionen in der Geschichte, Frankfurt am Main 2018, pp. 295–318.

Simon Gerhard, Der Umbruch des politischen Systems in der Sowjetunion, in: *Aus Politik und Zeitgeschichte* n.19–20 (1990), pp. 3–15.

Sitzler Katharina, Die Pentagonale aus ungarischer Sicht, in: *Südosteuropa* n.11–12 (1990), pp. 686–708.

Soutou Georges-Henri, Une histoire tourmentée : l'Allemagne unie ou désunie, in: *Questions internationales* n. 54 (mars-avril 2012), pp. 8–21.

Staffelmayr Emil, Die Dynamik der Entwicklung in Europa: Die Pentagonale als Beispiel einer neuen Nachbarschaftspolitik Österreichs, in: *Österreichisches Jahrbuch für Politik* (1990), pp. 711–722.

Stamm Rudolf, Die Pentagonale als Beitrag zu Annäherung in Europa, in: *Europäische Rundschau* Bd.19 n.2 (1991), pp. 35–41.

Steininger Rolf, „…Der Angelegenheit ein paneuropäisches Mäntelchen umhängen…". Das deutsch-österreichische Zollunionsprojekt von 1931, in: Michael Gehler/F. Rainer Schmidt/Harm-Heinrich Brandt/Rolf Steininger (eds.), Ungleiche Partner? Österreich und Deutschland im 19. und 20. Jahrhundert, Stuttgart 1996, pp. 441–479.

Sterpellone Alfonso, L'Europa e la questione tedesca, in: *Affari esteri rivista trimestrale* n. 66 (1985), pp.158–170.

Sucharipa Ernst, Die Pentagonale: eine neue Form regionaler Zusammenarbeit oder mitteleuropäische Nostalgie? in: *Internationale* 5/90 (1990), pp. 28–32.

Tavani Sara, La naissance d'une Ostpolitik de l'Europe de l'Est et de l'Ouest au début des années 1970 comme résultat d'une nouvelle solidarité européenne, in: *L'Europe en formation (revue d'étude sur la construction européenne et le fédéralisme)* n.353–354, 2009/3–4, pp. 75–91.

Tavani Sara, Alle origini dell'Ostpolitik italiana: l'evoluzione della politica orientale dell'Italia negli anni del «centrosinistra organico» di Aldo Moro, in: Renato Moro/Daniele Mezzana (eds), Una Vita un Paese: Aldo Moro e l'Italia del Novecento, Soveria Mannelli 2014, pp. 467–487.

Thiemeyer Guido, Economic Models in France and Germany and the Debates on the Maastricht Treaty, in: *Journal of European Integration History* vol. 19 (2013), pp. 85–104.

Valsalice Luigi, La Germania: è un problema per l'Europa?, in: *Affari esteri rivista trimestrale* n.73 (1987), pp. 65–86.

Varsori Antonio, La classe politique italienne et le couple franco-allemand, in: *Revue d'Allemagne et des pays de langue allemande* n.2 (april-juin 1997), pp. 243–257.

Varsori Antonio, The Andreotti Governments and the Maastricht Treaty: Between European Hopes and Domestic Constraints, in: *Journal of European Integration History* vol. 19 (2013), pp. 23–44.

Wilking Susanne, Das Italienbild in der bundesdeutschen Presse der 70er und 80er Jahre, in: Susanne Wilking (ed.), Deutsche und italienische Europapolitik-historische Grundlagen und aktuelle Fragen, Ergebnisse des deutsch-italienischen Gesprächsforums, Bonn, pp. 39–70.

Wilkens Andreas, L'Europe et la première crise monétaire, in: *Journal of European Integration History* vol. 18 (2012), pp. 221–244.

ITALIAN NEWSPAPERS:

La Stampa
Il Corriere della Sera
La Repubblica
L'Unità
Il Popolo

GERMAN NEWSPAPERS/MAGAZINES:

Frankfurter Allgemeine
Süddeutsche Zeitung
Die Welt
Die Zeit
Der Spiegel

STATISTICS:

Eurobarometer n. 32, 33, 34 (November 1989/December 1990)
Institut für Demoskopie Allensbach (September/November 1989)
USIA survey (November 1989)

Demopolis Survey: "La Caduta del Muro di Berlino venticinque anni dopo in Italia",

ISTAT, archivio storico, dati sul commercio estero relativi al periodo 1979–1990, https://www.coeweb.istat.it/

Oral Sources

INTERVIEWS WITH THE AUTHOR:

Alfredo Venturi (born 1939, Journalist)
-Correspondent in Bonn, Italian newspaper *La Stampa* (1986–1990)
-Correspondent in Bonn, Italian newspaper *Corriere della Sera* (1990–1996)
Interview in Arezzo, 3.2.2016

Luigi Guidobono Cavalchini (born 4 February 1934, Former Italian Ambassador)
-At the Foreign Ministry Cabinet (1979–1980)
-Vice-Head of the Foreign Ministry Cabinet (1980–1985)
-Head of the Foreign Ministry Cabinet (1985–1989)
-Secretary-General of the Presidency of the Council of Ministries (1989–1991)
Interview in Rome, 5.2.2016

Alessandro Quaroni (born 1934, Former Italian Ambassador)
-Ambassador to Vienna (1987–1992)
Interview in Rome, 12.2.2016

Alberto Indelicato[2] (born 25 July 1930, Former Italian Ambassador)
-Ambassador to Pankow DDR (1987–1990)

Roberto Nigido (born 17 October 1941, Former Italian Ambassador)
-First Counsellor and later Minister Counsellor at the Italian Permanent Representation in Brussels (1984–1988)
-In charge of the European section at the General Direction for Economic Affairs, Foreign Ministry (1988–1993)
Interview in Rome, 2.3.2016

Ezio Mauro (born 24 October 1948, Journalist)
-Correspondent in Moscow, Italian newspaper *Repubblica* (1988–1990)
-Co-director and then director, Italian newspaper *La Stampa* (1990–1996)
Interview in Rome, 11.3.2016

---

[2] Due to personal reasons a face-to face interview was not possible. The Ambassador kindly agreed to an exchange of messages.

Ludovico Ortona (born 1942, Former Italian Ambassador)
-Advisor and Head of the Press Office of Italian Head of State Cossiga (1985–1993)
Interview in Rome, 22.3.2016

Leonardo Visconti di Modrone (born 3 February 1947, Former Italian Ambassador)
-At the Presidency of the Council of Ministries (1981–1988)
Office of the diplomatic Counsellor (1981–1982)
Diplomatic Counsellor of the *presidente del Consiglio* (1983–1988)
-First Counsellor at the Embassy in London (1988–1992)
-Director of Villa Vigoni (2012–2017)
Interview in Rome, 12.5.2016

Luigi Vittorio Ferraris (born 20 March 1928 – death 13 November 2018, Former Italian Ambassador)
-Ambassador to Bonn (1980–1987)
Interview in Rome, 11.5.2016

Rudolf Seiters (born 13 October 1937, German politician)
-Chef des Bundeskanzleramtes (1989–1991)
Interview in Hildesheim, 30.6.2016

Pietro Calamia (born October 1930, Former Italian Ambassador)
-Counsellor Minister at the Italian Permanent Representation in Brussels (1978–1980)
-Ambassador at the Italian Permanent Representation in Brussels (1984–1990)
Interview in Rome, 29.9.2016

Ferdinando Salleo (born 2 October 1936, Former Italian Ambassador)
-Ambassador to Moscow (1989–1993)
Interview in Rome, 28.10.2016

INTERVIEWS:[3]

Bruno Bottai[4] (born 10 July 1930 – death 2 November 2014)

---

[3] Either for Italian Newspapers or as part of the Project Oral History of the European Commission.
[4] Voices on Europe, Oral History Collections, Historical Archives of the European Union (http://www.eui/HAEU/OralHistory/, last consulted 1.02.2016).

17.2.1998

Giulio Andreotti[5] (born 14 January 1919 – death 6 May 2013)
11.12.1998

Francesco Cossiga[6] (born 27 July 1928 – death 17 August 2010)
27.11.2009

Luigi Zanda[7] (born 28 November 1942)
14.3.2011

Filippo Maria Pandolfi[8] (born 1 November 1927)
23.9.2013

Alberto Indelicato[9] (born 25 July 1930)
10.11.2014

---

[5] Voices on Europe, Oral History Collections, Historical Archives of the European Union (http://www.eui/HAEU/OralHistory/, last consulted 1.02.2016).
[6] Full text of the interview in: Clio Pedone, Cossiga: *L'uomo che guardò oltre il Muro,* Rubbettino, Soveria Mannelli, 2013, ch. 8.
[7] Ibid.
[8]http://www.ecodibergamo.it/stories/Homepage/395105_pandolfi_racconta_la_germa-nia_i_miei_anni_con_schmidt_e_kohl/?mediaon.trackers.autorefresh.Homapage (last consulted 1.02.2016)
[9] Federico Ferraù, "MURO DI BERLINO. Dalle due Germanie di Andreotti alla 'guerra' di Kohl", in: https://www.ilsussidiario.net/news/cultura/2014/11/10/muro-di-berlino-dalle-due-germanie-di-andreotti-alla-guerra-di-kohl/552738/ (last consulted 05.10.2016).

Afterword by Maria Eleonora Guasconi

In the past few years, the large amount of literature existing on the end of the Cold War and on the German re-unification has mainly told these revolutionary events focusing its attention on the role played by 'key' actors – namely the two superpowers, the United States and the Soviet Union, but also other relevant European countries such as Germany, of course, France and the United Kingdom – and their political leaders: Mikhail Gorbachev, Ronald Reagan, George W. Bush, Helmut Kohl, François Mitterrand and Margaret Thatcher. Only scant attention has been, however, paid to the policy and the role played by other "smaller" European countries, as for example Italy.

Deborah Cuccia's volume aims at filling this historiographical gap by analysing the Italian political and diplomatic attitude towards the issue of German re-unification in 1989–1990, a difficult topic to investigate, due to the lack of Italian archival resources available for scholars' consultation.

To overcome this important obstacle, the author skillfully performs an exercise well known to historians who deal with Italian foreign policy, the so-called "game of mirrors", which consists in an analysis of the Italian foreign policy, seen mainly through the perception of other European countries. Thus, the book is based on a wide multi-archival research, pursued mainly in France and Germany, and on a series of interesting interviews with Italian diplomats and journalists, who played a prominent role during those extraordinary events.

The few studies, which have investigated the Italian reaction towards the 1989–1990 events, (as for example Gian Enrico Rusconi, *Italia e Germania 1945–2000: la costruzione dell'Europa*, Bologna 2005 and, more recently, Antonio Varsori, *L'Italia e la fine della Guerra fredda*, Bologna 2013) have mainly focused their attention on the famous statement uttered by the Italian Foreign Minister Giulio Andreotti in 1984, "*Esistono due stati germanici e due stati germanici devono rimanere*", as an example of the negative stance of the Italian Foreign Minister towards the unification of the two Germanies, describing how he slowly changed his attitude in 1990.

The consultation of Giulio Andreotti's papers has allowed Deborah Cuccia to evaluate the Italian actions and reactions towards the issue of the German unification in the broader framework of the relations between the two countries and in the European context of the 1980's.

Although absolute priority is given to the interaction between Italy and Western Germany, the development of an Italian *Ostpolitik* has also been addressed to better understand the Italian vision of the "German question".

Moreover, a specific focus has been laid on the Italian *Mitteleuropean* policy and on the *Quadrangolare* initiative, which was part of the Italian strategy to cope with the dynamics unfolded by the fall of the Wall.

In achieving these objectives, the author has pursued a multi-level analysis, aimed at investigating not only the political and diplomatic relations between Italy and Germany, the so-called "official Italy", but also the relevant role played by other "unofficial" actors, as the Italian main political parties, the DC (Democrazia Cristiana) and the PCI (Partito Comunista Italiano), the press, Italian public opinion and, last but not the least, the development of cultural relations between Rome and Bonn.

Furthermore, in spite of the fact that Giulio Andreotti has been one of the most important and well known Italian politicians, the books casts light also on the role played by other, less known abroad, but still relevant Italian political actors who payed particular attention to the German issue, as for example to the Demo-Christian Francesco Cossiga, who was President of the Republic from 1985 to 1992, and to the Socialist Gianni De Michelis, Italian Foreign Minister from 1989 to 1992.

In a long methodological introductory chapter, the book deals with the state of the art of the historiographical debate developed on the German question, showing an in-depth knowledge of the literature concerning this subject and giving much attention to the archival sources open for consultation in Italy and in other European countries.

The author accurately examines, linguistically and historically, a series of key terms, such as "reunification or unification", "German question" and "Mitteleuropa", which represent a key to understanding the leitmotiv of the volume.

The first part of the book is dedicated to a broad analysis of the relationship developed between Italy and Western Germany since the end of World War II. This remarkable effort, after an analysis of Italian-German relations during the well-known period of the 1950s, is mainly focused on the decade 1979–1989, and sheds some light on a series of turning points, that represent an original and important contribution to the historiographical debate as well as to the knowledge of the relationship between the two countries.

In particular, the author suggests an original and innovative interpretation of a breakthrough in the diplomatic relations between Italy and Western Germany which took place since 1979, by addressing the role played by Emilio Colombo and Francesco Cossiga, as well as by the Italian ambassador in Bonn, Luigi Vittorio Ferraris, who, together with the German Foreign minister Hans-Dietrich Genscher, strongly supported the improvement and the strengthening of the relations between the two countries.

Although the importance of Italian participation to the European Monetary System and the NATO's dual track decision have already been investigated by the literature, the book offers an original analysis of well known political initiatives as the Genscher-Colombo Plan of 1981, seen in a different light from the usual interpretation of a "missed opportunity" for the relaunch of European integration, or the projects *Arge* and *Alpe Adria*, which represent interesting examples of regional cooperation, or the establishment of a bilateral dialogue between Italy and Western Germany, similar to the French-German one, established in 1963 with the Élysée Treaty.

The book also addresses the "cultural diplomacy" deployed between the two countries in order to enhance their relationship, investigating on the active role played by the *Goethe-Institut* in Italy with the aim to improve the knowledge of the German language in the country, or describing the importance of the establishment of Villa Vigoni in 1986, a center devoted to the organization of Italo-German cultural initiatives. This part of the volume challenges a series of established stereotypes related to Italian-German relations, representing the necessary prerequisite for a better understanding of the reaction of important parts of the Italian society to the "German question", when it suddenly arose in 1989.

As a consequence, the famous sentence made by the Italian Foreign Minister Giulio Andreotti in 1984 is seen in a completely different light, representing mainly the Italian Foreign minister's attempt to preserve the Helsinki's order and placing the Italian perception of the German issue in a broader context.

The second part of the volume is focused on the Italian reaction to the unfolding of the revolutionary events which, between 1989 and 1990, led to the end of the Cold War and to the re-unification of Germany.

Also in this part of the volume, the author challenges the traditional interpretation that the Italian government was fully taken by surprise by these revolutionary events, describing the attention devoted by the Italian Foreign Ministry to the political transition started in Eastern Europe since 1985. Particularly interesting is the analysis of Mikail Gorbachev's project of a "European Common House", as well as of the Italian project named *Quadrangolare,* whose aim was to cope with the revolutionary dynamics unleashed by the end of the Cold War.

The author pays particular attention to the role played by Italian political actors as Giulio Andreotti, Francesco Cossiga and Gianni De Michelis, as well as by the Italian Ambassador in Bonn, Marcello Guidi, describing their different attitudes towards the issue of German re-unification and explaining the progressive development of an Italian strategy, based on three pillars: EEC, NATO and the CSCE, which would preserve the European order.

In this framework, the Italian government strategy to maintain "one nation and two states" in Germany, which crumbled between November 1989 and March 1990, and the Italian exclusion by the main table of negotiations are interpreted in a complete different light.

In conclusions, Deborah Cuccia successfully argues the provocative issue of a deterioration of Italian-German relations after the unification, challenging the definition coined by Gian Enrico Rusconi, of a "creeping estrangement" between Italy and Germany.

The book is the result of a Phd in History of International Relations, which Dr. Cuccia has brilliantly pursued at the Department of Political and Social Sciences of the University of Florence in co-tutelle with the University of Hildesheim, under my and Prof. Michael Gehler's supervision.

Maria Eleonora Guasconi

University of Genoa

This book is based on the PhD thesis which I presented in 2017. It was conceived within a co-tutelle agreement between the *Stiftung Universität Hildesheim* (Institut für Geschichte) and the *Università degli Studi di Firenze* (Dipartimento di Studi Politici e Sociali).

A grant of the *Deutsches Akademisches Austauschdient* (DAAD) provided me with the financial resources for a fruitful stay in Hildesheim. Another grant of the *Goethe-Institut* allowed me to attend further education courses in Munich in summer 2014.

A special thank is due to Elisa Anastassopulos for her suggestions and her help in checking my English.

It has been my decision and my responsibility to provide quotations in the text in their original language. Whenever necessary a translation in English has been added in the footnotes.

HISTORISCHE EUROPA-STUDIEN

Geschichte in Erfahrung, Gegenwart und Zukunft

herausgegeben vom Institut für Geschichte
der Stiftung Universität Hildesheim
unter der Leitung von Michael Gehler

Band 10: **Michael Gehler, Imke Scharlemann (Hg.): Zwischen Diktatur und Demokratie. Erfahrungen in Mittelost- und Südosteuropa. Hildesheimer Europagespräche II**
2013. 728 S. ISBN 978-3-487-14833-5

Band 11: **Michael Gehler, Marcus Gonschor, Hinnerk Meyer (Hg.): Banken, Finanzen und Wirtschaft im Kontext europäischer und globaler Krisen. Hildesheimer Europagespräche III**
Unter Mitarbeit von Severin Cramm und Miriam Hetzel.
2015. 687 S. ISBN 978-3-487-15041-3

Band 12: **Hinnerk Meyer: Formationsphasen der europäischen Integrationspolitik im Vergleich**
2014. 431 S. ISBN 978-3-487-15129-8

Band 13: **Michael Gehler, Marcus Gonschor, Severin Cramm, Miriam Hetzel (Hg.): Internationale Geschichte im globalen Wandel Hildesheimer Europagespräche IV**
2 Bände. 2018. XXII/1278 S. mit 82 Abb. ISBN 978-3-487-15568-5

Band 14: **Michael Gehler, Peter Müller, Peter Nitschke (Hg.): Europa-Räume. Von der Antike bis zur Gegenwart**
2016. 508 S. mit 43 Abb. ISBN 978-3-487-15482-4

Band 15: **Felix Hinz (Hg.): Kreuzzüge des Mittelalters und der Neuzeit. Realhistorie – Geschichtskultur – Didaktik**
2015. 389 S. ISBN 978-3-487-15267-7

Band 16: **Holm A. Leonhardt: Kartelltheorie und Internationale Beziehungen. Theoriegeschichtliche Studien**
2013. 861 S. ISBN 978-3-487-14840-3

Band 17: **Michael Gehler, Andrea Brait (Hg.): Am Ort des Geschehens in Zeiten des Umbruchs**
2018. 974 S. mit 30 Abb. ISBN 978-3-487-15622-4

Band 19: **Marcus Gonschor, Politik der Feder**
2017. 893 S. ISBN 978-3-487-15531-9

Band 20: **Michael Gehler, Paul Luif, Elisabeth Vyslonzil (Hg.): Die Dimension Mitteleuropa in der Europäischen Union**
2015. 499 S. mit 9 Abb. und 18 Tabellen. ISBN 978-3-487-15268-4

Band 22: **Deborah Cuccia: There are two German States and two must remain?**
2019. XIV/394 S. mit 18 Abb. ISBN 978-3-487-15810-5